P9-ASK-444

Everyman, I will go with thee, and be thy guide,
In thy most need to go by thy side.

This is No. 545 of Everyman's Library. A list of authors and their works in this series will be found at the end of this volume. The publishers will be pleased to send freely to all applicants a separate, annotated list of the Library.

J. M. DENT & SONS LIMITED
10–13 BEDFORD STREET LONDON W.C.2

E. P. DUTTON & CO. INC.
286–302 FOURTH AVENUE
NEW YORK

EVERYMAN'S LIBRARY
EDITED BY ERNEST RHYS

HISTORY

THE HISTORY OF ROME

BY THEODOR MOMMSEN · INTRODUCTION BY E. A. FREEMAN, LL.D.
TRANSLATED BY W. P. DICKSON
IN 4 VOLS. VOL. 4

THEODOR MOMMSEN, born in 1817 in Schleswig-Holstein. From 1848 was professor of Roman Law and Ancient History at Berlin and other universities. From 1873 to 1895 was secretary to the Berlin Academy of Sciences. From 1873 to 1888 was a member of the Prussian House of Representatives. Died in 1903.

THE HISTORY OF ROME

VOLUME FOUR

THEODOR MOMMSEN

LONDON: J. M. DENT & SONS LTD.
NEW YORK: E. P. DUTTON & CO. INC.

Made in Great Britain
at The Temple Press Letchworth
and decorated by Eric Ravilious
for
J. M. Dent & Sons Ltd.
Aldine House Bedford St. London
Toronto . Vancouver
Melbourne . Wellington
First Published in this Edition 1911
Reprinted 1921, 1930

CONTENTS

BOOK FIFTH

The Establishment of the Military Monarchy

BOOK FIFTH

THE ESTABLISHMENT OF THE MILITARY MONARCHY

Wie er sich sieht so um und um,
Kehrt es ihm fast den Kopf herum,
Wie er wollt' Worte zu allem finden?
Wie or möcht' so viel Schwall verbinden?
Wie er möcht' immer muthig bleiben
So fort und weiter fort zu schreiben?—Goethe.

THE HISTORY OF ROME

BOOK FIFTH

CHAPTER I

MARCUS LEPIDUS AND QUINTUS SERTORIUS

WHEN Sulla died in the year $\frac{676}{78}$, the oligarchy which he had restored ruled with absolute sway over the Roman state; but, as it had been established by force, it still needed force to maintain its ground against its numerous secret and open foes. It was opposed not by any single party with objects clearly expressed and under leaders distinctly acknowledged, but by a mass of multifarious elements, ranging themselves doubtless under the general name of the popular party, but in reality opposing the Sullan organisation of the commonwealth on very various grounds and with very different designs. There were the men of positive law, who neither mingled in nor understood politics, but who detested the arbitrary procedure of Sulla in dealing with the lives and property of the burgesses. Even during the regent's lifetime, when all other opposition was silent, the strict jurists were refractory; the Cornelian laws, for example, which deprived various Italian communities of the Roman franchise, were treated in judicial decisions as null and void; and in like manner the courts held that, where a burgess had been made a prisoner of war and sold into slavery during the revolution, his franchise was not forfeited. There was, further, the remnant of the old liberal minority in the senate, which in former times had sought a compromise with the reform party and the Italians, and was now in a similar spirit inclined to modify the rigidly oligarchic constitution of Sulla by concessions to the Populares. There were, moreover, the Populares strictly so called, the honest and credulous narrow-minded radicals, who staked property and life for the current watchwords of the party-programme, only to discover with painful surprise after the victory that they had been fighting not for a reality, but for a phrase. Their special aim was to re-establish the tribunician power, which Sulla had not abolished but had divested of its most essential prerogatives, and which exercised over the multitude a charm all the more mysterious because the institution had no obvious practical use and was in fact an empty phantom—the mere name of tribune of the people, more than a thousand years later, revolutionised Rome. There were, above all, the numerous and important classes whom the Sullan restoration had left unsatisfied, or whose political or private interests it had directly injured. Among those who for such reasons belonged to the opposition ranked the dense and prosperous population of the region between the Po and the Alps, which naturally regarded the bestowal of Latin rights in $\frac{665}{89}$ (iii. 234) as merely an instalment of the full Roman franchise, and so afforded a ready soil for agitation. To this category belonged also the freedmen, influential in numbers and wealth, and specially dangerous through their aggregation in the capital, who could not brook their having been reduced by the restoration to their earlier, practically useless, suffrage. In the same position stood, moreover, the great capitalists, who maintained a cautious silence, but still as before preserved their tenacity of resentment and their equal tenacity of power. The populace of the capital, which recognised true freedom in free bread-corn, was likewise discontented. Still deeper exasperation was felt by the class of burgesses affected by the Sullan confiscations—whether they, like those of Pompeii, lived on their property curtailed by the Sullan colonists, within the same ring-wall with the latter, and at perpetual variance with them; or, like the Arretines and Volaterrans, retained actual possession of their territory, but had the Damocles' sword of confiscation suspended over them by the Roman people; or, as was the case in Etruria especially, were reduced to be beggars in their former abodes, or robbers in the woods. Finally, the agitation extended to the whole family connections and freedmen of those democratic chiefs who had lost their lives in consequence of the restoration, or who were wandering along the Mauretanian coasts, or sojourning at the court and in the army of Mithradates, in all the misery of emigrant exile; for, according to the strict family associations that governed the political feeling of this age, it was accounted a point of honour [1] that those who were left behind should endeavour to procure for exiled relatives the

[1] It is a significant trait, that a distinguished teacher of literature, the freedman Staberius Eros, allowed the children of the proscribed to attend his course gratuitously.

privilege of returning to their native land, and, in the case of the dead, at least a removal of the stigma attaching to their memory and to their children, and a restitution to the latter of their paternal estate. More especially the immediate children of the proscribed, whom the regent had reduced in point of law to political Pariahs (iii. 330), had virtually received from the law itself a summons to rise in rebellion against the existing order of things.

To all these sections of the opposition there was added the whole body of men of ruined fortunes. All the rabble high and low, whose means and substance had been spent in refined or in vulgar debauchery; the aristocratic lords, who had no farther mark of quality than their debts; the Sullan soldiers whom the regent's fiat could transform into landholders but not into husbandmen, and who, after squandering the first inheritance of the proscribed, were longing to succeed to a second—all these waited only the unfolding of the banner which invited them to fight against the existing order of things, whatever else might be inscribed on it. From a like necessity all the aspiring men of talent, in search of popularity, attached themselves to the opposition; not only those to whom the strictly closed circle of the Optimates denied admission or at least opportunities for rapid promotion, and who therefore attempted to force their way into the phalanx and to break through the laws of oligarchic exclusiveness and seniority by means of popular favour, but also the more dangerous men, whose ambition aimed at something higher than helping to determine the destinies of the world within the sphere of collegiate intrigues. On the advocates' platform in particular—the only field of legal opposition left open by Sulla—even in the regent's life-time such aspirants waged lively war against the restoration with the weapons of formal jurisprudence and clever oratory: for instance, the adroit speaker Marcus Tullius Cicero (born 3rd January, $\frac{648}{106}$), son of a landholder of Arpinum, speedily made himself a name by the mingled caution and daring of his opposition to the dictator. Such efforts were not of much importance, if the opponent desired nothing farther than by their means to procure for himself a curule chair, and then to sit in it contentedly for the rest of his life. No doubt, if this chair should not satisfy a popular man and Gaius Gracchus should find a successor, a struggle for life or death was inevitable; but for the present at least no name could be mentioned the bearer of which had proposed to himself any such lofty aim.

Such was the sort of opposition with which the oligarchic government instituted by Sulla had to contend, when it had, earlier than Sulla himself probably expected, been thrown by his death on its own resources. The task was in itself far from easy, and it was farther complicated by the other social and political evils of this age—especially by the extraordinary double difficulty of keeping the military chiefs in the provinces in subjection to the supreme civil magistracy, and of dealing with the masses of the Italian and extra-Italian populace accumulating in the capital and of the slaves living there to a great extent in *de facto* freedom, without having troops at disposal. The senate was placed, as it were, in a fortress exposed and threatened on all sides, and serious conflicts could not be avoided. But the means of resistance organised by Sulla were considerable and lasting; and, although the majority of the nation was manifestly disinclined to the government which Sulla had installed, and even animated by hostile feelings towards it, that government might very well maintain itself for a long time in its stronghold against the distracted and confused mass of an opposition which was not agreed either as to end or means, was without a head, and was broken up into a hundred fragments. Only it was necessary that it should be determined to maintain its position, and should bring at least a spark of the energy which had built the fortress to its defence; for in the case of a garrison which will not defend itself, the greatest master of fortification constructs his walls and moats in vain.

The more everything ultimately depended on the personal character of the leading men on both sides, it was the more unfortunate that both, strictly speaking, wanted leaders. The politics of this period were thoroughly under the sway of the coterie-system in its worst form. This, indeed, was nothing new; close unions of families and clubs were inseparable from an aristocratic organisation of the state, and had for centuries prevailed in Rome. But it was not till this epoch that they became all-powerful, for it was only now (first in $\frac{690}{64}$) that their influence was substantiated rather than checked by legal measures of repression. All persons of quality, those of popular leanings no less than the oligarchy proper, met in Hetaeriae; the mass of the burgesses likewise, so far as they took any regular part in political events at all, formed according to their voting-districts close unions with an almost military organisation, which found their natural captains and agents in the "district-distributors" (*divisores tribuum*). With these political clubs everything was bought and sold; the vote of the elector especially, but also the votes of the senator and the judge, the fists too which produced the street riot, and the ringleaders who directed it. The associations of the upper and of the lower classes were distinguished merely in the matter of tariff. The Hetaeria decided the elections, the Hetaeria decreed the impeachments, the Hetaeria conducted the defence; it secured the distinguished advocate, and in case of need it contracted for an acquittal with one of the speculators who prosecuted on a great scale the lucrative traffic in judges' votes. The Hetaeria commanded by its compact bands the streets of the capital, and with the capital but too often the state. All these things were done in accordance with a certain rule, and, so to speak, publicly; the system of Hetaeriae was better arranged and managed than any branch of state administration; although there was, as is usual among civilised swindlers, a tacit understanding that there should be no direct mention of the nefarious proceedings, nobody made a secret of them, and advocates of repute were not ashamed to give open and intelligible hints of their relation to the Hetaeriae of their clients. If an individual was to be found here or there who kept aloof from such practices and yet mingled in public life, he was assuredly, like Marcus Cato, a political Don Quixote. Parties and party-strife were superseded by the clubs and their rivalry; government was superseded by intrigue. A more than equivocal character, Publius Cethegus, formerly one of the most zealous Marians, afterwards as a deserter received into favour by Sulla (iii. 312), acted a most influential part in the political proceedings of this period—unrivalled as a cunning tale-bearer and mediator between the sections of the senate and as having a statesman's acquaintance with the secrets of all cabals: at times the appointment to the most important posts of command was decided by a word from his mistress Praecia. Such a plight was only possible where none of the men taking part in politics rose above mediocrity: any man of more than ordinary talent would have swept away this system of factions like cobwebs; but there was in reality a sad lack of men of political or military capacity.

Of the older generation the civil wars had left not a single man of repute except the old shrewd and eloquent Lucius Philippus, consul in $\frac{663}{91}$, who, formerly of popular leanings (iii. 130), thereafter leader of the capitalist party against the senate (iii. 211), and closely associated with the Marians (iii. 306), and lastly passing over to the victorious oligarchy in sufficient time to earn thanks and commendation (iii. 312), had managed to escape between the parties. Among the men of the following generation the most notable chiefs of the pure aristocracy were Quintus Metellus Pius, consul in $\frac{674}{80}$, Sulla's comrade in dangers and victories; Quintus Lutatius Catulus, consul in the year of Sulla's death, $\frac{676}{78}$, the son of the victor of Vercellae; and two younger officers, the brothers Lucius and Marcus Lucullus, of whom the former had fought with distinction under Sulla in Asia, the latter in Italy; not to mention Optimates like Quintus Hortensius ($\frac{640-704}{114-50}$), who had importance only as a pleader, or men like Decimus Junius Brutus consul in $\frac{677}{77}$, Mamercus Aemilius Lepidus Livianus consul in $\frac{677}{77}$ and other such nullities, whose best quality was a euphonious aristocratic name. But even those four men rose little above the average calibre of the Optimates of this age. Catulus was like his father a man of refined culture and an honest aristocrat, but of moderate talents and no soldier. Metellus was not merely estimable in his personal character, but an able and experienced officer; and it was not so much on account of his close relations as a kinsman and colleague with the regent as because of his recognised ability that he was sent in $\frac{675}{79}$, after resigning the consulship, to Spain, where the Lusitanians and the Roman emigrants under Quintus Sertorius had begun fresh movements. The two Luculli were also able officers—particularly the elder, who combined very respectable military talents with thorough literary culture and a liking for authorship, and appeared honourable also as a man. But, as statesmen, even these better aristocrats were not much less remiss and shortsighted than the average senators of the time. In presence of an outward foe the more eminent among them, doubtless, proved themselves useful and brave; but no one of them evinced the desire or the skill to solve the problems of politics proper, and to guide the vessel of the state through the stormy seas of intrigue and faction with the hand of a true pilot. Their political wisdom was limited to a sincere belief in the oligarchy as the sole means of salvation, and to a cordial hatred and courageous execration of demagogism as well as of every individual authority which sought to emancipate itself. Their petty ambition was contented with little. The stories told of Metellus in Spain—that he not only allowed himself to be delighted with the far from harmonious lyre of the Spanish occasional poets, but even wherever he went had himself received like a god with libations of wine and odours of incense, and at table had his head crowned by descending Victories amidst theatrical thunder with the golden laurel of the conqueror—are no better attested than most historical anecdotes; but such gossip reflects the degenerate ambition of the race of Epigoni. Even the better men were content when they had gained not power and influence, but the consulship and a triumph and a place of honour in the senate; and at the very time when with right ambition they would have just begun to be truly useful to their country and their party, they retired from the political stage to spend their days in princely luxury. Men like Metellus and Lucius Lucullus were, even as generals, not more attentive to the enlargement of the Roman dominion by fresh conquests of kings and peoples than to the enlargement of the endless game, poultry, and dessert lists of Roman gastronomy by new delicacies from Africa and Asia Minor, and they wasted the best part of their lives in more or less intellectual idleness. The traditional aptitude and the individual self-denial, on which all oligarchic government is based, were lost in the decayed and artificially restored Roman aristocracy of this age; in its judgment universally the spirit of clique was accounted as patriotism, vanity as ambition, and narrow-mindedness as consistency. Had the Sullan constitution passed into the guardianship of such men as have sat in the Roman College of Cardinals or the Venetian Council of Ten, we cannot tell whether the opposition would have been able to shake it so soon; with such defenders every attack involved, at all events, a serious peril.

Of the men, who were neither unconditional adherents nor open opponents of the Sullan constitution, no one attracted more the eyes of the multitude than the young Gnaeus Pompeius, who was at the time of Sulla's death twenty-eight years of age (born 29th September, $\frac{648}{106}$). The fact was a misfortune for the admired as well as for the admirers; but it was natural. Sound in body and spirit, an excellent athlete, who even when a superior officer vied with his soldiers in leaping, running, and lifting, a vigorous and skilled rider and fencer, a bold leader of volunteer bands, the youth had become imperator and triumphator at an age which excluded him from every magistracy and from the senate, and had acquired the first place next to Sulla in public opinion; nay, had obtained from the indulgent regent himself—half in recognition, half in irony—the surname of the Great. Unhappily, his mental endowments by no means corresponded with these unprecedented successes. He was neither a bad nor an incapable man, but a man thoroughly ordinary, created by nature to be a good sergeant, called by circumstances to be a general and a statesman. An intelligent, brave and experienced, thoroughly excellent soldier, he was still, even in his military capacity, without trace of any higher gifts. It was characteristic of him as a general, as well as in other respects, to proceed with a caution bordering on timidity, and, if possible, to give the decisive blow only when he had established an immense superiority over his opponent. His culture was the average culture of the time; although entirely a soldier, he did not neglect, when he went to Rhodes, dutifully to admire and to make presents to the rhetoricians there. His integrity was that of a rich man who manages with discretion his considerable property inherited and acquired. He disdained not to make money in the usual senatorial way, but he was too cold and too rich to incur special risks, or draw down on himself conspicuous disgrace, on that account. The vice so much in vogue among his contemporaries, rather than any virtue of his own, procured for him the reputation—comparatively, no doubt, well warranted—of integrity and disinterestedness. His "honest countenance" became almost proverbial, and even after his death he was esteemed as a worthy and moral man; he was really a good neighbour, who did not join in the revolting schemes by which the grandees of that age extended the bounds of their domains through forced sales or measures still worse at the expense of their humbler neighbours, and in domestic life he displayed attachment to his wife and children: it redounds moreover to his credit that he was the first to depart from the barbarous custom of putting to death the captive kings and generals of the enemy after they had been exhibited in triumph. But this did not prevent him from separating from his beloved wife at the command of his lord and master Sulla, because she belonged to an outlawed family, nor from ordering with great composure that men who had stood by him and helped him in times of difficulty should be executed before his eyes at the nod of the same master (iii. 324): he was not cruel, though he was reproached with being so, but—what perhaps was worse—he was cold and, in good as in evil, unimpassioned. In the tumult of battle he faced the enemy fearlessly; in civil life he was a shy man, whose cheek flushed on the slightest occasion; he spoke in public not without embarrassment, and generally was angular, stiff, and awkward in intercourse. With all his haughty obstinacy he was—as indeed persons ordinarily are, who make a display of their independence—a pliant tool in the hands of men who knew how to manage him, especially of his freedmen and clients, by whom he had no fear of being controlled. For nothing was he less qualified than for a statesman. Uncertain as to his aims, unskilful in the choice of his means, alike in little and great matters shortsighted and helpless, he was wont to conceal his irresolution and indecision under a solemn silence, and, when he thought to play a subtle game, simply to deceive himself with the belief that he was deceiving others. By his military position and his territorial connections he acquired almost without any action of his own a considerable party personally devoted to him, with which the greatest things might have been accomplished; but Pompeius was in every respect incapable of leading and keeping together a party, and, if it still kept together, it did so—in like manner without his action—through the sheer force of circumstances. In this, as in other things, he reminds us of Marius; but Marius, with his nature of boorish roughness and sensual passion, was still less intolerable than this most tiresome and most starched of all artificial great men. His political position was utterly perverse. He was a Sullan officer and under obligation to serve the restored constitution, and yet again in opposition to Sulla personally as well as to the whole senatorial government. The *gens* of the Pompeii, which had only been named for some sixty years in the consular lists, had by no means acquired full standing in the eyes of the aristocracy; the father of this Pompeius had occupied a very invidious equivocal position towards the senate (iii. 255, 302), and he himself had once been in the ranks of the Cinnans (iii. 312)—recollections which were suppressed perhaps, but not forgotten. The prominent position which Pompeius acquired under Sulla set him at inward variance with the aristocracy, quite as much as it brought him into outward connection with it. Weak-headed as he was, Pompeius was seized with giddiness on the height of glory which he had climbed with such dangerous rapidity and ease. Just as if he wished to ridicule his dry prosaic nature by the parallel with the most poetical of all heroic figures, he began to compare himself with Alexander the Great, and to account himself a man of unique standing, whom it did not beseem to be merely one of the five hundred senators of Rome. In reality, no one was more fitted to take his place as a member of an aristocratic *régime* than Pompeius. His dignified outward appearance, his solemn formality, his personal bravery, his decorous private life, his want of all initiative might have gained for him, had he been born two hundred years earlier, an honourable place by the side of Quintus

Maximus and Publius Decius: this mediocrity, so characteristic of the genuine Optimate and the genuine Roman, contributed not a little to the special affinity which subsisted at all times between Pompeius and the mass of the burgesses and the senate. Even in his own age he would have had a definite and respectable position, had he contented himself with being the general of the senate—the office for which he was from the beginning destined. With this he was not content, and so he fell into the fatal plight of wishing to be something else than he could be. He was constantly aspiring to a special position in the state, and, when it offered itself, he could not make up his mind to occupy it; he was deeply indignant when persons and laws did not bend unconditionally before him, and yet he everywhere bore himself with no mere affectation of modesty as one of many peers, and trembled at the mere thought of undertaking anything unconstitutional. Thus constantly at fundamental variance with, and yet at the same time the obedient servant of, the oligarchy, constantly tormented by an ambition which was frightened at its own aims, his deeply-agitated life passed joylessly away in a perpetual inward contradiction.

Marcus Crassus cannot, any more than Pompeius, be reckoned among the unconditional adherents of the oligarchy. He is a personage highly characteristic of this epoch. Like Pompeius, whose senior he was by a few years, he belonged to the circle of the high Roman aristocracy, had obtained the usual culture befitting his rank, and had fought like Pompeius with distinction under Sulla in the Italian war. Far inferior to many of his peers in mental gifts, literary culture, and military talent, he outstripped them by his boundless activity, and by the perseverance with which he strove to possess all things and to become all-important. Above all, he threw himself into speculation. Purchases of estates during the revolution formed the foundation of his wealth; but he disdained no branch of gain; he carried on the business of building in the capital on an extensive scale and with prudence; he entered into partnership with his freedmen in the most varied undertakings; he acted as banker both in and out of Rome, in person or by his agents; he advanced money to his colleagues in the senate, and undertook—as it might happen—to execute works or to bribe the tribunals on their account. He was far from nice in the matter of making profit. On occasion of the Sullan proscriptions a forgery in the lists had been proved against him, for which reason Sulla made no more use of him thenceforward in affairs of state: he did not refuse to accept an inheritance, because the testamentary document which contained his name was notoriously forged; he made no objection, when his bailiffs by force or by fraud dislodged the petty holders from lands which adjoined his own. He avoided open collisions, however, with criminal justice, and lived himself like a genuine moneyed man in homely and simple style. In this way Crassus rose in the course of a few years from a man of ordinary senatorial fortune to be the master of wealth which not long before his death, after defraying enormous extraordinary expenses, still amounted to 170,000,000 sesterces (£1,700,000). He had become the richest of Romans and thereby, at the same time, a great political power. If, according to his expression, no one might call himself rich who could not maintain an army from his revenues, one who could do this was hardly any longer a mere citizen. In reality the views of Crassus aimed at a higher object than the possession of the fullest money-chest in Rome. He grudged no pains to extend his connections. He knew how to salute by name every burgess of the capital. He refused to no suppliant his assistance in court. Nature, indeed, had not done much for him as an orator: his speaking was dry, his delivery monotonous, he had difficulty of hearing; but his pertinacity, which no wearisomeness deterred and no enjoyment distracted, overcame such obstacles. He never appeared unprepared, he never extemporised, and so he became a pleader at all times in request and at all times ready; to whom it was no derogation that a cause was rarely too bad for him, and that he knew how to influence the judges not merely by his oratory, but also by his connections and, if necessary, by his gold. Half the senate was indebted to him; his habit of advancing to "friends" money without interest revocable at pleasure rendered a number of influential men dependent on him, and the more so that, like a genuine man of business, he made no distinction of parties, maintained connections on all hands, and readily lent to every one able to pay or otherwise useful. The most daring party-leaders, who made their attacks recklessly in all directions, were careful not to quarrel with Crassus; he was compared to the bull of the herd, whom it was advisable for none to provoke. That such a man, so situated, could not strive after lowly aims is clear; and, in a very different way from Pompeius, Crassus knew exactly like a banker the objects and the means of political speculation. From the origin of Rome capital was a political power there; the age was of such a sort, that everything seemed accessible to gold as to iron. If in the time of revolution a capitalist aristocracy might have thought of overthrowing the oligarchy of the *gentes*, a man like Crassus might raise his eyes higher than to the *fasces* and embroidered mantle of the triumphators. For the moment he was a Sullan and adherent of the senate; but he was too much of a financier to devote himself to a definite political party, or to pursue aught else than his personal advantage. Why should Crassus, the wealthiest and most intriguing man in Rome, and no penurious miser but a speculator on the greatest scale, not speculate also on the crown? Alone, perhaps, he could not attain this object; but he had already carried out many great transactions in partnership; it was not impossible that for this also a suitable partner might present himself. It is a trait characteristic of the time, that a mediocre orator and officer, a politician who took his activity for energy and his covetousness for ambition, one who at bottom had nothing but a colossal fortune and the mercantile talent of forming connections—that such a man, relying on the omnipotence of coteries and intrigues, could deem himself on a level with the first generals and statesmen of his day, and could contend with them for the highest prize which allures political ambition.

In the opposition proper, both among the liberal conservatives and among the Populares, the storms of revolution had made fearful havoc. Among the former, the only surviving man of note was Gaius Cotta ($\frac{630}{124}$—*c.* $\frac{681}{73}$), the friend and ally of Drusus and as such banished in $\frac{663}{91}$ (iii. 223), and then by Sulla's victory brought back to his native land (iii. 338); he was a shrewd man and an efficient advocate, but not called, either by the weight of his party or by that of his personal standing to act more than a respectable secondary part. In the democratic party, among the rising youth, Gaius Julius Cæsar, who was twenty-four years of age (born 12 July, $\frac{652}{102}$?[1]), drew towards him the

[1] It is usual to set down the year $\frac{654}{100}$ as that of Caesar's birth, because according to Suetonius (*Caes.* 88), Plutarch (*Caes.* 69), and Appian (*B. C.* ii. 149) he was at his death (15 March, $\frac{710}{44}$) in his 56th year; with which also the statement that he was 18 years old at the time of the Sullan proscription ($\frac{672}{82}$; Vell. ii. 41) nearly accords. But this view is utterly inconsistent with the facts that Caesar filled the aedileship in $\frac{689}{65}$, the praetorship in $\frac{692}{62}$, and the consulship in $\frac{695}{59}$, and that these offices could, according to the *leges annales*, be held at the very earliest in the 37-38th, 40-41st, and 43-44th years of a man's life respectively (Becker ii. 2, 24). We cannot conceive why Caesar should have filled all the curule offices two years before the legal time, and still less why there should be no mention anywhere of his having done so; these facts rather suggest the conjecture that,

eyes of friend and foe. His relationship with Marius and Cinna (his father's sister had been the wife of Marius, he himself had married Cinna's daughter); the courageous refusal of the youth who had scarce outgrown the age of boyhood to send a divorce to his young wife Cornelia at the bidding of the dictator, as Pompeius had in the like case done; his bold persistence in the priesthood conferred upon him by Marius, but revoked by Sulla; his wanderings during the proscription with which he was threatened, and which was with difficulty averted by the intercession of his relatives; his bravery in the conflicts before Mytilene and in Cilicia, a bravery which no one had expected from the tenderly reared and almost effeminately foppish boy; even the warnings of Sulla regarding the "boy in the petticoat" in whom more than a Marius lay concealed—all these were precisely so many recommendations in the eyes of the democratic party. But Caesar could only be the object of hopes for the future; and the men who from their age and their public position would have been called now to seize the reins of the party and the state, were all dead or in exile.

Thus the leadership of the democracy, in the absence of a

as his birthday fell undoubtedly on July 12, he was born not in $\frac{654}{100}$, but in $\frac{652}{102}$; so that in $\frac{672}{82}$ he was in his 20-21st year, and he died not in his 56th year, but at the age of 57 years 8 months. In favour of this latter view we may moreover adduce the circumstance, which has been strangely brought forward in opposition to it, that Caesar "*paene puer*" was appointed by Marius and Cinna as Flamen of Jupiter (Vell. ii. 43); for Marius died in January $\frac{668}{86}$, when Caesar was according to the usual view 13 years 6 months old, and therefore not "almost," as Velleius says, but actually still a boy, and most probably for this very reason not at all capable of holding such a priesthood. If, again, he was born in July, $\frac{652}{102}$, he was at the death of Marius in his 16th year; and with this the expression in Velleius agrees, as well as the general rule that civil positions were not assumed before the expiry of the age of boyhood. Further, with this latter view alone accords the fact that the *denarii* struck by Caesar about the outbreak of the civil war are marked with the number LII. probably the year of his life; for when it began, Caesar's age was according to this view somewhat over 52 years. Nor is it so rash as it appears to us who are accustomed to regular and official lists of births, to charge our authorities with an error in this respect. Those four statements may very well be all traceable to a common source; nor can they at all lay claim to any very high credibility, seeing that for the earlier period before the commencement of the *acta diurna* the statements as to the natal years of even the best known and most prominent Romans, *e.g.*, as to that of Pompeius, vary in the most surprising manner.

In the Life of Caesar by Napoleon III. (B. 2, ch. 1) it is objected to this view, first, that the *lex annalis* would point for Caesar's birth-year not to $\frac{652}{102}$, but to $\frac{651}{103}$; secondly and especially, that other cases are known where it was not attended to. But the first assertion rests on a mistake; for, as the example of Cicero shows, the *lex annalis* required only that at the enter-man with a true vocation for it, was to be had by any one who might please to give himself forth as the champion of oppressed popular freedom; and in this way it came to Marcus Aemilius Lepidus, a Sullan, who from motives more than equivocal deserted to the camp of the democracy. Once a zealous Optimate, and a large purchaser at the auctions of the proscribed estates, he had, as governor of Sicily, so scandalously plundered the province that he was threatened with impeachment, and, to evade it, threw himself into opposition. It was a gain of doubtful value. No doubt the opposition thus acquired a well-known name, a man of quality, a vehement orator in the Forum; but Lepidus was an insignificant and indiscreet personage, who did not deserve to become a leader either in council or in the field. Nevertheless the opposition welcomed him, and the new leader of the democrats succeeded not only in deterring his accusers from prosecuting the attack which they had begun, but also in carrying his election to the consulship for $\frac{676}{78}$; in

ing on office the 43rd year should be begun, not that it should be completed. None of the alleged exceptions to the rule, moreover, are pertinent. When Tacitus (*Ann.* xi. 22) says that formerly in conferring magistracies no regard was had to age, and that the consulate and dictatorship were entrusted to quite young men, he has in view, of course, as all commentators acknowledge, the earlier period before the issuing of the *leges annales*—the consulship of M. Valerius Corvus at twenty-three, and similar cases. The assertion that Lucullus received the supreme magistracy before the legal age is erroneous; it is only stated (Cicero, *Acad. Pr.* i. 1) that on the ground of an exceptional clause not more particularly known to us, in reward for some sort of act performed by him, he had a dispensation from the legal two years' interval between the aedileship and praetorship—in reality he was aedile in $\frac{675}{79}$, probably praetor in $\frac{677}{77}$, consul in $\frac{680}{74}$. That the case of Pompeius was a totally different one is obvious; but even as to Pompeius it is on several occasions expressly stated (Cicero, *de Imp. Pomp.* 21, 62; Appian iii. 88) that the senate released him from the laws as to age. That this should have been done with Pompeius, who had solicited the consulship as a commander-in-chief crowned with victory and a triumphator, at the head of an army and after his coalition with Crassus also of a powerful party, we can readily conceive. But it would be in the highest degree surprising, if the same thing should have been done with Caesar on his candidature for the minor magistracies, when he was of little more importance than other political beginners; and it would be, if possible, more surprising still, that, while there is mention of that—in itself readily understood—exception, there should be no notice of this more than strange deviation, however naturally such notices would have suggested themselves, especially with reference to Octavianus consul at 21 (comp. *e.g.*, Appian iii. 88). Of a piece with the examples adduced is the inference drawn from them, "that the law was little observed in Rome, where distinguished men were concerned." Anything more erroneous than this sentence was never uttered regarding Rome and the Romans. The greatness of the Roman commonwealth and not less that of its great generals and statesmen, depends above all things on the fact that the law held good for them as well as for others.

which he was helped not only by the treasures exacted in Sicily, but also by the foolish endeavour of Pompeius to show Sulla and the pure Sullans on this occasion what he could do. Now that the opposition had, on the death of Sulla, found a head once more in Lepidus, and now that this their leader had become the supreme magistrate of the state, the speedy outbreak of the new revolution in the capital might with certainty be foreseen.

But even before the democrats moved in the capital, the democratic emigrants had again bestirred themselves in Spain. The soul of this movement was Quintus Sertorius. This eminent man, a native of Nursia in the Sabine land, was from the first of a tender and even soft-hearted temperament—as his almost enthusiastic love for his mother, Raia, shows—and at the same time of the most chivalrous bravery, as was proved by the honourable scars which he brought home from the Cimbrian, Spanish, and Italian wars. Although wholly untrained as a speaker, he excited the admiration of learned advocates by the natural flow and the striking precision of his address. His remarkable military and statesmanly talent had found opportunity of shining by contrast, more particularly in the revolutionary war which the democrats so wretchedly and stupidly mismanaged; he was confessedly the only democratic officer who knew how to prepare and to conduct war, and the only democratic statesman who opposed the insensate and furious doings of his party with statesmanlike energy. His Spanish soldiers called him the new Hannibal, and this not merely because he had, like that hero, lost an eye in war. He in reality reminds us of the great Phoenician by his equally cunning and courageous strategy, by his rare talent of organising war by means of war, by his adroitness in attracting foreign nations to his interest and making them serviceable to his ends, by his prudence in success and misfortune, by the quickness of his ingenuity in turning to good account his victories and averting the consequences of his defeats. It may be doubted whether any Roman statesman of the earlier period, or of the present, can be compared in point of universal talent to Sertorius. After Sulla's generals had compelled him to quit Spain (iii. 324), he had led a restless life of adventure along the Spanish and African coasts, sometimes in league, sometimes at war, with the Cilician pirates who haunted these seas and with the chieftains of the wandering tribes of Libya. The victorious Roman restoration had pursued him even thither: when he besieged Tingis (Tangiers), a corps under Pacciaecus from Roman Africa had appeared to help the prince of the town; but Pacciaecus was totally defeated and Tingis was taken by Sertorius. On the report of such achievements by the Roman refugee spreading abroad, the Lusitanians, who, notwithstanding their pretended submission to the Roman supremacy, practically maintained their independence and annually fought with the governors of Further Spain, sent envoys to Sertorius in Africa, to invite him to their country and to commit to him the command of their militia.

Sertorius, who twenty years before had served under Titus Didius in Spain and knew the resources of the land, resolved to comply with the invitation, and, leaving behind a small detachment on the Mauretanian coast, embarked for Spain (about $\frac{674}{80}$). The straits separating Spain and Africa were occupied by a Roman squadron commanded by Cotta; to steal through it was impossible; so Sertorius fought his way through and succeeded in reaching the Lusitanians. There were not more than twenty Lusitanian communities that placed themselves under his orders; and of "Romans" he mustered only 2600 men, a considerable part of whom were deserters from the army of Pacciaecus or Africans armed after the Roman style. Sertorius saw that everything depended on his associating with the loose swarms of guerillas a strong nucleus of troops possessing Roman organisation and discipline: for this end he reinforced the band which he had brought with him by levying 4000 infantry and 700 cavalry, and with this one legion and the swarms of Spanish volunteers advanced against the Romans. The command in Further Spain was held by Lucius Fufidius, who through his absolute devotion to Sulla—so well-tried amidst the proscriptions—had risen from a subaltern to be propraetor; he was totally defeated on the Baetis; 2000 Romans covered the field of battle. Messengers in all haste summoned the governor of the adjoining province of the Ebro, Marcus Domitius Calvinus, to check the farther advance of the Sertorians; and there soon appeared ($\frac{675}{79}$) also the experienced general Quintus Metellus, sent by Sulla to relieve the incapable Fufidius in southern Spain. But they did not succeed in mastering the revolt. In the Ebro province not only was the army of Calvinus destroyed and he himself slain by Sertorius' lieutenant, the quaestor Lucius Hirtuleius, but Lucius Manlius, the governor of Transalpine Gaul, who had crossed the Pyrenees with three legions to help his colleague, was totally defeated by the same brave leader. With difficulty Manlius escaped with a few men to Ilerda (Lerida) and thence to his province, losing on the march his whole baggage through a sudden attack of the Aquitanian tribes. In Further Spain Metellus penetrated into the Lusitanian territory; but Sertorius succeeded during the siege of Longobriga (not far from the mouth of the Tagus) in alluring a division under Aquinus into an ambush, and thus compelling Metellus himself to raise the siege and to evacuate the Lusitanian territory. Sertorius followed him, defeated on the Anas (Guadiana) the corps of Thorius, and inflicted vast damage by guerilla warfare on the army of the commander-in-chief himself. Metellus, a methodical and somewhat clumsy tactician, was in despair as to this opponent, who obstinately declined a decisive battle, but cut off his supplies and communications and constantly hovered round him on all sides.

These extraordinary successes obtained by Sertorius in the two Spanish provinces were the more significant, that they were not achieved merely by arms and were not of a mere military nature. The emigrants as such were not formidable; nor were isolated successes of the Lusitanians under this or that foreign leader of much moment. But with the most decided political and patriotic tact Sertorius acted, whenever he could do so, not as *condottiere* of the Lusitanians in revolt against Rome, but as Roman general and governor of Spain, in which capacity he had in fact been sent thither by the former rulers. He began [1] to form the heads of the emigration into a senate, which was to increase to 300 members and to conduct affairs and to nominate magistrates in Roman form. He regarded his army as a Roman one, and filled the officers' posts, without exception, with Romans. With reference to the Spaniards he was the governor, who by virtue of his office levied troops and other support from them; but he was a governor who, instead of exercising the usual despotic sway, endeavoured to attach the provincials to Rome and to himself personally. His chivalrous character rendered it easy for him to enter into Spanish habits, and excited in the Spanish nobility the most ardent enthusiasm for the wonderful foreigner who had a spirit so kindred with their own. According to the warlike custom of personal following which subsisted in Spain as among the Celts and the Germans, thousands of the noblest Spaniards swore to stand faithfully by their Roman general unto death; and in them Sertorius found more trustworthy comrades than in his countrymen and party-associates.

[1] At least the outline of these organisations must be assigned to the years $\frac{674}{80}$, $\frac{675}{79}$, $\frac{676}{78}$, although the execution of them doubtless belonged, in great part, only to the subsequent years.

He did not disdain to turn to account the superstition of the ruder Spanish tribes, and to have his plans of war brought to him as commands of Diana by the white fawn of the goddess. Throughout he exercised a righteous and gentle rule. His troops, at least so far as his eye and his arm reached, had to maintain the strictest discipline. Gentle as he generally was in punishing, he showed himself inexorable when any outrage was perpetrated by his soldiers on friendly soil. Nor was he inattentive to the permanent relief of the condition of the provincials; he reduced the tribute, and directed the soldiers to construct winter barracks for themselves, so that the oppressive burden of quartering the troops was done away and thus a source of unspeakable mischief and annoyance was stopped. For the children of Spaniards of quality an academy was erected at Osca (Huesca), in which they received the higher instruction usual in Rome, learning to speak Latin and Greek, and to wear the toga—a remarkable measure, which was by no means designed merely to take from the allies in as gentle a form as possible the hostages that in Spain were inevitable, but was above all an emanation from, and an advance on, the great project of Gaius Gracchus and the democratic party for gradually Romanising the provinces. It was the first attempt to accomplish their Romanisation not by extirpating the old inhabitants and filling their places with Italian emigrants, but by Latinising the provincials themselves. The Optimates in Rome sneered at the wretched emigrants, the runaways from the Italian army, the relics of the robber-band of Carbo; the sorry taunt recoiled upon its authors. The masses that had been brought into the field against Sertorius were reckoned, including the Spanish general levy, at 120,000 infantry, 2000 archers and slingers, and 6000 cavalry. Against this enormous superiority of force Sertorius had not only held his ground in a series of successful conflicts and victories, but had also reduced the greater part of Spain under his power. In the Further province Metellus found himself confined to the districts immediately occupied by his troops; all the tribes, who could, had taken the side of Sertorius. In the Hither province, after the victories of Hirtuleius, there no longer existed a Roman army. Emissaries of Sertorius roamed through the whole territory of Gaul; there, too, the tribes began to stir, and bands gathering together began to make the Alpine passes insecure. The sea too belonged quite as much to the insurgents as to the legitimate government, since the allies of the former—the pirates—were almost as powerful in the Spanish waters as the Roman ships of war. At the promontory of Diana (between Valencia and Carthagena, opposite Ivica) Sertorius established for the corsairs a fixed station, where they lay in wait for such Roman ships as were conveying supplies to the Roman maritime towns and the army, carried away or delivered goods for the insurgents, and formed their medium of intercourse with Italy and Asia Minor. The constant readiness of these men moving to and fro to carry everywhere sparks from the scene of conflagration tended in a high degree to excite apprehension, especially at a time when so much combustible matter was everywhere accumulated in the Roman empire.

Amidst this state of matters the sudden death of Sulla took place ($\frac{676}{78}$). So long as the man lived at whose voice a trained and trustworthy army of veterans was ready any moment to rise, the oligarchy might tolerate the almost (as it seemed) definitive abandonment of the Spanish provinces to the emigrants, and the election of the leader of the opposition at home to be supreme magistrate, at all events as transient misfortunes; and in their shortsighted way, yet not wholly without reason, might cherish confidence either that the opposition would not venture to proceed to open conflict, or that, if it did venture, he who had twice saved the oligarchy would set it up a third time. Now the state of things was changed. The democratic Hotspurs in the capital, long impatient of the endless delay and inflamed by the brilliant news from Spain, urged that a blow should be struck; and Lepidus, with whom the decision at the moment lay, entered into the proposal with all the zeal of a renegade and with his own characteristic frivolity. For a moment it seemed as if the torch which kindled the funeral pile of the regent would also kindle civil war; but the influence of Pompey and the temper of the Sullan veterans induced the opposition to let the obsequies of the regent pass over in peace.

Yet all the more openly were arrangements thenceforth made for a fresh revolution. Daily the Forum resounded with accusations against the "mock Romulus" and his executioners. The overthrow of the Sullan constitution, the revival of the distributions of corn, the reinstating of the tribunes of the people in their former position, the recall of those who were banished contrary to law, the restoration of the confiscated lands, were openly indicated by Lepidus and his adherents as the objects at which they aimed. Communications were entered into with the proscribed; Marcus Perpenna, governor of Sicily in the days of Cinna (iii. 323), arrived in the capital. The sons of those whom

Sulla had declared guilty of treason—on whom the laws of the restoration bore with intolerable severity—and generally the more noted men of Marian views were invited to accede. Not a few, such as the young Lucius Cinna, joined the movement; others, however, followed the example of Gaius Caesar, who had returned home from Asia on receiving the accounts of the death of Sulla and of the plans of Lepidus, but after becoming more accurately acquainted with the character of the leader and of the movement prudently withdrew. Carousing and recruiting went on in behalf of Lepidus in the taverns and brothels of the capital. At length a conspiracy against the new order of things was concocted among the Etruscan malcontents.[1]

All this took place under the eyes of the government. The consul Catulus and the more judicious Optimates urged an immediate decisive interference and suppression of the revolt in the bud; the indolent majority, however, could not make up their minds to begin the struggle, but tried to deceive themselves as long as possible by a system of compromises and concessions. They yielded in respect to the corn law, and granted a limited renewal of the Gracchan distribution of grain, in doing which they probably returned to the mediating regulations made in the time of the Social war; according to these not all (as according to the Sempronian law) but only a definite number—it may be conjectured 40,000—of the poorer burgesses appear to have received the earlier largesses, as Gracchus had fixed them, of five *modii* monthly at the price of $6\frac{1}{3}$ *asses* (3*d.*)—a regulation which occasioned to the treasury an annual net loss of at least £40,000.[2] The opposition, naturally as little satisfied as it was

[1] The following narrative rests substantially on the account of Licinianus, which, fragmentary as it is at this very point, still gives important information as to the insurrection of Lepidus.

[2] Under the year $\frac{676}{78}$ Licinianus states (p. 23, Pertz; p. 42, Bonn); (*Lepidus ?*) [*le*]*gem frumentari*[*am*] *nullo resistente* [*adep ?*]*tus est, ut annon*[*ae*] *quinque modi popu*[*lo da*]*rentur*. According to this account, therefore, the law of the consuls of $\frac{681}{73}$ Marcus Terentius Lucullus and Gaius Cassius Varus, which Cicero mentions (*in Verr.* iii. 70, 136; v. 21, 52), and to which also Sallust refers (*Hist.* iii. 61, 19 Dietsch), did not first re-establish the five *modii*, but only secured the largesses of grain by regulating the purchases of Sicilian corn, and perhaps made various alterations of detail. That the Sempronian law (iii. 102) allowed every burgess domiciled in Rome to share in the largesses is certain; but this must have been subsequently departed from, for, seeing that the monthly corn of the Roman burgesses amounted to little more than 33,000 *medimni* = 198,000 *modii* (Cic. *Verr.* iii. 30, 72), only some 40,000 burgesses at that time received grain, whereas the number of burgesses domiciled in the capital was certainly far more considerable. This important alteration probably proceeded from the Octavian law, which introduced instead of the extravagant

decidedly emboldened by this partial concession, displayed all the more rudeness and violence in the capital; and in Etruria, the true centre of all insurrections of the Italian proletariate, civil war already broke out; the dispossessed Faesulans resumed possession of their lost estates by force of arms, and several of the veterans settled there by Sulla perished in the tumult. The senate on learning what had occurred, resolved to send the two consuls thither, in order to raise troops and suppress the insurrection.[1] It was impossible to adopt a more irrational course. The senate, in presence of the insurrection, evinced its pusillanimity and its fears by the re-establishment of the corn law; in order to be relieved from a street-riot, it furnished the notorious head of the insurrection with an army; and, when the two consuls were bound by the most solemn oath which could be contrived not to turn the arms entrusted to them against each other, it must have required the superhuman obduracy of oligarchic consciences to think of erecting such a bulwark against the impending insurrection. Of course Lepidus armed in Etruria not for the senate, but for the insurrection—sarcastically declaring that the oath which he had taken bound him only for the current year. The senate put the oracular machinery in motion to induce him to return, and committed to him the conduct of the impending consular elections; but Lepidus evaded compliance, and, while messengers passed to and fro and the official year drew to an end amidst proposals of accommodation, his force swelled to an army. When at length, in the beginning of the following year (677), the distinct injunction of the senate was issued to Lepidus to return without delay,

Sempronian amount "a moderate largess, tolerable for the state and necessary for the common people" (Cic. *de Off.* ii. 21, 72, *Brut.* 62, 222; see vol. iii. 223), and must have been again adopted in the law of $\frac{676}{78}$. The democracy was by no means content with this (Sallust, *l.c.*). The amount of loss is calculated on the basis of the grain being worth at least double (iii. 102); when piracy or other causes drove up the price of grain, a far more considerable loss must have ensued.

[1] From the fragments of the account of Licinianus (p. 44, Bonn) it is plain that the decree of the senate, *uti Lepidus et Catulus decretis exercitibus maturrime proficiscerentur* (Sallust, *Hist.* i. 44 Dietsch), is to be understood not of a despatch of the consuls before the expiry of their consulship to their proconsular provinces, for which there would have been no reason, but of their being sent to Etruria against the revolted Faesulans, just as in the Catilinarian war the consul Gaius Antonius was despatched to the same quarter. The statement of Philippus in Sallust (*Hist.* i. 48, 4) that Lepidus *ob seditionem provinciam cum exercitu adeptus est*, is entirely in harmony with this view; for the extraordinary consular command in Etruria was just as much a *provincia* as the ordinary proconsular command in Narbonese Gaul.

the proconsul haughtily refused obedience, and demanded in his turn the renewal of the former tribunician power, the reinstating of those who had been forcibly ejected from their civic rights and their property, and, besides this, his own re-election as consul for the current year or, in other words, the *tyrannis* in legal form.

Thus war was declared. The senatorial party could reckon, in addition to the Sullan veterans whose civil existence was threatened by Lepidus, upon the army assembled by the proconsul Catulus; and so, in compliance with the urgent warnings of the more sagacious, particularly of Philippus, Catulus was entrusted by the senate with the defence of the capital and the repelling of the main force of the democratic party stationed in Etruria. At the same time Gnaeus Pompeius was despatched with another corps to wrest from his former *protégé* the valley of the Po, which was held by Lepidus' lieutenant, Marcus Brutus. While Pompeius speedily accomplished his commission and shut up the enemy's general closely in Mutina, Lepidus appeared before the capital in order to conquer it for the revolution as Marius had formerly done by storm. The right bank of the Tiber fell wholly into his power, and he was able even to cross the river. The decisive battle was fought on the Campus Martius, close under the walls of the city. But Catulus conquered; and Lepidus was compelled to retreat to Etruria, while another division, under his son Scipio, threw itself into the fortress of Alba. The rising was substantially at an end. Mutina surrendered to Pompeius; and Brutus was, notwithstanding the safe-conduct promised to him, subsequently put to death by order of that general. Alba too was, after a long siege, reduced by famine, and the leader there was likewise executed. Lepidus, pressed on two sides by Catulus and Pompeius, fought another engagement on the coast of Etruria in order merely to procure the means of retreat, and then embarked at the port of Cosa for Sardinia, from which point he hoped to cut off the supplies of the capital, and to obtain communication with the Spanish insurgents. But the governor of the island opposed to him a vigorous resistance; and he himself died, not long after his landing, of consumption ($\frac{677}{77}$), whereupon the war in Sardinia came to an end. A part of his soldiers dispersed; with the flower of the insurrectionary army and with a well-filled chest the late praetor, Marcus Perpenna, proceeded to Liguria, and thence to Spain to join the Sertorians.

The oligarchy was thus victorious over Lepidus; but it found itself compelled by the dangerous turn of the Sertorian war to concessions, which violated the letter as well as the spirit of the Sullan constitution. It was absolutely necessary to send a strong army and an able general to Spain; and Pompeius indicated, very plainly, that he desired, or rather demanded, this commission. The pretension was bold. It was bad enough that they had allowed this secret opponent again to attain an extraordinary command in the pressure of the Lepidian revolution; but it was far more hazardous to set aside all the rules instituted by Sulla for the magisterial hierarchy, so as to invest a man who had hitherto filled no civil office with one of the most important ordinary provincial governorships, under circumstances in which the observance of the legal term of a year was not to be thought of. The oligarchy had thus, even apart from the respect due to their general Metellus, good reason to oppose with all earnestness this new attempt of the ambitious youth to perpetuate his exceptional position. But this was not easy. In the first place, they had not a single man fitted for the difficult post of general in Spain. Neither of the consuls of the year showed any desire to match himself against Sertorius; and what Lucius Philippus said in a full meeting of the senate had to be admitted as too true—that, among all the senators of note, not one was able and willing to command in a serious war. Yet they might, perhaps, have got over this, and after the manner of oligarchs, when they had no capable candidate, have filled the place with some makeshift, if Pompeius had merely desired the command and had not demanded it at the head of an army. He had already lent a deaf ear to the injunctions of Catulus that he should dismiss the army; it was at least doubtful whether those of the senate would find a better reception, and the consequences of a breach no one could calculate—the scale of aristocracy might very easily mount up, if the sword of a well-known general were thrown into the opposite scale. So the majority resolved on concession. Not from the people, which constitutionally ought to have been consulted in a case where a private man was to be invested with the supreme magisterial power, but from the senate, Pompeius received proconsular authority and the chief command in Hither Spain; and, forty days after he had received it, crossed the Alps in the summer of $\frac{677}{77}$.

First of all the new general found employment in Gaul, where no formal insurrection had broken out, but serious disturbances of the peace had occurred at several places; in consequence of which Pompeius deprived the cantons of the Volcae-Arecomici and the Helvii of their independence, and placed them under Massilia. He also laid out a new road over the Cottian Alps (Mont Genèvre, ii. 98), and so established a shorter communication between the valley of the Po and Gaul. Amidst this work the best season of the year passed away; it was not till late in autumn that Pompeius crossed the Pyrenees.

Sertorius had meanwhile not been idle. He had despatched Hirtuleius into the Further province to keep Metellus in check, and had himself endeavoured to follow up his complete victory in the Hither province, and to prepare for the reception of Pompeius. The isolated Celtiberian towns there, which still adhered to Rome, were attacked and reduced one after another; at last, in the very middle of winter, the strong Contrebia (south-east of Saragossa) had fallen. In vain the hard-pressed towns had sent message after message to Pompeius; he would not be induced by any entreaties to depart from his wonted course of slow progression. With the exception of the maritime towns, which were defended by the Roman fleet, and the districts of the Indigetes and Laletani in the north-east corner of Spain, where Pompeius established himself after he had at length crossed the Pyrenees, and made his raw troops bivouac throughout the winter to inure them to hardships, the whole of Hither Spain had at the end of $\frac{677}{77}$ become by treaty or force dependent on Sertorius, and the district on the upper and middle Ebro thenceforth continued the main stay of his power. Even the apprehension, which the fresh Roman force and the celebrated name of the general excited in the army of the insurgents, had a salutary effect on it. Marcus Perpenna, who hitherto as the equal of Sertorius in rank had claimed an independent command over the force which he had brought with him from Liguria, was, on the news of Pompeius' arrival in Spain, compelled by his soldiers to place himself under the orders of his abler colleague.

For the campaign of $\frac{678}{76}$ Sertorius again employed the corps of Hirtuleius against Metellus, while Perpenna with a strong army took up his position along the lower course of the Ebro to prevent Pompeius from crossing the river, if he should march, as was to be expected, in a southerly direction with the view of effecting a junction with Metellus, and along the coast for the sake of procuring supplies for his troops. The corps of Gaius Herennius was destined to the immediate support of Perpenna; farther inland on the upper Ebro Sertorius in person prosecuted meanwhile the subjugation of several districts friendly to Rome, and held himself at the same time ready to hasten according to circumstances to the aid of Perpenna or Hirtuleius. It was still his intention to avoid any pitched battle, and to annoy the enemy by petty conflicts and cutting off supplies.

Pompeius, however, not only forced the passage of the Ebro against Perpenna, but also totally defeated Herennius at Valentia (Valencia), and possessed himself of that important town. It was time that Sertorius should appear in person, and throw the superiority of his numbers and of his genius into the scale against the greater excellence of the soldiers of his opponent. For a considerable time the struggle was concentrated around the town of Lauro (on the Xucar, south of Valencia), which had declared for Pompeius and was on that account besieged by Sertorius. Pompeius exerted himself to the utmost to relieve it; but, after several of his divisions had already been assailed separately and cut to pieces, the great warrior found himself—just when he thought that he had surrounded the Sertorians, and when he had invited the besieged to be spectators of the capture of the besieging army—all of a sudden completely outmanœuvred; and in order that he might not be himself surrounded, he had to look on from his camp at the capture and burning of the allied town and the carrying off of its inhabitants to Lusitania—an event which induced a number of towns that were wavering in middle and eastern Spain to adhere anew to Sertorius.

Meanwhile Metellus fought with better fortune. In a sharp engagement near Italica (not far from Seville), which Hirtuleius had imprudently risked, and in which both generals fought hand to hand and Hirtuleius was wounded, Metellus defeated him and compelled him to evacuate the Roman territory proper, and to throw himself into Lusitania. This victory permitted Metellus in the next campaign ($\frac{679}{75}$) to enter on his march towards Hither Spain, with the view of joining Pompeius in the region of Valentia, and in concert with him offering battle to the main force of the enemy. Hirtuleius, with a hastily collected army, sought to intercept him at Segovia; he was, however, not merely defeated, but was himself slain along with his brother—an irreparable loss to the Sertorians. After this the union of the two Roman generals could no longer be prevented; but, while Metellus was advancing towards Valentia, Pompeius offered battle beforehand to the main army of the enemy, with a view to wipe out the stain of Lauro and to gain the expected laurels, if possible, alone. With joy Sertorius embraced the opportunity of fighting with Pompeius before Metellus arrived and the death of Hirtuleius transpired.

The armies met on the river Sucro (Xucar): after a sharp conflict Pompeius was beaten on the right wing, and was himself carried from the field severely wounded; Afranius conquered with the left and took the camp of the Sertorians, but during its pillage he was suddenly assailed by Sertorius and compelled also to give way. Had Sertorius been able to renew the battle on the following day, the army of Pompeius would perhaps have been annihilated. But meanwhile Metellus had come up, had overthrown the corps of Perpenna ranged against him, and taken his camp: it was not possible to resume the battle against the two armies united. The junction of the hostile forces, the certainty which thenceforth could no longer be concealed that the army of Hirtuleius had perished, the sudden stagnation after the victory, diffused terror among the Sertorians; and, as not unfrequently happened with Spanish armies, in consequence of this turn of things the greater portion of the Sertorian soldiers dispersed. But the despondency passed away as quickly as it had come; the white fawn, which represented in the eyes of the multitude the military plans of the general, was soon more popular than ever; in a short time Sertorius appeared with a new army confronting the Romans in the level country to the south of Saguntum (Murviedro), which firmly adhered to Rome, while the Sertorian privateers interfered with the Roman supplies by sea, and scarcity was already making itself felt in the Roman camp. Another battle took place in the plains of the river Turia (Guadalaviar), and the struggle was long undecided. Pompeius with the cavalry was defeated by Sertorius, and his brother-in-law and quaestor, the brave Lucius Memmius, was slain; on the other hand Metellus vanquished Perpenna, and victoriously repelled the attack of the enemy's main army directed against him, receiving himself a wound in the conflict. Once more the Sertorian army dispersed. Valentia, which Gaius Herennius held for Sertorius, was taken and razed to the ground. The Romans, probably for a moment, entertained a hope that they were done with their tough antagonist. The Sertorian army had disappeared; the Roman troops, penetrating far into the interior, besieged the general himself in the fortress Clunia on the upper Douro. But while they vainly invested this rocky stronghold, the contingents of the insurgent communities assembled elsewhere; Sertorius stole out of the fortress and stood once more as general at the head of an army, when the eventful year $\frac{679}{75}$ came to an end.

Yet the Romans at home had reason to be content with the results of this campaign. Southern and central Spain was delivered from the enemy in consequence of the destruction of the Hirtuleian army and the battles on the Xucar and Guadalaviar, and was permanently secured through the occupation of the Celtiberian towns Segobriga (between Toledo and Cuenca) and Bilbilis (near Calatayud) by Metellus. The struggle was thenceforth concentrated on the upper and middle Ebro, around the chief strongholds of the Sertorians, Calagurris, Osca, Ilerda, and on the coast around Tarraco. Although both Roman generals had fought bravely, it was not to Pompeius, but to Metellus that the success was mainly due.

But although not a little was gained, the Romans had by no means attained their object; and they had again to take up their winter quarters with the cheerless prospect of an inevitable renewal of their Sisyphean labours. It was not possible to choose quarters in the valley of the lower Ebro, so fearfully devastated by friend and foe; Pompeius spent the winter in the territory of the Vaccaei (about Valladolid), and Metellus even in Gaul. Reinforced by two fresh legions despatched from Italy, the two generals began their operations anew in the spring of $\frac{680}{74}$. No more battles, in the proper sense, were fought; Sertorius confined himself wholly to guerilla and siege warfare. Metellus reduced the places that still adhered to Sertorius in southern Spain, and everywhere, in order to stop the sources of insurrection, carried the whole male population away with him. Pompeius had a more difficult position in the province of the Ebro. Pallantia (Palencia above Valladolid), which he besieged, was relieved by Sertorius; in front of Calagurris (Calahorra, on the upper Ebro) he was defeated by Sertorius and compelled to leave those regions, although Metellus had united with him in order to the siege of that town. After Metellus had wintered in his province and Pompeius in Gaul, the campaign of $\frac{681}{73}$ was conducted in a similar fashion; but Pompeius gained in this year more permanent successes, and induced a considerable number of communities to withdraw from the insurrection.

To eight years the Sertorian war thus continued, and yet there seemed no prospect of its termination. The state suffered from it beyond description. The flower of the Italian youth perished amid the exhausting fatigues of Spanish warfare. The public treasury was not only deprived of the Spanish revenues, but had annually to send to Spain for the pay and maintenance of the Spanish armies very considerable sums, which the government hardly knew how to raise. Spain was devastated and impoverished, and the Roman civilisation, which presented so fair a promise there, received a severe shock; as was naturally to be expected in the case of an insurrectionary war waged with so much bitterness, and but too often occasioning the destruction of whole communities. Even the towns which adhered to the dominant party in Rome had countless hardships to endure; those situated on the coast had to be provided with necessaries by the Roman fleet, and the situation of the faithful communities in the interior was almost desperate. Gaul suffered hardly less, partly from the requisitions for contingents of infantry and cavalry, for grain and money, partly from the oppressive burden of the winter quarters, which rose to an intolerable degree in consequence of the bad harvest of $\frac{680}{74}$; almost all the local treasuries were compelled to betake themselves to the Roman bankers, and to burden themselves with a crushing load of debt. Generals and soldiers carried on the war with reluctance. The generals had encountered an opponent far superior in talent, a tediously pertinacious resistance, a warfare of very serious perils and of successes difficult to be attained, and far from brilliant; it was asserted that Pompeius was scheming to get himself recalled from Spain and entrusted with a more desirable command elsewhere. The soldiers, too, found little satisfaction in a campaign in which not only was there nothing to be got save hard blows and worthless booty, but their very pay was doled out to them with extreme irregularity. Pompeius reported to the senate, in the winter of $\frac{680}{74}-\frac{681}{73}$, that the pay was two years in arrear, and that the army threatened to disband if the senate did not devise ways and means; whereupon at length the needful sums came. The Roman government might certainly have obviated a considerable portion of these evils, if they could have prevailed on themselves to carry on the Spanish war with less remissness, to say nothing of better will. In the main, however, it was neither their fault nor the fault of their generals that a genius so superior as that of Sertorius was able to carry on this guerilla war year after year, despite of all numerical superiority, in a country so thoroughly favourable to insurrectionary and piratical warfare. So little could its end be foreseen, that the Sertorian insurrection seemed rather as if it would become intermingled with other contemporary revolts and thereby add to its dangerous character. Just at that time the Romans were contending on every sea with piratical fleets, in Italy with the revolted slaves, in Macedonia with the tribes of the lower Danube, in Asia Minor once more with king Mithradates. That Sertorius had formed connections with the Italian and Macedonian enemies of Rome cannot be distinctly affirmed, although he certainly was in constant intercourse with the Marians in Italy. With the pirates, on the other hand, he had previously formed an avowed league, and with the Pontic king—with whom he had long maintained relations through the medium of the Roman emigrants staying at his court—he now concluded a formal treaty of alliance, in which Sertorius ceded to the king the client-states of Asia Minor, but not the Roman province of Asia, and promised, moreover, to send him an officer qualified to lead his troops, and a number of soldiers, while the king, in turn, bound himself to transmit to Sertorius forty ships and 3000 talents (£720,000). The wise politicians in the capital were already recalling the time when Italy found itself threatened by Philip from the east and by Hannibal from the west; they conceived that the new Hannibal, just like his predecessor, after having by himself subdued Spain, could easily arrive with the forces of Spain in Italy sooner than Pompeius, in order that, like the Phoenician formerly, he might summon the Etruscans and Samnites to arms against Rome.

But this comparison was more ingenious than accurate. Sertorius was far from being strong enough to renew the gigantic enterprise of Hannibal. He was lost if he left Spain, where all his successes were bound up with the peculiarities of the country and the people; and even there he was more and more compelled to renounce the offensive. His admirable skill as a leader could not change the nature of his troops. The Spanish militia retained its character, untrustworthy as the wave or the wind; now collected in masses to the number of 150,000, now melting away again to a mere handful. The Roman emigrants, likewise, continued insubordinate, arrogant, and stubborn. Those kinds of armed force which require that a corps should keep together for a considerable time, such as cavalry especially, were of course very inadequately represented in his army. The war gradually swept off his ablest officers and the flower of his veterans; and even the most trustworthy communities, weary of being harassed by the Romans and ill-used by the Sertorian officers, began to show signs of impatience and wavering allegiance. It is remarkable that Sertorius, in this respect also like Hannibal, never deceived himself as to the hopelessness of his position; he allowed no opportunity for bringing about a compromise to pass, and was ready at any moment to lay down his command on the assurance of being allowed to live peacefully in his native land. But political orthodoxy knows nothing of compromise and conciliation. Sertorius might not recede or step aside; he was compelled inevitably to move on along the path which he had once entered, however narrow and giddy it might become. His military successes too, like those of Hannibal, of necessity became less and less considerable; people began to call in question his military talent; he was no longer, it was alleged, what he had been; he spent the day in feasting or over his cups, and squandered money as well as time.

The number of the deserters, and of communities falling away, increased. Soon projects formed by the Roman emigrants against the life of the general were reported to him; they sounded credible enough, especially as various officers of the insurgent army, and Perpenna in particular, had submitted with reluctance to the supremacy of Sertorius, and the Roman governors had for long promised amnesty and a high reward to any one who should kill him. Sertorius on hearing such allegations withdrew the charge of guarding his person from the Roman soldiers and entrusted it to select Spaniards. Against the suspected themselves he proceeded with fearful but necessary severity, and condemned various of the accused to death without resorting, as in other cases, to the advice of his council; he was now more dangerous—it was thereupon affirmed in the circles of the malcontents—to his friends than to his foes.

A second conspiracy was soon discovered, which had its seat in his own staff; whoever was denounced had to take flight or die; but all were not betrayed, and the remaining conspirators, including especially Perpenna, found in the circumstances only a new incentive to make haste. They were in the head-quarters at Osca. There, on the instigation of Perpenna, a brilliant victory was reported to the general as having been achieved by his troops; and at the festal banquet arranged by Perpenna to celebrate this victory Sertorius accordingly appeared, attended, as was his wont, by his Spanish retinue. Contrary to former custom in the Sertorian head-quarters, the feast soon became a revel; foul words passed at table, and it seemed as if some of the guests sought opportunity to begin an altercation. Sertorius threw himself back on his couch, and seemed desirous not to hear the disturbance. Then a wine-cup was dashed on the floor; Perpenna had given the concerted sign. Marcus Antonius, Sertorius' neighbour at table, dealt the first blow against him, and when Sertorius turned round and attempted to rise, the assassin flung himself upon him and held him down till the other guests at table, all of them implicated in the conspiracy, threw themselves on the struggling pair, and stabbed the defenceless general while his arms were pinioned ($\frac{682}{72}$). With him died his faithful attendants. So ended one of the greatest men, if not the very greatest man, that Rome had hitherto produced—a man who under more fortunate circumstances would perhaps have become the regenerator of his country—by the treason of the wretched band of emigrants whom he was condemned to lead against his native land. History loves not the Coriolani; nor has she made any exception even in the case of this the most magnanimous, most gifted, most deserving to be regretted of them all.

The murderers thought to succeed to the heritage of the murdered. After the death of Sertorius, Perpenna, as the highest among the Roman officers of the Spanish army, laid claim to the chief command. The army submitted, but with mistrust and reluctance. However men had murmured against Sertorius in his lifetime, death reinstated the hero in his rights, and vehement was the indignation of the soldiers when, on the publication of his testament, the name of Perpenna was read forth among the heirs. A part of the soldiers, especially the Lusitanians, dispersed; the remainder had a presentiment that with the death of Sertorius their spirit and their fortune had departed.

Accordingly, at the first encounter with Pompeius, the wretchedly led and despondent ranks of the insurgents were utterly broken, and Perpenna, among other officers, was taken prisoner. The wretch sought to purchase his life by delivering up the correspondence of Sertorius, which would have compromised numerous men of standing in Italy; but Pompeius ordered the papers to be burnt unread, and handed him, as well as the other chiefs of the insurgents, over to the executioner. The emigrants who had escaped dispersed; and most of them went into the Mauretanian deserts or joined the pirates. Soon afterwards the Plotian law, which was zealously supported by the young Caesar in particular, opened up to a portion of them the opportunity of returning home; but all those who had taken part in the murder of Sertorius, with but a single exception, died a violent death. Osca, and most of the towns which had still adhered to Sertorius in Hither Spain, now voluntarily opened their gates to Pompeius; Uxama (Osma), Clunia, and Calagurris alone had to be reduced by force. The two provinces were regulated anew; in the Further province, Metellus raised the annual tribute of the most guilty communities; in the Hither, Pompeius dispensed reward and punishment: Calagurris, for example, lost its independence and was placed under Osca. A band of Sertorian soldiers, which had collected in the Pyrenees, was induced by Pompeius to surrender, and was settled by him to the north of the Pyrenees near Lugudunum (St. Bertrand, in the department Haute-Garonne), as the community of the "assembled" (*convenae*). The Roman emblems of victory were erected at the summit of the pass of the Pyrenees; at the close of $\frac{683}{71}$, Metellus and Pompeius marched with their armies through the streets of the capital, to present the thanks of the nation to Father Jovis at the Capitol for the conquest of the Spaniards. The good fortune of Sulla seemed still to be with his creation after he had been laid in the grave, and to protect it better than the incapable and negligent watchmen appointed to guard it. The opposition in Italy had broken down from the incapacity and precipitation of its leader, and that of the emigrants from dissension within their own ranks. These defeats, although far more the result of their own perverseness and discordance than of the exertions of their opponents, were yet so many victories for the oligarchy. The curule chairs were rendered once more secure.

CHAPTER II

RULE OF THE SULLAN RESTORATION

When the suppression of the Cinnan revolution, which threatened the existence of the senate, rendered it possible for the restored senatorial government to devote the requisite attention to the internal and external security of the empire, various matters presented themselves, the settlement of which could not be postponed without injuring the most important interests and allowing present inconveniences to grow into future dangers. Apart from the very serious complications in Spain, it was absolutely necessary effectually to check the barbarians in Thrace and the regions of the Danube, whom Sulla on his march through Macedonia had only been able slightly to chastise (iii. 292), and to regulate, by military intervention, the disorderly state of things along the northern frontier of the Greek peninsula; thoroughly to suppress the bands of pirates infesting the seas everywhere, but especially the eastern waters; and to introduce better order into the unsettled relations of Asia Minor. The peace which Sulla had concluded in $\frac{670}{84}$ with Mithradates, king of Pontus (iii. 291), and of which the treaty with Murena in $\frac{673}{81}$ (iii. 325) was essentially a repetition, bore throughout the stamp of a provisional arrangement to meet the exigencies of the moment; and the relations of the Romans with Tigranes, king of Armenia, with whom they had *de facto* waged war, remained wholly untouched in this peace. Tigranes had with right regarded this as a tacit permission to bring the Roman possessions in Asia under his power. If these were not to be abandoned, it was necessary to come to terms amicably or by force with the new great king of Asia.

In the preceding chapter we have described the movements in Italy and Spain connected with the proceedings of the democracy, and their subjugation by the senatorial government. In the present chapter we shall review the external government, as the authorities installed by Sulla conducted, or failed to conduct, it.

We still recognise the vigorous hand of Sulla in the energetic measures which, in the last period of his regency, the senate adopted almost simultaneously against the Sertorians, the Dalmatians and Thracians, and the Cilician pirates.

The expedition to the Graeco-Illyrian peninsula was designed partly to reduce to subjection or at least to tame the barbarous tribes who ranged over the whole interior from the Black Sea to the Adriatic, and of whom the Bessi (in the great Balkan) especially were, as it was then said, notorious as robbers even among a race of robbers; partly to destroy the corsairs in their haunts, especially along the Dalmatian coast. As usual, the attack took place simultaneously from Dalmatia and from Macedonia, in which province an army of five legions was assembled for the purpose. In Dalmatia the former praetor Gaius Cosconius held the command, marched through the country in all directions, and took by storm the fortress of Salona after a two years' siege. In Macedonia the proconsul Appius Claudius ($\frac{676-678}{78-76}$) first attempted along the Macedono-Thracian frontier to make himself master of the mountain districts on the left bank of the Karasu. On both sides the war was conducted with savage ferocity; the Thracians destroyed the places which they took and massacred their captives, and the Romans returned like for like. But no results of importance were attained; the toilsome marches and the constant conflicts with the numerous and brave inhabitants of the mountains decimated the army to no purpose; the general himself sickened and died. His successor, Gaius Scribonius Curio ($\frac{679-681}{75-73}$), was induced by various obstacles, and particularly by a not inconsiderable military revolt, to desist from the difficult expedition against the Thracians, and to turn himself instead to the northern frontier of Macedonia, where he subdued the weaker Dardani (in Servia) and reached as far as the Danube. The brave and able Marcus Lucullus ($\frac{682}{72}$, $\frac{683}{71}$) again advanced eastward, defeated the Bessi in their mountains, took their capital Uscudama or Philippopolis (Adrianople), and compelled them to submit to the Roman supremacy. Sadalas king of the Odrysians, and the Greek towns on the east coast to the north and south of the Balkan chain—Istropolis, Tomi, Callatis, Odessus (near Varna), Mesembria, and others—became dependent on the Romans. Thrace, of which the Romans had hitherto held little more than the Attalic possessions on the Chersonese, now became a portion—though far from obedient—of the province of Macedonia.

But the predatory raids of the Thracians and Dardani, confined as they were to a small part of the empire, were far less injurious to the state and to individuals than the evil of piracy, which was continually spreading farther and acquiring more solid organisation. The commerce of the whole Mediterranean was in its power. Italy could neither export its own products nor import grain from the provinces; in the former the people were starving, in the latter the cultivation of the corn-fields ceased for want of a vent for the produce. No consignment of money, no traveller was longer safe; the public treasury suffered most serious losses; a great many Romans of rank were captured by the corsairs, and compelled to pay heavy sums for their ransom, except in special instances where it was the pleasure of the pirates to execute the sentence of death, seasoning their proceedings with a savage humour. The merchants, and even the divisions of Roman troops destined for the East, began to postpone their voyages chiefly to the unfavourable season of the year, and to be less afraid of the winter storms than of the piratical vessels, which indeed even at this season did not wholly disappear from sea. But severely as the closing of the sea was felt, it was more tolerable than the raids made on the islands and coasts of Greece and Asia Minor. Just as afterwards in the time of the Normans, piratical squadrons ran up to the maritime towns, and either compelled them to buy themselves off with large sums, or besieged and took them by storm. When Samothrace, Clazomenae, Samos, Iassus were pillaged by the pirates ($\frac{670}{84}$) under the eyes of Sulla after peace was concluded with Mithradates, we may conceive how matters went on where neither a Roman army nor a Roman fleet was at hand. All the old rich temples along the coasts of Greece and Asia Minor were plundered one after another; from Samothrace alone a treasure of 1000 talents (£240,000) is said to have been carried off. Apollo, according to a Roman poet of this period, was so impoverished by the pirates that, when the swallow paid him a visit, he could no longer produce to it out of all his treasures even a drachm of gold. More than four hundred townships were enumerated as having been taken or laid under contribution by the pirates, including cities like Cnidus, Samos, Colophon; from not a few places on islands or the coast, which were previously flourishing, the whole population migrated, that they might not be carried off by the pirates. Even inland districts were no longer safe from their attacks; they occasionally assailed places distant one or two days' march from the coast. The fearful debt, under which subsequently all the communities of the Greek East succumbed, proceeded in great part from these fatal times.

Piracy had totally changed its character. The pirates were no longer bold freebooters, who levied their tribute from the large Italo-Oriental traffic in slaves and luxuries, as it passed through the Cretan waters between Cyrene and the Peloponnesus—in the language of the pirates the "golden sea;" no longer even armed slave-catchers, who prosecuted "war, trade, and piracy" side by side; they formed now a piratical state, with a peculiar *esprit de corps*, with a solid and very respectable organisation, with a home of their own and the germs of a symmachy, and doubtless also with definite political designs. The pirates called themselves Cilicians; in fact their vessels were the rendezvous of desperadoes and adventurers from all countries—discharged mercenaries from the recruiting-grounds of Crete, burgesses from the destroyed townships of Italy, Spain, and Asia, soldiers and officers from the armies of Fimbria and Sertorius, in a word the ruined men of all nations, the hunted refugees of all vanquished parties, every one that was wretched and daring—and where was there not misery and violence in this unhappy age? It was no longer a gang of robbers who had flocked together, but a compact soldier-state, in which the freemasonry of exile and crime took the place of nationality, and within which crime redeemed itself, as it so often does in its own eyes, by displaying the most generous public spirit. In an abandoned age, when cowardice and insubordination had relaxed all the bonds of social order, the legitimate commonwealths might have taken a pattern from this state—the mongrel offspring of distress and violence—within which alone the inviolable determination to stand side by side, the sense of fellowship, respect for the pledged word and the self-chosen chiefs, valour and adroitness seemed to have taken refuge. If the banner of this state was inscribed with vengeance against the civil society which, rightly or wrongly, had ejected its members, it might be a question whether this device was much worse than those of the Italian oligarchy and the Oriental sultanship which seemed in the course of dividing the world between them. The corsairs at least felt themselves on a level with any legitimate state; their robber-pride, their robber-pomp, and their robber-humour are attested by many a genuine pirate's tale of outrageous merriment and chivalrous bandittism: they professed, and made it their boast, to live at righteous war with all the world: what they gained in that warfare they designated not as plunder, but as military spoil; and, while the captured corsair was sure of the cross in every Roman seaport, they too claimed the right of executing any of their captives. Their military-political organisation, especially since the Mithradatic war, was compact. Their ships, for the most part *myoparones,* that is, small open swift-sailing barks, with a smaller proportion of biremes and triremes, now regularly sailed associated in squadrons and under admirals, whose barges were wont to glitter in gold and purple. To a comrade in peril, though he might be totally unknown, no pirate captain refused the requested aid; an agreement concluded with any one of them was absolutely recognised by the whole society, and any injury inflicted on one was avenged by all. Their true home was the sea from the pillars of Hercules to the Syrian and Egyptian waters; the refuges which they needed for themselves and their floating houses on the mainland were readily furnished to them by the Mauretanian and Dalmatian coasts, by the island of Crete, and, above all, by the southern coast of Asia Minor, which abounded in headlands and hiding places, commanded the chief thoroughfare of the maritime commerce of that age, and was virtually without a master. The league of Lycian cities there, and the Pamphylian communities, were of little importance; the Roman station, which had existed in Cilicia since $\frac{652}{102}$, was far from adequate to command the extensive coast; the Syrian dominion over Cilicia had always been but nominal, and had recently been superseded by the Armenian, the holder of which, as a true great king, gave himself no concern about the sea and readily abandoned it to the pillage of the Cilicians. It was nothing wonderful, therefore, that the corsairs flourished there as they had never done elsewhere. Not only did they possess everywhere along the coast signal-places and stations, but farther inland—in the most remote recesses of the impassable and mountainous interior of Lycia, Pamphylia, and Cilicia—they had built their rock-castles, in which they concealed their wives, children, and treasures during their own absence at sea, and, doubtless, in times of danger found an asylum themselves. Great numbers of such corsair-castles existed especially in the Rough Cilicia, the forests of which at the same time furnished the pirates with the most excellent timber for ship-building; and there, accordingly, their principal dockyards and arsenals were situated. It was not to be wondered at that this organised military state gained a firm body of clients among the Greek maritime cities, which were more or less left to themselves and managed their own affairs: these cities entered into traffic with the pirates as with a friendly power on the basis of definite treaties, and did not comply with the summons of the Roman governors to furnish vessels against them. The not inconsiderable town of Side in Pamphylia, for instance, allowed the pirates to build ships on its quays, and to sell the free men whom they had captured in its market.

Such a society of pirates was a political power; and as a political power it gave itself out and was accepted from the time when the Syrian king Tryphon first employed it as such and supported his throne by it (iii. 62). We find the pirates as allies of Mithradates of Pontus as well as of the Roman democratic emigrants; we find them giving battle to the fleets of Sulla in the eastern and in the western waters; we find individual pirate princes ruling over a series of considerable coast towns. We cannot tell how far the internal political development of this floating state had already advanced; but its arrangements undeniably contained the germ of a sea-kingdom, which was already beginning to establish itself, and out of which, under favourable circumstances, a permanent state might have been developed.

This state of matters clearly shows, as we have partly indicated already (iii. 61), how the Romans kept—or rather did not keep—order on "their sea." The protectorate of Rome over the provinces consisted essentially in military guardianship; the provincials paid tax or tribute to the Romans for their defence by sea and land, which was concentrated in Roman hands. But never, perhaps, did a guardian more shamelessly defraud his ward than the Roman oligarchy defrauded the subject communities. Instead of Rome equipping a general fleet for the empire and centralising her marine police, the senate permitted the unity of superintendence—without which in this matter nothing could be done—to fall into abeyance, and left it to each governor and each client state to defend themselves against the pirates as each chose and was able. Instead of Rome providing for the fleet as she had bound herself to do, exclusively with her own blood and treasure and with those of the client states, which had remained formally sovereign, the senate allowed the Italian war-marine to decay, and learned to make shift with the vessels which the several mercantile towns were required to furnish, or still more frequently with the coast-guards everywhere organised—all the cost and burden falling, in either case, on the subjects. The provincials might deem themselves fortunate if their Roman governor applied the requisitions which he raised for the defence of the coast in reality solely to that object, and did not intercept them for himself; or if they were not, as very frequently happened, called on to pay ransom for some Roman of rank captured by the buccaneers. Measures undertaken perhaps with judgment, such as the occupation of Cilicia in $\frac{652}{102}$, were sure to be spoilt in the execution. Any Roman of this period, who was not wholly carried away by the current intoxicating idea of the national greatness must have wished that the ships' beaks might be torn down from the orator's platform in the Forum, that at least he might not be constantly reminded by them of the naval victories achieved in better times.

Nevertheless Sulla, who in the war against Mithradates had the opportunity of acquiring an adequate conviction of the dangers which the neglect of the fleet involved, took various steps seriously to check the evil. It is true that the instructions which he had left to the governors whom he appointed in Asia, to equip in the maritime towns a fleet against the pirates, had borne little fruit, for Murena preferred to begin war with Mithradates, and Gnaeus Dolabella, the governor of Cilicia, proved wholly incapable. Accordingly the senate resolved in $\frac{675}{79}$ to send one of the consuls to Cilicia; the lot fell on the able Publius Servilius. He defeated the piratical fleet in a bloody engagement, and then applied himself to destroy those towns on the south coast of Asia Minor which served them as anchorages and trading stations. The fortresses of the powerful maritime prince Zenicetes—Olympus, Corycus, Phaselis in eastern Lycia, Attalia in Pamphylia—were reduced, and the prince himself met his death in the flames of his stronghold Olympus. A movement was next made against the Isaurians, who in the north-west corner of the Rough Cilicia, on the northern slope of Mount Taurus, inhabited a labyrinth of steep mountain ridges, jagged rocks, and deep valleys, covered with magnificent oak forests—a region which is even at the present day filled with reminiscences of the old robber times. To reduce these Isaurian fastnesses, the last and most secure retreats of the freebooters, Servilius led the first Roman army over the Taurus, and broke up the stongholds of the enemy Oroanda, and above all Isaura itself—the ideal of a robber-town, situated on the summit of a scarcely accessible mountain chain, and completely overlooking and commanding the wide plain of Iconium. The three years' campaign ($\frac{676}{78}$–$\frac{678}{76}$), from which Publius Servilius acquired for himself and his descendants the surname of Isauricus, was not without fruit; a great number of pirates and piratical vessels fell in consequence of it into the power of the Romans; Lycia, Pamphylia, West Cilicia were severely devastated, the territories of the destroyed towns were confiscated, and the province of Cilicia was enlarged by their addition. But, in the nature of the case, piracy was far from being suppressed by these measures; on the contrary, it simply betook itself for the time to other regions, and particularly to Crete, the oldest harbour for the corsairs of the Mediterranean (iii. 61). Nothing but repressive measures carried out on a large scale and with unity of purpose—nothing, in fact, but the establishment of a standing maritime police—could in such a case afford thorough relief.

The affairs of the mainland of Asia Minor were connected by various relations with this maritime war. The variance which existed between Rome and the kings of Pontus and Armenia did not abate, but increased more and more. On the one hand Tigranes, king of Armenia, pursued his aggressive conquests in the most reckless manner. The Parthians, whose state was at this period torn by internal dissensions and enfeebled, were by constant hostilities driven farther and farther back into the interior of Asia. Of the countries between Armenia, Mesopotamia, and Iran, the kingdoms of Corduene (northern Kurdistan), and Media Atropatene (Azerbijan), were converted from Parthian into Armenian fiefs, and the kingdom of Nineveh (Mosul), or Adiabene, was likewise compelled, at least temporarily, to become a dependency of Armenia. In Mesopotamia, too, particularly in and around Nisibis, the Armenian rule was established; but the southern half, which was in great part desert, seems not to have passed into the firm possession of the new great king, and Seleucia, on the Tigris, in particular, appears not to have been subject to him. The kingdom of Edessa or Osroene he handed over to a tribe of wandering Arabs, which he transplanted from southern Mesopotamia and settled in this region, with the view of commanding by its means the passage of the Euphrates and the great route of traffic.[1]

[1] The foundation of the kingdom of Edessa is placed by native chronicles in $\frac{620}{134}$ (iii. 59), but it was not till some time after its rise that it passed into the hands of the Arabic dynasty bearing the names of Abgarus and Mannus, which we afterwards find there. This dynasty is obviously connected with the settlement of many Arabs by Tigranes the Great in the region of Edessa, Callirrhoe, Carrhae (Plin. *H. N.* v. 20, 85; 21, 86; vi. 28, 142); respecting which Plutarch also (*Luc.* 21) states that Tigranes, changing the habits of the tent-Arabs, settled them nearer to his kingdom in order by their means to possess himself of the trade. We may probably take this to mean that

But Tigranes by no means confined his conquests to the eastern bank of the Euphrates. Cappadocia especially was the object of his attacks, and, defenceless as it was, suffered destructive blows from its too potent neighbour. Tigranes wrested the most easterly province Melitene from Cappadocia, and united it with the opposite Armenian province Sophene, by which means he obtained command of the passage of the Euphrates with the great thoroughfare of traffic between Asia Minor and Armenia. After the death of Sulla the armies of Tigranes even advanced into Cappadocia proper, and carried off to Armenia the inhabitants of the capital Mazaca (afterwards Caesarea) and eleven other towns of Greek organisation.

Nor could the kingdom of the Seleucids, already in the course of dissolution, oppose greater resistance to the new great king. The south from the Egyptian frontier to Straton's Tower (Caesarea) was under the rule of the Jewish prince Alexander Jannaeus, who extended and strengthened his dominion step by step in conflict with the Syrian, Egyptian, and Arabic neighbours and with the imperial cities. The larger towns of Syria—Gaza, Straton's Tower, Ptolemais, Beroea—attempted to maintain themselves by their own resources, sometimes as free communities, sometimes under so-called tyrants; the capital, Antioch, in particular, was virtually independent. Damascus and the valleys of Lebanon had submitted to the Nabataean prince, Aretas of Petra. Lastly, in Cilicia the pirates or the Romans bore sway. And for this crown breaking into a thousand fragments the Seleucid princes continued perseveringly to quarrel with each other, as though it were their object to make royalty ridiculous and offensive to all; nay more, while this family, doomed like the house of Laius to perpetual discord, had its own subjects all in revolt, it even raised claims to the throne of Egypt vacant by the decease of king Alexander II. without heirs. Accordingly king Tigranes fell to work there without ceremony. Eastern Cilicia was easily subdued by him, and the citizens of Soli and other towns were carried off, just like the Cappadocians, to Armenia. In like manner the province of Upper Syria, with the exception of the bravely-defended town of Seleucia at the mouth of the Orontes, and the greater part

the Bedouins, who were accustomed to open routes for traffic through their territory and to levy on these routes fixed transit-dues (Strabo, xvi. 748), were to serve the great king as a sort of toll-supervisors, and to levy tolls for him and themselves at the passage of the Euphrates. These Osroenian Arabs (*Orei Arabes*), as Pliny calls them, must also be the Arabs on Mount Amanus, whom Afranius subdued (Plut. *Pomp.* 39).

of Phoenicia were reduced by force; Ptolemais was occupied by the Armenians about $\frac{680}{74}$, and the Jewish state was already seriously threatened by them. Antioch, the old capital of the Seleucids, became one of the residences of the great king. Already from $\frac{671}{83}$, the year following the peace between Sulla and Mithradates, Tigranes is designated in the Syrian annals as the sovereign of the country, and Cilicia and Syria appear as an Armenian satrapy under Magadates, the lieutenant of the great king. The age of the kings of Nineveh, of the Salmanezers and Sennacheribs, seemed to be renewed; again Oriental despotism pressed heavily on the trading population of the Syrian coast, as it did formerly on Tyre and Sidon; again great states of the interior threw themselves on the provinces along the Mediterranean; again Asiatic hosts, said to number half a million combatants, appeared on the Cilician and Syrian coasts. As Salmanezer and Nebuchadnezzar had formerly carried the Jews to Babylon, so now from all the frontier provinces of the new kingdom — from Corduene, Adiabene, Assyria, Cilicia, Cappadocia—the inhabitants, especially the Greek or half-Greek citizens of the towns, were compelled to settle with their whole goods and chattels (under penalty of the confiscation of everything that they left behind) in the new capital, one of those gigantic cities proclaiming rather the nothingness of the people than the greatness of the rulers, which sprang up in the countries of the Euphrates on every change in the supreme sovereignty at the fiat of the new grand sultan. The new "city of Tigranes," Tigranocerta, situated in the most southern province of Armenia, not far from the Mesopotamian frontier,[1] was a city like Nineveh and Babylon, with walls fifty yards high, and the appendages of palace, garden, and park that were appropriate to sultanism. In other respects, too, the new great king proved faithful to his part. As amidst the perpetual childhood of the East the child-like conceptions of kings with real crowns on their heads have never disappeared, Tigranes, when he showed himself in public, appeared in the state and the costume of a successor of Darius and Xerxes, with the purple caftan, the half-white half-purple tunic, the long plaited trousers, the high turban, and the royal diadem—attended moreover and served in slavish fashion, wherever he went or stood, by four "kings."

King Mithradates acted with greater moderation. He

[1] The town was situated not at Diarbekir, but between Diarbekir and the Lake of Van, nearer to the latter, on the Nicephorius (Jezidchaneh Su), one of the northern affluents of the Tigris.

refrained from aggressions in Asia Minor, and contented himself with—what no treaty forbade—placing his dominion along the Black Sea on a firmer basis, and gradually bringing into more definite dependence the regions which separated the Bosporan kingdom, now ruled under his supremacy by his son Machares, from that of Pontus. But he too applied every effort to render his fleet and army efficient, and especially to arm and organise the latter after the Roman model; in which the Roman emigrants, who stayed in great numbers at his court, rendered him essential service.

The Romans had no desire to become further involved in Oriental affairs than they were already. This appears with striking clearness in the fact, that the opportunity, which at this time presented itself, of peacefully bringing the kingdom of Egypt under the immediate dominion of Rome was spurned by the senate. The legitimate descendants of Ptolemy Lagides had come to an end when the king installed by Sulla after the death of Ptolemy Soter II. Lathyrus—Alexander II., a son of Alexander I.—was killed, a few days after he had ascended the throne, on occasion of a tumult in the capital ($\frac{673}{81}$). This Alexander had in his testament[1] appointed the Roman community his heir. The genuineness of this document was no doubt disputed; but the senate acknowledged it by assuming in virtue of it the sums deposited on account of the deceased king in Tyre. Nevertheless it allowed two notoriously illegitimate sons of king Lathyrus, Ptolemy XI., who was styled the new Dionysos or the

[1] The disputed question, whether this alleged or real testament proceeded from Alexander I. (+ $\frac{666}{88}$) or Alexander II. (+ $\frac{673}{81}$), is usually decided in favour of the former alternative. But the reasons are inadequate; for Cicero (*de L. Agr.* i. 4, 12; 15, 38; 16, 41) does not say that Egypt fell to Rome in $\frac{666}{88}$, but that it did so in or after this year; and while the circumstance that Alexander I. died abroad, and Alexander II. in Alexandria, has led some to infer that the treasures mentioned in the testament in question as lying in Tyre must have belonged to the former, they have overlooked that Alexander II. was killed nineteen days after his arrival in Egypt (Letronne, *Inscr. de l'Egypte*, ii. 20), when his treasure might still very well be in Tyre. On the other hand the circumstance that the second Alexander was the last genuine Lagid is decisive, for in the similar acquisitions of Pergamus, Cyrene, and Bithynia, it was always by the last scion of the legitimate ruling family that Rome was appointed heir. The ancient constitutional law, as it applied at least to the Roman client-states, seems to have given to the reigning prince the right of ultimate disposal of his kingdom not absolutely, but only in the absence of *agnati* entitled to succeed.

Whether the testament was genuine or spurious cannot be ascertained, and is of no great moment; there are no special reasons for assuming a forgery.

Flute-blower (Auletes), and Ptolemy the Cyprian, to take practical possession of Egypt and Cyprus respectively. They were not indeed expressly recognised by the senate, but no distinct summons to surrender their kingdoms was addressed to them. The reason why the senate allowed this state of uncertainty to continue, and did not commit itself to a definite renunciation of Egypt and Cyprus, was undoubtedly the considerable rent which these kings ruling, as it were, on sufferance, regularly paid for the continuance of the uncertainty to the heads of the Roman coteries. But the motive for waiving that attractive acquisition altogether was different. Egypt, by its peculiar position and its financial organisation, placed in the hands of any governor commanding it a pecuniary and naval power and generally an independent authority, which were absolutely incompatible with the suspicious and feeble government of the oligarchy: in this point of view it was judicious to forego the direct possession of the country of the Nile.

Less justifiable was the failure of the senate to interfere directly in the affairs of Asia Minor and Syria. The Roman government did not indeed recognise the Armenian conqueror as king of Cappadocia and Syria; but it did nothing to drive him back, although the war, which under pressure of necessity it began in $\frac{676}{78}$ against the pirates in Cilicia, naturally suggested its interference more especially in Syria. In fact, by tolerating the loss of Cappadocia and Syria without declaring war, the government abandoned not merely those committed to its protection, but the most important foundations of its own ascendancy. It adopted a hazardous course, even when it sacrificed the outworks of its dominion in the Greek settlements and kingdoms on the Euphrates and Tigris; but when it allowed the Asiatics to establish themselves on the Mediterranean which was the political basis of its empire, such a course was not a proof of love of peace, but a confession that the oligarchy had been rendered by the Sullan restoration more oligarchical doubtless, but neither wiser nor more energetic, and it was for the universal power of Rome the beginning of the end.

On the other side, too, there was no desire for war. Tigranes had no reason to wish it, when Rome even without war abandoned to him all its allies. Mithradates, who was no mere sultan and had enjoyed opportunity enough, amidst good and bad fortune, of gaining experience regarding friends and foes, knew very well that in a second Roman war he would very probably stand quite as much alone as in the first, and that he could follow no more prudent course than to keep quiet and to strengthen his kingdom in the interior. That he was in earnest with his peaceful declarations, he had sufficiently proved in the conference with Murena (iii. 325). He continued to avoid everything which would compel the Roman government to abandon its passive attitude.

But as the first Mithradatic war had arisen without either of the parties properly desiring it, so now there grew out of the opposition of interests mutual suspicion, and out of this suspicion mutual preparations for defence; and these, by their very gravity, ultimately led to an open breach. That distrust of her own readiness to fight and preparation for fighting, which had for long governed the policy of Rome—a distrust which the want of standing armies and the far from exemplary character of the collegiate rule render sufficiently intelligible—made it, as it were, an axiom of her policy to pursue every war not merely to the vanquishing, but to the annihilation of her opponents; in this point of view the Romans were from the outset as little content with the peace of Sulla, as they had formerly been with the terms which Scipio Africanus had granted to the Carthaginians. The apprehension often expressed that a second attack by the Pontic king was imminent, was in some measure justified by the singular resemblance between the present circumstances and those which existed twelve years before. Once more a dangerous civil war coincided with serious military preparations by Mithradates; once more the Thracians overran Macedonia, and piratical fleets covered the Mediterranean; emissaries were coming and going—as formerly between Mithradates and the Italians—so now between the Roman emigrants in Spain and those at the court of Sinope. As early as the beginning of $\frac{677}{77}$ it was declared in the senate that the king was only waiting for the opportunity of falling upon Roman Asia during the Italian civil war; the Roman armies in Asia and Cilicia were reinforced to meet possible emergencies.

Mithradates on his part followed with growing apprehension the development of the Roman policy. He could not but feel that a war between the Romans and Tigranes, however much the feeble senate might dread it, was in the long run almost inevitable, and that he would not be able to avoid taking part in it. His attempt to obtain from the Roman senate the documentary record of the terms of peace, which was still wanting, had fallen amidst the disturbances attending the revolution of Lepidus and remained without result; Mithradates found in this an indication of the impending renewal of the conflict. The expedition against the pirates, which directly concerned also the kings of the East whose allies they were, seemed the preliminary to such a war. Still more suspicious were the claims which Rome held in suspense over Egypt and Cyprus: it is significant that the king of Pontus betrothed his two daughters Mithradatis and Nyssa to the two Ptolemies, to whom the senate continued to refuse recognition. The emigrants urged him to strike: the position of Sertorius in Spain, as to which Mithradates despatched envoys under convenient pretexts to the head-quarters of Pompeius to obtain information, and which was about this very time really imposing, opened up to the king the prospect of fighting not, as in the first Roman war, against both the Roman parties, but in concert with the one against the other. A more favourable moment could hardly be hoped for, and after all it was always better to declare war than to let it be declared against him. In $\frac{679}{75}$ Nicomedes III. Philopator king of Bithynia, died, and as the last of his race—for the son of his marriage with Nysa was, or was said to be, supposititious—bequeathed his kingdom to the Romans, who delayed not to take possession of a country bordering on the Roman province and long ago filled with Roman officials and merchants. At the same time Cyrene, which had been already bequeathed to the Romans in $\frac{658}{96}$ (iii. 257), was at length constituted a province, and a Roman governor was sent thither ($\frac{679}{75}$). These measures, in connection with the attacks carried out about the same time against the pirates on the south coast of Asia Minor, must have excited apprehensions in the king; the annexation of Bithynia in particular made the Romans—for Paphlagonia was hardly to be taken into account—immediate neighbours of the Pontic kingdom; and this, it may be presumed, turned the scale. The king took the decisive step and declared war against the Romans in the winter of $\frac{679-680}{75-74}$.

Gladly would Mithradates have avoided undertaking so arduous a work singlehanded. His nearest and natural ally was the great king Tigranes; but that shortsighted man declined the proposal of his father-in-law. So there remained only the insurgents and the pirates. Mithradates was careful to place himself in communication with both, by despatching strong squadrons to Spain and to Crete. A formal treaty was concluded with Sertorius (p. 31), by which Rome ceded to the king Bithynia, Paphlagonia, Galatia, and Cappadocia—all of them, it is true, acquisitions which had to be ratified on the field of battle. More important was the support which the Spanish general gave to the king, by sending Roman officers to lead his armies and fleets. The most active of the emigrants in the east, Lucius Magius and Lucius Fannius, were appointed by Sertorius as his representatives at the court of Sinope. From the pirates also came help; they flocked largely to the kingdom of Pontus, and by their means especially the king seems to have succeeded in forming a naval force imposing by the number as well as by the quality of the ships. His main support still lay in his own forces, with which the king hoped, before the Romans should arrive in Asia, to make himself master of their possessions there; especially as the financial distress produced in the province of Asia by the Sullan war-tribute, the aversion in Bithynia towards the new Roman government, and the elements of combustion left behind by the desolating war recently brought to a close in Cilicia and Pamphylia, opened up favourable prospects to a Ponti invasion. There was no lack of stores; 2,000,000 *medimni* of grain lay in the royal granaries. The fleet and the men were numerous and well exercised, particularly the Bastarnian mercenaries, a select corps which was a match even for Italian legionaries. On this occasion also it was the king who took the offensive. A corps under Diophantus advanced into Cappadocia, to occupy the fortresses there and to close the way to the kingdom of Pontus against the Romans; the leader sent by Sertorius, the propraetor Marcus Marius, went in company with the Pontic officer Eumachus to Phrygia, with a view to rouse the Roman province and the Taurus mountains to revolt; the main army, above 100,000 men with 16,000 cavalry and 100 scythe-chariots, led by Taxiles and Hermocrates under the personal superintendence of the king, and the war-fleet of 400 sail commanded by Aristonicus, moved along the north coast of Asia Minor to occupy Paphlagonia and Bithynia.

On the Roman side there was selected for the conduct of the war in the first rank the consul of $\frac{680}{74}$, Lucius Lucullus, who as governor of Asia and Cilicia was placed at the head of the four legions stationed in Asia Minor and of a fifth brought by him from Italy, and was directed to penetrate with this army, amounting to 30,000 infantry and 1600 cavalry, through Phrygia into the kingdom of Pontus. His colleague Marcus Cotta proceeded with the fleet and another Roman corps to the Propontis, to cover Asia and Bithynia. A general arming of the coasts and particularly of the Thracian coast more immediately threatened by the Pontic fleet, was enjoined; and the task of clearing all the seas and coasts from the pirates and their Pontic allies was, by extraordinary decree, entrusted to a single magistrate, the choice falling on the praetor Marcus Antonius, the son of the man who thirty years before had first chastised the Cilician corsairs (iii. 131). Moreover, the senate placed at the disposal of Lucullus a sum of 72,000,000 sesterces (£720,000), in order to build a fleet; which, however, Lucullus declined. From all this we see that the Roman government recognised the root of the evil in the neglect of their marine, and showed earnestness in the matter at least so far as their decrees went.

Thus the war began in $\frac{680}{74}$ at all points. It was a misfortune for Mithradates that at the very moment of his declaring war the Sertorian struggle reached its crisis, by which one of his principle hopes was from the outset destroyed, and the Roman government was enabled to apply its whole power to the maritime and Asiatic contest. In Asia Minor on the other hand Mithradates reaped the advantage of the offensive, and of the great distance of the Romans from the immediate seat of war. A considerable number of cities in Asia Minor opened their gates to the Sertorian propraetor who was placed at the head of the Roman province, and they massacred, as in $\frac{666}{88}$, the Roman families settled among them: the Pisidians, Isaurians, and Cilicians took up arms against Rome. The Romans for the moment had no troops at the points threatened. Individua energetic men attempted no doubt at their own hand to check this mutiny of the provincials; thus on receiving accounts of these events the young Gaius Caesar left Rhodes where he was staying on account of his studies, and with a hastily-collected band opposed himself to the insurgents; but not much could be effected by such volunteer corps. Had not Deiotarus, the brave tetrarch of the Tolistobogi—a Celtic tribe settled around Pessinus—embraced the side of the Romans and fought with success against the Pontic generals, Lucullus would have had to begin with recapturing the interior of the Roman province from the enemy. But even as it was, he lost in pacifying the province and driving back the enemy precious time, for which the slight successes achieved by his cavalry were far from affording compensation. Still more unfavourable than in Phrygia was the aspect of things for the Romans on the north coast of Asia Minor. Here the great Pontic army and the fleet had completely mastered Bithynia, and compelled the Roman consul Cotta to take shelter with his far from numerous force and his ships within the walls and port of Chalcedon, where Mithradates kept them blockaded.

This blockade, however, was so far a favourable event for the Romans, as, if Cotta detained the Pontic army before Chalcedon and Lucullus proceeded also thither, the whole Roman forces might unite at Chalcedon and compel the decision of arms there rather than in the distant and impassable region of Pontus. Lucullus did take the route for Chalcedon; but Cotta, with the view of executing a great feat at his own hand before the arrival of his colleague, ordered his admiral Publius Rutilius Nudus to make a sally, which not only ended in a bloody defeat of the Romans, but also enabled the Pontic force to attack the harbour, to break the chain which closed it, and to burn all the Roman vessels of war which were there, nearly seventy in number. On the news of these misfortunes reaching Lucullus at the river Sangarius, he accelerated his march to the great discontent of his soldiers, in whose opinion Cotta was of no moment, and who would far rather have plundered an undefended country than have taught their comrades to conquer. His arrival made up in part for the misfortunes sustained: the king raised the siege of Chalcedon, but did not retreat to Pontus; he went southward into the old Roman province, where he spread his army along the Propontis and the Hellespont, occupied Lampsacus, and began to besiege the large and wealthy town of Cyzicus. He thus entangled himself more and more deeply in the *cul de sac* which he had chosen to enter, instead of—which alone promised success for him—bringing the wide distances into play against the Romans.

In few places had the old Hellenic adroitness and ability preserved themselves so pure as in Cyzicus; its citizens, although they had suffered great loss of men and ships in the unfortunate double battle of Chalcedon, made the most resolute resistance. Cyzicus lay on an island directly opposite the mainland and connected with it by a bridge. The besiegers possessed themselves not only of the line of heights on the mainland terminating at the bridge and of the suburb situated there, but also of the celebrated Dindymene heights on the island itself; and alike on the mainland and on the island the Greek engineers put forth all their art to pave the way for an assault. But the breach which they at length made was closed again during the night by the besieged, and the exertions of the royal army remained as fruitless as did the barbarous threat of the king to put to death the captured Cyzicenes before the walls, if the citizens still refused to surrender. The Cyzicenes continued the defence with courage and success; they fell little short of capturing the king himself in the course of the siege.

Meanwhile Lucullus had possessed himself of a very strong position in rear of the Pontic army, which, although not permitting him directly to relieve the hard-pressed city, gave him the means of cutting off all supplies by land from the enemy. Thus the enormous army of Mithradates, estimated with the camp-followers at 300,000 persons, was not in a position either to fight or to march, firmly wedged in between the impregnable city and the immovable Roman army, and dependent for all its supplies solely on the sea, which fortunately for the Pontic troops was exclusively commanded by their fleet. But the bad season set in; a storm destroyed a great part of the siege-works; the scarcity of provisions and above all of fodder for the horses began to become intolerable. The beasts of burden and the baggage were sent off under convoy of the greater portion of the Pontic cavalry, with orders to steal away or break through at any cost; but at the river Rhyndacus, to the east of Cyzicus, Lucullus overtook them and cut to pieces the whole body. Another division of cavalry under Metrophanes and Lucius Fannius was obliged, after wandering long in the west of Asia Minor, to return to the camp before Cyzicus. Famine and disease made fearful ravages in the Pontic ranks. When spring came on ($\frac{681}{73}$), the besieged redoubled their exertions and took the trenches constructed on Dindymon: nothing remained for the king but to raise the siege and with the aid of his fleet to save what he could. He went in person with the fleet to the Hellespont, but suffered considerable loss partly at its departure, partly through storms on the voyage. The land army under Hermaeus and Marius likewise set out thither, with the view of embarking at Lampsacus under the protection of its walls. They left behind their baggage as well as the sick and wounded, who were all put to death by the exasperated Cyzicenes; Lucullus inflicted on them very considerable loss by the way at the passage of the rivers Aesepus and Granicus; but they attained their object. The Pontic ships carried off the remains of the great army and the citizens of Lampsacus themselves beyond the reach of the Romans.

The consistent and discreet conduct of the war by Lucullus had not only repaired the errors of his colleague, but had also destroyed without a pitched battle the flower of the enemy's army—it was said 200,000 soldiers. Had he still possessed the fleet which was burnt in the harbour of Chalcedon, he would have annihilated the whole army of his opponent. As it was, the work of destruction continued incomplete; and while he was obliged to remain passive, the Pontic fleet notwithstanding the disaster of Cyzicus took its station in the Propontis, Perinthus and Byzantium were blockaded by it on the European coast and Priapus pillaged on the Asiatic, and the head-quarters of the king were established in the Bithynian port of Nicomedia. In fact a select squadron of fifty sail, which carried 10,000 select troops including Marcus Marius and the flower of the Roman emigrants, sailed forth even into the Aegean; it was destined, according to report, to effect a landing in Italy and there re-kindle the civil war. But the ships, which Lucullus after the disaster off Chalcedon had demanded from the Asiatic communities, began to appear, and a squadron ran forth in pursuit of the enemy's fleet which had gone into the Aegean. Lucullus himself, experienced as an admiral (iii. 290), took the command. Thirteen quinqueremes of the enemy on their voyage to Lemnos, under Isidorus, were assailed and sunk off the Achaean harbour in the waters between the Trojan coast and the island of Tenedos. At the small island of Neae, between Lemnos and Scyros, at which little-frequented point the Pontic flotilla of thirty-two sail lay drawn up on the shore, Lucullus found it, immediately attacked the ships and the crews scattered over the island, and possessed himself of the whole squadron. Here Marcus Marius and the ablest of the Roman emigrants met their death, either in conflict or subsequently by the axe of the executioner. The whole Aegean fleet of the enemy was annihilated by Lucullus. The war in Bithynia was meanwhile continued by Cotta and by Voconius, Barba, and Gaius Valerius Triarius the legates of Lucullus with the land army reinforced by fresh arrivals from Italy, and a squadron collected in Asia. Barba captured in the interior Prusa on Olympus and Nicaea, while Triarius along the coast captured Apamea (formerly Myrlea) and Prusa on the sea (formerly Cius). They then united for a joint attack on Mithradates himself in Nicomedia; but the king without even attempting battle escaped to his ships and sailed homeward, and in this he was successful only because the Roman admiral Voconius, who was entrusted with the blockade of the port of Nicomedia, arrived too late. On the voyage the important Heraclea was indeed betrayed to the king and occupied by him; but a storm in these waters sank more than sixty of his ships and dispersed the rest; the king arrived almost alone at Sinope.

The offensive on the part of Mithradates ended in a complete and very far from honourable (least of all for the supreme leader) defeat of the Pontic forces by land and sea.

Lucullus now in turn resorted to the aggressive. Triarius received the command of the fleet, with orders first of all to blockade the Hellespont and lie in wait for the Pontic ships returning from Crete and Spain; Cotta was charged with the siege of Heraclea; the difficult task of providing supplies was entrusted to the faithful and active princes of the Galatians and to Ariobarzanes king of Cappadocia; Lucullus himself advanced in the autumn of $\frac{681}{73}$ into the favoured land of Pontus, which had long been untrodden by an enemy. Mithradates, now resolved to maintain the strictest defensive, retired without giving battle from Sinope to Amisus, and from Amisus to Cabira (afterwards Neocaesarea, now Niksar) on the Lycus, a tributary of the Iris; he contented himself with drawing the enemy after him farther and farther into the interior, and obstructing their supplies and communications. Lucullus rapidly followed; Sinope was passed by; the Halys, the old limit of Scipio, was crossed, and the considerable towns of Amisus, Eupatoria (on the Iris), and Themiscyra (on the Thermodon) were invested, till at length winter put an end to the onward march, though not to the investment of the towns. The soldiers of Lucullus murmured at the constant advance which did not allow them to reap the fruits of their exertions, and at the tedious and—amidst the severity of that season—burdensome blockades. But it was not the habit of Lucullus to listen to such complaints: in the spring of $\frac{682}{72}$ he immediately advanced against Cabira, leaving behind two legions before Amisus under Lucius Murena. The king had made an attempt during the winter to induce the great king of Armenia to take part in the struggle; it remained like the former attempt fruitless, or led only to empty promises. Still less did the Parthians show any desire to interfere in the forlorn cause. Nevertheless a considerable army, chiefly raised by enlistments in Scythia, had again assembled under Diophantus and Taxiles at Cabira. The Roman army, which still numbered only three legions and was decidedly inferior to the Pontic in cavalry, found itself compelled to avoid as far as possible the plains, and arrived, not without toil and loss, by difficult by-paths in the vicinity of Cabira. At this town the two armies lay for a considerable period confronting each other. The chief struggle was for supplies, which were on both sides scarce: for this purpose Mithradates formed the flower of his cavalry and a division of select infantry under Diophantus and Taxiles into a flying corps, which was intended to scour the country between the Lycus and the Halys and to seize the Roman trains of provisions coming from Cappadocia. But the lieutenant of Lucullus, Marcus Fabius Hadrianus, who escorted such a train, not only completely defeated the band which lay in wait for him in the defile where it expected to surprise him, but after being reinforced from the camp defeated also the army of Diophantus and Taxiles itself, so that it totally broke up. It was an irreparable loss for the king, when his cavalry, on which alone he relied, was thus overthrown.

As soon as he received through the first fugitives that arrived at Cabira from the field of battle—significantly enough, the beaten generals themselves—the fatal news, earlier even than Lucullus got tidings of the victory, he resolved on an immediate farther retreat. But the resolution taken by the king spread with the rapidity of lightning among those immediately around him; and, when the soldiers saw the confidants of the king packing in all haste, they too were seized with a panic. No one was willing to be the hindmost; all, high and low, ran pell-mell like startled deer; no authority, not even that of the king, was longer heeded; and the king himself was carried away amidst the wild tumult. Lucullus, perceiving the confusion, made his attack, and the Pontic troops allowed themselves to be massacred almost without offering resistance. Had the legions been able to maintain discipline and to restrain their eagerness for spoil, hardly a man would have escaped them, and the king himself would doubtless have been taken. With difficulty Mithradates escaped along with a few attendants through the mountains to Comana (not far from Tocat and the source of the Iris); from which, however, a Roman corps under Marcus Pompeius soon scared him off and pursued him, till, attended by not more than 2000 cavalry, he crossed the frontier of his kingdom at Talaura in Lesser Armenia. In the empire of the great king he found a refuge, but nothing more (end of $\frac{682}{72}$). Tigranes, it is true, ordered royal honours to be shown to his fugitive father-in-law; but he did not invite him to his court, and detained him in the remote border-province to which he had come in a sort of decorous captivity.

The Roman troops overran all Pontus and Lesser Armenia, and as far as Trapezus the flat country submitted without resistance to the conqueror. The commanders of the royal treasure-stores also surrendered after more or less delay, and delivered up their contents. The king ordered that the women of the royal harem—his sisters, his numerous wives and concubines—as it was not possible to secure their flight, should all be put to death by one of his eunuchs at Pharnacea (Kerasunt). The towns alone offered obstinate resistance. It is true that the few in the interior—Cabira, Amasia, Eupatoria—were now in the power of the Romans; but the larger maritime towns, Amisus and Sinope in Pontus, Amastris in Paphlagonia, Tius and the Pontic Heraclea in Bithynia, defended themselves with desperation, partly animated by attachment to the king and to their free Hellenic constitution which he had protected, partly overawed by the bands of corsairs whom the king had called to his aid. Sinope and Heraclea even sent forth vessels against the Romans; and the squadron of Sinope seized a Roman flotilla which was bringing corn from the Tauric peninsula for the army of Lucullus. Heraclea did not succumb till after a two years' siege, when the Roman fleet had cut off the city from intercourse with the Greek towns on the Tauric peninsula and treason had broken out in the ranks of the garrison. When Amisus was reduced to extremities, the garrison set fire to the town, and under cover of the flames took to their ships. In Sinope, where the daring pirate-captain Seleucus and the royal eunuch Bacchides conducted the defence, the garrison plundered the houses before it withdrew, and set the ships which it could not take along with it on fire; it is said that, although the greater portion of the defenders were enabled to embark, 8000 corsairs were there put to death by Lucullus. These sieges of towns lasted for two whole years and more after the battle of Cabira ($\frac{682-684}{72-70}$); Lucullus prosecuted them in great part by means of his lieutenants, while he himself regulated the affairs of the province of Asia, which demanded and obtained a thorough reform.

Remarkable, in an historical point of view, as was that obstinate resistance of the Pontic mercantile towns to the victorious Romans, it was of little immediate use; the cause of Mithradates was none the less lost. The great king had evidently, for the present at least, no intention at all of restoring him to his kingdom. The Roman emigrants in Asia had lost their best men by the destruction of the Aegean fleet; of the survivors not a few, such as the active leaders Lucius Magius and Lucius Fannius, had made their peace with Lucullus; and with the death of Sertorius, who perished in the year of the battle of Cabira, the last hope of the emigrants vanished. Mithradates' own power was totally shattered, and one after another his remaining supports gave way; his squadrons returning from Crete and Spain, to the number of seventy sail, were attacked and destroyed by Triarius at the island of Tenedos; even the governor of the Bosporan kingdom, the king's own son Machares, deserted him, and as independent prince of the Tauric Chersonese concluded on his own behalf peace and friendship with the Romans ($\frac{684}{70}$). The king himself, after a not too glorious resistance, was confined in a remote Armenian mountain-stronghold, a fugitive from his kingdom and almost a prisoner of his son-in-law. Although the bands of corsairs might still hold out in Crete, and such as had escaped from Amisus and Sinope might make their way along the hardly-accessible east coast of the Black Sea to the Sanegae and Lazi, the skilful conduct of the war by Lucullus and his judicious moderation, which did not disdain to remedy the just grievances of the provincials and to employ the repentant emigrants as officers in his army, had at a moderate sacrifice delivered Asia Minor from the enemy and annihilated the Pontic kingdom, so that it might be converted from a Roman client-state into a Roman province. A commission of the senate was expected, to settle in concert with the commander-in-chief the new provincial organisation.

But the relations with Armenia were not yet settled. That a declaration of war by the Romans against Tigranes was in itself justified and even demanded, we have already shown. Lucullus, who looked at the state of affairs from a nearer point of view and with a higher spirit than the senatorial college in Rome, perceived clearly the necessity of confining Armenia within its bounds and of re-establishing the lost dominion of Rome over the Mediterranean. He showed himself in the conduct of Asiatic affairs no unworthy successor of his instructor and friend Sulla. A Philhellene above most Romans of his time, he was not insensible to the obligation which Rome had come under when taking up the heritage of Alexander—the obligation to be the shield and sword of the Greeks in the East. Personal motives—the wish to earn laurels also beyond the Euphrates, irritation at the fact that the great king in a letter to him had omitted the title of Imperator—may doubtless have partly influenced Lucullus; but it is unjust to assume paltry and selfish motives for actions, which motives of duty quite suffice to explain. The Roman governing college at any rate—timid, indolent, ill-informed, and above all beset by perpetual financial embarrassments—could never be expected, without direct compulsion, to take the initiative in an expedition so vast and costly. About the year $\frac{682}{72}$ the legitimate representatives of the Seleucid dynasty, Antiochus called the Asiatic and his brother, moved by the favourable turn of the Pontic war, had gone to Rome to procure a Roman intervention in Syria, and at the same time a recognition of their hereditary claims on Egypt. If the latter demand might not be granted, there could not, at any rate, be found a more favourable moment or occasion for beginning the war which had long been necessary against Tigranes; but the senate, while it recognised the princes doubtless as the legitimate kings of Syria, could not make up its mind to decree the armed intervention. If the favourable opportunity was to be employed and Armenia was to be dealt with in earnest, Lucullus had to undertake the war, without any proper orders from the senate, at his own hand and his own risk; he found himself, just like Sulla, compelled to execute what he did in the most manifest interest of the existing government, not with its sanction, but in spite of it. His resolution was facilitated by the uncertainty of the relations, wavering between peace and war, which had long subsisted between Rome and Armenia—an uncertainty which screened in some measure the arbitrariness of his proceedings, and readily suggested formal grounds for war. The state of matters in Cappadocia and Syria afforded pretexts enough; and already in the pursuit of the king of Pontus Roman troops had violated the territory of the great king. As, however, the commission of Lucullus had reference to the conduct of the war against Mithradates, and he wished to connect what he did with that commission, he preferred to send one of his officers, Appius Claudius, to the great king at Antioch to demand the surrender of Mithradates, which in fact could not but lead to war.

The resolution was a grave one, especially considering the condition of the Roman army. It was indispensable during the campaign in Armenia to keep the extensive territory of Pontus strongly occupied—otherwise the army in Armenia might lose its communications with home; and besides it might be easily foreseen that Mithradates would attempt an inroad into his former kingdom. The army, at the head of which Lucullus had ended the Mithradatic war, amounting to about 30,000 men, was obviously inadequate for this double task. Under ordinary circumstances the general would have asked and obtained from his government the despatch of a second army; but as Lucullus wished, and was in some measure compelled,

to take up the war over the head of the government, he found himself necessitated to renounce that plan and—although he himself incorporated the captured Thracian mercenaries of the Pontic king with his troops—to carry the war over the Euphrates with not more than two legions, or at most 15,000 men. This was itself hazardous; but the smallness of the number might be in some degree compensated by the tried valour of the army consisting throughout of veterans. A much worse circumstance was the temper of the soldiers, to which Lucullus, in his high aristocratic fashion, had given far too little heed. Lucullus was an able general, and—according to the aristocratic standard—an upright and benevolent man, but very far from being a favourite with his soldiers. He was unpopular, as a decided adherent of the oligarchy; unpopular, because he had vigorously checked the monstrous usury of the Roman capitalists in Asia Minor; unpopular, on account of the toils and fatigues which he inflicted on his troops; unpopular, because he demanded strict discipline in his soldiers and prevented as far as possible the pillage of the Greek towns by his men, but withal caused many a waggon and many a camel to be laden with the treasures of the East for himself; unpopular too on account of his manner, which was polished, stately, Hellenising, not at all familiar, and inclining, wherever it was possible, to ease and pleasure. There was no trace in him of the charm which creates a personal bond between the general and the soldier. Moreover, a large portion of his ablest soldiers had reason to complain of the unmeasured prolongation of their term of service. His two best legions were the same which Flaccus and Fimbria had led in 668/86
to the East (iii. 289); notwithstanding that shortly after the battle of Cabira they had been promised their discharge well earned by thirteen campaigns, Lucullus now led them beyond the Euphrates to face a new incalculable war—it seemed as though the victors of Cabira were to be treated worse than the vanquished of Cannae (ii. 128, 169). It was in fact more than rash that, with troops so weak and so much out of humour, a general should at his own hand and, strictly speaking, in the face of the constitution, undertake an expedition to a distant and unknown land, full of rapid streams and snow-clad mountains—a land which from the very vastness of its extent rendered any lightly-undertaken attack fraught with danger. The conduct of Lucullus was therefore much and not unreasonably censured in Rome; but amidst the censure the fact should not have been concealed, that the perversity of the government was

the prime occasion of this venturesome project of the general, and, if it did not justify it, rendered it at least excusable.

The mission of Appius Claudius was intended not only to furnish a diplomatic pretext for the war, but also to induce the princes and cities of Syria especially to take arms against the king: in the spring of $\frac{685}{69}$ the formal attack began. During the winter the king of Cappadocia had silently provided vessels for transport; with these the Euphrates was crossed, and the march was directed through the province of Sophene, without losing time with the siege of smaller places, straight towards Tigranocerta, whither the great king had shortly before returned from Syria, after having temporarily deferred the prosecution of his plans of conquest on the Mediterranean on account of the embroilment with the Romans. He was just projecting an inroad into Roman Asia from Cilicia and Lycaonia, and was considering whether the Romans would at once evacuate Asia or would previously give him battle, possibly at Ephesus, when a messenger interrupted him with the tidings of the advance of Lucullus. He ordered the messenger to be hanged, but the disagreeable reality remained unaltered; so he left his capital and resorted to the interior of Armenia, to raise a force—which had not yet been done—against the Romans. Meanwhile Mithrobarzanes with the troops actually at his disposal and in concert with the neighbouring Bedouin tribes, who were called out in all haste, was to give employment to the enemy. But the corps of Mithrobarzanes was dispersed by the Roman vanguard, and the Arabs by a detachment under Sextilius; and, while the Armenian main force assembling in the mountains to the north-east of Tigranocerta (about Bitlis) was held in check by a Roman division—which had been pushed forward—in a well-chosen position where its skirmishing was successful, Lucullus vigorously prosecuted the siege of Tigranocerta.

The exhaustless showers of arrows which the garrison poured upon the Roman army, and the setting fire to the besieging machines by means of naphtha, initiated the Romans into the new dangers of Iranian warfare; and the brave commandant Mancaeus maintained the city, till at length the great royal army of relief had assembled from all parts of the vast empire and the adjoining countries that were open to Armenian recruiting officers, and had advanced through the north-eastern passes to the rescue of the capital. The leader Taxiles, experienced in the wars of Mithradates, advised Tigranes to avoid a battle, and to surround and starve out the small Roman army by means of his cavalry. But when the king saw the Roman general, who had determined to give battle without raising the siege, move out with not much more than 10,000 men against a force twenty times superior, and boldly cross the river which separated the two armies; when he surveyed on the one side this little band, "too many for an embassy, too few for an army," and on the other side his own immense host, in which the peoples of the Black Sea and the Caspian met with those of the Mediterranean and of the Persian Gulf, in which the dreaded iron-clad lancers alone were more numerous than the whole army of Lucullus, and in which even infantry armed after the Roman fashion were not wanting; he resolved promptly to accept the battle desired by the enemy. But while the Armenians were still forming their array, the quick eye of Lucullus perceived that they had neglected to occupy a height which commanded the whole position of their cavalry. He hastened to occupy it with two cohorts, while at the same time his weak cavalry by a flank attack diverted the attention of the enemy from this movement; and as soon as he had reached the height, he led his little band against the rear of the enemy's cavalry. They were totally broken and threw themselves on the not yet fully formed infantry, which fled without striking a blow. The bulletin of the victor —that 100,000 Armenians and five Romans had fallen and that the king, throwing away his turban and diadem, had galloped off unrecognised with a few horsemen—is composed in the style of his master Sulla. Nevertheless the victory achieved on the 6th October $\frac{685}{69}$ before Tigranocerta remains one of the most brilliant in the glorious history of Roman warfare; and it was not less momentous than brilliant.

All the provinces wrested from the Parthians or Syrians were now strategically lost to the Armenians, and passed, for the most part, without delay into the possession of the victor. The newly-built capital of the great kingdom itself set the example. The Greeks, who had been forced in such numbers to settle there, rose against the garrison and opened to the Roman army the gates of the city, which was abandoned to the pillage of the soldiers. From Cilicia and Syria all the troops had already been withdrawn by the Armenian satrap Magadates to reinforce the relieving army before Tigranocerta. Lucullus advanced into Commagene, the most northern province of Syria, and stormed Samosata, the capital; he did not reach Syria proper, but envoys arrived from the dynasts and communities as far as the Red Sea—from Hellenes, Syrians, Jews, Arabs—to do homage to the Romans as their new sovereigns. Even the prince of Corduene, the province situated to the east of Tigranocerta, submitted; while, on the other hand, Guras the brother of the great king maintained himself in Nisibis, and thereby in Mesopotamia. Lucullus everywhere came forward as the protector of the Hellenic princes and municipalities: in Commagene he placed Antiochus, a prince of the Seleucid house, on the throne; he recognised Antiochus Asiaticus, who after the withdrawal of the Armenians had returned to Antioch, as king of Syria; he sent away the forced settlers of Tigranocerta once more to their homes. The immense stores and treasures of the great king—the grain amounted to 30,000,000 *medimni*, the money in Tigranocerta alone to 8000 talents (nearly £2,000,000)—enabled Lucullus to defray the expenses of the war without making any demand on the state-treasury, and to bestow on each of his soldiers, besides the amplest maintenance, a present of 800 *denarii* (£33).

The great king was deeply humbled. He was of a feeble character, arrogant in prosperity, faint-hearted in adversity. Probably an agreement would have been come to between him and Lucullus—an agreement which there was every reason that the great king should purchase by considerable sacrifices, and the Roman general should grant under tolerable conditions—had not the old Mithradates interfered. The latter had taken no part in the conflicts around Tigranocerta. Liberated after twenty months' captivity about the middle of $\frac{684}{70}$ in consequence of the variance that had occurred between the great king and the Romans, he had been despatched with 10,000 Armenian cavalry to his former kingdom, to threaten the communications of the enemy. Recalled even before he could accomplish anything there, when the great king summoned his whole force to relieve the capital which he had built, Mithradates was met on his arrival before Tigranocerta by the multitudes just fleeing from the field of battle. To every one, from the great king down to the common soldier, all seemed lost. But if Tigranes should now make peace, not only would Mithradates lose the last chance of being reinstated in his kingdom, but his surrender would be beyond doubt the first condition of peace; and certainly Tigranes would not have acted otherwise towards him than Bocchus had formerly acted towards Jugurtha. The king accordingly staked his whole personal weight to prevent things from taking this course, and to induce the Armenian court to continue the war, in which he had nothing to lose and everything to gain; and, fugitive and dethroned as was Mithradates, his influence on the court was not inconsiderable. He was still a stately and powerful man, who, although upwards of sixty years old, vaulted on horseback in full armour, and in hand-to-hand conflict stood his ground like the best. Years and vicissitudes seemed to have steeled his spirit: while in earlier times he sent forth generals to lead his armies and took no direct part in war himself, we find him henceforth as an old man commanding in person and fighting in person on the field of battle. To one who, during his fifty years of rule, had witnessed so many unexampled vicissitudes, the cause of the great king appeared by no means lost through the defeat of Tigranocerta; whereas the position of Lucullus was very difficult, and, if peace should not now take place and the war should be judiciously continued, even in a high degree precarious.

The veteran of varied experience, who stood towards the great king almost as a father, and was now able to exercise a personal influence over him, overpowered by his energy that weak man, and induced him not only to resolve on the continuance of the war, but also to entrust Mithradates with its political and military management. The war was now to be changed from a cabinet contest into a national Asiatic struggle; the kings and peoples of Asia were to unite for this purpose against the domineering and haughty Occidentals. The greatest exertions were made to reconcile the Parthians and Armenians, and to induce them to make common cause against Rome. At the suggestion of Mithradates, Tigranes offered to give back to the Arsacid Phraates the God (who had reigned since $\frac{684}{70}$) the provinces conquered by the Armenians—Mesopotamia, Adiabene, the "great valleys"—and to enter into friendship and alliance with him. But, after all that had previously taken place, this offer could scarcely reckon on a favourable reception; Phraates preferred to secure the boundary of the Euphrates by a treaty not with the Armenians, but with the Romans, and to look on, while the hated neighbour and the inconvenient foreigner fought out their strife. Greater success attended the application of Mithradates to the peoples of the East than to the kings. It was not difficult to represent the war as a national one of the East against the West, for such it was; it might very well be made a religious war also, and the report might be spread that the object aimed at by the army of Lucullus was the temple of the Persian Nanaea or Anaitis in Elymais or the modern Luristan, the most celebrated and the richest shrine in the whole region of the Euphrates.[1] From far and near the Asiatics flocked in crowds to the banner of the kings, who summoned them to protect the East and its gods from the impious foreigners. But facts had shown not only that the mere assemblage of enormous hosts was of little avail, but that the troops really capable of marching and fighting were by their very incorporation in such a mass rendered useless and involved in the general ruin. Mithradates sought above all to develop the arm which was at once weakest among the Occidentals and strongest among the Asiatics, the cavalry; in the army newly formed by him half of the force was mounted. For the ranks of the infantry he carefully selected, out of the mass of recruits called forth or volunteering, those fit for service, and caused them to be drilled by his Pontic officers. The considerable army, however, which soon assembled under the banner of the great king was destined not to measure its strength with the Roman veterans on the first chance field of battle, but to confine itself to defence and petty warfare. Mithradates had conducted the last war in his empire on the system of constantly retreating and avoiding battle; similar tactics were adopted on this occasion, and Armenia proper was destined as the theatre of war—the hereditary land of Tigranes, still wholly untouched by the enemy, and excellently adapted for this sort of warfare both by its physical character and by the patriotism of its inhabitants.

The year $\frac{686}{68}$ found Lucullus in a position of difficulty, which daily assumed a more dangerous aspect. In spite of his brilliant victories, people in Rome were not at all satisfied with him. The senate felt the arbitrary nature of his conduct; the capitalist party, sorely offended by him, set all means of intrigue and corruption at work to effect his recall. Daily the Forum echoed with just and unjust complaints regarding the foolhardy, the covetous, the un-Roman, the traitorous general. The senate so far yielded to the complaints regarding the union of such unlimited power—two ordinary governorships and an important extraordinary command—in the hands of such a man as to assign the province of Asia to one of the praetors, and the province of Cilicia along with three newly-raised legions to the consul Quintus Marcius Rex, and to restrict the general to the command against Mithradates and Tigranes.

[1] Cicero (*De Imp. Pomp.* 9, 23) hardly means any other than one of the rich temples of the province Elymais, whither the predatory expeditions of the Syrian and Parthian kings were regularly directed (Strabo, xvi. 744; Polyb. xxxi. 11; 1 Maccab. 6, etc.), and probably this as the best known; on no account can the allusion be to the temple of Comana or any shrine at all in the kingdom of Pontus.

These accusations springing up against the general in Rome found a dangerous echo in the soldiers' quarters on the Iris and on the Tigris; and the more so that several officers including the general's own brother-in-law, Publius Clodius, worked upon the soldiers with this view. The report beyond doubt designedly circulated by these, that Lucullus now thought of combining with the Pontic-Armenian war an expedition against the Parthians, augmented the exasperation of the troops.

But while the troublesome temper of the government and of the soldiers thus threatened the victorious general with recall and mutiny, he himself continued like a desperate gambler to increase his stake and his risk. He did not march against the Parthians; but when Tigranes showed himself neither ready to make peace nor disposed, according to the wish of Lucullus, to risk a second pitched battle, Lucullus resolved to advance from Tigranocerta, through the difficult mountain-country along the eastern shore of the lake of Van, into the valley of the eastern Euphrates (or the Arsanias, now Myrad-Chaï), and thence into that of the Araxes, where, on the northern slope of Ararat, lay Artaxata the capital of Armenia proper, with the hereditary castle and the harem of the king. He hoped, by threatening the king's hereditary residence, to compel him to fight either on the way or at any rate before Artaxata. It was inevitably necessary to leave behind a division at Tigranocerta; and, as the marching army could not possibly be further reduced, no course was left but to weaken the position in Pontus and to summon troops thence to Tigranocerta. The main difficulty, however, was the shortness of the Armenian summer, so inconvenient for military enterprises. On the table-land of Armenia, which lies 5000 feet and more above the level of the sea, the corn at Erzeroum only germinates in the beginning of June, and the winter sets in with the harvest in September; Artaxata had to be reached and the campaign had to be ended in four months at the utmost.

At midsummer, $\frac{686}{68}$, Lucullus set out from Tigranocerta, and—passing doubtless through the valley of the Karasu, a stream flowing in a south-easterly direction to join the eastern arm of the Euphrates, the only valley which connects the plains of Mesopotamia with the table-land of interior Armenia—arrived on the plateau of Musch and at the Euphrates. The march went on—amidst constant and very troublesome skirmishing with the enemy's cavalry, and especially with the mounted archers—slowly, but without material hindrance; and the passage of the Euphrates, which was seriously defended by the Armenian cavalry, was secured by a successful engagement; the Armenian infantry showed itself, but the attempt to involve it in the conflict did not succeed. Thus the army reached the table-land, properly so called, of Armenia, and continued its march into the unknown country. They had suffered no actual misfortune; but the mere inevitable retardation of the march by the difficulties of the ground and the horsemen of the enemy was itself a very serious disadvantage. Long before they had reached Artaxata, winter set in; and when the Italian soldiers saw snow and ice around them, the bow of military discipline that had been far too tightly stretched gave way.

A formal mutiny compelled the general to order a retreat, which he effected with his usual skill. When he had safely reached the plain where the season still permitted farther operations, Lucullus crossed the Tigris, and threw himself with the mass of his army on Nisibis, the capital of Armenian Mesopotamia. The great king, rendered wiser by the experience acquired before Tigranocerta, left the city to itself: notwithstanding its brave defence it was stormed in a dark, rainy night by the besiegers, and the army of Lucullus found there booty not less ample and winter-quarters no less comfortable than the year before in Tigranocerta.

But, meanwhile, the whole weight of the enemy's offensive fell on the weak Roman divisions left behind in Pontus and at Tigranocerta. Tigranes compelled the Roman commander of the latter corps, Lucius Fannius—the same who had formerly been the medium of communication between Sertorius and Mithradates (pp. 49, 56)—to throw himself into a fortress, and kept him beleaguered there. Mithradates advanced into Pontus with 4000 Armenian horsemen and 4000 of his own, and as liberator and avenger summoned the nation to rise against the common foe. All joined him; the scattered Roman soldiers were everywhere seized and put to death: when Hadrianus, the Roman commandant in Pontus (p. 55), led his troops against him, the former mercenaries of the king and the numerous natives of Pontus following the army as slaves made common cause with the enemy. For two successive days the unequal conflict lasted; it was only the circumstance that the king after receiving two wounds had to be carried off from the field of battle, which gave the Roman commander the opportunity of breaking off the virtually lost battle, and throwing himself with the small remnant of his troops into Cabira. Another of

Lucullus' lieutenants who accidentally came into this region, the resolute Triarius, again gathered round him a body of troops and fought a successful engagement with the king; but he was much too weak to expel him afresh from Pontic soil, and had to acquiesce while the king took up winter-quarters in Comana.

So the spring of $\frac{687}{67}$ came on. The reunion of the army in Nisibis, the idleness of winter-quarters, the frequent absence of the general, had meanwhile increased the insubordination of the troops; not only did they vehemently demand to be led back, but it was already tolerably evident that, if the general refused to lead them home, they would break up of themselves. The supplies were scanty; Fannius and Triarius, in their distress, sent the most urgent entreaties to the general to furnish aid. With a heavy heart Lucullus resolved to yield to necessity, to give up Nisibis and Tigranocerta, and, renouncing all the brilliant hopes of his Armenian expedition, to return to the right bank of the Euphrates. Fannius was relieved; but in Pontus the help was too late. Triarius, not strong enough to fight with Mithradates, had taken up a strong position at Gaziura (Turksal on the Iris, to the west of Tokat), while the baggage was left behind at Dadasa. But when Mithradates laid siege to the latter place, the Roman soldiers, apprehensive for their property, compelled their leader to leave his secure position, and to give battle to the king between Gaziura and Ziela (Zilleh) on the Scotian heights.

What Triarius had foreseen occurred. In spite of the stoutest resistance the wing which the king commanded in person broke the Roman line and huddled the infantry together into a clayey ravine, where it could make neither a forward nor a lateral movement and was cut to pieces without pity. The king indeed was dangerously wounded by a Roman centurion, who sacrificed his life for it; but the defeat was not the less complete. The Roman camp was taken; the flower of the infantry, and almost all the staff and subaltern officers, strewed the ground; the dead were left lying unburied on the field of battle, and, when Lucullus arrived on the right bank of the Euphrates, he learned the defeat not from his own soldiers, but through the reports of the natives.

Along with this defeat came the outbreak of the military conspiracy. At this very time news arrived from Rome that the people had resolved to grant a discharge to the soldiers whose legal term of service had expired, to wit, to the Fimbrians, and to entrust the chief command in Pontus and Bithynia to one of the consuls of the current year: the successor of Lucullus, the consul Manius Acilius Glabrio, had already landed in Asia Minor. The disbanding of the bravest and most turbulent legions and the recall of the commander-in-chief, in connection with the impression produced by the defeat of Ziela, dissolved all the bonds of authority in the army just when the general had most urgent need of their aid. Near Talaura in Lesser Armenia he confronted the Pontic troops, at whose head Tigranes' son-in-law, Mithradates of Media, had already engaged the Romans successfully in a cavalry conflict; the main force of the great king was advancing to the same point from Armenia. Lucullus sent to Quintus Marcius the new governor of Cilicia, who had just arrived on the way to his province with three legions in Lycaonia, to ask him for aid; Marcius declared that his soldiers refused to march to Armenia. He sent to Glabrio with the request that he would take up the supreme command committed to him by the people; Glabrio showed still less inclination to undertake this task, which had now become so difficult and hazardous. Lucullus, compelled to retain the command, with the view of not being obliged to fight at Talaura against the Armenian and the Pontic armies conjoined, ordered a movement against the advancing Armenians.

The soldiers obeyed the order to march; but, when they reached the point where the routes to Armenia and Cappadocia diverged, the bulk of the army took the latter, and proceeded to the province of Asia. There the Fimbrians demanded their immediate discharge; and although they desisted from this at the urgent entreaty of the commander-in-chief and the other corps, they yet persevered in their purpose of disbanding if the winter should come on without an enemy confronting them; which accordingly was the case. Mithradates not only occupied once more almost his whole kingdom, but his cavalry ranged over all Cappadocia and as far as Bithynia; king Ariobarzanes sought help equally in vain from Quintus Marcius, from Lucullus, and from Glabrio. It was a strange almost incredible issue for a war conducted in a manner so glorious. If we look merely to military achievements, hardly any other Roman general accomplished so much with so trifling means as Lucullus; the talent and the fortune of Sulla seemed to have devolved on this his disciple. That under the circumstances the Roman army should have returned from Armenia to Asia Minor uninjured, is a military miracle which, so far as we can judge, far excels the retreat of Xenophon; and, although mainly doubtless to be explained by the solidity of the Roman, and the inefficiency of the Oriental, system of war, it at all events secures to the leader of this expedition an honourable name in the foremost rank of men of military capacity. If the name of Lucullus is not usually included among these, it is to all appearance simply owing to the fact that no narrative of his campaigns which is in a military point of view even tolerable has come down to us, and to the circumstance that in everything, and particularly in war, nothing is taken into account but the final result; and this, in reality, was equivalent to a complete defeat. Through the last unfortunate turn of things, and principally through the mutiny of the soldiers, all the results of an eight years' war had been lost; in the winter of $\frac{687-688}{67-66}$ the Romans again stood exactly at the same spot as in the winter of $\frac{679-680}{75-74}$.

The maritime war against the pirates, which began at the same time with the continental war and was all along most closely connected with it, yielded no better results. It has been already mentioned (p. 50) that the senate in $\frac{680}{74}$ adopted the judicious resolution to entrust the task of clearing the seas from the corsairs to a single admiral in supreme command, the praetor Marcus Antonius. But at the very outset they had made an utter mistake in the choice of the leader; or rather those who had carried this measure, so appropriate in itself, had not taken into account that in the senate all personal questions were decided by the influence of Cethegus (p. 7) and similar coterie-considerations. They had moreover neglected to furnish the admiral of their choice with money and ships in a manner befitting his comprehensive task, so that with his enormous requisitions he was almost as burdensome to the provincials whom he befriended as were the corsairs. The results were corresponding. In the Campanian waters the fleet of Antonius captured a number of piratical vessels. But an engagement took place with the Cretans, who had entered into friendship and alliance with the pirates and abruptly rejected his demand that they should desist from such fellowship; and the chains, with which the foresight of Antonius had provided his vessels for the purpose of placing the captive buccaneers in irons, served to fasten the quaestor and the other Roman prisoners to the masts of the captured Roman ships, when the Cretan generals Lasthenes and Panares steered back in triumph to Cydonia from the naval combat in which they had engaged the Romans off their island. Antonius, after having squandered immense sums and accomplished not the slightest result by his inconsiderate mode of warfare, died in $\frac{683}{71}$ at Crete. The bad success of his expedition, the costliness of building a fleet, and the repugnance of the oligarchy to confer any powers of a more comprehensive kind on the magistrates, led them, after the practical termination of this enterprise by Antonius' death, to make no farther nomination of an admiral in chief, and to revert to the old system of leaving each governor to look after the suppression of piracy in his own province: the fleet equipped by Lucullus for instance (p. 53) was actively employed for this purpose in the Aegean sea.

So far however as the Cretans were concerned, a disgrace like that endured off Cydonia seemed even to the degenerate Romans of this age as if it could be answered only by a declaration of war. Yet the Cretan envoys, who in the year $\frac{684}{70}$ appeared in Rome soliciting that the prisoners might be taken back and the old alliance re-established, had almost obtained a favourable decree of the senate; what the whole corporation termed a disgrace, the individual senator was ready to sell for a substantial price. It was not till a formal resolution of the senate rendered the loans of the Cretan envoys among the Roman bankers non-actionable—that is, not until the senate had incapacitated itself for undergoing bribery—that a decree passed to the effect that the Cretan communities, if they wished to avoid war, should hand over not only the Roman deserters but the authors of the outrage perpetrated off Cydonia—the leaders Lasthenes and Panares—to the Romans for befitting punishment should deliver up all ships and boats of four or more oars, should furnish 400 hostages, and should pay a fine of 4000 talents (£975,000). When the envoys declared that they were not empowered to enter into such terms, one of the consuls of the next year was appointed to depart on the expiry of his official term for Crete, in order either to receive there what was demanded or to begin the war.

Accordingly in $\frac{686}{68}$ the proconsul Quintus Metellus appeared in the Cretan waters. The communities of the island, with the larger towns Gortyna, Cnossus, Cydonia at their head were resolved rather to defend themselves in arms than to submit to those excessive demands. The Cretans were a nefarious and degenerate people (iii. 61), with whose public and private existence piracy was as intimately associated as robbery with the commonwealth of the Aetolians; but they resembled the Aetolians in valour as in many other respects, and accordingly these two were the only Greek communities that waged a courageous and honourable struggle for independence. At

Cydonia, where Metellus landed his three legions, a Cretan army of 24,000 men under Lasthenes and Panares was ready to receive him; a battle took place in the open field, in which the victory after a hard struggle remained with the Romans. Nevertheless the towns bade defiance from behind their walls to the Roman general; Metellus had to make up his mind to besiege them in succession. First Cydonia, in which the remains of the beaten army had taken refuge, was after a long siege surrendered by Panares in return for the promise of a free departure for himself. Lasthenes, who had escaped from the town, had to be besieged a second time in Cnossus; and, when this fortress also was on the point of falling, he destroyed its treasures and escaped once more to places which still continued their defence, such as Lyctus, Eleutherna, and others. Two years ($\frac{686}{68}$, $\frac{687}{67}$) elapsed before Metellus became master of the whole island, and the last spot of free Greek soil thereby passed under the control of the dominant Romans; the Cretan communities, as they were the first of all Greek commonwealths to develop the free urban constitution and the dominion of the sea, were also to be the last of all the Greek maritime states formerly filling the Mediterranean to succumb to the Roman continental power.

All the legal conditions were fulfilled for celebrating another of the usual pompous triumphs; the *gens* of the Metelli could add to its Macedonian, Numidian, Dalmatian, Balearic titles with equal right to the new title of Creticus, and Rome possessed another name of pride. Nevertheless the power of the Romans in the Mediterranean was never lower, that of the corsairs never higher than in those years. Well might the Cilicians and Cretans of the seas, who are said to have numbered at this time 1000 ships, mock the Isauricus and the Creticus, and their empty victories. With what effect the pirates interfered in the Mithradatic war, and how the obstinate resistance of the Pontic maritime towns derived its best resources from the corsair-state has been already related. But that state transacted business on a hardly less grand scale on its own behoof. Almost under the eyes of the fleet of Lucullus, the pirate Athenodorus surprised in $\frac{685}{69}$ the island of Delos, destroyed its far-famed shrines and temples, and carried off the whole population into slavery. The island Lipara near Sicily paid to the pirates a fixed tribute annually, to remain exempt from like attacks. Another pirate chief Heracleon destroyed in $\frac{682}{72}$ the squadron equipped in Sicily against him, and ventured with no more than four open boats to sail into the harbour of Syracuse. Two years later his colleague Pyrganion even landed at the same port, established himself there and sent forth flying parties into the island, till the Roman governor at last compelled him to re-embark. People grew at length quite accustomed to the fact that all the provinces equipped squadrons and raised coastguards, or were at any rate taxed for both; and yet the pirates appeared to plunder the provinces with as much regularity as the Roman governors. But even the sacred soil of Italy was now no longer respected by the shameless transgressors: from Croton they carried off with them the temple-treasures of the Lacinian Hera; they landed in Brundisium, Misenum, Caieta, in the Etruscan ports, even in Ostia itself; they seized the most eminent Roman officers as captives, among others the admiral of the Cilician army and two praetors with their whole retinue, with the dreaded *fasces* themselves and all the insignia of their dignity; they carried away from a villa at Misenum the very sister of the Roman admiral-in-chief Antonius, who was sent forth to annihilate the pirates; they destroyed in the port of Ostia the Roman war fleet equipped against them and commanded by a consul. The Latin husbandman, the traveller on the Appian highway, the genteel visitor at the terrestrial paradise of Baiae were no longer secure of their property or their life for a single moment; all traffic and all intercourse were suspended; the most dreadful scarcity prevailed in Italy, and especially in the capital, which subsisted on transmarine corn. The contemporary world and history indulge freely in complaints of the insupportable distress; in this case the epithet may have been appropriate.

We have already described how the senate restored by Sulla carried out its guardianship of the frontier in Macedonia, its discipline over the client kings of Asia Minor, its marine police; the results were nowhere satisfactory. Nor did better success attend the government in another and perhaps even more urgent matter, the supervision of the provincial, and above all of the Italian proletariate. The gangrene of a slave-proletariate gnawed at the vitals of all the states of antiquity, and the more so, the more vigorously they had risen and prospered; for the power and riches of the state regularly led, under the existing circumstances, to a disproportionate increase of the body of slaves. Rome naturally suffered more severely from this cause than any other state of antiquity. Even the government of the sixth century had been under the necessity of sending troops against the gangs of runaway herdsmen and rural slaves. The plantation system, spreading more and more among the Italian speculators, had infinitely increased the dangerous evil: in the time of the Gracchan and Marian crises and in close connection with them servile revolts had taken place at numerous points of the Roman empire, and in Sicily had even grown into two bloody wars ($\frac{619-622}{135-132}$ and $\frac{652-654}{102-100}$; iii. 76-78, 131-134). But the ten years of the rule of the restoration after Sulla's death formed the golden age both for the buccaneers at sea and for bands of a similar character on land, above all in the Italian peninsula, which had hitherto been comparatively well regulated. The land could hardly be said any longer to enjoy peace. In the capital and the less populous districts of Italy robberies were of every-day occurrence, murders were frequent. A special decree of the people was issued—perhaps at this epoch—against kidnapping of foreign slaves and of free men; a special summary action was about this time introduced against violent deprivation of landed property. These crimes could not but appear specially dangerous, because, while they were usually perpetrated by the proletariate, the higher class were to a great extent also concerned in them as moral originators and partakers in the gain. The abduction of men and of estates was very frequently suggested by the overseers of the large estates and carried out by the gangs of slaves, frequently armed, that were collected there: and many a man even of high respectability did not disdain what one of his officious slave-overseers thus acquired for him as Mephistopheles acquired for Faust the lime-trees of Philemon. The state of things is shown by the aggravated punishment for outrages on property committed by armed bands, which was introduced by one of the better Optimates, Marcus Lucullus, as presiding over the administration of justice in the capital about the year $\frac{676}{78}$,[1] with the express object of inducing the proprietors of large bands of slaves to exercise a more strict superintendence over them and thereby avoid the penalty of seeing them judicially condemned. Where pillage and murder were thus carried on by order of the world of quality, it was natural for these masses of slaves and proletarians to prosecute the same business on their own account; a spark was sufficient to set fire to so inflammable materials, and to convert the proletariate into an insurrectionary army. An occasion was soon found.

The gladiatorial games, which now held the first rank among the popular amusements in Italy, had led to the institution of

[1] These enactments gave rise to the conception of robbery as a separate crime, while the older law comprehended robbery under theft.

numerous establishments, more especially in and around Capua, designed partly for the custody, partly for the training of those slaves who were destined to kill or be killed for the amusement of the sovereign multitude. These were naturally in great part brave men captured in war, who had not forgotten that they had once faced the Romans in the field. A number of these desperadoes broke out of one of the Capuan gladiatorial schools ($\frac{681}{73}$), and sought refuge on Mount Vesuvius. At their head were two Celts, who are designated by their slave-names Crixus and Oenomaus, and the Thracian Spartacus. The latter, perhaps a scion of the noble family of the Spartocids which attained even to royal honours in its Thracian home and in Panticapaeum, had served among the Thracian auxiliaries in the Roman army, had deserted and gone as a brigand to the mountains, and had been there recaptured and destined for the gladiatorial games.

The inroads of this little band, numbering at first only seventy-four persons, but rapidly swelling by concourse from the surrounding country, soon became so troublesome to the inhabitants of the rich region of Campania, that these, after having vainly attempted themselves to repel them, sought help against them from Rome. A division of 3000 men hurriedly collected appeared under the leadership of Clodius Glaber, and occupied the approaches of Vesuvius with the view of starving out the slaves. But the brigands in spite of their small number and their defective armament had the boldness to scramble down steep declivities and to fall upon the Roman posts; and when the wretched militia saw the little band of desperadoes unexpectedly assail them, they took to their heels and fled on all sides. This first success procured for the robbers arms and large accessions to their ranks. Although even now a great portion of them carried nothing but pointed clubs, the new and stronger division of the militia—two legions under the praetor Publius Varinius—which advanced from Rome into Campania, found them encamped almost like a regular army in the plain. Varinius had a difficult position. His militia, compelled to bivouac opposite the enemy, were severely weakened by the damp autumn weather and the diseases which it engendered; and, worse than the epidemics, cowardice and insubordination thinned the ranks. At the very outset one of his divisions broke up entirely, so that the fugitives did not fall back on the main corps, but went straight home. Thereupon, when the order was given to advance against the enemy's entrenchments and attack them, the greater portion of the troops refused to comply with it. Nevertheless Varinius set out with those who kept their ground against the robber-band; but it was no longer to be found where he sought it. It had broken up in the deepest silence and had turned to the south towards Picentia (Vicenza near Amalfi), where Varinius overtook it, but could not prevent it from retiring over the Silarus to the interior of Lucania, the chosen land of shepherds and robbers. Varinius followed thither, and there at length the despised enemy arrayed themselves for battle. All the circumstances under which the combat took place were to the disadvantage of the Romans: the soldiers, vehemently as they had demanded battle a little before, fought ill; Varinius was completely vanquished; his horse and the insignia of his official dignity fell with the Roman camp itself into the enemy's hand. The south-Italian slaves, especially the brave half-savage herdsmen, flocked in crowds to the banner of the deliverers who had so unexpectedly appeared; according to the most moderate estimates the number of armed insurgents rose to 40,000 men. Campania, just evacuated, was speedily reoccupied, and the Roman corps which was left behind there under Gaius Thoranius, the quaestor of Varinius, was broken and destroyed. In the whole south and south-west of Italy the open country was in the hands of the victorious bandit-chiefs; even considerable towns, such as Consentia in the Bruttian country, Thurii and Metapontum in Lucania, Nola and Nuceria in Campania, were stormed by them, and suffered all the atrocities which victorious barbarians could inflict on defenceless civilised men, and unshackled slaves on their former masters. That a conflict like this should be altogether abnormal and more a massacre than a war, was unhappily a matter of course: the masters duly crucified every captured slave; the slaves naturally killed their prisoners also, or with still more sarcastic retaliation even compelled their Roman captives to slaughter each other in gladiatorial sport; as was subsequently done with three hundred of them at the obsequies of a robber-captain who had fallen in combat.

In Rome people were with reason apprehensive as to the destructive power of a conflagration which was daily spreading. It was resolved next year ($\frac{682}{72}$) to send both consuls against the formidable leaders of the gang. The praetor Quintus Arrius, a lieutenant of the consul Lucius Gellius, actually succeeded in seizing and destroying at Mount Garganus in Apulia the Celtic band, which under Crixus had separated from the mass of the robber-army and was levying contributions for itself. But Spartacus achieved all the more brilliant victories in the Apennines and in northern Italy, where first the consul Gnaeus Lentulus who had thought to surround and capture the robbers, then his colleague Gellius and the so recently victorious praetor Arrius, and lastly at Mutina the governor of Cisalpine Gaul Gaius Cassius (consul 681) and the praetor Gnaeus Manlius, one after another succumbed to his blows. The scarcely armed gangs of slaves were the terror of the legions; the series of defeats recalled the first years of the Hannibalic war.

What might have come of it, had the national kings from the mountains of Auvergne or of the Balkan, and not runaway gladiatorial slaves, been at the head of the victorious bands, it is impossible to say; as it was, the movement remained notwithstanding its brilliant victories a rising of robbers, and succumbed less to the superior force of its opponents than to internal discord and the want of regular plan. The unity in confronting the common foe, which was so remarkably conspicuous in the earlier servile wars of Sicily, was wanting in this Italian war—a difference probably due to the fact that, while the Sicilian slaves found a quasi-national point of union in the common Syrohellenism, the Italian slaves were separated into the two bodies of Helleno-Barbarians and Celto-Germans. The rupture between the Celtic Crixus and the Thracian Spartacus—Oenomaus had fallen in one of the earliest conflicts—and other similar quarrels hindered them from turning the successes achieved to good account, and procured for the Romans several important victories. But the want of a definite plan and aim produced far more injurious effects on the enterprise than the insubordination of the Celto-Germans. Spartacus doubtless—to judge by the little which we learn regarding that remarkable man—stood in this respect above his party. Along with his strategic ability he displayed no ordinary talent for organisation, as indeed from the very outset the uprightness with which he presided over his band and distributed the spoil had directed the eyes of the multitude to him quite as much at least as his valour. To remedy the severely felt want of cavalry and of arms, he tried with the help of the herds of horses seized in Lower Italy to train and discipline a cavalry, and, so soon as he got the port of Thurii into his hands, to procure from that quarter iron and copper, doubtless through the medium of the pirates. But he was unable in the main to induce the wild hordes whom he led to pursue any definite ulterior aims.

Gladly would he have checked the frantic orgies of cruelty, in which the robbers indulged on the capture of towns, and which formed the chief reason why no Italian city voluntarily made common cause with the insurgents; but the obedience which the bandit-chief found in battle ceased with the victory, and his representations and entreaties were in vain. After the victories obtained in the Appenines in $\frac{682}{72}$ the slave army was free to move in any direction. Spartacus himself is said to have intended to cross the Alps, with a view to open to himself and his followers the means of return to their Celtic or Thracian home: if the statement is well-founded, it shows how little the conqueror overrated his successes and his power. When his men refused so speedily to forsake the riches of Italy, Spartacus took the route for Rome, and is said to have meditated blockading the capital. The troops, however, showed themselves also averse to this desperate but yet methodical enterprise; they compelled their leader, when he was desirous to be a general, to remain a mere captain of banditti and aimlessly to wander to and fro in search of plunder. Rome might think herself fortunate that the matter took this turn; but even as it was, the perplexity was great. There was a want of trained soldiers and experienced generals; Quintus Metellus and Gnaeus Pompeius were employed in Spain, Marcus Lucullus in Thrace, Lucius Lucullus in Asia Minor; and none but raw militia and, at best, mediocre officers were available. The extraordinary supreme command in Italy was given to the praetor Marcus Crassus, who was not a general of much reputation, but had fought with honour under Sulla and had at least character; and an army of eight legions, imposing if not by its quality, at any rate by its numbers, was placed at his disposal. The new commander-in-chief began by treating the first division which again threw away its arms and fled before the banditti with all the severity of martial law, and causing every tenth man in it to be executed; whereupon the legions in reality grew somewhat more manly. Spartacus, vanquished in the next engagement, retreated and sought to reach Rhegium through Lucania.

Just at that time the pirates commanded not merely the Sicilian waters, but even the port of Syracuse (p. 71); with the help of their boats Spartacus proposed to throw a corps into Sicily, where the slaves only waited for instigation to break out a third time. The march to Rhegium was accomplished; but the corsairs, perhaps terrified by the coastguards established in Sicily by the praetor Gaius Verres, perhaps also bribed by the Romans, took from Spartacus the stipulated hire without performing the service for which it was given. Crassus meanwhile had followed the robber-army nearly as far as the mouth of the Crathis, and, like Scipio before Numantia, ordered his soldiers, seeing that they did not fight as they ought, to construct an entrenched wall of the length of thirty-two miles, which shut off the Bruttian peninsula from the rest of Italy,[1] intercepted the insurgent army on the return from Rhegium, and cut off its supplies. But in a dark winter night Spartacus broke through the lines of the enemy, and in the spring of $\frac{683}{71}$ [2] was once more in Lucania. The laborious work had thus been in vain. Crassus began to despair of accomplishing his task and demanded that the senate should for his support recall to Italy the armies stationed in Macedonia under Marcus Lucullus and in Hither Spain under Gnaeus Pompeius.

This extreme step however was not needed; the disunion and the arrogance of the robber-bands sufficed again to frustrate their successes. Once more the Celts and Germans broke off from the league of which the Thracian was the head and soul, in order that, under leaders of their own nation Gannicus and Castus, they might separately fall victims to the sword of the Romans. Once, at the Lucanian lake, the opportune appearance of Spartacus saved them, and thereupon they pitched their camp near to his; nevertheless Crassus succeeded in giving employment to Spartacus by means of the cavalry, and meanwhile surrounded the Celtic bands and compelled them to a separate engagement, in which the whole body—numbering it is said 12,300 combatants—fell fighting bravely all on the spot and with their wounds in front. Spartacus then attempted to throw himself with his division into the mountains round Petelia (near Strongoli in Calabria), and signally defeated the Roman vanguard, which followed his retreat. But this victory proved more injurious to the victor than to the vanquished. Intoxicated by success, the robbers refused to retreat farther, and compelled their general to lead them through Lucania towards Apulia to face the last decisive struggle. Before the

[1] As the line was thirty-two miles long (Sallust, *Hist.* iv. 19, Dietsch; Plutarch, *Crass.* 10), it probably passed not from Squillace to Pizzo, but more to the north, somewhere near Castrovillari and Cassano, over the peninsula which is here in a straight line about twenty-seven miles broad.

[2] That Crassus was invested with the supreme command in $\frac{682}{72}$, follows from the setting aside of the consuls (Plutarch, *Crass.* 10); that the winter of $\frac{682-683}{72-71}$ was spent by the two armies at the Bruttian wall, follows from the "snowy night" (Plut. *l. c.*).

battle Spartacus stabbed his horse: as in prosperity and adversity he had faithfully kept by his men, he now by that act showed them that the issue for him and for all was victory or death. In the battle he fought with the courage of a lion; two centurions fell by his hand; wounded and on his knees he still wielded his spear against the assailing foe. Thus the great robber-captain and with him the best of his comrades died the death of free men and of honourable soldiers ($\frac{683}{71}$). After the dearly-bought victory the troops who had achieved it, and those of Pompeius that had meanwhile after conquering the Sertorians arrived from Spain, instituted throughout Apulia and Lucania a man-hunt, such as there had never been before, to crush out the last sparks of the mighty conflagration. Although in the southern districts, where for instance the little town of Tempsa was seized in $\frac{683}{71}$ by a gang of robbers, and in Etruria, which was severely affected by Sulla's evictions, there was by no means as yet general tranquillity, peace was officially considered as re-established in Italy. At least the disgracefully lost eagles were recovered—after the victory over the Celts alone five of them were brought in; and along the road from Capua to Rome the six thousand crosses bearing captured slaves testified to the re-establishment of order, and to the renewed victory of acknowledged right over its living property that had rebelled.

Let us look back on the events which fill up the decennium of the Sullan restoration. No one of the movements, external or internal, which occurred during this period—neither the insurrection of Lepidus, nor the enterprises of the Spanish emigrants, nor the wars in Thrace and Macedonia and in Asia Minor, nor the risings of the pirates and the slaves—constituted of itself a great danger necessarily affecting the life-springs of the nation; and yet the state had in all these struggles well-nigh fought for its very existence. The reason was that the tasks were everywhere left unperformed, so long as they might still have been performed with ease; the neglect of the simplest precautionary measures produced the most dreadful mischiefs and misfortunes, and transformed dependent classes and impotent kings into antagonists on a footing of equality. The democracy and the servile insurrection were doubtless subdued; but such as the victories were, the victor was neither inwardly elated nor outwardly strengthened by them. It was no credit to Rome, that the two most celebrated generals of the government-party had during a struggle of eight years marked by more defeats than victories failed to master the insurgent chief

Sertorius and his Spanish guerillas, and that it was only the dagger of his friends that decided the Sertorian war in favour of the legitimate government. As to the slaves, it was far less an honour to have conquered them than a disgrace to have been pitted against them in equal strife for years. Little more than a century had elapsed since the Hannibalic war; it must have brought a blush to the cheek of the honourable Roman, when he reflected on the fearfully rapid decline of the nation since that great age. Then the Italian slaves stood like a wall against the veterans of Hannibal; now the Italian militia were scattered like chaff before the bludgeons of their runaway serfs. Then every plain captain acted in case of need as general, and fought often without success, but always with honour; now it was difficult to find among all the officers of rank a leader of even ordinary efficiency. Then the government preferred to take the last farmer from the plough rather than forego the acquisition of Spain and Greece; now they were on the eve of again abandoning both regions long since acquired, merely that they might be able to defend themselves against the insurgent slaves at home. Spartacus too as well as Hannibal had traversed Italy with an army from the Po to the Sicilian straits, beaten both consuls, and threatened Rome with blockade; the enterprise which it required the greatest general of antiquity to undertake against the Rome of former days could be undertaken against the Rome of the present by a daring captain of banditti. Was there any wonder that no fresh life sprang out of such victories over insurgents and robber-chiefs?

The external wars, however, had produced a result still less satisfactory. It is true that the Thraco-Macedonian war yielded a result not directly unfavourable, although far from corresponding to the considerable expenditure of men and money. In the wars in Asia Minor and with the pirates on the other hand, the government had exhibited utter failure. The former ended with the loss of the whole conquests made in eight bloody campaigns, the latter with the total driving of the Romans from "their own sea." Once Rome, fully conscious of the irresistibleness of her power by land, had transferred her superiority also to the other element; now the mighty state was powerless at sea and, as it seemed, on the point of losing its dominion at least over the Asiatic continent. The material benefits which a state exists to confer—security of frontier, undisturbed peaceful intercourse, legal protection, and regulated administration—began all of them to vanish for the whole of the nations united in the

Roman state; the gods of blessing seemed all to have ascended to Olympus and to have left the miserable earth at the mercy of official or volunteer plunderers and tormentors. Nor was this decay of the state felt as a public misfortune merely perhaps by such as had political rights and public spirit; the insurrection of the proletariate, and the brigandage and piracy which remind us of the times of the Neapolitan Ferdinands, carried the sense of this decay into the remotest valley and the humblest hut of Italy, and made every one who pursued trade and commerce, or who bought even a bushel of wheat, feel it as a personal calamity.

If enquiry was made as to the authors of this dreadful and unexampled misery, it was not difficult to charge the blame of it with good reason on many. The slaveholders whose heart was in their money-bags, the insubordinate soldiers, the generals cowardly, incapable, or foolhardy, the demagogues of the market-place mostly pursuing a mistaken aim, bore their share of the blame; or, to speak more truly, who was there that did not share it? It was instinctively felt that this misery, this disgrace, this disorder were too colossal to be the work of any one man. As the greatness of the Roman commonwealth was the work not of prominent individuals, but rather of a soundly-organised community of burgesses, so the decay of this mighty structure was the result not of the destructive genius of individuals, but of a general disorganisation. The great majority of the burgesses were good for nothing, and every rotten stone in the building helped to bring about the ruin of the whole; the whole nation suffered for what was the whole nation's fault. It was unjust to hold the government, as the ultimate tangible organ of the state, responsible for all its curable and incurable diseases; but it certainly was true that the government shared to a very grave extent the general culpability. In the Asiatic war, for example, where no individual of the ruling lords conspicuously failed, and Lucullus, in a military point of view at least, behaved with ability and even glory, it was all the more clear that the blame of failure lay in the system and in the government as such—mainly, so far as that war was concerned, in the remissness with which Cappadocia and Syria were at first abandoned, and in the awkward position of the able general with reference to a governing college incapable of any energetic resolution. In maritime police likewise the true idea which the senate had taken up as to a general hunting out of the pirates was first spoilt by it in the execution and then totally dropped, in order to revert to the old foolish system of sending legions against the coursers of the seas. The expeditions of Servilius and Marcius to Cilicia, and of Metellus to Crete, were undertaken on this system; and in accordance with it Triarius had the island of Delos surrounded by a wall for protection against the pirates. Such attempts to secure the dominion of the seas remind us of the Persian great king, who ordered the sea to be scourged with rods to make it subject to him. Doubtless therefore the nation had good reason for laying the blame of its failure primarily on the government of the restoration. A similar misrule had indeed previously accompanied the re-establishment of the oligarchy, after the fall of the Gracchi as after that of Marius and Saturninus; yet never before had it borne itself with such violence and at the same time such laxity, never had it appeared so corrupt and pernicious. But, when a government cannot govern, it ceases to be legitimate, and whoever has the power has also the right to overthrow it. It is, no doubt, unhappily true that an incapable and flagitious government may for a long period trample under foot the welfare and honour of the land, before the men are found who are able and willing to wield against that government the formidable weapons of its own forging, and to evoke out of the moral revolt of the good and the distress of the many the revolution which such circumstances legitimise. But if the game with the fortunes of nations may be a merry one and may be played perhaps for a long time without molestation, it is a treacherous game, which in its own time entraps the players; and no one then blames the axe, if it is laid to the root of the tree that bears such fruits. For the Roman oligarchy this time had now come. The Pontic-Armenian war and the affair of the pirates became the proximate grounds for the overthrow of the Sullan constitution and for the establishment of a revolutionary military dictatorship.

CHAPTER III

THE FALL OF THE OLIGARCHY AND THE RULE OF POMPEIUS

THE Sullan constitution still stood unshaken. The assault, which Lepidus and Sertorius had ventured to make on it, had been repulsed with little loss. The government had neglected, it is true, to finish the half-completed building in the energetic spirit of its author. It is characteristic of the government, that it neither distributed the lands which Sulla had destined for allotment but had not yet parcelled out, nor directly abandoned the claim to them, but tolerated the former owners in provisional possession without regulating their title, and indeed even allowed various still undistributed tracts of Sullan domain-land to be arbitrarily taken possession of by individuals according to the old system of occupation which was *de jure* and *de facto* set aside by the Gracchan reforms (iii. 336). Whatever in the Sullan enactments was indifferent or inconvenient for the Optimates, was without scruple ignored or cancelled; for instance, the sentences by which whole communities were deprived of the state-franchise, the prohibition against conjoining the new farms, and several of the charters conferred by Sulla on particular communities—naturally, however, without giving back to the communities the sums paid for these exemptions. But though these violations of the ordinances of Sulla by the government itself contributed to shake the foundations of his structure, the Sempronian laws were substantially abolished and remained so.

There was no lack, indeed, of men who had in view the re-establishment of the Gracchan constitution, or of projects to attain piecemeal in the way of constitutional reform what Lepidus and Sertorius had attempted by the path of revolution. The government had already under the pressure of the agitation of Lepidus immediately after the death of Sulla consented to a limited revival of the largesses of grain ($\frac{676}{78}$); and it did, moreover, what it could to satisfy the proletariate of the capital in regard to this vital question. When, notwithstanding those distributions, the high price of grain occasioned chiefly by piracy produced so oppressive a dearth in Rome as to lead to a violent tumult in the streets in $\frac{679}{75}$, extraordinary purchases of Sicilian grain on account of the government relieved for the time the most severe distress; and a corn-law brought in by the consuls of $\frac{681}{73}$ regulated for the future the purchases of Sicilian grain and furnished the government, although at the expense of the provincials, with better means of obviating similar evils. But the less material points of difference also—the restoration of the tribunician power in its old compass, and the setting aside of the senatorial tribunals—ceased not to form subjects of popular agitation; and in their case the government offered more decided resistance. The dispute regarding the tribunician magistracy was opened as early as $\frac{678}{76}$, immediately after the defeat of Lepidus, by the tribune of the people Lucius Sicinius, perhaps a descendant of the man of the same name who had first filled this office more than four hundred years before; but it failed before the opposition made to it by the active consul Gaius Curio. In $\frac{680}{74}$ Lucius Quinctius resumed the agitation, but was induced by the authority of the consul Lucius Lucullus to desist from his purpose. The matter was taken up in the following year with greater zeal by Gaius Licinius Macer, who—in a way characteristic of the period—carried his literary studies into public life, and counselled the burgesses, just as he had read in the Annals, to refuse the conscription.

Complaints also, only too well founded, prevailed respecting the bad administration of justice by the senatorial jurymen. The condemnation of a man of any influence could hardly be obtained. Not only did colleague feel reasonable compassion for colleague, those who had been or were likely to be accused for the poor sinner under accusation at the moment; the sale also of the votes of jurymen was hardly any longer exceptional. Several senators had been judicially convicted of this crime: men pointed with the finger at others equally guilty; the most respected Optimates, such as Quintus Catulus, granted in the open senate that the complaints were quite well-founded; individual specially striking cases compelled the senate on several occasions, *e.g.* in $\frac{680}{74}$, to deliberate on measures to check the venalities of juries, but only of course till the first outcry had subsided and the matter could be allowed to slip out of sight. The consequences of this wretched administration of justice appeared especially in a system of plundering and torturing the provincials, compared with which previous outrages even seemed tolerable and moderate. Stealing and robbing had been in some measure legitimised by custom; the commission on extortions might be regarded as an institution for taxing the senators returning from the provinces for the benefit of their colleagues that remained at home. But when a respectable Siceliot, because he had not been ready to help the governor in a crime, was by the latter condemned to death in his absence and unheard: when even Roman burgesses, if they were not equites or senators, were in the provinces no longer safe from the rods and axes of the Roman magistrate, and the oldest acquired right of the Roman democracy—security of life and person—began to be trodden under foot by the ruling oligarchy; then even the public in the Forum at Rome had an ear for the complaints regarding its magistrates in the provinces, and regarding the unjust judges who morally shared the responsibility of such misdeeds. The opposition of course did not omit to assail its opponents in—what was almost the only ground left to it—the tribunals. The young Gaius Caesar, who also, so far as his age allowed, took zealous part in the agitation for the revival of the tribunician power, brought to trial in 677/77 one of the most distinguished partisans of Sulla the consular Gnaeus Dolabella, and in the following year another Sullan officer Gaius Antonius; and Marcus Cicero in 684/70 called to account Gaius Verres, one of the most wretched of the creatures of Sulla, and one of the worst scourges of the provincials. Again and again were the pictures of that dark period of the proscriptions, the fearful sufferings of the provincials, the disgraceful state of Roman criminal justice, unfolded before the assembled multitude with all the parade of Italian rhetoric, and with all the bitterness of Italian sarcasm, and the mighty dead as well as his living instruments were unrelentingly exposed to their wrath and scorn. The re-establishment of the full tribunician power, with the continuance of which the freedom, might, and prosperity of the republic seemed bound up as by a charm of primeval sacredness, the reintroduction of the "stern" equestrian tribunals, the renewal of the censorship, which Sulla had set aside, for the purifying of the supreme governing board from its corrupt and pernicious elements, were daily demanded with a loud voice by the orators of the popular party.

But with all this no progress was made. There was scandal and outcry enough, but no real result was attained by this exposure of the government according to and beyond its deserts. The material power still lay, so long as there was no military interference, in the hands of the burgesses of the capital; and the "people" that thronged the streets of Rome and made magistrates and laws in the Forum, was in fact nowise better than the governing senate. The government no doubt had to come to terms with the multitude, where its own immediate interest was at stake; this was the reason for the renewal of the Sempronian corn-law. But it was not to be imagined that this populace would display earnestness on behalf of an idea or even of a judicious reform. What Demosthenes said of his Athenians was justly applied to the Romans of this period—the people were very zealous for action, so long as they stood round the platform and listened to proposals of reforms; but when they went home, no one thought further of what he had heard in the market-place. However those democratic agitators might stir the fire, it was to no purpose, for the inflammable material was wanting. The government knew this, and allowed no concession to be wrung from it on important questions of principle; at the utmost it consented about $\frac{682}{72}$ to grant amnesty to a portion of those who had become exiles with Lepidus. Any concessions that did take place, came not so much from the pressure of the democracy as from the attempts at mediation of the moderate aristocracy. But of the two laws which the single still surviving leader of this section Gaius Cotta carried in his consulate of $\frac{679}{75}$, that which concerned the tribunals was again set aside in the very next year; and the second, which abolished the Sullan enactment that those who had held the tribunate should be disqualified for undertaking other magistracies, but allowed the other limitations to continue, merely excited—like every half measure—the displeasure of both parties. The party of conservatives friendly to reform which lost its most eminent head by the early death of Cotta occurring soon after (about $\frac{681}{73}$) dwindled away more and more—crushed between the extremes, which were becoming daily more marked. But of these the party of the government, wretched and indolent as it was, necessarily retained the advantage in presence of the equally wretched and equally indolent opposition.

But this state of matters so favourable to the government was altered, when the differences became more distinctly developed which subsisted between it and those of its partisans whose hopes aspired to higher objects than the seat of honour in the senate and the aristocratic villa. In the first rank of these stood Gnaeus Pompeius. He was a Sullan; but we have already shown (p. 11) how little he was at home among his own party, how his lineage, his past history, his hopes still separated him from the nobility as whose protector and champion he was officially regarded. The breach already apparent had been widened irreparably during the Spanish campaigns of the general ($\frac{677-683}{77-71}$). With reluctance and semi-compulsion the government had associated him as colleague with their true representative Quintus Metellus; and in turn he accused the senate, probably not without ground, of having by its neglect of the Spanish armies, whether from carelessness or malice, occasioned their defeats and placed the fortunes of the expedition in jeopardy. Now he returned as victor over his open and his secret foes, at the head of an army inured to war and wholly devoted to him, requiring assignments of land for his soldiers, a triumph and consulship for himself. The latter demands came into collision with the law. Pompeius, although several times invested in an extraordinary way with supreme official authority, had not yet filled any ordinary magistracy, not even the quaestorship, and was still not a member of the senate; and none but one who had passed through the round of lesser ordinary magistracies could be consul, none but one who had been invested with the ordinary supreme power could triumph. The senate was legally entitled, if he became a candidate for the consulship, to bid him begin with the quaestorship; if he requested a triumph, to remind him of the great Scipio, who under like circumstances had renounced his triumph over conquered Spain. Nor was Pompeius less dependent constitutionally on the good will of the senate as respected the lands promised to his soldiers. But, although the senate—as with its feebleness even in animosity was very conceivable—should yield those points and concede to the victorious general in return for his acting as executioner against the democratic chiefs the triumph, the consulate, and the assignations of land, an honourable annihilation in senatorial indolence among the long series of peaceful senatorial *imperatores* was the most favourable lot which the oligarchy was able to assign to the general of thirty-six. That which his heart really longed for—the command in the Mithradatic war—he could never expect to obtain from the voluntary bestowal of the senate: in their own well-understood interest the oligarchy could not permit him to add to his African and European trophies those of a third continent; the laurels which were to be plucked copiously and easily in the East were reserved at all events for the pure aristocracy. But if the celebrated general did not find his account in the ruling oligarchy, there remained—for neither was the time ripe, nor was the temperament of Pompeius at all fitted, for a purely personal outspoken dynastic policy—no alternative save to make common cause with the democratic party. No special interest bound him to the Sullan constitution; he could pursue his personal objects quite as well, if not better, with one more democratic. On the other hand he found all that he needed in the democratic party. Its active and adroit leaders were ready and able to relieve the helpless and somewhat awkward hero of the trouble of political leadership, and yet much too insignificant to be able or even willing to dispute with the celebrated general the first place and especially the military supremacy. Even Gaius Caesar, by far the most important of them, was simply a young man whose daring exploits and fashionable debts far more than his fiery democratic eloquence had gained him a name, and who could not but feel himself greatly honoured when the world-renowned Imperator allowed him to be his political adjutant. That popularity, to which men like Pompeius, with pretensions greater than their abilities, usually attach more value than they are willing to confess, could not but fall in the highest measure to the lot of the young general whose accession should give victory to the almost forlorn cause of the democracy. The reward of victory claimed by him for himself and his soldiers would then follow of itself. In general it seemed, if the oligarchy were overthrown, that amidst the total want of other considerable chiefs of the opposition it would depend solely on Pompeius himself to determine his future position. And of this much there could hardly be a doubt, that the accession of the general of the army, which had just returned victorious from Spain and still stood unbroken in Italy, to the party of opposition must have as its consequence the fall of the existing order of things. Government and opposition were equally powerless; so soon as the latter no longer fought merely with the weapons of declamation, but had the sword of a victorious general ready to back its demands, the government would be overcome at all events, and that perhaps even without a struggle.

Pompeius and the democrats thus found themselves urged into coalition. Personal dislikings were probably not wanting on either side: it was not possible that the victorious general could love the street orators, nor could these hail with pleasure as their chief the executioner of Carbo and Brutus; but political necessity outweighed at least for the moment all moral scruples.

The democrats and Pompeius, however, were not the sole parties to the league. Marcus Crassus was in a similar situation with Pompeius. Although a Sullan like the latter, his politics were quite as in the case of Pompeius pre-eminently of a personal kind, and by no means those of the ruling oligarchy; and he too was now in Italy at the head of a large and victorious army, with which he had just suppressed the slave insurrection. He had to choose whether he would ally himself with the oligarchy against the coalition, or enter that coalition: he chose the latter, which was doubtless the safer course. With his colossal wealth and his influence on the clubs of the capital he was in any case a valuable ally; but under existing circumstances it was an incalculable gain, when the only army, with which the senate could have met the troops of Pompeius, joined the attacking force. The democrats moreover, who were probably somewhat uneasy at their alliance with that too powerful general, were not displeased to see a counterpoise and perhaps a future rival associated with him in the person of Marcus Crassus.

Thus in the summer of $\frac{683}{71}$ the first coalition took place between the democracy on the one hand, and the two Sullan generals Gnaeus Pompeius and Marcus Crassus on the other. The generals adopted the party-programme of the democracy; and they were promised immediately in return the consulship for the coming year, while Pompeius was to have also a triumph and the desired allotments of land for his soldiers, and Crassus as the conqueror of Spartacus at least the honour of a solemn entrance into the capital.

To the two Italian armies, the great capitalists, and the democracy, which thus came forward in league for the overthrow of the Sullan constitution, the senate had nothing to oppose save perhaps the second Spanish army under Quintus Metellus Pius. But Sulla had truly predicted that what he did would not be done a second time; Metellus, by no means inclined to involve himself in a civil war, had discharged his soldiers immediately after crossing the Alps. So nothing was left for the oligarchy but to submit to what was inevitable. The senate granted the dispensations requisite for the consulship and triumph; Pompeius and Crassus were, without opposition, elected consuls for $\frac{684}{70}$, while their armies, on pretext of awaiting their trumph, encamped before the city. Pompeius thereupon, even before entering on office, gave his public and formal adherence to the democratic programme in an assembly of the people held by the tribune Marcus Lollius Palicanus. The change of the constitution was thus in principle decided.

They now set to work in earnest to abolish the Sullan institutions. First of all the tribunician magistracy regained its earlier authority. Pompeius himself as consul introduced the law which gave back to the tribunes of the people their time-honoured prerogatives, and in particular the initiative of legislation—a singular gift indeed, from the hand of a man who had done more than any one living to wrest from the community its ancient privileges.

With respect to the jury tribunals, the regulation of Sulla, that the roll of the senators was to serve as the list of jurymen, was abolished; but this by no means led to a simple restoration of the Gracchan equestrian courts. In future—it was enacted by the new Aurelian law—the colleges of jurymen were to consist one-third of senators and two-thirds of men of equestrian census, and of the latter the half must have filled the office of district-presidents (the so-called *tribuni aerarii*). This last alteration was a farther concession made to the democrats, inasmuch as at least a third of the criminal *iudices*, just like the civil *iudices* of the court of the *centumviri*, were indirectly derived from the elections of the tribes. The reason, again, why the senate was not totally excluded from the tribunals is probably to be sought partly in the relations of Crassus to the senate, partly in the accession of the senatorial middle party to the coalition; with which is doubtless connected the circumstance that this law was brought in by the praetor Lucius Cotta, the brother of their lately deceased leader.

Not less important was the abolition of the arrangements as to taxation established for Asia by Sulla (iii. 337), which in all probability likewise took place this year. The governor of Asia at that time, Lucius Lucullus, was directed to re-establish the system of farming the revenue introduced by Gaius Gracchus; and thus this important source of money and power was restored to the great capitalists.

Lastly, not only was the censorship renewed, but probably at the same time the earlier limitation of the magistracy to a term of eighteen months was abolished, and the censors were allowed, in case they found it necessary, to hold office for five years—the professedly original term, namely that assigned to the first pair of censors in the Annals falsified in the interest of democracy. The elections which the new consuls fixed shortly after entering on their office fell, in evident mockery of the senate, on the two consuls of $\frac{682}{72}$, Gnaeus Lentulus Clodianus and Lucius Gellius, who had been removed by the senate from their commands on account of their wretched management of the war against Spartacus (p. 76). It may readily be conceived that these men put in motion all the means which their important and grave office placed at their command, for the purpose of doing homage to the new holders of power and of annoying the senate. At least an eighth part of the senate, sixty-four senators, a number hitherto unparalleled, were deleted from the roll, including Gaius Antonius, formerly impeached without success by Gaius Caesar (p. 85), Publius Lentulus Sura, the consul of $\frac{683}{71}$, and in all probability not a few of the most obnoxious creatures of Sulla.

Thus in $\frac{684}{70}$ they had reverted in the main to the arrangements that subsisted before the Sullan restoration. Again the multitude of the capital was fed from the state-chest, in other words from the provinces; again the tribunician authority gave to every demagogue a legal licence to overturn the arrangements of the state; again the moneyed nobility, as farmers of the revenue and possessed of the judicial control over the governors, raised their heads alongside of the government as powerfully as ever; again the senate trembled before the verdict of jurymen of the equestrian order and before the censorial censure. The system of Sulla, which had based the monopoly of power by the nobility on the political annihilation of the mercantile aristocracy and of demagogism, was thus completely overthrown. Leaving out of view some subordinate enactments the abolition of which was not overtaken till afterwards, such as the restoration of the right of self-completion to the priestly colleges (iii. 341), nothing of the general ordinances of Sulla survived except on the one hand concessions which he himself found it necessary to make to the opposition, such as the recognition of the Roman citizenship of all the Italians, and, on the other hand, enactments without any marked partisan tendency, and with which therefore even judicious democrats found no fault—such as, among others, the restriction of the freedmen, the regulation of the functions of the magistrates, and the material alterations in criminal law.

The coalition was more agreed regarding these questions of principle than with respect to the personal questions which such a political revolution raised. As might be expected, the democrats were not content with the general recognition of their programme; but they now demanded a restoration in their own sense—revival of the commemoration of their dead, punishment of the murderers, recall of the proscribed from exile, removal of the political disqualification that lay on their children, restoration of the estates confiscated by Sulla, indemnification at the expense of the heirs and assistants of the dictator. These were certainly the logical consequences which ensued from a pure victory of the democracy; but the victory of the coalition of $\frac{683}{71}$ was very far from being such. The democracy gave to it their name and their programme, but it was the officers who had joined the movement, and above all Pompeius, that gave to it power and completion; and these could never yield their consent to a reaction which would not only have shaken the existing state of things to its foundations, but would have ultimately turned against themselves—men still had a lively recollection whose blood Pompeius had shed, and how Crassus had laid the foundation of his enormous fortune. It was natural therefore, but at the same time significant of the weakness of the democracy, that the coalition of $\frac{683}{71}$ took not the slightest step towards procuring for the democrats revenge or even rehabilitation. The supplementary collection of all the purchase money still outstanding for confiscated estates bought by auction, or even remitted to the purchasers by Sulla—for which the censor Lentulus provided in a special law—can hardly be regarded as an exception; for though not a few Sullans were thereby severely affected in their personal interests, yet the measure itself was essentially a confirmation of the confiscations undertaken by Sulla.

The work of Sulla was thus destroyed; but what the future order of things was to be was a question raised rather than decided by that destruction. The coalition, kept together solely by the common object of setting aside the work of restoration, dissolved of itself, if not in name, at any rate in reality, when that object was attained; while the question to what quarter the preponderance of power was in the first instance to fall seemed approaching an equally speedy and violent solution. The armies of Pompeius and Crassus still lay before the gates of the city. The former had indeed promised to disband his soldiers after his triumph (last day of December, $\frac{683}{71}$); but he had left his promise unperformed, in order that the revolution in the state might be completed without hindrance under the pressure which the Spanish army in front of the capital exercised over the city and the senate—a precedent which in like manner applied to the army of Crassus. This reason now existed no longer; but still the dissolution of the armies was postponed. Matters looked as if one of the two generals allied with the democracy would seize the military dictatorship and place oligarchs and democrats in the same chains; and this one could only be Pompeius. From the first Crassus had played a subordinate part in the coalition; he had been obliged to propose himself, and owed even his election to the consulship mainly to the proud intercession of Pompeius. Far the stronger, Pompeius was evidently master of the situation; if he availed himself of it, it seemed as if he could not but become what the instinct of the multitude even now designated him—the absolute ruler of the mightiest state in the civilised world. Already the whole mass of the servile crowded around the future monarch. Already his weaker opponents were seeking their last resource in a new coalition; Crassus, full of old and recent jealousy towards the younger rival who so thoroughly outstripped him, made approaches to the senate and attempted by unprecedented largesses to attach to himself the multitude of the capital—as if the oligarchy which Crassus himself had helped to break down, and the ever ungrateful multitude, would have been able to afford any protection whatever against the veterans of the Spanish army. For a moment it seemed as if the armies of Pompeius and Crassus would come to blows before the gates of the capital.

But the democrats averted this catastrophe by their sagacity and their pliancy. For their party too, as well as for the senate and Crassus, it was all-important that Pompeius should not seize the dictatorship; but with a truer discernment of their own weakness and of the character of their powerful opponent their leaders tried the method of conciliation. Pompeius lacked no condition for grasping at the crown except the first of all—true kingly courage. We have already described the man—with his effort to be at once loyal republican and master of Rome, with his vacillation and indecision, with his pliableness that concealed itself under the boasting of independent resolution. This was the first great trial to which destiny subjected him; and he failed to stand it. The pretext under which Pompeius refused to dismiss the army was, that he distrusted Crassus and therefore could not take the initiative in disbanding the soldiers. The democrats induced Crassus to make gracious advances in the matter, and to present overtures of peace to his colleague before the eyes of all; in public and in private they besought the latter that to the double merit of having vanquished the enemy and reconciled the parties he would add the third and yet greater service of preserving internal peace to his country, and banishing the fearful spectre of civil war with which they were threatened. Whatever could tell on a vain, unskilful, vacillating man—all the flattering arts of diplomacy, all the theatrical apparatus of patriotic enthusiasm—was put in motion to obtain the desired result; and—which was the main point—things had by the well-timed compliances of Crassus assumed such a shape, that Pompeius had no alternative but either to come forward openly as tyrant of Rome or to retire. So he at length yielded and consented to disband the troops. The command in the Mithradatic war, which he doubtless hoped to obtain when he allowed himself to be chosen consul for $\frac{684}{70}$, he could not now desire, since Lucullus seemed to have practically ended that war with the campaign of $\frac{683}{71}$. He deemed it beneath his dignity to accept the consular province assigned him by the senate in accordance with the Sempronian law, and Crassus in this followed his example. Accordingly when Pompeius after discharging his soldiers resigned his consulship on the last day of $\frac{684}{70}$, he retired for the time wholly from public affairs, and declared that he wished thenceforth to live a quiet life as a simple citizen. He had put himself into such a position that he was obliged to grasp at the crown; and, seeing that he was not willing to do this, no part was left to him but the empty one of a candidate resigning his pretensions to a throne.

The retirement of the man, to whom as things stood the first place belonged, from the political stage produced in the first instance nearly the same position of parties which we found in the Gracchan and Marian epochs. Sulla had merely strengthened the senatorial government, not created it; so, after the bulwarks erected by Sulla had fallen, the government nevertheless remained primarily with the senate, although, no doubt, the constitution with which it governed—in the main the restored Gracchan constitution—was pervaded by a spirit hostile to the oligarchy. The democracy had effected the re-establishment of the Gracchan constitution; but without a new Gracchus it was a body without a head, and that neither Pompeius nor Crassus could be permanently such a head, was in itself clear and had been made still clearer by the recent events. So the democratic opposition, for want of a leader who could have directly seized the helm, had to content itself for the time being with hindering and annoying the government at every step. Between the oligarchy, however, and the democracy there rose into new consideration the capitalist party, which in the recent crisis had made common cause with the latter, but which the oligarchs now zealously endeavoured to draw over to their side so as to acquire in it a counterpoise to the democracy. Thus courted on both sides the moneyed lords did not neglect to turn their advantageous position to account, and to have the only one of their former privileges which they had not yet regained—the fourteen benches reserved for the equestrian order in the theatre—now ($\frac{687}{67}$) restored to them by decree of the people. On the whole, without abruptly breaking with the democracy, they again drew closer to the government. The very relations of the senate with Crassus and his clients point in this direction; but a better understanding between the senate and the moneyed aristocracy seems to have been chiefly brought about by the fact, that in $\frac{686}{68}$ the senate withdrew from Lucius Lucullus the ablest of the senatorial officers, at the instance of the capitalists whom he had sorely annoyed, the administration of the province of Asia so important for their purposes (p. 64).

But while the factions of the capital were indulging in their wonted mutual quarrels which they were never able to bring to any proper decision, events in the East followed their fatal course, as we have already described; and it was these events that brought the dilatory course of the politics of the capital to a crisis. The war both by land and by sea had there taken a most unfavourable turn. In the beginning of $\frac{687}{67}$ the Pontic army of the Romans was destroyed, and their Armenian army was utterly breaking up on its retreat; all their conquests were lost, the sea was exclusively in the power of the pirates, and the price of grain in Italy was thereby so raised that they were afraid of an actual famine. No doubt, as we saw, the faults of the generals, especially the utter incapacity of the admiral Marcus Antonius and the temerity of the otherwise able Lucius Lucullus, were in part the occasion of these calamities; no doubt also the democracy had by its revolutionary agitations materially contributed to the breaking up of the Armenian army. But of course the government was now held cumulatively responsible for all the mischief which itself and others had occasioned, and the indignant hungry multitude desired only an opportunity to settle accounts with the senate.

It was a decisive crisis. The oligarchy, though degraded and disarmed, was not yet overthrown, for the management of public affairs was still in the hands of the senate; but it would fall, if its opponents should appropriate to themselves that management and more especially the superintendence of military affairs; and now this was possible. If proposals for another and better management of the war by land and sea were now submitted to the comitia, the senate was obviously—looking to the temper of the burgesses—not in a position to prevent their passing; and an interference of the burgesses in these supreme questions of administration was practically the deposition of the senate and the transference of the management of the state to the leaders of opposition. Once more the concatenation of events brought the decision into the hands of Pompeius. For more than two years the famous general had lived as a private citizen in the capital. His voice was seldom heard in the senate-house or in the Forum; in the former he was unwelcome and without influence, in the latter he was afraid of the stormy proceedings of the parties. But when he did show himself, it was with the full retinue of his clients high and low, and the very fact of his solemn reserve imposed on the multitude. If he, who was still surrounded with the undiminished lustre of his extraordinary successes, should now offer to go to the East, he would beyond doubt be readily invested by the burgesses with all the plenitude of military and political power which he might ask. For the oligarchy, which saw in the popular military dictatorship their certain ruin, and in Pompeius himself since the coalition of $\frac{683}{71}$ their most hated foe, this was an overwhelming blow; but the democratic party also could have little comfort in the prospect. However desirable the putting an end to the government of the senate could not but be in itself, it was, if it took place in this way, far less a victory for their party than a personal victory for their overpowerful ally. In the latter there might easily arise a far more dangerous opponent to the democratic party than the senate had been. The danger fortunately avoided a few years before by the disbanding of the Spanish army and the retirement of Pompeius would recur in an increased measure, if Pompeius should now be placed at the head of the armies of the East.

On this occasion, however, Pompeius acted or at least allowed others to act in his behalf. In $\frac{687}{67}$ two projects of law were introduced, one of which, besides decreeing the discharge—long demanded by the democracy—of the soldiers of the Asiatic army who had served their term, decreed the recall of its commander-in-chief Lucius Lucullus and the supplying of his place by one of the consuls of the current year, Gaius Piso or Manius Glabrio; while the second revived and extended the plan proposed seven years before by the senate itself for clearing the seas from the pirates. A single general to be named by the senate from the consulars was to be appointed, to hold by sea exclusive command over the whole Mediterranean from the Pillars of Hercules to the coasts of Pontus and Syria, and to exercise by land, concurrently with the respective Roman governors, supreme command over the whole coasts for fifty miles inland. The office was secured to him for three years. He was surrounded by a staff, such as Rome had never seen, of five-and-twenty lieutenants of senatorial rank, all invested with praetorian insignia and praetorian powers, and of two under-treasurers with quaestorian prerogatives, all of them selected by the exclusive will of the commander-in-chief. He was allowed to raise as many as 120,000 infantry, 7000 cavalry, 500 ships of war, and for this purpose to dispose absolutely of the means of the provinces and client-states; moreover, the existing vessels of war and a considerable number of troops were at once handed over to him. The treasures of the state in the capital and in the provinces as well as those of the dependent communities were to be placed absolutely at his command, and in spite of the severe financial distress a sum of £1,400,000 (144,000,000 sesterces) was at once to be paid to him from the state-chest.

It is clear that by these projects of law, especially by that which related to the expedition against the pirates, the government of the senate was set aside. Doubtless the ordinary supreme magistrates nominated by the burgesses were of themselves the proper generals of the commonwealth, and the extraordinary magistrates needed, at least according to strict law, confirmation by the burgesses in order to act as generals; but in the appointment to particular commands no influence constitutionally belonged to the community, and it was only on the proposition of the senate, or at any rate on the proposition of a magistrate entitled in himself to exercise the office of general, that the comitia had hitherto occasionally interfered in this matter and assigned the special sphere of office. On this point, ever since there had existed a Roman free state, the practical decision pertained to the senate, and this its prerogative had in the course of time obtained full recognition. No doubt the democracy had already assailed it; but even in the most doubtful of the cases which had hitherto occurred—the transference of the African command to Gaius Marius in $\frac{647}{107}$ (iii. 149)—it was only a magistrate constitutionally entitled to hold the office of general that was entrusted by the resolution of the burgesses with a definite expedition. But now the burgesses were to invest any private man at their pleasure not merely with the extraordinary authority of the supreme magistracy, but also with a sphere of office definitely settled by them. That the senate had to choose this man from the ranks of the consulars, was a mitigation only in form; for the selection was left to it simply because there was really no choice, and in presence of the vehemently excited multitude the senate could entrust the chief command of the seas and coasts to no other save Pompeius alone. But more dangerous still than this negation in principle of the senatorial control was its practical abolition by the institution of an office of almost unlimited military and financial powers. While the office of general was formerly restricted to a term of one year, to a definite province, and to military and financial resources strictly measured out, the new extraordinary office had from the outset a duration of three years secured to it—which of course did not preclude a farther prolongation; had the greater portion of all the provinces, and even Italy itself which was formerly free from military jurisdiction, subordinated to it; had the soldiers, ships, treasures of the state placed almost without restriction at its disposal. Even the primitive fundamental principle in the state-law of the Roman republic which we have just mentioned—that the highest military and civil authority could not be conferred without the co-operation of the burgesses—was infringed in favour of the new commander-in-chief. Inasmuch as the law conferred beforehand on the twenty-five adjutants whom he was to nominate praetorian rank and praetorian prerogatives,[1] the highest office of republican

[1] The extraordinary magisterial power (*pro consule, pro praetore, pro quaestore*) might according to Roman state-law originate in three ways. It might arise out of the principle which applied to the non-urban magistracies that the magistracy continued up to the appointed legal term but the official authority up to the arrival of the successor, which was the oldest, simplest, and most frequent case. Or it might arise in consequence of the appropriate organs—especially the comitia, and in later times also perhaps the senate—nominating a chief magistrate not contemplated in the constitution, who was otherwise on a parity with the ordinary magistrate, but in token of the extraordinary nature of his office designated himself merely "in stead of a praetor" or "of a consul." To this class belong also the magistrates nominated in the ordinary way as quaestors, and then extraordinarily furnished with praetorian or even consular authority (*quaestores pro praetore* or *pro consule;* Becker-Marquardt, iii. 1, 284), in which quality, for example, Publius Lentulus Marcellinus went in $\frac{679}{75}$ to Cyrene (Sallust, *Hist.* ii. 39 Dietsch), Gnaeus Piso in $\frac{689}{65}$ to Hither Spain (Sallust, *Cat.* 19), and Cato in $\frac{696}{58}$ to Cyprus (Vell. ii. 45). Or, lastly, the extraordinary magisterial authority might rest on the right of delegation vested in the supreme magistrate. If he left the bounds of his province or otherwise was prevented from administering his office, he was entitled to nominate

Rome became subordinate to a newly created office, for which it was left to the future to find the fitting name, but which in reality even now involved in it the monarchy. It was a total revolution in the existing order of things, for which the foundation was laid in this project of law.

These measures of a man who had just given so striking proofs of his vacillation and weakness surprise us by their decisive energy. Nevertheless the fact that Pompeius acted on this occasion more resolutely than during his consulate is very capable of explanation. The point at issue was not that he should come forward at once as monarch, but only that he should prepare the way for the monarchy by a military exceptional measure, which, revolutionary as it was in its nature, could still be accomplished under the forms of the existing constitution, and which directly led Pompeius towards the old object of his wishes, the command against Mithradates and Tigranes. Important reasons of expediency also might be urged for the emancipation of the military power from the senate. Pompeius could not have forgotten that a plan designed on exactly similar principles for the suppression of piracy had a few years before failed through the mismanagement of the senate, and that the issue of the Spanish war had been placed in extreme jeopardy by the neglect of the armies on the part of the senate and its injudicious conduct of the finances; he could not fail to see what were the feelings with which the great majority of the aristocracy regarded him as a renegade Sullan, and what fate was in store for him, if he allowed himself to be sent as general of the government with the usual powers to the East. It was natural therefore that he should indicate a position independent of the senate as the first condition of his undertaking the command, and that the burgesses should readily agree to it. It is moreover in a high degree probable that Pompeius was on this occasion urged to more

one of those about him as his substitute, who was then called *legatus pro praetore* (Sallust, *Iug.* 36, 37, 38), or, if the choice fell on the quaestor, *quaestor pro praetore* (Sallust, *Iug.* 103). In like manner he was entitled, if he had no quaestor, to cause the quaestorial duties to be discharged by one of his suite, who was then called *legatus pro quaestore*, a name which is to be met with, perhaps for the first time, on the Macedonian tetradrachms of Sura, lieutenant of the governor of Macedonia in $\frac{665-667}{89-87}$. But it was contrary to the nature of delegation and therefore according to the older state-law inadmissible, that the highest magistrate should, without having met with any hindrance to the discharge of his functions, immediately upon his entering on office invest one or more of his subordinates with supreme authority; and thus the *legati pro praetore* of the proconsul Pompeius were an innovation, and already similar in kind to those who played so great a part in the times of the empire.

rapid action by those around him, who were, it may be presumed, not a little indignant at his retirement two years before. The projects of law regarding the recall of Lucullus and the expedition against the pirates were introduced by the tribune of the people Aulus Gabinius, a man ruined in finances and morals, but a dexterous negotiator, a bold orator, and a brave soldier. Little as the assurances of Pompeius, that he had no wish at all for the chief command in the war with the pirates and only longed for domestic repose, were meant in earnest, there was probably this much of truth in them, that the bold and active client, who was in confidential intercourse with Pompeius and his more immediate friends and who completely saw through the situation and the men, took the decision to a considerable extent out of the hands of his shortsighted and helpless patron.

The democracy, discontented as its leaders might be in secret, could not well come publicly forward against the project of law. It would, to all appearance, have been in no case able to hinder the carrying of the law; but it would have openly broken with Pompeius and thereby compelled him either to make approaches to the oligarchy or regardlessly to pursue his personal policy in the face of both parties. No course was left to the democrats but still to adhere to their alliance with Pompeius, hollow as it was, and to embrace the present opportunity of at least definitively overthrowing the senate and passing over from opposition into government, leaving the ulterior issue to the future and to the well-known weakness of Pompeius' character. Accordingly their leaders—the praetor Lucius Quinctius, the same who seven years before had exerted himself for the restoration of the tribunician power (p. 84), and the late quaestor Gaius Caesar—supported the Gabinian proposals.

The privileged classes were furious—not merely the nobility, but also the mercantile aristocracy, which felt its exclusive rights endangered by so thorough a state-revolution and once more recognised its true patron in the senate. When the tribune Gabinius after the introduction of his proposals appeared in the senate-house, the fathers of the city were almost on the point of strangling him with their own hands, without considering in their zeal how extremely disadvantageous to them this method of arguing must have ultimately proved. The tribune escaped to the Forum and summoned the multitude to storm the senate-house, when just at the right time the sitting terminated. The consul Piso, the champion of the oligarchy, who accidentally fell into the hands of the multitude, would have certainly become a victim to popular fury, had not Gabinius come up and, in order that his certain success might not be endangered by unseasonable acts of violence, liberated the consul. Meanwhile the exasperation of the multitude remained undiminished and constantly found fresh nourishment in the high prices of grain and the numerous rumours more or less absurd which were in circulation —such as that Lucius Lucullus had invested the money entrusted to him for carrying on the war at interest in Rome, or had attempted with its aid to withdraw the praetor Quinctius from the cause of the people; that the senate intended to prepare for the "second Romulus," as they called Pompeius, the fate of the first,[1] and other reports of a like character.

Amidst this state of things the day of voting arrived. The multitude stood densely packed in the Forum; all the buildings, whence the rostra could be seen, were covered even on the roofs with men. All the colleagues of Gabinius had promised their veto to the senate; but in presence of the surging masses all were silent except the single Lucius Trebellius, who had sworn to himself and the senate rather to die than yield. When the latter exercised his veto, Gabinius immediately interrupted the voting on his projects of law and proposed to the assembled people to deal with his refractory colleague, as Octavius had formerly been dealt with on the proposition of Tiberius Gracchus (iii. 87), namely, to depose him immediately from office. The vote was taken and the reading out of the voting tablets began; when the first seventeen tribes, which came to be read out, had declared for the proposal and the next affirmative vote would give it the majority, Trebellius, forgetting his oath, pusillanimously withdrew his veto. In vain the tribune Otho then endeavoured to procure at least the election of two generals —the old *duumviri navales* (i. 412)—instead of one; in vain the aged Quintus Catulus, the most respected man in the senate, exerted his last energies to secure that the lieutenant-generals should not be nominated by the commander-in-chief, but chosen by the people. Otho could not even procure a hearing amidst the noise of the multitude; the well-calculated complaisance of Gabinius procured a hearing for Catulus, and in respectful silence the multitude listened to the old man's words; but they were nevertheless thrown away. The proposals were not merely converted into law with all the clauses unaltered, but the special supplementary requests made by Pompeius were instantaneously and completely agreed to.

[1] According to the legend king Romulus was torn in pieces by the senators.

With high-strung hopes men saw the two generals Pompeius and Glabrio depart for their destinations. The price of grain had fallen immediately after the passing of the Gabinian laws to the ordinary rates—an evidence of the hopes attached to the grand expedition and its glorious leader. These hopes were, as we shall have afterwards to relate, not merely fulfilled, but surpassed: in three months the clearing of the seas was completed. Since the Hannibalic war the Roman government had displayed no such energy in external action; as compared with the lax and incapable administration of the oligarchy, the democratic-military opposition had almost brilliantly made good its title to grasp and wield the reins of the state. The equally unpatriotic and unskilful attempts of the consul Piso to put paltry obstacles in the way of the arrangements of Pompeius for the suppression of piracy in Narbonese Gaul only increased the exasperation of the burgesses against the oligarchy and their enthusiasm for Pompeius; it was nothing but the personal intervention of the latter that prevented the assembly of the people from summarily removing the consul from his office.

Meanwhile the confusion on the Asiatic continent had become still worse. Glabrio, who was to take up in the stead of Lucullus the chief command against Mithradates and Tigranes, had remained stationary in the west of Asia Minor and, while instigating the soldiers by various proclamations against Lucullus, had not entered on the supreme command, so that Lucullus was forced to retain it. Against Mithradates, of course, nothing was done; the Pontic cavalry plundered fearlessly and with impunity in Bithynia and Cappadocia. Pompeius had been led by the piratical war to proceed with his army to Asia Minor; nothing seemed more natural than to invest him with the supreme command in the Pontic-Armenian war, to which he himself had long aspired. But the democratic party did not, as may be readily conceived, share the wishes of its general, and carefully avoided taking the initiative in the matter. It is very probable that it had induced Gabinius not to entrust both the war with Mithradates and that with the pirates from the outset to Pompeius, but to entrust the former to Glabrio; upon no account could it now desire to increase and perpetuate the exceptional position of the already too powerful general. Pompeius himself retained according to his custom a passive attitude; and perhaps he would in reality have returned home after fulfilling the commission which he had received, but for the occurrence of an incident unexpected by all parties.

One Gaius Manilius, an utterly worthless and insignificant man, had when tribune of the people by his unskilful projects of legislation lost favour both with the aristocracy and with the democracy. In the hope of sheltering himself under the wing of the powerful general, if he should procure for the latter what every one knew that he eagerly desired but had not the boldness to ask, Manilius proposed to the burgesses to recall the governors Glabrio from Bithynia and Pontus and Marcius Rex from Cilicia, and to entrust their offices as well as the conduct of the war in the East, apparently without any fixed limit as to time and at any rate with the freest authority to conclude peace and alliance, to the proconsul of the seas and coasts in addition to his previous office (beginning of $\frac{688}{66}$). This occurrence very clearly showed how disorganised was the machinery of the Roman constitution, when the power of legislation was placed as respected the initiative in the hands of any demagogue however insignificant, and as respected the final determination in the hands of the incapable multitude, while it at the same time was extended to the most important questions of administration. The Manilian proposal was acceptable to none of the political parties; yet it scarcely anywhere encountered serious resistance. The democratic leaders, for the same reasons which had forced them to acquiesce in the Gabinian law, could not venture earnestly to oppose the Manilian; they kept their displeasure and their fears to themselves and spoke in public for the general of the democracy. The moderate Optimates declared themselves for the Manilian proposal, because after the Gabinian law resistance in any case was vain, and far-seeing men already perceived that the true policy for the senate was to make approaches as far as possible to Pompeius and to draw him over to their side on occasion of the breach which might be foreseen between him and the democrats. The trimmers blessed the day when they too seemed to have an opinion and could come forward decidedly without losing favour with either of the parties—it is significant that Marcus Cicero first appeared as an orator on the political platform in defence of the Manilian proposal. The strict Optimates alone, with Quintus Catulus at their head, showed at least their colours and spoke against the proposition. Of course it was converted into law by a majority bordering on unanimity. Pompeius thus obtained, in addition to his earlier extensive powers, the administration of the most important provinces of Asia Minor—so that there scarcely remained a spot of land within the wide Roman domains that had not obeyed him—and the conduct of a war as to which, like the expedition of Alexander, men could tell where and when it began, but not where and when it might end. Never since Rome stood had such power been united in the hands of a single man.

The Gabinio-Manilian proposals terminated the struggle between the senate and the popular party, which the Sempronian laws had begun sixty-seven years before. As the Sempronian laws first constituted the revolutionary party into a political opposition, the Gabinio-Manilian first converted it from the opposition into the government; and as it had been a great moment when the first breach in the existing constitution was made by disregarding the veto of Octavius, it was a moment no less full of significance when the last bulwark of the senatorial rule fell with the withdrawal of Trebellius. This was felt on both sides and even the indolent souls of the senators were convulsively roused by this death-struggle; but yet the war as to the constitution terminated in a very different and far more pitiful fashion than it had begun. A youth in every sense noble had commenced the revolution; it was concluded by pert intriguers and demagogues of the lowest type. On the other hand, while the Optimates had begun the struggle with a measured resistance and with a defence which earnestly maintained even the forlorn posts, they ended with taking the initiative in club-law, with grandiloquent weakness, and with pitiful perjury. What had once appeared a daring dream was now attained; the senate had ceased to govern. But when the few old men, who had seen the first storms of revolution and heard the words of the Gracchi, compared that time with the present, they found that everything had in the interval changed—countrymen and citizens, state-law and military discipline, life and manners; and well might those painfully smile, who compared the ideals of the Gracchan period with their realisation. Such reflections however belonged to the past. For the present and perhaps also for the future the fall of the aristocracy was an accomplished fact. The oligarchs resembled an army utterly broken up, whose scattered bands might serve to reinforce another body of troops, but could no longer themselves keep the field or risk a combat on their own account. But as the old struggle came to an end, a new one was simultaneously beginning—the struggle between the two powers hitherto leagued for the overthrow of the aristocratic constitution, the civil-democratic opposition and the military power daily aspiring to greater ascendancy. The exceptional position of Pompeius even under the Gabinian, and much more under the Manilian, law was incompatible with a republican organisation. He had been, as even then his opponents urged with good reason, appointed by the Gabinian law not as admiral, but as regent of the empire; not unjustly was he designated by a Greek familiar with Eastern affairs "kings of kings." If he should hereafter, on returning from the East once more victorious and with increased glory, with well-filled chests, and with troops ready for battle and devoted to his cause, stretch forth his hand to seize the crown—who would then arrest his arm? Was the consular Quintus Catulus, forsooth, to summon forth the senators against the first general of his time and his experienced legions? or was the designated aedile Gaius Caesar to call forth the civic multitude, whose eyes he had just feasted on his three hundred and twenty pairs of gladiators with their silver equipments? Soon, exclaimed Catulus, it would be necessary once more to flee to the rocks of the Capitol, in order to save liberty. It was not the fault of the prophet, that the storm came not as he expected from the East, but that on the contrary fate, fulfilling his words more literally than he himself anticipated, brought on the destroying tempest a few years later from Gaul.

CHAPTER IV

POMPEIUS AND THE EAST

We have already seen how wretched was the state of the affairs of Rome by land and sea in the East, when at the commencement of $\frac{687}{67}$ Pompeius, with an almost absolute plenitude of power, undertook the conduct of the war against the pirates. He began by dividing the immense field committed to him into thirteen districts and assigning to each of these districts a lieutenant, for the purpose of equipping ships and men there, of searching the coasts, and of capturing piratical vessels or chasing them into the meshes of a colleague. He himself went with the best part of the ships of war that were available—among which on this occasion also those of Rhodes were distinguished—early in the year to sea, and swept in the first place the Sicilian, African, and Sardinian waters, with a view especially to re-establish the supply of grain from these provinces to Italy. His lieutenants meanwhile addressed themselves to the clearing of the Spanish and Gallic coasts. It was on this occasion that the consul Piso attempted from Rome to prevent the levies which Marcus Pomponius the legate of Pompeius instituted by virtue of the Gabinian law in the province of Narbo—an imprudent proceeding, to check which, and at the same time to keep the just indignation of the multitude against the consul within legal bounds, Pompeius temporarily reappeared in Rome (p. 102). When at the end of forty days the navigation had been everywhere set free in the western basin of the Mediterranean, Pompeius proceeded with sixty of his best vessels to the eastern seas, and first of all to the original and main seat of piracy, the Lycian and Cilician waters. On the news of the approach of the Roman fleet the piratical barks everywhere disappeared from the open sea; and even the strong Lycian fortresses of Anticragus and Cragus surrendered without offering serious resistance. The well-calculated moderation of Pompeius helped more than fear to open the gates of these scarcely accessible marine strongholds. His predecessors had ordered every captured freebooter to be nailed to the cross; without hesitation he gave quarter to all, and treated in particular the common rowers found in the captured piratical vessels with unusual indulgence. The bold Cilician sea-kings alone ventured on an attempt to maintain at least their own waters by arms against the Romans; after having placed their children and wives and their rich treasures for security in the mountain-fortresses of the Taurus, they awaited the Roman fleet at the western frontier of Cilicia, in the offing of Coracesium. But the ships of Pompeius, well manned and well provided with all implements of war, achieved a complete victory. Without farther hindrance he landed and began to storm and break up the mountain-castles of the corsairs, while he continued to offer to themselves freedom and life as the price of submission. Soon the great multitude desisted from the continuance of a hopeless war in their strongholds and mountains, and consented to submit. Forty-nine days after Pompeius had appeared in the eastern seas, Cilicia was subdued and the war at an end.

The rapid suppression of piracy was a great relief, but not a grand achievement; the corsairs could as little cope with the resources of the Roman state which had been called forth in lavish measure as the combined gangs of thieves in a great city can cope with a well-organised police. It was a naïve proceeding to celebrate such a razzia as a victory. But when compared with the prolonged continuance and the vast and daily increasing extent of the evil, it was natural that the surprisingly rapid subjugation of the dreaded pirates should make a most powerful impression on the public; and the more so, that this was the first trial of rule centralised in a single hand, and the parties were eagerly waiting to see whether that hand would understand the art of ruling better than the collegiate body had done. Nearly 400 ships and boats, including 90 war vessels properly so called, were either taken by Pompeius or surrendered to him; in all about 1300 piratical vessels are said to have been destroyed; besides which the richly filled arsenals and magazines of the buccaneers were burnt. Of the pirates about 10,000 perished; upwards of 20,000 fell into the hands of the victor alive; while Publius Clodius the admiral of the Roman army stationed in Cilicia, and a multitude of other individuals carried off by the pirates, some of them long believed at home to be dead, obtained once more their freedom through Pompeius. In the summer of $\frac{687}{67}$, three months after the beginning of the compaign commerce resumed its wonted course, and instead of the former famine abundance prevailed in Italy.

A disagreeable interlude in the island of Crete, however, disturbed in some measure this pleasing success of the Roman arms. There Quintus Metellus was stationed in the second year of his command, and was employed in finishing the subjugation—already substantially effected—of the island (p. 71), when Pompeius appeared in the eastern waters. A collision was natural, for according to the Gabinian law the command of Pompeius extended concurrently with that of Metellus over the whole island, which stretched to a great length but was nowhere more than eighty miles broad; but Pompeius was considerate enough not to assign it to any of his lieutenants. The still resisting Cretan communities however, who had seen their subdued countrymen taken to task by Metellus with the most cruel severity and had learned on the other hand the gentle terms which Pompeius was in the habit of imposing on the places which surrendered to him in the south of Asia Minor, preferred to give in their joint surrender to Pompeius. He accepted it in Pamphylia, where he was at the moment, from their envoys, and sent along with them his legate Lucius Octavius to announce to Metellus the conclusion of the conventions and to take over the towns. This proceeding was, no doubt, not like that of a colleague; but formal right was wholly on the side of Pompeius, and Metellus was most evidently in the wrong when, utterly ignoring the convention of the cities with Pompeius, he continued to treat them as hostile. In vain Octavius protested; in vain, as he had himself come without troops, he summoned from Achaia Lucius Sisenna, the lieutenant of Pompeius stationed there; Metellus, not troubling himself about either Octavius or Sisenna, besieged Eleutherna and took Lappa by storm, where Octavius in person was taken prisoner and ignominiously dismissed, while the Cretans who were taken with him were consigned to the executioner. Accordingly formal conflicts took place between the troops of Sisenna, at whose head Octavius placed himself after that leader's death, and those of Metellus; even when the former had been commanded to return to Achaia, Octavius continued the war in concert with the Cretan Aristion, and Hierapytna, where both made a stand, was only subdued by Metellus after the most obstinate resistance.

In reality the zealous Optimate Metellus had thus begun formal civil war at his own hand against the generalissimo of the democracy. It shows the indescribable disorganisation in the Roman state, that these incidents led to nothing farther than a bitter correspondence between the two generals, who a couple of years afterwards were sitting once more peacefully and even " amicably " side by side in the senate.

Pompeius during these events remained in Cilicia; preparing for the next year, as it seemed, a compaign against the Cretans or rather against Metellus, in reality waiting for the signal which should call him to interfere in the utterly confused affairs of the continent of Asia Minor. The portion of the Lucullan army that was still left after the losses which it had suffered and the departure of the Fimbrian legions remained inactive on the upper Halys in the country of the Trocmi bordering on the Pontic territory. Lucullus still held provisionally the chief command, as his nominated successor Glabrio continued to linger in the west of Asia Minor. The three legions commanded by Quintus Marcius Rex lay equally inactive in Cilicia. The Pontic territory was again wholly in the power of king Mithradates, who made the individuals and communities that had joined the Romans, such as the town of Eupatoria, pay for their revolt with cruel severity. The kings of the East did not proceed to any serious offensive movement against the Romans, either because it formed no part of their plan, or—as was asserted—because the landing of Pompeius in Cilicia induced Mithradates and Tigranes to desist from advancing farther. The Manilian law realised the secretly cherished hopes of Pompeius more rapidly than he probably himself anticipated; Glabrio and Rex were recalled and the governorships of Pontus-Bithynia and Cilicia with the troops stationed there, as well as the management of the Pontic-Armenian war along with authority to make war, peace, and alliance with the dynasts of the East at his own discretion, were transferred to Pompeius. Amidst the prospect of honours and spoils so ample Pompeius was glad to forego the chastising of an ill-humoured Optimate who enviously guarded his scanty laurels; he abandoned the expedition against Crete and the farther pursuit of the corsairs, and destined his fleet also to support the attack which he projected on the kings of Pontus and Armenia. Yet amidst this land-war he by no means wholly lost sight of piracy which was perpetually raising its head afresh. Before he left Asia ($\frac{691}{63}$) he caused the necessary ships to be fitted out there against the corsairs; on his proposal in the following year a similar measure was resolved on for Italy, and the sum needed for the purpose was granted by the senate. They continued to protect the coasts with guards of cavalry and small squadrons, and though, as the expeditions to be mentioned afterwards against Cyprus in $\frac{696}{58}$ and Egypt in $\frac{699}{55}$ show, piracy was not thoroughly mastered, it yet after the expedition of Pompeius amidst all the vicissitudes and political crises of Rome could never again so raise its head and so totally dislodge the Romans from the sea, as it had done under the government of the mouldering oligarchy.

The few months which still remained before the commencement of the campaign in Asia Minor, were employed by the new commander-in-chief with strenuous activity in diplomatic and military preparations. Envoys were sent to Mithradates, rather to reconnoitre than to attempt a serious mediation. There was a hope at the Pontic court that Phraates king of the Parthians would be induced by the recent considerable successes which the allies had achieved over Rome to enter into the Pontic-Armenian alliance. To counteract this, Roman envoys proceeded to the court of Ctesiphon; and the internal troubles, which distracted the Armenian ruling house, came to their aid. A son of the great king Tigranes, bearing the same name, had rebelled against his father, either because he was unwilling to wait for the death of the old man, or because his father's suspicion, which had already cost several of his brothers their lives, led him to discern his only chance of safety in open insurrection. Vanquished by his father, he had taken refuge with a number of Armenians of rank at the court of the Arsacid, and intrigued against his father there. It was partly due to his exertions, that Phraates preferred to take the reward which was offered to him by both sides for his accession—the secured possession of Mesopotamia—from the hand of the Romans, renewed with Pompeius the agreement concluded with Lucullus respecting the boundary of the Euphrates (p. 63), and even consented to operate in concert with the Romans against Armenia. But the younger Tigranes occasioned still greater damage than that which arose out of his promoting the alliance between the Romans and the Parthians, for his insurrection produced a variance between the kings Tigranes and Mithradates themselves. The great king cherished in secret the suspicion that Mithradates might have had a hand in the insurrection of his grandson—Cleopatra the mother of the younger Tigranes was the daughter of Mithradates—and, though no open rupture took place, the good understanding between the two monarchs was disturbed at the very moment when it was most urgently needed.

At the same time Pompeius prosecuted his warlike preparations with energy. The Asiatic allied and client communities were warned to furnish the stipulated contingents. Public notices summoned the discharged veterans of the legions of Fimbria to return to the standards as volunteers, and by great promises and the name of Pompeius a considerable portion of them were induced in reality to obey the call. The whole force united under the orders of Pompeius may have amounted, exclusive of the auxiliaries, to between 40,000 and 50,000 men.[1]

In the spring of $\frac{688}{66}$ Pompeius proceeded to Galatia, to take the chief command of the troops of Lucullus and to advance with them into the Pontic territory, whither the Cilician legions were directed to follow. At Danala, a place belonging to the Trocmi, the two generals met; but the reconciliation, which mutual friends had hoped to effect, was not accomplished. The preliminary courtesies soon passed into bitter discussions, and these into violent altercation: they parted in worse mood than they had met. As Lucullus continued to make presents and to distribute lands just as if he were still in office, Pompeius declared all the acts performed by his predecessor subsequent to his own arrival null and void. Formally he was in the right; befitting tact in the treatment of a meritorious and more than sufficiently mortified opponent was not to be looked for from him.

So soon as the season allowed, the Roman troops crossed the frontier of Pontus. There they were opposed by Mithradates with 30,000 infantry and 3000 cavalry. Left in the lurch by his ally and attacked by Rome with reinforced power and energy, he made an attempt to procure peace; but he would not listen to the unconditional submission which Pompeius demanded—what worse issue could the most unsuccessful campaign bring? That he might not expose his army, mostly archers and horsemen, to the formidable shock of the Roman infantry of the line, he slowly retired before the enemy, and compelled the Romans to follow him in his various cross-marches; making a stand, wherever there was opportunity, with his superior cavalry against that of the enemy, and occasioning no small hardship to the Romans by impeding their supplies. At last Pompeius in his impatience desisted from following the Pontic army, and, letting the king alone, proceeded to subdue the land; he marched to the upper Euphrates, crossed it, and entered the eastern provinces of the Pontic empire. But Mithradates followed along the left bank of the Euphrates, and when he had arrived

[1] Pompeius distributed among his soldiers and officers as presents 384,000,000 sesterces (=16,000 talents, App. *Mithr.* 116); as the officers received 100,000,000 (Plin. *H. N.* xxxvii. 2, 16) and each of the common soldiers 6,000 sesterces (Plin., App.), the army still numbered at its triumph about 40,000 men.

in the Anaitic or Acilisenian province, he intercepted the route of the Romans at the castle of Dasteira, which was strong and well provided with water, and from which with his light troops he commanded the plain. Pompeius, still wanting the Cilician legions and not strong enough to maintain himself in this position without them, had to retire over the Euphrates and to seek protection from the cavalry and archers of the king in the wooded ground of Pontic Armenia extensively intersected by rocky ravines and deep valleys. It was not till the troops from Cilicia arrived and rendered it possible to resume the offensive with a superiority of force, that Pompeius again advanced, invested the camp of the king with a chain of posts of almost eighteen miles in length, and kept him formally blockaded there, while the Roman detachments scoured the country far and wide. The distress in the Pontic camp was great; the draught animals even had to be killed; at length after remaining for forty-five days the king caused his sick and wounded, whom he could not save and was unwilling to leave in the hands of the enemy, to be put to death by his own troops, and departed during the night with the utmost secrecy towards the east. Cautiously Pompeius followed through the unknown land: the march was now approaching the boundary which separated the dominions of Mithradates and Tigranes. When the Roman general perceived that Mithradates intended not to bring the contest to a decision within his own territory, but to draw the enemy away after him into the far distant regions of the East, he determined not to permit this.

The two armies lay close to each other. During the rest at noon the Roman army set out without the enemy observing the movement, made a circuit, and occupied the heights which lay in front and commanded a defile to be passed by the enemy on the southern bank of the river Lycus (Jeschil-Irmak) not far from the modern Enderes, at the point where Nicopolis was afterwards built. The following morning the Pontic troops broke up in their usual manner, and, supposing that the enemy was as hitherto behind them, after accomplishing the day's march they pitched their camp in the very valley whose encircling heights the Romans had occupied. Suddenly in the silence of the night there sounded all around them the dreaded battle-cry of the legions, and missiles from all sides poured on the Asiatic host, in which soldiers and camp-followers, chariots, horses, and camels jostled each other; and amidst the dense throng, notwithstanding the darkness, not a missile failed to take effect. When the Romans had expended their darts, they charged down from the heights on the masses which had now become visible by the light of the newly-risen moon, and which were abandoned to them almost defenceless; those that did not fall by the steel of the enemy were trodden down in the fearful pressure under the hoofs and wheels. It was the last battle-field on which the grey-haired king fought with the Romans. With three attendants—two of his horsemen, and a concubine who was accustomed to follow him in male attire and to fight bravely by his side—he made his escape to the fortress of Sinoria, whither a portion of his trusty followers found their way to him. He divided among them his treasures preserved there, 6000 talents of gold (£1,400,000); furnished them and himself with poison; and hastened with the band that was left to him up the Euphrates to unite with his ally, the great king of Armenia.

This hope likewise was vain; the alliance, on the faith of which Mithradates took the route for Armenia, already by that time existed no longer. During the conflicts between Mithradates and Pompeius just narrated, the king of the Parthians, yielding to the urgency of the Romans and above all of the exiled Armenian prince, had invaded the kingdom of Tigranes by force of arms, and had compelled him to withdraw into the inaccessible mountains. The invading army even began the siege of the capital Artaxata; but, on its becoming protracted, king Phraates took his departure with the greater portion of his troops; whereupon Tigranes overpowered the Parthian corps left behind and the Armenian emigrants led by his son, and re-established his dominion throughout the kingdom. Naturally, however, the king was under such circumstances little inclined to fight with the freshly victorious Romans, and least of all to sacrifice himself for Mithradates; whom he trusted less than ever, since information had reached him that his rebellious son intended to betake himself to his grandfather. So he entered into negotiations with the Romans for a separate peace; but he did not wait for the conclusion of the treaty to break off the alliance which linked him to Mithradates. The latter, when he had arrived at the frontier of Armenia, was doomed to learn that the great king Tigranes had set a price of 100 talents (£24,000) on his head, had arrested his envoys, and had delivered them to the Romans. King Mithradates saw his kingdom in the hands of the enemy, and his allies on the point of coming to an agreement with them; it was not possible to continue the war; he might deem himself fortunate, if he succeeded in effecting his escape along the eastern and northern shores of the Black Sea, in perhaps dislodging his son Machares—who had revolted and entered into connection with the Romans (p. 57)—once more from the Bosporan kingdom, and in finding on the Maeotis a fresh soil for fresh projects. So he turned northward. When the king in his flight had crossed the Phasis, the ancient boundary of Asia Minor, Pompeius for the time discontinued his pursuit; but instead of returning to the region of the sources of the Euphrates, he turned aside into the region of the Araxes to settle matters with Tigranes.

Almost without meeting resistance he arrived in the region of Artaxata (not far from Erivan) and pitched his camp thirteen miles from the city. There he was met by the son of the great king, who hoped after the fall of his father to receive the Armenian diadem from the hand of the Romans, and therefore had endeavoured in every way to prevent the conclusion of the treaty between his father and the Romans. The great king was only the more resolved to purchase peace at any price. On horseback and without his purple robe, but adorned with the royal diadem and the royal turban, he appeared at the gate of the Roman camp and desired to be conducted to the presence of the Roman general. After having given up at the bidding of the lictors, as the regulations of the Roman camp required, his horse and his sword, he threw himself in barbarian fashion at the feet of the proconsul, and in token of unconditional surrender placed the diadem and tiara in his hands. Pompeius, highly delighted at a victory which cost nothing, raised the humbled king of kings, invested him again with the insignia of his dignity, and dictated the peace. Besides a payment of £1,400,000 (6000 talents) to the war-chest and a present to the soldiers, out of which each of them received 50 *denarii* (£2 2*s*.), the king ceded all the conquests which he had made, not merely his Phoenician, Syrian, Cilician, and Cappadocian possessions, but also Sophene and Corduene on the right bank of the Euphrates; he was again restricted to Armenia proper, and his position of great king was, of course, at an end. In a single campaign Pompeius had totally subdued the two mighty kings of Pontus and Armenia. At the beginning of $\frac{688}{66}$ there was not a Roman soldier beyond the bounds of the old Roman possessions; at its close king Mithradates was wandering as an exile and without an army in the ravines of the Caucasus, and king Tigranes sat on the Armenian throne no longer as king of kings, but as a vassal of Rome. The whole domain of Asia Minor to the west of the Euphrates unconditionally obeyed the Romans; the victorious army took up its winter quarters to the east of that stream on Armenian soil, in the country from the upper Euphrates to the river Kur, from which the Italians then for the first time watered their horses.

But the new field, on which the Romans here set foot, raised up for them new conflicts. The brave peoples of the middle and eastern Caucasus saw with indignation the remote Occidentals encamping on their territory. There—in the fertile and well-watered table land of the modern Georgia—dwelt the Iberians, a brave, well-organised, agricultural nation, whose clan-cantons under their patriarchs cultivated the soil according to the system of common possession, without any separate ownership of the individual cultivators. Army and people were one; the people were headed partly by the ruling clans—out of which the eldest always presided over the whole Iberian nation as king, and the next eldest as judge and leader of the army—partly by special families of priests, on whom chiefly devolved the duty of preserving a knowledge of the treaties concluded with other peoples and of watching over their observance. The mass of the non-freemen were regarded as serfs of the king. Their eastern neighbours, the Albanians or Alans, who were settled on the lower Kur as far as the Caspian Sea, were in a far lower stage of culture. Chiefly a pastoral people they tended, on foot or on horseback, their numerous herds in the luxuriant meadows of the modern Shirvan; their few tilled fields were still cultivated with the old wooden plough without iron share. Coined money was unknown, and they did not count beyond a hundred. Each of their tribes, twenty-six in all, had its own chief and spoke its distinct dialect. Far superior in number to the Iberians, the Albanians could not at all cope with them in bravery. The mode of fighting was on the whole the same with both nations; they fought chiefly with arrows and light javelins, which they frequently after the Indian fashion discharged from their lurking-places in the woods behind the trunks of trees, or hurled down from the tops of trees on the foe; the Albanians had also numerous horsemen partly mailed after the Medo-Armenian manner with heavy cuirasses and greaves. Both nations lived on their lands and pastures in a complete independence preserved from time immemorial. Nature itself, as it were, seems to have raised the Caucasus between Europe and Asia as a rampart against the tide of national movements; there the arms of Cyrus and of Alexander had formerly found their limit; now the brave garrison of this partition-wall set themselves to defend it also against the Romans.

Alarmed by the information that the Roman commander-in-chief intended next spring to cross the mountains and to pursue the Pontic king beyond the Caucasus—for Mithradates, they heard, was passing the winter in Dioscurias (Iskuria between Suchum Kale and Anaklia) on the Black Sea—the Albanians under their prince Oroizes first crossed the Kur in the middle of the winter of $\frac{688-689}{66-65}$ and threw themselves on the army, which was divided for the sake of its supplies into three larger corps under Quintus Metellus Celer, Lucius Flaccus, and Pompeius in person. But Celer, on whom the chief attack fell, made a brave stand, and Pompeius, after having delivered himself from the division sent to attack him, pursued the barbarians beaten at all points as far as the Kur. Artoces the king of the Iberians kept quiet and promised peace and friendship; but Pompeius, informed that he was secretly arming so as to fall upon the Romans on their march in the passes of the Caucasus, advanced in the spring of $\frac{689}{65}$, before resuming the pursuit of Mithradates, to the two fortresses just two miles distant from each other, Harmozica (Horum Ziche or Armazi) and Seusamora (Tsumar) which a little above the modern Tiflis command the two valleys of the river Kur and its tributary the Aragua, and with these the only passes leading from Armenia to Iberia. Artoces, surprised by the enemy before he was aware of it, hastily burnt the bridge over the Kur and retreated negotiating into the interior. Pompeius occupied the fortresses and followed the Iberians to the other bank of the Kur; by which he hoped to induce them to immediate submission. But Artoces retired farther and farther into the interior, and, when at length he halted on the river Pelorus, he did so not to surrender but to fight. The Iberian archers however withstood not for a moment the onset of the Roman legions, and, when Artoces saw the Pelorus also crossed by the Romans, he submitted at length to the conditions which the victor proposed, and sent his children as hostages.

Pompeius now, agreeably to the plan which he had formerly projected, marched through the Sarapana pass from the region of the Kur to that of the Phasis and thence down that river to the Black Sea, where the fleet under Servilius already awaited him on the Colchian coast. But it was for an uncertain idea—

for an aim almost unsubstantial—that the army and fleet were thus brought to the fabled shores of Colchis. The laborious march just completed through unknown and mostly hostile nations was nothing when compared with what still awaited them; and if they should really succeed in conducting the force from the mouth of the Phasis to the Crimea, through warlike and poor barbarian tribes, on inhospitable and unknown waters, along a coast where at certain places the mountains sink perpendicularly into the sea and it would have been absolutely necessary to embark in the ships—if such a march should be successfully accomplished, which was perhaps more difficult than the campaigns of Alexander and Hannibal—what was gained by it even at the best, corresponding at all to its toils and dangers? The war doubtless was not ended, so long as the old king was still among the living; but who could guarantee that they would really succeed in catching the royal game for the sake of which this unparalleled chase was to be instituted? Was it not better, even at the risk of Mithradates once more throwing the torch of war into Asia Minor, to desist from a pursuit which promised so little gain and so much peril? Doubtless numerous voices in the army, and still more numerous voices in the capital, urged the general to continue the pursuit incessantly and at any price; but they were the voices partly of foolhardy Hotspurs, partly of those perfidious friends, who would gladly at any price have kept the too powerful Imperator aloof from the capital and entangled him amidst interminable undertakings in the East. Pompeius was too experienced and too discreet an officer to hazard his fame and his army in obstinate adherence to so injudicious an expedition; an insurrection of the Albanians in rear of the army furnished a pretext for abandoning the pursuit of the king and ordering his return. The fleet received instructions to cruise in the Black Sea, to protect the northern coast of Asia Minor against any hostile invasion, and strictly to blockade the Cimmerian Bosporus under the threat of death to any trader who should break the blockade. Pompeius conducted the land troops not without great hardships through the Colchian and Armenian territory to the lower course of the Kur and onward, crossing the stream, into the Albanian plain.

For several days the Roman army had to march in the glowing heat through this almost waterless flat country, without encountering the enemy; it was only on the left bank of the Abas (probably the river elsewhere named Alazonius, now Alasan) that the force of the Albanians under the leadership of Coses, brother of the king Oroizes, was drawn up against the Romans; they are said to have amounted, including the contingent which had arrived from the inhabitants of the Transcaucasian steppes, to 60,000 infantry and 12,000 cavalry. Yet they would hardly have risked the battle, unless they had supposed that they had merely to fight with the Roman cavalry; but the cavalry had only been placed in front, and on its retiring the masses of Roman infantry showed themselves from their concealment behind. After a short conflict the army of the barbarians was driven into the woods, which Pompeius gave orders to invest and set on fire. The Albanians thereupon consented to make peace; and, following the example of the more powerful peoples, all the tribes settled between the Kur and the Caspian concluded a treaty with the Roman general. The Albanians, Iberians, and generally the peoples settled to the south along, and at the foot of, the Caucasus, thus entered at least for the moment into a relation of dependence on Rome. When, on the other hand, the peoples between the Phasis and the Maeotis—Colchians, Soani, Heniochi, Jazyges, Achaeans, even the remote Bastarnae—were inscribed in the long list of the nations subdued by Pompeius, the notion of subjugation was evidently employed in a manner very far from exact. The Caucasus once more verified its significance in the history of the world; the Roman conquest, like the Persian and the Hellenic, found its limit there.

Accordingly king Mithradates was left to himself and to destiny. As formerly his ancestor, the founder of the Pontic state, had first entered his future kingdom as a fugitive from the executioners of Antigonus and attended only by six horsemen, so had Mithradates now been compelled once more to cross the frontier of his kingdom and to turn his back on his own and his fathers' conquests. But to no one had the lottery of fate turned up the highest gains and the greatest losses more frequently and more capriciously than to the old sultan of Sinope; and the fortunes of men in the East changed rapidly and incalculably. Well might Mithradates now in the evening of his life accept each new vicissitude with the thought that it too was only in its turn paving the way for a fresh revolution, and that the only thing constant was the perpetual change of fortune. Inasmuch as the Roman rule was at bottom utterly intolerable to the Orientals, and Mithradates himself was in good and in evil a true prince of the East, it might well happen that amidst the laxity of the rule exercised by the Roman senate over the provinces, and amidst the dissensions of the political parties in Rome fermenting and ripening into civil war, Mithradates might, if he was fortunate enough to bide his time, re-establish his dominion for the third time. For this very reason—because he hoped and planned while still there was life in him—he remained dangerous to the Romans so long as he lived, as an aged refugee no less than when he had marched forth with his hundred thousands to wrest Hellas and Macedonia from the Romans. The restless old man made his way in the year $\frac{689}{65}$ from Dioscurias amidst unspeakable hardships partly by land, partly by sea, to the kingdom of Panticapaeum, where by his reputation and his numerous retainers he drove his renegade son Machares from the throne and compelled him to put himself to death. From this point he attempted once more to negotiate with the Romans; he besought that his paternal kingdom might be restored to him, and declared himself ready to recognise the supremacy of Rome and to pay tribute as a vassal. But Pompeius refused to grant the king a position in which he would have begun the old game afresh, and insisted on his personal submission.

Mithradates, however, had no thought of giving himself into the hands of the enemy, but was projecting new and still more extravagant plans. Straining all the resources with which the treasures that he had saved and the remnant of his states supplied him, he equipped a new army of 36,000 men consisting partly of slaves which he armed and exercised after the Roman fashion, and a war-fleet; according to rumour he designed to march westward through Thrace, Macedonia, and Pannonia, to carry along with him the Scythians in the Sarmatian steppes and the Celts on the Danube as allies, and with this avalanche of peoples to throw himself on Italy. This has been deemed a grand idea, and the plan of war of the Pontic king has been compared with the military march of Hannibal; but the same project, which is a stroke of genius in a man of genius, becomes an absurdity in one who is wrong-headed. This intended invasion of Italy by the Orientals was simply ridiculous, and the mere offspring of the impotent imagination of despair. Through the prudent coolness of their leader the Romans were prevented from Quixotically pursuing their Quixotic antagonist and warding off in the distant Crimea an attack, which, if it were not nipped of itself in the bud, would still be soon enough met at the foot of the Alps.

In fact, while Pompeius, without troubling himself further

as to the threats of the impotent giant, was employed in organising the territory which he had gained, the destinies of the aged king drew on to their fulfilment without his aid in the remote north. His extravagant preparations had produced the most violent excitement among the Bosporans, whose houses were torn down, and whose oxen were taken from the plough and put to death, in order to procure beams and sinews for constructing engines of war. The soldiers too were disinclined to enter on the hopeless Italian expedition. Mithradates had constantly been surrounded by suspicion and treason; he had not the gift of calling forth affection and fidelity among those around him. As in earlier years he had compelled his distinguished general Archelaus to seek protection in the Roman camp; as during the campaigns of Lucullus his most trusted officers Diocles, Phoenix, and even the most notable of the Roman emigrants had passed over to the enemy; so now, when his star grew pale and the old, infirm, embittered sultan was accessible to no one else save his eunuchs, desertion followed still more rapidly on desertion. Castor, the commandant of the fortress Phanagoria (on the Asiatic coast opposite Kertch), first raised the standard of revolt; he proclaimed the freedom of the town and delivered the sons of Mithradates that were in the fortress into the hands of the Romans. While the insurrection spread among the Bosporan towns, and Chersonesus (not far from Sebastopol), Theudosia (Caffa), and others joined the Phanagorites, the king allowed his suspicion and his cruelty to have free course. On the information of despicable eunuchs his most confidential adherents were nailed to the cross; the king's own sons were the least sure of their lives. The son who was his father's favourite and was probably destined by him as his successor, Pharnaces, took his resolution and headed the insurgents. The servants whom Mithradates sent to arrest him, and the troops despatched against him, passed over to his side; the corps of Italian deserters, perhaps the most efficient among the divisions of Mithradates' army and for that very reason the least inclined to take part in the romantic—and for the deserters peculiarly hazardous—expedition against Italy, declared itself *en masse* for the prince; the other divisions of the army and the fleet followed the example thus set.

After the country and the army had abandoned the king, the capital Panticapaeum at length opened its gates to the insurgents and delivered over to them the old king enclosed in his palace. From the high wall of his castle the latter besought his son at least to grant him life and not imbrue his hands in his father's blood; but the request came ill from the lips of a man whose own hands were stained with the blood of his mother and with the recently shed blood of his innocent son Xiphares; and in heartless severity and inhumanity Pharnaces even outstripped his father. Seeing therefore he had now to die, the sultan resolved at least to die as he had lived; his wives, his concubines, and his daughters, including the youthful brides of the kings of Egypt and Cyprus, had all to suffer the bitterness of death and drain the poisoned cup before him; then he seized it, but, as the draught did not take effect quickly enough, he presented his neck for the fatal stroke to a Celtic mercenary Betuitus. So died in 691/63 Mithradates Eupator, in the sixth-eighth year of his life and the fifty-seventh of his reign, twenty-six years after he had for the first time taken the field against the Romans. The dead body, which king Pharnaces sent as a voucher of his merits and of his loyalty to Pompeius, was by order of the latter laid in the royal sepulchre of Sinope.

The death of Mithradates was looked on by the Romans as equivalent to a victory: the messengers who reported to the general the catastrophe appeared crowned with laurel, as if they had a victory to announce, in the Roman camp before Jericho. In him a great enemy was borne to the tomb, greater than had ever yet withstood the Romans in the indolent East. Instinctively the multitude felt this: as formerly Scipio had triumphed even more over Hannibal than over Carthage, so the conquest of the numerous tribes of the East and of the great king himself was almost forgotten in the death of Mithradates; and at the solemn entry of Pompeius nothing attracted more the eyes of the multitude than the pictures, in which they saw king Mithradates as a fugitive leading his horse by the rein and thereafter sinking down in death between the dead bodies of his daughters. Whatever judgment may be formed as to the idiosyncrasy of the king, he is a figure of world-historical importance—in the full sense of the expression. He was not a personage of genius, probably not even of rich endowments; but he possessed the very respectable gift of hating, and out of his hatred he sustained an unequal conflict against superior foes throughout half a century, without success doubtless, but still with honour. He became still more significant through the position in which history had placed him than through his individual character. As the advanced post of the national reaction of the East against the Occidentals, he opened the new conflict of the East against the West; and the feeling remained with the vanquished as with the victors, that his death was not so much the end as the beginning.

Meanwhile Pompeius, after his warfare in $\frac{689}{65}$ with the peoples of the Caucasus, had returned to the kingdom of Pontus, and there reduced the last castles still offering resistance; these were razed in order to check the evils of brigandage, and the castle wells were rendered unserviceable by rolling blocks of rock into them. Thence he set out in the summer of $\frac{690}{64}$ for Syria, to regulate its affairs.

It is difficult to present a clear view of the state of disorganisation which then prevailed in the Syrian provinces. It is true that in consequence of the attacks of Lucullus the Armenian governor Magadates had evacuated these provinces in $\frac{685}{69}$ (p. 61), and that the Ptolemies, gladly as they would have renewed the attempts of their predecessors to attach the Syrian coast to their kingdom, were yet afraid to provoke the Roman government by the occupation of Syria; the more so, as that government had not yet regulated their more than doubtful legal title even in the case of Egypt, and had been several times solicited by the Syrian princes to recognise them as the legitimate heirs of the extinct house of the Lagidae. But, though the greater powers all at the moment refrained from interference in the affairs of Syria, the land suffered far more than it would have suffered amidst a great war, through the endless and aimless feuds of the princes, knights, and cities.

The actual masters in the Seleucid kingdom were at this time the Bedouins, the Jews, and the Nabataeans. The inhospitable sandy steppe destitute of springs and trees, which, stretching from the Arabian peninsula up to and beyond the Euphrates, reaches towards the west as far as the Syrian mountain-chain and its narrow belt of coast, towards the east as far as the rich lowlands of the Tigris and lower Euphrates—this Asiatic Sahara—was the primitive home of the sons of Ishmael; from the commencement of tradition we find the "Bedouin," the "son of the desert," pitching his tents there and pasturing his camels, or mounting his swift horse in pursuit now of the foe of his tribe, now of the travelling merchant. Favoured formerly by king Tigranes who made use of them for his plans half commercial half political (p. 43), and subsequently by the total absence of any master in the Syrian land, these children of the desert spread themselves over northern Syria. Well-nigh the leading part in a political point of view was enacted by those tribes which had appropriated the first rudiments of a settled existence from the vicinity of the civilised Syrians. The most noted of these emirs were Abgarus, chief of the Arab tribe of the Mardani, whom Tigranes had settled about Edessa and Carrhae in upper Mesopotamia (p. 42); then to the west of the Euphrates Sampsiceramus, emir of the Arabs of Hemesa (Hems) between Damascus and Antioch, and master of the strong fortress Arethusa; Azizus the head of another horde roaming in the same region; Alchaudonius, the prince of the Rhambaeans, who had already put himself into communication with Lucullus; and several others.

Alongside of these Bedouin princes there had everywhere appeared bold cavaliers, who equalled or excelled the children of the desert in the noble trade of waylaying. Such was Ptolemaeus son of Mennaeus, perhaps the most powerful among these Syrian robber-chiefs and one of the richest men of this period, who ruled over the territory of the Ityraeans—the modern Druses—in the valleys of the Libanus as well as on the coast and over the plain of Massyas to the northward with the cities of Heliopolis (Baalbec) and Chalcis, and maintained 8000 horsemen at his own expense; such were Dionysius and Cinyras, the masters of the maritime cities Tripolis (Tarablus) and Byblus (between Tarablus and Beirout); such was the Jew Silas in Lysias, a fortress not far from Apamea on the Orontes.

In the south of Syria, on the other hand, the race of the Jews seemed as though it would about this time consolidate itself into a political power. Through the devout and bold defence of the primitive Jewish national worship, which was imperilled by the levelling Hellenism of the Syrian kings, the family of the Hasmonaeans or the Makkabi had not only attained to their hereditary principality and gradually to kingly honours (iii. 57); but these princely high priests had also spread their conquests to the north, south, and east. When the brave Jannaeus Alexander died ($\frac{675}{79}$), the Jewish kingdom stretched towards the south over the whole Philistian territory as far as the Egyptian frontier, towards the south-east as far as the Nabataean kingdom of Petra, from which Jannaeus had wrested considerable tracts on the right bank of the Jordan and the Dead Sea, towards the north over Samaria and Decapolis up to the lake of Gennesareth; here he was already making arrangements to occupy Ptolemais (Acco) and victoriously to repel the aggressions of the Ityraeans. The coast obeyed the Jews from Mount Carmel as far as Rhinocorura, including the important Gaza—Ascalon alone was still free; so that the territory of the Jews, once almost cut off from the sea, could now be enumerated among the asylums of piracy. Now that the Armenian invasion, just as it approached the borders of Judaea, was averted by the intervention of Lucullus (p. 60), the gifted rulers of the Hasmonaean house would probably have carried their arms still farther, had not the development of the power of that remarkable conquering sacerdotal state been arrested by internal divisions.

The spirit of religious independence, and the national patriotism—the energetic union of which had called the Maccabee state into life—very soon became dissociated and even antagonistic. The Jewish orthodoxy gaining fresh strength in the times of the Maccabees, or Pharisaism as it was called, proposed as its practical aim a community of Jews composed of the orthodox in all lands essentially irrespective of the secular government—a community which found its visible points of union in the tribute to the temple at Jerusalem obligatory on every conscientious Jew and in the schools of religion and spiritual courts, and its canonical superintendence in the great temple consistory at Jerusalem, which was reconstituted in the first period of the Maccabees and may be compared as respects its sphere of jurisdiction to the Roman pontifical college. Against this orthodoxy, which was becoming more and more ossified into theological formalism and a painful ceremonial service, was arrayed the opposition of the so-called Sadducees—partly dogmatic, in so far as these innovators acknowledged only the sacred books themselves and conceded authority merely, not canonicity, to the "bequests of the scribes," that is, canonical tradition;[1] partly political, in so far as instead of a fatalistic waiting for the strong arm of the Lord of Zebaoth they taught that the salvation of the nation was to be expected from the weapons of this world, and above all from the internal and external strengthening of the kingdom of David as re-established in the glorious times of the Maccabees. The partisans of orthodoxy found their support in the priesthood and the multitude, and fought against the noxious heretics with all the unscrupulous implacability with which the pious are often

[1] Thus the Sadducees rejected the doctrine of angels and spirits and the resurrection of the dead. Most of the traditional points of difference between Pharisees and Sadducees relate to subordinate questions of ritual, jurisprudence, and the calendar. It is a characteristic fact, that the victorious Pharisees have introduced those days, on which they definitively obtained the superiority in particular controversies or ejected heretical members from the supreme consistory, into the list of the memorial and festival days of the nation.

found to contend for the possession of earthly goods. The innovators on the other hand relied for support on intelligence brought into contact with the influences of Hellenism, on the army, in which numerous Pisidian and Cilician mercenaries served, and on the abler kings, who here strove with the ecclesiastical power much as a thousand years later the Hohenstaufen strove with the Papacy. Jannaeus had kept down the priesthood with a strong hand; under his two sons there arose ($\frac{685}{69}$ *et seq.*) a civil and fraternal war, since the Pharisees opposed the vigorous Aristobulus and attempted to obtain their objects under the nominal rule of his brother, the good-natured and indolent Hyrcanus. This dissension not merely put a stop to the Jewish conquests, but gave also foreign nations opportunity to interfere and to obtain a commanding position in southern Syria.

This was the case first of all with the Nabataeans. This remarkable nation has often been confounded with its eastern neighbours, the wandering Arabs, but it is more closely related to the Aramaean branch than to the proper children of Ishmael. This Aramaean or, according to the designation of the Occidentals, Syrian stock must have in very early times sent forth from its most ancient settlements about Babylon a colony, probably for the sake of trade, to the northern end of the Arabian gulf; these were the Nabataeans on the Sinaitic peninsula, between the gulf of Suez and Aila, and in the region of Petra (Wadi Mousa). In their ports the wares of the Mediterranean were exchanged for those of India; the great southern caravan-route, which ran from Gaza to the mouth of the Euphrates and the Persian gulf, passed through the capital of the Nabataeans—Petra—whose still magnificent rock-palaces and rock-tombs furnish clearer evidence of the Nabataean civilisation than does an almost extinct tradition. The party of the Pharisees, to whom after the manner of priests the victory of their faction seemed not too dearly bought at the price of the independence and integrity of their country, solicited Aretas the king of the Nabataeans for aid against Aristobulus, in return for which they promised to give back to him all the conquests wrested from him by Jannaeus. Thereupon Aretas had advanced with, it was said, 50,000 men into Judaea and, reinforced by the adherents of the Pharisees, he kept king Aristobulus besieged in his capital.

Amidst the system of violence and feud which thus prevailed from one end of Syria to another, the larger cities were of course the principal sufferers; such as Antioch, Seleucia, Damascus, whose citizens found themselves paralysed in their husbandry as well as in their maritime and caravan trade. The citizens of Byblus and Berytus (Beirout) were unable to protect their fields and their ships from the Ityraeans, who issuing from their mountain and maritime strongholds rendered land and sea equally insecure. Those of Damascus sought to ward off the attacks of the Ityraeans and Ptolemaeus by handing themselves over to the more remote kings of the Nabataeans or of the Jews. In Antioch Sampsiceramus and Azizus mingled in the internal feuds of the citizens, and the Hellenic great city had well-nigh become even now the seat of an Arab emir. The state of things reminds us of the kingless times of the German middle ages, when Nuremberg and Augsburg found their protection not in the sovereign jurisdiction of the king, but in their own walls alone; impatiently the merchant-citizens of Syria awaited the strong arm, which should restore to them peace and security of intercourse.

There was no want, however, of a legitimate king of Syria; there were even two or three of them. A prince Antiochus from the house of the Seleucids had been appointed by Lucullus as ruler of the most northern province in Syria, Commagene (p. 62). Antiochus Asiaticus, whose claims on the Syrian throne had met with recognition both from the senate and from Lucullus (pp. 58, 62), had been received in Antioch after the retreat of the Armenians and there acknowledged as king. A third Seleucid prince Philippus had immediately confronted him there as a rival; and the great population of Antioch, excitable and delighting in opposition almost like that of Alexandria, as well as one or two of the neighbouring Arab emirs had interfered in the family strife which now seemed inseparable from the rule of the Seleucids. Was there any wonder that legitimacy became ridiculous and loathsome to its subjects; and that the so-called rightful kings were of even somewhat less importance in the land than the petty princes and robber-chiefs?

To create order amidst this chaos did not require either brilliance of conception or a mighty display of force, but it required a clear insight into the interests of Rome and of her subjects, and vigour and consistency in establishing and maintaining the institutions which were seen to be necessary. The policy of the senate in support of legitimacy had sufficiently degraded itself; the general whom the opposition had brought into power was not to be guided by dynastic considerations, but had only to see that the Syrian kingdom should not be withdrawn from the clientship of Rome in future either by the quarrels of pretenders or by the covetousness of neighbours. But to secure this end there was only one course; that the Roman community should send a satrap to grasp with a vigorous hand the reins of government, which had long since practically slipped from the hands of the kings of the ruling house more through their own fault than through outward misfortunes. This course Pompeius took. Antiochus the Asiatic, on requesting to be acknowledged as the hereditary ruler of Syria, received the answer that Pompeius would not give back the sovereignty to a king who knew neither how to maintain nor how to govern his kingdom, even at the request of his subjects, much less against their distinctly expressed wishes. With this letter of the Roman proconsul the house of Seleucus was ejected from the throne which it had occupied for two hundred and fifty years. Antiochus soon after lost his life through the artifice of the emir Sampsiceramus, as whose client he played the ruler in Antioch; thenceforth there is no further mention of these mock-kings and their pretensions.

But, to establish the new Roman government and introduce any tolerable order into the confusion of affairs, it was further necessary to advance into Syria with a military force and to terrify or subdue all the disturbers of the peace, who had sprung up during the many years of anarchy, by means of the Roman legions. Already during the campaigns in the kingdom of Pontus and on the Caucasus Pompeius had turned his attention to the affairs of Syria and directed detached commissioners and corps to interfere, where there was need. Aulus Gabinius—the same who as tribune of the people had sent Pompeius to the East—had in $\frac{689}{65}$ marched along the Tigris and then across Mesopotamia to Syria, to adjust the complicated affairs of Judaea. In like manner the severely pressed Damascus had already been occupied by Lollius and Metellus. Soon afterwards another adjutant of Pompeius, Marcus Scaurus, arrived in Judaea, to allay the feuds ever breaking out afresh there. Lucius Afranius also, who during the expedition of Pompeius to the Caucasus held the command of the Roman troops in Armenia, had proceeded from Corduene (the northern Kurdistan) to upper Mesopotamia, and, after he had successfully accomplished the perilous march through the desert with the sympathising help of the Hellenes settled in Carrhae, brought the Arabs in Osroene to submission. Towards the end of $\frac{690}{64}$

Pompeius in person arrived in Syria,[1] and remained there till the summer of the following year, resolutely interfering and regulating matters for the present and the future. He sought to restore the kingdom to its state in the better times of the Seleucid rule; all usurped powers were set aside, the robber-chiefs were summoned to give up their castles, the Arab sheiks were again restricted to their desert domains, the affairs of the several communities were definitively regulated.

The legions stood ready to procure obedience to these stern orders, and their interference proved especially necessary against the audacious robber-chiefs. Silas the ruler of Lysias, Dionysius the ruler of Tripolis, Cinyras the ruler of Byblus were taken prisoners in their fortresses and executed, the mountain and maritime strongholds of the Ityraeans were broken up, Ptolemaeus son of Mennaeus was forced to purchase his freedom and his lordship with a ransom of 1000 talents (£240,000). Elsewhere the commands of the new master met for the most part with unresisting obedience.

The Jews alone hesitated. The mediators formerly sent by Pompeius, Gabinius and Scaurus, had—both, as it was said, bribed with considerable sums—decided the dispute between the brothers Hyrcanus and Aristobulus in favour of the latter, and had also induced king Aretas to raise the siege of Jerusalem and to proceed homeward, in doing which he sustained a defeat at the hands of Aristobulus. But, when Pompeius arrived in Syria, he cancelled the orders of his subordinates and directed the Jews to resume their old constitution of high priests, as the senate had recognised it about $\frac{593}{161}$ (iii. 57), and to renounce along with the hereditary principality itself all the conquests made by the Hasmonaean princes. It was the Pharisees, who had sent an embassy of two hundred of their most eminent men to the Roman general and procured from him the overthrow of the kingdom; not to the advantage of their own nation, but doubtless to that of the Romans, who from the nature of the case could not but here revert to the old rights of the Seleucids,

[1] Pompeius spent the winter of $\frac{689}{65}-\frac{690}{64}$ still in the neighbourhood of the Caspian Sea (Dio. xxxvii. 7). In $\frac{690}{64}$ he first reduced the last strongholds still offering resistance in the kingdom of Pontus, and then moved slowly, regulating matters everywhere, towards the south. That the organisation of Syria began in $\frac{690}{64}$ is confirmed by the fact that the Syrian provincial era begins with this year, and by Cicero's statement as to Commagene (*Ad Q. fr.* ii. 12, 2; comp. Dio. xxxvii. 7). During the winter of $\frac{690}{64}-\frac{691}{63}$ Pompeius seems to have had his head-quarters in Damascus (Joseph. xiv. 3, 1, 2, where, however, there is much confusion; Diodorus, *Fr. Vat.* p. 139).

and could not tolerate a conquering power like that of Jannaeus within the limits of their empire. Aristobulus was uncertain whether it was better patiently to acquiesce in his inevitable doom or to meet his fate with arms in hand; at one time he seemed on the point of submitting to Pompeius, at another he seemed as though he would summon the national party among the Jews to a struggle with the Romans. When at length, with the legions already at the gates, he yielded to the enemy, the more resolute or more fanatical portion of his army refused to comply with the orders of a king who was not free. The capital submitted; the steep temple-rock was defended by that fanatical band for three months with an obstinacy ready to brave death, till at last the besiegers effected an entrance while the besieged were resting on the sabbath, possessed themselves of the sanctuary, and handed over the authors of that desperate resistance, so far as they had not fallen under the sword of the Romans, to the axes of the lictors. Thus ended the last resistance of the territories newly annexed to the Roman state.

The work began by Lucullus had been completed by Pompeius; the hitherto formally independent states of Bithynia, Pontus, and Syria were united with the Roman state; the exchange—which had been recognised for more than a hundred years as necessary—of the feeble system of a protectorate for that of direct sovereignty over the more important dependent territories (iii. 21), had at length been realised, as soon as the senate had been overthrown and the Gracchan party had come to the helm. Rome had obtained in the East new frontiers, new neighbours, new friendly and hostile relations. There were now added to the indirect territories of Rome the kingdom of Armenia and the principalities of the Caucasus, and also the kingdom on the Cimmerian Bosporus, the small remnant of the extensive conquests of Mithradates Eupator, now a client-state of Rome under the government of his son and murderer Pharnaces; the town of Phanagoria alone, whose commandant Castor had given the signal for the revolt, was on that account recognised by the Romans as free and independent.

No like successes could be boasted of against the Nabataeans. King Aretas had indeed, yielding to the desire of the Romans, evacuated Judaea; but Damascus was still in his hands, and the Nabataean land had not yet been trodden by any Roman soldier. To subdue that region or at least to show to their new neighbours in Arabia that the Roman eagles were now dominant on the Orontes and on the Jordan, and that the time had gone by when any one was free to levy contributions in the Syrian provinces as a domain without a master, Pompeius began in 691/63 an expedition against Petra; but detained by the revolt of the Jews, which broke out during this expedition, he was not reluctant to leave to his successor Marcus Scaurus the carrying out of the difficult enterprise against the Nabataean city situated far off amidst the desert.[1] In reality Scaurus also soon found himself compelled to return without having accomplished his object. He had to content himself with making war on the Nabataeans in the deserts on the left bank of the Jordan, where he could lean for support on the Jews; and he gained but very trifling successes. Ultimately the dexterous Jewish minister Antipater from Idumaea persuaded Aretas to purchase a guarantee for all his possessions, Damascus included, from the Roman governor for a sum of money; and this is the peace celebrated on the coins of Scaurus, where king Aretas appears—leading his camel—as a suppliant offering the olive branch to the Romans.

Far more important than these new relations of the Romans to the Armenians, Iberians, Bosporans, and Nabataeans was the proximity into which through the occupation of Syria they were brought with the Parthian state. Complaisant as had been the demeanour of Roman diplomacy towards Phraates while the Pontic and Armenian states still subsisted, willingly as both Lucullus and Pompeius had then conceded to him the possession of the regions beyond the Euphrates (pp. 63, 110), the new neighbour now sternly took up his position by the side of the Arsacids; and Phraates, if the royal art of forgetting his own faults allowed him, might well recall now the warning words of Mithradates that the Parthian by his alliance with the Occidentals against the kingdoms of kindred race paved the way first for their destruction and then for his own. Romans and Parthians in league had brought Armenia to ruin; when it was overthrown Rome true to her old policy now reversed the parts and favoured the humbled foe at the expense of the powerful ally. The singular preference, which the father Tigranes experienced from Pompeius as contrasted with his son the ally and son-in-law of

[1] Orosius indeed (vi. 6) and Dio (xxxvii. 15), both of them doubtless following Livy, make Pompeius get to Petra and occupy the city or even reach the Red Sea; but that he, on the contrary, soon after receiving the news of the death of Mithradates, which came to him on his march towards Jerusalem, returned from Syria to Pontus, is stated by Plutarch (*Pomp.* 41, 42) and is confirmed by Florus (i. 39) and Josephus (xiv. 3, 3, 4). The figuring of king Aretas in the bulletins among those conquered by Pompeius is sufficiently accounted for by the fact that it was Pompeius who occasioned his withdrawal from Jerusalem.

the Parthian king, was already part of this policy; it was a direct offence, when soon afterwards by the orders of Pompeius the younger Tigranes and his family were arrested and were not released even on Phraates interceding with the friendly general for his daughter and his son-in-law. But Pompeius paused not here. The province of Corduene, to which both Phraates and Tigranes laid claim, was at the command of Pompeius occupied by Roman troops for the latter, and the Parthians who were found in possession were driven beyond the frontier and pursued even as far as Arbela in Adiabene, without the government of Ctesiphon having been previously heard ($\frac{689}{65}$). Far the most suspicious circumstance however was, that the Romans seemed not at all inclined to respect the boundary of the Euphrates fixed by treaty. On several occasions Roman divisions destined from Armenia for Syria marched across Mesopotamia; the Arab emir Abgarus of Osroene was received under singularly favourable conditions into Roman protection; nay, Oruros, situated in upper Mesopotamia somewhere between Nisibis and the Tigris 220 miles eastward from the Commagenian passage of the Euphrates, was designated as the eastern limit of the Roman dominion—apparently their indirect dominion, inasmuch as the larger and more fertile northern half of Mesopotamia had been assigned by the Romans in like manner with Corduene to the Armenian empire. The boundary between Romans and Parthians thus became the great Syro-Mesopotamian desert instead of the Euphrates; and this too seemed only provisional. To the Parthian envoys, who came to insist on the maintenance of the agreements—which certainly, as it would seem, were only concluded orally—respecting the Euphrates boundary, Pompeius gave the ambiguous reply that the territory of Rome extended as far as her rights. The remarkable intercourse between the Roman commander-in-chief and the Parthian satraps of the region of Media and even of the distant province Elymais (between Susiana, Media, and Persia, in the modern Luristan) seemed a commentary on this speech.[1] The

[1] This view rests on the narrative of Plutarch (*Pomp.* 36) which is supported by Strabo's (xvi. 744) description of the position of the satrap of Elymais. It is an embellishment of the matter, when in the lists of the countries and kings conquered by Pompeius Media and its king Darius are enumerated (Diodorus *Fr. Vat.* p. 140; Appian, *Mithr.* 117); and from this there has been further concocted the war of Pompeius with the Medes (Vell. ii. 40; Appian, *Mithr.* 106, 114) and then even his expedition to Ecbatana (Oros vi. 5). A confusion with the fabulous town of the same name on Carmel has hardly taken place here; it is simply that intolerable exaggeration—apparently originating in the grandiloquent and designedly

viceroys of this latter mountainous, warlike, and remote land had always exerted themselves to acquire a position independent of the great king; it was the more offensive and menacing to the Parthian government, when Pompeius accepted the proffered homage of this dynast. Not less significant was the fact that the title of "king of kings," which had been hitherto conceded to the Parthian king by the Romans in official intercourse, was now all at once exchanged by them for the simple title of king. This was even more a threat than a violation of etiquette. Since Rome had entered on the heritage of the Seleucids, it seemed almost as if the Romans had a mind to revert at a convenient moment to those old times when all Iran and Turan were ruled from Antioch, and there was as yet no Parthian empire but merely a Parthian satrapy. The court of Ctesiphon would thus have had reason enough for going to war with Rome; it seemed the prelude to its doing so, when in $\frac{690}{64}$ it declared war on Armenia on account of the question of the frontier. But Phraates had not the courage to come to an open rupture with the Romans at a time when the dreaded general with his strong army was on the borders of the Parthian empire. When Pompeius sent commissioners to settle amicably the dispute between Parthia and Armenia, Phraates yielded to the Roman mediation forced upon him and acquiesced in their award, which assigned to the Armenians Corduene and northern Mesopotamia. Soon afterwards his daughter with her son and her husband graced the triumph of the Roman general. Even the Parthians trembled before the superior power of Rome; and, if they had not, like the inhabitants of Pontus and Armenia, succumbed to the Roman arms, the reason seemed only to be that they had not ventured to stand the conflict.

There still devolved on the general the duty of regulating the internal relations of the newly-acquired provinces and of removing as far as possible the traces of a thirteen years' desolating war. The work of organisation begun in Asia Minor by Lucullus and the commission associated with him, and in Crete by Metellus, received its conclusion from Pompeius. The former province of Asia, which embraced Mysia, Lydia, Phrygia, Caria, and Lycia, was converted from a frontier province into a central one. The newly-erected provinces were, that of

ambiguous bulletins of Pompeius—which has converted his razzia against the Gaetulians (iii. 324) into a march to the west coast of Africa (Plut. *Pomp.* 38), his abortive expedition against the Nabataeans into a conquest of the city of Petra, and his award as to the boundaries of Armenia into a fixing of the boundary of the Roman empire beyond Nisibis.

Bithynia and Pontus, which was formed out of the whole former kingdom of Nicomedes and the western half of the former Pontic state as far as and beyond the Halys; that of Cilicia, which indeed was older, but was now for the first time enlarged and organised in a manner befitting its name, and comprehended also Pamphylia and Isauria; that of Syria, and that of Crete. Much was no doubt wanting to render that mass of countries capable of being regarded as the territorial possession of Rome in the modern sense of the term. The form and order of the government remained substantially as they were; only the Roman community came in place of the former monarchs. Those Asiatic provinces consisted as formerly of a motley mixture of domanial possessions, civic territories *de facto* or *de jure* autonomous, lordships pertaining to princes and priests, and kingdoms, all of which were as regards internal administration more or less left to themselves, and in other respects were dependent, sometimes in milder sometimes in stricter form, on the Roman government and its proconsuls very much as formerly on the great king and his satraps.

The first place, in rank at least, among the dependent dynasts was held by the king of Cappadocia, whose territory Lucullus had already enlarged by investing him with the province of Melitene (about Malatia) as far as the Euphrates, and to whom Pompeius farther granted on the western frontier some districts taken off Cilicia from Castabala as far as Derbe near Iconium, and on the eastern frontier the province of Sophene situated on the left bank of the Euphrates opposite Melitene and at first destined for the Armenian prince Tigranes; so that the most important passage of the Euphrates thus came wholly into the power of the Cappadocian prince. The small province of Commagene between Syria and Cappadocia with its capital Samosata (Samsat) remained a dependent kingdom in the hands of the already named Seleucid Antiochus;[1] to him too were assigned the important fortress of Seleucia (near Biradjik) commanding the more southern passage of the Euphrates, and the adjoining tracts on the left bank of that river; and thus care was taken that the two chief passages of the Euphrates with a corresponding territory on the eastern bank were left in the hands of two

[1] The war which this Antiochus is alleged to have waged with Pompeius (Appian. *Mithr.* 106, 117) is not very consistent with the treaty which he concluded with Lucullus (Dio xxxvi. 4), and his undisturbed continuance in his sovereignty; probably it was concocted simply from the circumstance, that Antiochus of Commagene figured among the kings subdued by Pompeius.

dynasts wholly dependent on Rome. Alongside of the kings of Cappadocia and Commagene, and in real power far superior to them, the new king Deiotarus ruled in Asia Minor. One of the tetrarchs of the Celtic stock of the Tolistobogi settled round Pessinus, and summoned by Lucullus and Pompeius to render military service with the other small Roman clients, Deiotarus had in these campaigns so brilliantly proved his trustworthiness and his energy as contrasted with all the indolent Orientals that the Roman generals conferred upon him, in addition to his Galatian heritage and his possessions in the rich country between Amisus and the mouth of the Halys, the eastern half of the former Pontic empire with the maritime towns of Pharnacia and Trapezus and the Pontic Armenia as far as the Colchian and Great-Armenian frontier, to form the kingdom of Lesser Armenia. Soon afterwards he increased his already considerable territory by the country of the Celtic Trocmi, whose tetrarch he dispossessed. Thus the petty feudatory became one of the most powerful dynasts of Asia Minor, to whom might be entrusted the guardianship of an important part of the frontier of the empire.

Vassals of lesser importance were the other numerous Galatian tetrarchs, one of whom, Bogodiatarus prince of the Trocmi, was on account of his tried valour in the Mithradatic war presented by Pompeius with the formerly Pontic frontier-town of Mithradatium; Attalus prince of Paphlagonia, who traced back his lineage to the old ruling house of the Pylaemenidae; Aristarchus and other petty lords in the Colchian territory; Tarcondimotus who ruled in eastern Cilicia in the mountain-valleys of the Amanus; Ptolemaeus son of Mennaeus who continued to rule in Chalcis on the Libanus; Aretas king of the Nabataeans as lord of Damascus; lastly, the Arabic emirs in the countries on either side of the Euphrates, Abgarus in Osroene, whom the Romans endeavoured in every way to draw over to their interest with the view of using him as an advanced post against the Parthians, Sampsiceramus in Hemesa, Alchaudonius the Rhambaean, and another emir in Bostra.

To these fell to be added the spiritual lords who in the East frequently ruled over land and people like secular dynasts, and whose authority firmly established in that native home of fanaticism the Romans prudently refrained from disturbing, as they refrained from even robbing the temples of their treasures: the high priest of the Mother of the Gods in Pessinus; the two high priests of the goddess Ma in the Cappadocian Comana (on the upper Sarus) and in the Pontic city of the same name (Gumenek near Tocat), both lords who were in their countries inferior only to the king in power, and each of whom even at a much later period possessed extensive estates with special jurisdiction and about six thousand slaves—Archelaus, son of the general of that name who passed over from Mithradates to the Romans, was invested by Pompeius with the Pontic high priesthood; the high priest of the Venasian Zeus in the Cappadocian district of Morimene, whose revenues amounted annually to £3600 (15 talents); the "arch-priest and ruler" of that territory in Cilicia Trachea, where Teucer the son of Ajax had founded a temple to Zeus, over which his descendants presided by virtue of hereditary right; the "arch-priest and ruler of the people" of the Jews, to whom Pompeius, after having razed the walls of the capital and the royal treasuries and strongholds in the land, gave back the presidency of the nation with a serious admonition to keep the peace and no longer to aim at conquests.

Alongside of these secular and spiritual potentates stood the urban communities. These were partly associated into larger unions which rejoiced in a comparative independence, such as in particular the league of the twenty-three Lycian cities, which was well organised and constantly kept aloof from participation in the disorders of piracy; whereas the numerous detached communities, even if they had their self-government secured by charter, were in practice wholly dependent on the Roman governors.

The Romans failed not to see that with the task of representing Hellenism and protecting and extending the domain of Alexander in the East there devolved on them the primary duty of elevating the urban system; for, while cities are everywhere the pillars of civilisation, the antagonism between Orientals and Occidentals was most distinctly embodied in the contrast between the Oriental, military-despotic, feudal hierarchy and the Helleno-Italian urban commonwealth prosecuting trade and commerce. Lucullus and Pompeius, however little they in other respects aimed at the reduction of things to one level in the East, and however much the latter was disposed in questions of detail to censure and alter the arrangements of his predecessor, were yet completely agreed in the principle of promoting as far as they could an urban life in Asia Minor and Syria. Cyzicus, on whose vigorous resistance the first violence of the last war had spent itself, received from Lucullus a considerable extension of its domain. The Pontic Heraclea, energetically as it had resisted the Romans, yet recovered its territory and its harbours; and the barbarous fury of Cotta against the unhappy city met with the sharpest censure in the senate. Lucullus had deeply and sincerely regretted that fate had refused him the happiness of rescuing Sinope and Amisus from devastation by the Pontic soldiery and his own; he did at least what he could to restore them, extended considerably their territories, peopled them afresh—partly with the old inhabitants, who at his invitation returned in troops to their beloved homes, partly with new settlers of Hellenic descent—and provided for the reconstruction of the buildings destroyed. Pompeius acted in the same spirit and on a greater scale. Even after the subjugation of the pirates he had, instead of following the example of his predecessors and crucifying his prisoners, whose number exceeded 20,000, settled them partly in the desolated cities of the Plain Cilicia, such as Mallus, Adana, Epiphaneia, and especially in Soli, which thenceforth bore the name of Pompeius' city (Pompeiupolis), partly at Dyme in Achaia, and even at Tarentum. This colonising by means of pirates met with manifold censure,[1] as it seemed in some measure to set a premium on crime; in reality it was politically and morally justifiable, for, as things then stood, piracy was something different from robbery and the prisoners might fairly be treated according to martial law.

But Pompeius made it his business above all to promote urban life in the new Roman provinces. We have already observed how poorly provided with towns the Pontic empire was (iii. 264); most districts of Cappadocia even a century after this had no towns, but merely mountain fortresses as a refuge for the agricultural population in war; the whole east of Asia Minor, apart from the sparse Greek colonies on the coasts, must have been at this time in a similar plight. The number of towns newly established by Pompeius in these provinces is, including the Cilician settlements, stated at thirty-nine, several of which attained great prosperity. The most notable of these townships in the former kingdom of Pontus were Nicopolis, the "city of victory," founded on the spot where Mithradates sustained the last decisive defeat (p. 112)—the fairest memorial of a general rich in similar trophies; Megalopolis, named from Pompeius'

[1] To this Cicero's reproach probably points (De Off. iii. 12, 49): *piratas immunes habemus, socios vectigales*; in so far, namely, as those pirate-colonies probably had the privilege of immunity conferred on them by Pompeius, while, as is well known, the provincial communities dependent on Rome were in general liable to taxation.

surname, on the frontier of Cappadocia and Lesser Armenia, the subsequent Sebasteia (now Siwas); Ziela, where the Romans fought the unfortunate battle (p. 67), a place which had arisen round the temple of Anaitis there and hitherto had belonged to its high priest, and to which Pompeius now gave the form and privileges of a city, Diospolis, formerly Cabira, afterwards Neocaesarea (Niksar), likewise one of the battle-fields of the late war; Magnopolis or Pompeiupolis, the restored Eupatoria at the confluence of the Lycus and the Iris, originally built by Mithradates, but again destroyed by him on account of its defection to the Romans (p. 109); Neapolis, formerly Phazemon, between Amasia and the Halys. Most of the towns thus established were formed not by bringing colonists from a distance, but by the suppression of villages and the collection of their inhabitants within the new ring-wall; in Nicopolis Pompeius settled the invalids and veterans of his army, who preferred to establish a home for themselves there at once rather than afterwards in Italy. But in other places also there arose at the beck of the regent new centres of Hellenic civilisation. In Paphlagonia a third Pompeiupolis marked the spot where the army of Mithradates in $\frac{666}{88}$ achieved the great victory over the Bithynians (iii. 276). In Cappadocia, which perhaps had suffered more than any other province by the war, the royal residence Mazaca (afterwards Caesarea, now Kaisarieh) and seven other townships were restored by Pompeius and received urban institutions. In Cilicia and Coelesyria there were enumerated twenty cities laid out by Pompeius. In the districts ceded by the Jews, Gadara in the Decapolis rose from its ruins at the command of Pompeius, and the city of Seleucia was founded. By far the greater portion of the domain land at his disposal on the Asiatic continent must have been applied by Pompeius for his new settlements; whereas in Crete, about which Pompeius troubled himself little or not at all, the Roman domanial possessions seemed to have continued tolerably extensive.

Pompeius was no less intent on regulating and elevating the existing communities than on founding new ones. The abuses and usurpations which prevailed were reformed as far as lay in his power; copious ordinances drawn up carefully with reference to the different provinces regulated the municipal system in detail. A number of the most considerable cities had fresh privileges conferred on them. Autonomy was bestowed on Antioch on the Orontes, the most important city of Roman Asia and but little inferior to the Egyptian Alexandria and to the Bagdad of antiquity, the city of Seleucia in the Parthian empire; as also on the neighbour of Antioch, the Pierian Seleucia, which was thus rewarded for its courageous resistance to Tigranes; on Gaza and generally on all the towns liberated from the Jewish rule; on Mytilene in the west of Asia Minor; and on Phanagoria on the Black Sea.

Thus was completed the structure of the Roman state in Asia, which with its feudatory kings and vassals, its sacerdotal princes, and its series of free and half-free cities puts us vividly in mind of the Holy Roman Empire of the German nation. It was no miraculous work, either as respects the difficulties overcome or as respects the result obtained; nor was it rendered such by all the high-sounding words which the Roman world of quality lavished in favour of Lucullus and the artless multitude in praise of Pompeius. Pompeius in particular consented to be praised, and praised himself, in such a fashion that people might almost have reckoned him still more weak-minded than he really was. His triumphal inscriptions enumerated twelve millions of people as subjugated and 1538 cities and strongholds as conquered—it seemed as if quantity was to make up for quality—and made the circle of his victories extend from the Maeotic Sea to the Caspian and from the Caspian to the Red Sea, when his eyes had never seen any one of the three; nay farther, if he did not exactly say so, he at any rate induced the public to suppose that the annexation of Syria, which in truth was no heroic deed, had added the whole East as far as Bactria and India to the Roman empire—so dim was the distance amidst which according to his statements the boundary line of his eastern conquests was lost. The democratic servility, which has at all times rivalled that of courts, readily entered into these insipid extravagances. It was not satisfied by the pompous triumphal procession, which moved through the streets of Rome on the 28th and 29th September $\frac{693}{61}$—the forty-sixth birthday of Pompeius the Great—adorned, to say nothing of jewels of all sorts, by the crown insignia of Mithradates and by the children of the three mightiest kings of Asia, Mithradates, Tigranes, and Phraates; it rewarded its general, who had conquered twenty-two kings, with regal honours and bestowed on him the golden chaplet and the insignia of the magistracy for life. The coins struck in his honour exhibit the globe itself placed amidst the triple laurels brought home from the three continents, and surmounted by the golden chaplet conferred by the burgesses on the man who had triumphed over Africa, Spain, and Asia. It need excite no surprise, if in presence of such childish acts of homage voices were heard of an opposite import. Among the Roman world of quality it was currently affirmed that the true merit of having subdued the East belonged to Lucullus, and that Pompeius had only gone thither to supplant Lucullus and to plait the laurels which another hand had plucked around his own brow. Both statements were totally erroneous: it was not Pompeius but Glabrio that was sent to Asia to relieve Lucullus, and, bravely as Lucullus had fought, it was a fact that, when Pompeius took the supreme command, the Romans had forfeited all their earlier successes and had not a foot's breadth of Pontic soil in their possession. More pointed and effective was the ridicule of the inhabitants of the capital, who failed not to nickname the mighty conqueror of the globe after the great powers which he had conquered and saluted him now as "conqueror of Salem," now as "emir" (*Arabarches*), now as the Roman Sampsiceramus.

The unprejudiced judge will not agree either with those exaggerations or with these disparagements. Lucullus and Pompeius, in subduing and regulating Asia, showed themselves to be, not heroes and state-creators, but sagacious and energetic commanders and governors. As general Lucullus displayed no common talents and a self-confidence bordering on rashness, while Pompeius displayed military judgment and a rare self-restraint; for hardly has any general with such forces and a position so wholly free ever acted so cautiously as Pompeius in the East. The most brilliant undertakings, as it were, offered themselves to him on all sides; he was free to start for the Cimmerian Bosporus and for the Red Sea; he had opportunity of declaring war against the Parthians; the revolted provinces of Egypt invited him to dethrone king Ptolemy who was not recognised by the Romans, and to carry out the testament of Alexander; but Pompeius marched neither to Panticapaeum nor to Petra, neither to Ctesiphon nor to Alexandria; throughout he plucked only those fruits which spontaneously came to his hand. In like manner he fought all his battles by sea and land with a crushing superiority of force. Had this moderation proceeded from the strict observance of the instructions given to him, as Pompeius was wont to profess, or even from a perception that the conquests of Rome must somewhere find a limit and that fresh accessions of territory were not advantageous to the state, it would deserve a higher praise than history confers on the most talented officer; but constituted as Pompeius was, his self-restraint was beyond doubt solely the result of his peculiar want of decision and of initiative—defects, indeed, which were in his case far more useful to the state than the opposite excellences of his predecessor. Certainly very grave errors were perpetrated both by Lucullus and by Pompeius. Lucullus reaped their fruits himself, when his imprudent conduct wrested from him all the results of his victories; Pompeius left it to his successors to bear the consequences of his false policy towards the Parthians. He might either have made war on the Parthians, if he had had the courage to do so, or have maintained peace with them and recognised, as he had promised, the Euphrates as boundary; he was too timid for the former course, too vain for the latter, and so he resorted to the silly perfidy of rendering the good neighbourhood, which the court of Ctesiphon desired and on its part practised, impossible through the most unbounded aggressions, and yet allowing the enemy to choose of themselves the time for rupture and retaliation. As administrator of Asia Lucullus acquired a more than princely wealth; and Pompeius also received as reward for its organisation large sums in cash and still more considerable promissory notes from the king of Cappadocia, from the rich city of Antioch, and from other lords and communities. But such exactions had become almost a customary tribute; and both generals showed themselves at any rate to be not altogether venal in questions of greater importance, but if possible got themselves paid by the party whose interests coincided with those of Rome. Looking to the times, this does not prevent us from characterising the administration of both as comparatively commendable and conducted primarily in the interest of Rome, secondarily in that of the provincials.

The conversion of the clients into subjects, the better regulation of the eastern frontier, the establishment of a single and strong government, were full of blessing for the rulers as well as for the ruled. The financial gain acquired by Rome was immense; the new property tax, which with the exception of some specially exempted communities all those princes, priests, and cities had to pay to Rome, raised the Roman state-revenues almost by a half above their former amount. Asia indeed suffered severely. Pompeius brought in money and jewels an amount of £2,000,000 (200,000,000 sesterces) into the state-chest and distributed £3,900,000 (16,000 talents) among his officers and soldiers; if we add to this the considerable sums brought home by Lucullus, the non-official exactions of the Roman army, and the amount of the damage done by the war, the financial exhaustion of the land may be readily conceived. The Roman taxation of Asia was perhaps in itself not worse than that of its earlier rulers, but it formed a heavier burden on the land in so far as the taxes thenceforth went out of the country and only the lesser portion of the proceeds was again expended in Asia; and at any rate it was, in the old as well as the newly-acquired provinces, based on a systematic plundering of the provinces for the benefit of Rome. But the responsibility for this rests far less on the generals personally than on the parties at home, whom these had to consider; Lucullus had even exerted himself energetically to set limits to the usurious dealings of the Roman capitalists in Asia, and this essentially contributed to bring about his fall. How much both men earnestly sought to revive the prosperity of the reduced provinces, is shown by their action in cases where no considerations of party policy tied their hands, and especially in their care for the cities of Asia Minor. Although for centuries afterwards many an Asiatic village lying in ruins recalled the times of the great war, Sinope might well begin a new era with the date of its restoration by Lucullus, and almost all the more considerable inland towns of the Pontic kingdom might gratefully honour Pompeius as their founder. The organisation of Roman Asia by Lucullus and Pompeius may with all its undeniable defects be described as on the whole judicious and praiseworthy; serious as were the evils that might still adhere to it, it could not but be welcome to the sorely tormented Asiatics for the very reason that it came attended by the inward and outward peace, the absence of which had been so long and so painfully felt.

Peace continued substantially in the East, till the idea—merely indicated by Pompeius with his characteristic timidity—of joining the regions eastward of the Euphrates to the Roman empire was taken up again energetically but unsuccessfully by the new triumvirate of Roman regents, and soon thereafter the civil war drew the eastern provinces as well as all the rest into its fatal vortex. In the interval the governors of Cilicia had to fight constantly with the mountain-tribes of the Amanus and those of Syria with the hordes of the desert, and in the latter war against the Bedouins more especially many Roman troops were destroyed; but these movements had no further significance. More remarkable was the obstinate resistance, which the tough Jewish nation opposed to the conquerors. Alexander son of the deposed king Aristobulus, and Aristobulus himself who after a time succeeded in escaping from captivity, excited during the governorship of Aulus Gabinius ($\frac{697-700}{57-54}$) three different revolts against the new rulers, to each of which the government of the high priest Hyrcanus installed by Rome impotently succumbed. It was not political conviction, but the invincible repugnance of the Oriental towards the unnatural yoke, which compelled them to kick against the pricks; as indeed the last and most dangerous of these revolts, for which the withdrawal of the Syrian army of occupation in consequence of the Egyptian crisis furnished the immediate impulse, began with the murder of the Romans settled in Palestine. It was not without difficulty that the able governor succeeded in rescuing the few Romans, who had escaped the same fate and found a temporary refuge on Mount Gerizim, from the insurgents who kept them blockaded there, and in overpowering the revolt after several severely contested battles and tedious sieges. In consequence of this the monarchy of the high priests was abolished and the Jewish land was broken up, as Macedonia had formerly been, into five independent districts administered by governing colleges with an optimate organisation; Samaria and other places razed by the Jews were restored, to form a counterpoise to Jerusalem; and lastly a heavier tribute was imposed on the Jews than on the other Syrian subjects of Rome.

It still remains that we should glance at the kingdom of Egypt along with the last dependency that remained to it of the extensive conquests of the Lagidae, the fair island of Cyprus. Egypt was now the only state of the Hellenic East that was still at least nominally independent; just as formerly, when the Persians established themselves along the eastern half of the Mediterranean, Egypt was their last conquest, so now the mighty conquerors from the West long delayed the annexation of that opulent and peculiar country. The reason lay, as was already indicated, neither in any fear of the resistance of Egypt nor in the want of a fitting occasion. Egypt was nearly as powerless as Syria, and had already in $\frac{673}{81}$ fallen in all due form of law to the Roman community (p. 45.) The control exercised over the court of Alexandria by the royal guard—which appointed and deposed ministers and occasionally kings, took for itself what it pleased, and, if it was refused a rise of pay, besieged the king in his palace—was by no means liked in the country or rather in the capital (for the country with its population of agricultural slaves was hardly taken into account); and at least a party there wished for the annexation of Egypt by Rome, and even took steps to procure it. But the less the kings of Egypt could think of contending in arms against Rome, the more energetically Egyptian gold resisted the Roman plans of union; and in consequence of the peculiar despotico-communistic centralisation of the Egyptian finances the revenues of the court of Alexandria were still nearly equal to the public income of Rome even after its augmentation by Pompeius. The suspicious jealousy of the oligarchy, which was chary of allowing any individual either to conquer or to administer Egypt, operated in the same direction. So the *de facto* rulers of Egypt and Cyprus were enabled by bribing the leading men in the senate not merely to respite their tottering crowns, but even to fortify them afresh and to purchase from the senate the confirmation of their royal title. But with this they had not yet obtained their object. Formal state-law required a decree of the Roman burgesses; until this was issued, the Ptolemies were dependent on the caprice of every democratic ruler, and they had thus to commence the warfare of bribery also against the other Roman party, which as the more powerful stipulated for far higher prices.

The result in the two cases was different. The annexation of Cyprus was decreed in $\frac{696}{58}$ by the people, that is, by the leaders of the democracy, the support given to piracy by the Cypriots being alleged as the official reason why that course should now be adopted. Marcus Cato, entrusted by his opponents with the execution of this measure, came to the island without an army; but he had no need of one. The king took poison; the inhabitants submitted without offering resistance to their inevitable fate, and were placed under the governor of Cilicia. The ample treasure of nearly 7000 talents (£1,700,000), which the equally covetous and miserly king could not prevail on himself to apply for the bribes requisite to save his crown, fell along with the latter to the Romans, and filled after a desirable fashion the empty vaults of their treasury.

On the other hand the brother who reigned in Egypt succeeded in purchasing his recognition by decree of the people from the new masters of Rome in $\frac{695}{59}$; the purchase-money is said to have amounted to 6000 talents (£1,460,000). The citizens indeed, long exasperated against their good flute-player and bad ruler, and now reduced to extremities by the definitive loss of Cyprus and the pressure of the taxes which were raised to an intolerable degree in consequence of the transactions with the Romans ($\frac{696}{58}$), chased him on that account out of the country. When the king thereupon applied, as if on account of his eviction from the estate which he had purchased, to those who sold it, these were reasonable enough to see that it was their duty as honest men of business to get back his kingdom for Ptolemaeus; only the parties could not agree as to the person to whom the important charge of occupying Egypt by force along with the perquisites thence to be expected should be assigned. It was only when the triumvirate was confirmed anew at the conference of Luca, that this affair was also arranged, after Ptolemaeus had agreed to a further payment of 10,000 talents (£2,400,000); the governor of Syria, Aulus Gabinius, now obtained orders from those in power to take the necessary steps immediately for restoring the king. The citizens of Alexandria had meanwhile placed the crown on the head of Berenice the eldest daughter of the ejected king, and given her a husband in the person of one of the spiritual princes of Roman Asia, Archelaus the high priest of Comana (p. 135), who possessed ambition enough to hazard his secure and respectable position in the hope of mounting the throne of the Lagidae. His attempts to gain the Roman regents to his interests remained without success; but he did not recoil before the idea of being obliged to maintain his new kingdom with arms in hand even against the Romans.

Gabinius, without ostensible powers to undertake war against Egypt but directed to do so by the regents, made a pretext out of the alleged support of piracy by the Egyptians and the building of a fleet by Archelaus, and started without delay for the Egyptian frontier ($\frac{699}{55}$). The march through the sandy desert between Gaza and Pelusium, in which so many invasions previously directed against Egypt had broken down, was on this occasion successfully accomplished—a result especially due to the quick and skilful leader of the cavalry Marcus Antonius. The frontier fortress of Pelusium also was surrendered without resistance by the Jewish garrison stationed there. In front of this city the Romans met the Egyptians, defeated them—on which occasion Antonius again distinguished himself—and arrived, as the first Roman army, at the Nile. Here the fleet and army of the Egyptians were drawn up for the last decisive struggle; but the Romans once more conquered, and Archelaus himself with many of his followers perished in the combat. Immediately after this battle the capital surrendered, and therewith all resistance was at an end. The unhappy land was handed over to its legitimate oppressor; the hanging and beheading, with which, but for the intervention of the chivalrous Antonius, Ptolemaeus would have already in Pelusium begun to celebrate the restoration of the legitimate government, now took its course unhindered, and first of all the innocent daughter was sent by her father to the scaffold. The payment of the reward agreed upon with the regents broke down through the absolute impossibility of exacting from the exhausted land the enormous sums required, although they took from the poor people the last penny; but care was taken that the country should at least be kept quiet by the garrison of Roman infantry and Celtic and German cavalry left in the capital, which took the place of the native praetorians and otherwise emulated them not unsuccessfully. The previous hegemony of Rome over Egypt was thus converted into a direct military occupation, and the nominal continuance of the native monarchy was not so much a privilege granted to the land as a double burden imposed on it.

CHAPTER V

THE STRUGGLE OF PARTIES DURING THE ABSENCE OF POMPEIUS

With the passing of the Gabinian law the parties in the capital changed positions. From the time that the elected general of the democracy held in his hand the sword, his party, or what was reckoned such, had the preponderance in the capital. The nobility doubtless still stood in compact array, and still as before there issued from the comitial machinery none but consuls who according to the expression of the democrats were already designated to the consulate in their cradles; to command the elections and break down the influence of the old families over them was beyond the power even of the regents. But unfortunately the consulate, at the very moment when they had got the length of virtually excluding the "new men" from it, began itself to grow pale before the newly-risen star of the exceptional military power. The aristocracy felt this though they did not exactly confess it; they gave themselves up as lost. Except Quintus Catulus, who with honourable firmness, persevered at his far from pleasant post as champion of a vanquished party down to his death ($\frac{694}{60}$), no Optimate could be named from the highest ranks of the nobility, who sustained the interests of the aristocracy with courage and steadfastness. Their very men of most talent and fame, such as Quintus Metellus Pius and Lucius Lucullus, practically abdicated and retired, so far as they could at all do so with propriety, to their villas, in order to forget as much as possible the Forum and the senate-house amidst their gardens and libraries, their aviaries and fish-ponds. Still more, of course, was this the case with the younger generation of the aristocracy, which was either wholly absorbed in luxury and literature or turning towards the rising sun.

There was among the younger men a single exception; it was Marcus Porcius Cato (born in $\frac{659}{95}$), a man of the best intentions and of rare devotedness, and yet one of the most Quixotic and one of the most melancholy phenomena in this age so abounding in political caricatures. Honourable and steadfast, earnest in purpose and in action, full of attachment to his country and to its hereditary constitution, but dull in intellect and sensually as well as morally destitute of passion, he might certainly have made a tolerable master of finance. But unfortunately he fell early under the power of formalism, and swayed partly by the phrases of the Stoa, which in their abstract baldness and spiritless isolation were current among the genteel world of that day, partly by the example of his great-grandfather whom he deemed it his especial task to reproduce, he began to walk about in the sinful capital as a model burgess and mirror of virtue, to rebuke the times like the old Cato, to travel on foot instead of riding, to take no interest, to decline badges of distinction as a soldier, and to introduce the restoration of the good old days by going after the precedent of king Romulus without a shirt. A strange caricature of his ancestor—the grey-haired yeoman whom hatred and anger made an orator, who wielded in masterly style the plough as well as the sword, who with his narrow, but original and sound common sense ordinarily hit the nail on the head—was this young and shallow pedant from whose lips dropped scholastic wisdom and who was everywhere seen sitting book in hand, this philosopher who understood neither the art of war nor any other art whatever, this cloud-walker in the realm of abstract moral philosophy. Yet he attained to moral and thereby even to political importance. In an utterly wretched and cowardly age his courage and his negative virtues told powerfully on the multitude; he even formed a school, and there were individuals—it is true they were but few—who in their turn copied and caricatured afresh the living pattern of a philosopher. On the same cause depended also his political influence. As he was the only conservative of note who possessed if not talent and insight, at any rate integrity and courage, and was always ready to throw himself into the breach whether it was necessary to do so or not, he soon became the recognised champion of the Optimate party, although neither his age nor his rank nor his intellect entitled him to be so. Where the perseverance of a single resolute man could decide, he no doubt sometimes achieved a success, and in questions of detail, more particularly of a financial character, he often judiciously interfered, for he was absent from no meeting of the senate; in fact his quaestorship formed an epoch, and as long as he lived he checked the details of the public budget, regarding which he was of course at constant warfare with the farmers of the taxes. For the rest, he wanted simply every ingredient of a statesman. He was incapable of even comprehending a political aim and of surveying political relations; his whole tactics consisted in setting his face against every one who deviated or seemed to him to deviate from the traditionary moral and political catechism of the aristocracy, and thus of course he worked as often into the hands of his opponents as into those of his own party. The Don Quixote of the aristocracy, he proved by his character and his actions that at this time, while there was certainly still an aristocracy in existence, the aristocratic policy was nothing more than a chimera.

To continue the conflict with this aristocracy brought little honour. Yet the attacks of the democracy on the vanquished foe naturally did not cease. The pack of the Populares threw themselves on the broken ranks of the nobility like the sutlers on a conquered camp, and the surface at least of politics was ruffled by this agitation into high waves of foam. The multitude entered into the matter the more readily, as Gaius Caesar kept them in good humour by the extravagant magnificence of his games ($\frac{689}{65}$)—in which all the equipments, even the cages of the wild beasts, appeared of massive silver—and generally by a liberality which was all the more princely that it was based solely on the contraction of debt. The attacks on the nobility were of the most varied kind. The abuses of aristocratic rule afforded copious materials; magistrates and advocates who were liberal or assumed a liberal hue, like Gaius Cornelius, Aulus Gabinius, Marcus Cicero, continued systematically to unveil the most offensive and scandalous aspects of the Optimate doings and to propose laws against them. The senate was directed to give access to foreign envoys on set days, with the view of preventing the usual postponement of audiences. Loans borrowed from foreign ambassadors in Rome were declared non-actionable, as this was the only means of seriously checking the corruptions which formed the order of the day in the senate ($\frac{687}{67}$). The right of the senate to give dispensation in particular cases from the laws was restricted ($\frac{687}{67}$); as was also the abuse whereby every noble Roman, who had private business to attend to in the provinces, got himself invested with the character of a Roman envoy thither ($\frac{691}{63}$). They heightened the penalties against the purchase of votes and electioneering intrigues ($\frac{687}{67}$, $\frac{691}{63}$); which latter were especially increased in a scandalous fashion by the attempts of the individuals ejected from the senate (p. 90) to get back to it through re-election. What had hitherto been understood as a matter of course was now expressly laid down as a law, that the praetors were bound to administer justice in conformity with the rules set forth by them, as was the Roman use and wont, at their entering on office ($\frac{687}{67}$).

But, above all, efforts were made to complete the democratic restoration and to realise the leading ideas of the Gracchan period in a form suitable to the times. The election of the priests by the comitia, which Gnaeus Domitius had introduced (iii. 192) and Sulla had again done away (iii. 341), was restored by a law of the tribune of the people Titus Labienus in $\frac{691}{63}$. The democrats were fond of pointing out how much was still wanting towards the restoration of the Sempronian corn-laws in their full extent, and at the same time passed over in silence the fact that under the altered circumstances—with the straitened condition of the public finances and the great increase in the number of fully privileged Roman citizens—that restoration was absolutely impracticable. In the country between the Po and the Alps they zealously fostered the agitation for political equality with the Italians. As early as $\frac{686}{68}$ Gaius Caesar travelled from place to place there for this purpose; in $\frac{689}{65}$ Marcus Crassus as censor made arrangements to enrol the inhabitants directly in the burgess-roll—which was only frustrated by the resistance of his colleague; in the following censorships this attempt seems regularly to have been repeated. As formerly Gracchus and Flaccus had been the patrons of the Latins, so the present leaders of the democracy gave themselves forth as protectors of the Transpadanes, and Gaius Piso (consul in $\frac{687}{67}$) had bitterly to regret that he had ventured to outrage one of these clients of Caesar and Crassus. On the other hand the same leaders appeared by no means disposed to advocate the political equalisation of the freedmen; the tribune of the people Gaius Manilius, who in a thinly attended assembly had procured the renewal (31 December $\frac{687}{67}$) of the Sulpician law as to the suffrage of freedmen (iii. 244), was immediately disavowed by the leading men of the democracy, and with their consent the law was cancelled on the very day after its passing by the senate. In the same spirit all the strangers, who possessed neither Roman nor Latin burgess-rights, were ejected from the capital by decree of the people in $\frac{689}{65}$. It is obvious that the intrinsic inconsistency of the Gracchan policy—in abetting at once the effort of the excluded to obtain admission into the circle of the privileged, and the effort of the privileged to maintain their distinctive rights—had passed over to their successors; while Caesar and his friends on the one hand held forth to the Transpadanes the prospect of the franchise, they on the other hand gave their assent to the continuance of the disabilities of the freedmen, and to the barbarous setting aside of the rivalry which the industry and trading skill of the Hellenes and Orientals maintained with the Italians in Italy itself.

The mode in which the democracy dealt with the ancient criminal jurisdiction of the comitia was characteristic. It had not been properly abolished by Sulla, but practically the jury-commissions on high treason and murder had superseded it (iii. 350), and no rational man could think of seriously restoring the old procedure which long before Sulla had been thoroughly impracticable. But as the idea of the sovereignty of the people appeared to require a recognition at least in principle of the criminal jurisdiction of the burgesses, the tribune of the people Titus Labienus in $\frac{691}{63}$ brought the old man, who thirty-eight years before had slain or was alleged to have slain the tribune of the people Lucius Saturninus (iii. 202), before the same high court of criminal jurisdiction, by virtue of which, if the annals reported truly, king Tullus had procured the acquittal of the Horatius who had killed his sister. The accused was one Gaius Rabirius, who, if he had not killed Saturninus, had at least paraded with his cut-off head at the tables of the nobles, and who moreover was notorious among the Apulian landholders for his kidnapping and his bloody deeds. The object, if not of the accuser himself, at any rate of the more sagacious men who backed him, was not at all to make this pitiful wretch die the death of the cross; they were not unwilling to acquiesce, when first the form of the impeachment was materially modified by the senate, and then the assembly of the people called to pronounce sentence on the guilty was dissolved under some pretext by the opposite party—so that the whole procedure was set aside. At all events by this process the two palladia of Roman freedom, the right of the citizens to appeal and the inviolability of the tribunes of the people, were once more established as practical rights, and the legal basis on which the democracy rested was vindicated afresh.

The democratic reaction manifested still greater vehemence in all personal questions, wherever it could and dared. Prudence indeed enjoined it not to urge the restoration of the estates confiscated by Sulla to their former owners, that it might not quarrel with its own allies and at the same time get into a conflict with material interests, for which a policy based on theory is rarely a match; the recall of the emigrants was too closely connected with this question of property not to appear equally unadvisable. On the other hand great exertions were made to restore to the children of the proscribed the political rights withdrawn from them ($\frac{691}{63}$), and the heads of the senatorial party were incessantly subjected to personal attacks. Thus Gaius Memmius instituted a party process against Marcus Lucullus in $\frac{688}{66}$. Thus they allowed his more famous brother to wait for three years before the gates of the capital for his well-deserved triumph ($\frac{688-691}{66-63}$). Quintus Rex and the conqueror of Crete Quintus Metellus were similarly insulted. It produced a still greater sensation, when the young leader of the democracy Gaius Caesar in $\frac{691}{63}$ not merely presumed to compete with the two most distinguished men of the nobility, Quintus Catulus and Publius Servilius the victor of Isaura, in the candidature for the supreme pontificate, but even carried the day among the burgesses. The heirs of Sulla, especially his son Faustus, found themselves constantly threatened with an action for the refunding of the public moneys which, it was alleged, had been embezzled by the regent. They talked even of resuming the democratic impeachments suspended in $\frac{664}{90}$ on the basis of the Varian law (iii. 223). The individuals who had taken part in the Sullan executions were, as may readily be conceived, judicially prosecuted with most zeal. When the quaestor Marcus Cato, in his awkard integrity, himself made a beginning by demanding back from them the rewards which they had received for murder as property illegally alienated from the state ($\frac{689}{65}$), it can excite no surprise that in the following year ($\frac{690}{64}$) Gaius Caesar, as president of the commission regarding murder, summarily treated the clause in the Sullan ordinance, which declared that a proscribed person might be killed with impunity, as null and void, and caused the most noted of Sulla's executioners, Lucius Catilina, Lucius Bellienus, Lucius Luscius to be brought before his jurymen and, partially, to be condemned.

Lastly, they did not hesitate now to name once more in public the long-proscribed names of the heroes and martyrs of the democracy, and to celebrate their memory. We have already mentioned how Saturninus was rehabilitated by the process directed against his murderer. But a different sound had the name of Gaius Marius, at the mention of which all hearts once had thrilled; and it happened that the man, to whom Italy owed her deliverance from the northern barbarians, was at the same time the uncle of the present leader of the democracy. Loudly had the multitude rejoiced, when in $\frac{686}{68}$ Gaius Caesar ventured in spite of the prohibitions publicly to show the honoured features of the hero in the Forum at the interment of the widow of Marius. But when, three years afterwards ($\frac{689}{65}$), the emblems of victory, which Marius had caused to be erected in the Capitol and Sulla had ordered to be thrown down, one morning unexpectedly glittered afresh in gold and marble at the old spot, the veterans from the African and Cimbrian wars crowded, with tears in their eyes, around the statue of their beloved general; and in presence of the rejoicing masses the senate did not venture to seize the trophies which the same bold hand had renewed in defiance of the laws.

But all these doings and disputes, however much noise they made, were, politically considered, of but very subordinate importance. The oligarchy was vanquished; the democracy had attained the helm. That underlings of various grades should hasten to inflict an additional kick on the prostrate foe; that the democrats also should have their groundwork of law and their worship of principles; that their *doctrinaires* should not rest till the whole privileges of the commons were in all particulars restored, and should in that respect occasionally make themselves ridiculous, as legitimists are wont to do—all this was just as much to be expected as it was matter of indifference. Taken as a whole, the agitation was aimless; and we discern in it the perplexity of its authors to find an object for their activity, for it turned almost wholly on things already essentially settled or on subordinate matters.

It could not be otherwise. In the struggle with the aristocracy the democrats had remained victors; but they had not conquered alone, and the fiery trial still awaited them—the reckoning not with their former foe, but with their too powerful ally, to whom in the struggle with the aristocracy they were substantially indebted for victory, and to whose hands they had now entrusted an unexampled military and political power, because they dared not refuse it to him. The general of the East and of the seas was still employed in appointing and deposing kings. How long time he would take for that work, or when he would declare the business of the war to be ended, no one could tell but himself; since like everything else the time of his return to Italy, or in other words the day of decision, was left in his own hands. The parties in Rome meanwhile sat and waited. The Optimates indeed looked forward to the arrival of the dreaded general with comparative calmness; by the rupture between Pompeius and the democracy, which they saw to be approaching, they could not lose, but could only gain. The democrats on the contrary waited with painful anxiety, and sought, during the interval still allowed to them by the absence of Pompeius, to lay a counter mine against the impending explosion.

In this policy they again coincided with Crassus, to whom no course was left for encountering his envied and hated rival but that of allying himself afresh, and more closely than before, with the democracy. Already in the first coalition a special approximation had taken place between Caesar and Crassus as the two weaker parties; a common interest and a common danger tightened yet more the bond which joined the richest and the most insolvent of Romans in closest alliance. While in public the democrats described the absent general as the head and pride of their party and seemed to direct all their arrows against the aristocracy, preparations were secretly made against Pompeius; and these attempts of the democracy to escape from the impending military dictatorship have historically a far higher significance than the noisy agitation, for the most part employed only as a mask, against the nobility. It is true that they were carried on amidst a darkness, upon which our tradition allows only some stray gleams of light to fall; for not the present alone, but the succeeding age also had its reasons for throwing a veil over the matter. But in general both the course and the object of these efforts are completely clear. The military power could only be effectually checkmated by another military power. The design of the democrats was to possess themselves of the reins of government after the example of Marius and Cinna, then to entrust one of their leaders either with the conquest of Egypt or with the governorship of Spain or some similar ordinary or extraordinary office, and thus to find in him and his troops a counterpoise to Pompeius and his army. For this they required a revolution, which was directed immediately against the nominal government, but in reality against Pompeius as the designated monarch;[1] and, to effect this revolution, there was from the passing of the Gabinio-Manilian laws down to the return of Pompeius ($\frac{688-692}{66-62}$) perpetual conspiracy in Rome. The capital was in anxious suspense; the depressed temper of the capitalists,

[1] Any one who surveys the whole state of the political relations of this period will need no special proofs to help him to see that the ultimate object of the democratic machinations in $\frac{688}{66}$ *et seq.* was the overthrow not of the senate, but of Pompeius. Yet such proofs are not wanting. Sallust states that the Gabinio-Manilian laws inflicted a mortal blow on the democracy (*Cat.* 39); that the conspiracy of $\frac{688-689}{66-65}$ and the Servilian rogation were specially directed against Pompeius, is likewise attested (Sallust, *Cat.* 19; Val. Max. vi. 2, 4; Cic. *de Lege Agr.* ii. 17, 46). Besides the attitude of Crassus in relation to the conspiracy alone shows sufficiently that it was directed against Pompeius.

the suspensions of payment, the frequent bankruptcies were heralds of the fermenting revolution, which seemed as though it must at the same time produce a totally new position of parties. The project of the democracy, which pointed beyond the senate at Pompeius, suggested an approximation between that general and the senate. The democracy moreover, in attempting to oppose to the dictatorship of Pompeius that of a man more agreeable to it, recognised, strictly speaking, in its turn the military government, and in reality drove out Satan by Beelzebub; the question of principles became in its hands a question of persons.

The first step therefore towards the revolution projected by the leaders of the democracy was to be the overthrow of the existing government by means of an insurrection primarily instigated in Rome by democratic conspirators. The moral condition of the lowest as of the highest ranks of society in the capital presented the materials for this purpose in lamentable abundance. We need not here repeat what was the character of the free and the servile proletariate of the capital. The significant saying was already heard, that only the poor man was qualified to represent the poor; the idea was thus suggested, that the mass of the poor might constitute itself an independent power as well as the oligarchy of the rich, and instead of allowing itself to be tyrannised over, might in its own turn play the tyrant. But even in the circles of the young men of rank similar ideas found an echo. The fashionable life of the capital deranged not merely the fortunes of men, but also their vigour of body and mind. That elegant world of fragrant ringlets, of fashionable mustachios and ruffles—merry as were its doings in the dance and with the harp, and early and late at the wine-cup—yet concealed in its bosom an alarming abyss of moral and economic ruin, of well or ill concealed despair, and frantic or knavish resolves. These circles sighed without disguise for a return of the time of Cinna with its proscriptions and confiscations and its annihilation of creditors' claims; there were people enough, including not a few of no mean descent and unusual abilities, who only waited the signal to fall like a gang of robbers on civil society and to recruit by pillage the fortune which they had squandered. Where a band gathers, leaders are not wanting; and in this case the men were soon found who were fitted to be captains of banditti.

The late praetor Lucius Catilina, and the quaestor Gnaeus Piso, were distinguished among their fellows not merely by their noble birth and their superior rank. They had broken down the bridge completely behind them, and impressed their accomplices by their dissoluteness quite as much as by their talents. Catilina in particular was one of the most nefarious men in that nefarious age. His villanies belong to the records of crime, not to history; but his very outward appearance—the pale countenance, the wild glance, the gait by turns sluggish and hurried—betrayed his dismal past. He possessed in a high degree the qualities which are required in the leader of such a band—the faculty of enjoying all pleasures and of bearing all privations, courage, military talent, knowledge of men, the energy of a felon, and that horrible mastery of vice which knows how to bring the weak to fall, and how to train the fallen to crime.

To form out of such elements a conspiracy for the overthrow of the existing order of things could not be difficult to men who possessed money and political influence. Catilina, Piso, and their fellows entered readily into any plan which gave the prospect of proscriptions and cancelling of debts; the former had moreover special hostility to the aristocracy, because it had opposed the candidature of that infamous and dangerous man for the consulship. As he had formerly in the character of an executioner of Sulla hunted the proscribed at the head of a band of Celts and had killed among others his own aged father-in-law with his own hand, he now readily consented to promise similar services to the opposite party. A secret league was formed. The number of individuals received into it is said to have exceeded 400; it included associates in all the districts and urban communities of Italy; besides which, as a matter of course, numerous recruits would flock unbidden from the ranks of the dissolute youth to an insurrection which inscribed on its banner the seasonable programme of the abolition of debts.

In December $\frac{688}{66}$—so we are told—the leaders of the league thought that they had found the fitting occasion for striking a blow. The two consuls chosen for $\frac{689}{65}$, Publius Cornelius Sulla and Publius Autronius Paetus, had recently been judicially convicted of electoral bribery, and therefore had according to legal rule forfeited their expectancy of the highest office. Both thereupon joined the league. The conspirators resolved to procure the consulship for them by force, and so to put themselves in possession of the supreme power in the state. On the day when the new consuls should enter on their office—the 1st January $\frac{689}{65}$—the senate-house was to be assailed by armed men, the new consuls and the victims otherwise designated were to be put to death, and Sulla and Paetus were to be proclaimed as consuls after the cancelling of the judicial sentence which excluded them. Crassus was then to be invested with the dictatorship and Caesar with the mastership of the horse, doubtless with a view to raise an imposing military force, while Pompeius was employed afar off at the Caucasus. Captains and common soldiers were hired and instructed; Catilina waited on the appointed day in the neighbourhood of the senate-house for the concerted signal, which was to be given him by Caesar on a hint from Crassus. But he waited in vain; Crassus was absent from the decisive sitting of the senate, and for this once the projected insurrection failed. A similar still more comprehensive plan of murder was then agreed on for the 5th February; but this too was frustrated, because Catilina gave the signal too early, before the bandits who were bespoken had all arrived. Thereupon the secret was divulged. The government did not venture openly to proceed against the conspiracy, but it assigned a guard to the consuls who were immediately threatened, and it opposed to the band of the conspirators a band paid by the government. To remove Piso, the proposal was made that he should be sent as quaestor with praetorian powers to Hither Spain; to which Crassus consented, in the hope of securing the resources of that important province for the insurrection. Proposals going farther were prevented by the tribunes.

So runs the account that has come down to us, which evidently gives the version current in the government circles, and the credibility of which in detail must, in the absence of any means of checking it, be left an open question. As to the main matter—the participation of Caesar and Crassus—the testimony of their political opponents certainly cannot be regarded as sufficient evidence of it. But their notorious action at this epoch corresponds with striking exactness to the secret action which this report ascribes to them. The attempt of Crassus, who in this year was censor, officially to enrol the Transpadanes in the burgess-list (p. 149) was itself directly a revolutionary enterprise. It is still more remarkable, that Crassus on the same occasion made preparations to enrol Egypt and Cyprus in the list of Roman domains,[1] and that Caesar about

[1] Plutarch, *Crass.* 13; Cicero, *de Lege Agr.* ii. 17, 44. To this year ($\frac{689}{65}$) belongs Cicero's oration *de Rege Alexandrino*, which has been incorrectly assigned to the year $\frac{698}{56}$. In it Cicero refutes, as the fragments clearly

the same time ($\frac{689}{65}$ or $\frac{690}{64}$) got a proposal submitted by some tribunes to the burgesses to send him to Egypt, in order to reinstate king Ptolemaeus whom the Alexandrians had expelled. These machinations suspiciously coincide with the charges made by their antagonists. Certainty cannot be attained on the point; but there is a great probability that Crassus and Caesar had projected a plan to possess themselves of the military dictatorship during the absence of Pompeius; that Egypt was selected as the basis of this democratic military power; and that, in fine, the insurrectionary attempt of $\frac{689}{65}$ had been contrived to realise these projects, and Catilina and Piso had thus been tools in the hands of Crassus and Caesar.

For a moment the conspiracy came to a standstill. The elections for $\frac{690}{64}$ took place without Crassus and Caesar renewing their attempt to get possession of the consulate; which may have been partly owing to the fact that a relative of the leader of the democracy, Lucius Caesar, a weak man who was not unfrequently employed by his kinsman as a tool, was on this occasion a candidate for the consulship. But the reports from Asia urged them to make haste. The affairs of Asia Minor and Armenia were already completely arranged. However clearly the democratic strategists showed that the Mithradatic war could only be regarded as terminated by the capture of the king, and that it was therefore necessary to undertake the pursuit round the Black Sea, and above all things to keep aloof from Syria (p. 117)—Pompeius, not concerning himself about such talk, had set out in the spring of $\frac{690}{64}$ from Armenia and marched towards Syria. If Egypt was really selected as the headquarters of the democracy, there was no time to be lost; otherwise Pompeius might easily arrive in Egypt sooner than Caesar. The conspiracy of $\frac{688}{66}$, far from being broken up by the lax and timid measures of repression, was again active when the consular elections for $\frac{691}{63}$ approached. The persons were, it is probable, substantially the same, and the plan was but little altered. The leaders of the movement again kept in the background. On this

show, the assertion of Crassus, that Egypt had been rendered Roman property by the testament of king Alexander. This question of law might and must have been discussed in $\frac{689}{65}$; but in $\frac{698}{56}$ it had been deprived of its significance through the Julian law of $\frac{695}{59}$. In $\frac{698}{56}$ moreover the discussion related not to the question to whom Egypt belonged, but to the restoration of the king driven out by a revolt, and in this transaction which is well known to us Crassus played no part. Lastly, Cicero after the conference of Luca was not at all in a position seriously to oppose one of the triumvirs.

occasion they had set up as candidates for the consulship Catilina himself and Gaius Antonius, the younger son of the orator and a brother of the general notorious for his failure at Crete. They were sure of Catilina; Antonius, originally a Sullan like Catilina and like the latter brought to trial on that account some years before by the democratic party and ejected from the senate (pp. 85, 91)—otherwise an indolent, insignificant man, in no respect called to be a leader, and utterly bankrupt—willingly lent himself as a tool to the democrats for the prize of the consulship and the advantages attached to it. Through these consuls the heads of the conspiracy intended to seize the government, to arrest the children of Pompeius who remained in the capital as hostages, and to arm in Italy and the provinces against Pompeius. On the first news of the blow struck in the capital, the governor Gnaeus Piso was to raise the banner of insurrection in Hither Spain. Communication could not be held with him by way of the sea, since Pompeius commanded the seas. To procure this they reckoned on the Transpadanes the old clients of the democracy—among whom there was great agitation, and who would of course have at once received the franchise—and, further, on different Celtic tribes.[1] The threads of this combination reached as far as Mauretania. One of the conspirators, the Roman speculator Publius Sittius from Nuceria, compelled by financial embarrassments to keep aloof from Italy, had armed a troop of desperadoes there and in Spain, and with these wandered about as a leader of free-lances in western Africa, where he had old business connections.

The party put forth all its energies for the struggle of the election. Crassus and Caesar staked their money—whether their own or borrowed—and their connections to procure the consulship for Catilina and Antonius; the comrades of Catilina strained every nerve to bring to the helm the man who promised them the magistracies and priesthoods, the palaces and estates of their opponents, and above all deliverance from their debts, and who, they knew, would keep his word. The aristocracy was in great perplexity, chiefly because it could not even start counter-candidates. That such a candidate risked his head, was obvious; and the times were past when the post of danger allured the burgess—now even ambition was hushed in presence of fear. Accordingly the nobility contented themselves with making a feeble attempt to check electioneering intrigues by

[1] The *Ambrani* (Suet. *Caes.* 9) are probably not the Ligurian Ambrones (Plutarch, *Mar.* 19), but a mistake of the pen for *Arverni*.

issuing a new law respecting bribery—which, however, was thwarted by the veto of a tribune of the people—and with turning over their votes to a candidate who, although not acceptable to them, was at least inoffensive. This was Marcus Cicero, notoriously a political trimmer,[1] accustomed to flirt at times with the democrats, at times with Pompeius, at times from a somewhat greater distance with the aristocracy, and to lend his services as an advocate to every influential man under impeachment without distinction of person or party (he numbered even Catilina among his clients); belonging properly to no party or—which was much the same—to the party of material interests which was dominant in the courts and was pleased with the eloquent pleader and the polite and witty companion. He had connections enough in the capital and the country towns to have a chance alongside of the candidates proposed by the democracy; and as the nobility, although with reluctance, and the Pompeians voted for him, he was elected by a great majority. The two candidates of the democracy obtained almost the same number of votes; but a few more fell to Antonius, whose family was of more consideration than that of his fellow-candidate. This accident frustrated the election of Catilina, and saved Rome from a second Cinna. A little before this Piso had—it was said at the instigation of his political and personal enemy Pompeius—been put to death in Spain by his native escort.[2] With the consul Antonius alone nothing could be done; Cicero broke the loose bond which attached him to the conspiracy, even before they entered on their offices, inasmuch as he renounced his legal privilege of having the consular provinces determined by lot, and handed over to his deeply-embarrassed colleague the lucrative governorship of Macedonia. The essential preliminary conditions of this project also had therefore miscarried.

Meanwhile the aspect of Oriental affairs grew daily more perilous for the democracy. The settlement of Syria rapidly advanced; already invitations had been addressed to Pompeius from Egypt to march thither and occupy the country for Rome; they could not but be afraid that they would next hear of Pompeius in person having taken possession of the valley of the

[1] This cannot well be expressed more naïvely than is done by his own brother (*De Pet Cons.* 1, 5; 13, 51, 53; in $\frac{690}{64}$). In proof of this, unprejudiced persons will read not without interest the second oration against Rullus, where the "first democratic consul," gulling the friendly public in a very delectable fashion, unfolds to it the "true democracy."

[2] His epitaph still extant runs: *Cn. Calpurnius Cn. f. Piso quaestor pro pr. ex s. c. provinciam Hispaniam citeriorem optinuit.*

Nile. It was by this very apprehension probably that the attempt of Caesar to get himself sent by the people to Egypt for the purpose of aiding the king against his rebellious subjects (p. 157) was called forth: it failed, apparently through the disinclination of great and small to undertake anything whatever against the interest of Pompeius. His return home, and the probable catastrophe which it involved, were always drawing the nearer; often as the string of the bow had been broken, it was necessary that there should be a fresh attempt to bend it. The city was in sullen ferment; frequent conferences of the heads of the movement indicated that some step was again contemplated.

What they wished became manifest when the new tribunes of the people entered on their office (10th December $\frac{690}{64}$), and one of them, Publius Servilius Rullus, immediately proposed an agrarian law, which was designed to procure for the leaders of the democrats a position similar to that which Pompeius occupied in consequence of the Gabinio-Manilian proposals. The nominal object was the founding of colonies in Italy. The ground for these, however, was not to be gained by dispossession; on the contrary all existing private rights were guaranteed, and even the illegal occupations of the most recent times (p. 83) were converted into full property. The leased Campanian domain alone was to be parcelled out and colonised; in other cases the government was to acquire the land destined for assignation by ordinary purchase. To procure the sums necessary for this purpose, the remaining Italian, and more especially all the extra-Italian, domain-land was successively to be brought to sale; which was understood to include the former royal hunting domains in Macedonia, the Thracian Chersonese, Bithynia, Pontus, Cyrene, and also the territories of the cities acquired in full property by right of war in Spain, Africa, Sicily, Hellas, and Cilicia. Everything was likewise to be sold which the state had acquired in movable and immovable property since the year $\frac{666}{88}$, and of which it had not previously disposed; this was aimed chiefly at Egypt and Cyprus. For the same purpose all subject communities, with the exception of the towns with Latin rights and the other free cities, were burdened with very high rates of taxes and tithes. Lastly there was likewise destined for those purchases the produce of the new provincial revenues, to be reckoned from $\frac{692}{62}$, and the proceeds of the whole booty not yet legally applied; which regulation had reference to the new sources of taxation opened up by Pompeius in the East and to the public moneys that might be found in the hands of Pompeius and the heirs of Sulla. For the execution of this measure decemvirs with a special jurisdiction and special *imperium* were to be nominated, who were to remain five years in office and to surround themselves with 200 subalterns from the equestrian order; but in the election of the decemvirs only those candidates who should personally announce themselves were to be taken into account, and, as in the elections of priests (iii. 409), only seventeen tribes to be fixed by lot out of the thirty-five were to make the election. It needed no great acuteness to discern that in this decemviral college it was intended to create a power after the model of that of Pompeius, only with somewhat less of a military and more of a democratic hue. The jurisdiction was especially needed for the sake of deciding the Egyptian question, the military power for the sake of arming against Pompeius; the clause, which forbade the choice of an absent person, excluded Pompeius; and the diminution of the tribes entitled to vote as well as the manipulation of the balloting were designed to facilitate the management of the election in accordance with the views of the democracy.

But this attempt totally missed its aim. The multitude, finding it more agreeable to have their corn measured out to them under the shade of Roman porticoes from the public magazines than to cultivate it for themselves in the sweat of their brow, received even the proposal in itself with complete indifference. They soon came also to feel that Pompeius would never acquiesce in such a resolution offensive to him in every respect, and that matters could not stand well with a party which in its painful alarm condescended to offers so extravagant. Under such circumstances it was not difficult for the government to frustrate the proposal; the new consul Cicero seized the opportunity of exhibiting in this case his talent for giving a finishing stroke to the beaten party; even before the tribunes who stood ready exercised their veto, the author himself withdrew his proposal (1 January $\frac{691}{63}$). The democracy had gained nothing but the unpleasant lesson, that the great multitude out of love or fear still continued to adhere to Pompeius, and that every proposal was certain to fail which the public perceived to be directed against him.

Wearied by all this vain agitation and scheming without result, Catilina determined to push the matter to a decision and make an end of it once for all. He took his measures in the course of the summer to open the civil war. Faesulae

(Fiesole), a very strong town situated in Etruria—which swarmed with the impoverished and conspirators—and fifteen years before the centre of the rising of Lepidus, was again selected as the head-quarters of the insurrection. Thither were despatched the consignments of money, for which the ladies of quality in the capital implicated in the conspiracy furnished the means; there arms and soldiers were collected; and there an old Sullan captain, Gaius Manlius, as brave and as free from scruples of conscience as was ever any soldier of fortune, took temporarily the chief command. Similar though less extensive warlike preparations were made at other points of Italy. The Transpadanes were so excited that they seemed only waiting for the signal to strike. In the Bruttian country, on the east coast of Italy, in Capua—wherever great bodies of slaves were accumulated—a second slave insurrection like that of Spartacus seemed on the eve of arising. Even in the capital there was something brewing; those who saw the haughty bearing with which the summoned debtors appeared before the urban praetor, could not but remember the scenes which had preceded the murder of Asellio (iii. 244). The capitalists were in unutterable anxiety; it seemed needful to enforce the prohibition of the export of gold and silver, and to place the principal ports under surveillance. The plan of the conspirators was—on occasion of the consular election for $\frac{692}{62}$, for which Catilina had again announced himself—summarily to put to death the consul conducting the election as well as the inconvenient rival candidates, and to carry the election of Catilina at any price; in case of necessity, even to bring armed bands from Faesulae and the other rallying points against the capital, and with their help to crush resistance.

Cicero, who was constantly and completely informed by his agents male and female of the transactions of the conspirators, on the day fixed for the election (20th October) denounced the conspiracy in the full senate and in presence of its principal leaders. Catilina did not condescend to deny it; he answered haughtily that, if the election for consul should fall on him, the great headless party would certainly no longer want a leader against the small party led by wretched heads. But as palpable evidences of the plot were not before them, nothing farther was to be got from the timid senate, except that it gave its previous sanction in the usual way to the exceptional measures which the magistrates might deem suitable (21st October). Thus the election battle approached—on this occasion more a battle than an election; for Cicero too had formed for himself an armed body-guard out of the younger men, more especially of the mercantile order; and it was his armed force that covered and commanded the Campus Martius on the 28th October, the day to which the election had been postponed by the senate. The conspirators were not successful either in killing the consul conducting the election, or in deciding the elections according to their mind.

But meanwhile the civil war had begun. On the 27th October Gaius Manlius had planted at Faesulae the eagle round which the army of the insurrection was to flock—it was one of the Marian eagles from the Cimbrian war—and he had summoned the robbers from the mountains as well as the country people to join him. His proclamations, following the old traditions of the popular party, deemed liberation from the oppressive load of debt and a modification of the procedure in insolvency, which, if the amount of the debt actually exceeded the clear estate, certainly still involved in law the forfeiture of the debtor's freedom. It seemed as though the rabble of the capital, in coming forward as if it were the legitimate successor of the old plebeian farmers and fighting its battles under the glorious eagles of the Cimbrian war, wished to cast a stain not only on the present but on the past of Rome. This rising, however, remained isolated; at the other places of rendezvous the conspiracy did not go beyond the collection of arms and the institution of secret conferences, as resolute leaders were everywhere wanting. This was fortunate for the government; for, although the impending civil war had been for a considerable time openly announced, its own irresolution and the clumsiness of the rusty machinery of administration had not allowed it to make any military preparations whatever. It was only now that the general levy was called out, and superior officers were ordered to the several regions of Italy that each might suppress the insurrection in his own district; while at the same time the gladiatorial slaves were ejected from the capital, and patrols were ordered on account of the apprehension of incendiarism.

Catilina was in a painful position. According to his design there should have been a simultaneous rising in the capital and in Etruria on occasion of the consular elections; the failure of the former and the outbreak of the latter movement endangered his person as well as the whole success of his undertaking. Now that his partisans at Faesulae had once risen in arms against the government, he could no longer remain in the capital; and yet not only did everything depend on his inducing the conspirators of the capital now at least to strike quickly, but this had to be done even before he left Rome—for he knew his helpmates too well to rely on them for that matter. The more considerable of the conspirators—Publius Lentulus Sura consul in $\frac{683}{71}$, afterwards expelled from the senate and now, in order to get back into the senate, praetor for the second time, and the two former praetors Publius Autronius and Lucius Cassius—were incapable men; Lentulus an ordinary aristocrat of big words and great pretensions, but slow in conception and irresolute in action; Autronius distinguished for nothing but his powerful screaming voice; while as to Lucius Cassius no one comprehended how a man so corpulent and so simple had fallen among the conspirators. But Catilina could not venture to place his abler partisans, such as the young senator Gaius Cethegus and the equites Lucius Statilius and Publius Gabinius Capito, at the head of the movement; for even among the conspirators the traditional hierarchy of rank held its ground, and the very anarchists thought that they should be unable to carry the day unless a consular or at least a praetorian were at their head. Therefore, however urgently the army of the insurrection might long for its general, and however perilous it was for the latter to remain longer at the seat of government after the outbreak of the revolt, Catilina nevertheless resolved still to remain for a time in Rome. Accustomed to impose on his cowardly opponents by his audacious insolence, he showed himself publicly in the Forum and in the senate-house and replied to the threats which were there addressed to him, that they should beware of pushing him to extremities; that, if they should set his house on fire, he would be compelled to extinguish the conflagration in ruins. In reality neither private persons nor officials ventured to lay hands on the dangerous man; it was almost a matter of indifference when a young nobleman brought him to trial on account of violence, for long before the process could come to an end, the question could not but be decided elsewhere. But the projects of Catilina failed; chiefly because the agents of the government had made their way into the circle of the conspirators and kept it accurately informed of every detail of the plot. When, for instance, the conspirators appeared before the important fortress of Praeneste (1 November), which they had hoped to surprise by a *coup de main*, they found the garrison warned and strengthened; and in a similar way everything miscarried. Catalina with all his temerity now found it advisable to fix his departure for one of the ensuing

New World, and the third with *Beyond the Mexique Bay,* and that is all. Dr. Praz makes it clear that he prefers what he calls Mr. Huxley's "master hand" in fixing the iridescence of contemporary social nonsense to his later excursions into satire of a heavier kind.

As regards Mr. Eliot, to whose *Criterion* Dr. Praz was an occasional contributor, the position is different. There are only two articles in the first volume, dated respectively 1934 and 1948, of which the first is comparatively slight, being mainly an account of *The Rock,* while the second is an extremely interesting article of the affinities between the poetry of Mr. Eliot and that of Eugenio Montale. It was Dr. Praz himself who introduced the work of each to the other. However, in the consecutive series of articles which concludes the "Cronache inglesi" in the second volume, the achievement and influence of Mr. Eliot as the leading poet of a particular age and tendency is present whenever poetry is discussed. These articles are balanced in the "Cronache americane" by the two studies of Hawthorne, the two articles on

SOVIET FOREIGN POLICY

Sir,—To my utter amazement I find in the article on "Soviet Foreign Policy" (in your issue of August 17) the statement that Mommsen celebrated the exploits of Bismarck in the person of Caesar. May I point out that this is a chronological impossibility since the first three volumes of Mommsen's *Roemische Geschichte* were published long before Bismarck's rise to prominence and power? But your contributor's suggestion represents also an intrinsical absurdity, for Mommsen was one of the few German historians of that generation who never became reconciled to the anti-democratic policy of the Iron Chancellor.

If the German liberal tradition in which Mommsen occupies a place of honour were strong and deeply rooted, rash and ill-informed remarks of this sort could perhaps be ignored. As things are, they must not be allowed to pass unchallenged. I am thinking in this context also of Bertrand Russell's somewhat distorted picture of German political trends in the nineteenth century, where he links Mommsen with Treitschke as protagonists of German-Prussian nationalism (*History of Western Philosophy*, page 748).

MARTIN BRAUN.

*** We regret that our reviewer, in an *obiter dictum* irrelevant to his main theme, should have fallen into a popular fallacy.

(Other Letters to the Editor on page 554.)

days; but previously on his urgent exhortation, at a last conference of the conspirators in the night between the 6th and 7th November it was resolved to assassinate the consul Cicero who was the principal director of the counter mine, before the departure of their leader, and, in order to obviate any treachery, to carry the resolve at once into execution. Early on the morning of the 7th November, accordingly, the selected murderers knocked at the house of the consul; but they found the guard reinforced and themselves repulsed—on this occasion too the spies of the government had outdone the conspirators.

On the following day Cicero convoked the senate. Even now Catilina ventured to appear and to attempt a defence against the indignant attacks of the consul, who unveiled before his face the events of the last few days; but men no longer listened to him, and in the neighbourhood of the place where he sat the benches became empty. He left the sitting, and proceeded, as he would doubtless have done even apart from this incident, in accordance with the agreement, to Etruria. Here he proclaimed himself consul, and assumed a position of readiness to put his troops in motion against the capital at the first announcement of the outbreak of the insurrection. The government declared the two leaders Catilina and Manlius, as well as those of their comrades who should not have laid down their arms by a certain day, to be outlaws, and called out new levies; but at the head of the army destined against Catilina was placed the consul Gaius Antonius, who was notoriously implicated in the conspiracy, and with whose character it was wholly a matter of accident whether he would lead his troops against Catilina or over to his side. They seemed to have directly aimed at converting this Antonius into a second Lepidus. As little were steps taken against the leaders of the conspiracy who had remained behind in the capital, although every one pointed the finger at them and the insurrection in the capital was far from being abandoned by the conspirators—on the contrary the plan of it had been settled by Catilina himself before his departure from Rome. A tribune was to give the signal by calling an assembly of the people; in the following night Cethegus was to despatch the consul Cicero; Gabinius and Statilius were to set the city simultaneously on fire at twelve places; and a communication was to be established as speedily as possible with the army of Catilina, which should have meanwhile advanced. Had the urgent representations of Cethegus borne fruit and had Lentulus, who after Catilina's departure was placed at the head of the conspirators, resolved on rapidly striking a blow, the conspiracy might still have been successful. But the conspirators were just as incapable and as cowardly as their opponents; weeks elapsed and the matter came to no decisive issue.

At length the counter mine brought about a decision. Lentulus in his tedious fashion, which sought to cover negligence in regard to what was immediate and necessary by the projection of large and distant plans, had entered into relations with the deputies of a Celtic canton, the Allobroges, now present in Rome; had attempted to implicate these—the representatives of a thoroughly disorganised commonwealth and themselves deeply involved in debt—in the conspiracy; and had given them on their departure messages and letters to his confidants. The Allobroges left Rome, but were arrested in the night between the 2nd and 3rd December close to the gates by the Roman authorities, and their papers were taken from them. It was obvious that the Allobrogian deputies had lent themselves as spies to the Roman government, and had carried on the negotiations only with a view to convey into the hands of the latter the desired evidences against the ringleaders of the conspiracy. On the following morning orders were issued with the utmost secrecy by Cicero for the arrest of the most dangerous leaders of the plot, and executed in regard to Lentulus, Cethegus, Gabinius, and Statilius, while some others escaped from seizure by flight. The guilt of those arrested as well as of the fugitives was completely evident. Immediately after the arrest the letters seized, the seals and handwriting of which the prisoners could not avoid acknowledging, were laid before the senate, and the captives and witnesses were heard; further confirmatory proofs, deposits of arms in the houses of the conspirators, threatening expressions which they had employed, were presently forthcoming; the facts of the conspiracy were fully and validly established, and the most important documents were immediately on the suggestion of Cicero published as news-sheets.

The indignation against the anarchist conspiracy was general. Gladly would the oligarchic party have made use of the revelations to settle accounts with the democracy generally and Caesar in particular, but it was far too thoroughly broken to be able to accomplish this, and to prepare for him the fate which it had formerly prepared for the two Gracchi and Saturninus; in this respect the matter went no farther than good will. The multitude of the capital was especially shocked by the incendiary schemes of the conspirators. The merchants and the whole party of material interests naturally perceived in this war of the debtors against the creditors a struggle for their very existence; in tumultuous excitement their youth crowded, with swords in their hands, round the senate-house and brandished them against the open and secret partisans of Catilina. In fact, the conspiracy was for the moment paralysed; though its ultimate authors perhaps were still at liberty, the whole staff entrusted with its execution were either captured or had fled; the band assembled at Faesulae could not possibly accomplish much, unless supported by an insurrection in the capital.

In a tolerably well-ordered commonwealth the matter would now have been politically at an end, and the military and the tribunals would have undertaken the rest. But in Rome matters had come to such a pitch, that the government was not even in a position to keep a couple of noblemen of note in safe custody. The slaves and freedmen of Lentulus and of the others arrested were stirring; plans, it was alleged, were contrived to liberate them by force from the private houses in which they were detained; there was no lack—thanks to the anarchist doings of recent years—of ringleaders in Rome who contracted at a certain rate for riots and deeds of violence; Catilina, in fine, was informed of what had occurred, and was near enough to attempt a *coup de main* with his bands. How much of these rumours was true, we cannot tell; but there was ground for apprehension, because, agreeably to the constitution, neither troops nor even a respectable police force were at the command of the government in the capital, and it was in reality left at the mercy of every gang of banditti. The idea was suggested of precluding all possible attempts at liberation by the immediate execution of the prisoners. Constitutionally, this was not possible. According to the ancient and sacred right of appeal, a sentence of death could only be pronounced against the Roman burgess by the whole body of burgesses, and not by any other authority; and, as the courts formed by the body of burgesses had themselves become antiquated, a capital sentence was no longer pronounced at all. Cicero would gladly have rejected the hazardous suggestion; indifferent as in itself the legal question might be to the advocate, he knew well how very useful it is to an advocate to be called liberal, and he showed little desire to separate himself for ever from the democratic party by shedding this blood. But those around him, and particularly his aristocratic wife, urged him to crown his services to his country by this bold step; the consul like all cowards anxiously endeavouring to avoid the appearance of cowardice, and yet trembling before the formidable responsibility, in his distress convoked the senate, and left it to that body to decide as to the life or death of the four prisoners. This indeed had no meaning; for as the senate was constitutionally even less entitled to act than the consul, all the responsibility still devolved rightfully on the latter: but when was cowardice ever consistent? Caesar made every exertion to save the prisoners, and his speech, full of covert threats as to the future inevitable vengeance of the democracy, made the deepest impression. Although all the consulars and the great majority of the senate had already declared for the execution, most of them, with Cicero at their head, seemed now once more inclined to keep within the limits of the law. But when Cato in pettifogging fashion brought the champions of the milder view into suspicion of being accomplices of the plot, and pointed to the preparations for liberating the prisoners by a street-riot, he succeeded in throwing the waverers into a fresh alarm, and in securing a majority for the immediate execution of the transgressors.

The execution of the decree naturally devolved on the consul, who had called it forth. Late on the evening of the 5th of December the prisoners were brought from their previous quarters, and conducted across the market-place still densely crowded by men to the prison in which criminals condemned to death were wont to be kept. It was a subterranean vault, twelve feet deep, at the foot of the Capitol, which formerly had served as a well-house. The consul himself conducted Lentulus, and praetors the others, all attended by strong guards; but the attempt at rescue, which had been expected, did not take place. No one knew whether the prisoners were being conveyed to a secure place of custody or to the scene of execution. At the door of the prison they were handed over to the triumvirs who conducted the executions, and were strangled in the subterranean vault by torchlight. The consul had waited before the door till the executions were accomplished, and then with his loud well-known voice proclaimed over the Forum to the multitude waiting in silence, "They are dead." Till far on in the night the crowds moved through the streets and exultingly saluted the consul, to whom they believed that they owed the security of their houses and their property. The senate ordered public festivals of gratitude, and the first men of the nobility, Marcus Cato and Quintus Catulus, saluted the author of the sentence of death with the name—now heard for the first time —of a "father of his fatherland."

But it was a dreadful deed, and all the more dreadful that it appeared to a whole people great and commendable. Never perhaps has a commonwealth more lamentably declared itself bankrupt than did Rome through this resolution—adopted in cold blood by the majority of the government and approved by public opinion—to put to death in all haste a few political prisoners, who were no doubt culpable according to the laws, but had not forfeited life; because, forsooth, the security of the prisons was not to be trusted, and there was no sufficient police. It was the humorous trait seldom wanting to an historical tragedy that this act of the most brutal tyranny had to be carried out by the most unstable and timid of all Roman statesmen, and that the "first democratic consul" was selected to destroy the palladium of the ancient freedom of the Roman commonwealth, the right of *provocatio*.

After the conspiracy had been thus stifled in the capital, even before it came to an outbreak, there remained the task of putting an end to the insurrection in Etruria. The army amounting to about 2000 men, which Catilina found on his arrival, had increased nearly fivefold by the numerous recruits who flocked in, and already formed two tolerably full legions, in which however only about a fourth part of the men were sufficiently armed. Catilina had thrown himself with his force into the mountains and avoided a battle with the troops of Antonius, with the view of completing the organisation of his bands and awaiting the outbreak of the insurrection in Rome. But the news of its failure broke up the army of the insurgents; the mass of the less compromised thereupon returned home. The remnant of resolute, or rather desperate, men that were left made an attempt to cut their way through the Apennine passes into Gaul; but when the little band arrived at the foot of the mountains near Pistoria (Pistoja), it found itself caught between two armies. In front of it was the corps of Quintus Metellus, which had come up from Ravenna and Ariminum to occupy the northern slope of the Apennines; behind it was the army of Antonius, who had at length yielded to the urgency of his officers and agreed to a winter campaign. Catilina was wedged in on both sides, and his supplies came to an end; nothing was left but to throw himself on the nearest foe, which was Antonius. In a narrow valley enclosed by rocky mountains the conflict took place between the insurgents and the troops of Antonius, which—in order that he might not be obliged at least personally to perform execution on his former allies—he had under a pretext entrusted for this day to a brave officer who had grown grey under arms, Marcus Petreius. The superior strength of the government army was of little account, owing to the nature of the field of battle. Both Catilina and Petreius placed their most trusty men in the foremost ranks; quarter was neither given nor received. The conflict lasted long, and many brave men fell on both sides; Catilina, who before the beginning of the battle had sent back his horse and those of all his officers, showed on this day that nature had destined him for no ordinary things, and that he knew at once how to command as a general and how to fight as a soldier. At length Petreius with his guard broke the centre of the enemy, and, after having overthrown this, attacked the two wings from within. This decided the victory. The corpses of the Catilinarians—there were counted 3000 of them—covered, as it were in rank and file, the ground where they had fought; the officers and the general himself had, when all was lost, thrown themselves headlong on the enemy and thus sought and found death (beginning of $\frac{692}{62}$). Antonius was on account of this victory stamped by the senate with the title of Imperator, and new thanksgiving-festivals showed that the government and the governed were beginning to become accustomed to civil war.

The anarchist plot had thus been suppressed in the capital and in Italy with bloody violence; people were reminded of it merely by the criminal processes which in the Etruscan country towns and in the capital thinned the ranks of those affiliated to the beaten party, and by the large accessions to the robber-bands of Italy—one of which, for instance, formed out of the remains of the armies of Spartacus and Catilina, was destroyed by a military force in $\frac{694}{60}$ in the territory of Thurii. But it is important to keep in view that the blow fell by no means merely on the anarchists proper, who had conspired to set the capital on fire and had fought at Pistoria, but on the whole democratic party. That this party, and in particular Crassus and Caesar, had a hand in the game on the present occasion as well as in the plot of $\frac{688}{66}$, may be regarded—not in a juristic, but in an historical, point of view—as an ascertained fact. The circumstance, indeed, that Catulus and the other heads of the senatorial party accused the leader of the democrats of complicity in the anarchist plot, and that the latter as senator spoke and voted against the brutal judicial murder contemplated by the oligarchy, could only be urged by partisan sophistry as any valid proof of his participation in the plans of Catilina. But a series of other facts is of more weight. According to express and irrefragable testimonies it was especially Crassus and Caesar that supported the candidature of Catilina for the consulship. When Caesar in $\frac{690}{64}$ brought the executioners of Sulla before the commission for murder (p. 151) he allowed the rest to be condemned, but the most guilty and infamous of all, Catilina, to be acquitted. In the revelations of the 3rd of December, it is true, Cicero did not include among the names of the conspirators of whom he had information those of the two influential men; but it is notorious that the informers denounced not merely those against whom subsequently investigation was directed, but "many innocent" persons besides, whom the consul Cicero thought proper to erase from the list; and in later years, when he had no reason to disguise the truth, he expressly named Caesar among the accomplices. An indirect but very intelligible inculpation is implied also in the circumstance, that of the four persons arrested on the 3rd of December the two least dangerous, Statilius and Gabinius, were handed over to be guarded by the senators Caesar and Crassus; it was manifestly intended that these should either, if they allowed them to escape, be compromised in the view of public opinion as accessories, or, if they really detained them, be compromised in the view of their fellow-conspirators as renegades.

The following scene which occurred in the senate shows significantly how matters stood. Immediately after the arrest of Lentulus and his comrades, a messenger despatched by the conspirators in the capital to Catilina was seized by the agents of the government, and, after having been assured of impunity, was induced to make a comprehensive confession in a full meeting of the senate. But when he came to the critical portions of his confession and in particular named Crassus as having commissioned him, he was interrupted by the senators, and on the suggestion of Cicero it was resolved to cancel the whole statement without further inquiry, and to imprison its author notwithstanding the amnesty assured to him, until such time as he should have not merely retracted the statement, but have also confessed who had instigated him to give such false testimony. Here it is abundantly clear, not merely that that man had a very accurate knowledge of the state of matters who, when summoned to make an attack upon Crassus, replied that he had no desire to provoke the bull of the herd, but also that the majority of the senate with Cicero at their head were agreed in not permitting the revelations to go beyond a certain limit. The public was not so nice; the young men, who had taken up arms to ward off the incendiaries, were exasperated against no one so much as against Caesar; on the 5th of December, when he left the senate, they pointed their swords at his breast, and even now he narrowly escaped with his life on the same spot where the fatal blow fell on him seventeen years afterwards; he did not again for a considerable time enter the senate-house. Any one who impartially considers the course of the conspiracy will not be able to resist the suspicion that during all this time Catilina was backed by more powerful men, who—relying on the want of a legally complete chain of evidence and on the lukewarmness and cowardice of the majority of the senate, which was but half-initiated and greedily caught at any pretext for inaction—knew how to hinder any serious interference with the conspiracy on the part of the authorities, to procure free departure for the chief of the insurgents, and even so to manage the declaration of war and the sending of troops against the insurrection that it was almost equivalent to the sending of an auxiliary army. While the course of the events themselves thus testifies that the threads of the Catilinarian plot reached far higher than Lentulus and Catilina, it deserves also to be noticed, that at a much later period, when Caesar had got to the head of the state, he was in the closest alliance with the only Catilinarian still surviving, Publius Sittius the leader of the Mauretanian free bands, and that he modified the law of debt quite in the sense that the proclamations of Manlius demanded.

All these pieces of evidence speak clearly enough; but, even were it not so, the desperate position of the democracy in presence of the military power—which since the Gabinio-Manilian laws assumed alongside of it an attitude more threatening than ever—renders it almost a certainty that, as usually happens in such cases, it sought a last resource in secret plots and in alliance with anarchy. The circumstances were very similar to those of the Cinnan times. While in the East Pompeius occupied a position nearly such as Sulla then did, Crassus and Caesar sought to raise a counter-power in Italy like that which Marius and Cinna had possessed, with the view of employing it if possible better than they had done. The way to this result lay once more through terrorism and anarchy, and to pave that way Catilina was certainly the fitting man.

Naturally the more reputable leaders of the democracy kept themselves as far as possible in the background, and left to their unclean associates the execution of the unclean work, the political results of which they hoped afterwards to appropriate. Still more naturally, when the enterprise had failed, the partners of higher position applied every effort to conceal their participation in it. And at a later period, when the former conspirator had himself become the target of political plots, the veil was for that very reason drawn only the more closely over those darker years in the life of the great man, and even special apologies for him were written with that very object.[1]

For five years Pompeius was in the East at the head of his armies and fleets; for five years the democracy at home conspired to overthrow him. The result was discouraging. With unspeakable exertions they had not merely attained nothing, but had suffered morally as well as materially enormous loss. Even the coalition of $\frac{683}{71}$ was probably regarded by democrats of pure water as a scandal, although the democracy at that time only coalesced with two distinguished men of the opposite party and bound these to its programme. But now the democratic party had made common cause with a band of murderers and bankrupts, who were almost all likewise deserters from the camp of the aristocracy; and had at least for the time being accepted their programme, that is to say, the terrorism of Cinna. The party of material interests, one of the chief elements of the coalition of $\frac{683}{71}$, was thereby alienated from the democracy, and driven into the arms of the Optimates in the first instance, or of any power at all which would and could give protection against anarchy. Even the multitude of the capital, who, although having no objection to a street-riot, found it inconvenient to have their houses set on fire over their heads, were in some measure alarmed. It is remarkable that in this very year ($\frac{691}{63}$)

[1] Such an apology is the *Catilina* of Sallust, which was published by the author, a notorious Caesarian, after the year $\frac{708}{46}$, either under the monarchy of Caesar or more probably under the triumvirate of his heirs; evidently as a treatise with a political drift, which endeavours to bring into credit the democratic party—on which in fact the Roman monarchy was based—and to clear Caesar's memory from the blackest stain that rested on it; and with the collateral object of whitewashing as much as possible the uncle of the triumvir Marcus Antonius. The *Jugurtha* of the same author is in an exactly similar way designed partly to expose the pitifulness of the oligarchic government, partly to glorify the Coryphaeus of the democracy, Gaius Marius. The circumstance that the adroit author keeps the apologetic and inculpatory character of these writings of his in the background, proves, not that they are not partisan treatises, but that they are good ones.

the full restoration of the Sempronian corn-largesses took place, and was effected by the senate on the proposal of Cato. The league of the democratic leaders with anarchy had obviously created a breach between the former and the burgesses of the city; and the oligarchy sought, not without at least momentary success, to enlarge the chasm and to draw over the masses to their side. Lastly, Gnaeus Pompeius had been partly warned, partly exasperated, by all these cabals; after all that had occurred, and after the democracy had itself virtually torn asunder the ties which connected it with Pompeius, it could no longer with propriety make the request—which in $\frac{684}{70}$ had had a certain amount of reason on its side—that he should not himself destroy with the sword the democratic power which he had raised, and which had raised him.

Thus the democracy was disgraced and weakened; but above all it had become ridiculous through the merciless exposure of its perplexity and weakness. Where the humiliation of the overthrown government and similar matters of little moment were concerned, it was great and potent; but every one of its attempts to attain a real political success had proved a downright failure. Its relation to Pompeius was as false as pitiful. While it was loading him with panegyrics and demonstrations of homage, it was concocting against him one intrigue after another; and one after another, like soap bubbles, they burst of themselves. The general of the East and of the seas, far from standing on his defence against them, appeared not even to observe all the busy agitation, and to obtain his victories over the democracy as Herakles gained his over the Pygmies, without being himself aware of it. The attempt to kindle civil war had miserably failed; if the anarchist section had at least displayed some energy, the pure democracy, while knowing doubtless how to hire conspirators, had not known how to lead them or to save them or to die with them. Even the old languid oligarchy, strengthened by the masses passing over to it from the ranks of the democracy and above all by the—in this affair unmistakable—identity of its interests and those of Pompeius, had been enabled to suppress this attempt at revolution and thereby to achieve yet a last victory over the democracy. Meanwhile king Mithradates had died, Asia Minor and Syria were regulated, and the return of Pompeius to Italy might be every moment expected. The decision was not far distant; but was there in fact still room to speak of a decision between the general, who returned more famous and mightier than ever, and the democracy humbled beyond parallel and utterly powerless? Crassus prepared to embark his family and his gold and to seek an asylum somewhere in the East; and even so elastic and so energetic a nature as that of Caesar seemed on the point of giving up the game as lost. In this year ($\frac{691}{63}$) occurred his candidature for the place of *pontifex maximus* (p. 151); when he left his house on the morning of the election, he declared that, if he should fail in this also, he would never again cross its threshold.

CHAPTER VI

RETIREMENT OF POMPEIUS AND COALITION OF THE PRETENDERS

When Pompeius, after having transacted the affairs committed to his charge, again turned his eyes towards home, he found for the second time the diadem at his feet. For long the development of the Roman commonwealth had been tending towards such a catastrophe; it was evident to every unbiassed observer, and had been remarked a thousand times, that, if the rule of the aristocracy should be brought to an end, monarchy was inevitable. The senate had now been overthrown at once by the civil democratic opposition and by the military power; the only question remaining was to settle the persons, names, and forms for the new order of things; and these were already clearly enough indicated in the partly democratic, partly military elements of the revolution. The events of the last five years had set, as it were, the final seal on this impending transformation of the commonwealth. In the newly-erected Asiatic provinces, which gave regal honours to their organiser as the successor of Alexander the Great, and received even his favourite freedmen like princes, Pompeius had laid the foundations of his dominion, and found at once the treasures, the army, and the halo of glory which the future prince of the Roman state required. The anarchist conspiracy, moreover, in the capital, and the civil war connected with it, had made it palpably clear to every one who studied political or even merely material interests, that a government without authority and without military power, like that of the senate, exposed the state to the equally ludicrous and formidable tyranny of political sharpers, and that a change of constitution, which should connect the military power more closely with the government, was an indispensable necessity if social order was to be maintained. So the ruler had arisen in the East, the throne had been erected in Italy; to all appearance the year $\frac{692}{62}$ was the last of the republic, the first of monarchy.

This goal, it is true, was not to be reached without a struggle. The constitution, which had endured for five hundred years, and under which the insignificant town on the Tiber had risen to unprecedented greatness and glory, had sunk its roots into the soil to a depth beyond human ken, and no one could at all calculate to what extent the attempt to overthrow it would penetrate and convulse civil society. Several rivals had been outrun by Pompeius in the race towards the great goal, but had not been wholly set aside. It was not altogether impossible that all these elements might combine to overthrow the new holder of power, and that Pompeius might find Quintus Catulus and Marcus Cato united in opposition to him with Marcus Crassus, Gaius Caesar, and Titus Labienus. But the inevitable and undoubtedly serious struggle could not well be undertaken under circumstances more favourable. It was in a high degree probable that, under the fresh impression of the Catilinarian revolt, a rule which promised order and security, although at the price of freedom, would receive the submission of the whole middle party—embracing especially the merchants who concerned themselves only about their material interests, but including also a great part of the aristocracy, which, disorganised in itself and politically hopeless, had to rest content with securing for itself riches, rank, and influence by a timely compromise with the prince; perhaps even a portion of the democracy, so sorely smitten by the recent blows, might submit to hope for the realisation of a portion of its demands from a military chief raised to power by itself. But, whatever might be the feeling of parties, of what importance, in the first instance at least, were the parties in Italy at all in presence of Pompeius and his victorious army? Twenty years previously Sulla, after having concluded a temporary peace with Mithradates, had with his five legions been able to carry a restoration running counter to the natural development of things in the face of the whole liberal party which had been arming *en masse* for years, from the moderate aristocrats and the liberal mercantile class down to the anarchists. The task of Pompeius was far less difficult. He returned, after having fully and conscientiously performed his different functions by sea and land. He might expect to encounter no other serious opposition save that of the various extreme parties, each of which by itself could do nothing, and which even when leagued together were still nothing more than a coalition of factions that remained vehemently hostile to each other and were inwardly at thorough variance. Completely unarmed, they were without a military force and without a head, without organisation in Italy, without support in the provinces, above all, without a general; there was in their ranks hardly a soldier—to say nothing of an officer—of note, who could have ventured to call forth the burgesses to a conflict with Pompeius. The circumstance might further be taken into account, that the volcano of revolution, which had been now incessantly blazing for seventy years and feeding on its own flame, was visibly burning out and verging of itself to extinction. It was very doubtful whether the attempt to arm the Italians for party interests would now succeed as it had succeeded with Cinna and Carbo. If Pompeius exerted himself, how could he fail to effect a revolution of the state, which was chalked out by a certain necessity of nature in the organic development of the Roman commonwealth?

Pompeius had seized the right moment when he undertook his mission to the East; he seemed desirous to go forward. In the autumn of $\frac{691}{63}$, Quintus Metellus Nepos arrived from the camp of Pompeius in the capital, and came forward as a candidate for the tribuneship, with the express design of employing that position to procure for Pompeius the consulship for the year $\frac{693}{61}$ and more immediately, by special decree of the people, the conduct of the war against Catilina. The excitement in Rome was great. It was not to be doubted that Nepos was acting under the direct or indirect orders of Pompeius; the desire of Pompeius to appear in Italy as general at the head of his Asiatic legions, and to administer simultaneously the supreme military and the supreme civil power there, was conceived to be a farther step on the way to the throne, and the mission of Nepos a semi-official proclamation of the monarchy.

Everything turned on the attitude which the two great political parties should assume towards these overtures; their future position and the future of the nation depended on this. But the reception which Nepos met with was itself in its turn determined by the then existing relation of the parties to Pompeius, which was of a very peculiar kind. Pompeius had gone to the East as general of the democracy. He had reason enough to be discontented with Caesar and his adherents, but no open rupture had taken place. It is probable that Pompeius, who was at a great distance and occupied with other things, and who besides was wholly destitute of the gift of political divination, by no means saw through, at least at that time, the extent and mutual connection of the democratic intrigues contrived against him; perhaps even in his haughty and shortsighted manner he had a certain pride in ignoring these underground proceedings. Then there came the fact, which with a character of Pompeius' sort had much weight, that the democracy never lost sight of outward respect for the great man, and even now ($\frac{691}{63}$) spontaneously (as was his wish) it had granted to him by a special decree of the people unprecedented honours and decorations (p. 138). But, even if all this had not been the case, it lay in Pompeius' own well-understood interest to continue his adherence, at least outwardly, to the popular party; democracy and monarchy stand so closely related that Pompeius, in aspiring to the crown, could scarcely do otherwise than call himself, as hitherto, the champion of popular rights. While personal and political reasons, therefore, co-operated to keep Pompeius and the leaders of the democracy, despite of all that had taken place, in their previous connection, nothing was done on the opposite side to fill up the chasm which separated him since his desertion to the camp of the democracy from his Sullan partisans. His personal quarrel with Metellus and Lucullus transferred itself to their extensive and influential coteries. A paltry opposition of the senate—but, to a character of so paltry a mould, all the more exasperating by reason of its very paltriness—had attended him through his whole career as a general. He felt it keenly, that the senate had not taken the smallest step to honour the extraordinary man according to his desert, that is, by extraordinary means. Lastly, it is not to be forgotten, that the aristocracy was just then intoxicated by its recent victory and the democracy deeply humbled, and that the aristocracy was led by the pedantically stiff and half-witless Cato, and the democracy by the most supple master of intrigue, Caesar.

Such was the state of parties amidst which the emissary sent forth by Pompeius appeared. The aristocracy not only regarded the proposals which he announced in favour of Pompeius as a declaration of war against the existing constitution, but treated them openly as such, and took not the slightest pains to conceal their alarm and their indignation. With the express design of combating these proposals, Marcus Cato had himself elected as tribune of the people along with Nepos, and abruptly repelled the repeated attempts of Pompeius to approach him personally. Nepos naturally after this found himself under no inducement to spare the aristocracy, but attached himself the more readily to the democrats, when these, pliant as ever, submitted to what was inevitable and chose freely to concede the office of general in Italy as well as the consulate rather than let the concession be wrung from them by force of arms. The cordial understanding soon showed itself. Nepos publicly accepted (December $\frac{691}{63}$) the democratic view of the executions recently decreed by the majority of the senate, as unconstitutional judicial murders; and that his lord and master looked on them in no other light, was shown by his significant silence respecting the voluminous vindication of them which Cicero had sent to him. On the other hand, the first act with which Caesar began his praetorship was to call Quintus Catulus to account for the moneys alleged to have been embezzled by him in the rebuilding of the Capitoline temple, and to transfer the completion of the temple to Pompeius. This was a masterstroke. Catulus had already been building at the temple for fifteen years, and seemed very much disposed to die as he had lived superintendent of the Capitoline buildings; an attack on this abuse of a public commission—an abuse covered only by the reputation of the noble commissioner—was in reality entirely justified and in a high degree popular. But when the prospect was simultaneously opened up to Pompeius of being allowed to delete the name of Catulus and engrave his own on this proudest spot of the proudest city of the globe, there was offered to him the very thing which most of all delighted him and did no harm to the democracy—abundant but empty honour; while at the same time the aristocracy, which could not possibly allow its best man to fall, was brought into the most annoying collision with Pompeius.

Meanwhile Nepos had brought his proposals concerning Pompeius before the burgesses. On the day of voting Cato and his friend and colleague, Quintus Minucius, interposed their veto. When Nepos did not regard this and continued the reading out, a formal conflict took place; Cato and Minucius threw themselves on their colleague and forced him to stop; an armed band liberated him, and drove the aristocratic section from the Forum; but Cato and Minucius returned, now supported likewise by armed bands, and ultimately maintained the field of battle for the government. Encouraged by this victory of their bands over those of their antagonist, the senate suspended the tribune Nepos as well as the praetor Caesar, who had vigorously supported him in the bringing in of the law, from their offices; their deposition, which was proposed in the senate, was prevented by Cato, more, doubtless, because it was unconstitutional than because it was injudicious. Caesar did not regard the decree, and continued his official functions till the senate used violence against him. As soon as this was known, the multitude appeared before his house and placed itself at his disposal; it depended solely on him whether the struggle in the streets should be begun, or whether at least the proposals made by Metellus should now be resumed and the military command in Italy desired by Pompeius should be procured for him; but this was not in Caesar's interest, and so he induced the crowds to disperse, whereupon the senate recalled the penalty decreed against him. Nepos himself had, immediately after his suspension, left the city and embarked for Asia, in order to report to Pompeius the result of his mission.

Pompeius had every reason to be content with the turn which things had taken. The way to the throne now lay necessarily through civil war; and he owed it to Cato's incorrigible perversity that he could begin this war with good reason. After the illegal condemnation of the adherents of Catalina, after the unparalleled acts of violence against the tribune of the people Metellus, Pompeius might wage war at once as defender of the two palladia of Roman public freedom—the right of appeal and the inviolability of the tribunate of the people—against the aristocracy, and as champion of the party of order against the Catilinarian band. It seemed almost impossible that Pompeius should neglect this opportunity and with his eyes open put himself a second time into the painful position, in which the dismissal of his army in $\frac{684}{70}$ had placed him, and from which only the Gabinian law had released him. But near as seemed the opportunity of placing the white chaplet around his brow, and much as his own soul longed after it, when the question of action presented itself, his heart and his hand once more failed him. This man, altogether ordinary in every respect excepting only his pretensions, would doubtless gladly have placed himself above the law, if only he could have done so without forsaking legal ground. His very lingering in Asia betrayed a misgiving of this sort. He might, had he wished, have very well arrived in January $\frac{692}{62}$ with his fleet and army at the port of Brundisium, and have received Nepos there. His tarrying the whole winter of $\frac{691}{63}-\frac{692}{62}$ in Asia had proximately the injurious consequence, that the aristocracy, which of course accelerated the campaign against Catilina as it best could, had meanwhile got rid of his bands, and had thus set aside the most feasible pretext for keeping together the Asiatic legions in Italy. For a man of Pompeius' character, who for want of faith in himself and in his star timidly clung in public life to formal right, and with whom the pretext was nearly of as much importance as the motive, this circumstance was of serious weight. He probably said to himself, moreover, that, even if he dismissed his army, he did not let it wholly out of his hand, but could in case of need raise a force ready for battle sooner at any rate than any other party-chief; that the democracy was waiting in submissive attitude for his signal, and that he could deal with the refractory senate even without soldiers; and other similar considerations that suggested themselves, in which there was exactly enough of truth to make them appear plausible to one who wished to deceive himself. The very peculiar temperament of Pompeius naturally turned once more the scale. He was one of those men who are capable it may be of a crime, but not of insubordination; in a good as in a bad sense, he was thoroughly a soldier. Men of mark respect the law as a moral necessity, ordinary men as a traditional every-day rule; for this very reason military discipline, in which more than anywhere else law takes the form of habit, binds every man not entirely self-reliant as with a magic spell. It has often been observed that the soldier, even where he has determined to refuse obedience to his commander, involuntarily when that obedience is demanded resumes his place in the ranks. It was this feeling that made Lafayette and Dumouriez hesitate at the last moment before the breach of faith and fail in their design; and to this too Pompeius succumbed.

In the autumn of $\frac{692}{62}$ Pompeius embarked for Italy. While in the capital all was preparation for receiving the new monarch, news came that Pompeius, when barely landed at Brundisium, had broken up his legions and with a small escort had entered on his journey to the capital. If it is a piece of good fortune to gain a crown without trouble, fortune never did more for mortal than it did for Pompeius; but on those who lack courage the gods lavish every favour and every gift in vain.

The parties breathed freely. Pompeius had abdicated a second time; his already vanquished competitors might once more begin the race—in which doubtless the strangest thing was, that Pompeius was again a rival runner. In January $\frac{693}{61}$ he came to Rome. His position was an awkward one and vacillated with so much uncertainty between the parties, that people gave him the nickname of Gnaeus Cicero. He had in fact lost favour with all. The anarchists saw in him an adversary, the democrats an inconvenient friend, Marcus Crassus a rival, the wealthy class an untrustworthy protector, the aristocracy a declared foe.[1]

[1] The impression of the first address, which Pompeius made to the burgesses after his return, is thus described by Cicero (*ad Att.* i. 14); *prima contio Pompei non iucunda miseris* (the rabble), *inanis improbis* (the demo-

He was still indeed the most powerful man in the state; his military adherents scattered throughout Italy, his influence in the provinces, particularly those of the East, his military fame, his enormous riches gave him a weight which no other possessed; but instead of the enthusiastic reception on which he had counted, the reception which he met with was more than cool, and still cooler was the treatment given to the demands which he presented. He requested for himself, as he had already caused to be announced by Nepos, a second consulship; demanding also, of course, a confirmation of the arrangements made by him in the East and a fulfilment of the promise which he had given to his soldiers to furnish them with lands. Against these demands a systematic opposition arose in the senate, the chief elements of which were furnished by the personal exasperation of Lucullus and Metellus Creticus, the old resentment of Crassus, and the conscientious folly of Cato. The desired second consulship was at once and bluntly refused. The very first request which the returning general addressed to the senate, that the election of the consuls for $\frac{693}{61}$ might be put off till after his entry into the capital, had been rejected; much less was there any likelihood of obtaining from the senate the necessary dispensation from the law of Sulla as to re-election (iii. 342). As to the arrangements which he had made in the Eastern provinces, Pompeius naturally asked their confirmation as a whole; Lucullus carried a proposal that every ordinance should be separately discussed and voted upon, which opened the door for endless annoyances and a multitude of defeats in detail. The promise of a grant of land to the soldiers of the Asiatic army was ratified indeed in general by the senate, but was at the same time extended to the Cretan legions of Metellus; and —what was worse—it was not executed, because the public chest was empty and the senate was not disposed to meddle with the domains for this purpose. Pompeius, in despair of mastering the persistent and spiteful opposition of the senate, turned to the burgesses. But he understood still less how to conduct his movements on this field. The democratic leaders, although they did not openly oppose him, had no cause at all to make his interests their own, and so kept aloof. Pompeius' own instruments—such as the consuls elected by his influence and partly by his money, Marcus Pupius Piso for $\frac{693}{61}$ and Lucius Afranius for $\frac{694}{60}$—showed themselves unskilful and useless.

crats), *beatis* (the wealthy) *non grata*, *bonis* (the aristocrats) *non gravis*; *itaque frigebat*.

When at length the assignation of land for the veterans of Pompeius was submitted to the burgesses by the tribune of the people Lucius Flavius in the form of a general agrarian law, the proposal, not supported by the democrats, openly combated by the aristocrats, was left in a minority (beginning of $\frac{694}{60}$). The exalted general now sued almost humbly for the favour of the masses, for it was on his instigation that the Italian tolls were abolished by a law introduced by the praetor Metellus Nepos ($\frac{694}{60}$). But he played the demagogue without skill and without success; his reputation suffered from it, and he did not obtain what he desired. He had completely run himself into a noose. One of his opponents summed up his political position at that time by saying that he had endeavoured "to conserve by silence his embroidered triumphal mantle." In fact nothing remained for him but to fret.

Then a new combination offered itself. The leader of the democratic party had actively employed in his own interest the political calm which had immediately followed on the retirement of the previous holder of power. When Pompeius returned from Asia, Caesar had been little more than what Catilina was—the chief of a political party which had dwindled almost into a club of conspirators, and a bankrupt. But since that event he had, after administering the praetorship ($\frac{692}{62}$), been invested with the governorship of Further Spain, and thereby had found means partly to rid himself of his debts, partly to lay the foundation for a military position and a military renown. His old friend and ally Crassus had been induced by the hope of finding the support against Pompeius, which he had lost in Piso (p. 159), once more in Caesar, to relieve him even before his departure to the province from the most oppressive portion of his load of debt. He himself had energetically employed his brief sojourn there. Returning from Spain in the year $\frac{694}{60}$ with filled chests and as Imperator with well-founded claims to a triumph, he came forward for the following year as a candidate for the consulship; for the sake of which, as the senate refused him permission to announce himself as a candidate for the consular election in absence, he without hesitation abandoned the honour of the triumph. For years the democracy had striven to raise one of its partisans to the possession of the supreme magistracy, that by this means it might attain a military power of its own. It had long been clear to discerning men of all shades that the strife of parties could not be settled by civil conflict, but only by military power; but the course of the coalition between the democracy and the powerful military chiefs, through which the rule of the senate had been terminated, showed with inexorable clearness that every such alliance ultimately issued in a subordination of the civil under the military elements, and that the popular party, if it would really rule, must not ally itself with generals properly foreign and even hostile to it, but must make generals of its own leaders themselves. The attempts made with this view to carry the election of Catilina as consul, and to gain a military support in Spain or Egypt, had failed; now a possibility presented itself of procuring for their most important man the consulship and the consular province in the usual constitutional way, and of rendering themselves independent of their dubious and dangerous ally Pompeius by the establishment, if we may so speak, of a home power in their own democratic household.

But the more the democracy could not but desire to open up for itself this path, which offered not so much the most favourable as the only prospect of real successes, the more certainly it might reckon on the resolute resistance of its political opponents. Everything depended on whom it found opposed to it in this matter. The aristocracy isolated was not formidable; but it had just been rendered evident in the Catilinarian affair that it could certainly still exert some influence, where it was more or less openly supported by the men of material interests and by the adherents of Pompeius. It had several times frustrated Catilina's candidature for the consulship, and that it would attempt the like against Caesar was sufficiently certain. But, even though Caesar should perhaps be chosen in spite of it, his election alone did not suffice. He needed at least some years of undisturbed working out of Italy, in order to gain a firm military position; and the nobility assuredly would leave no means untried to thwart his plans during this time of preparation. The idea naturally occurred, whether the aristocracy might not be again successfully isolated as in $\frac{683}{71}-\frac{684}{70}$, and an alliance firmly based on mutual advantage might not be established between the democrats with their ally Crassus on the one side and Pompeius and the great capitalists on the other. For Pompeius such a coalition was certainly a political suicide. His weight hitherto in the state rested on the fact, that he was the only party-leader who at the same time disposed of legions—which, though now dissolved, might still in a certain sense be said to be at his disposal. The plan of the democracy was directed to the very object of depriving him of this preponderance, and of placing by his side in their own chief a military rival. Never could he consent to this, and least of all personally help to a post of supreme command a man like Caesar, who already as a mere political agitator had given him trouble enough and had just furnished the most brilliant proofs also of military capacity in Spain. But on the other hand, in consequence of the cavilling opposition of the senate and the indifference of the multitude to Pompeius and Pompeius' wishes, his position, particularly with reference to his old soldiers, had become so painful and so humiliating, that people might well expect from his character to gain him for such a coalition at the price of releasing him from that disagreeable situation. And as to the so-called equestrian party, it was to be found on whatever side the power lay; and as a matter of course it would not let itself be long waited for, if it saw Pompeius and the democracy combining anew in earnest. It happened, moreover, that on account of Cato's severity—otherwise very laudable—towards the lessees of the taxes, the great capitalists were just at this time once more at vehement variance with the senate.

So the second coalition was concluded in the summer of $\frac{694}{60}$. Caesar was assured of the consulship for the following year and a governorship in due course; to Pompeius was promised the ratification of his arrangements made in the East, and an assignation of lands for the soldiers of the Asiatic army; to the equites Caesar likewise promised to procure for them by means of the burgesses what the senate had refused; Crassus in fine—the inevitable—was allowed at least to join the league, although without obtaining the promise of a definite equivalent for an accession which he could not refuse. It was exactly the same elements, and indeed the same persons, who concluded the league with one another in the autumn of $\frac{683}{71}$ and in the summer of $\frac{694}{60}$; but how entirely different was the position of the parties then and now! Then the democracy was nothing but a political party, while its allies were victorious generals at the head of their armies; now the leader of the democracy was himself an Imperator crowned with victory and full of magnificent military schemes, while his allies were retired generals without any army. Then the democracy conquered in questions of principle, and in return for that victory conceded the highest offices of state to its two confederates; now it had become more practical and grasped the supreme civil and military power for itself, while concessions were made to its allies only in subordinate points and, significantly enough, not even the old demand of Pompeius for a second consulship was attended to. Then the democracy sacrificed itself to its allies; now these had to entrust themselves to it. All the circumstances were completely changed, most of all, however, the character of the democracy itself. No doubt it had, ever since it existed at all, contained at its core a monarchic element; but the ideal of a constitution, which floated in more or less clear outline before its best intellects, was always that of a civil commonwealth, a Periclean organisation of the state, in which the power of the prince rested on the fact that he represented the burgesses in the noblest and most accomplished manner, and the most accomplished and noblest part of the burgesses recognised him as the man in whom they thoroughly confided. Caesar too set out with such views; but they were simply ideals, which might have some influence on realities, but could not be directly realised. Neither the simple civil power, as Gaius Gracchus possessed it, nor the arming of the democratic party, such as Cinna though in a very inadequate fashion had attempted, was able to maintain a permanent superiority in the Roman commonwealth; the military machine fighting not for a party but for a general, the rude force of the *condottieri*—which had first appeared on the stage in the service of the restoration—soon showed itself absolutely superior to all political parties. Caesar could not but acquire a conviction of this amidst the practical workings of party, and accordingly he matured the momentous resolution of making this military machine itself serviceable to his ideals, and of erecting such a commonwealth as he had in his mind by the power of *condottieri*. With this design he concluded in $\frac{683}{71}$ the league with the generals of the opposite party, which, notwithstanding that they had accepted the democratic programme, yet brought the democracy and Caesar himself to the brink of destruction. With the same design he himself came forward eleven years afterwards as a *condottiere*. It was done in both cases with a certain naïveté—with good faith in the possibility of his being able to found a free commonwealth, if not by the swords of others, at any rate by his own. We perceive without difficulty that this faith was fallacious, and that no one takes an evil spirit into his service without becoming himself enslaved to it; but the greatest men are not those who err the least. If we still after so many centuries bow in reverence before what Caesar willed and did, it is not because he desired and gained a crown (to do which is, abstractly, as little of a great thing as the crown itself), but because his mighty ideal—of a free commonwealth under one ruler—never forsook him, and preserved him even when monarch from sinking into vulgar royalty.

The election of Caesar as consul for $\frac{695}{59}$ was carried without difficulty by the united parties. The aristocracy had to rest content with giving to him—by means of a bribery, for which the whole order of lords contributed the funds, and which excited surprise even in that period of deepest corruption—a colleague in the person of Marcus Bibulus, whose narrow-minded obstinacy was regarded in their circles as conservative energy, and whose good intentions at least were not at fault if the noble lords did not get a fit return for their patriotic expenditure.

As consul Caesar first submitted to discussion the requests of his confederates, among which the assignation of land to the veterans of the Asiatic army was by far the most important. The agrarian law projected for this purpose by Caesar adhered in general to the principles set forth in the project of law, which was introduced in the previous year at the suggestion of Pompeius but not carried (p. 184). There was destined for distribution only the Italian domain land, that is to say, substantially, the territory of Capua, and, if this should not suffice, other Italian estates were to be purchased out of the revenue of the new eastern provinces at the taxable value recorded in the censorial rolls; all existing rights of property and heritable possession thus remained unaffected. The individual allotments were small. The receivers of land were to be poor burgesses, fathers of at least three children; the dangerous principle, that the rendering of military service gave a claim to landed estate, was not laid down, but, as was reasonable and had been done at all times, the old soldiers as well as the temporary lessees to be ejected were simply recommended to the special consideration of the land-distributors. The execution of the measure was entrusted to a commission of twenty, into which Caesar distinctly declared that he did not wish to be himself elected.

The opposition had a difficult task in resisting this proposal. It could not rationally be denied, that the state finances ought after the erection of the provinces of Pontus and Syria to be in a position to dispense with the moneys from the Campanian leases; that it was unwarrantable to withhold one of the finest districts of Italy, and one peculiarly fitted for small holdings, from private enterprise; and, lastly, that it was as unjust as it was ridiculous, after the extension of the franchise to all Italy, still to withhold municipal rights from the township of Capua.

The whole proposal bore the stamp of moderation, honesty, and solidity, with which a democratic party-character was very dexterously combined; for in substance it amounted to the re-establishment of the Capuan colony founded in the time of Marius and again done away by Sulla (iii. 306, 335). In form too Caesar observed all possible respect. He laid the project of the agrarian law, as well as the proposal to ratify collectively the ordinances issued by Pompeius in the East, and the petition of the farmers of the taxes for remission of a third of the sums payable by them, in the first instance before the senate for approval, and declared himself ready to receive and discuss proposals for alterations. The corporation had now opportunity of convincing itself how foolishly it had acted in driving Pompeius and the equites into the arms of the adversary by refusing these requests. Perhaps it was the secret sense of this, that drove the high-born lords to the most vehement opposition, which contrasted ill with the calm demeanour of Caesar. The agrarian law was rejected by them nakedly and even without discussion. The decree as to Pompeius' arrangements in Asia found quite as little favour in their eyes. Cato attempted, in accordance with the disreputable custom of Roman parliamentary debate, to kill the proposal regarding the farmers of the taxes by speaking, that is, to prolong his speech up to the legal hour for closing the sitting; when Caesar threatened to have the stubborn man arrested, this proposal too was at length rejected.

Of course all the proposals were now brought before the burgesses. Without deviating far from the truth, Caesar could tell the multitude that the senate had scornfully rejected most rational and most necessary proposals submitted to it in the most respectful form, simply because they came from the democratic consul. When he added that the aristocrats had contrived a plot to procure the rejection of the proposals, and summoned the burgesses, and more especially Pompeius himself and his old soldiers, to stand by him against fraud and force, this too was by no means a mere invention. The aristocracy, with the obstinate weak creature Bibulus and the unbending dogmatical fool Cato at their head, in reality intended to push the matter to open violence. Pompeius, instigated by Caesar to proclaim his position with reference to the pending question, declared bluntly, as was not his wont on other occasions, that if any one should venture to draw the sword, he too would grasp his, and in that case would not leave the shield at home; Crassus expressed himself to the same effect. The old soldiers of

Pompeius were directed to appear on the day of the vote—which in fact primarily concerned them—in great numbers, and with arms under their dress, at the place of voting.

The nobility however left no means untried to frustrate the proposals of Caesar. On each day when Caesar appeared before the people, his colleague Bibulus instituted the well-known political observations of the weather which interrupted all public business (iii. 409); Caesar did not trouble himself about the skies, but continued to prosecute his terrestrial occupation. The tribunician veto was interposed; Caesar contented himself with disregarding it. Bibulus and Cato sprang to the rostra, harangued the multitude, and instigated the usual riot; Caesar ordered that they should be led away by lictors from the Forum, and took care that otherwise no harm should befall them—it was for his interest that the political comedy should remain such as it was.

Notwithstanding all the chicanery and all the blustering of the nobility, the agrarian law, the confirmation of the Asiatic arrangements, and the remission to the lessees of taxes were adopted by the burgesses; and the commission of twenty was elected with Pompeius and Crassus at its head, and installed in office. With all their exertions the aristocracy had gained nothing, save that their blind and spiteful antagonism had drawn the bonds of the coalition still tighter, and their energy, which they were soon to need for matters more important, had exhausted itself on affairs that were at bottom indifferent. They congratulated each other on the heroic courage which they had displayed; the declaration of Bibulus that he would rather die than yield, the peroration which Cato still continued to deliver when in the hands of the lictors, were great patriotic feats; otherwise they resigned themselves to their fate. The consul Bibulus shut himself up for the remainder of the year in his house, while he at the same time intimated by public placard that he had the pious intention of watching the signs of the sky on all the days appropriate for public assemblies during that year. His colleagues once more admired the great man who, as Ennius had said of the old Fabius, "saved the state by wise delay," and they followed his example; most of them, Cato included, no longer appeared in the senate, but within their four walls helped their consul to fret over the fact that the history of the world went on in spite of political astronomy. To the public this passive attitude of the consul as well as of the aristocracy in general appeared, as it fairly might, a political abdication; and the coalition were naturally very well content that they were left to take their farther steps almost undisturbed.

The most important of these steps was the regulating of the future position of Caesar. Constitutionally it devolved on the senate to fix the functions of the second consular year of office before the election of the consuls took place; accordingly it had, in prospect of the election of Caesar, selected with that view for $\frac{696}{58}$ two provinces in which the governor should find no other employment than the construction of roads and other such works of utility. Of course the matter could not so remain; it was determined among the confederates, that Caesar should obtain by decree of the people an extraordinary command formed on the model of the Gabinio-Manilian laws. Caesar however had publicly declared that he would introduce no proposal in his own favour; the tribune of the people Publius Vatinius therefore undertook to submit the proposal to the burgesses, who naturally gave their unconditional assent. By this means Caesar obtained the governorship of Cisalpine Gaul and the supreme command of the three legions which were stationed there and were already experienced in border warfare under Lucius Afranius, along with the same rank of propraetor for his adjutants which those of Pompeius had enjoyed; this office was secured to him for five years—a longer period than had ever before been assigned to any general whose appointment was limited to a definite time at all. The Transpadanes, who for years had in hope of the franchise been the clients of the democratic party in Rome and of Caesar in particular (p. 149), formed the main portion of his province. His jurisdiction extended south as far as the Arnus and the Rubico, and included Luca and Ravenna. Subsequently there was added to Caesar's official district the province of Narbo with the one legion stationed there—a resolution adopted by the senate on the proposal of Pompeius, that it might at least not see this command also pass to Caesar by extraordinary decree of the burgesses. What was wished was thus attained. As no troops could constitutionally be stationed in Italy proper (iii. 347), the commander of the legions of northern Italy and Gaul dominated at the same time Italy and Rome for the next five years; and he who was master for five years was master for life. The consulship of Caesar had attained its object. As a matter of course, the new holders of power did not neglect withal to keep the multitude in good humour by games and amusements of all sorts, and they embraced every opportunity of filling their exchequer; in the case of the king of Egypt, for instance, the decree of the people, which recognised him as legitimate ruler (p. 143), was sold to him by the coalition at a high price, and in like manner other dynasts and communities acquired charters and privileges on this occasion.

The permanence of the arrangements made seemed also sufficiently secured. The consulship was, at least for the next year, entrusted to safe hands. The public believed at first, that it was destined for Pompeius and Crassus themselves; the regents however preferred to procure the election of two subordinate but trustworthy men of their party—Aulus Gabinius, the best among Pompeius' adjutants, and Lucius Piso, who was less important but was Caesar's father-in-law—as consuls for $\frac{696}{58}$. Pompeius personally undertook to watch over Italy, where at the head of the commission of twenty he prosecuted the execution of the agrarian law and furnished nearly 20,000 burgesses, in great part old soldiers from his army, with land in the territory of Capua. Caesar's north-Italian legions served to back him against the opposition in the capital. There existed no prospect, immediately at least, of a rupture among the regents themselves. The laws issued by Caesar as consul, in the maintenance of which Pompeius was as much interested as Caesar, formed a guarantee for the continuance of the breach between Pompeius and the aristocracy—whose heads, and Cato in particular, continued to treat these laws as null—and thereby a guarantee for the subsistence of the coalition. Moreover, the personal bonds of connection between its chiefs were drawn closer. Caesar had honestly and faithfully kept his word to his confederates without curtailing or cheating them of what he had promised, and in particular had fought to secure the agrarian law proposed in the interest of Pompeius just as if the case had been his own with dexterity and energy; Pompeius was not insensible to upright dealing and good faith, and was kindly disposed towards the man who had helped him to get quit at a blow of the sorry part of a suppliant which he had been playing for three years. Frequent and familiar intercourse with a man of the irresistible amiableness of Caesar did what was farther requisite to convert the alliance of interests into an alliance of friendship. The result and the pledge of this friendship—at the same time, doubtless, a public announcement which could hardly be misunderstood of the newly established conjoint rule—was the marriage of Pompeius with Caesar's only daughter, three-and-twenty years of age. Julia, who had inherited the charm of her father, lived in the happiest domestic relations with her husband, who was nearly twice as old; and the burgesses longing for rest and order after so many troubles and crises, saw in this nuptial alliance the guarantee of a peaceful and prosperous future.

The more firmly and closely the alliance was thus cemented between Pompeius and Caesar, the more hopeless grew the cause of the aristocracy. They felt the sword suspended over their head and knew Caesar sufficiently to have no doubt that he would, if necessary, use it without hesitation. "On all sides," wrote one of them, "we are checkmated; we have already through fear of death or of banishment despaired of 'freedom;' every one sighs, no one ventures to speak." More the confederates could not desire. But though the majority of the aristocracy was in this desirable frame of mind, there was, of course, no lack of Hotspurs among the party. Hardly had Caesar laid down the consulship, when some of the most violent aristocrats, Lucius Domitius and Gaius Memmius, proposed in a full senate the annulling of the Julian laws. This indeed was simply a piece of folly, which redounded only to the benefit of the coalition; for, when Caesar now himself insisted that the senate should investigate the validity of the laws assailed, the latter could not but formally recognise their legality. But, as may readily be conceived, the regents found in this a new call to make an example of some of the most notable and noisiest of their opponents, and thereby to assure themselves that the remainder would adhere to that fitting policy of sighing and silence. At first there had been a hope that the clause of the agrarian law, which as usual required all the senators to take an oath to the new law on pain of forfeiting their political rights, would induce its most vehement opponents to banish themselves, after the example of Metellus Numidicus (iii. 198), by refusing the oath. But these did not show themselves so complaisant; even the rigid Cato submitted to the oath, and his Sanchos followed him. A second, far from honourable, attempt to threaten the heads of the aristocracy with criminal impeachments on account of an alleged plot for the murder of Pompeius, and so to drive them into exile, was frustrated by the incapacity of the instruments; the informer, one Vettius, exaggerated and contradicted himself so grossly, and the tribune Vatinius, who directed the foul scheme, showed his complicity with that Vettius so clearly, that it was found advisable to strangle the latter in prison and to let the whole matter drop. On this occasion however they had obtained sufficient evidence of the total disorganisation of the aristocracy and the boundless alarm of the grandees: even a man like Lucius Lucullus had thrown himself in person at Caesar's feet and publicly declared that he found himself compelled by reason of his great age to withdraw from public life.

Ultimately therefore they were content with a few isolated victims. It was of primary importance to remove Cato, who made no secret of his conviction as to the nullity of all the Julian laws, and who was a man to act as he thought. Such a man Marcus Cicero was certainly not, and they did not give themselves the trouble to fear him. But the democratic party, which played the leading part in the coalition, could not possibly after its victory leave unpunished the judicial murder of the 5th December $\frac{691}{63}$, which it had so loudly and so justly censured. Had they wished to bring to account the real authors of the fatal decree, they ought to have seized not on the pusillanimous consul, but on the section of the strict aristocracy which had urged the timorous man to that execution. But in formal law it was certainly not the advisers of the consul, but the consul himself, that was responsible for it, and it was above all the gentler course to call the consul alone to account and to leave the senatorial college wholly out of the case; for which reason in the grounds of the proposal directed against Cicero the decree of the senate, in virtue of which he ordered the execution, was directly described as supposititious. Even against Cicero the regents would gladly have avoided steps that attracted attention; but he could not prevail on himself either to give to the regents the guarantees which they required, or to banish himself from Rome under one of the feasible pretexts on several occasions offered to him, or even to keep silence. With the utmost desire to avoid any offence and the most sincere alarm, he yet had not self-control enough to be prudent; the word had to come out, when a petulant witticism stung him, or when his self-conceit almost rendered crazy by the praise of so many noble lords gave vent to the well-cadenced periods of the plebeian advocate.

The execution of the measures resolved on against Cato and Cicero was committed to the loose and dissolute, but clever and pre-eminently audacious Publius Clodius, who had lived four years in the bitterest enmity with Cicero, and, with the view of satisfying that enmity and playing a part as demagogue, had got himself converted under the consulship of Caesar by a hasty adoption from a patrician into a plebeian, and then chosen as tribune of the people for the year $\frac{696}{58}$. To support Clodius, the proconsul Caesar remained in the immediate vicinity of the capital till the blow was struck against the two victims. Agreeably to the instructions which he had received, Clodius proposed to the burgesses to entrust Cato with the regulation of the complicated municipal affairs of the Byzantines and with the annexation of the kingdom of Cyprus, which as well as Egypt had fallen to the Romans by the testament of Alexander II., but had not like Egypt bought off the Roman annexation, and the king of which, moreover, had formerly given personal offence to Clodius. As to Cicero, Clodius brought in a project of law which characterised the execution of a burgess without trial and sentence as a crime to be punished with banishment. Cato was thus removed by an honourable mission, while Cicero was visited with at least the gentlest possible punishment—and besides was not designated by name in the proposal. But they did not refuse themselves the pleasure, on the one hand, of punishing a man notoriously timid and belonging to the class of political weathercocks for the conservative energy which he displayed, and, on the other hand, of investing the bitter opponent of all interferences of the burgesses in administration and of all extraordinary commands with such a command conferred by decree of the burgesses themselves; and in a similar spirit the proposal respecting Cato was based on the ground of the abnormal virtue of the man, which made him appear pre-eminently qualified to execute so delicate a commission, as was the confiscation of the considerable crown-treasure of Cyprus, without embezzlement. Both proposals bear generally the same character of respectful deference and cool irony, which marks throughout the bearing of Caesar in reference to the senate. They met with no resistance. It was naturally of no avail, that the majority of the senate, with the view of protesting in some way against the mockery and censure of their decree in the matter of Catilina, publicly put on mourning, and that Cicero himself, now when it was too late, fell on his knees and besought mercy from Pompeius; he had to banish himself even before the passing of the law which debarred him from his native land (April $\frac{696}{58}$). Cato likewise did not venture to provoke sharper measures by declining the commission which he had received, but accepted it and embarked for the East (p. 143). What was most immediately necessary was done; Caesar too might leave Italy to devote himself to more serious tasks.

CHAPTER VII

THE SUBJUGATION OF THE WEST

When the course of history turns from the miserable monotony of the political selfishness, which fought its battles in the senate-house and in the streets of the capital, to matters of greater importance than the question whether the first monarch of Rome should be called Gnaeus, Gaius, or Marcus, we may well be allowed—on the threshold of an event, the effects of which still at the present day influence the destinies of the world—to look round us for a moment, and to indicate the point of view under which the conquest of what is now France by the Romans, and their first contact with the inhabitants of Germany and of Great Britain, are to be regarded in connection with the general history of the world.

By virtue of the law, that a people which has grown into a state absorbs its neighbours who are in political nonage, and a civilised people absorbs its neighbours who are in intellectual nonage—by virtue of this law, which is as universally valid and as much a law of nature as the law of gravity—the Italian nation (the only one in antiquity which was able to combine a superior political development and a superior civilisation, though it presented the latter only in an imperfect and external manner) was entitled to reduce to subjection the Greek states of the East which were ripe for destruction, and to dispossess the peoples of lower grades of culture in the West—Libyans, Iberians, Celts, Germans—by means of its settlers; just as England with equal right has in Asia reduced to subjection a civilisation of rival standing but politically impotent, and in America and Australia has marked and ennobled, and still continues to mark and ennoble, extensive barbarian countries with the impress of its nationality. The Roman aristocracy had accomplished the preliminary condition required for this task—the union of Italy; the task itself it never solved, but always regarded the extra-Italian conquests either as simply a necessary evil, or as a fiscal possession virtually beyond the pale of the state. It is the imperishable glory of the Roman democracy or monarchy—for the two coincide—to have correctly apprehended and vigorously realised this its highest destination. What the irresistible force of circumstances had paved the way for, through the senate establishing against its will the foundations of the future Roman dominion in the West as in the East; what thereafter the Roman emigration to the provinces—which came as a public calamity, no doubt, but also in the western regions at any rate as a pioneer of a higher culture—instinctively apprehended; the creator of the Roman democracy Gaius Gracchus recognised and began to carry out with statesmanlike clearness and decision. The two fundamental ideas of the new policy—to reunite the territories under the power of Rome, so far as they were Hellenic, and to colonise them, so far as they were not Hellenic—had already in the Gracchan age been practically recognised by the annexation of the kingdom of Attalus and by the Transalpine conquests of Flaccus: but the reaction which carried the day threw them again into the shade. The Roman state remained a chaotic mass of countries without thorough occupation and without proper limits. Spain and the Graeco-Asiatic possessions were separated from the mother country by wide territories, of which barely the borders along the coast were subject to the Romans; on the north coast of Africa the domains of Carthage and Cyrene alone were occupied like oases; large tracts even of the subject territory, especially in Spain, were but nominally subject to the Romans. Absolutely nothing was done on the part of the government towards concentrating and rounding off their dominion, and the decay of the fleet seemed at length to dissolve the last bond of connection between the distant possessions. The democracy no doubt attempted, so soon as it again raised its head, to shape its external policy in the spirit of Gracchus—Marius in particular cherished such ideas—but as it did not for any length of time attain the helm, its projects were left unfulfilled. It was not till the democracy practically took in hand the government on the overthrow of the Sullan constitution in $\frac{684}{70}$, that a revolution in this respect occurred. First of all their sovereignty on the Mediterranean was restored—the most vital question for a state like that of Rome. Towards the East, moreover, the boundary of the Euphrates was secured by the annexation of the provinces of Pontus and Syria. But there still remained beyond the Alps the task of at once rounding off the Roman territory towards the north and west, and of gaining a fresh virgin soil there for Hellenic civilisation and for the yet unbroken vigour of the Italic race.

This task Gaius Caesar undertook. It is more than an error, it is an outrage upon the sacred spirit dominant in history, to regard Gaul solely as the parade ground on which Caesar exercised himself and his legions for the impending civil war. Though the subjugation of the West was for Caesar so far a means to an end that he laid the foundations of his later height of power in the Transalpine wars, it is the especial privilege of a statesman of genius that his means themselves are ends in their turn. Caesar needed no doubt for his party aims a military power, but he did not conquer Gaul as a partisan. There was a direct political necessity for Rome to meet the perpetually threatened invasion of the Germans thus early beyond the Alps, and to construct a rampart there which should secure the peace of the Roman world. But even this important object was not the highest and ultimate reason for which Gaul was conquered by Caesar. When their old home had become too narrow for the Roman burgesses and they were in danger of decay, the senate's policy of Italian conquest saved them from ruin. Now the Italian home had become in its turn too narrow; once more the state languished under the same social evils repeating themselves in similar fashion only on a greater scale. It was a brilliant idea, a grand hope, which led Caesar over the Alps—the idea and the confident expectation that he should gain there for his fellow burgesses a new boundless home, and regenerate the state a second time by placing it on a broader basis.

The campaign which Caesar undertook in $\frac{693}{61}$ in Further Spain, may be in some sense included among the enterprises which aimed at the subjugation of the West. Long as Spain had obeyed the Romans, its western shore had remained substantially independent of them even after the expedition of Decimus Brutus against the Gallaeci (iii. 17), and they had not even set foot on the northern coast; while the predatory raids to which the subject provinces found themselves continually exposed from those quarters did no small injury to the civilisation and Romanising of Spain. Against these the expedition of Caesar along the west coast was directed. He crossed the chain of the Herminian mountains (Sierra de Estrella) bounding the Tagus on the north; after having defeated their inhabitants and transplanted them in part to the plain, he reduced the country on both sides of the Douro and arrived at the northwest point of the peninsula, where with the aid of a flotilla brought up from Gades he occupied Brigantium (Corunna). By this means the peoples adjoining the Atlantic Ocean, Lusitanians and Gallaecians, were forced to acknowledge the Roman supremacy, while the conqueror was at the same time careful to render the position of the subjects generally more tolerable by reducing the tribute to be paid to Rome and regulating the financial affairs of the communities.

But, although in this military and administrative outset of the great general and statesman the same talents and the same leading ideas are discernible which he afterwards evinced on a greater stage, his agency in the Iberian peninsula was much too transient to have any deep effect; the more especially as, owing to its physical and national peculiarities, nothing but action steadily continued for a considerable time could exert any durable influence there.

A more important part in the Romanic development of the West was reserved by destiny for the country which stretches between the Pyrenees and the Rhine, the Mediterranean and the Atlantic Ocean, and which since the Augustan age has been especially designated by the name of the land of the Celts—Gallia—although strictly speaking the land of the Celts was partly narrower, partly much more extensive, and the country so called never formed a national unity and did not form a political unity before Augustus. For this very reason it is not easy to present a clear picture of the very heterogeneous state of things which Caesar encountered on his arrival there in $\frac{696}{58}$.

In the region on the Mediterranean, which, embracing approximately Languedoc on the west of the Rhone, on the east Dauphiné and Provence, had been for sixty years a Roman province, the Roman arms had seldom been at rest since the Cimbrian invasion which had swept over it. In $\frac{664}{90}$ Gaius Caelius had fought with the Salyes about Aquae Sextiae, and in $\frac{674}{80}$ Gaius Flaccus (iii. 324), on his march to Spain, with other Celtic nations. When in the Sertorian war the governor Lucius Manlius, compelled to hasten to the aid of his colleagues beyond the Pyrenees, returned defeated from Ilerda (Lerida) and on his way home was vanquished a second time by the western neighbours of the Roman province, the Aquitani (about 676; p. 19), this seems to have provoked a general rising of the provincials between the Pyrenees and the Rhone, perhaps even of those between the Rhone and Alps. Pompeius had to make his way with the sword through the insurgent Gaul to Spain (p. 25), and by way of penalty for their rebellion gave the territories of the Volcae-Arecomici and the Helvii (dep. Gard and Ardêche) over to the Massiliots: the governor Marcius Fonteius

($\frac{678-680}{76-74}$) carried out these arrangements and restored tranquillity in the province by subduing the Vocontii (dep. Drôme), protecting Massilia from the insurgents, and liberating the Roman capital Narbo which they invested. Despair, however, and the financial embarrassment which the participation in the sufferings of the Spanish war (p. 30) and generally the official and non-official exactions of the Romans brought upon the Gallic provinces, did not allow them to be tranquil; and in particular the canton of the Allobroges, the most remote from Narbo, was in a perpetual ferment, which was attested by the "pacification" that Gaius Piso undertook there in $\frac{688}{66}$ as well as by the conduct of the Allobrogian embassy in Rome on occasion of the anarchist plot in $\frac{691}{63}$ (p. 166), and which soon afterwards ($\frac{693}{61}$) broke into open revolt. Catugnatus the leader of the Allobroges in this war of despair, who had at first fought not unsuccessfully, was conquered at Solonium after a glorious resistance by the governor Gaius Pomptinus.

Notwithstanding all these conflicts the bounds of the Roman territory were not materially advanced; Lugudunum Convenarum, where Pompeius had settled the remnant of the Sertorian army (p. 34), Tolosa, Vienna, and Geneva were still the most remote Roman townships towards the west and north. But at the same time the importance of these Gallic possessions for the mother country was continually on the increase. The glorious climate, akin to that of Italy, the favourable nature of the ground, the large and rich region behind so advantageous for commerce with its mercantile routes reaching as far as Britain, the easy intercourse by land and sea with the mother country, rapidly gave to southern Gaul an economic importance for Italy, which much older possessions, such as those in Spain, had not acquired in the course of centuries; and as the Romans who had suffered political shipwreck at this period sought an asylum especially in Massilia, and there found once more Italian culture and Italian luxury, voluntary emigrants from Italy also were attracted more and more to the Rhone and the Garonne. "The province of Gaul," it was said in a sketch drawn ten years before Caesar's arrival, "is full of merchants; it swarms with Roman burgesses. No native of Gaul transacts a piece of business without the intervention of a Roman; every penny that passes from one hand to another in Gaul goes through the account books of the Roman burgesses." From the same description it appears that in addition to the colonists of Narbo there were Roman farmers and graziers resident in great numbers in Gaul; as to which, however, it must not be overlooked that most of the provincial land possessed by Romans, just like the greater part of the English possessions in the earliest times in America, was in the hands of the high nobility living in Italy, and those farmers and graziers consisted for the most part of their stewards—slaves or freedmen.

It is easy to understand how under such circumstances civilisation and Romanising rapidly spread among the natives. The Celts were not fond of agriculture; but their new masters compelled them to exchange the sword for the plough, and it is very credible that the bitter resistance of the Allobroges was provoked in part by some such ordinances. In earlier times Hellenism had also to a certain degree influenced those regions; the elements of a higher culture, the stimulus to the cultivation of the vine and the olive (iii. 157), to the use of writing,[1] and to the coining of money, came to them from Massilia. The Hellenic culture was in this case far from being set aside by the Romans; Massilia gained through them more influence than it lost, and even in the Roman period Greek physicians and rhetoricians were publicly employed in Gallic cantons. But, as may readily be conceived, Hellenism in southern Gaul acquired through the agency of the Romans the same character as in Italy; the distinctively Hellenic civilisation gave place to the Latino-Greek mixed culture, which soon made proselytes here in great numbers. The "Gauls in the breeches," as the inhabitants of southern Gaul were called by way of contrast to the "Gauls in the toga" of northern Italy, were not indeed like the latter already completely Romanised, but they were even now very perceptibly distinguished from the "long-haired Gauls" of the northern regions still unsubdued. The semi-culture becoming naturalised among them furnished, doubtless, materials enough for ridicule of their barbarous Latin, and people did not fail to suggest to any one suspected of Celtic descent his "relationship with the breeches," but this bad Latin was yet sufficient to enable even the remote Allobroges to transact business with the Roman authorities, and even to give testimony in the Roman courts without an interpreter.

While the Celtic and Ligurian population of these regions was thus in the course of losing its nationality, and was languishing

[1] There was found, for instance, at Vaison in the Vocontian canton an inscription in the Celtic language with the ordinary Greek alphabet. It runs thus: *σεγομαρος ουιλλονεος τοουτιους ναμανατιο ειωρουβηλησαμισοειν νεμητον*. The last word means "holy."

and pining withal under a political and economic oppression, the intolerable nature of which is sufficiently attested by their hopeless insurrections, the decline of the native population there went hand in hand with the naturalising of the same higher culture which we find at this period in Italy. Aquae Sextiae and Narbo especially were considerable places, which might probably be named by the side of Beneventum and Capua, and Massilia, the best organised, most free, most capable of self-defence, and most powerful of all the Greek cities dependent on Rome, under its rigidly aristocratic government to which the Roman conservatives probably pointed as the model of a good urban constitution, in possession of an important territory which had been considerably enlarged by the Romans and of an extensive trade, stood by the side of those Latin towns as Rhegium and Neapolis stood in Italy by the side of Beneventum and Capua. Matters wore a different aspect when one crossed the Roman frontier. The great Celtic nation, which in the southern districts already began to be crushed by the Roman immigration, still moved to the north of Cevennes in its ancient freedom. It is not the first time that we meet it: the Italians had already fought with the offsets and advanced posts of this vast stock on the Tiber and on the Po, in the mountains of Castile and Carinthia, and even in the heart of Asia Minor; but it was here that the main stock was first assailed at its very core by their attacks. The Celtic race had on its settlement in central Europe diffused itself chiefly over the rich river-valleys and the pleasant hill-country of the present France including the western districts of Germany and Switzerland, and from thence had occupied the southern part of England, perhaps even at this time all Great Britain and Ireland;[1] it formed here more than anywhere else a broad, geographically compact mass of peoples. In spite of the differences in language and manners which naturally were to be found within this wide territory, a lively mutual intercourse, an innate sense of fellowship, seems to have knit together the tribes from the Rhone and Garonne to the Rhine and the Thames; whereas, although these doubtless were in a certain measure locally connected with the Celts in

[1] An immigration of Belgic Celts to Britain continuing for a considerable time seems indicated by the names of English tribes on both banks of the Thames borrowed from Belgic cantons; such as the Atrebates, the Belgae, and even the Britanni themselves, which word appears to have been transferred from the Brittones settled on the Somme below Amiens first to an English canton and then to the whole island. The English gold coinage was also derived from the Belgic and originally identical with it.

Spain and in the modern Austria, the mighty mountain walls of the Pyrenees and the Alps on the one hand, and the encroachments of the Romans and the Germans which also operated here on the other, interrupted the intercourse and the intrinsic connection of the cognate peoples far otherwise than the narrow arm of the sea interrupted the relations of the continental and the British Celts. Unhappily we are not permitted to trace stage by stage the history of the internal development of this remarkable people in these its chief seats; we must be content with presenting at least some outline of its historical culture and political condition, as it here meets us in the time of Caesar.

Gaul was, according to the reports of the ancients, comparatively well peopled. Certain statements lead us to infer that in the Belgic districts there were some 200 persons to the square mile—a proportion such as nearly holds at present for Wales and for Livonia—in the Helvetic canton about 245;[1] it is probable that in the districts which were more cultivated than the Belgic and less mountainous than the Helvetian, as among the Bituriges, Arverni, Haedui, the number rose still higher. Agriculture was no doubt practised in Gaul, for even the contemporaries of Caesar were surprised in the region of the Rhine by the custom of manuring with marl,[2] and the primitive Celtic

[1] The first levy of the Belgic cantons exclusive of the Remi, that is, of the country between the Seine and the Scheldt and eastward as far as the vicinity of Rheims and Andernach, from 9000 to 10,000 square miles, is reckoned at about 300,000 men; in accordance with which, if we regard the proportion of the first levy to the whole men capable of bearing arms specified for the Bellovaci as holding good generally, the number of the Belgae capable of bearing arms would amount to 500,000, and the whole population accordingly to at least 2,000,000. The Helvetii with the adjoining peoples numbered before their migration 336,000; if we assume that they were at that time already dislodged from the right bank of the Rhine, their territory may be estimated at nearly 1350 square miles. Whether the serfs are included in this, we can the less determine, as we do not know the form which slavery assumed amongst the Celts; what Caesar relates (i. 4) as to the slaves, clients, and debtors of Orgetorix tells rather in favour of, than against, their being included.

That, moreover, every such attempt to supply the statistical basis, in which ancient history is especially deficient, by means of calculation must be received with due caution, will be at once apprehended by the intelligent reader, while he will not absolutely reject it on that account.

[2] "In the interior of Transalpine Gaul on the Rhine," says Scrofa in Varro, *De R. R.* i. 7, 8, "when I commanded there, I traversed some districts, where neither the vine nor the olive nor the fruit-tree appears, where they manure the fields with white pit-chalk, where they have neither rock nor sea-salt, but make use of the saline ashes of certain burnt wood instead of salt." This description refers probably to the period before Caesar and to the eastern districts of the old province, such as the country of the Allobroges; subsequently Pliny (*H. N.* xvii. 6, 42 *seq.*) describes at length the Gallo-Britannic manuring with marl.

custom of preparing beer (*cervesia*) from barley is likewise an evidence of the early and wide diffusion of the culture of grain; but it was not held in estimation. Even in the more civilised south it was reckoned not becoming for the free Celts to handle the plough. In far higher estimation among the Celts stood pastoral husbandry, for which the Roman land-holders of this epoch very gladly availed themselves both of the Celtic breed of cattle, and of the brave Celtic slaves skilled in riding and familiar with the rearing of animals.[1] Particularly in the northern Celtic districts pastoral husbandry was thoroughly predominant. Brittany was in Caesar's time a country poor in corn. In the north-east dense forests, attaching themselves to the heart of the Ardennes, stretched almost without interruption from the German Ocean to the Rhine; and on the plains of Flanders and Lorraine, now so fertile, the Menapian and Treverian shepherd then fed his half-wild swine in the impenetrable oak-forest. Just as in the valley of the Po the Romans made the production of wool and the culture of corn supersede the Celtic feeding of pigs on acorns, so the rearing of sheep and the agriculture in the plains of the Scheldt and the Maas are traceable to their influence. In Britain even the threshing of corn was not yet usual; and in its more northern districts agriculture was not practised, and the rearing of cattle was the only known mode of turning the soil to account. The culture of the olive and vine, which yielded rich produce to the Massiliots, was not yet prosecuted beyond the Cevennes in the time of Caesar.

The Gauls were from the first disposed to settle in groups; there were open villages everywhere, and the Helvetic canton alone numbered in $\frac{696}{58}$ four hundred of these, besides a multitude of single homesteads. But there were not wanting also walled towns, whose walls of alternate layers surprised the Romans both by their suitableness and by the elegant combination of timber and stones; while, it is true, even in the towns of the Allobroges the buildings were erected solely of wood. Of such towns the Helvetii had twelve and the Suessiones an equal number; whereas in the more northern districts, such as among

[1] "The Gallic oxen especially are of good repute in Italy, for field labour forsooth; whereas the Ligurian are good for nothing" (Varro, *De R. R.* ii. 5, 9). Here, no doubt, Cisalpine Gaul is referred to, but the pastoral husbandry there doubtless goes back to the Celtic epoch. Plautus already mentions the "Gallic ponies" (*Gallici canterii*, *Aul.* iii. 5, 21). "It is not every race that is suited for the business of herdsmen; neither the Bastulians nor the Turdulians" (both in Andalusia) "are fit for it; the Celts are the best, especially as respects beasts for riding and burden (*iumenta*)" (Varro, *De R. R.* ii. 10, 4).

the Nervii, while there were doubtless also towns, the population during war sought protection in the morasses and forests rather than behind their walls, and beyond the Thames the primitive defence of the wooden abatis altogether took the place of towns and was in war the only place of refuge for men and herds.

In close association with the comparatively considerable development of urban life stands the activity of intercourse by land and by water. Everywhere there were roads and bridges. The river-navigation, which streams like the Rhone, Garonne, Loire, and Seine, of themselves invited, was considerable and lucrative. But far more remarkable was the maritime navigation of the Celts. Not only were the Celts, to all appearance, the nation that first regularly navigated the Atlantic ocean, but we find that the art of building and of managing vessels had attained among them a remarkable development. The navigation of the peoples of the Mediterranean had, as may readily be conceived from the nature of the waters traversed by them, for a comparatively long period adhered to the oar; the war-vessels of the Phoenicians, Hellenes, and Romans were at all times oared galleys, in which the sail was applied only as an occasional aid to the oar; the trading vessels alone were in the epoch of developed ancient civilisation "sailers" properly so called.[1] But, while the Gauls employed in the channel in Caesar's time, as for long afterwards, a species of portable leathern skiffs, which seem to have been in the main common oared boats, on the west coast of Gaul the Santones, the Pictones, and above all the Veneti sailed in large though clumsily built ships, which were not impelled by oars but were provided with leathern sails and iron anchor-chains; and they employed these not only for their traffic with Britain, but also in naval combat. Here therefore we not only meet for the first time with navigation in the open ocean, but we find that here the sailing vessel first fully took the place of the oared boat—an improvement, it is true, which the declining activity of the old world did not know how to turn to account, and the immeasurable results of which our own epoch of renewed culture is employed in gradually reaping.

With this regular maritime intercourse between the British

[1] We are led to this conclusion by the designation of the trading or "round" as contrasted with the "long" or war vessel, and the similar contrast of the "oared ships" (ἐπίκωποι νῆες) and the "merchantmen" (ὁλκάδες, Dionys. iii. 44); and moreover by the smallness of the crew in the trading vessels, which in the very largest amounted to not more than 200 men (Rhein. Mus. N. F. xi. 625), while in the ordinary galley of three decks there were employed 170 rowers (ii. 36). Comp. Movers, *Phoen.* ii. 3, 167 *seq.*

and Gallic coasts, the very close political connection between the inhabitants on both sides of the Channel is as easily explained as the flourishing of transmarine commerce and of fisheries. It was the Celts of Brittany, in particular, that brought the tin of the mines of Cornwall from England and carried it by the river and land routes of Gaul to Narbo and Massilia. The statement, that in Caesar's time certain tribes at the mouth of the Rhine subsisted on fish and birds' eggs, may probably refer to the circumstance that marine fishing and the collection of the eggs of sea-birds were prosecuted there on an extensive scale. When we put together and endeavour to fill up the isolated and scanty statements which have reached us regarding the Celtic commerce and intercourse, we come to see why the tolls of the river and maritime ports play a great part in the budgets of certain cantons, such as those of the Haedui and the Veneti, and why the chief god of the nation was regarded by them as the protector of the roads and of commerce, and at the same time as the inventor of manufactures. Accordingly the Celtic industry cannot have been wholly undeveloped; indeed the singular dexterity of the Celts, and their peculiar skill in imitating any model and executing any instructions, are noticed by Caesar. In most branches, however, their handicraft does not appear to have risen above the ordinary level; the manufacture of linen and woollen stuffs, that subsequently flourished in central and northern Gaul, was demonstrably called into existence only by the Romans. The elaboration of metals forms an exception, and so far as we know the only one. The copper implements not unfrequently of excellent workmanship and even now malleable, which are brought to light in the tombs of Gaul, and the carefully adjusted Arvernian gold coins, are still at the present day striking witnesses of the skill of the Celtic workers in copper and gold; and with this the reports of the ancients well accord, that the Romans learned the art of tinning from the Bituriges and that of silvering from the Alesini—inventions, the first of which was naturally suggested by the traffic in tin, and both of which were probably made in the period of Celtic freedom.

Hand in hand with dexterity in the elaboration of the metals went the art of procuring them, which had attained, more especially in the iron mines on the Loire, such a degree of professional skill that the miners played an important part in the sieges. The opinion prevalent among the Romans of this period, that Gaul was one of the richest gold countries in the world, is no doubt refuted by the well-known nature of the soil and by the character of the articles discovered in the Celtic tombs, in which gold appears but sparingly and with far less frequency than in the similar repositories of the true native regions of gold; the idea no doubt had its origin merely from the descriptions which Greek travellers and Roman soldiers, doubtless not without strong exaggeration, gave to their countrymen of the magnificence of the Arvernian kings (iii. 158), and of the treasures of the Tolosan temples (iii. 172). But their stories were not pure fictions. It may well be believed that in and near the rivers which flow from the Alps and the Pyrenees gold-washing and searches for gold, which are unprofitable at the present value of labour, were worked with profit and on a considerable scale in ruder times and with a system of slavery; besides, the commercial relations of Gaul may, as is not unfrequently the case with half-civilised peoples, have favoured the accumulation of a dead stock of the precious metals.

The low state of the arts of design is remarkable, and is the more striking by the side of this mechanical skill in handling the metals. The fondness for parti-coloured and brilliant ornaments shows the want of a proper taste, which is sadly confirmed by the Gallic coins with their representations sometimes exceedingly simple, sometimes odd, but always childish, in design, and almost without exception rude beyond parallel in their execution. It is perhaps unexampled that a coinage practised for centuries with a certain technical skill should have essentially limited itself to always imitating two or three Greek dies, and always with increasing deformity. On the other hand the art of poetry was highly valued by the Celts, and intimately blended with the religious and even with the political institutions of the nation; we find religious poetry, as well as that of the court and of the mendicant, flourishing (iii. 158). Natural science and philosophy also found, although subject to the forms and fetters of the theology of the country, a certain amount of attention among the Celts; and Hellenic humanism met with a ready reception wherever and in whatever shape it approached them. The knowledge of writing was general at least among the priests. For the most part in free Gaul the Greek writing was made use of in Caesar's time, as was done among others by the Helvetii; but in its most southern districts even then, in consequence of intercourse with the Romanised Celts, the Latin attained predominance—we meet with it, for instance, on the Arvernian coins of this period.

The political development of the Celtic nation also presents very remarkable phenomena. The constitution of the state was based in this case, as everywhere, on the clan-canton, with its prince, its council of the elders, and its community of freemen capable of bearing arms; but the peculiarity in this case was that it never got beyond this cantonal constitution. Among the Greeks and Romans the canton was very early superseded by the ringwall as the basis of political unity; where two cantons met within the same walls, they amalgamated into one commonwealth; where a body of burgesses assigned to a portion of their fellow burgesses a new ringwall, there regularly arose in this way a new state connected with the mother-community only by the ties of piety or at most of clientship. Among the Celts on the other hand the "burgess-body" continued at all times to be the clan; prince and council presided over the canton and not over any town, and the general diet of the canton formed the authority of last resort in the state. The town had, as in the East, merely mercantile and strategic, not political importance; for which reason the Gallic townships, even when walled and very considerable such as Vienna and Genava, were in the view of the Greeks and Romans merely villages. In the time of Caesar the original clan-constitution still subsisted substantially unaltered among the insular Celts and in the northern cantons of the mainland; the general assembly held the supreme authority; the prince was in essential questions bound by its decrees; the common council was numerous—it numbered in certain clans six hundred members—but does not appear to have had more importance than the senate under the Roman kings. In the more stirring southern portion of the land, again, one or two generations before Caesar—the children of the last kings were still living in his time—there had occurred, at least among the larger clans, the Arverni, Haedui, Sequani, Helvetii, a revolution which set aside the royal dominion and gave the power into the hands of the nobility.

It is simply the reverse side of the total want of urban commonwealths among the Celts just noticed, that the opposite pole of political development, knighthood, so thoroughly preponderates in the Celtic clan-constitution. The Celtic aristocracy was to all appearance a high nobility, for the most part perhaps the members of the royal or formerly royal families; as indeed it is remarkable that the heads of the opposite parties in the same clan very frequently belong to the same house. These great families combined in their hands financial, warlike, and political ascendency. They monopolised the leases of the profitable rights of the state. They compelled the common freemen, who were oppressed by the load of debt, to borrow from them, and to surrender their freedom first *de facto* as debtors, then *de jure* as bondmen. They developed the system of retainers, that is, the privilege of the nobility to surround themselves with a number of hired mounted servants—the *ambacti* as they were called [1]—and thereby to form a state within the state; and, resting on the support of these troops of their own, they defied the legal authorities and the common levy and practically broke up the commonwealth. If in a clan, which numbered about 80,000 men capable of arms, a single noble could appear at the diet with 10,000 retainers, not reckoning the bondmen and the debtors, it is clear that such an one was an independent dynast rather than a burgess of his clan. Moreover, the leading families of the different clans were closely connected and through intermarriages and special treaties formed virtually a compact league, in presence of which the single clan was powerless.

[1] This remarkable word must have been in use as early as the sixth century of Rome among the Celts in the valley of the Po; for Ennius is already acquainted with it, and it can only have reached the Italians at so early a period from that quarter. It is not merely Celtic, however, but also German, the root of our "Amt," as indeed the retainer-system itself is common to the Celts and the Germans. It would be of great historical importance to ascertain whether the word—and therefore the thing—came to the Celts from the Germans, or to the Germans from the Celts. If, as is usually supposed, the word is originally German and primarily signified the servant standing in battle "against the back" (*and*=against, *bak*=back) of his master, this is not wholly irreconcilable with the singularly early occurrence of this word among the Celts. According to all analogy the right to keep *ambacti*, that is, δοῦλοι μισθωτοί, cannot have belonged to the Celtic nobility from the outset, but must only have developed itself gradually in antagonism to the older monarchy and to the equality of the free commons. If thus the system of *ambacti* among the Celts was not an ancient and national, but a comparatively recent institution, it is—looking to the relation which had subsisted for centuries between the Celts and Germans, and which is to be explained further on —not merely possible but even probable that the Celts, in Italy as in Gaul, employed Germans chiefly as those hired servants-at-arms. The "Swiss guard" would therefore in that case be some thousands of years older than people suppose. Should the term by which the Romans, perhaps after the example of the Celts, designate the Germans as a nation—the name *Germani*—be really of Celtic origin (ii. 72), this obviously accords very well with that hypothesis. No doubt these assumptions must necessarily give way, should the word *ambactus* be explained in a satisfactory way from a Celtic root; as in fact Zeuss (*Gramm.* p. 761), though doubtfully, traces it to *ambi*=around and *aig*=*agere*, viz. persons moving round or moved round, and so attendants, servants. The circumstance that the word occurs also as a Celtic proper name (Zeuss, p. 89), and is perhaps preserved in the Cambrian *amaeth*=peasant, labourer (Zeuss, p. 179), cannot decide the point either way.

Therefore the communities were no longer able to maintain the public peace, and sword-law reigned throughout. The dependent found protection only from his master, whom duty and interest compelled to redress the injury inflicted on his client; the state had no longer the power to protect those who were free, and consequently these gave themselves over in numbers to some powerful man as clients.

The common assembly lost its political importance; and even the power of the prince, which should have checked the encroachments of the nobility, succumbed to it among the Celts as well as in Latium. In place of the king came the "judgment-worker" or *Vergobretus*,[1] who was like the Roman consul nominated only for a year. So far as the canton still held together at all, it was led by the common council, in which naturally the heads of the aristocracy usurped the government. Of course under such circumstances there was agitation in the several clans much in the same way as there had been agitation in Latium for centuries after the expulsion of the kings: while the nobility of the different communities combined to form a separate alliance hostile to the power of the community, the multitude ceased not to desire the restoration of the monarchy; and not unfrequently an eminent nobleman attempted, as Spurius Cassius had done in Rome, with the support of the mass of those belonging to the canton to break down the power of his peers, and to reinstate the crown in its rights for his own special benefit.

While the individual cantons were thus irremediably declining, the sense of unity was at the same time powerfully stirring in the nation and seeking in various ways to take shape and hold. That combination of the whole Celtic nobility in contra-distinction to the individual canton-unions, while disturbing the existing order of things, awakened and fostered the idea of the collective unity of the nation. The attacks directed against the nation from without, and the continued diminution of its territory in war with its neighbours, operated in the same direction. Like the Hellenes in their wars with the Persians, and the Italians in their wars with the Celts, the Transalpine Gauls seem to have become conscious of the existence and the power of their national unity in the wars against Rome. Amidst the dissensions of rival clans and all their feudal quarreling there might still be heard the voices of those who were ready

[1] From the Celtic words *guerg*=worker and *breth*=judgment.

to purchase the independence of the nation at the cost of the independence of the several cantons, and even at that of the independence of the nobility. The thorough popularity of the opposition to a foreign yoke was shown by the wars of Caesar, with reference to whom the Celtic patriot party occupied a position entirely similar to that of the German patriots towards Napoleon; its extent and organisation are attested, among other things, by the telegraphic rapidity with which news was communicated from one point to another.

The universality and the strength of the Celtic national feeling would be inexplicable but for the circumstance that, amidst the greatest political division, the Celtic nation had for long been centralised in respect of religion and even of theology. The Celtic priesthood or, to use the native name, the corporation of the Druids, certainly embraced the British islands and all Gaul, and perhaps also other Celtic countries, in a common religious-national bond. It possessed a special head elected by the priests themselves; special schools, in which its very comprehensive tradition was transmitted; special privileges, particularly exemption from taxation and military service, which every clan respected; annual councils, which were held near Chartres at the "centre of the Celtic earth;" and above all, a believing people, who in painful devotion and blind obedience to their priests seem to have been nowise inferior to the Irish of modern times. It may readily be conceived that such a priesthood attempted to usurp, as it partially did usurp, the secular government; where the annual monarchy subsisted, it conducted the elections in the event of an interregnum; it successfully laid claim to the right of excluding individuals and whole communities from religious, and consequently also from civil, society; it was careful to draw to itself the most important civil causes, especially processes as to boundaries and inheritance; on the ground, apparently, of its right to exclude from the community and perhaps also of the national custom that criminals should be taken by preference for the usual human sacrifices, it developed an extensive priestly criminal jurisdiction, which was co-ordinate with that of the kings and vergobrets; it even claimed the right of deciding on war and peace. The Gauls were not far removed from an ecclesiastical state with its pope and councils, its immunities, interdicts, and spiritual courts; only this ecclesiastical state did not, like that of recent times, stand aloof from the nations, but was on the contrary pre-eminently national.

But while the sense of mutual relationship was thus vividly awakened among the Celtic tribes, the nation was still precluded from attaining a basis of political centralisation, such as Italy found in the Roman burgesses, and the Hellenes and Germans in the Macedonian and Frank kings. The Celtic priesthood and likewise the nobility—although both in a certain sense represented and combined the nation—were yet, on the one hand, incapable of uniting it in consequence of their peculiar class-interests, and, on the other hand, sufficiently powerful to allow no king and no canton to accomplish the work of union. Attempts at this work were not wanting; they followed, as the cantonal constitution suggested, the system of hegemony. A powerful canton induced a weaker to become subordinate, on such a footing that the leading canton acted for the other as well as for itself in its external relations and stipulated for it in state-treaties, while the dependent canton bound itself to render military service and sometimes also to pay a tribute. In this way a series of separate leagues arose; but there was no leading canton for all Gaul—no tie, however loose, combining the nation as a whole.

It has been already mentioned (iii. 158) that the Romans at the commencement of their Transalpine conquests found in the north a Britanno-Belgic league under the leadership of the Suessiones, and in central and southern Gaul the confederation of the Arverni, with which latter the Haedui, although having a weaker body of clients, carried on a rivalry. In Caesar's time we find the Belgae in north-eastern Gaul between the Seine and the Rhine still forming such an association, which, however, apparently no longer extends to Britain; by their side there appears, in the modern Normandy and Brittany, the league of the Aremorican or the maritime cantons: in central or proper Gaul two parties as formerly contended for the hegemony, the one headed by the Haedui, the other by the Sequani after the Arvernians weakened by the wars with Rome had retired. These different confederacies subsisted independently side by side; the leading states of central Gaul appear never to have extended their clientship to the north-east nor, seriously, even to the north-west of Gaul.

The impulse of the nation towards unity found doubtless a certain gratification in these cantonal unions; but they were in every respect unsatisfactory. The union was of the loosest kind, constantly fluctuating between alliance and hegemony; the representation of the whole body in peace by the federal diets, in war by the general,[1] was in the highest degree feeble. The Belgian confederacy alone seems to have been bound together somewhat more firmly; the national enthusiasm, from which the successful repulse of the Cimbri proceeded (iii. 178), may have proved beneficial to it. The contests for the hegemony made a breach in every league, which time did not close but widened, because the victory of any one competitor still left its opponents in possession of political existence, and it always remained open to them, even though they had submitted to clientship, subsequently to renew the struggle. The rivalry among the more powerful cantons not only set these at variance, but spread into every dependent clan, into every village, often indeed into every house, for each individual chose his side according to his personal relations. As Hellas exhausted its strength not so much in the struggle of Athens against Sparta as in the internal strife of the Athenian and Lacedaemonian factions in every dependent community, and even in Athens itself, so the rivalry of the Arverni and Haedui with its repetitions on a smaller and smaller scale destroyed the Celtic people.

The defensive capacity of the nation felt the reflex influence of these political and social relations. The cavalry was throughout the predominant arm; alongside of which among the Belgae, and still more in the British islands, the old national war-chariots appear in remarkable efficiency. These equally numerous and efficient bands of combatants on horseback and in chariots were formed from the nobility and its vassals; for the nobles had a genuine knightly delight in dogs and horses, and were at much expense to procure noble horses of foreign breed. It is characteristic of the spirit and the mode of fighting of these nobles that, when the levy was called out, whoever could keep his seat on horseback, even the grey-haired old man, took the field, and that, when on the point of beginning a combat with an enemy of whom they made little account, they swore man by man that they would keep aloof from house and homestead, unless their band should charge at least twice through the enemy's line. Among the hired warriors the freelance spirit prevailed with all its demoralised and stolid indifference towards their own life and that of others. This is apparent from the stories—however anecdotic their colouring—of the Celtic custom of tilting by way

[1] The position which such a federal general occupied with reference to his troops, is shown by the accusation of high treason raised against Vercingetorix (Caesar, *B. G.*, vii. 20).

of sport and now and then fighting for life or death at a banquet, and of the usage (which prevailed among the Celts, and outdid even the Roman gladiatorial games) of selling themselves to be killed for a set sum of money or a number of casks of wine, and voluntarily accepting the fatal blow stretched on their shield before the eyes of the whole multitude.

By the side of these mounted warriors the infantry fell into the background. In the main it essentially resembled the bands of Celts with whom the Romans had fought in Italy and Spain. The large shield was, as then, the principal weapon of defence; among the offensive arms, on the other hand, the long thrusting lance now played the chief part in room of the sword. Where several cantons waged war in league, they naturally encamped and fought clan against clan; there is no trace of their giving to the levy of each canton military organisation and forming smaller and more regular tactical subdivisions. A long train of waggons still dragged the baggage of the Celtic army; instead of an entrenched camp, such as the Romans pitched every night, the poor substitute of a barricade of waggons still sufficed. In the case of certain cantons, such as the Nervii, the efficiency of their infantry is noticed as exceptional; it is remarkable that these had no cavalry, and perhaps were not even a Celtic but an immigrant German tribe. But in general the Celtic infantry of this period appears as an unwarlike and unwieldy levy *en masse*; most of all in the more southern provinces, where along with barbarism valour had also disappeared. The Celt, says Caesar, ventures not to face the German in battle. The Roman general passed a censure still more severe than this judgment on the Celtic infantry, seeing that, after having become acquainted with them in his first campaign, he never again employed them in connection with Roman infantry.

If we survey the whole condition of the Celts as Caesar found it in the Transalpine regions, there is an unmistakable advance in civilisation, as compared with the stage of culture at which the Celts came before us a century and a half previously in the valley of the Po. Then the militia, excellent of its kind, thoroughly preponderated in their armies (i. 325); now the cavalry occupies the first place. Then the Celts dwelt in open villages; now well-constructed walls surrounded their towns. The objects too found in the tombs of Lombardy are, especially as respects articles of copper and glass, far inferior to those of northern Gaul. Perhaps the most trustworthy measure of the increase of culture is the sense of a common relationship in the nation; so little of it comes to light in the Celtic battles fought on the soil of what is now Lombardy, while it strikingly appears in the struggles against Caesar. To all appearance the Celtic nation, when Caesar encountered it, had already reached the maximum of the culture allotted to it, and was even now on the decline. The civilisation of the Transalpine Celts in Caesar's time presents, even for us who are but very imperfectly informed regarding it, several aspects that are estimable, and yet more that are interesting; in some respects it is more akin to the modern than to the Hellenic-Roman culture, with its sailing vessels, its knighthood, its ecclesiastical constitution, above all with its attempts, however imperfect, to build the state not on the city, but on the tribe and in a higher degree on the nation. But just because we here meet the Celtic nation at the culminating point of its development, its lesser degree of moral endowment or, which is the same thing, its lesser capacity of culture, comes more distinctly into view. It was unable to produce from its own resources either a national art or a national state; it attained at the utmost a national theology and a peculiar order of nobility. The original simple valour was no more; the military courage based on higher morality and judicious organisation, which comes in the train of increased civilisation, had only made its appearance in a very stunted form among the knights. Barbarism in the strict sense was doubtless outlived; the times had gone by when in Gaul the fat haunch was assigned to the bravest of the guests, but each of his fellow-guests who thought himself offended thereby was at liberty to challenge the receiver on that score to combat, and when the most faithful retainers of a deceased chief were burnt along with him. But human sacrifices still continued, and the maxim of law, that torture was inadmissible in the case of the free man but allowable in that of the free woman as well as of slaves, throws a far from agreeable light on the position which the female sex held among the Celts even in their period of culture. The Celts had lost the advantages which specially belong to the primitive epoch of nations, but had not acquired those which civilisation brings with it when it intimately and thoroughly pervades a people.

Such was the internal condition of the Celtic nation. It remains that we set forth their external relations with their neighbours, and describe the part which they sustained at this moment in the mighty rivalry and competitive struggle of nations, in which it is everywhere still more difficult to maintain than to acquire. Along the Pyrenees the relations of the peoples had for long been peaceably settled, and the times had long gone by when the Celts there pressed hard on, and to some extent supplanted, the Iberian, that is, the Basque, original population. The valleys of the Pyrenees as well as the mountains of Bearn and Gascony, and also the coast-steppes to the south of the Garonne, were at the time of Caesar in the undisputed possession of the Aquitani, a great number of small tribes of Iberian descent, coming little into contact with each other and still less with the outer world; in this quarter only the mouth of the Garonne with the important port of Burdigala (Bordeaux) was in the hands of a Celtic tribe, the Bituriges-Vivisci.

Of far greater importance was the contact of the Celtic nation with the Roman people, and with the Germans. We need not here repeat—what has been related already—how the Romans in their slow advance had gradually pressed back the Celts, had at last occupied the seaboard between the Alps and the Pyrenees, and had thereby totally cut them off from Italy, Spain, and the Mediterranean Sea—a catastrophe for which the way had already been prepared centuries before by the construction of the Hellenic stronghold at the mouth of the Rhone. But we must here recall the fact that it was not merely the superiority of the Roman arms which pressed hard on the Celts, but quite as much that of Roman culture, which ultimately reaped the benefit of the respectable nucleus of Hellenic civilisation in Gaul. Here too, as so often happens, trade and commerce paved the way for conquest. The Celt after northern fashion was fond of fiery drinks; the fact that like the Scythian he drank the generous wine unmingled and to intoxication, excited the surprise and the disgust of the temperate southern; but the trader has no objection to deal with such customers. Soon the wine trade to Gaul became a mine of gold for the Italian merchant; it was nothing unusual there for a jar of wine to be exchanged for a slave. Other articles of luxury, such as Italian horses, found advantageous sale in Gaul. There were instances even already of Roman burgesses acquiring landed property beyond the Roman frontier, and turning it to profit after the Italian fashion; there is mention, for example, of Roman estates in the canton of the Segusiavi (near Lyons) as early as about $\frac{673}{61}$. Beyond doubt it was a consequence of this that, as already mentioned (p. 207), in free Gaul itself, *e.g.* among the Arverni, the Roman language was not unknown even before the conquest; although this knowledge was probably still restricted to few, and even the leading men of the allied canton of the Haedui had to be conversed with through interpreters. Just as the traffickers in fire-water and the squatters led the way in the occupation of North America, so these Roman wine-traders and landlords paved the way for, and beckoned onward, the future conqueror of Gaul. How vividly this was felt even on the opposite side, is shown by the prohibition which one of the most energetic tribes of Gaul, the canton of the Nervii, like some German peoples, issued against trafficking with the Romans.

Still more violent even than the pressure of the Romans from the Mediterranean was that of the Germans downward from the Baltic and the North Sea—a fresh stock from the great cradle of peoples in the East, which made room for itself by the side of its elder brethren with youthful vigour, although also with youthful rudeness. Though the tribes of this stock dwelling nearest to the Rhine—the Usipetes, Tencteri, Sugambri, Ubii—had begun to be in some degree civilised, and had at least ceased voluntarily to change their abodes, all accounts yet agree that farther inland agriculture was of little importance, and the several tribes had hardly yet attained fixed abodes. It is significant in this respect that their western neighbours at this time hardly knew how to name any one of the peoples of the interior of Germany by its cantonal name; these were only known to them under the general appellations of the Suebi, that is, the wandering people or nomads, and the Marcomanni, that is, the border-warriors [1]—names which were hardly cantonal names in Caesar's time, although they appeared as such to the Romans and subsequently became in various cases names of cantons.

The most violent pressure of this great nation fell upon the Celts. The struggles, in which the Germans probably engaged with the Celts for the possession of the regions to the east of the

[1] Caesar's Suebi were probably the Chatti; but that designation certainly belonged in Caesar's time, and even much later, to every other German stock which could be described as a regularly wandering one. Accordingly if, as is not to be doubted, the "king of the Suebi" in Mela (iii. 1) and Pliny (*H. N.* ii. 67, 170) was Ariovistus, it by no means therefore follows that Ariovistus was a Chattan. The Marcomanni cannot be demonstrated as a distinct people before Marbod; it is very possible that the word up to that point indicates nothing but what it etymologically signifies—the land, or frontier, guard. When Caesar (i. 51) mentions Marcomanni among the peoples fighting in the army of Ariovistus, he may in this instance have misunderstood a merely appellative designation, just as he has decidedly done in the case of the Suebi.

Rhine, are wholly withdrawn from our view. We are only able to perceive, that about the end of the seventh century of Rome all the land as far as the Rhine was already lost to the Celts; that the Boii, who were probably once settled in Bavaria and Bohemia (iii. 163), were homeless wanderers; and that even the Black Forest formerly possessed by the Helvetii (iii. 182), if not taken possession of by the German tribes dwelling in the vicinity, was at least waste debatable border-land, and was in all likelihood even then, what it was afterwards called, the Helvetian desert. The barbarous strategy of the Germans—which secured them from hostile attacks by laying waste the neighbourhood for miles—seems to have been applied here on the greatest scale.

But the Germans had not remained stationary at the Rhine. The march of the Cimbrian and Teutonic host, composed, as respects its flower, of German tribes, which had swept with such force fifty years before over Pannonia, Gaul, Italy, and Spain, seemed to have been nothing but a grand *reconnaissance*. Already different German tribes had formed permanent settlements to the west of the Rhine, especially of its lower course; having intruded as conquerors, these settlers continued to demand hostages and to levy annual tribute from the Gallic inhabitants in their neighbourhood, as if from subjects. Among these German tribes were the Aduatuci, who from a fragment of the Cimbrian horde (iii. 178) had grown into a considerable canton, and a number of other tribes afterwards comprehended under the name of the Tungri on the Maas in the region of Liège; even the Treveri (about Treves) and the Nervii (in Hainault), two of the largest and most powerful peoples of this region, are directly designated by respectable authorities as Germans. The complete credibility of these accounts must certainly remain doubtful, since, as Tacitus remarks in reference to the two peoples last mentioned, it was subsequently, at least in these regions, reckoned an honour to be descended of German blood and not to belong to the little-esteemed Celtic nation; yet the population in the region of the Scheldt, Maas, and Moselle seems certainly to have become, in one way or another, largely mingled with German elements, or at any rate to have come under German influences. The German settlements themselves were perhaps small; they were not unimportant, for amidst the chaotic obscurity, through which we see the stream of peoples on the right bank of the Rhine ebbing and flowing about this period, we can well perceive that larger German hordes were preparing to cross the Rhine in the track of these advanced posts. Threatened on two sides by foreign domination and torn by internal dissension, it was scarcely to be expected that the unhappy Celtic nation would now rally and save itself by its own vigour. Dismemberment, and decay in virtue of dismemberment, had hitherto been its history; how should a nation, which could name no day like those of Marathon and Salamis, of Aricia and the Raudine field—a nation which, even in its time of vigour, had made no attempt to destroy Massilia by a united effort—now when evening had come, defend itself against so formidable foes?

The less the Celts, left to themselves, were a match for the Germans, the more reason had the Romans carefully to watch over the complications in which the two nations might be involved. Although the movements thence arising had not up to the present time directly affected them, they and their most important interests were yet concerned in the issue of those movements. As may readily be conceived, the internal condition of the Celtic nation had become speedily and permanently mixed up with its outward relations. As in Greece the Lacedaemonian party combined with Persia against the Athenians, so the Romans from their first appearance beyond the Alps had found a support against the Arverni, who were then the ruling power among the southern Celts, in their rivals for the hegemony, the Haedui; and with the aid of these new "brothers of the Roman nation" they had not merely reduced to subjection the Allobroges and a great portion of the indirect territory of the Arverni, but had also, in the Gaul that remained free, occasioned by their influence the transference of the hegemony from the Arverni to these Haedui. But while the Greeks were threatened with danger to their nationality only from one side, the Celts found themselves hard pressed simultaneously by two national foes; and it was natural that they should seek from the one protection against the other, and that, if the one Celtic party attached itself to the Romans, their opponents should on the contrary form alliance with the Germans. This course was most natural for the Belgae, who were brought by neighbourhood and manifold intermixture into closer relation to the Germans who had crossed the Rhine, and moreover, with their less-developed culture, probably felt themselves at least as much akin to the Suebian of alien race as to their cultivated Allobrogian or Helvetic countryman. But the southern Celts also, among whom now, as already mentioned, the considerable canton of the Sequani (about Besançon) stood at the head of the party hostile to the Romans, had every reason at this very time to call in the Germans against the Romans who immediately threatened them; the remiss government of the senate and the signs of the revolution preparing in Rome, which had not remained unknown to the Celts, made this very moment seem suitable for ridding themselves of the Roman influence and primarily for humbling the Roman clients, the Haedui. A rupture had taken place between the two cantons respecting the tolls on the Saone, which separated the territory of the Haedui from that of the Sequani, and about the year $\frac{683}{71}$ the German prince Ariovistus with some 15,000 armed men had crossed the Rhine as *condottiere* of the Sequani.

The war was prolonged for some years with varying success; on the whole the results were unfavourable to the Haedui. Their leader Eporedorix at length called out their whole clients, and marched forth with an enormous superiority of force against the Germans; but these obstinately refused battle, and kept themselves under cover of morasses and forests. It was not till the clans, weary of waiting, began to break up and disperse, that the Germans appeared in the open field, and then Ariovistus compelled a battle at Admagetobriga, in which the flower of the cavalry of the Haedui were left on the field. The Haedui, forced by this defeat to conclude peace on the terms which the victor proposed, were obliged to renounce the hegemony, and to consent with their whole adherents to become clients of the Sequani; they had to bind themselves to pay tribute to the Sequani or rather to Ariovistus, and to furnish the children of their principal nobles as hostages; and lastly they had to swear that they would never demand back these hostages nor invoke the intervention of the Romans.

This peace was concluded apparently about $\frac{693}{61}$.[1] Honour and advantage enjoined the Romans to come forward in opposition to it; the noble Haeduan Divitiacus, the head of the Roman party in his clan, and for that reason now banished by his countrymen, went in person to Rome to solicit their intervention. A still more serious warning was the insurrection of the Allobroges in $\frac{693}{61}$ (p. 200)—the neighbours of the Sequani—which was beyond doubt connected with these events. In

[1] The arrival of Ariovistus in Gaul has been placed, according to Caesar, i. 36, in $\frac{683}{71}$, and the battle of Admagetobriga (for such was the name of the place now usually, in accordance with a false inscription, called Magetobriga) according to Caesar i. 35 and Cicero *Ad. Att.* i. 19 in $\frac{693}{61}$.

reality orders were issued to the Gallic governors to assist the Haedui; they talked of sending consuls and consular armies over the Alps; but the senate, to whose decision these affairs primarily fell, at length here also crowned great words with little deeds. The insurrection of the Allobroges was suppressed by arms, but nothing was done for the Haedui; on the contrary, Ariovistus was even enrolled in $\frac{695}{59}$ in the list of kings friendly with the Romans.[1]

The German warlike prince naturally took this as a renunciation by the Romans of the Celtic land which they had not occupied; he accordingly took up his abode there, and began to establish a German principality on Gallic soil. It was his intention that the numerous bands which he had brought with him, and the still more numerous bands that afterwards followed at his call from home—it was reckoned that up to $\frac{696}{58}$ some 120,000 Germans had crossed the Rhine—this whole mighty immigration of the German nation, which poured through the once opened sluices like a stream over the beautiful West, should become settled there and form a basis on which he might build his dominion over Gaul. The extent of the German settlements which he called into existence on the left bank of the Rhine cannot be determined; beyond doubt it was great, and his projects were far greater still. The Celts were treated by him as a wholly subjugated nation, and no distinction was made between the several cantons. Even the Sequani, as whose hired commander-in-chief he had crossed the Rhine, were obliged, as if they were vanquished enemies, to cede to him for his people a third of their territory—probably upper Alsace afterwards inhabited by the Triboci—where Ariovistus permanently settled with his followers; nay, as if this were not enough, a second third was afterwards demanded of them for the Harudes who arrived subsequently. Ariovistus seemed as if he wished to take up in Gaul the part of Philip of Macedonia, and to play the master over the Celts who were friendly to the Germans no less than over those who adhered to the Romans.

The appearance of the energetic German prince in so dangerous proximity, which could not but in itself excite the most serious apprehension in the Romans, appeared still more threatening, inasmuch as it stood by no means alone. The Usipetes and

[1] That we may not deem this course of things incredible, or even impute to it deeper motives than political ignorance and laziness, we shall do well to realise the frivolous tone in which a distinguished senator like Cicero expresses himself in his correspondence respecting these important Transalpine affairs.

Tencteri settled on the right bank of the Rhine, weary of the incessant devastation of their territory by the overbearing Suebian tribes, had, the year before Caesar arrived in Gaul ($\frac{695}{59}$), set out from their previous abodes to seek others at the mouth of the Rhine. They had already taken away from the Menapii there the portion of their territory situated on the right bank, and it might be foreseen that they would make the attempt to establish themselves also on the left. Suebian bands, moreover, assembled between Cologne and Mayence, and threatened to appear as uninvited guests in the opposite Celtic canton of the Treveri. Lastly, the territory of the most easterly clan of the Celts, the warlike and numerous Helvetii, was visited with growing frequency by the Germans, so that the Helvetii, who perhaps even apart from this were suffering from over-population through the reflux of their settlers from the territory which they had lost to the north of the Rhine, and besides were liable to be completely isolated from their kinsmen by the settlement of Ariovistus in the territory of the Sequani, conceived the desperate resolution of voluntarily evacuating the territory hitherto in their possession to the Germans, and acquiring larger and more fertile abodes to the west of the Jura, along with, if possible, the hegemony in the interior of Gaul—a plan which some of their districts had already formed and attempted to execute during the Cimbrian invasion (iii. 171). The Rauraci whose territory (Basle and southern Alsace) was similarly threatened, the remains of the Boii who had already at an earlier period been compelled by the Germans to forsake their homes and were now unsettled wanderers, and other smaller tribes, made common cause with the Helvetii. As early as $\frac{693}{61}$ their flying parties came over the Jura and even as far as the Roman province; their departure itself could not be much longer delayed; inevitably German settlers would then advance into the important region between the lakes of Constance and Geneva forsaken by its defenders. From the sources of the Rhine to the Atlantic Ocean the German tribes were in motion; the whole line of the Rhine was threatened by them; it was a moment like that when the Alamanni and the Franks threw themselves on the falling empire of the Caesars; and even now there seemed on the eve of being carried into effect against the Celts that very movement which was successful five hundred years afterwards against the Romans.

Under these circumstances the new governor Gaius Caesar arrived in the spring of $\frac{696}{58}$ in Narbonese Gaul, which had been added by decree of the senate to his original province embracing Cisalpine Gaul along with Istria and Dalmatia. His office, which was committed to him first for five years (to the end of $\frac{700}{54}$), then in $\frac{699}{55}$ for five more (to the end of $\frac{705}{49}$), gave him the right to nominate ten lieutenants of propraetorian rank, and (at least according to his own interpretation) to fill up his legions, or even to form new ones at his discretion out of the burgess-population—who were especially numerous in Cisalpine Gaul—of the territory under his sway. The army, which he received in the two provinces, consisted, as regards infantry of the line, of four legions trained and inured to war, the seventh, eighth, ninth, and tenth, or at the utmost 24,000 men, to which fell to be added, as usual, the contingents of the subjects. The cavalry and light-armed troops, moreover, were represented by horsemen from Spain, and by Numidian, Cretan, and Balearic archers and slingers. The staff of Caesar—the *élite* of the democracy of the capital—contained, along with not a few useless young men of rank, some able officers, such as Publius Crassus the younger son of the old political ally of Caesar, and Titus Labienus, who followed the chief of the democracy as a faithful adjutant from the Forum to the battle-field. Caesar had not received definite instructions; to one who was discerning and courageous these were implied in the circumstances with which he had to deal. The negligence of the senate had to be retrieved, and first of all the stream of German invasion had to be checked.

Just at this time the Helvetic invasion, which was closely interwoven with the German and had been in preparation for years, began. That they might not make a grant of their abandoned huts to the Germans and might render their own return impossible, the Helvetii had burnt their towns and villages; and their long trains of waggons, laden with women, children, and the best part of their movables, arrived from all sides at the Leman lake near Genava (Geneva), where they and their comrades had fixed their rendezvous for the 28th of March [1] of this year. According to their own reckoning the whole body consisted of 368,000 persons, of whom about a fourth part were able to bear arms. As the mountain chain of the Jura, stretching from the Rhine to the Rhone, almost completely closed in

[1] According to the uncorrected calendar. According to the current rectification, which however here by no means rests on sufficiently trustworthy data, this day corresponds to the 16th of April of the Julian calendar.

the Helvetic country on the west, and its narrow defiles were as ill adapted for the passage of such a caravan as they were well adapted for defence, the leaders had resolved to go round in a southerly direction, and to open up for themselves a way to the west at the point where the Rhone has broken through the mountain-chain between the south-western and highest part of the Jura and the Savoy mountains, near the modern Fort de l'Ecluse. But on the right bank here the rocks and precipices come so close to the river that there remained only a narrow path which could easily be blocked up, and the Sequani, to whom this bank belonged, could with ease intercept the route of the Helvetii. They preferred therefore to pass over, above the point where the Rhone breaks through, to the left Allobrogian bank, with the view of regaining the right bank farther down the stream where the Rhone enters the plain, and then marching on towards the level west of Gaul, where the fertile canton of the Santones (Saintonge, the valley of the Charente) on the Atlantic Ocean was selected by the wanderers for their new abode. This march led, where it touched the left bank of the Rhone, through Roman territory; and Caesar, otherwise not disposed to acquiesce in the establishment of the Helvetii in western Gaul, was firmly resolved not to permit their passage. But of his four legions three were stationed far off at Aquileia; although he called out in haste the militia of the Transalpine province, it seemed scarcely possible with so small a force to hinder the innumerable Celtic host from crossing the Rhone, between its exit from the Leman lake at Geneva and the point of its breaking through the mountains, over a distance of more than fourteen miles. Caesar, however, by negotiations with the Helvetii, who would gladly have effected by peaceable means the crossing of the river and the march through the Allobrogian territory, gained a respite of fifteen days, which was employed in breaking down the bridge over the Rhone at Genava, and barring the southern bank of the Rhone against the enemy by an entrenchment nearly nineteen miles long: it was the first application of the system—afterwards carried out on so immense a scale by the Romans—of guarding the frontier of the empire in a military point of view by a chain of forts connected with each other by ramparts and ditches. The attempts of the Helvetii to gain the other bank at different places in boats or by means of fords were successfully frustrated by the Romans in these lines, and the Helvetii were compelled to desist from the passage of the Rhone.

On the other hand, the party in Gaul hostile to the Romans, which hoped to obtain a powerful reinforcement in the Helvetii, more especially the Haeduan Dumnorix brother of Divitiacus, and at the head of the national party in his canton as the latter was at the head of the Romans, procured for them a passage through the passes of the Jura and the territory of the Sequani. The Romans had no legal title to forbid this; but other and higher interests were at stake for them in the Helvetic expedition than the question of the formal integrity of the Roman territory—interests which could only be defended, if Caesar, instead of confining himself, as all the governors of the senate and even Marius (iii. 179) had done, to the modest task of watching the frontier, should cross what had hitherto been the frontier at the head of a considerable army. Caesar was general not of the senate, but of the state; he showed no hesitation. He had immediately proceeded from Genava in person to Italy, and with characteristic speed brought up the three legions cantoned there as well as two newly formed legions of recruits.

These troops he united with the corps stationed at Genava, and crossed the Rhone with his whole force. His unexpected appearance in the territory of the Haedui naturally at once restored the Roman party there to power, which was not unimportant as regarded supplies. He found the Helvetii employed in crossing the Saone, and moving from the territory of the Sequani into that of the Haedui; those of them that were still on the left bank of the Saone, especially the corps of the Tigorini, were caught and destroyed by the Romans rapidly advancing. The bulk of the expedition, however, had already passed to the right bank of the river; Caesar followed them and effected the passage, which the unwieldy host of the Helvetii had not been able to accomplish in twenty days, in twenty-four hours. The Helvetii, prevented by this passage of the river on the part of the Roman army from continuing their march westward, turned in a northerly direction, doubtless under the supposition that Caesar would not venture to follow them far into the interior of Gaul, and with the intention, if he should desist from following them, of turning again toward their proper destination. For fifteen days the Roman army marched behind that of the enemy at a distance of about four miles, clinging to its rear, and hoping for an advantageous opportunity of assailing the Helvetian host under conditions favourable to victory, and destroying it. But this moment came not: unwieldy as was the march of the Helvetic caravan, the leaders knew how to guard against a surprise, and appeared to be copiously provided with supplies as well as most accurately informed through their spies of every event in the Roman camp. On the other hand the Romans began to suffer from want of necessaries, especially when the Helvetii removed from the Saone and the means of river-transport ceased. The non-arrival of the supplies promised by the Haedui, from which this embarrassment primarily arose, excited the more suspicion, as both armies were still moving about in their territory. Moreover the considerable Roman cavalry, numbering almost 4000 horse, proved utterly untrustworthy—which doubtless admitted of explanation, for they consisted almost wholly of Celtic horsemen, especially of the mounted retainers of the Haedui, under the command of Dumnorix the well-known enemy of the Romans, and Caesar himself had taken them still more as hostages than as soldiers. There was good reason to believe that a defeat which they suffered at the hands of the far weaker Helvetian cavalry was occasioned by themselves, and that the enemy was informed by them of all occurrences in the Roman camp. The position of Caesar grew critical; it was becoming disagreeably evident, how much the Celtic patriot party could effect even with the Haedui in spite of their official alliance with Rome, and of the distinctive interests of this canton inclining it towards the Romans; what was to be the issue, if they ventured deeper and deeper into a country full of excitement and removed daily farther from their means of communication? The armies were just marching past Bibracte (Autun), the capital of the Haedui, at a moderate distance; Caesar resolved to seize this important place by force before he continued his march into the interior; and it is very possible that he intended to desist altogether from farther pursuit and to establish himself in Bibracte. But when he ceased from the pursuit and turned against Bibracte, the Helvetii thought that the Romans were making preparations for flight, and now attacked in their turn.

Caesar desired nothing better. The two armies posted themselves on two parallel chains of hills; the Celts began the engagement, broke the Roman cavalry which advanced into the plain, and ran onward against the Roman legions posted on the slope of the hill, but were there obliged to give way before Caesar's veterans. When the Romans thereupon, following up their advantage, descended in their turn to the plain, the Celts again advanced against them, and a reserved Celtic corps took them at the same time in flank. The reserve of the Roman attacking column was pushed forward against the latter; it forced it away from the main body upon the baggage and the barricade of waggons, where it was destroyed. The bulk of the Helvetic host was at length brought to give way, and compelled to beat a retreat in an easterly direction—the opposite of that towards which their expedition led them. This day had frustrated the scheme of the Helvetii to establish for themselves new settlements on the Atlantic Ocean, and handed them over to the pleasure of the victor; but it had been a hot day also for the conquerors. Caesar, who had reason for not altogether trusting his staff of officers, had at the very outset sent away all the officers' horses, so as to make the necessity of holding their ground thoroughly clear to his troops; in fact the battle, had the Romans lost it, would have probably occasioned the annihilation of the Roman army. The Roman troops were too much exhausted to pursue the conquered with vigour; but in consequence of the proclamation of Caesar that he would treat all who should support the Helvetii as like the Helvetii themselves enemies of the Romans, all support was refused to the beaten army whithersoever it went—in the first instance, in the canton of the Lingones (about Langres)—and, deprived of all supplies and of their baggage and burdened by the mass of camp-followers incapable of fighting, they were under the necessity of submitting to the Roman general.

The lot of the vanquished was a comparatively mild one. The Haedui were directed to concede settlements in their territory to the homeless Boii; and this settlement of the conquered foe in the midst of the most powerful Celtic cantons rendered almost the services of a Roman colony. The survivors of the Helvetii and Rauraci, something more than a third of the men that had marched forth, were naturally sent back to their former territory, to defend, under Roman supremacy, the frontier along the upper Rhine against the Germans. Only the south-western point of the Helvetic canton was taken possession of by the Romans, and there subsequently, on the charming shores of the Leman lake, the old Celtic town Noviodunum (now Nyon) was converted into a Roman frontier-fortress, the "Julian equestrian colony." [1]

Thus the threatening invasion of the Germans on the upper

[1] *Julia Equestris*, where the last surname is to be taken as in other colonies of Caesar the surnames of *sextanorum*, *decimanorum*, etc. It was Celtic or German horsemen of Caesar who, of course with the bestowal of the Roman or, at any rate, Latin franchise, received land allotments there.

Rhine was obviated, and, at the same time, the party hostile to the Romans among the Celts was humbled. On the middle Rhine also, where the Germans had already crossed years ago, and where the power of Ariovistus which vied with that of Rome in Gaul was daily spreading, there was need of similar action, and the occasion for a rupture was easily found. In comparison with the yoke threatened or already imposed on them by Ariovistus, the Roman supremacy probably now appeared to the greater part of the Celts in this quarter the lesser evil; the minority, who retained their hatred of the Romans, had at least to keep silence. A diet of the Celtic tribes of central Gaul, held under Roman influence, requested the Roman general in name of the Celtic nation for aid against the Germans. Caesar consented. At his suggestion the Haedui stopped the payment of the tribute stipulated to be paid to Ariovistus, and demanded back the hostages furnished; and when Ariovistus on account of this breach of treaty attacked the clients of Rome, Caesar took occasion thereby to enter into direct negotiation with him and specially to demand, in addition to the return of the hostages and a promise to keep peace with the Haedui, that Ariovistus should bind himself to allure no more Germans over the Rhine. The German general replied to the Roman in the full consciousness of equal power and equal right, that northern Gaul had become subject to him by right of war as fairly as southern Gaul to the Romans; and that, as he did not hinder the Romans from taking tribute from the Allobroges, so they should not prevent him from taxing his subjects. In later secret overtures it appeared that the prince was well aware of the circumstances of the Romans; he mentioned the invitations which had been addressed to him from Rome to put Caesar out of the way, and offered, if Caesar would leave to him northern Gaul, to assist him in turn to obtain the sovereignty of Italy. As the quarrels of the Celtic nation had opened up an entrance for him into Gaul, he seemed to expect the consolidation of his rule there from the quarrels of the Italian nation. For centuries no such language of power completely on a footing of equality and bluntly and carelessly expressing its independence had been held in presence of the Romans, as was now heard from the king of the German host; he summarily refused to come, when the Roman general suggested that he should appear personally before him according to the usual practice with client-princes.

It was the more necessary not to delay; Caesar immediately set out against Ariovistus. A panic seized his troops, especially his officers, when they were to measure their strength with the flower of the German troops that for fourteen years had not come under shelter of a roof: it seemed as if the deep decay of Roman moral and military discipline would show itself and provoke desertion and mutiny even in Caesar's camp. But the general, while declaring that in case of need he would march with the tenth legion alone against the enemy, knew not merely how to influence these by such an appeal to honour, but also how to bind the other regiments to their eagles by warlike emulation, and to inspire the troops with something of his own energy. Without leaving them time for reflection, he led them onward in rapid marches, and fortunately anticipated Ariovistus in the occupation of Vesontio (Besançon), the capital of the Sequani. A personal conference between the two generals, which took place at the request of Ariovistus, seemed as if solely meant to cover an attempt against the person of Caesar; arms alone could decide between the two oppressors of Gaul. The war came temporarily to a stand. In lower Alsace somewhere in the region of Mühlhausen, five miles from the Rhine,[1] the two armies lay at a little distance from each other, till Ariovistus with his very superior force succeeded in marching past the Roman camp, placing himself in its rear, and cutting off the Romans from their base and their supplies. Caesar attempted to free himself from his painful situation by a battle; but Ariovistus did not accept it. Nothing remained for the Roman general but, in spite of his inferior strength, to imitate the movement of the Germans, and to recover his communications by making two

[1] Göler (*Caesars gall. Krieg*, p. 45, etc.) thinks that he has found the field of battle at Cernay not far from Mühlhausen, which, on the whole, agrees with Napoleon's (*Précis*, p. 35) placing of the battle-field in the district of Belfort. This hypothesis, although not certain, suits the circumstances of the case; for the fact that Caesar required seven days' march for the short space from Besançon to that point, is explained by his own remark (i. 41) that he had taken a circuit of fifty miles to avoid the mountain paths; and the whole description of the pursuit continued as far as the Rhine, and evidently not lasting for several days but ending on the very day of the battle, decides—the authority of tradition being equally balanced—in favour of the view that the battle was fought five, not fifty, miles from the Rhine. The proposal of Rüstow (*Einleitung zu Caesars Comm.* p. 117) to transfer the field of battle to the upper Saar rests on a misunderstanding. The corn expected from the Sequani, Leuci, Lingones was not to come to the Roman army in the course of their march against Ariovistus, but to be delivered at Besançon before their departure, and taken by the troops along with them; as is clearly apparent from the fact that Caesar, while pointing his troops to those supplies, comforts them at the same time with the hope of corn to be brought in on the route. From Besançon Caesar commanded the region of Langres and Epinal, and, as may be well conceived, preferred to levy his requisitions there rather than in the exhausted districts from which he came.

legions march past the enemy and take up a position beyond the camp of the Germans, while four legions remained in the former camp. Ariovistus, when he saw the Romans divided, attempted an assault on their lesser camp; but the Romans repulsed it. Under the impression made by this success, the whole Roman army was led on to the attack; and the Germans also placed themselves in battle array, in a long line, each tribe for itself, the cars of the army with the baggage and women being placed behind them to render flight more difficult. The right wing of the Romans, led by Caesar himself, threw itself rapidly on the enemy, and drove them before it; the right wing of the Germans was in like manner successful. The balance still stood equal; but the tactics of the reserve, which had decided so many other conflicts with barbarians, decided the conflict with the Germans also in favour of the Romans; their third line, which Publius Crassus seasonably sent to render help, restored the battle on the left wing and thereby decided the victory. The pursuit was continued to the Rhine; only a few, including the king, succeeded in escaping to the other bank ($\frac{696}{58}$).

Thus brilliantly the Roman rule announced its advent to the mighty stream, which the Italian soldiers here saw for the first time; by a single fortunate battle the line of the Rhine was won. The fate of the German settlements on the left bank of the Rhine lay in the hands of Caesar; the victor could destroy them, but he did not do so. The neighbouring Celtic cantons—the Sequani, Leuci, Mediomatrici—were neither capable of self-defence nor trustworthy; the transplanted Germans promised to become not merely braver guardians of the frontier but also better subjects of Rome, for their nationality severed them from the Celts, and their own interest in the preservation of their newly-won settlements severed them from their countrymen across the Rhine, so that in their isolated position they could not avoid adhering to the central power. Caesar here as everywhere, preferred conquered foes to doubtful friends; he left the Germans settled by Ariovistus along the left bank of the Rhine—the Triboci about Strassburg, the Nemetes about Spires, the Vangiones about Worms—in possession of their new abodes, and entrusted them with the guarding of the Rhine-frontier against their countrymen.[1]

[1] This seems the simplest hypothesis regarding the origin of these Germanic settlements. That Ariovistus settled those peoples on the middle Rhine is probable, because they fight in his army (*Caes.* i. 51) and do not appear earlier; that Caesar left them in possession of their settlements is probable, because he in presence of Ariovistus declared himself

The Suebi, who threatened the territory of the Treveri on the middle Rhine, on receiving news of the defeat of Ariovistus, again retreated into the interior of Germany; on which occasion they sustained considerable loss by the way at the hands of the adjoining tribes.

The consequences of this one campaign were immense; they were felt for many centuries after. The Rhine had become the boundary of the Roman empire against the Germans. In Gaul, which was no longer able to govern itself, the Romans had hitherto ruled on the south coast, while lately the Germans had attempted to establish themselves farther up. The recent events had decided that Gaul was to succumb not merely in part but wholly to the Roman supremacy, and that the natural boundary presented by the mighty river was also to become the political boundary. The senate in its better times had not rested till the dominion of Rome had reached the natural bounds of Italy—the Alps and the Mediterranean—and its adjacent islands. The enlarged empire also needed a similar military rounding off; but the present government left the matter to accident, and the object of its highest care was, not that the frontiers might be defended, but that they should not need to be defended quite immediately by itself. People felt that now another spirit and another arm had begun to guide the destinies of Rome.

The foundations of the future edifice were laid; but in order to finish the building and completely to secure the recognition of the Roman rule by the Gauls, and that of the Rhine-frontier by the Germans, very much still remained to be done. All central Gaul indeed from the Roman frontier as far up as Chartres and Treves submitted without objection to the new regent; and on the upper and middle Rhine also no attack was for the present to be apprehended from the Germans. But the northern provinces—as well the Aremorican cantons in Brittany and Normandy as the more powerful confederation of the Belgae—were not affected by the blows directed against central Gaul, and found no occasion to submit to the conqueror of Ariovistus. Moreover, as was already remarked, very close relations subsisted between the Belgae and the Germans over the Rhine, and at the mouth of the Rhine also Germanic tribes

ready to tolerate the Germans already settled in Gaul (*Caes.* i. 35, 43), and because we find them afterwards in these abodes. Caesar does not mention the directions given after the battle concerning these Germanic settlements, because he keeps silence on principle regarding all the organic arrangements made by him in Gaul.

were making ready to cross the stream. In consequence of this Caesar set out with his army, now increased to eight legions, in the spring of $\frac{697}{57}$ against the Belgic cantons. Mindful of the brave and successful resistance which fifty years before they had conjointly presented to the Cimbri on the borders of their country (iii. 179), and stimulated by the patriots who had fled to them in numbers from central Gaul, the confederacy of the Belgae sent their whole first levy—300,000 armed men under the leadership of Galba the king of the Suessiones—to their southern frontier to receive Caesar there. A single canton alone, that of the powerful Remi (about Rheims) discerned in this invasion of the foreigners an opportunity to shake off the rule which their neighbours the Suessiones exercised over them, and prepared to take up in the north the part which the Haedui had played in central Gaul. The Roman and the Belgic armies arrived in their territory almost at the same time.

Caesar did not venture to give battle to the brave enemy six times as strong; to the north of the Aisne, not far from the modern Pontavert between Rheims and Laon, he pitched his camp on a plateau rendered almost unassailable on all sides partly by the river and by morasses, partly by fosses and redoubts, and contented himself with thwarting by defensive measures the attempts of the Belgae to cross the Aisne and thereby to cut him off from his communications. When he counted on the likelihood that the coalition would speedily collapse under its own weight, he had reckoned rightly. King Galba was an honest man, held in universal respect; but he was not equal to the management of an army of 300,000 men on hostile soil. No progress was made, and provisions began to fail; discontent and dissension began to insinuate themselves into the camp of the confederates. The Bellovaci in particular, equal to the Suessiones in power, and already dissatisfied that the supreme command of the confederate army had not fallen to them, could no longer be detained after news had arrived that the Haedui as allies of the Romans were making preparations to enter the Bellovacic territory. They determined to break up and go home; though for honour's sake all the cantons at the same time bound themselves to hasten with their united strength to the help of the one first attacked, the miserable dispersion of the confederacy was but miserably palliated by such impracticable stipulations. It was a catastrophe vividly reminding us of that which occurred almost on the same spot in 1792; and, just as with the campaign in Champagne, the defeat was all the more severe that it took place without a battle. The bad leadership of the retreating army allowed the Roman general to pursue it as if it were beaten, and to destroy a portion of the contingents that had remained to the last. But the consequences of the victory were not confined to this. As Caesar advanced into the western cantons of the Belgae, one after another gave themselves up as lost almost without resistance; the powerful Suessiones (about Soissons), as well as their rivals, the Bellovaci (about Beauvais) and the Ambiani (about Amiens). The towns opened their gates when they saw the strange besieging machines, the towers rolling up to their walls; those who would not submit to the foreign masters sought a refuge beyond the sea in Britain.

But in the eastern cantons the national feeling was more energetically roused. The Viromandui (about Arras), the Atrebates (about St. Quentin), the German Aduatuci (about Namur), but above all the Nervii (in Hainault) with their considerable body of clients, little inferior in number to the Suessiones and Bellovaci, far superior to them in valour and vigorous patriotic spirit, concluded a second and closer league, and assembled their forces on the upper Sambre. Celtic spies informed them most accurately of the movements of the Roman army; their own local knowledge, and the high hedges which were formed everywhere in these districts to obstruct the bands of mounted depredators who often visited them, allowed the allies to conceal their own operations for the most part from the view of the Romans. When these arrived on the Sambre not far from Bavay, and the legions were occupied in pitching their camp on the crest of the left bank, while the cavalry and light infantry were exploring the opposite heights, the latter were all at once assailed by the whole mass of the enemy's forces and driven down the hill into the river. In a moment the enemy had crossed this also, and stormed the heights of the left bank with a determination that braved death. Scarcely was there time left for the entrenching legionaries to exchange the mattock for the sword; the soldiers, many without helmets, had to fight just as they stood, without line of battle, without plan, without proper command; for, owing to the suddenness of the attack and the intersection of the ground by tall hedges, the several divisions had wholly lost their communications. Instead of a battle there arose a number of unconnected conflicts. Labienus with the left wing overthrew the Atrebates and pursued them even across the river. The Roman central division forced the Viromandui down the declivity. But the right wing, where the general himself was present, was outflanked by the far more numerous Nervii the more easily, as the central division carried away by its own success had evacuated the ground alongside of it, and even the half-ready camp was occupied by the Nervii; the two legions, each separately rolled together into a dense mass and assailed in front and on both flanks, deprived of most of their officers and their best soldiers, appeared on the point of being broken and cut to pieces. The Roman camp-followers and the allied troops were already fleeing in all directions; of the Celtic cavalry whole divisions, like the contingent of the Treveri, galloped off at full speed, that from the battle-field itself they might announce at home the welcome news of the defeat which had been sustained. Everything was at stake. The general himself seized his shield and fought among the foremost; his example, his call even now inspiring enthusiasm, induced the wavering ranks to rally. They had already in some measure extricated themselves and had at least restored the connection between the two legions of this wing, when help arrived—partly down from the crest of the bank, where in the interval the Roman rearguard with the baggage had appeared, partly from the other bank of the river, where Labienus had meanwhile penetrated to the enemy's camp and taken possession of it, and now, perceiving at length the danger that menaced the right wing, despatched the victorious tenth legion to the aid of his general. The Nervii, separated from their confederates and simultaneously assailed on all sides, now showed, when fortune turned, the same heroic courage as when they believed themselves victors; still over the pile of corpses of their fallen comrades they fought to the last man. According to their own statement, of their six hundred senators only three survived this day.

After this annihilating defeat the Nervii, Atrebates, and Viromandui were obliged doubtless to recognise the Roman supremacy. The Aduatuci, who arrived too late to take part in the fight on the Sambre, attempted still to hold their ground in the strongest of their towns (on the mount Falhize near the Maas not far from Huy), but they too soon submitted. A nocturnal attack on the Roman camp in front of the town, which they ventured after the surrender, miscarried; and the perfidy was avenged by the Romans with fearful severity. The clients of the Aduatuci, consisting of the Eburones between the Maas and Rhine and other small adjoining tribes, were declared independent by the Romans, while the Aduatuci taken prisoners were sold under the hammer *en masse* for the benefit of the Roman treasury. It seemed as if the fate which had befallen the Cimbri still pursued even this last Cimbrian fragment. Caesar contented himself with imposing on the other subject tribes a general disarmament and furnishing of hostages. The Remi became naturally the leading canton in Belgic, like the Haedui in central Gaul; even in the latter several clans at enmity with the Haedui preferred to rank among the clients of the Remi. Only the remote maritime cantons of the Morini (Artois) and the Menapii (Flanders and Brabant), and the country between the Scheldt and the Rhine inhabited in great part by Germans, remained still for the present exempt from Roman invasion and in possession of their hereditary freedom.

The turn of the Aremorican cantons came. In the autumn of $\frac{697}{57}$ Publius Crassus was sent thither with a Roman corps; he induced the Veneti—who as masters of the ports of the modern Morbihan and of a respectable fleet occupied the first place among all the Celtic cantons in navigation and commerce—and generally the coast-districts between the Loire and Seine, to submit to the Romans and give them hostages. But they soon repented. When in the following winter ($\frac{697}{57}$–$\frac{698}{56}$) Roman officers came to these regions to levy requisitions of grain there, they were detained by the Veneti as counter-hostages. The example thus set was quickly followed not only by the Aremorican cantons, but also by the maritime cantons of the Belgae that still remained free; where, as in some cantons of Normandy, the common council refused to join the insurrection, the multitude put them to death and attached itself with redoubled zeal to the national cause. The whole coast from the mouth of the Loire to that of the Rhine rose against Rome; the most resolute patriots from all the Celtic cantons hastened thither to co-operate in the great work of liberation; they already calculated on the rising of the whole Belgic confederacy, on aid from Britain, on the arrival of Germans from beyond the Rhine.

Caesar sent Labienus with all the cavalry to the Rhine, with a view to hold in check the agitation in the Belgic province, and in case of need to prevent the Germans from crossing the river; another of his lieutenants, Quintus Titurius Sabinus, went with three legions to Normandy, where the main body of the insurgents assembled. But the powerful and intelligent Veneti were the true centre of the insurrection; the chief attack by land and sea was directed against them. Caesar's lieutenant,

Decimus Brutus, brought up the fleet formed partly of the ships of the subject Celtic cantons, partly of a number of Roman galleys hastily built on the Loire and manned with rowers from the Narbonese province; Caesar himself advanced with the flower of his infantry into the territory of the Veneti. But these were prepared beforehand, and had with equal skill and resolution availed themselves of the favourable circumstances which the nature of the ground in Brittany and the possession of a considerable naval power presented. The country was much intersected and poorly furnished with grain, the towns were situated for the most part on cliffs and tongues of land, and were accessible from the mainland only by shoals which it was difficult to cross; the provision of supplies and the conducting of sieges were equally difficult for the army attacking by land, while the Celts by means of their vessels could furnish the towns easily with everything needful, and in the event of the worst could accomplish their evacuation. The legions expended their time and strength in the sieges of the Venetian towns, only to see the substantial fruits of victory ultimately carried off in the vessels of the enemy.

Accordingly when the Roman fleet, long detained by storms at the mouth of the Loire, arrived at length on the coast of Brittany, it was left to decide the struggle by a naval battle. The Celts, conscious of their superiority on this element, brought forth their fleet against that of the Romans commanded by Brutus. Not only did it number 220 sail, far more than the Romans had been able to bring up, but their high-built strong sailing-vessels with flat bottoms were also far better adapted for the high-running waves of the Atlantic Ocean than the low, lightly-built oared galleys of the Romans with their sharp keels. Neither the missiles nor the boarding-bridges of the Romans could reach the high deck of the enemy's vessels, and the iron beaks recoiled powerless from the strong oaken planks. But the Roman mariners cut the ropes, by which the yards were fastened to the masts, by means of sickles fastened to long poles; the yards and sails fell down, and, as they did not know how to repair the damage speedily, the ship was thus rendered a wreck just as it is at the present day by the falling of the masts, and the Roman boats easily succeeded by a joint attack in mastering the maimed vessel of the enemy. When the Gauls perceived this manœuvre, they attempted to move from the coast on which they had taken up the combat with the Romans, and to gain the high seas, whither the Roman galleys could not follow them;

but unhappily for them there suddenly set in a dead calm, and the immense fleet, towards the equipment of which the maritime cantons had applied all their energies, was almost wholly destroyed by the Romans. Thus was this naval battle—so far as historical knowledge reaches, the earliest fought on the Atlantic Ocean—just like the engagement at Mylae two hundred years before (ii. 37), notwithstanding the most unfavourable circumstances, decided in favour of the Romans by a lucky invention suggested by necessity. The consequence of the victory achieved by Brutus was the surrender of the Veneti and of all Brittany. More with a view to impress the Celtic nation, after so manifold evidences of clemency towards the vanquished, by an example of fearful severity now against those whose resistance had been obstinate, than with the view of punishing the breach of treaty and the arrest of the Roman officers, Caesar caused the whole common council to be executed and the people of the Venetian canton to the last man to be sold into slavery. By this dreadful fate, as well as by their intelligence and their patriotism, the Veneti have more than any other Celtic clan acquired a title to the sympathy of posterity.

Sabinus meanwhile opposed to the levy of the coast-states assembled on the Channel the same tactics by which Caesar had in the previous year conquered the Belgic general levy on the Aisne; he stood on the defensive till impatience and want invaded the ranks of the enemy, and then managed by deceiving them as to the temper and strength of his troops, and above all by means of their own impatience, to allure them to an imprudent assault upon the Roman camp, in which they were defeated; whereupon the militia dispersed and the country as far as the Seine submitted.

The Morini and Menapii alone persevered in withholding their recognition of the Roman supremacy. To compel them to this, Caesar appeared on their borders; but, rendered wiser by the experiences of their countrymen, they avoided accepting battle on the borders of their land, and retired into the forests which then stretched almost without interruption from the Ardennes towards the German Ocean. The Romans attempted to make a road through the forest with the axe, ranging the felled trees on each side as a barricade against the enemy's attacks; but even Caesar, daring as he was, found it advisable after some days of most laborious marching, especially as it was verging towards winter, to order a retreat, although but a small portion of the Morini had submitted and the more powerful Menapii had not been reached at all. In the following year ($\frac{699}{55}$), while Caesar himself was employed in Britain, the greater part of the army was sent afresh against these tribes; but this expedition also remained in the main unsuccessful. Nevertheless the result of the last campaigns was the almost complete reduction of Gaul under the dominion of the Romans. While central Gaul had submitted to it without resistance, during the campaign of $\frac{697}{57}$ the Belgic, and during that of the following year the maritime, cantons had been compelled by force of arms to acknowledge the Roman rule. The lofty hopes, with which the Celtic patriots had begun the last campaign, had nowhere been fulfilled. Neither Germans nor Britons had come to their aid; and in Belgia the presence of Labienus had sufficed to prevent the renewal of the conflicts of the previous year.

While Caesar was thus forming the Roman domain in the West by force of arms into a compact whole, he did not neglect to open up for the newly-conquered country—which was destined in fact to fill up the wide gap in that domain between Italy and Spain—communications both with the Italian home and with the Spanish provinces. The communication between Gaul and Italy had certainly been materially facilitated by the military road laid out by Pompeius in $\frac{677}{77}$ over Mont Genèvre (p. 26); but since the whole of Gaul had been subdued by the Romans, there was need of a route crossing the ridge of the Alps from the valley of the Po, not in a westerly but in a northerly direction, and furnishing a shorter communication between Italy and central Gaul. The way which leads over the great St. Bernard into the Valais and along the lake of Geneva had long served the merchant for this purpose; to get this road into his power, Caesar as early as the autumn of $\frac{697}{57}$ caused Octodurum (Martigny) to be occupied by Servius Galba, and the inhabitants of the Valais to be reduced to subjection—a result which was, of course, merely postponed, not prevented, by the brave resistance of these mountain-peoples.

To gain communication with Spain, moreover, Publius Crassus was sent in the following year ($\frac{698}{56}$) to Aquitania with instructions to compel the Iberian tribes dwelling there to acknowledge the Roman rule. The task was not without difficulty; the Iberians were united more compactly than the Celts and knew better than these how to learn from their enemies. The tribes beyond the Pyrenees, especially the valiant Cantabri, sent a contingent to their threatened countrymen; with this there came experienced officers trained under the leadership of Sertorius in the Roman fashion, who introduced as far as possible the principles of the Roman art of war, and especially of encampment, among the Aquitanian levy already respectable from its numbers and its valour. But the excellent officer who led the Romans knew how to surmount all difficulties, and after some hardly contested but successful battles he induced the peoples from the Garonne to the vicinity of the Pyrenees to submit to the new master.

One of the objects which Caesar had proposed to himself—the subjugation of Gaul—had been in substance, with exceptions scarcely worth mentioning, attained so far as it could be attained at all by the sword. But the other half of the work undertaken by Caesar was still far from being satisfactorily accomplished, and the Germans had by no means as yet been everywhere compelled to recognise the Rhine as their limit. Even now in the winter of $\frac{698-699}{56-55}$ a fresh crossing of the boundary had taken place on the lower course of the river, whither the Romans had not yet penetrated. The German tribes of the Usipetes and Tencteri whose attempts to cross the Rhine in the territory of the Menapii have been already mentioned (p. 222), had at length, eluding the vigilance of their opponents by a feigned retreat, crossed in the vessels belonging to the Menapii—an enormous host, which is said, including women and children, to have amounted to 430,000 persons. They still lay, apparently, in the region of Nimeguen and Cleves; but it was said that, following the invitations of the Celtic patriot party, they intended to advance into the interior of Gaul; and the rumour was confirmed by the fact that bands of their horsemen already roamed as far as the borders of the Treveri. But when Caesar with his legions arrived opposite to them, the sorely harassed emigrants seemed not desirous of fresh conflicts, but very ready to accept land from the Romans and to till it under their supremacy in peace. While negotiations as to this were going on, a suspicion arose in the mind of the Roman general that the Germans only sought to gain time till the bands of horsemen sent out by them had returned. Whether this suspicion was well founded or not, we cannot tell; but confirmed in it by an attack, which in spite of the *de facto* suspension of arms a troop of the enemy made on his vanguard, and exasperated by the severe loss thereby sustained, Caesar believed himself entitled to disregard every consideration of international law. When on the second morning the princes and elders of the Germans appeared in the Roman camp to apologise for the attack made without their knowledge, they were arrested, and the multitude anticipating no assault and deprived of their leaders were suddenly fallen upon by the Roman army. It was rather a man-hunt than a battle; those that did not fall under the sword of the Romans were drowned in the Rhine; almost none but the divisions detached at the time of the attack escaped the massacre and succeeded in recrossing the Rhine, where the Sugambri gave them an asylum in their territory, apparently on the Lippe. The behaviour of Caesar towards these German immigrants met with severe and merited censure in the senate; but, however little it can be excused, the German encroachments were emphatically checked by the terror which it occasioned. Caesar however found it advisable to take yet a further step and to lead the legions over the Rhine. He was not without connections beyond the river. The Germans at the stage of culture which they had then reached, had as yet no national union; in political disorganisation they—though from other causes—fell nothing short of the Celts. The Ubii (on the Sieg and Lahn), the most civilised among the German tribes, had recently been made subject and tributary by a powerful Suebian canton of the interior, and had as early as $\frac{697}{57}$ through their envoys entreated Caesar to free them like the Gauls from the Suebian rule. It was not Caesar's design seriously to respond to this suggestion, which would have involved him in endless enterprises; but it seemed advisable, with the view of preventing the appearance of the Germanic arms on the south of the Rhine, at least to show the Roman arms beyond it. The protection which the fugitive Usipetes and Tencteri had found among the Sugambri afforded a suitable occasion. In the region, apparently between Coblentz and Andernach, Caesar erected a bridge of piles over the Rhine and led his legions across from the Treverian to the Ubian territory. Some small cantons gave in their submission; but the Sugambri, against whom the expedition was primarily directed, withdrew, on the approach of the Roman army, with those under their protection into the interior. In like manner the powerful Suebian canton which oppressed the Ubii—probably the same which subsequently appears under the name of the Chatti—caused the districts immediately adjoining the Ubian territory to be evacuated and the non-combatant portion of the people to be placed in safety, while all the men capable of arms were directed to assemble at the centre of the canton. The Roman general had neither occasion nor desire to accept this challenge; his object—partly to reconnoitre, partly to produce an impressive effect if possible upon the Germans, or at least on the Celts and his countrymen at home, by an expedition over the Rhine—was substantially attained; after remaining eighteen days on the right bank of the Rhine he again arrived in Gaul and broke down the Rhine bridge behind him ($\frac{699}{55}$).

There remained the insular Celts. From the close connection between them and the Celts of the continent, especially the maritime cantons, it may readily be conceived that they had at least sympathised with the national resistance; and if they did not grant armed assistance to the patriots, they gave at any rate an honourable asylum in their sea-protected isle to every one who was no longer safe in his native land. This certainly involved a danger, if not for the present, at any rate for the future; it seemed judicious—if not to undertake the conquest of the island itself—at any rate to conduct there also defensive operations by offensive means, and to show the islanders by a landing on the coast that the arm of the Romans reached even across the Channel. The first Roman officer who entered Brittany, Publius Crassus, had already ($\frac{697}{57}$) crossed from thence to the "tin-islands" at the south-west point of England (Scilly islands); in the summer of $\frac{699}{55}$ Caesar himself with only two legions crossed the Channel at its narrowest part.[1] He found the coast covered with masses of the enemy's troops and sailed onward with his vessels; but the British war-chariots

[1] The nature of the case as well as Caesar's express statement proves that the passages of Caesar to Britain were made from ports of the coast between Calais and Boulogne to the coast of Kent. A more exact determination of the localities has often been attempted, but without success. All that is recorded is, that on the first voyage the infantry embarked at one port, the cavalry at another distant from the former eight miles in an easterly direction (iv. 22, 23, 28), and that the second voyage was made from that one of those two ports which Caesar had found most convenient, the (otherwise not further mentioned) Portus Itius, distant from the British coast 30 (so according to the MSS. of Caesar v. 2) or 40 miles (=320 stadia, according to Strabo iv. 5, 2, who doubtless drew his account from Caesar). From Caesar's words (iv. 21) that he had chosen "the shortest crossing," we may doubtless reasonably infer that he crossed not the Channel but the Straits of Calais, but by no means that he crossed the latter by the mathematically shortest line. It requires the implicit faith of local topographers to proceed to the determination of the locality with such data in hand—data of which the best in itself becomes almost useless from the variation of the authorities as to the number; but among the many possibilities most may perhaps be said in favour of the view that the Itian port (which Strabo *l.c.* is probably right in identifying with that from which the infantry crossed in the first voyage) is to be sought near Ambleteuse to the west of Cape Gris Nez, and the cavalry-harbour near Ecale (Wissant) to the east of the same promontory, and that the landing took place to the east of Dover near Walmer Castle.

moved on quite as fast by land as the Roman galleys by sea, and it was only with the utmost difficulty that the Roman soldiers succeeded in gaining the shore in the face of the enemy, partly by wading, partly in boats, under the protection of the ships of war, which swept the beach with missiles thrown from machines and by the hand. In the first alarm the nearest villages submitted; but the islanders soon perceived how weak the enemy was, and how he did not venture to move far from the shore. The natives disappeared into the interior and returned only to threaten the camp; and the fleet, which had been left in the open roads, suffered very considerable damage from the first tempest that burst upon it. The Romans had to reckon themselves fortunate in repelling the attacks of the barbarians till they had bestowed the necessary repairs on the ships, and in regaining with these the Gallic coast before the bad season of the year came on.

Caesar himself was so dissatisfied with the results of this expedition undertaken inconsiderately and with inadequate means, that he immediately (in the winter of $\frac{699}{55}$–$\frac{700}{54}$) ordered a transport fleet of 800 sail to be fitted out, and in the spring of $\frac{700}{54}$ sailed a second time for the Kentish coast, on this occasion with five legions and 2000 cavalry. The forces of the Britons, assembled this time also on the shore, retired before the mighty armada without risking a battle; Caesar immediately set out on his march into the interior, and after some successful conflicts crossed the river Stour; but he was obliged to halt very much against his will, because the fleet in the open roads had been again half destroyed by the storms of the Channel. Before they got the ships drawn up upon the beach and the extensive arrangements made for their repair, precious time was lost, which the Celts wisely turned to account.

The brave and cautious prince Cassivellaunus, who ruled in what is now Middlesex and the surrounding district—formerly the terror of the Celts to the south of the Thames, but now the protector and champion of the whole nation—had headed the defence of the land. He soon saw that nothing at all could be done with the Celtic infantry against the Roman, and that the mass of the general levy—which it was difficult to feed and difficult to control—was only a hindrance to the defence; he therefore dismissed it and retained only the war-chariots, of which he collected 4000, and in which the warriors, accustomed to leap down from their chariots and fight on foot, could be employed in a two-fold manner like the burgess-cavalry of the earliest Rome. When Caesar was once more able to continue his march, he met with no interruption to it; but the British war-chariots moved always in front and alongside of the Roman army, induced the evacuation of the country (which from the absence of towns proved no great difficulty), prevented the sending out of detachments, and threatened the communications. The Thames was crossed—apparently between Kingston and Brentford above London—by the Romans; they moved forward, but made no real progress; the general achieved no victory, the soldiers made no booty, and the only actual result, the submission of the Trinobantes in the modern Essex, was less the effect of a dread of the Romans than of the deep hostility between this canton and Cassivellaunus. The danger increased with every onward step, and the attack, which the princes of Kent by the orders of Cassivellaunus made on the Roman naval camp, although it was repulsed, was an urgent warning to turn back. The taking by storm of a great British abatis, in which a multitude of cattle fell into the hands of the Romans, furnished a passable conclusion to the aimless advance and a tolerable pretext for returning. Cassivellaunus was sagacious enough not to drive the dangerous enemy to extremities, and promised, as Caesar desired him, to abstain from disturbing the Trinobantes, to pay tribute, and to furnish hostages; nothing was said of delivering up arms or leaving behind a Roman garrison, and even those promises were, it may be presumed, so far as they concerned the future, neither given nor received in earnest. After receiving the hostages Caesar returned to the naval camp and thence to Gaul. If he, as it would certainly seem, had hoped on this occasion to conquer Britain, the scheme was totally thwarted partly by the wise defensive system of Cassivellaunus, partly and chiefly by the unserviceableness of the Italian oared fleet in the waters of the North Sea; for it is certain that the stipulated tribute was never paid. But the immediate object—of rousing the islanders out of their haughty security and inducing them in their own interest no longer to allow their island to be a rendezvous for continental emigrants—seems certainly to have been attained; at least no complaints are afterwards heard as to the bestowal of such protection.

The work of repelling the Germanic invasion and of subduing the continental Celts was completed. But it is often easier to subdue a free nation than to keep a subdued one in subjection. The rivalry for the hegemony, by which more even than by the attacks of Rome the Celtic nation had been ruined, was in some measure set aside by the conquest, inasmuch as the conqueror took the hegemony to himself. Separate interests were silent; under the common oppression at any rate they felt themselves again as one people; and the infinite value of that which they had with indifference gambled away when they possessed it—freedom and nationality—was now, when it was too late, fully appreciated by their infinite longing. But was it indeed too late? With indignant shame they confessed to themselves that a nation, which numbered at least a million of men capable of arms, a nation of ancient and well-founded warlike renown, had allowed the yoke to be imposed on it by, at the most, 50,000 Romans. The submission of the confederacy of central Gaul without having struck even a blow; the submission of the Belgic confederacy without having done more than merely shown a wish to strike; the heroic fall on the other hand of the Nervii and the Veneti, the sagacious and successful resistance of the Morini, and of the Britons under Cassivellaunus—all that in each case had been done or neglected, had failed or had succeeded—spurred the minds of the patriots to new attempts, if possible, more united and more successful. Especially among the Celtic nobility there prevailed an excitement, which seemed every moment as if it must break out into a general insurrection. Even before the second expedition to Britain in the spring of $\frac{700}{54}$ Caesar had found it necessary to go in person to the Treveri, who, since they had compromised themselves in the Nervian conflict in $\frac{697}{57}$, had no longer appeared at the general diets and had formed more than suspicious connections with the Germans beyond the Rhine. At that time Caesar had contented himself with carrying the men of most note among the patriot party, particularly Indutiomarus, along with him to Britain in the ranks of the Treverian cavalry-contingent; he did his utmost to overlook the conspiracy, that he might not by strict measures ripen it into insurrection. But when the Haeduan Dumnorix, who likewise was present in the army destined for Britain, nominally as a cavalry officer, but really as a hostage, peremptorily refused to embark and rode home instead, Caesar could not do otherwise than have him pursued as a deserter; he was accordingly overtaken by the division sent after him and, when he stood on his defence, was cut down ($\frac{700}{54}$). That the most illustrious knight of the most powerful and the least dependent of the Celtic cantons should have been put to death by the Romans, was a thunder-clap for the whole Celtic nobility; every one who was conscious of similar sentiments—and they formed the great majority—saw in that catastrophe the picture of what was in store for himself.

If patriotism and despair had induced the heads of the Celtic nobility to conspire, fear and self-defence now drove the conspirators to strike. In the winter of $\frac{700}{54}-\frac{701}{53}$, with the exception of a legion stationed in Brittany and a second in the very unsettled canton of the Carnutes (near Chartres), the whole Roman army numbering six legions was encamped in the Belgic territory. The scantiness of the supplies of grain had induced Caesar to station his troops farther apart than he was otherwise wont to do—in six different camps constructed in the cantons of the Bellovaci, Ambiani, Morini, Nervii, Remi, and Eburones. The fixed camp placed farthest towards the east in the territory of the Eburones, probably not far from the later Aduatuca (the modern Tongern), the strongest of all, consisting of a legion under one of the most distinguished of Caesar's leaders of division, Quintus Titurius Sabinus, besides different detachments led by the brave Lucius Aurunculeius Cotta[1] and amounting together to the strength of half a legion, found itself all of a sudden surrounded by the general levy of the Eburones under the kings Ambiorix and Catuvolcus. The attack came so unexpectedly, that the very men absent from the camp could not be recalled and were cut off by the enemy; otherwise the immediate danger was not great, as there was no lack of provisions, and the assault, which the Eburones attempted, recoiled powerless from the Roman intrenchments. But king Ambiorix informed the Roman commander that all the Roman camps in Gaul were similarly assailed on the same day, and that the Romans would undoubtedly be lost if the several corps did not quickly set out and effect a junction; that Sabinus had the more reason to make haste, as the Germans too from beyond the Rhine were already advancing against him; that he himself out of friendship for the Romans would promise them a free

[1] That Cotta, although not lieutenant-general of Sabinus, but like him legate, was yet the younger and less noted general and was probably directed in the event of a difference to yield, may be inferred both from the earlier services of Sabinus and from the fact that, where the two are mentioned together (iv. 22, 38; v. 24, 26, 52; vi. 32; otherwise in vi. 37) Sabinus regularly takes precedence, as also from the narrative of the catastrophe itself. Besides we cannot possibly suppose that Caesar should have placed over a camp two officers with equal authority, and have made no arrangement at all for the case of a difference of opinion. The five cohorts are not counted as part of a legion (comp. vi. 32, 33) any more than the twelve cohorts at the Rhine bridge (vi. 29, comp. 32, 33), and appear to have consisted of detachments of other portions of the army, which had been assigned to reinforce this camp situated nearest to the Germans.

retreat as far as the nearest Roman camp, only two days' march distant. Some things in these statements seemed no fiction; that the little canton of the Eburones specially favoured by the Romans (p. 234) should have undertaken the attack of its own accord was in reality incredible, and, owing to the difficulty of effecting a communication with the other far distant camps, the danger of being attacked by the whole mass of the insurgents and destroyed in detail was by no means to be esteemed slight; nevertheless it could not admit of the smallest doubt that both honour and prudence required them to reject the capitulation offered by the enemy and to maintain the post entrusted to them. Yet, although in the council of war numerous voices and especially the weighty voice of Lucius Aurunculeius Cotta supported this view, the commandant determined to accept the proposal of Ambiorix. The Roman troops accordingly marched off next morning; but when they had arrived at a narrow valley about two miles from the camp they found themselves surrounded by the Eburones and every outlet closed. They attempted to open a way for themselves by force of arms; but the Eburones would not enter into any close combat, and contented themselves with discharging their missiles from their unassailable positions into the dense mass of the Romans. Bewildered, as if seeking deliverance from treachery at the hands of the traitor, Sabinus requested a conference with Ambiorix; it was granted, and he and the officers accompanying him were first disarmed and then slain. After the fall of the commander the Eburones threw themselves from all sides at once on the exhausted and despairing Romans, and broke their ranks; most of them, including Cotta who had already been wounded, met their death in this attack; a small portion, who had succeeded in regaining the abandoned camp, flung themselves on their own swords during the following night. The whole corps was annihilated.

This success, such as the insurgents themselves had hardly ventured to expect, increased the excitement among the Celtic patriots so greatly that the Romans were no longer sure of a single district with the exception of the Haedui and Remi, and the insurrection broke out at the most diverse points. First of all the Eburones followed up their victory. Reinforced by the levy of the Aduatuci, who gladly embraced the opportunity of requiting the injury done to them by Caesar, and of the powerful and still unsubdued Menapii, they appeared in the territory of the Nervii, who immediately joined them, and the whole host thus swelled to 60,000 came before the Roman camp formed in the Nervian canton. Quintus Cicero, who commanded there, had with his weak corps a difficult position, especially as the besiegers, learning from their foes, constructed ramparts and trenches, *testudines* and movable towers after the Roman fashion, and showered fire-balls and burning spears over the straw-covered huts of the camp. The only hope of the besieged rested on Caesar, who lay not so very far off with three legions in his winter encampment in the region of Amiens; but—a significant proof of the feeling that prevailed in Gaul—for a considerable time not the slightest indication reached the general either of the disaster of Sabinus or of the perilous situation of Cicero.

At length a Celtic horseman from Cicero's camp succeeded in stealing through the enemy to Caesar. On receiving the startling news Caesar immediately set out, although only with two weak legions, together numbering about 7000, and 400 horsemen; nevertheless the announcement that Caesar was advancing sufficed to induce the insurgents to raise the siege. It was time; not one tenth of the men in Cicero's camp remained unwounded. Caesar, against whom the insurgent army had turned, deceived the enemy, in the way which he had already on several occasions successfully applied, as to his strength; under the most unfavourable circumstances they ventured an assault upon the Roman camp and suffered a defeat. It is singular, but characteristic of the Celtic nation, that in consequence of this one lost battle, or perhaps rather in consequence of Caesar's appearance in person on the scene of conflict, the insurrection, which had commenced so victoriously and extended so widely, suddenly and pitiably broke off the war. The Nervii, Menapii, Aduatuci, Eburones, returned to their homes. The forces of the maritime cantons, who had made preparations for assailing the legion in Brittany, did the same. The Treveri, through whose leader Indutiomarus the Eburones, the clients of the powerful neighbouring canton, had been chiefly induced to that so successful attack, had taken arms on the news of the disaster of Aduatuca and advanced into the territory of the Remi with the view of attacking the legion cantoned there under the command of Labienus; they too desisted for the present from continuing the struggle. Caesar not unwillingly postponed farther measures against the revolted districts till the spring, in order not to expose his troops which had suffered much to the whole severity of the Gallic winter, and with the view of only reappearing in the field when the fifteen cohorts destroyed should have been replaced in an imposing manner by the levy of thirty new cohorts which he had ordered. The insurrection meanwhile pursued its course, although there was for the moment a suspension of arms. Its chief seats in central Gaul were, partly the districts of the Carnutes and the neighbouring Senones (about Sens), the latter of whom drove the king appointed by Caesar out of their country; partly the region of the Treveri, who invited the whole Celtic emigrants and the Germans beyond the Rhine to take part in the impending national war, and called out their whole force, with a view to advance in the spring a second time into the territory of the Remi, to capture the corps of Labienus, and to seek a communication with the insurgents on the Seine and Loire. The deputies of these three cantons remained absent from the diet convoked by Caesar in central Gaul, and thereby declared war just as openly as a part of the Belgic cantons had done by the attacks on the camps of Sabinus and Cicero.

The winter was drawing to a close when Caesar set out with his army, which meanwhile had been considerably reinforced, against the insurgents. The attempts of the Treveri to concentrate the revolt had not succeeded; the agitated districts were kept in check by the marching in of Roman troops, and those in open rebellion were attacked in detail. First the Nervii were routed by Caesar in person. The Senones and Carnutes met the same fate. The Menapii, the only canton which had never submitted to the Romans, were compelled by a grand attack simultaneously directed against them from three sides to renounce their long-preserved freedom. Labienus meanwhile was preparing the same fate for the Treveri. Their first attack had been paralysed, partly by the refusal of the adjoining German tribes to furnish them with mercenaries, partly by the fact that Indutiomarus, the soul of the whole movement, had fallen in a skirmish with the cavalry of Labienus. But they did not on this account abandon their projects. With their whole force they appeared in front of Labienus and waited for the German bands that were to follow, for their recruiting agents found a better reception than they had met with from the dwellers on the Rhine, among the warlike tribes of the interior of Germany, especially, as it would appear, among the Chatti. But when Labienus seemed as if he wished to avoid these and to march off in all haste, the Treveri attacked the

Romans even before the Germans arrived and in a most unfavourable spot, and were completely defeated. Nothing remained for the Germans who came up too late but to return, nothing for the Treverian canton but to submit; its government reverted to the head of the Roman party Cingetorix, the son-in-law of Indutiomarus. After these expeditions of Caesar against the Menapii and of Labienus against the Treveri the whole Roman army was again united in the territory of the latter. With the view of rendering the Germans disinclined to come back, Caesar once more crossed the Rhine, in order if possible to strike a vigorous blow against the troublesome neighbours; but, as the Chatti, faithful to their tried tactics, assembled not on their western boundary, but far in the interior, apparently at the Harz mountains, for the defence of the land, he immediately turned back and contented himself with leaving behind a garrison at the passage of the Rhine.

Accounts had thus been settled with all the tribes that took part in the rising; the Eburones alone were passed over but not forgotten. Since Caesar had met with the disaster of Aduatuca, he had worn mourning and had sworn that he would only lay it aside when he should have avenged his soldiers, who had not fallen in honourable war, but had been treacherously murdered. Helpless and passive the Eburones sat in their huts and looked on, as the neighbouring cantons one after another submitted to the Romans, till the Roman cavalry from the Treverian territory advanced through the Ardennes into their land. So little were they prepared for the attack, that the cavalry had almost seized the king Ambiorix in his house; with great difficulty, while his attendants sacrificed themselves on his behalf, he escaped into the neighbouring thicket. Ten Roman legions soon followed the cavalry. At the same time an invitation was issued to the surrounding tribes to hunt the outlawed Eburones and pillage their land in concert with the Roman soldiers; not a few complied with the call, including even an audacious band of Sugambrian horsemen from the other side of the Rhine, who for that matter treated the Romans no better than the Eburones, and had almost by a daring *coup de main* surprised the Roman camp at Aduatuca. The fate of the Eburones was dreadful. However they might hide themselves in forests and morasses, there were more hunters than game. Many put themselves to death like the grey-haired prince Catuvolcus; only a few saved life and liberty, but among these few was the man whom the Romans sought above all to seize, the prince Ambiorix; with but four horsemen he escaped over the Rhine. This execution against the canton which had transgressed above all the rest was followed in the other districts by processes of high treason against individuals. The season for clemency was past. At the bidding of the Roman proconsul the eminent Carnutic knight Acco was beheaded by Roman lictors ($\frac{701}{53}$) and the rule of the *fasces* was thus formally inaugurated. Opposition was silent; tranquillity everywhere prevailed. Caesar went as he was wont towards the end of the year ($\frac{701}{53}$) over the Alps, that through the winter he might observe more closely the daily-increasing complications in the capital.

The sagacious calculator had on this occasion miscalculated. The fire was smothered, but not extinguished. The stroke, under which the head of Acco fell, was felt by the whole Celtic nobility. At this very moment the position of affairs presented better prospects than ever. The insurrection of the last winter had evidently failed only through Caesar himself appearing on the scene of action; now he was at a distance, detained on the Po by the imminence of civil war, and the Gallic army, which was collected on the upper Seine, was far separated from its dreaded leader. If a general insurrection now broke out in central Gaul, the Roman army might be surrounded, and the almost undefended old Roman province be overrun, before Caesar reappeared beyond the Alps, even if the Italian complications did not altogether prevent him from further concerning himself about Gaul.

Conspirators from all the cantons of central Gaul assembled; the Carnutes, as most directly affected by the execution of Acco, offered to take the lead. On a set day in the winter of $\frac{701}{53}-\frac{702}{52}$ the Carnutian knights Gutruatus and Conconnetodumnus gave at Cenabum (Orleans) the signal for the rising, and put to death all the Romans who happened to be there. The most vehement agitation seized the length and breadth of Gaul; the patriots everywhere bestirred themselves. But nothing stirred the nation so deeply as the insurrection of the Arverni. The government of this community, which had formerly under its kings been the first in southern Gaul, and had still after the fall of its princedom occasioned by the unfortunate wars against Rome (iii. 158) continued to be one of the wealthiest, most civilised, and most powerful in all Gaul, had hitherto inviolably adhered to Rome. Even now the patriot party in the governing common council was in the minority; an attempt to induce it to join the insurrection was in vain. The attacks of the patriots were therefore directed against the common council and the existing constitution itself; and the more so, that the change of constitution which among the Arvernians had substituted the common council for the prince (p. 208) had taken place after the victories of the Romans and probably under their influence.

The leader of the Arvernian patriots Vercingetorix, one of those nobles whom we meet with among the Celts, of almost regal authority in and beyond his canton, and a stately, brave, sagacious man to boot, left the capital and summoned the country people, who were as hostile to the ruling oligarchy as to the Romans, at once to re-establish the Arvernian monarchy and to go to war with Rome. The multitude quickly joined him; the restoration of the throne of Luerius and Betuitus was at the same time the declaration of a national war against Rome. The centre of unity, from the want of which all previous attempts of the nation to shake off the foreign yoke had failed, was now found in the new self-nominated king of the Arvernians. Vercingetorix became for the Celts of the continent what Cassivellaunus was for the insular Celts; the feeling strongly pervaded the masses that he, if any one, was the man to save the nation.

The west from the mouth of the Garonne to that of the Seine was rapidly infected by the insurrection, and Vercingetorix was recognised by all the cantons there as commander-in-chief; where the common council made any difficulty, the multitude compelled it to join the movement; only a few cantons, such as that of the Bituriges, required compulsion to join it, and these perhaps only for appearance' sake. The insurrection found a less favourable soil in the regions to the east of the upper Loire. Everything here depended on the Haedui; and these wavered. The patriotic party was very strong in this canton; but the old antagonism to the hegemony of the Arvernians counterbalanced their influence—to the most serious detriment of the insurrection, as the accession of the eastern cantons, particularly of the Sequani and Helvetii, was conditional on the accession of the Haedui, and generally in this part of Gaul the decision rested with them. While the insurgents were thus labouring partly to induce the cantons that still hesitated, especially the Haedui, to join them, partly to get possession of Narbo—one of their leaders, the daring Lucterius, had already appeared on the Tarn within the limits of the old province—the Roman commander-in-chief suddenly presented himself in the depth of winter, unexpected alike by friend and foe, on this side of the Alps. He quickly made the necessary preparations to cover the old province, and not only so, but sent also a corps over the snow-covered Cevennes into the Arvernian territory; but he could not remain here, where the accession of the Haedui to the Gallic alliance might any moment cut him off from his army encamped about Sens and Langres. With all secresy he went to Vienna, and thence, attended by only a few horsemen, through the territory of the Haedui to his troops. The hopes, which had induced the conspirators to declare themselves, vanished; peace continued in Italy, and Caesar was once more at the head of his army.

But what were they to do? It was folly under such circumstances to let the matter come to the decision of arms; for these had already decided irrevocably. They might as well attempt to shake the Alps by throwing stones at them as to shake the legions by means of the Celtic bands, whether these might be congregated in huge masses or sacrificed in detail canton after canton. Vercingetorix despaired of defeating the Romans. He adopted a system of warfare similar to that by which Cassivellaunus had saved the insular Celts. The Roman infantry was not to be vanquished; but Caesar's cavalry consisted almost exclusively of the contingent of the Celtic nobility, and was practically dissolved by the general revolt. It was possible for the insurrection, which was in fact essentially composed of the Celtic nobility, to develop such a superiority in this arm, that it could lay waste the land far and wide, burn down towns and villages, destroy the magazines, and endanger the supplies and the communications of the enemy, without his being able seriously to hinder it. Vercingetorix accordingly directed all his efforts to the increase of his cavalry, and of the infantry-archers who were according to the mode of fighting of that time regularly associated with it. The immense and self-obstructing masses of the militia of the line he did not indeed send home, but he did not allow them to face the enemy, and attempted to impart to them gradually some capacity of intrenching, marching, and manœuvring, and some perception that the soldier is not destined merely for single combat. Learning from the enemy, he adopted in particular the Roman system of encampment on which depended the whole secret of the tactical superiority of the Romans; for in consequence of it every Roman corps conbined all the advantages of the garrison of a fortress with all the advantages of an offensive army.[1] It is true that a system completely adapted to Britain which had few towns and to its rude, resolute, and on the whole united inhabitants was not absolutely transferable to the rich regions on the Loire and their indolent inhabitants on the eve of utter political dissolution. Vercingetorix at least accomplished this much, that they did not attempt as hitherto to hold every town with the result of holding none; they agreed to destroy the places not capable of defence before attack reached them, but to defend with all their might the strong fortresses. At the same time the Arvernian king did what he could to bind to the cause of their country the cowardly and backward by stern severity, the hesitating by entreaties and representations, the covetous by gold, the decided opponents by force, and to compel or allure the rabble high or low to some manifestation of patriotism.

Even before the winter was at an end, he threw himself on the Boii settled by Caesar in the territory of the Haedui, with the view of annihilating these, almost the sole trustworthy allies of Rome, before Caesar came up. The news of this attack induced Caesar, leaving behind the baggage and two legions in the winter quarters of Agedincum (Sens), to march immediately and earlier than he would doubtless otherwise have done against the insurgents. He remedied the sorely-felt want of cavalry and light infantry in some measure by gradually bringing up German mercenaries, who instead of using their own small and weak ponies were furnished with Italian and Spanish horses partly bought, partly procured by requisition from the officers. Caesar, after having caused Cenabum, the capital of the Carnutes, which had given the signal for the revolt, to be pillaged and laid in ashes, moved over the Loire into the country of the Bituriges. He thereby induced Vercingetorix to abandon the siege of the town of the Boii, and to resort likewise to the Bituriges. Here the new mode of warfare was first to be tried. By order of Vercingetorix more than twenty townships of the Bituriges perished in the flames on one day; the general decreed a similar self-devastation as to the neighbouring cantons, so far as they could be reached by the Roman foraging parties.

According to his intention, Avaricum (Bourges), the rich

[1] This, it is true, was only possible so long as offensive weapons chiefly aimed at cutting and stabbing. In the modern mode of warfare, as Napoleon has excellently explained, this system has become inapplicable, because with our offensive weapons operating from a distance the deployed position is more advantageous than the concentrated. In Caesar's time the reverse was the case.

and strong capital of the Bituriges, was to meet the same fate; but the majority of the war-council yielded to the suppliant entreaties of the Biturigian authorities, and resolved rather to defend that city with all their energy. Thus the war was concentrated in the first instance around Avaricum. Vercingetorix placed his infantry amidst the morasses adjoining the town in a position so unapproachable, that even without being covered by the cavalry they needed not to fear the attack of the legions. The Celtic cavalry covered all the roads and obstructed the communication. The town was strongly garrisoned, and the connection between it and the army before the walls was kept open. Caesar's position was very awkward. The attempt to induce the Celtic infantry to fight was unsuccessful; it stirred not from its unassailable lines. Bravely as his soldiers in front of the town trenched and fought, the besieged vied with them in ingenuity and courage, and they had almost succeeded in setting fire to the siege apparatus of their opponents. The task withal of supplying an army of nearly 60,000 men with provisions in a country devastated far and wide and scoured by far superior bodies of cavalry became daily more difficult. The slender stores of the Boii were soon used up; the supply promised by the Haedui failed to appear; the corn was already consumed, and the soldier was placed exclusively on flesh-rations. But the moment was approaching when the town, with whatever contempt of death the garrison fought, could be held no longer. Still it was not impossible to withdraw the troops secretly by night and to destroy the town, before the enemy occupied it. Vercingetorix made arrangements for this purpose, but the cry of distress raised at the moment of evacuation by the women and children left behind attracted the attention of the Romans; the departure miscarried. On the following gloomy and rainy day the Romans scaled the walls, and, exasperated by the obstinate defence, spared neither age nor sex in the conquered town. The ample stores, which the Celts had accumulated in it, were welcome to the starved soldiers of Caesar. With the capture of Avaricum (spring of $\frac{702}{52}$) a first success had been achieved over the insurrection, and according to former experience Caesar might well expect that it would now dissolve, and that it would only be requisite to deal with the cantons individually. After he had therefore shown himself with his whole army in the canton of the Haedui and had by this imposing demonstration compelled the patriot party agitating there to keep themselves quiet at least for the moment, he divided his army and sent Labienus back to Agedincum, that in combination with the troops left there he might at the head of four legions suppress the movement in the territory of the Carnutes and Senones, who on this occasion once more took the lead; while he himself with the six remaining legions turned to the south and prepared to carry the war into the Arvernian mountains, the proper territory of Vercingetorix.

Labienus moved from Agedincum up the left bank of the Seine with a view to possess himself of Lutetia (Paris), the town of the Parisii situated on an island in the Seine, and from this well secured position in the heart of the insurgent country to reduce it again to subjection. But behind Melodunum (Melun) he found his route barred by the whole army of the insurgents, which had here taken up a position between unassailable morasses under the leadership of the aged Camulogenus. Labienus retreated a certain distance, crossed the Seine at Melodunum, and moved up its right bank unhindered towards Lutetia; Camulogenus caused this town to be burnt and the bridges leading to the left bank to be broken down, and took up a position over against Labienus, in which the latter could neither bring him to battle nor effect a passage under the eyes of the hostile army.

The Roman main army in its turn advanced along the Allier down into the canton of the Arverni. Vercingetorix attempted to prevent it from crossing to the left bank of the Allier, but Caesar overreached him and after some days stood before the Arvernian capital Gergovia.[1] Vercingetorix however, doubtless even while he was confronting Caesar on the Allier, had caused sufficient stores to be collected in Gergovia and a fixed camp provided with strong stone ramparts to be constructed for his troops in front of the walls of the town, which was situated on the summit of a pretty steep hill; and, as he had a sufficient start, he arrived before Caesar at Gergovia and awaited the attack in the fortified camp under the wall of the fortress. Caesar

[1] This place has been sought on a rising ground which is still named Gergoie, a league to the south of the Arvernian capital Nemetum, the modern Clermont; and both the remains of rude fortress-walls brought to light in excavations there, and the tradition of the name which is traced in documents up to the tenth century, leave no room for doubt as to the correctness of this determination of the locality. Moreover it accords, as with the other statements of Caesar, so especially with the fact that he pretty clearly indicates Gergovia as the chief place of the Arverni (vii. 4). We shall have accordingly to assume, that the Arvernians after their defeat were compelled to transfer their settlement from Gergovia to the neighbouring less strong Nemetum.

with his comparatively weak army could neither regularly besiege the place nor even sufficiently blockade it; he pitched his camp below the rising ground occupied by Vercingetorix, and was compelled to preserve an attitude as inactive as his opponent. It was almost a victory for the insurgents that Caesar's career of advance from triumph to triumph had been suddenly checked on the Seine and on the Allier. In fact the consequences of this check for Caesar were almost equivalent to those of a defeat.

The Haedui, who had hitherto continued vacillating, now made preparations in earnest to join the patriotic party; the body of men, whom Caesar had ordered to Gergovia, had on the march been induced by its officers to declare for the insurgents; at the same time they had begun in the canton itself to plunder and kill the Romans settled there. Caesar, who had gone with two-thirds of the blockading army to meet that corps of the Haedui which was being brought up to Gergovia, had by his sudden appearance recalled it to nominal obedience; but it was more than ever a hollow and fragile relation, the continuance of which had been almost too dearly purchased by the great peril of the two legions left behind in front of Gergovia. For Vercingetorix, rapidly and resolutely availing himself of Caesar's departure, had during his absence made an attack on them, which had well nigh ended in their being overpowered, and the Roman camp being taken by storm. Caesar's unrivalled celerity alone averted a second catastrophe like that of Aduatuca. Though the Haedui made once more fair promises, it might be foreseen that, if the blockade should still be prolonged without result, they would openly range themselves on the side of the insurgents and would thereby compel Caesar to raise it; for their accession would interrupt the communication between him and Labienus, and expose the latter especially in his isolation to the greatest peril. Caesar was resolved not to let matters come to this pass, but, however painful and even dangerous it was to retire from Gergovia without having accomplished his object, nevertheless, if it must be done, rather to set out immediately and by marching into the canton of the Haedui to prevent at any cost their formal desertion.

Before entering however on this retreat, which was far from agreeable to his quick and sanguine temperament, he made yet a last attempt to free himself from his painful perplexity by a brilliant success. While the bulk of the garrison of Gergovia was occupied in entrenching the side on which the assault was expected, the Roman general watched his opportunity to surprise another access less conveniently situated but at the moment left bare. In reality the Roman storming columns scaled the camp-wall, and occupied the nearest quarters of the camp; but the whole garrison was already alarmed, and owing to the small distances Caesar found it not advisable to risk the second assault on the city-wall. He gave the signal for retreat; but the foremost legions, carried away by the impetuosity of victory, heard not or did not wish to hear, and pushed forward without halting, up to the city-wall, some even into the city. But masses more and more dense threw themselves in front of the intruders; the foremost fell, the columns stopped; in vain centurions and legionaries fought with the most devoted and heroic courage; the assailants were chased with very considerable loss out of the town and down the hill, where the troops stationed by Caesar in the plain received them and prevented greater mischief. The expected capture of Gergovia had been converted into a defeat, and the considerable loss in killed and wounded—there were counted 700 soldiers that had fallen, including 46 centurions—was the least part of the misfortune.

The imposing position of Caesar in Gaul depended essentially on the halo of victory that surrounded him; and this began to grow pale. The conflicts around Avaricum, Caesar's vain attempts to compel the enemy to fight, the resolute defence of the city and its almost accidental capture by storm bore a stamp different from that of the earlier Celtic wars, and had strengthened rather than impaired the confidence of the Celts in themselves and their leader. Moreover, the new system of warfare—the making head against the enemy in entrenched camps under the protection of fortresses—had completely approved itself at Lutetia as well as at Gergovia. Lastly, this defeat, the first which Caesar in person had suffered from the Celts, crowned their success, and it accordingly gave as it were the signal for a second outbreak of the insurrection. The Haedui now broke formally with Caesar and entered into union with Vercingetorix. Their contingent, which was still with Caesar's army, not only deserted from it, but also took occasion to carry off the depôts of the army of Caesar at Noviodunum on the Loire, whereby the chests and magazines, a number of fresh horses, and all the hostages furnished to Caesar, fell into the hands of the insurgents. It was of at least equal importance, that on this news the Belgae, who had hitherto kept aloof from the whole movement, began to bestir themselves. The powerful canton of the Bellovaci rose with the view of attacking in the rear the corps of Labienus, while it confronted at Lutetia the levy of the surrounding cantons of central Gaul. Everywhere else too men were taking to arms; the strength of patriotic enthusiasm carried along with it even the most decided and most favoured partisans of Rome, such as Commius king of the Atrebates, who on account of his faithful services had received from the Romans important privileges for his community and the hegemony over the Morini. The threads of the insurrection ramified even into the old Roman province: they cherished the hope, perhaps not without ground, of inducing the Allobroges themselves to take arms against the Romans. With the single exception of the Remi and of the districts—dependent immediately on the Remi—of the Suessiones, Leuci, and Lingones, whose peculiar isolation was not affected even amidst this general enthusiasm, the whole Celtic nation from the Pyrenees to the Rhine was now in reality, for the first and for the last time, in arms for its freedom and nationality; whereas, singularly enough, the whole German communities, who in the former struggles had held the foremost rank, kept aloof. In fact, the Treveri, and as it would seem the Menapii also, were prevented by their feuds with the Germans from taking an active part in the national war.

It was a grave and momentous crisis, when after the retreat from Gergovia and the loss of Noviodunum a council of war was held in Caesar's head-quarters regarding the measures now to be adopted. Various voices expressed themselves in favour of a retreat over the Cevennes into the old Roman province, which now lay open on all sides to the insurrection and certainly was in urgent need of the legions that had been sent from Rome primarily for its protection. But Caesar rejected this timid strategy suggested not by the position of affairs, but by government instructions and fear of responsibility. He contented himself with calling the general levy of the Romans settled in the province to arms, and having the frontiers guarded by that levy to the best of its ability. On the other hand he himself set out in the opposite direction and advanced by forced marches to Agedincum, to which he ordered Labienus to retreat in all haste. The Celts naturally endeavoured to prevent the junction of the two Roman armies. Labienus might by crossing the Marne and marching down the right bank of the Seine have reached Agedincum, where he had left his reserve and his baggage; but he preferred not to allow the Celts again to witness the retreat of Roman troops. He therefore instead of crossing the Marne crossed the Seine under the eyes of the deluded enemy, and on its left bank fought a battle with the hostile forces, in which he conquered, and among many others the Celtic general himself, the old Camulogenus, was left on the field. Nor were the insurgents more successful in detaining Caesar on the Loire; Caesar gave them no time to assemble larger masses there, and without difficulty dispersed the militia of the Haedui, which alone he found at that point.

Thus the junction of the two divisions of the army was happily accomplished. The insurgents meanwhile had consulted as to the farther conduct of the war at Bibracte (Autun) the capital of the Haedui; the soul of these consultations was again Vercingetorix, to whom the nation was enthusiastically attached after the victory of Gergovia. Particular interests were not, it is true, even now silent; the Haedui still in this death-struggle of the nation asserted their claims to the hegemony, and made a proposal in the national assembly to substitute a leader of their own for Vercingetorix. But the national representatives had not merely declined this and confirmed Vercingetorix in the supreme command, but had also adopted his plan of war without alteration. It was substantially the same as that on which he had operated at Avaricum and at Gergovia. As the base of the new position there was selected the strong city of the Mandubii, Alesia (Alise Sainte Reine near Semur in the department Côte d'Or),[1] and another entrenched camp was constructed under its walls. Immense stores were here accumulated, and the army was ordered thither from Gergovia, having its cavalry raised by resolution of the national assembly to 15,000 horse. Caesar with the whole strength of his army after it was reunited at Agedincum took the direction of Besançon, with the view of now approaching the alarmed province and protecting it from an invasion, for in fact bands of insurgents had already shown themselves in the territory of the Helvii on the south slope of the Cevennes. Alesia lay almost on his way; the cavalry of the Celts, the only arm with which Vercingetorix chose to operate, attacked him on the route, but to the surprise of all was worsted by the new German squadrons of Caesar and the Roman infantry drawn up in support of them.

Vercingetorix hastened the more to shut himself up in Alesia; and if Caesar was not disposed altogether to renounce the offen-

[1] The question so much discussed of late, whether Alesia is not rather to be identified with Alaise (25 kilometres to the south of Besançon, Dep. Doubs), has been rightly answered in the negative by all judicious inquirers.

sive, no course was left to him but for the third time in this campaign to proceed by way of attack with a far weaker force against an army encamped under a well-garrisoned and well-provisioned fortress and supplied with immense masses of cavalry. But, while the Celts had hitherto been opposed by only a part of the Roman legions, the whole forces of Caesar were united in the lines round Alesia, and Vercingetorix did not succeed, as he had succeeded at Avaricum and Gergovia, in placing his infantry under the protection of the walls of the fortress and keeping his external communications open for his own benefit by his cavalry, while he interrupted those of the enemy. The Celtic cavalry, already discouraged by that defeat inflicted on them by their despised opponents, was beaten by Caesar's German horse in every encounter. The line of circumvallation of the besiegers extending about ten miles invested the whole town, including the camp attached to it. Vercingetorix had been prepared for a struggle under the walls, but not for being besieged in Alesia; in that point of view the accumulated stores, considerable as they were, were yet far from sufficient for his army—which was said to amount to 80,000 infantry and 15,000 cavalry—and for the numerous inhabitants of the town. Vercingetorix could not but perceive that his plan of warfare had on this occasion turned to his own destruction, and that he was lost unless the whole nation hastened up to the rescue of its blockaded general. The existing provisions were still, when the Roman circumvallation was closed, sufficient for a month and perhaps something more; at the last moment, when there was still free passage at least for horsemen, Vercingetorix dismissed his whole cavalry, and sent at the same time to the heads of the nation instructions to call forth all their forces and lead them to the relief of Alesia. He himself, resolved to bear in person the responsibility for the plan of war which he had projected and which had miscarried, remained in the fortress, to share in good or evil the fate of his followers. But Caesar made up his mind at once to besiege and to be besieged. He prepared his line of circumvallation for defence also on its outer side, and furnished himself with provisions for a longer period. The days passed; they had no longer a boll of grain in the fortress, and they were obliged to drive out the unhappy inhabitants of the town to perish miserably between the entrenchments of the Celts and of the Romans, pitilessly rejected by both.

At the last hour there appeared behind Caesar's lines the interminable array of the Celto-Belgic relieving army, said to amount to 250,000 infantry and 8000 cavalry. From the Channel to the Cevennes the insurgent cantons had strained every nerve to rescue the flower of their patriots and the general of their choice—the Bellovaci alone had answered that they were disposed to fight against the Romans, but not beyond their own bounds. The first assault, which the besieged of Alesia and the relieving troops without made on the Roman double line, was repulsed; but, when after a day's rest it was repeated, the Celts succeeded—at a spot where the line of circumvallation ran over the slope of a hill and could be assailed from the height above—in filling up the trenches and hurling the defenders down from the rampart. Then Labienus, sent thither by Caesar, collected the nearest cohorts and threw himself with four legions on the foe. Under the eyes of the general, who himself appeared at the most dangerous moment, the assailants were driven back in a desperate hand-to-hand conflict, and the squadrons of cavalry that came with Caesar, taking the fugitives in rear, completed the defeat.

It was more than a great victory; the fate of Alesia, and indeed of the Celtic nation, was thereby irrevocably decided. The Celtic army, utterly disheartened, dispersed at once from the battlefield and went home. Vercingetorix might perhaps have even now taken to flight, or at least have saved himself by the last means open to a free man; he did not do so, but declared in a council of war that, since he had not succeeded in breaking off the alien yoke, he was ready to give himself up as a victim and to avert as far as possible destruction from the nation by bringing it on his own head. This was done. The Celtic officers delivered their general—the solemn choice of the whole nation—to the enemy of their country for such punishment as might be thought fit. Mounted on his steed and in full armour the king of the Arvernians appeared before the Roman proconsul and rode round his tribunal; then he surrendered his horse and arms, and sat down in silence on the steps at Caesar's feet ($\frac{702}{52}$). Five years afterwards he was led in triumph through the streets of the Italian capital, and, while his conqueror was offering solemn thanks to the gods on the summit of the Capitol, Vercingetorix was beheaded at its foot as guilty of high treason against the Roman nation. As after a day of gloom the sun breaks through the clouds at its setting, so destiny bestows on nations in their decline a last great man. Thus Hannibal stands at the close of the Phoenician history, and Vercingetorix at the close of the Celtic. They were not able to save the nations to which they belonged from a foreign yoke, but they spared them the last remaining disgrace—an inglorious fall. Vercingetorix, just like the Carthaginian, was obliged to contend not merely against the public foe, but also and above all against that anti-national opposition of wounded egotists and startled cowards, which regularly accompanies a degenerate civilisation; for him too a place in history is secured, not by his battles and sieges, but by the fact that he was able to furnish in his own person a centre and rallying-point to a nation distracted and ruined by the rivalry of individual interests. And yet there can hardly be a more marked contrast than between the sober townsman of the Phoenician mercantile city, whose plans were directed towards one great object with unchanging energy throughout fifty years, and the bold prince of the Celtic land, whose mighty deeds and high-minded self-sacrifice fall within the compass of one brief summer. The whole ancient world presents no more genuine knight, whether as regards his essential character or his outward appearance. But man ought not to be a mere knight, and least of all the statesman. It was the knight, not the hero, who disdained to escape from Alesia, when he alone was of more consequence to the nation than a hundred thousand ordinary brave men. It was the knight, not the hero, who gave himself up as a sacrifice, when the only thing gained by that sacrifice was that the nation publicly dishonoured itself and with equal cowardice and absurdity employed its last breath in proclaiming that its great historical death-struggle was a crime against its oppressor. How very different was the conduct of Hannibal in similar positions! It is impossible to part from the noble king of the Arverni without a feeling of historical and human sympathy; but it is characteristic of the Celtic nation, that its greatest man was after all merely a knight.

The fall of Alesia and the capitulation of the army enclosed in it were fearful blows for the Celtic insurrection; but blows quite as heavy had befallen the nation and yet the conflict had been renewed. The loss of Vercingetorix, however, was irreparable. With him unity had come to the nation; with him it seemed also to have departed. We do not find that the insurgents made any attempt to continue their joint defence and to appoint another generalissimo; the league of patriots fell to pieces of itself, and every clan was left to fight or come to terms with the Romans as it pleased. Naturally the desire after rest everywhere prevailed. Caesar too had an interest in bringing the war quickly to an end. Of the ten years of his governorship seven had elapsed, and the last was called in question by his political opponents in the capital; he could only reckon with some degree of certainty on two more summers, and, while his interest as well as his honour required that he should hand over the newly-acquired regions to his successor in a condition of tolerable peace and tranquillity, there was in truth but scanty time to bring about such a state of things. To exercise mercy was in this case still more a necessity for the victor than for the vanquished; and he might thank his stars that the internal dissensions and the easy temperament of the Celts met him in this respect half way. Where—as in the two most eminent cantons of central Gaul, those of the Haedui and Arverni—there existed a strong party well disposed to Rome, the cantons obtained immediately after the fall of Alesia a complete restoration of their former relations with Rome, and even their captives, 20,000 in number, were released without ransom, while those of the other clans passed into the hard bondage of the victorious legionaries. The greater portion of the Gallic districts submitted like the Haedui and Arverni to their fate, and allowed their inevitable punishment to be inflicted without farther resistance. But not a few clung in foolish frivolity or sullen despair to the lost cause, till the Roman troops of execution appeared within their borders. Such expeditions were in the winter of $\frac{702-703}{52-51}$ undertaken against the Bituriges and the Carnutes.

More serious resistance was offered by the Bellovaci, who in the previous year had kept aloof from the relief of Alesia; they seem to have wished to show that their absence on that decisive day at least did not proceed from want of courage or of love for freedom. The Atrebates, Ambiani, Caletes, and other Belgic cantons took part in this struggle; the brave king of the Atrebates Commius, whose accession to the insurrection the Romans had least of all forgiven, and against whom recently Labienus had even directed a repulsive attempt at assassination, brought to the Bellovaci 500 German horse, whose value the campaign of the previous year had shown. The resolute and talented Bellovacian Correus, to whom the chief conduct of the war had fallen, waged warfare as Vercingetorix had waged it, and with no small success. Although Caesar had gradually brought up the greater part of his army, he could neither bring the infantry of the Bellovaci to a battle, nor even prevent it from taking up other positions which afforded better protection against his augmented forces; while the Roman horse, especially the Celtic contingents, suffered most severe losses in various combats at the hands of the enemy's cavalry, especially of the German cavalry of Commius. But after Correus had met his death in a skirmish with the Roman foragers, the resistance here too was broken; the victor proposed tolerable conditions, to which the Bellovaci along with their confederates submitted. The Treveri were reduced to obedience by Labienus, and incidentally the territory of the outlawed Eburones was once more traversed and laid waste. Thus the last resistance of the Belgic confederacy was broken. The maritime cantons still made an attempt to defend themselves against the Roman domination in concert with their neighbours on the Loire. Insurgent bands from the Andian, Carnutic, and other surrounding cantons assembled on the lower Loire and besieged in Lemonum (Poitiers) the prince of the Pictones who was friendly to the Romans. But here too a considerable Roman force soon appeared against them; the insurgents abandoned the siege, and retreated with the view of placing the Loire between themselves and the enemy, but were overtaken on the march and defeated; whereupon the Carnutes and the other revolted cantons, including even the maritime ones, sent in their submission.

The resistance was at an end; save that an isolated leader of free bands still here and there upheld the national banner. The bold Drappes and the brave comrade in arms of Vercingetorix Lucterius, after the breaking up of the army united on the Loire, gathered together the most resolute men, and with these threw themselves into the strong mountain-town of Uxellodunum on the Lot,[1] which amidst severe and fatal conflicts they succeeded in sufficiently provisioning. In spite of the loss of their leaders, of whom Drappes had been taken prisoner, and Lucterius had been cut off from the town, the garrison resisted to the uttermost; it was not till Caesar appeared in person, and under his orders the spring from which the besieged derived their water was diverted by means of subterranean drains, that the fortress, the last stronghold of the Celtic nation, fell. To distinguish the last champions of the cause of freedom, Caesar ordered that the whole garrison should have their hands cut off and should then be dismissed, each one to his home. Caesar, who felt it all-important to put an end at least to open resistance

[1] This is usually sought at Capdenac not far from Figeac; Göler has recently declared himself in favour of Luzech to the west of Cahors, a site which had been previously suggested.

throughout Gaul, allowed king Commius, who still held out in the region of Arras and maintained desultory warfare with the Roman troops there down to the winter of $\frac{703}{51}-\frac{704}{50}$, to make his peace, and even acquiesced when the irritated and justly distrustful man haughtily refused to appear in person in the Roman camp. It is very probable that Caesar in a similar way allowed himself to be satisfied with a merely nominal submission, perhaps even with a *de facto* armistice, in the less accessible districts of the north-west and north-east of Gaul.[1]

Thus was Gaul—or, in other words, the land west of the Rhine and north of the Pyrenees—rendered subject after only eight years of conflict ($\frac{696}{58}-\frac{703}{51}$) to the Romans. Hardly a year after the full pacification of the land, at the beginning of $\frac{705}{49}$, the Roman troops had to be withdrawn over the Alps in consequence of the civil war which at length broke out in Italy, and there remained nothing but at the most some weak divisions of recruits in Gaul. Nevertheless the Celts did not again rise against the foreign yoke; and, while in all the old provinces of the empire there was fighting against Caesar, the newly-acquired country alone remained continuously obedient to its conqueror. Even the Germans did not during those decisive years repeat their attempts to conquer new settlements on the left bank of the Rhine. As little did there occur in Gaul any national insurrection or German invasion during the subsequent crises, although these offered most favourable opportunities. If disturbances broke out anywhere, such as the rising of the Bellovaci against the Romans in $\frac{708}{46}$, the movements were so isolated and so unconnected with the complications in Italy, that they were suppressed without material difficulty by the Roman governors. Certainly this state of peace was most probably, just as was the peace of Spain for centuries, purchased by provisionally allowing the regions that were most remote and most strongly pervaded by national feeling—Brittany, the districts on the Scheldt, the region of the Pyrenees—to withdraw themselves *de facto* in a more or less definite manner from the Roman allegiance. Nevertheless the building of Caesar—however scanty the time which he found for it amidst other and at the moment still more urgent labours, however unfinished and but provisionally rounded off he may have left it—in substance

[1] This indeed, as may readily be conceived, is not recorded by Caesar himself; but an intelligible hint of it is given by Sallust (*Hist.* i. 9 Kritz), although he wrote as a partisan of Caesar. Further proofs are furnished by the coins.

stood the test of this fiery trial, as respected both the repelling of the Germans and the subjugation of the Celts.

As to superintendence, the territories newly acquired by the governor of Narbonese Gaul remained for the time being united with the province of Narbo; it was not till Caesar gave up this office ($\frac{710}{44}$) that two new governorships—Gaul proper and Belgia—were formed out of the territory which he conquered. That the individual cantons lost their political independence was implied in the very nature of conquest. They became throughout tributary to the Roman community. Their system of tribute however was, of course, not that by means of which the nobles and financial aristocracy turned Asia to profitable account; but, as was the case in Spain, a tribute fixed once for all was imposed on each individual community, and the levying of it was left to itself. In this way forty million sesterces (£400,000) flowed annually from Gaul into the chests of the Roman government; which, no doubt, undertook in return the cost of defending the frontier of the Rhine. Moreover, the masses of gold accumulated in the temples of the gods and the treasuries of the grandees found their way, as a matter of course, to Rome; when Caesar offered his Gallic gold throughout the Roman empire and brought such masses of it at once into the money market that gold as compared with silver fell about 25 per cent., we may guess what sums Gaul lost through the war.

The former cantonal constitutions with their hereditary kings, or their ruling feudal-oligarchies, continued in the main to subsist after the conquest, and even the system of clientship, which made certain cantons dependent on others more powerful, was not abolished, although no doubt with the loss of political independence its edge was taken off. The sole object of Caesar was, while making use of the existing dynastic, feudalist, and hegemonic divisions, to arrange matters in the interest of Rome, and to bring everywhere into power the men favourably disposed to the foreign rule. Caesar spared no pains to form a Roman party in Gaul; extensive rewards in money and specially in confiscated estates were bestowed on his adherents, and places in the common council and the first offices of state in their cantons were procured for them by Caesar's influence. Those cantons in which a sufficiently strong and trustworthy Roman party existed, such as the Remi, the Lingones, the Haedui, were favoured by the bestowal of a freer communal constitution—the right of alliance, as it was called—and by preferences in the regulation of the matter of hegemony. The national worship and its priests seem to have been spared by Caesar from the outset as far as possible; no trace is found in his case of measures such as were adopted in later times by the Roman regents against the Druidical system, and with this is probably connected the fact that his Gallic wars, so far as we see, do not at all bear the character of religious warfare after the fashion which formed so prominent a feature of the Britannic wars subsequently.

While Caesar thus showed to the conquered nation every allowable consideration and spared their national, political, and religious institutions as far as was at all compatible with their subjection to Rome, he did so, not as renouncing the fundamental idea of his conquest, the Romanisation of Gaul, but with a view to realise it in the most indulgent way. He did not content himself with leaving the same circumstances, which had already in great part Romanised the south province, to produce their effect likewise in the north; but, like a genuine statesman, he stimulated the natural course of development and sought to shorten as far as possible the always painful period of transition. To say nothing of the admission of a number of Celts of rank into Roman citizenship and even of several perhaps into the Roman senate, it was probably Caesar who introduced, although with certain restrictions, the Latin instead of the native tongue as the official language within the several cantons in Gaul, and who introduced the Roman instead of the national monetary system on the footing of reserving the coinage of gold and of *denarii* to the Roman authorities, while the smaller money was to be coined by the several cantons but only for circulation within the cantonal bounds, and this too in accordance with the Roman standard. We may smile at the Latin jargon, which the dwellers by the Loire and the Seine henceforth employed in accordance with orders;[1] but these barbarisms were pregnant with a greater future than the correct Latin of the capital. Perhaps too, if the cantonal constitution in Gaul afterwards appears more closely to approach the Italian urban constitution, and the chief places of the canton as well as the common councils attain a more marked prominence in it than was probably the case in the original Celtic organisation, the change may be referred to Caesar. No one probably felt

[1] Thus we read on a *semis*, which a Vergobretus of the Lexovii (Lisieux, dep. Calvados) caused to be struck, the following inscription: *Cisiambos Cattos vercobreto; simissos* (sic) *publicos Lixovio.* The often scarcely legible writing and the incredibly wretched stamping of these coins are in excellent harmony with their stammering Latin.

more than the political heir of Gaius Gracchus and of Marius, how desirable in a military as well as in a political point of view it would have been to establish a series of Transalpine colonies as bases of support for the new rule and centres of the new civilisation. If nevertheless he confined himself to the settlement of his Celtic or German horsemen in Noviodunum (p. 227) and to that of the Boii in the canton of the Haedui (p. 227)—which latter settlement already rendered quite the services of a Roman colony in the war with Vercingetorix—the reason was merely that his farther plans did not permit him to put the plough instead of the sword into the hands of his legions. What he did in later years for the old Roman province in this respect will be explained in its own place; it is probable that the want of time alone prevented him from extending the same system to the regions which he had recently subdued.

All was over with the Celtic nation. Its political annihilation had been completed by Caesar; its national annihilation was begun and in regular progress. This was no accidental destruction, such as destiny sometimes prepares even for peoples capable of development, but a self-incurred and in some measure historically necessary catastrophe. The very course of the last war proves this, whether we view it as a whole or in detail. When the establishment of the foreign rule was in contemplation, only single districts—mostly, moreover, German or half-German—offered energetic resistance. When the foreign rule was actually established, the attempts to shake it off were either undertaken altogether without judgment, or they were to an undue extent the work of certain prominent nobles, and were therefore immediately and entirely brought to an end with the death or capture of an Indutiomarus, Camulogenus, Vercingetorix, or Correus. The sieges and guerrilla warfare, in which elsewhere the whole moral depth of national struggles displays itself, were throughout this Celtic struggle of a peculiarly pitiable character. Every page of Celtic history confirms the severe saying of one of the few Romans who had the judgment not to despise the so-called barbarians—that the Celts boldly challenge danger while future, but lose their courage before its presence. In the mighty vortex of the world's history, which inexorably crushes all peoples that are not as hard and as flexible as steel, such a nation could not permanently maintain itself; with reason the Celts of the continent suffered the same fate at the hands of the Romans, as their kinsmen in Ireland suffer down to our own day at the hands of the Saxons—the fate of becoming merged as a leaven of future development in a politically superior nationality. On the eve of parting from this remarkable nation we may be allowed to call attention to the fact, that in the accounts of the ancients as to the Celts on the Loire and Seine we find almost every one of the characteristic traits which we are accustomed to recognise as marking the Irish. Every feature reappears: the laziness in the culture of the fields; the delight in tippling and brawling; the ostentation—we may recall that sword of Caesar hung up in the sacred grove of the Arvernians after the victory of Gergovia, which its alleged former owner viewed with a smile at the consecrated spot and ordered the sacred property to be carefully spared; the language full of comparisons and hyperboles, of allusions and quaint turns; the droll humour—an excellent example of which was the rule that if any one interrupted a person speaking in public a substantial and very visible hole should be cut, as a measure of police, in the coat of the disturber of the peace; the hearty delight in singing and reciting the deeds of past ages, and the most decided talent for rhetoric and poetry; the curiosity—no trader was allowed to pass, before he had told in the open street what he knew, or did not know, in the shape of news—and the extravagant credulity which acted on such accounts, for which reason in the better regulated cantons travellers were prohibited on pain of severe punishment from communicating unauthenticated reports to others than the public magistrates; the childlike piety, which sees in the priest a father and asks him for his advice in all things; the unsurpassed fervour of national feeling, and the closeness with which those who are fellow-countrymen cling together almost like one family in opposition to the stranger; the inclination to rise in revolt under the first chance leader that presents himself and to form bands, but at the same time the utter incapacity to preserve a self-reliant courage equally remote from presumption and from pusillanimity, to perceive the right time for waiting and for striking, to attain or even barely to tolerate any organisation, any sort of fixed military or political discipline. It is, and remains, at all times and places the same indolent and poetical, irresolute and fervid, inquisitive, credulous, amiable, clever, but —in a political point of view—thoroughly useless nation; and therefore its fate has been always and everywhere the same.

But the fact that this great people was ruined by the Transalpine wars of Caesar was not the most important result of that grand enterprise; far more momentous than the negative was the positive result. It hardly admits of a doubt that, if the rule of the senate had prolonged its semblance of life for some generations longer, the migration of peoples, as it is called, would have occurred four hundred years sooner than it did, and would have occurred at a time when the Italian civilisation had not become naturalised either in Gaul, or on the Danube, or in Africa and Spain. Inasmuch as the great general and statesman of Rome with sure glance perceived in the German tribes the rival antagonists of the Romano-Greek world; inasmuch as with firm hand he established the new system of aggressive defence down even to its details, and taught men to protect the frontiers of the empire by rivers or artificial ramparts, to colonise the nearest barbarian tribes along the frontier with the view of warding off the more remote, and to recruit the Roman army by enlistment from the enemy's country; he gained for the Hellenic-Italian culture the interval necessary to civilise the West just as it had already civilised the East. Ordinary men see the fruits of their action; the seed sown by men of genius germinate slowly. Centuries elapsed before men understood that Alexander had not merely erected an ephemeral kingdom in the East, but had carried Hellenism to Asia; centuries again elapsed before men understood that Caesar had not merely conquered a new province for the Romans, but had laid the foundation for the Romanising of the regions of the West. It was only a late posterity that perceived the meaning of those expeditions to England and Germany, so inconsiderate in a military point of view, and so barren of immediate result. An immense circle of peoples, whose existence and condition hitherto were known barely through the reports—mingling some truth with much fiction—of the mariner and the trader, was disclosed by this means to the Greek and Roman world. "Daily," it is said in a Roman writing of May $\frac{698}{56}$, "the letters and messages from Gaul are announcing names of peoples, cantons, and regions hitherto unknown to us." This enlargement of the historical horizon by the expeditions of Caesar beyond the Alps was as much an event in the world's history as the exploring of America by European bands. To the narrow circle of the Mediterranean states were added the peoples of central and northern Europe, the dwellers on the Baltic and North seas; to the old world was added a new one, which thenceforth was influenced by the old and influenced it in turn. What the Gothic Theodoric afterwards succeeded in, came very near to being already carried out by Ariovistus. Had it so happened, our civilisation would have hardly stood in any more intimate relation to the Romano-Greek than to the Indian and Assyrian culture. That there is a bridge connecting the past glory of Hellas and Rome with the prouder fabric of modern history; that Western Europe is Romanic, and Germanic Europe classic; that the names of Themistocles and Scipio have to us a very different sound from those of Asoka and Salmanassar; that Homer and Sophocles are not merely like the Vedas and Kalidasa attractive to the literary botanist, but bloom for us in our own garden—all this is the work of Caesar; and, while the creation of his great predecessor in the East has been almost wholly reduced to ruin by the tempests of the Middle Ages, the structure of Caesar has outlasted those thousands of years which have changed religion and polity for the human race and even shifted the centre of civilisation itself, and it stands erect for what we may term perpetuity.

To complete the sketch of the relations of Rome to the peoples of the North at this period, it remains that we cast a glance at the countries which stretch to the north of the Italian and Greek peninsulas, from the sources of the Rhine to the Black Sea. It is true that the torch of history does not illumine the mighty stir and turmoil of peoples which probably prevailed at that time there, and the solitary gleams of light that fall on this region are, like a faint glimmer amidst deep darkness, more fitted to bewilder than to enlighten. But it is the duty of the historian to indicate also the gaps in the record of the history of nations; he may not deem it beneath him to mention, by the side of Caesar's magnificent system of defence, the paltry arrangements by which the generals of the senate professed to protect on this side the frontier of the empire.

North-eastern Italy was still as before (iii. 164) left exposed to the attacks of the Alpine tribes. The strong Roman army encamped at Aquileia in $\frac{696}{58}$, and the triumph of the governor of Cisalpine Gaul, Lucius Afranius, lead us to infer that about this time an expedition to the Alps took place, and it may have been in consequence of this that we find the Romans soon afterwards in closer connection with a king of the Noricans. But that even subsequently Italy was not at all secure on this side, is shown by the sudden assault of the Alpine barbarians on the flourishing town of Tergeste in $\frac{702}{52}$, when the Transalpine insurrection had compelled Caesar to divest upper Italy wholly of troops.

The turbulent peoples also, who had possession of the district along the Illyrian coast, gave their Roman masters constant employment. The Dalmatians, even at an earlier period the most considerable people of this region, enlarged their power so much by admitting their neighbours into their union, that the number of their townships rose from twenty to eighty. With respect to the town of Promona (not far from the river Kerka), which they had wrested from the Liburnians and refused to surrender, they fell into a quarrel with the Romans, and defeated the general levy which Caesar called forth against them; a defeat which the outbreak of the civil war prevented him from avenging. Partly on this account Dalmatia became in that war a rendezvous of the party hostile to Caesar, and the inhabitants in concert with the Pompeians and with the pirates offered an energetic resistance to the generals of Caesar both by land and by water.

Lastly Macedonia along with Epirus and Hellas lay in greater desolation and decay than almost any other part of the Roman empire. Dyrrhachium, Thessalonica, and Byzantium had still some trade and commerce; Athens attracted travellers and students by its name and its philosophical school; but on the whole there lay over the formerly populous little towns of Hellas, and her seaports once swarming with men, the calm of the grave. But if the Greeks stirred not, the inhabitants of the hardly accessible Macedonian mountains on the other hand continued after the old fashion their predatory raids and feuds; for instance about $\frac{697-698}{57-56}$ Agraeans and Dolopians overran the Aetolian towns, and in $\frac{700}{54}$ the Pirustae dwelling in the valleys of the Drin overran southern Illyria. The neighbouring peoples did likewise. The Dardani on the northern frontier as well as the Thracians in the east had no doubt been humbled by the Romans in the eight years' conflicts from $\frac{676}{78}$ to $\frac{683}{71}$; the most powerful of the Thracian princes, Cotys, the ruler of the old Odrysian kingdom, was thenceforth numbered among the client kings of Rome. Nevertheless the pacified land had still as before to suffer invasions from the north and east. The governor Gaius Antonius was severely handled both by the Dardani and by the tribes settled in the modern Dobrudscha, who, with the help of the dreaded Bastarnae brought up from the left bank of the Danube, inflicted on him an important defeat ($\frac{692-693}{62-61}$) at Istropolis (Istere, not far from Kustendji). Gaius Octavius fought with better fortune against the Bessi and Thracians ($\frac{694}{60}$). Marcus Piso again ($\frac{697-998}{57-56}$) as general in chief wretchedly mismanaged matters; which was no wonder, seeing that he gave friends and foes whatever they wished for money. The Thracian Dentheletae (on the Strymon) under his governorship plundered Macedonia far and wide, and even stationed their posts on the great Roman military road leading from Dyrrhachium to Thessalonica; the people in Thessalonica made up their minds to stand a siege from them, for the strong Roman army in the province seemed to be present only as an onlooker while the inhabitants of the mountains and the neighbouring peoples levied contributions from the peaceful subjects of Rome.

Such attacks could not indeed endanger the power of Rome, and a fresh disgrace had long ago ceased to occasion concern. But just about this period a people began to acquire political consolidation beyond the Danube in the wide Dacian steppes—a people which seemed destined to play a different part in history from that of the Bessi and the Dentheletae. Among the Getae or Dacians in primeval times there had been associated with the king of the people a holy man called Zamolxis, who, after having explored the ways and wonders of the gods in distant travel in foreign lands, and having thoroughly studied in particular the wisdom of the Egyptian priests and of the Greek Pythagoreans, had returned to his native country to end his life as a pious hermit in a cavern of the "holy mountain." He remained accessible only to the king and his servants, and gave forth to the king and through him to the people his oracles with reference to every important undertaking. He was regarded by his countrymen at first as priest of the supreme god and ultimately as himself a god, just as it is said of Moses and Aaron that the Lord had made Aaron the prophet and Moses the god of the prophet. This had become a permanent institution; there was regularly associated with the king of the Getae such a god, from whose mouth everything which the king ordered proceeded or appeared to proceed. This peculiar constitution, in which the theocratic idea had become subservient to the apparently absolute power of the king, probably gave to the kings of the Getae some such position with respect to their subjects as the caliphs had with respect to the Arabs; and one result of it was the marvellous religious-political reform of the nation, which was carried out about this time by the king of the Getae, Boerebistas, and the god Dekaeneos. The people, which had morally and politically fallen into utter decay through unexampled drunkenness, was as it were metamorphosed by the new gospel of temperance and valour; with his bands under the influence, so to speak, of puritanic discipline and enthusiasm king Boerebistas founded within a few years a mighty kingdom, which extended along both banks of the Danube and reached southward far into Thrace, Illyria, and Noricum. No direct contact with the Romans had yet taken place, and no one could tell what might come out of this singular state, which reminds us of the early times of Islam; but this much it needed no prophetic gift to foretell, that proconsuls like Antonius and Piso were nowise fitted to contend with gods.

CHAPTER VIII

THE JOINT RULE OF POMPEIUS AND CAESAR

AMONG the democratic chiefs, who from the time of the consulate of Caesar were recognised officially, so to speak, as the joint rulers of the commonwealth, as the governing "triumvirs," Pompeius in public opinion occupied decidedly the first place. It was he who was called by the Optimates the "private dictator;" it was before him that Cicero prostrated himself in vain; against him were directed the sharpest sarcasms in the placards of Bibulus, and the most envenomed arrows of the conversation in the saloons of the opposition. This was only to be expected. According to the facts before the public Pompeius was indisputably the first general of his time; Caesar was a dexterous party leader and party orator, of undeniable talents, but as notoriously of unwarlike, and indeed of effeminate temperament. Such opinions had been long current; it could not be expected of the rabble in high quarters, that they should trouble themselves about the real state of things and abandon platitudes once established because of some obscure feats of heroism on the Tagus. Caesar evidently played in the league the mere part of the adjutant who executed for his chief the work which Flavius, Afranius, and other less capable instruments had attempted and not performed. It seemed as if even his governorship could not alter this state of things. Afranius had only recently occupied a very similar position, without thereby acquiring any special importance; several provinces at once had been of late years repeatedly placed under one governor, and often far more than four legions had been united in one hand; as matters were again quiet beyond the Alps and prince Ariovistus was recognised by the Romans as a friend and neighbour, there was no prospect of conducting a war of any moment there. It was natural to compare the position which Pompeius had obtained by the Gabinio-Manilian law with that which Caesar had obtained by the Vatinian; but the comparison did not turn out to Caesar's advantage. Pompeius ruled over nearly the whole Roman empire; Caesar over two provinces. Pompeius had the soldiers and the treasures of the state almost absolutely at his disposal; Caesar had only the sums assigned to him and an army of 24,000 men. It was left to Pompeius himself to fix the point of time for his retirement; Caesar's command was secured to him for a long period no doubt, but yet only for a limited term. Pompeius, in fine, had been entrusted with the most important undertakings by sea and land; Caesar was sent to the north, to watch over the capital from upper Italy and to take care that Pompeius should rule it undisturbed.

But when Pompeius was appointed by the coalition to be ruler of the capital, he undertook a task far exceeding his powers. Pompeius understood nothing more of ruling than might be summed up in the word of command. The waves of agitation in the capital were swelled at once by past and by future revolutions; the problem of ruling this city—which in many respects might be compared to the Paris of the nineteenth century—without an armed force was infinitely difficult, and for that stiff and stately pattern-soldier altogether insoluble. Very soon matters reached such a pitch that friends and foes, both equally inconvenient to him, could, so far as he was concerned, do what they pleased; after Caesar's departure from Rome the coalition ruled doubtless still the destines of the world, but not the streets of the capital. The senate too, to whom there still belonged a sort of nominal government, allowed things in the capital to follow their natural course; partly because the section of this body controlled by the coalition lacked the instructions of the regents, partly because the angry opposition kept aloof out of indifference or pessimism, but chiefly because the whole aristocratic corporation began to feel at any rate, if not to comprehend, its utter impotence. For the moment therefore there was nowhere at Rome any power of resistance in any sort of government, nowhere a real authority. Men were living in an interregnum between the ruin of the aristocratic, and the rise of the military, rule; and, if the Roman commonwealth has presented all the different political functions and organisations more purely and normally than any other in ancient or modern times, it has also exhibited political disorganisation—anarchy—with an unenviable clearness. It is a strange coincidence that in the same years in which Caesar was creating beyond the Alps a work to last for ever, there was enacted in Rome one of the most extravagant political farces that was ever produced upon the stage of the world's history. The new regent of the commonwealth did not rule, but shut himself up in his house and sulked in silence. The former half-deposed government likewise did not rule, but sighed, sometimes in private amidst the confidential circles of the villas, sometimes in chorus in the senate house. The portion of the burgesses which had still at heart freedom and order was disgusted with the reign of confusion, but utterly without leaders and helpless it maintained a passive attitude—not merely avoiding all political activity, but keeping aloof, as far as possible, from the political Sodom itself.

On the other hand the rabble of every sort never had better days, never found a merrier arena. The number of little great men was legion. Demagogism became quite a trade, which accordingly did not lack its professional insignia—the threadbare mantle, the shaggy beard, the long streaming hair, the deep bass voice; and not seldom it was a trade with golden soil. For the standing declamations the tried gargles of the theatrical staff were an article in much request;[1] Greeks and Jews, freedmen and slaves, were the most regular attenders and the loudest criers in the public assemblies; frequently, even when it came to a vote, only a minority of those voting consisted of burgesses constitutionally entitled to do so. "Next time," it is said in a letter of this period, "we may expect our lackeys to outvote the emancipation-tax." The real powers of the day were the compact and armed bands, the battalions of anarchy raised by adventurers of rank out of gladiatorial slaves and blackguards. Their possessors had from the outset been mostly numbered among the popular party; but since the departure of Caesar, who alone understood how to impress the democracy, and alone knew how to manage it, all discipline had departed from them and every partisan adopted his politics at his own hand. Even now, no doubt, these men fought with most pleasure under the banner of freedom; but, strictly speaking, they were neither of democratic nor of anti-democratic views; they inscribed on the—in itself indispensable—banner, as it happened, now the name of the people, anon that of the senate or that of a party chief; Clodius for instance fought or professed to fight in succession for the ruling democracy, for the senate, and for Crassus. The leaders of these bands kept to their colours only so far as they inexorably persecuted their personal enemies—as in the case of Clodius against Cicero and Milo against Clodius—while their partisan position served them merely as a handle in these personal feuds. We might as well seek to set a charivari to music as to write the history of this political witches' revel;

[1] This is the meaning of *cantorum convitio contiones celebrare* (Cic. *pro Sest.* 55, 118).

nor is it of any moment to enumerate all the deeds of murder, besiegings of houses, acts of incendiarism, and other scenes of violence within a great capital, and to reckon up how often the scale was traversed from hissing and shouting to spitting on and trampling down opponents, and thence to throwing stones and drawing swords.

The principal performer in this theatre of political rascality was that Publius Clodius, of whose services, as already mentioned (p. 194), the regents availed themselves against Cato and Cicero. Left to himself, this influential, talented, energetic, and—in his trade—really exemplary partisan pursued during his tribunate of the people ($\frac{696}{58}$) an ultra-democratic policy, gave the citizens corn gratis, restricted the right of the censors to stigmatise immoral burgesses, prohibited the magistrates from obstructing the course of the comitial machinery by religious formalities, set aside the limits which had shortly before ($\frac{690}{64}$), for the purpose of checking the system of bands, been imposed on the right of association of the lower classes, and re-established the "street-clubs" (*collegia compitalicia*) at that time abolished, which were nothing else than a formal organisation—subdivided according to the streets, and with an almost military arrangement—of the whole free or slave proletariate of the capital. If in addition the further law, which Clodius had likewise already projected and purposed to introduce when praetor in $\frac{702}{52}$, should give to freedmen and to slaves living in *de facto* possession of freedom the same political rights with the freeborn, the author of all these brave improvements of the constitution might declare his work complete, and as a second Numa of freedom and equality might invite the sweet rabble of the capital to see him celebrate high mass in honour of the arrival of the democratic millennium in the temple of Liberty which he had erected on the site of one of his burnings at the Palatine. Of course these exertions in behalf of freedom did not exclude a traffic in decrees of the burgesses; like Caesar himself, Caesar's ape kept governorships and other posts great and small on sale for the benefit of his fellow-citizens, and sold the sovereign rights of the state for the benefit of subject kings and cities.

At all these things Pompeius looked on without stirring. If he did not perceive how seriously he thus compromised himself, his opponent perceived it. Clodius had the hardihood to engage in a dispute with the regent of Rome on a question of little moment, as to the sending back of a captive Armenian prince; and the variance soon became a formal feud, in which the utter helplessness of Pompeius was displayed. The head of the state knew not how to encounter the partisan otherwise than with his own weapons, only wielded with far less dexterity. If he had been tricked by Clodius respecting the Armenian prince, he offended him in turn by releasing Cicero, who was pre-eminently obnoxious to Clodius, from the exile into which Clodius had sent him; and he attained his object so thoroughly, that he converted his opponent into an implacable foe. If Clodius made the streets insecure with his bands, the victorious general likewise set slaves and pugilists to work; in the frays which ensued the general naturally was worsted by the demagogue and defeated in the streets, and Gaius Cato was kept almost constantly under siege in his garden by Clodius and his comrades. It is not the least remarkable feature in this remarkable spectacle, that the regent and the rogue amidst their quarrel vied in courting the favour of the fallen government; Pompeius, partly to please the senate, permitted Cicero's recall, Clodius on the other hand declared the Julian laws null and void, and called on Marcus Bibulus publicly to testify to their having been unconstitutionally passed.

Naturally no positive result could issue from this imbroglio of dark passions; its most distinctive character was just its utterly ludicrous want of object. Even a man of Caesar's genius had to learn by experience that democratic agitation was completely worn out, and that even the way to the throne lay no longer through demagogism. It was nothing more than an historical makeshift, if now, in the interregnum between republic and monarchy, some whimsical fellow dressed himself out with the prophet's mantle and staff which Caesar had long laid aside, and the great ideals of Gaius Gracchus came once more upon the stage distorted into a parody; the so-called party from which this democratic agitation proceeded was so little such in reality, that afterwards it had no part at all allotted to it in the decisive struggle. It cannot even be asserted that by means of this anarchical state of things the desire after a strong government based on military power had been vividly kindled in the minds of those who were indifferent to politics. Even apart from the fact that such neutral burgesses were chiefly to be sought outside of Rome, and thus were not directly affected by the rioting in the capital, those minds which could be at all influenced by such motives had been already by their former experience, and especially by the Catilinarian conspiracy, thoroughly converted to the principle of authority; but those that were really alarmed were affected far more emphatically by a dread of the gigantic crisis inseparable from an overthrow of the constitution, than by dread of the mere continuance of the—at bottom withal very superficial—anarchy in the capital. The only result of it which historically deserves notice was the painful position in which Pompeius was placed by the attacks of the Clodians, and which had a material share in determining his farther steps.

Little as Pompeius liked and understood taking the initiative, he was yet on this occasion compelled by the change of his position towards both Clodius and Caesar to depart from his previous inaction. The irksome and disgraceful situation to which Clodius had reduced him, could not but at length arouse even his sluggish nature to hatred and anger. But far more important was the change which took place in his relation to Caesar. While, of the two confederate regents, Pompeius had utterly failed in the functions which he had undertaken, Caesar had the skill to turn his official position to an account which left all calculations and all fears far behind. Without much inquiry as to permission, Caesar had doubled his army by levies in his southern province inhabited in great measure by Roman burgesses; had with this army crossed the Alps instead of keeping watch over Rome from Northern Italy; had crushed in the bud a new Cimbrian invasion, and within two years ($\frac{696}{58}$, $\frac{697}{57}$) had carried the Roman arms to the Rhine and the Channel. In presence of such facts even the aristocratic tactics of ignoring and disparaging were baffled. He who had often been scoffed at as effeminate was now the idol of the army, the celebrated victory-crowned hero, whose fresh laurels outshone the faded laurels of Pompeius, and to whom even the senate as early as $\frac{697}{57}$ accorded the demonstrations of honour usual after successful campaigns in richer measure than had ever fallen to the share of Pompeius. Pompeius stood towards his former adjutant precisely as after the Gabinio-Manilian laws the latter had stood towards him. Caesar was now the hero of the day and the master of the most powerful Roman army; Pompeius was an ex-general who had once been famous. It is true that no collision had yet occurred between father-in-law and son-in-law, and their relation was externally undisturbed; but every political alliance is inwardly broken up when the relative proportions of the power of the parties are materially altered. While the quarrel with Clodius was merely annoying, the change in the position of Caesar involved a very serious danger for Pompeius; just as Caesar and his confederates had formerly sought a military support against him, he found himself now compelled to seek a military support against Caesar, and laying aside his haughty privacy to come forward as a candidate for some extraordinary magistracy, which would enable him to hold his place by the side of the governor of the two Gauls with equal, and, if possible, with superior power. His tactics, like his position, were exactly those of Caesar during the Mithradatic war. To balance the military power of a superior but still remote adversary by the obtaining of a similar command, Pompeius required in the first instance the official machinery of government. A year and a half ago this had been absolutely at his disposal. The regents then ruled the state both by the comitia, which absolutely obeyed them as the masters of the street, and by the senate, which was energetically overawed by Caesar; as representative of the coalition in Rome and as its acknowledged head, Pompeius would have doubtless obtained from the senate and from the burgesses any decree which he wished, even if it were against Caesar's interest. But by the awkward quarrel with Clodius, Pompeius had lost the command of the streets, and could not expect to carry a proposal in his favour in the popular assembly. Things were not quite so unfavourable for him in the senate; but even there it was doubtful whether Pompeius after that long and fatal inaction still held the reins of the majority firmly enough in hand to procure such a decree as he required.

The position of the senate also, or rather of the nobility generally, had meanwhile undergone a change. From the very fact of its complete abasement it drew fresh energy. In the coalition of $\frac{694}{60}$ various things had been revealed which were by no means ripe for the light. The banishment of Cato and Cicero—which public opinion, however much the regents kept themselves in the background and even professed to lament it, referred with unerring tact to its real authors—and the marriage-relationship formed between Caesar and Pompeius suggested to men's minds with disagreeable clearness monarchical decrees of banishment and family alliances. The larger public too, which stood more aloof from political events, observed the foundations of the future monarchy coming more and more distinctly into view. From the moment when the public perceived that Caesar's object was not a modification of the republican constitution, but that the question at stake was the existence or non-existence of the republic, many of the best men, who had hitherto reckoned themselves of the popular party and honoured in Caesar its head, must infallibly have passed over to the opposite side. It was no longer in the saloons and the country houses of the governing nobility alone that men talked of the "three dynasts," of the "three-headed monster." The dense crowds of people listened to the consular orations of Caesar without a sound of acclamation or approval; not a hand stirred to applaud when the democratic consul entered the theatre. But they hissed when one of the tools of the regent showed himself in public, and even staid men applauded when an actor uttered an anti-monarchic sentence or an allusion against Pompeius. Nay, when Cicero was to be banished, a great number of burgesses—it is said twenty thousand—mostly of the middle classes, put on mourning after the example of the senate. "Nothing is now more popular," it is said in a letter of this period, "than hatred of the popular party." The regents dropped hints, that through such opposition the equites might easily lose their new special places in the theatre, and the commons their bread-corn; people were therefore somewhat more guarded perhaps in the expression of their displeasure, but the feeling remained the same. The lever of material interests was applied with better success. Caesar's gold flowed in streams. Men of seeming riches whose finances were in disorder, influential ladies who were in pecuniary embarrassment, insolvent young nobles, merchants and bankers in difficulties, either went in person to Gaul with the view of drawing from the fountain head, or applied to Caesar's agents in the capital; and rarely was any man outwardly respectable—Caesar avoided dealings with vagabonds who were utterly lost—rejected in either quarter. To this fell to be added the enormous buildings which Caesar caused to be executed on his account in the capital—and by which a countless number of men of all ranks from the consular down to the common porter found opportunity of profiting—as well as the immense sums expended for public amusements. Pompeius did the same on a more limited scale; to him the capital was indebted for the first theatre of stone, and he celebrated its dedication with a magnificence never seen before. Of course such distributions reconciled a number of men who were inclined towards opposition, more especially in the capital, to the new order of things up to a certain extent; but the marrow of the opposition was not to be reached by this system of corruption. Every day more and more clearly showed how deeply the existing constitution had struck root among the people, and how little, in particular, the circles more aloof from direct party agitation, especially the country towns, were inclined towards monarchy or even ready to submit to it.

If Rome had had a representative constitution, the discontent of the burgesses would have found its natural expression in the elections, and have increased by so expressing itself; under the existing circumstances nothing was left for those true to the constitution but to place themselves under the senate, which, degraded as it was, still appeared the representative and champion of the legitimate republic. Thus it happened that the senate, now when it had been overthrown, suddenly found at its disposal an army far more considerable and far more earnestly faithful, than when in its power and splendour it overthrew the Gracchi and under the protection of Sulla's sword restored the state. The aristocracy felt this; it began to bestir itself afresh. Just at this time Marcus Cicero, after having bound himself to join the obsequious party in the senate and not only to offer no opposition, but to work with all his might for the regents, had obtained from them permission to return. Although Pompeius in this matter only made an incidental concession to the oligarchy, and intended first of all to play a trick on Clodius, and secondly to acquire in the fluent consular a tool rendered pliant by sufficient blows, the opportunity afforded by the return of Cicero was embraced for republican demonstrations, just as his banishment had been a demonstration against the senate. With all possible solemnity, protected moreover against the Clodians by the band of Titus Annius Milo, the two consuls, following out a resolution of the senate, submitted a proposal to the burgesses to permit the return of the consular Cicero, and the senate called on all burgesses true to the constitution not to be absent from the vote. An unusual number of worthy men, especially from the country towns, actually assembled in Rome on the day of voting (4th August $\frac{697}{57}$). The journey of the consular from Brundisium to the capital gave occasion to a series of similar, not less brilliant, manifestations of public feeling. The new alliance between the senate and the burgesses faithful to the constitution was on this occasion as it were publicly proclaimed, and a sort of review of the latter was held, the singularly favourable result of which contributed not a little to revive the sunken courage of the aristocracy.

The helplessness of Pompeius in presence of these daring demonstrations as well as the undignified and almost ridiculous position into which he had fallen with reference to Clodius, deprived him and the coalition of their credit; and the section of the senate which adhered to the regents, demoralised by the singular inaptitude of Pompeius and helplessly left to itself, could not prevent the republican-aristocratic party from regaining completely the ascendancy in the corporation. The game of this party really at that time—$\frac{697}{57}$—was still by no means desperate for a courageous and dexterous player. It had now —what it had not possessed for a century past—a firm support in the people; if it trusted the people and itself, it might attain its object in the shortest and most honourable way. Why not attack the regents openly and avowedly? Why should not a resolute and eminent man at the head of the senate cancel the extraordinary powers as unconstitutional, and summon all the republicans of Italy to arms against the tyrants and their following? It was possible perhaps in this way once more to restore the rule of the senate. Certainly the republicans would thus play a bold game; but perhaps in this case, as often, the most courageous resolution might have been at the same time the most prudent. Only, it is true, the indolent aristocracy of this period was scarcely capable of so simple and bold a resolution. There was however another way perhaps more sure, at any rate better adapted to the character and nature of these constitutionalists; they might labour to set the two regents at variance and through this variance to attain ultimately to the helm themselves. The relations between the two men ruling the state had become altered and relaxed, now that Caesar had acquired a standing of preponderant power by the side of Pompeius and had compelled the latter to canvass for a new position of command; it was probable that, if he obtained it, there would arise in one way or other a rupture and struggle between them. If Pompeius remained unsupported in this, his defeat was scarcely doubtful, and the constitutional party would in that event find themselves after the close of the conflict under the rule of one master instead of two. But if the nobility employed against Caesar the same means by which the latter had won his previous victories, and entered into alliance with the weaker competitor, victory would probably, with a general like Pompeius, and with an army such as that of the constitutionalists, fall to the coalition; and to settle matters with Pompeius after the victory could not—judging from the proofs of political incapacity which he had already given—appear a specially difficult task.

Things had taken such a turn as naturally to suggest an understanding between Pompeius and the republican party.

Whether such an approximation was to take place, and what shape the mutual relations of the two regents and of the aristocracy, which had become utterly enigmatical, were next to assume, fell necessarily to be decided, when in the autumn of $\frac{697}{57}$ Pompeius came to the senate with the proposal to entrust him with extraordinary official power. He based his proposal once more on that by which he had eleven years before laid the foundations of his power, the price of bread in the capital, which had just then—as previously to the Gabinian law—reached an oppressive height. Whether it had been forced up by special machinations, such as Clodius imputed sometimes to Pompeius, sometimes to Cicero, and these in their turn charged on Clodius, cannot be determined; the continuance of piracy, the emptiness of the public chest, and the negligent and disorderly supervision of the supplies of corn by the government were already quite sufficient of themselves, even without political forestalling, to produce scarcities of bread in a great city dependent almost solely on transmarine supplies. The plan of Pompeius was to get the senate to commit to him the superintendence of the matters relating to corn throughout the whole Roman empire, and, with a view to this ultimate object, to entrust him on the one hand with the unlimited disposal of the Roman state-treasure, and on the other hand with an army and fleet, as well as a command which not only stretched over the whole Roman empire, but was superior in each province to that of the governor—in short he designed to institute an improved edition of the Gabinian law, to which the conduct of the Egyptian war just then pending (p. 139) would therefore quite as naturally have been annexed as the conduct of the Mithradatic war to the razzia against the pirates. However much the opposition to the new dynasts had gained ground in recent years, the majority of the senate was still, when this matter came to be discussed in September $\frac{697}{57}$, under the constraint of the terror excited by Caesar. It obsequiously accepted the project in principle, and that on the proposition of Marcus Cicero, who was expected to give, and gave, in this case the first proof of the pliableness learned by him in exile. But in the settlement of the details very material portions were abated from the original plan, which the tribune of the people Gaius Messius submitted. Pompeius obtained neither free control over the treasury, nor legions and ships of his own, nor even an authority superior to that of the governors; but they contented themselves with granting to him, for the purpose of his organising due supplies for the capital, considerable sums, fifteen adjutants, and in all affairs relating to the supply of grain full proconsular power throughout the Roman dominions for the next five years, and with having this decree confirmed by the burgesses. There were many different reasons which led to this alteration, almost equivalent to a rejection, of the original plan: a regard to Caesar, with reference to whom the most timid could not but have the greatest scruples in investing his colleague not merely with equal but with superior authority in Gaul itself; the concealed opposition of Pompeius' hereditary enemy and reluctant ally Crassus, to whom Pompeius himself attributed or professed to attribute primarily the failure of his plan; the antipathy of the republican opposition in the senate to any decree which really or nominally enlarged the authority of the regents; lastly and mainly, the incapacity of Pompeius himself, who even after having been compelled to act could not prevail on himself to acknowledge his own action, but chose always to bring forward his real design as it were in incognito by means of his friends, while he himself in his well-known modesty declared his willingness to be content with even less. No wonder that they took him at his word, and gave him the less.

Pompeius was nevertheless glad to have found at any rate a serious employment, and above all a fitting pretext for leaving the capital. He succeeded, moreover, in providing it with ampler and cheaper supplies, although not without the provinces severely feeling the reflex effect. But he had missed his real object; the proconsular title, which he had a right to bear in all the provinces, remained an empty name, so long as he had not troops of his own at his disposal. Accordingly he soon afterwards got a second proposition made to the senate, that it should confer on him the charge of conducting back the expelled king of Egypt, if necessary by force of arms, to that country. But the more that his urgent need of the senate became evident, the senators received his wishes with a less pliant and less respectful spirit. It was immediately discovered in the Sibylline oracles that it was impious to send a Roman army to Egypt; whereupon the pious senate almost unanimously resolved to abstain from armed intervention. Pompeius was already so humbled, that he would have accepted the mission even without an army; but in his incorrigible dissimulation he left this also to be declared merely by his friends, and spoke and voted for the despatch of another senator. Of course the senate rejected a proposal which wantonly risked a life so precious to his country;

and the ultimate issue of the endless discussions was the resolution not to interfere in Egypt at all (January $\frac{698}{56}$).

These repeated repulses which Pompeius met with in the senate and, what was worse, had to acquiesce in without retaliation, were naturally regarded—come from what side they would—by the public at large as so many victories of the republicans and defeats of the regents generally; the tide of republican opposition was accordingly always on the increase. Already the elections for $\frac{698}{56}$ had gone but partially according to the mind of the dynasts; Caesar's candidates for the praetorship, Publius Vatinius and Gaius Alfius, had failed, while two decided adherents of the fallen government, Gnaeus Lentulus Marcellinus and Gnaeus Domitius Calvinus, had been elected, the former as consul, the latter as praetor. But for $\frac{699}{55}$ there even appeared as candidate for the consulship Lucius Domitius Ahenobarbus, whose election it was difficult to prevent owing to his influence in the capital and his colossal wealth, and who, it was sufficiently well known, would not be content with a concealed opposition. The comitia thus rebelled; and the senate chimed in. It solemnly deliberated over an opinion, which Etruscan soothsayers of acknowledged wisdom had furnished respecting certain signs and wonders at its special request. The celestial revelation announced that through the dissension of the upper classes the whole power over the army and treasure threatened to pass to one ruler, and the state to incur loss of freedom—it seemed that the gods pointed primarily at the proposal of Gaius Messius. The republicans soon descended from heaven to earth. The law as to the domain of Capua and the other laws issued by Caesar as consul had been constantly described by them as null and void, and an opinion had been expressed in the senate as early as December $\frac{697}{57}$ that it was necessary to cancel them for their informalities. On the 6th April $\frac{698}{56}$ the consular Cicero proposed in a full senate to put the consideration of the Campanian land distribution in the order of the day for the 15th May. It was the formal declaration of war; and it was the more significant, that it came from the mouth of one of those men who only show their colours when they think that they can do so with safety. Evidently the aristocracy held that the moment had come for beginning the struggle not with Pompeius against Caesar, but against the *tyrannis* generally. What would further follow might easily be seen. Domitius made no secret that he intended as consul to propose to the burgesses the immediate recall of Caesar from

Gaul. An aristocratic restoration was at work; and with the attack on the colony of Capua the nobility threw down the gauntlet to the regents.

Caesar, although receiving from day to day detailed accounts of the events in the capital and, whenever military considerations allowed, watching their progress from as near a point of his southern province as possible, had not hitherto, visibly at least, interfered in them. But now war had been declared against him as well as his colleague, in fact against him especially; he was compelled to act, and he acted quickly. He happened to be in the very neighbourhood; the aristocracy had not even found it advisable to delay the rupture, till he should have again crossed the Alps. In the beginning of April $\frac{698}{56}$ Crassus left the capital, to concert the necessary measures with his more powerful colleague; he found Caesar in Ravenna. Thence both proceeded to Luca, and there they were joined by Pompeius, who had departed from Rome soon after Crassus (April 11), ostensibly for the purpose of procuring supplies of grain from Sardinia and Africa. The most noted adherents of the regents, such as Metellus Nepos the proconsul of Hither Spain, Appius Claudius the propraetor of Sardinia, and many others, followed them; a hundred and twenty lictors and upwards of two hundred senators were counted at this conference, where already the new monarchical senate was represented in contradistinction to the republican. In every respect the decisive voice lay with Caesar. He used it to re-establish and consolidate the existing joint rule on a new basis of more equal distribution of power. The governorships of most importance in a military point of view, next to that of the two Gauls, were assigned to his two colleagues—that of the two Spains to Pompeius, that of Syria to Crassus; and these offices were to be secured to them by decree of the people for five years ($\frac{700}{54}-\frac{704}{50}$), and to be suitably provided for in a military and financial point of view. On the other hand Caesar stipulated for the prolongation of his command, which expired with the year $\frac{700}{54}$, to the close of $\frac{705}{49}$, as well as for the prerogative of increasing his legions to ten and of charging the pay for the troops arbitrarily levied by him on the state-chest. Pompeius and Crassus were moreover promised a second consulship for the next year ($\frac{699}{55}$) before they departed for their governorships, while Caesar kept it open to himself to administer the supreme magistracy a second time after the termination of his governorship in $\frac{706}{48}$, when the ten years' interval legally requisite between two consulships should have in his case elapsed. The military support, which Pompeius and Crassus required for regulating the affairs of the capital all the more that the legions of Caesar originally destined for this purpose could not now be withdrawn from Transalpine Gaul, was to be found in new legions, which they were to raise for the Spanish and Syrian armies and were not to despatch from Italy to their several destinations until it should seem to themselves to be convenient. The main questions were thus settled; subordinate matters, such as the settlement of the tactics to be followed against the opposition in the capital, the regulation of the candidatures for the ensuing years, and the like, did not long detain them. The great master of mediation composed the personal differences which stood in the way of an agreement with his wonted ease, and compelled the most refractory elements to act in concert. An understanding befitting colleagues was restored, externally at least, between Pompeius and Crassus. Even Publius Clodius was induced to keep himself and his pack quiet, and to give no farther annoyance to Pompeius—not the least marvellous feat of the mighty magician.

That this whole settlement of the pending questions proceeded, not from a compromise among independent and rival regents meeting on equal terms, but solely from the good will of Caesar, is evident from the circumstances. Pompeius appeared at Luca in the painful position of a powerless refugee, who comes to ask aid from his opponent. Whether Caesar chose to dismiss him and to declare the coalition dissolved, or to receive him and to let the league continue just as it stood—Pompeius was in either view politically annihilated. If he did not in this case break with Caesar, he became the powerless client of his confederate. If again he did break with Caesar and, which was not very probable, effected even now a coalition with the aristocracy, this alliance between opponents, concluded under pressure of necessity and at the last moment, was so little formidable that it was hardly for the sake of averting it that Caesar agreed to those concessions. A serious rivalry on the part of Crassus with Caesar was utterly impossible. It is difficult to say what motives induced Caesar to surrender without necessity his superior position, and now voluntarily to concede—what he had refused to his rival even on the conclusion of the league of $\frac{694}{60}$, and what the latter had since, with the evident design of being armed against Caesar, vainly striven in different ways to attain without, nay against, Caesar's will—

the second consulate and military power. Certainly it was not Pompeius alone that was placed at the head of an army, but also his old enemy and Caesar's ally throughout many years, Crassus; and undoubtedly Crassus obtained his respectable military position merely as a counterpoise to the new power of Pompeius. Nevertheless Caesar was a great loser, when his rival exchanged his former powerlessness for an important command. It is possible that Caesar did not yet feel himself sufficiently master of his soldiers to lead them with confidence to warfare against the formal authorities of the land, and was therefore anxious not to be forced to civil war now by being recalled from Gaul; but whether civil war should arise or not depended at the moment far more on the aristocracy of the capital than on Pompeius, and this would have been at most a reason for Caesar not breaking openly with Pompeius, so that the opposition might not be emboldened by the rupture, but not a reason for conceding to him what he did concede. Purely personal motives may have contributed to the result; it may be that Caesar recollected how he had once stood in a position of similar powerlessness in presence of Pompeius, and had been saved from destruction only by his—pusillanimous, it is true, rather than magnanimous—retirement; it is probable that Caesar hesitated to break the heart of his beloved daughter who was sincerely attached to her husband—in his soul there was room for much besides the statesman. But the decisive reason was doubtless the consideration of Gaul. Caesar—differing from his biographers—regarded the subjugation of Gaul not as an incidental enterprise useful to him for the gaining of the crown, but as one on which depended the external security and the internal reorganisation, in a word the future, of his country. That he might be enabled to complete this conquest undisturbed and might not be obliged to take in hand just at once the extrication of Italian affairs, he unhesitatingly gave up his superiority over his rivals and granted to Pompeius sufficient power to settle matters with the senate and its adherents. This was a grave political blunder, if Caesar had no other object than to become as quickly as possible king of Rome; but the ambition of that rare man was not confined to the vulgar aim of a crown. He had the boldness to prosecute side by side, and to complete, two labours equally vast—the settlement of the internal affairs of Italy, and the acquisition and securing of a new and fresh soil for Italian civilisation. These tasks of course interfered with each other; his Gallic conquests hindered much more than helped him on his way to the throne. It yielded him bitter fruit, that he postponed the Italian revolution to $\frac{706}{48}$ instead of settling it in $\frac{698}{56}$. But as a statesman as well as a general Caesar was a peculiarly daring player, who, confiding in himself and despising his opponents, gave them always great and sometimes extravagant odds.

It was now therefore the turn of the aristocracy to make good their high gage, and to wage war as boldly as they had boldly declared it. But there is no more pitiable spectacle than when cowardly men have the misfortune to take a bold resolution. They had simply exercised no foresight at all. It seemed to have occurred to nobody that Caesar would possibly stand on his defence, or that even now Pompeius and Crassus might combine with him afresh and more closely than ever. This seems incredible; but it becomes intelligible when we glance at the persons who then led the constitutionalist opposition in the senate. Cato was still absent;[1] the most influential man in the senate at this time was Marcus Bibulus, the hero of passive resistance, the most obstinate and most stupid of all consulars. They had taken up arms only to lay them down, so soon as the adversary merely put his hand to the sheath; the bare news of the conferences of Luca sufficed to suppress all thought of a serious opposition and to bring the mass of the timid—that is, the immense majority of the senate—back to their duty as subjects, which in an unhappy hour they had abandoned. There was no further talk of the appointed discussion to try the validity of the Julian laws; the legions raised by Caesar on his own behalf were charged by decree of the senate on the public chest; the attempts on occasion of regulating the next consular provinces to take away both Gauls or one of them by decree from Caesar were rejected by the majority (end of May $\frac{698}{56}$). Thus the corporation did public penance. Secretly the lords, one after another, thoroughly frightened at their own temerity, came to make their peace and vow unconditional obedience—none more quickly than Marcus Cicero, who repented too late

[1] Cato was not yet in Rome when Cicero spoke on 11th March $\frac{698}{56}$ in favour of Sestius (*Pro Sest.* 28, 60) and when the discussion took place in the senate in consequence of the resolutions of Luca respecting Caesar's legions (Plut. *Caes.* 21); it is not till the discussions at the beginning of $\frac{699}{55}$ that we find him once more busy, and, as he travelled in winter (Plut. *Cato Min.* 38), he must have returned to Rome in the end of $\frac{698}{56}$. He cannot therefore, as has been mistakenly inferred from Asconius (p. 35, 53), have defended Milo in February $\frac{698}{56}$.

of his perfidy, and with reference to the most recent period of his life applied to himself epithets which were altogether more appropriate than flattering.[1] Of course the regents agreed to be pacified; they refused nobody pardon, for there was nobody who was worth the trouble of making him an exception. That we may see how suddenly the tone in aristocratic circles changed after the resolutions of Luca became known, it is worth while to compare the pamphlets given forth by Cicero shortly before with the palinode which he issued publicly to evince his repentance and his good intentions.[2]

The regents could thus regulate Italian affairs at their pleasure and more thoroughly than before. Italy and the capital obtained practically a garrison although not assembled in arms, and one of the regents as commandant. Of the troops levied for Syria and Spain by Crassus and Pompeius, those destined for the East no doubt took their departure; but Pompeius caused the two Spanish provinces to be administered by his lieutenants with the garrison hitherto stationed there, while he dismissed the officers and soldiers of the legions which were newly raised—nominally for despatch to Spain—on furlough, and remained himself with them in Italy.

Doubtless the tacit opposition of public opinion increased, the more clearly and generally men perceived that the regents were working to put an end to the old constitution and with as much gentleness as possible to accommodate the existing condition of the government and administration to the forms of the monarchy; but they submitted, because they were obliged to submit. First of all, all the more important affairs, and particularly all that related to military matters and external relations, were disposed of without consulting the senate, sometimes by decree of the people, sometimes by the mere good pleasure of the rulers. The arrangements agreed on at Luca respecting the military command of Gaul were submitted directly to the burgesses by Crassus and Pompeius, those relating to Spain and Syria by the tribune of the people Gaius Trebonius,

[1] *Me asinum germanum fuisse* (*Ad Att.* iv. 5, 3).

[2] This palinode is the still extant oration on the Provinces to be assigned to the consuls of $\frac{699}{55}$. It was delivered in the end of May $\frac{698}{56}$. The pieces contrasting with it are the orations for Sestius and against Vatinius and that upon the opinion of the Etruscan soothsayers, dating from the months of March and April, in which the aristocratic regime is glorified to the best of his ability and Caesar in particular is treated in a very cavalier tone. It was but reasonable that Cicero should, as he himself confesses (*Ad Att.* iv. 5, 1), be ashamed to transmit even to intimate friends that attestation of his resumed allegiance.

and in other instances the more important governorships were frequently filled up by decree of the people. That the regents did not need the consent of the authorities to increase their troops at pleasure, Caesar had already sufficiently shown: as little did they hesitate mutually to borrow troops; Caesar for instance received such collegiate support from Pompeius for the Gallic, and Crassus from Caesar for the Parthian, war. The Transpadanes, who possessed according to the existing constitution only Latin rights, were treated by Caesar during his administration practically as full burgesses of Rome.[1] While formerly the organisation of newly-acquired territories had been managed by a senatorial commission, Caesar organised his extensive Gallic conquests altogether according to his own judgment, and founded, for instance, without having received any farther powers burgess-colonies, particularly Novum-Comum (Como) with five thousand colonists. Piso conducted the Thracian, Gabinius the Egyptian, Crassus the Parthian war, without consulting the senate, and even without reporting, as was usual, to that body; in like manner triumphs and other marks of honour were accorded and carried out without the senate being asked about them. Obviously this did not arise from a mere neglect of forms, which would be the less intelligible, seeing that in the great majority of cases no opposition from

[1] This is not stated by our authorities. But the view that Caesar levied no soldiers at all from the Latin communities, that is to say from by far the greater part of his province, is in itself utterly incredible, and is directly refuted by the fact that the opposition party slightingly designates the force levied by Caesar as "for the most part natives of the Transpadane colonies" (Caes. *B. C.* iii. 87); for here the Latin colonies of Strabo (Ascon. *in Pison.* p. 3; Sueton. *Caes.* 8) are evidently meant. Yet there is no trace of Latin cohorts in Caesar's Gallic army; on the contrary according to his express statements all the recruits levied by him in Cisalpine Gaul were added to the legions or distributed into legions. It is possible that Caesar combined with the levy the bestowal of the franchise; but more probably he adhered in this matter to the standpoint of his party, which instead of seeking to procure for the Transpadanes the Roman franchise rather regarded it as already legally belonging to them (p. 149). Only thus could the report spread, that Caesar had introduced of his own authority the Roman municipal constitution among the Transpadane communities (Cic. *Ad Att.* v. 3, 2; *Ad Fam.* viii. 1, 2). This hypothesis too explains why Hirtius designates the Transpadane towns as "colonies of Roman burgesses" (*B. G.* viii. 24), and why Caesar treated the colony of Comum founded by him as a burgess-colony (Sueton. *Caes.* 28; Strabo, v. 1, p. 213; Plutarch, *Caes.* 29) while the moderate party of the aristocracy conceded to it only the same rights as to the other Transpadane colonies, viz. Latin rights, and the ultras even declared the civic rights conferred on the settlers as altogether null, and consequently did not concede to the Comenses the privileges attached to the holding of a Latin municipal magistracy (Cic. *Ad Att.* v. 11, 2; Appian, *B. C.* ii. 26).

the senate was to be expected. On the contrary, it was a well-calculated design to dislodge the senate from the domain of military arrangements and higher politics, and to restrict its administrative action to financial questions and internal affairs; and the opponents of the regents plainly saw this and protested, so far as they could, against this conduct of theirs by means of senatorial decrees and criminal actions. While the regents thus in the main set aside the senate, they still made some use of the less dangerous popular assemblies—care was taken that in these the lords of the street should put no farther difficulty in the way of the lords of the state; in many cases however they dispensed with this empty shadow, and employed without disguise autocratic forms.

The humbled senate had to submit to its position whether it would or not. The leader of the compliant majority continued to be Marcus Cicero. He was useful on account of his lawyer's talent of finding reasons, or at any rate words, for everything; and there was a genuine Caesarian irony in employing the man, by means of whom mainly the aristocracy had conducted their demonstrations against the regents, as the mouthpiece of servility. Accordingly they pardoned him for his brief desire to kick against the pricks, not however without having previously assured themselves of his submissiveness in every way. His brother had been obliged to take the position of an officer in the Gallic army to answer in some measure as a hostage for him; Pompeius had compelled Cicero himself to accept a lieutenant-generalship under him, which furnished a handle for politely banishing him at any moment. Clodius had certainly been instructed to leave him meanwhile at peace, but Caesar as little threw off Clodius on account of Cicero as he threw off Cicero on account of Clodius; and the great saviour of his country and the no less great hero of liberty entered into an antechamber rivalry in the head-quarters of Samarobriva, for the befitting illustration of which there lacked, unfortunately, a Roman Aristophanes. But not only was the same rod kept in suspense over Cicero's head, which had once already descended on him so severely; golden fetters were also laid upon him. Amidst the serious embarrassment of his finances the loans of Caesar free of interest, and the joint overseership of those buildings which occasioned the circulation of enormous sums in the capital, were in a high degree welcome to him; and many an immortal oration for the senate was nipped in the bud by the thought that the agent of Caesar might present a bill to him after the close of the sitting. Consequently he vowed "in future to ask no more after right and honour, but to strive for the favour of the regents," and "to be as flexible as an ear-lap." They used him accordingly as—what he was good for—an advocate; in which capacity it was on various occasions his lot to be obliged to defend his very bitterest foes at a higher bidding, and that especially in the senate, where he almost regularly served as the organ of the dynasts and submitted the proposals "to which others probably consented, but not he himself;" indeed, as recognised leader of the majority of the compliant, he obtained even a certain political importance. They dealt with the other members of the governing corporation accessible to fear, flattery, or gold in the same way as they had dealt with Cicero, and succeeded in keeping it on the whole in subordination.

Certainly there remained a section of their opponents, who at least kept to their colours and were neither to be terrified nor to be won. The regents had become convinced that exceptional measures, such as those against Cato and Cicero, did their cause more harm than good, and that it was a lesser evil to tolerate an unpleasant republican opposition than to convert their opponents into martyrs for the republic. Therefore they allowed Cato to return (end of $\frac{698}{56}$) and thenceforward in the senate and in the Forum, often at the peril of his life, to offer a continued opposition to the regents, which was doubtless deserving of honour, but unhappily was at the same time ridiculous. They allowed him on occasion of the proposals of Trebonius to push matters once more to a hand-to-hand conflict in the Forum, and to submit to the senate a proposal that the proconsul Caesar should be given over to the Usipetes and Tencteri on account of his perfidious conduct towards those barbarians (p. 239). They were patient when Marcus Favonius, Cato's Sancho, after the senate had adopted the resolution to charge the legions of Caesar on the state-chest, sprang to the door of the senate-house and proclaimed to the streets the danger of the country; when the same person in his scurrilous fashion called the white bandage, which Pompeius wore round his weak leg, a misplaced diadem; when the consular Lentulus Marcellinus, on being applauded, called out to the assembly to make diligent use of this privilege of expressing their opinion while they were still allowed to do so; when the tribune of the people Gaius Ateius Capito consigned Crassus on his departure for Syria, with all the formalities of the theology of the day, publicly to the evil spirits. These were, on the whole, vain demonstrations of an irritated minority; yet the little party from which they issued was so far of importance, that it on the one hand fostered and gave the watchword to the republican opposition fermenting in secret, and on the other hand sometimes dragged the majority of the senate, which withal cherished at bottom quite the same sentiments with reference to the regents, into isolated decrees directed against them. For even the majority felt the need of giving vent, at least sometimes and in subordinate matters to their suppressed indignation, and especially—after the manner of those who are servile with reluctance—of exhibiting their resentment towards the great foes in rage against the small. Wherever it was possible, a gentle blow was administered to the instruments of the regents; thus Gabinius was refused the thanksgiving-festival that he asked ($\frac{698}{56}$); thus Piso was recalled from his province; thus mourning was put on by the senate, when the tribune of the people Gaius Cato hindered the elections for $\frac{699}{55}$ as long as the consul Marcellinus belonging to the constitutional party was in office. Even Cicero, however humbly he always bowed before the regents, issued an equally envenomed and insipid pamphlet against Caesar's father-in-law. But both these feeble signs of opposition by the majority of the senate and the ineffectual resistance of the minority show only the more clearly that the government had now passed from the senate to the regents as it formerly passed from the burgesses to the senate; and that the senate was already not much more than a monarchical council of state employed also to absorb the anti-monarchical elements. "No man," the adherents of the fallen government complained, "is of the slightest account except the three; the regents are all-powerful, and they take care that no one shall remain in doubt about it; the whole state is virtually transformed and obeys the dictators; our generation will not live to see a change of things." They were living in fact no longer under the republic, but under monarchy.

But if the guidance of the state was at the absolute disposal of the regents, there remained still a political domain separated in some measure from the government proper, which it was more easy to defend and more difficult to conquer; that of the ordinary elections of magistrates, and of the jury-courts. That the latter, although not coming directly under politics, are greatly influenced everywhere, and were so above all in Rome, by the spirit that rules state-affairs, is of itself clear. The elections of magistrates certainly belonged by right to the government proper of the state; but, as at this period the state was administered substantially by extraordinary magistrates or by men wholly without title, and even the supreme ordinary magistrates, if they belonged to the anti-monarchical party, could not in any tangible way influence the state-machinery, the ordinary magistrates sank more and more into mere puppets —as, in fact, even those of them who were most disposed to opposition described themselves frankly and with entire justice as powerless ciphers—and their elections therefore sank into mere demonstrations. Thus, after the opposition had already been wholly dislodged from the proper field of battle, hostilities might nevertheless be continued in that of elections and processes. The regents spared no pains to remain victors also in this field. As to the elections, they had already at Luca settled between themselves the lists of candidates for the next years, and they left no means untried to carry the candidates agreed upon there. They expended their gold primarily for the purpose of influencing the elections. A great number of soldiers were dismissed annually on furlough from the armies of Caesar and Pompeius to take part in the voting of Rome. Caesar was wont himself to guide, and watch over, the election movements from as near a point as possible of Upper Italy. Yet the object was but very imperfectly attained. For $\frac{699}{55}$ no doubt Pompeius and Crassus were elected consuls, agreeably to the convention of Luca, and Lucius Domitius, the only candidate of the opposition who persevered, was set aside; but this had been effected only by open violence, on which occasion Cato was wounded and other extremely scandalous incidents occurred. In the next consular elections for $\frac{700}{54}$, in spite of all the exertions of the regents, Domitius was actually elected, and Cato likewise now prevailed in the candidature for the praetorship, in which to the scandal of the whole burgesses Caesar's client Vatinius had during the previous year beaten him off the field. At the elections for $\frac{701}{53}$ the opposition succeeded in so indisputably convicting the candidates of the regents along with others of the most shameful electioneering intrigues that the regents, on whom the scandal recoiled, could not do otherwise than abandon them. These repeated and severe defeats of the dynasts on the battle-field of the elections may be traceable in part to the unmanageableness of the rusty machinery, to the incalculable accidents of the polling, to the opposition at heart of the middle classes, to the various private considerations that interfere in such cases and often strangely clash with those of party; but the main cause lies elsewhere. The elections were at this time essentially in the power of the different clubs into which the aristocracy had grouped themselves; the system of bribery was organised by them on the most extensive scale and with the utmost method. The same aristocracy therefore, which was represented in the senate, ruled the elections; but while in the senate it yielded with a grudge, it worked and voted here—in secret and secure from all reckoning—absolutely against the regents. That the influence of the nobility in this field was by no means broken by the strict penal law against the electioneering intrigues of the clubs, which Crassus when consul in $\frac{699}{55}$ caused to be confirmed by the burgesses, is self-evident, and is shown by the elections of the succeeding years.

The jury-courts occasioned equally great difficulty to the regents. As they were then composed, while the senatorial nobility was here also influential, the decisive voice lay chiefly with the middle class. The fixing of a high-rated census for jurymen by a law proposed by Pompeius in $\frac{699}{55}$ is a remarkable proof that the opposition to the regents had its chief seat in the middle class properly so called, and that the great capitalists showed themselves here, as everywhere, more compliant than the latter. Nevertheless the republican party was not yet deprived of all hold in the courts, and it was never weary of directing political impeachments, not indeed against the regents themselves, but against their prominent instruments. This warfare of prosecutions was waged the more keenly, that according to usage the duty of accusation belonged to the senatorial youth, and, as may readily be conceived, there was more of republican passion, fresh talent, and bold delight in attack to be found among these youths than among the older members of their order. Certainly the courts were not free; if the regents were in earnest, the courts ventured as little as the senate to refuse obedience. None of their antagonists were prosecuted by the opposition with such hatred—so furious that it almost passed into a proverb—as Vatinius, by far the most audacious and unscrupulous of the closer adherents of Caesar; but his master gave the command, and he was acquitted in all the processes raised against him. But impeachments by men who knew how to wield the sword of dialectics and the lash of sarcasm as did Gaius Licinius Calvus and Gaius Asinius Pollio, did not miss their mark even when they failed; nor were isolated successes wanting. They were mostly, no doubt, obtained over subordinate individuals, but even one of the highest and

most hated adherents of the dynasts, the consular Gabinius, was overthrown in this way. Certainly in his case the implacable hatred of the aristocracy, which as little forgave him for the law regarding the conducting of the war with the pirates as for his disparaging treatment of the senate during his Syrian governorship, was combined with the rage of the great capitalists, against whom he had when governor of Syria ventured to defend the interests of the provincials, and even with the resentment of Crassus, with whom he had stood on ceremony in handing over to him the province. His only protection against all these foes was Pompeius, and the latter had every reason to defend his ablest, boldest, and most faithful adjutant at any price; but here, as everywhere, he knew not how to use his power and to defend his clients, as Caesar defended his; in the end of 700/54
the jurymen found Gabinius guilty of extortions and sent him into banishment.

On the whole, therefore, in the sphere of the popular elections and of the jury-courts it was the regents that fared worst. The elements which ruled in these were less tangible, and therefore more difficult to be terrified or corrupted than the direct organs of government and administration. The holders of power encountered here, especially in the popular elections, the tough energy of a close oligarchy—grouped in coteries—which is by no means finally disposed of when its rule is overthrown, and which is the more difficult to vanquish the more covert its action. They encountered here too, especially in the jury-courts, the repugnance of the middle classes towards the new monarchical rule, which with all the perplexities springing out of it they were as little able to remove. They suffered in both quarters a series of defeats. The election-victories of the opposition had, it is true, merely the value of demonstrations, since the regents possessed and employed the means of practically annulling any magistrate whom they disliked; but the criminal trials in which the opposition carried condemnations deprived them, in a way keenly felt, of useful auxiliaries. As things stood, the regents could neither set aside nor adequately control the popular elections and the jury-courts, and the opposition, however much it felt itself straitened even here, maintained to a certain extent the field of battle.

It proved, however, yet a more difficult task to encounter the opposition in a field, to which they turned with the greater zeal the more they were precluded from direct political action. This was literature. Even the judicial opposition was at the same time a literary one, and indeed pre-eminently so, for the orations were regularly published and served as political pamphlets. The arrows of poetry hit their mark still more rapidly and sharply. The lively youth of the high aristocracy, and still more energetically perhaps the cultivated middle class in the Italian country towns, waged the war of pamphlets and epigrams with zeal and success. There fought side by side on this field the noble senator's son Gaius Licinius Calvus ($\frac{672}{82}$–$\frac{706}{48}$) who was as much feared in the character of an orator and pamphleteer as of a versatile poet, and the municipals of Cremona and Verona Marcus Furius Bibaculus ($\frac{652}{102}$–$\frac{691}{63}$) and Quintus Valerius Catullus ($\frac{667}{87}$-*c.* $\frac{700}{54}$) whose elegant and pungent epigrams flew swiftly like arrows through Italy and were sure to hit their mark. An oppositional tone prevails throughout the literature of these years. It is full of indignant sarcasm against the "great Caesar," "the unique general," against the affectionate father-in-law and son-in-law, who ruin the whole globe in order to give their dissolute favourites opportunity to parade the spoils of the long-haired Celts through the streets of Rome, to furnish royal banquets with the booty of the farthest isles of the west, and as rivals showering gold to supplant honest youths at home in the favour of their mistresses. There is in the poems of Catullus[1] and the other fragments of the literature of this period something of that fervour of personal and political hatred, of that republican agony overflowing in riotous humour or in stern despair, which are more prominently and powerfully apparent in Aristophanes and Demosthenes.

The most sagacious of the three rulers at least saw well that it was as impossible to despise this opposition as to suppress it by word of command. So far as he could, Caesar tried rather personally to gain over the more eminent authors. Cicero himself had to thank his literary reputation in good part for the respectful treatment which he especially experienced from

[1] The collection handed down to us is full of references to the events of $\frac{699}{55}$ and $\frac{700}{54}$ and was doubtless published in the latter year; the most recent event which it mentions is the prosecution of Vatinius (August $\frac{700}{54}$). The statement of Hieronymus that Catullus died in $\frac{697}{57}$–$\frac{698}{56}$ requires therefore to be altered only by a few years. From the circumstance that Vatinius "swears falsely by his consulship," it has been erroneously inferred that the collection did not appear till after the consulate of Vatinius ($\frac{707}{47}$); it only follows from it that Vatinius, when the collection appeared, might already reckon on becoming consul in a definite year, for which he had every reason as early as $\frac{700}{54}$; for his name certainly stood on the list of candidates agreed on at Luca (Cicero, *Ad Att.* iv. 8 *b.* 2).

Caesar; but the governor of Gaul did not disdain to conclude a special peace even with Catullus through the intervention of his father who had become personally known to him in Verona; and the young poet, who had just heaped upon the powerful general the bitterest and most personal sarcasms, was treated by him with the most flattering distinction. In fact Caesar had genius enough to follow his literary opponents on their own domain and to publish—as an indirect defence against manifold attacks—a detailed report on the Gallic wars, which set forth before the public, with happily assumed naïveté, the necessity and constitutional propriety of his military operations. But it is freedom alone that is absolutely and exclusively poetical and creative; it and it alone is able even in its most wretched caricature, even with its latest breath, to inspire fresh enthusiasm. All the sound elements of literature were and remained anti-monarchical; and, if Caesar himself could venture on this domain without proving a failure, the reason was merely that even now he still cherished at heart the magnificent dream of a free commonwealth, although he was unable to transfer it either to his adversaries or to his adherents. Practical politics were not more absolutely controlled by the regents than literature by the republicans.[1]

[1] The well-known poem of Catullus numbered xxix. was written in $\frac{699}{55}$ or $\frac{700}{54}$ after Caesar's Britannic expedition and before the death of Julia:

> *Quis hoc potest videre, quis potest pati,*
> *Nisi impudicus et vorax et aleo,*
> *Mamurram habere quod comata Gallia*
> *Habebat ante et ultima Britannia? etc.*

Mamurra of Formiae, Caesar's favourite and for a time during the Gallic wars an officer in his army, had, probably a short time before the composition of this poem, returned to the capital and was in all likelihood then occupied with the building of his much-talked-of marble palace furnished with lavish magnificence on the Caelian hill. The Pontic booty mentioned in the poem is that of Mytilene, of which Caesar had a share as one of the officers serving in $\frac{675}{79}$ in the army of the governor of Bithynia and Pontus (iii. 325); the Iberian spoil is that which was acquired in the governorship of Further Spain (p. 184).

More innocent than this virulent invective, which was bitterly felt by Caesar (Suet. *Caes.* 73), is another nearly contemporary poem of the same author (xi.) to which we may here refer, because with its pathetic introduction to an anything but pathetic commission it very cleverly quizzes the staff of the new regents—the Gabiniuses, Antoniuses, and such like, suddenly advanced from the lowest haunts to head-quarters. Let it be remembered that it was written at a time when Caesar was fighting on the Rhine and on the Thames, and when the expeditions of Crassus to Parthia and of Gabinius to Egypt were in preparation. The poet, as if he too expected one of the vacant posts from one of the regents, gives to two of his clients their last instructions before departure:

> *Furi et Aureli, comites Catulli, etc.*

It became necessary to take serious steps against this impotent, but still troublesome and audacious opposition. The condemnation of Gabinius, apparently, turned the scale (end of $\frac{700}{54}$). The regents agreed to introduce a dictatorship, though only a temporary one, and by means of this to carry new coercive measures, especially respecting the elections and the jury-courts. Pompeius, as the regent on whom primarily devolved the government of Rome and Italy, was charged with the execution of this resolve; which accordingly bore the impress of the awkwardness in resolution and action that characterised him, and of his singular incapacity of speaking out frankly, even where he would and could command. Already at the close of $\frac{700}{54}$ the demand for a dictatorship was brought forward in the senate in the form of hints, and that not by Pompeius himself. There served as its ostensible ground the continuance of the system of clubs and bands in the capital, which by acts of bribery and violence certainly exercised the most pernicious influence on the elections as well as on the jury-courts and perpetuated a state of disturbance; we must allow that this rendered it easy for the regent to justify their exceptional measures. But, as may well be conceived, even the servile majority shrank from granting what the future dictator himself seemed to shrink from openly asking. When the unparalleled agitation regarding the elections for the consulship of $\frac{701}{53}$ led to the most scandalous scenes, so that the elections were postponed a full year beyond the fixed time and only took place after a seven months' interregnum in July $\frac{701}{53}$, Pompeius found in this state of things the desired occasion for indicating still more distinctly to the senate that the dictatorship was the only means of cutting, if not of loosing the knot; but the decisive word of command was not even yet spoken. Perhaps it would have still remained for long unuttered, had not the most audacious partisan of the republican opposition Titus Annius Milo stepped into the field at the consular elections for $\frac{702}{52}$ as a candidate in opposition to the candidates of the regents, Quintus Metellus Scipio and Publius Plautius Hypsaeus, both men closely connected with Pompeius personally and thoroughly devoted to him.

Milo, endowed with physical courage, with a certain talent for intrigue and for contracting debt, and above all with an ample amount of native assurance which had been carefully cultivated, had made himself a name among the political adventurers of the time, and was the most famous man in his trade next to Clodius, and naturally therefore through rivalry at the most deadly feud with the latter. As the Achilles of the streets had been acquired by the regents and with their permission was again playing the ultra-democrat, the Hector of the streets became as a matter of course an aristocrat; and the republican opposition, which now would have concluded an alliance with Catilina in person, had he presented himself to them, readily acknowledged Milo as their legitimate champion in all riots. In fact the few successes, which they carried off in this field of battle, were the work of Milo and of his well-trained band of gladiators. So Cato and his friends in return supported the candidature of Milo for the consulship; even Cicero could not avoid recommending one who had been his enemy's enemy and his own protector during many years; and as Milo himself spared neither money nor violence to carry his election, it seemed secure. For the regents it would have been not only a new and keenly felt defeat, but also an imminent danger; for it was to be foreseen that the bold partisan would not allow himself as consul to be reduced to insignificance so easily as Domitius and other men of the respectable opposition. It happened that Achilles and Hector accidently encountered each other not far from the capital on the Appian Way, and a fray arose between their respective bands, in which Clodius himself received a sword-cut on the shoulder and was compelled to take refuge in a neighbouring house. This had occurred without orders from Milo; but, as the matter had gone so far, and as the storm had now to be encountered at any rate, the whole crime seemed to Milo more desirable and even less dangerous than the half; he ordered his men to drag Clodius forth from his lurking place and to put him to death (13th January $\frac{702}{52}$).

The street leaders of the regents' party—the tribunes of the people Titus Munatius Plancus, Quintus Pompeius Rufus, and Gaius Sallustius Crispus—saw in this occurrence a fitting opportunity to thwart in the interest of their masters the candidature of Milo and carry the dictatorship of Pompeius. The dregs of the populace, especially the freedmen and slaves, had lost in Clodius their patron and future deliverer (p. 278); the necessary excitement was thus easily aroused. After the bloody corps had been exposed for show at the orators' platform in the Forum and the speeches appropriate to the occasion had been made, the riot broke forth. The seat of the perfidious aristocracy was destined as a funeral pile for the great liberator; the mob carried the body to the senate-house, and set the building on fire. Thereafter the multitude proceeded to the front of Milo's house and kept it under siege, till his band drove off the assailants by a discharge of arrows. They passed on to the house of Pompeius and of his consular candidates, of whom the former was saluted as dictator and the latter as consuls, and thence to the house of the interrex Marcus Lepidus, on whom devolved the conduct of the consular elections. When the latter, as in duty bound, refused to make arrangements for the elections immediately, as the clamorous multitude demanded, he was kept during five days under siege in his dwelling house.

But the instigators of these scandalous scenes had over-acted their part. Certainly their lord and master was resolved to employ this favourable episode in order not merely to set aside Milo, but also to seize the dictatorship; he wished, however, to receive it not from a mob of bludgeon-men, but from the senate. Pompeius brought up troops to put down the anarchy which prevailed in the capital, and which had in reality become intolerable to everybody; at the same time he now enjoined what he had hitherto requested, and the senate complied. It was merely an empty subterfuge, that on the proposal of Cato and Bibulus the proconsul Pompeius, retaining his former offices, was nominated as "consul without colleague" instead of dictator (on the 25th of the intercalary month [1] $\frac{702}{52}$) —a subterfuge, which admitted an appellation labouring under a double incongruity [2] for the mere purpose of avoiding one which expressed the simple fact, and which vividly reminds us of the sagacious resolution of the waning patriciate to concede to the plebeians not the consulship, but only the consular power (i. 287).

Thus in legal possession of full power, Pompeius set to work and proceeded with energy against the republican party which was powerful in the clubs and jury-courts. The existing enactments as to elections were repeated and enforced by a special law; and by another against electioneering intrigues, which obtained retrospective force for all offences of this sort committed since $\frac{684}{70}$, the penalties hitherto imposed were augmented. Still more important was the enactment, that the governorships, which were by far the more important and especially by far the more lucrative half of official life, should be conferred on the consuls and praetors not immediately on their retirement from

[1] In this year the January with 29 and the February with 23 days were followed by the intercalary month with 28, and then by March.

[2] *Consul* signifies "colleague" (i. 246), and a consul who is at the same time proconsul is at once an actual consul and a consul's substitute.

the consulate or praetorship, but only after the expiry of other five years; an arrangement which of course could only come into effect after four years, and therefore made the filling up of the governorships for the next few years substantially dependent on decrees of senate which were to be issued for the regulation of this interval, and thus practically on the person or section ruling the senate at the moment. The jury-commissions were left in existence, but limits were put to the right of counter-plea, and—what was perhaps still more important—the liberty of speech in the courts was done away; for both the number of the advocates and the time of speaking apportioned to each were restricted by fixing a maximum, and the bad habit which had prevailed of adducing, in addition to the witnesses as to facts, witnesses to character or *laudatores*, as they were called, in favour of the accused was prohibited. The obsequious senate further decreed on the suggestion of Pompeius that the country had been placed in peril by the quarrel on the Appian Way; accordingly a special commission was appointed by an exceptional law for all crimes connected with it, the members of which were directly nominated by Pompeius. An attempt was also made to give once more a serious importance to the office of the censors, and by that agency to purge the deeply disordered burgess-body of its worst elements.

All these measures were adopted under the pressure of the sword. In consequence of the declaration of the senate that the country was in danger, Pompeius called the men capable of service throughout Italy to arms and made them swear allegiance for all contingencies; an adequate and trustworthy corps was temporarily stationed at the Capitol; at every stirring of opposition Pompeius threatened armed intervention, and during the proceedings at the trial respecting the murder of Clodius stationed, contrary to all precedent, a guard over the place of trial itself.

The scheme for the revival of the censorship failed, because among the servile majority of the senate no one possessed sufficient moral courage and authority even to become a candidate for such an office. On the other hand Milo was condemned by the jurymen (8th April, $\frac{702}{52}$) and Cato's candidature for the consulship of $\frac{703}{51}$ was frustrated. The opposition of speeches and pamphlets received through the new judicial ordinances a blow from which it never recovered; the dreaded forensic eloquence was thereby driven from the field of politics, and thenceforth felt the restraints of monarchy. Opposition of course had not disappeared either from the minds of the great majority of the nation or even wholly from public life—to effect that end the popular elections, the jury-courts, and literature must have been not merely restricted, but annihilated. Indeed, in these very transactions themselves, Pompeius by his unskilfulness and perversity helped the republicans to gain even under his dictatorship several triumphs which he severely felt. The special measures, which the rulers took to strengthen their power, were of course officially characterised as enactments made in the interest of public tranquillity and order, and every burgess, who did not desire anarchy, was described as substantially concurring in them. But Pompeius pushed this transparent fiction so far, that instead of putting safe instruments into the special commission for the investigation of the late tumult, he chose the most respectable men of all parties, including even Cato, and applied his influence over the court essentially to maintain order, and to render it impossible for his adherents as well as for his opponents to indulge in the scenes of disturbance customary in the trials of this period. This neutrality of the regent was discernible in the judgments of the special court. The jurymen did not venture to acquit Milo himself; but most of the subordinate persons accused belonging to the party of the republican opposition were acquitted, while condemnation inexorably befell those who in the late riot had taken part for Clodius, or in other words for the regents, including not a few of Caesar's and of Pompeius's own most intimate friends—even Hypsaeus his candidate for the consulship, and the tribunes of the people Plancus and Rufus, who had directed the *émeute* in his interest. That Pompeius did not prevent their condemnation for the sake of appearing impartial, was one specimen of his folly; and a second was, that he withal in matters quite indifferent violated his own laws to favour his friends—appearing for example as a witness to character in the trial of Plancus, and in fact protecting from condemnation several accused persons specially connected with him, such as Metellus Scipio. As usual, he wished here also to accomplish opposite things; in attempting to satisfy the duties at once of the impartial regent and of the party chief, he fulfilled neither the one nor the other, and was regarded by public opinion with justice as a despotic regent, and by his adherents with equal justice as a leader who either could not or would not protect his followers.

But, although the republicans were still stirring and were even refreshed by an isolated success here and there, chiefly through the blundering of Pompeius, the object which the regents had proposed to themselves in that dictatorship was on the whole attained, the reins were drawn tighter, the republican party was humbled, and the new monarchy was strengthened. The public began to reconcile themselves to it. When Pompeius not long after recovered from a serious illness, his restoration was celebrated throughout Italy with the befitting demonstrations of joy which are usual on such occasions in monarchies. The regents showed themselves satisfied; as early as the 1st of August $\frac{702}{52}$ Pompeius resigned his dictatorship, and shared the consulship with his client Metellus Scipio.

CHAPTER IX

DEATH OF CRASSUS—RUPTURE BETWEEN THE JOINT RULERS

MARCUS CRASSUS had for years been reckoned among the heads of the "three-headed monster," without any proper title to be so included. He served as a makeweight to trim the balance between the real regents Pompeius and Caesar, or, to speak more accurately, he threw his weight into the scale of Caesar against Pompeius. The part of a supernumerary colleague is not a very honourable one; but Crassus was never hindered by any keen sense of honour from pursuing his own advantage. He was a merchant and was open to negotiation. What was offered to him was not much; but, as more was not to be got, he accepted it, and sought to forget the ambition that fretted him, and his chagrin at occupying a position so near to power and yet so powerless, amidst his always accumulating piles of gold. But the conference at Luca changed the state of matters also for him; with the view of still retaining the preponderance as compared with Pompeius after concessions so extensive, Caesar gave to his old confederate Crassus an opportunity of attaining in Syria through the Parthian war the same position to which Caesar had attained by the Celtic war in Gaul. It was difficult to say whether these new prospects proved more attractive to the ardent thirst for gold which had now become at the age of sixty a second nature and grew only the more intense with every newly won million, or to the ambition which had been long repressed with difficulty in the old man's breast and now glowed in it with restless fire. He arrived in Syria as early as the beginning of $\frac{700}{54}$; he had not even waited for the expiry of his consulship to depart. Full of impatient ardour he seemed desirous to redeem every minute with the view of making up for what he had lost, of gaining the treasures of the East in addition to those of the West, of achieving the power and glory of a general as rapidly as Caesar, and with as little trouble as Pompeius.

He found the Parthian war already commenced. The faithless conduct of Pompeius towards the Parthians has been already mentioned (p. 131); he had not respected the stipulated frontier of the Euphrates and had wrested several provinces from the

Parthian empire for the benefit of Armenia, which was now a client state of Rome. King Phraates had submitted to this treatment; but after he had been murdered by his two sons Mithradates and Orodes, the new king Mithradates immediately declared war on the king of Armenia, Artavasdes, son of the recently deceased Tigranes (about $\frac{698}{56}$).[1] This was at the same time a declaration of war against Rome; as soon therefore as the revolt of the Jews was suppressed, Gabinius, the able and spirited governor of Syria, led the legions over the Euphrates. Meanwhile, however, a revolution had occurred in the Parthian empire; the grandees of the kingdom, with the young, bold, and talented grand vizier at their head, had overthrown king Mithradates and placed his brother Orodes on the throne. Mithradates therefore made common cause with the Romans and resorted to the camp of Gabinius. Everything promised the best results to the enterprise of the Roman governor, when he unexpectedly received orders to restore the king of Egypt by force of arms to Alexandria (p. 144). He was obliged to obey; but, in the expectation of soon coming back, he induced the dethroned Parthian prince who solicited aid from him to commence the war in the meanwhile at his own hand. Mithradates did so; and Seleucia and Babylon declared for him; but the vizier captured Seleucia by assault, having been in person the first to mount the battlements, and in Babylon Mithradates himself was forced by famine to surrender, whereupon he was by his brother's orders put to death. His death was a palpable loss to the Romans; but it by no means put an end to the agitation in the Parthian empire, and the Armenian war continued. Gabinius, after ending the Egyptian campaign, was just on the eve of turning to account the still favourable opportunity and resuming the interrupted Parthian war, when Crassus arrived in Syria and along with the command took up also the plans of his predecessor. Full of high-flown hopes he estimated the difficulties of the march as slight, and the power of resistance in the armies of the enemy as yet slighter; he not only spoke confidently of the subjugation of the Parthians, but was already in imagination the conqueror of the kingdoms of Bactria and India.

The new Alexander, however, was in no haste. Before he carried into effect these great plans, he found leisure for very

[1] Tigranes was still living in February $\frac{698}{56}$ (Cic. *pro Sest.* 27, 59); on the other hand Artavasdes was already reigning before $\frac{700}{54}$ (Justin, xlii. 2, 4; Plut. *Crass.* 49).

tedious and very lucrative subordinate transactions. The temples of Derceto at Hierapolis Bambyce and of Jehovah at Jerusalem and other rich shrines of the Syrian province, were by order of Crassus despoiled of their treasures; and contingents or, still better, sums of money instead were levied from all the subjects. The military operations of the first summer were limited to an extensive reconnaissance in Mesopotamia; the Euphrates was crossed, the Parthian satrap was defeated at Ichnae (on the Belik to the north of Rakkah), and the neighbouring towns, including the considerable one of Nicephorium (Rakkah), were occupied, after which the Romans having left garrisons behind in them returned to Syria. They had hitherto been in doubt whether it was more advisable to march to Parthia by the circuitous route of Armenia or by the direct route through the Mesopotamian desert. The first route, leading through mountainous regions under the control of trustworthy allies, commended itself by its greater safety; king Artavasdes came in person to the Roman head-quarters to advocate this plan of campaign. But that reconnaissance decided in favour of the march through Mesopotamia. The numerous and flourishing Greek and half-Greek towns in the regions along the Euphrates and Tigris, above all the great city of Seleucia, were altogether averse to the Parthian rule; all the Greek townships with which the Romans came into contact had now, like the citizens of Carrhae at an earlier time (p. 127), practically shown how ready they were to shake off the intolerable foreign yoke and to receive the Romans as deliverers, almost as countrymen. The Arab prince Abgarus, who commanded the desert of Edessa and Carrhae and thereby the usual route from the Euphrates to the Tigris, had arrived in the camp of the Romans to assure them in person of his devotedness. The Parthians had appeared to be wholly unprepared.

Accordingly ($\frac{701}{53}$) the Euphrates was crossed (near Biradjik). To reach the Tigris from this point they had the choice of two routes; either the army might move downward along the Euphrates to the latitude of Seleucia where the Euphrates and Tigris are only a few miles distant from each other; or they might immediately after crossing take the shortest line to the Tigris right across the great Mesopotamian desert. The former route led directly to the Parthian capital Ctesiphon, which lay opposite Seleucia on the other bank of the Tigris; several weighty voices were raised in favour of this route in the Roman council of war; in particular the quaestor Gaius Cassius pointed to the difficulties of the march in the desert, and to the suspicious reports arriving from the Roman garrisons on the left bank of the Euphrates as to the Parthian warlike preparations. But in opposition to this the Arab prince Abgarus announced that the Parthians were employed in evacuating their western provinces. They had already packed up their treasures and put themselves in motion to flee to the Hyrcanians and Scythians; only through a forced march by the shortest route was it at all possible still to reach them; but by such a march the Romans would probably succeed in overtaking and cutting up at least the rear guard of the great army under Sillaces and the vizier, and obtaining enormous spoil. These reports of the friendly Bedouins decided the direction of the march; the Roman army, consisting of seven legions, 4000 cavalry, and 4000 slingers and archers, turned off from the Euphrates and away into the inhospitable plains of northern Mesopotamia.

Far and wide no enemy appeared; only hunger and thirst, and the endless sandy desert, seemed to keep watch at the gates of the East. At length, after many days of toilsome marching, not far from the first river which the Roman army had to cross, the Balissus (Belik), the first horsemen of the enemy were descried. Abgarus with his Arabs was sent out to reconnoitre; the Parthian squadrons retired up to and over the river and vanished in the distance, pursued by Abgarus and his followers. With impatience the Romans waited for his return and for more exact information. The general hoped here at length to come upon the constantly retreating foe; his young and brave son Publius, who had fought with the greatest distinction in Gaul under Caesar (pp. 223, 235), and had been sent by the latter at the head of a Celtic squadron of horse to take part in the Parthian war, was inflamed with a vehement desire for the fight. When no tidings came, they resolved to advance at a venture; the signal for starting was given, the Balissus was crossed, the army after a brief insufficient rest at noon was led on without delay at a rapid pace. Then suddenly the kettledrums of the Parthians sounded all around; on every side their silken gold-embroidered banners were seen waving, and their iron helmets and coats of mail glittering in the blaze of the hot noonday sun; and by the side of the vizier stood prince Abgarus with his Bedouins.

The Romans saw too late the net in which they had allowed themselves to be ensnared. With sure glance the vizier had thoroughly seen both the danger and the means of meeting it. Nothing could be accomplished against Roman infantry of the line with Oriental infantry; so he had got rid of this arm, and by sending a mass which was useless in the main field of battle under the personal leadership of king Orodes to Armenia, he had prevented king Artavasdes from allowing the promised 10,000 heavy cavalry to join the army of Crassus, who now painfully felt the want of them. On the other hand the vizier met the Roman tactics, unsurpassed of their kind, with a system entirely different. His army consisted exclusively of cavalry; the line was formed of the heavy horsemen armed with long thrusting-lances, and protected, man and horse, by a coat of mail of metallic plates or a leathern doublet and by similar greaves; the mass of the troops consisted of mounted archers. As compared with these, the Romans were thoroughly inferior in the corresponding arms both as to number and excellence. Their infantry of the line, excellent as they were in close combat, whether at a short distance with the heavy javelin or in hand-to-hand combat with the sword, could not compel an army consisting wholly of cavalry to come to an engagement with them; and they found, even when they did come to a hand-to-hand conflict, an equal if not superior adversary in the ironclad hosts of lancers. As compared with an army like this Parthian one, the Roman army was at a disadvantage strategically, because the cavalry commanded the communications; and at a disadvantage tactically, because every weapon of close combat must succumb to that which is wielded from a distance, unless the struggle becomes an individual one, man against man. The concentrated position, on which the whole Roman method of war was based, increased the danger in presence of such an attack; the closer the ranks of the Roman column, the more irresistible certainly was its onset, but the less also could the missiles fail to hit their mark. Under ordinary circumstances, where towns have to be defended and difficulties of the ground have to be considered, such a system of tactics operating with mere cavalry against infantry could never be completely carried out; but in the Mesopotamian desert, where the army almost like a ship on the high seas neither encountered an obstacle nor met with a basis for strategic dispositions during many days' march, this mode of warfare was irresistible for the very reason that circumstances allowed it to be developed there in all its purity and therefore in all its power. There everything combined to put the foreign infantry at a disadvantage against the native cavalry. Where the heavily-laden Roman foot-soldier dragged himself toilsomely through the sand or the steppe, and perished from hunger or still more from thirst amid the pathless route marked only by water-springs that were far apart and difficult to find, the Parthian horseman, accustomed from childhood to sit on his fleet steed or camel, nay almost to spend his life in the saddle, easily traversed the desert whose hardships he had long learned how to lighten or in case of need to bear. There no rain fell to mitigate the intolerable heat, and to slacken the bow-strings and leathern thongs of the enemy's archers and slingers; there amidst the deep sand at many places ordinary ditches and ramparts could hardly be formed for the camp. Imagination can scarcely conceive a situation in which all the military advantages were more on the one side, and all the disadvantages more thoroughly on the other.

To the question, under what circumstances this new style of tactics, the first national system that on its own proper ground showed itself superior to the Roman, arose among the Parthians, we can only reply by conjectures. The lancers and mounted archers were of great antiquity in the East, and already formed the flower of the armies of Cyrus and Darius; but hitherto these arms had been employed only as secondary, and essentially to cover the thoroughly useless Oriental infantry. The Parthian armies also by no means differed in this respect from the other Oriental ones; armies are mentioned, five-sixths of which consisted of infantry. In the campaign of Crassus, on the other hand, the cavalry for the first time came forward independently, and this arm obtained quite a new application and quite a different value. The irresistible superiority of the Roman infantry in close combat seems to have led the adversaries of Rome in very different parts of the world independently of each other—at the same time and with similar success—to meet it with cavalry and distant weapons. What was completely successful with Cassivellaunus in Britain (p. 242) and partially successful with Vercingetorix in Gaul (p. 252)—what was to a certain degree attempted even by Mithradates Eupator (p. 64)—the vizier of Orodes carried out only on a larger scale and more completely. And in doing so he had special advantages: for he found in the heavy cavalry the means of forming a line; the bow which was national in the East and was handled with masterly skill in the Persian provinces gave him an effective weapon for distant combat; and lastly the peculiarities of the country and the people enabled him freely to realise his brilliant idea. Here, where the Roman weapons of close combat and the Roman system of concentration yielded for the first time before the weapons of more distant warfare and the system of deploying, was initiated that military revolution which only reached its completion with the introduction of fire-arms.

Under such circumstances the first battle between the Romans and Parthians was fought amidst the sandy desert thirty miles to the south of Carrhae (Harran) where there was a Roman garrison, and at a somewhat less distance to the north of Ichnae. The Roman archers were sent forward, but retired immediately before the enormous numerical superiority and the far greater elasticity and range of the Parthian bows. The legions, which, in spite of the advice of the more sagacious officers that they should be deployed as much as possible against the enemy, had been drawn up in a dense square of twelve cohorts on each side, were soon outflanked and overwhelmed with the formidable arrows, which under such circumstances hit their man even without special aim, and against which the soldiers had no means of retaliation. The hope that the enemy might expend his missiles vanished with a glance at the endless range of camels laden with arrows. The Parthians were still extending their line. That the outflanking might not end in surrounding, Publius Crassus advanced to the attack with a select corps of cavalry, archers, and infantry of the line. The enemy in fact abandoned the attempt to close the circle, and retreated, hotly pursued by the impetuous leader of the Romans. But, when the corps of Publius had totally lost sight of the main army, the heavy cavalry made a stand against it, and the Parthian host hastening up from all sides closed in like a net round it. Publius, who saw his troops falling thickly and vainly around him under the arrows of the mounted archers, threw himself in desperation with his Celtic cavalry unprotected by any coats of mail on the iron-clad lancers of the enemy; but the fearless valour of his Celts, who seized the lances with their hands or sprang from their horses to stab the enemy, performed its marvels in vain. The remains of the corps, including their leader wounded in the sword-arm, were driven to a slight eminence, where they only served for an easier mark to the enemy's archers. Mesopotamian Greeks, who were accurately acquainted with the country, adjured Crassus to ride off with them and make an attempt to escape; but he refused to separate his fate from that of the brave men whom his too daring courage had led to death, and he caused himself to be stabbed by the hand of his shield-bearer. Following his example, most of the still surviving officers put themselves to death. Of the whole division, about

6000 strong, not more than some 500 were taken prisoners; no one was able to escape. Meanwhile the attack on the main army had slackened, and the Romans were but too glad to rest. When at length the absence of any tidings from the corps sent out startled them out of the deceitful calm, and they drew near to the scene of the battle for the purpose of learning its fate, the head of the son was displayed on a pole before his father's eyes; and the terrible onslaught began once more against the main army with the same fury and the same hopeless uniformity. They could neither break the ranks of the lancers nor reach the archers; night alone put an end to the slaughter. Had the Parthians bivouacked on the battle-field, hardly a man of the Roman army would have escaped. But not trained to fight otherwise than on horseback, and therefore afraid of a surprise, they were wont never to encamp close to the enemy; jeeringly they shouted to the Romans that they would give the general a night to bewail his son, and galloped off to return next morning and despatch the game that lay bleeding on the ground.

Of course the Romans did not wait for the morning. The lieutenant-generals Cassius and Octavius—Crassus himself had completely lost his judgment—ordered the men still capable of marching to set out immediately and with the utmost silence (leaving behind the whole—said to amount to 4000—of the wounded and stragglers), with the view of seeking protection within the walls of Carrhae. It happened that the Parthians, when they returned on the following day, applied themselves first of all to seek out and massacre the scattered Romans left behind, and that the garrison and inhabitants of Carrhae, early informed of the disaster by fugitives, had marched forth in all haste to meet the beaten army; the remnant was thus saved from what seemed inevitable destruction.

The Parthian cavalry could not think of undertaking the siege of Carrhae. But the Romans soon voluntarily departed, whether compelled by want of provisions, or in consequence of the desponding precipitation of their commander-in-chief, whom the soldiers had vainly attempted to remove from the command and to replace by Cassius. They moved in the direction of the Armenian mountains; marching by night and resting by day. Octavius, with a band of 5000 men, reached the fortress of Sinnaca, which was only a day's march distant from the heights that would give shelter, and liberated even at the peril of his own life the commander-in-chief, whom a guide had led astray and given up to the enemy. Then the vizier rode in front of the Roman camp to offer, in the name of his king, peace and friendship to the Romans, and to propose a personal conference between the two generals. The Roman army, demoralised as it was, adjured and indeed compelled its leader to accept the offer. The vizier received the consular and his staff with the usual honours, and offered anew to conclude a compact of friendship; only, with just bitterness recalling the fate of the agreements concluded with Lucullus and Pompeius respecting the Euphrates boundary (p. 131), he demanded that it should be immediately reduced to writing. A richly adorned horse was produced; it was a present from the king to the Roman commander-in-chief; the servants of the vizier crowded round Crassus, zealous to mount him on the steed. It seemed to the Roman officers as if there was a design to seize the person of the commander-in-chief; Octavius, unarmed as he was, pulled the sword of one of the Parthians from its sheath and stabbed the groom. In the tumult which thereupon arose, the Roman officers were all put to death; the grey-haired commander-in-chief also, like his grand-uncle (iii. 52), was unwilling to serve as a living trophy to the enemy, and sought and found death. The multitude left behind in the camp without a leader were partly taken prisoners, partly dispersed. What the day of Carrhae had begun, the day of Sinnaca completed (June 9, $\frac{701}{53}$); the two took their place side by side with the days of the Allia, of Cannae, and of Arausio. The army of the Euphrates was no more. Only the squadron of Gaius Cassius, which had been broken off from the main army on the retreat from Carrhae, and some other scattered bands and isolated fugitives succeeded in escaping from the Parthians and Bedouins and separately finding their way back to Syria. Of above 40,000 Roman legionaries, who had crossed the Euphrates, not a fourth part returned; the half had perished; nearly 10,000 Roman prisoners were settled by the victors in the extreme east of their kingdom—in the oasis of Merv—as bondsmen compelled after the Parthian fashion to render military service. For the first time since the eagles had headed the legions, they had become in the same year trophies of victory in the hands of foreign nations, almost contemporaneously of a German tribe in the West (p. 246) and of the Parthians in the East. As to the impression which the defeat of the Romans produced in the East, unfortunately no adequate information has reached us; but it must have been deep and lasting. King Orodes was just celebrating the marriage of his son Pacorus with the sister of his new ally, Artavasdes the king of Armenia, when the announcement of the victory of his vizier arrived, and along with it, according to Oriental usage, the cut-off head of Crassus. The tables were already removed; one of the wandering companies of actors from Asia Minor, numbers of which at that time existed and carried Hellenic poetry and the Hellenic drama far into the East, was just performing before the assembled court the Bacchae of Euripides. The actor playing the part of Agave, who in her Dionysiac frenzy has torn in pieces her son and returns from Cithaeron carrying his head on the thyrsus, exchanged this for the bloody head of Crassus, and to the infinite delight of his audience of half-Hellenised barbarians began afresh the well-known song:

φέρομεν ἐξ ὄρεος
ἕλικα νεότομον ἐπὶ μέλαθρα
μακαρίαν θήραν.

It was, since the times of the Achaemenidae, the first serious victory which the Orientals had achieved over the West; and there was a deep significance in the fact that, by way of celebrating his victory, the fairest product of the western world—Greek tragedy—parodied itself through its degenerate representatives in that hideous burlesque. The civic spirit of Rome and the genius of Hellas began simultaneously to accommodate themselves to the chains of sultanism.

The disaster, terrible in itself, seemed also as though it was to be dreadful in its consequences, and to shake the foundations of the Roman power in the East. It was among the least of its results that the Parthians now had absolute sway beyond the Euphrates; that Armenia, after having fallen away from the Roman alliance even before the disaster of Crassus, was reduced by it into entire dependence on Parthia; that the faithful citizens of Carrhae were bitterly punished for their adherence to the Occidentals by the new master appointed over them by the Parthians, one of the treacherous guides of the Romans, named Andromachus. The Parthians now prepared in earnest to cross the Euphrates in their turn, and, in union with the Armenians and Arabs, to dislodge the Romans from Syria. The Jews and various other Occidentals awaited emancipation from the Roman rule there, no less impatiently than the Hellenes beyond the Euphrates awaited relief from the Parthian; in Rome civil war was at the door; an attack at this particular place and time was a grave peril. But fortunately for Rome the leaders on each side had changed. Sultan Orodes was too much indebted to the heroic prince, who had first placed the crown on his head and then cleared the land from the enemy, not to get rid of him as soon as possible by the executioner. His place as commander-in-chief of the invading army destined for Syria was filled by a prince, the king's son Pacorus, with whom on account of his youth and inexperience the prince Osaces had to be associated as military adviser. On the other side the *interim* command in Syria in room of Crassus was taken up by the prudent and resolute quaestor Gaius Cassius.

The Parthians were, just like Crassus formerly, in no haste to attack, but during the years $\frac{701}{53}$ and $\frac{702}{52}$ sent only weak flying bands, who were easily repulsed, across the Euphrates; so that Cassius obtained time to reorganise the army in some measure, and with the help of the faithful adherent of the Romans, Herodes Antipater, to reduce to obedience the Jews, whom their resentment at the spoliation of the temple perpetrated by Crassus had already driven to arms. The Roman government had thus full time to send fresh troops for the defence of the threatened frontier; but this was left undone amidst the convulsions of the incipient revolution, and, when at length in $\frac{703}{51}$ the great Parthian invading army appeared on the Euphrates, Cassius had still nothing to oppose to it but the two weak legions formed from the remains of the army of Crassus. Of course with these he could neither prevent the crossing nor defend the province. Syria was overrun by the Parthians, and all Western Asia trembled. But the Parthians did not understand the besieging of towns. They not only retreated from Antioch, into which Cassius had thrown himself with his troops, without having accomplished their object, but they were on their retreat along the Orontes allured into an ambush by Cassius' cavalry and there severely handled by the Roman infantry; prince Osaces was himself among the slain. Friend and foe thus perceived that the Parthian army under an ordinary general and on ordinary ground was not capable of much more than any other Oriental army. However, the attack was not abandoned. Pacorus lay encamped during the winter of $\frac{703}{51}$–$\frac{704}{50}$ in Cyrrhestica on this side of the Euphrates; and the new governor of Syria, Marcus Bibulus, as wretched a general as he was an incapable statesman, knew no better course of action than to shut himself up in his fortresses. It was generally expected that the war would break out in $\frac{704}{50}$ with renewed fury. But instead of turning his arms against the Romans Pacorus turned against his own father, and accordingly even entered into an understanding with the Roman governor. Thus the stain was not wiped from the shield of Roman honour, nor was the reputation of Rome restored in the East; but the Parthian invasion of Western Asia was over, and the Euphrates boundary was, for the time being at least, retained.

In Rome meanwhile the periodical volcano of revolution was whirling upward its clouds of stupefying smoke. The Romans began to have no longer a soldier or a denarius to be employed against the public foe—no longer a thought for the destinies of the nations. It is one of the most dreadful signs of the times, that the huge national disaster of Carrhae and Sinnaca gave the politicians of that time far less to think and speak of than that wretched tumult on the Appian road, in which, a couple of months after Crassus, Clodius the partisan-leader perished; but it is easily conceivable and almost excusable. The breach between the two regents, long felt as inevitable and often announced as near, was now assuming such a shape that it could not be stopped. Like the boat of the ancient Greek mariners' tale, the vessel of the Roman community now found itself as it were between two rocks swimming towards each other; expecting every moment the crash of collision, those whom it was bearing tortured by nameless anguish into the eddying surge that rose higher and higher, were benumbed; and, while every slightest movement there attracted a thousand eyes, no one ventured to give a glance to the right or the left.

After Caesar had, at the conference of Luca in April 698/56, agreed to considerable concessions as regarded Pompeius, and the regents had thus placed themselves substantially on a level, their relation was not without the outward conditions of durability, so far as a division of the monarchical power—in itself indivisible—could be lasting at all. It was a different question whether the regents, at least for the present, were determined to keep together and mutually to acknowledge without reserve their title to rank as equals. That this was the case with Caesar, in so far as he had acquired the interval necessary for the conquest of Gaul at the price of equalisation with Pompeius, has been already set forth. But Pompeius was hardly ever, even provisionally, in earnest with the collegiate scheme. His was one of those petty and mean natures, towards which it is dangerous to practise magnanimity; to his paltry spirit it appeared certainly a dictate of prudence to supplant at the first opportunity his reluctantly acknowledged rival, and his mean soul thirsted after a possibility of retaliating on Caesar for the humiliation which he had suffered through Caesar's indulgence. But while it is probable that Pompeius in accordance with his heavy and sluggish nature never properly consented to let Caesar hold a position of equality by his side, yet the design of breaking up the alliance doubtless came only by degrees to be distinctly entertained by him. At any rate the public, which usually saw better through the views and intention of Pompeius than he did himself, could not be mistaken in thinking that at least with the death of the beautiful Julia—who died in the bloom of womanhood in the autumn of $\frac{700}{54}$ and was soon followed by her only child to the tomb—the personal relation between her father and her husband was broken up. Caesar attempted to re-establish the ties of affinity which fate had severed; he asked for himself the hand of the only daughter of Pompeius, and offered Octavia, his sister's grand-daughter, who was now his nearest relative, in marriage to his fellow-regent; but Pompeius left his daughter to her existing husband Faustus Sulla the son of the regent, and he himself married the daughter of Quintus Metellus Scipio. The personal breach had unmistakably begun, and it was Pompeius who drew back his hand. It was expected that a political breach would at once follow; but in this people were mistaken; in public affairs a collegiate understanding continued for a time to subsist. The reason was, that Caesar did not wish publicly to dissolve the relation before the subjugation of Gaul was accomplished, and Pompeius did not wish to dissolve it before the governing authorities and Italy should be wholly reduced under his power by his investiture with the dictatorship. It is singular, but yet readily admits of explanation, that the regents under these circumstances supported each other; Pompeius after the disaster of Aduatuca in the winter of $\frac{700}{54}$ handed over one of his Italian legions that were dismissed on furlough by way of loan to Caesar; on the other hand Caesar granted his consent and his moral support to Pompeius in the repressive measures which the latter took against the stubborn republican opposition.

It was only after Pompeius had in this way procured for himself at the beginning of $\frac{702}{52}$ the undivided consulship and an influence in the capital thoroughly outweighing that of Caesar, and after all the men capable of arms in Italy had tendered their military oath to himself personally and in his name, that he formed the resolution to break as soon as possible formally with Caesar; and the design became distinctly enough apparent. That the judicial prosecution which took place after the tumult on the Appian Way lighted with unsparing severity precisely on the old democratic partisans of Caesar (p. 306), might perhaps pass as a mere awkwardness. That the new law against electioneering intrigues, which had retrospective effect as far as $\frac{684}{70}$, included also the dubious proceedings at Caesar's candidature for the consulship (p. 304), might likewise be nothing more, although not a few Caesarians thought that they perceived in it a definite design. But people could no longer shut their eyes, however willing they might be to do so, when Pompeius did not select for his colleague in the consulship his former father-in-law Caesar, as was fitting in the circumstances of the case and was in many quarters demanded, but associated with himself a puppet wholly dependent on him in his new father-in-law Scipio (p. 307); and still less, when Pompeius at the same time got the governorship of the two Spains continued to him for five years more, that is to $\frac{709}{45}$, and a considerable fixed sum appropriated from the state-chest for the payment of his troops, not only without stipulating for a like prolongation of command and a like grant of money to Caesar, but even while labouring ulteriorly to effect the recall of Caesar before the term formerly agreed on through the new regulations which were issued at the same time regarding the holding of the governorships. These encroachments were unmistakably calculated to undermine Caesar's position and eventually to overthrow him. The moment could not be more favourable. Caesar had conceded so much to Pompeius at Luca, only because Crassus and his Syrian army would necessarily, in the event of any rupture with Pompeius, be thrown into Caesar's scale; for upon Crassus —who since the times of Sulla had been at the deepest enmity with Pompeius and almost as long politically and personally allied with Caesar, and who from his peculiar character at all events, if he could not himself be king of Rome, would have been content to be the new king's banker—Caesar could always reckon, and could have no apprehension at all of seeing Crassus enter into an alliance with his enemies. The catastrophe of June $\frac{701}{53}$, by which army and general in Syria perished, was therefore a terribly severe blow for Caesar. A few months later the national insurrection burst forth more violently than ever in Gaul, just when it had seemed completely subdued, and for the first time Caesar there encountered an equal opponent in the Arvernian king Vercingetorix. Once more fate had been working for Pompeius; Crassus was dead, all Gaul was in revolt,

Pompeius was practically dictator of Rome and master of the senate. What might have happened, if he had now, instead of remotely intriguing against Caesar, summarily compelled the burgesses or the senate to recall Caesar at once from Gaul! But Pompeius never understood how to take advantage of fortune. He heralded the breach clearly enough; already in $\frac{702}{52}$ his acts left no doubt about it, and in the spring of $\frac{703}{51}$ he openly expressed his purpose of breaking with Caesar; but he did not break with him, and allowed the months to slip away unemployed.

But however Pompeius might delay, the crisis was incessantly urged on by the mere force of circumstances. The impending war was not eventually a struggle between republic and monarchy—for that had been virtually decided years before—but a struggle between Pompeius and Caesar for the possession of the crown of Rome. But neither of the pretenders found his account in uttering the plain truth; he would have thereby driven all that very respectable portion of the burgesses, which desired the continuance of the republic and believed in its possibility, directly into the camp of his opponent. The old battle-cries raised by Gracchus and Drusus, Cinna and Sulla, used up and meaningless as they were, remained still good enough for watchwords in the struggle of the two generals contending for sole power; and, though for the moment both Pompeius and Caesar ranked themselves officially with the so-called popular party, it could not be for a moment doubtful that Caesar would inscribe on his banner the people and democratic progress, Pompeius the aristocracy and the legitimate constitution.

Caesar had no choice. He was from the outset and very earnestly a democrat; the monarchy as he understood it differed more in name than in reality from the Gracchan government of the people; and he was too magnanimous and too profound a statesman to conceal his colours and to fight under any other escutcheon than his own. The immediate advantage no doubt, which this battle-cry brought to him, was trifling; it was confined mainly to the circumstance that he was thereby relieved from the inconvenience of directly naming the kingdom, and so alarming the mass of the lukewarm and his own adherents by that detested word. The democratic banner hardly yielded farther positive gain, since the ideals of Gracchus had been rendered infamous and ridiculous by Clodius; for where was there now—laying aside perhaps the Transpadanes—any class of any sort of importance, which would have been induced by the battle-cries of the democracy to take part in the struggle?

This state of things would have decided the part of Pompeius in the impending struggle, even if apart from this it had not been self-evident that he could only enter into it as the general of the legitimate republic. Nature had destined him, if ever any one, to be a member of an aristocracy; and nothing but very accidental and very selfish motives had carried him over as a deserter from the aristocratic to the democratic camp. That he should now revert to his Sullan traditions was not merely natural, but in every respect of essential advantage. Effete as was the democratic cry, the conservative cry could not but have the more potent effect if it proceeded from the right man. Perhaps the majority, at any rate the flower of the burgesses, belonged to the constitutional party; and as respected its numerical and moral strength might well be called to interfere powerfully, perhaps decisively, in the impending struggle of the pretenders. It wanted nothing but a leader. Marcus Cato, its present head, did the duty, as he understood it, of its leader amidst daily peril of his life and perhaps without hope of success; his fidelity to duty deserves respect, but to be the last at a forlorn post is commendable in the soldier, not in the general. He had not the skill either to organise or to bring into action at the proper time the powerful reserve, which had sprung up as it were spontaneously in Italy for the party of the overthrown government; and he had for good reasons never made any pretension to the military leadership, on which everything ultimately depended. If instead of this man, who knew not how to act either as party chief or as general, a man of the political and military mark of Pompeius should raise the banner of the existing constitution, the municipals of Italy would necessarily flock towards it in crowds, that under it they might help to fight, if not indeed for the kingship of Pompeius, at any rate against the kingship of Caesar.

To this was added another consideration at least as important. It was characteristic of Pompeius, even when he had formed a resolve, not to be able to find his way to its execution. While he knew perhaps how to conduct war but certainly not how to declare it, the Catonian party, although assuredly unable to conduct it, was very able and above all very ready to furnish reasons for war against the monarchy which was in course of being established. According to the intention of Pompeius, while he kept himself aloof and in his peculiar way now talked as though he would immediately depart for his Spanish provinces, now made preparations as though he would set out to take the command on the Euphrates, the legitimate governing board, namely the senate, were to break with Caesar, to declare war against him, and to entrust the conduct of it to Pompeius, who then, yielding to the general desire, was to come forward as the protector of the constitution against demagogico-monarchical plots, as an upright man and champion of the existing order of things against the profligates and anarchists, as the duly installed general of the senate against the Imperator of the street, and so once more to save his country. Thus Pompeius gained by the alliance with the conservatives both a second army in addition to his personal adherents, and a suitable war-manifesto—advantages which certainly were purchased at the high price of coalescing with those who were in principle opposed to him. Of the countless evils involved in this coalition, there was developed in the meantime only one—but that already a very grave one—that Pompeius surrendered the power of commencing hostilities against Caesar when and how he pleased, and in this decisive point made himself dependent on all the accidents and caprices of an aristocratic corporation.

Thus the republican opposition, after having been for years obliged to rest content with the part of a mere spectator and having hardly ventured to whisper, was now brought back once more to the political stage by the impending rupture between the regents. It consisted primarily of the circle which rallied round Cato—those republicans who were resolved to venture on the struggle for the republic and against the monarchy under all circumstances, and the sooner the better. The pitiful issue of the attempt made in $\frac{698}{56}$ (p. 291) had taught them that they by themselves alone were not in a position either to conduct war or even to call it forth; it was known to every one that even in the senate, while the whole corporation with a few isolated exceptions was averse to monarchy, the majority would still only restore the oligarchic government if it might be restored without danger—in which case, to be sure, it might have a good while to wait. In presence of the regents on the one hand, and on the other hand of this indolent majority, which desired peace above all things, and at any price, and was averse to any decided action and most of all to a decided rupture with one or other of the regents, the only possible course for the Catonian party to obtain a restoration of the old rule lay in a coalition with the less dangerous of the rulers.

If Pompeius acknowledged the oligarchic constitution and offered to fight for it against Caesar, the republican opposition might and must recognise him as its general, and in alliance with him compel the timid majority to a declaration of war. That Pompeius was not quite in earnest with his fidelity to the constitution could indeed escape nobody; but, undecided as he was in everything, he had by no means arrived like Caesar at a clear and firm conviction that it must be the first business of the new monarch to sweep off thoroughly and conclusively the oligarchic lumber. At any rate the war would train a really republican army and really republican generals; and, after the victory over Caesar, they might proceed with more favourable prospects to set aside not merely one of the monarchs, but the monarchy itself, which was in the course of formation. Desperate as was the cause of the oligarchy, the offer of Pompeius to become its ally was the most favourable arrangement possible for it.

The conclusion of the alliance between Pompeius and the Catonian party was effected with comparative rapidity. Already during the dictatorship of Pompeius a remarkable approximation had taken place between them. The whole behaviour of Pompeius in the Milonian crisis, his abrupt repulse of the mob that offered him the dictatorship, his distinct declaration that he would accept this office only from the senate, his unrelenting severity against disturbers of the peace of every sort and especially against the ultra-democrats, the surprising complaisance with which he treated Cato and those who shared his views, appeared as much calculated to gain the men of order as they were offensive to the democratic Caesar. On the other hand Cato and his followers, instead of combating with their wonted sternness the proposal to confer the dictatorship on Pompeius, had made it with immaterial alterations of form their own; Pompeius had received the undivided consulship immediately from the hands of Bibulus and Cato. While the Catonian party and Pompeius had thus at least a tacit understanding as early as the beginning of $\frac{702}{52}$, the alliance might be held as formally concluded, when at the consular elections for $\frac{703}{51}$ there was elected not Cato himself indeed, but—along with an insignificant man belonging to the majority of the senate—one of the most decided adherents of Cato, Marcus Claudius Marcellus. Marcellus was no furious zealot and still less a genius, but a steadfast and strict aristocrat, just the right man to declare war if war was to be begun with Caesar. As the case stood, this election, so surprising after the repressive measures adopted immediately before against the republican opposition, can hardly have occurred otherwise than with the consent, or at least under the tacit permission, of the regent of Rome for the time being. Slowly and awkwardly, as was his wont, but surely and steadily Pompeius moved onward to the rupture.

It was not the intention of Caesar on the other hand to fall out at this moment with Pompeius. He could not indeed desire seriously and permanently to share the ruling power with any colleague, least of all with one of so secondary a sort as was Pompeius; and beyond doubt he had long resolved after terminating the conquest of Gaul to take the sole power for himself, and in case of need to extort it by force of arms. But a man like Caesar, in whom the officer was thoroughly subordinate to the statesman, could not fail to perceive that the regulation of the political organism by force of arms does in its consequences deeply and often permanently disorganise it; and therefore he could not but seek to solve the difficulty, if at all possible, by peaceful means or at least without open civil war. But even if civil war was not to be avoided, he could not desire to be driven to it at a time, when in Gaul the rising of Vercingetorix imperilled afresh all that had been obtained and occupied him without interruption from the winter of $\frac{701-702}{53-52}$ to the winter of $\frac{703}{51}$, and when Pompeius and the constitutional party opposed to him on principle were dominant in Italy. Accordingly he sought to preserve the relation with Pompeius and thereby the peace unbroken, and to attain, if at all possible, by peaceful means to the consulship for $\frac{706}{48}$ already promised to him at Luca. If he should then after a conclusive settlement of Celtic affairs be placed in a regular manner at the head of the state, he, who was still more decidedly superior to Pompeius as a statesman than as a general, might well reckon on outmanœuvring the latter in the senate-house and in the Forum without special difficulty. Perhaps it was possible to find out for his awkward, vacillating, and arrogant rival some sort of honourable and uninfluential position, in which the latter might be content to sink into a nullity; the repeated attempts of Caesar to keep himself related by marriage to Pompeius may have been designed to pave the way for such a solution and to bring about a final settlement of the old quarrel through the succession of offspring inheriting the blood of both competitors. The republican opposition would then remain without a leader and therefore probably quiet, and peace would be preserved.

If this should not be successful, and if there should be, as was certainly possible, a necessity for ultimately resorting to the decision of arms, Caesar would then as consul in Rome dispose of the compliant majority of the senate; and he could impede or perhaps frustrate the coalition of the Pompeians and the republicans, and conduct the war far more suitably and more advantageously, than if he now as proconsul of Gaul gave orders to march against the senate and its general. Certainly the success of this plan depended on Pompeius being good-natured enough to let Caesar still obtain the consulship for $\frac{706}{48}$ promised to him at Luca; but, even if it failed, it would be always of advantage for Caesar to have given practical and repeated evidence of the most yielding disposition. On the one hand time would thus be gained for attaining his object meanwhile in Gaul; on the other hand his opponents would be left with the odium of initiating the rupture and consequently the civil war—which was of the utmost moment for Caesar with reference to the majority of the senate and the party of material interests, and more especially with reference to his own soldiers.

On these views he acted. He armed certainly; the number of his legions was raised through new levies in the winter of $\frac{702-703}{52-51}$ to eleven, including that borrowed from Pompeius. But at the same time he expressly and openly approved of Pompeius' conduct during the dictatorship and the restoration of order in the capital which he had effected, rejected the warnings of officious friends as calumnies, reckoned every day by which he succeeded in postponing the catastrophe a gain, overlooked whatever could be overlooked and bore whatever could be borne—immovably adhering only to the one decisive demand that, when his governorship of Gaul came to an end with $\frac{705}{49}$, the second consulship, admissible by republican state-law and promised to him according to agreement by his colleague, should be granted to him for the year $\frac{706}{48}$.

This very demand became the battle-field of the diplomatic war which now began. If Caesar were compelled either to resign his office of governor before the last day of December $\frac{705}{49}$, or to postpone the assumption of the magistracy in the capital beyond the 1st January $\frac{706}{48}$, so that he should remain for a time between the governorship and the consulate without office, and consequently liable to criminal impeachment—which according to Roman law was only allowable against one who was not in office—the public had good reason to prophesy for him in this case the fate of Milo, because Cato had for long been ready to impeach him and Pompeius was a more than doubtful protector.

Now, to attain that object, Caesar's opponents had a very simple means. According to the existing ordinance as to elections, every candidate for the consulship was obliged to announce himself personally to the presiding magistrate, and to cause his name to be inscribed on the official list of candidates before the election, that is half a year before entering on office. It had probably been regarded in the conferences at Luca as a matter of course that Caesar would be released from this obligation, which was purely formal and was very often dispensed with; but the decree to that effect had not yet been issued, and, as Pompeius was now in possession of the decretive machinery, Caesar depended in this respect on the good will of his rival. Pompeius incomprehensibly abandoned of his own accord this completely secure position; with his consent and during his dictatorship ($\frac{702}{52}$) the personal appearance of Caesar was dispensed with by a tribunican law. When however soon afterwards the new election-ordinance (p. 304) was issued, the obligation of candidates personally to enroll themselves was repeated in general terms, and no exception was inserted in favour of those released from it by earlier resolution of the people; according to strict form the privilege granted in favour of Caesar was cancelled by the later general law. Caesar complained, and the clause was subsequently appended but not confirmed by special decree of the people, so that this enactment inserted by mere interpolation in the already promulgated law could only be looked on *de jure* as a nullity. Where Pompeius, therefore, might have simply kept by the law, he had preferred first to make a spontaneous concession, then to recall it, and lastly to palliate this recall in a manner most illegal.

While in this way the shortening of Caesar's governorship was only aimed at indirectly, the regulations as to the governorships issued at the same time sought the same object directly. The ten years for which the governorship had been secured to Caesar, latterly through the law proposed by Pompeius himself in concert with Crassus, ran according to the usual mode of reckoning from 1st March $\frac{695}{59}$ to the last day of February $\frac{705}{49}$. As, however, according to the earlier practice, the proconsul or propraetor had the right of entering on his provincial magistracy immediately after the termination of his first year of office, the successor of Caesar was to be nominated, not from the urban magistrates of $\frac{704}{50}$, but from those of $\frac{705}{49}$, and could not therefore enter before 1st January $\frac{706}{48}$. So far Caesar had still during the last ten months of $\frac{705}{49}$ a right to the command, not on the ground of the Pompeio-Licinian law, but on the ground of the old rule that a command with a set term still continued after the expiry of the term up to the arrival of the successor. But now, since the new regulation of $\frac{702}{52}$ called to the governorships not the consuls and praetors going out, but those who had gone out five years ago, or more, and thus prescribed an interval between the civil magistracy and the command instead of the previous immediate sequence, there was no longer any difficulty in straightway filling up from another quarter every legally vacant governorship. The pitiful dissimulation and procrastinating artifice of Pompeius are after a remarkable manner mixed up, in these arrangements, with the wily formalism and the constitutional erudition of the republican party. Years before these weapons of state-law could be employed, they had them duly prepared, and put themselves in a condition on the one hand to compel Caesar to the resignation of his command from the day when the term secured to him by Pompeius' own law expired, that is from the 1st March $\frac{705}{49}$, by sending successors to him, and on the other hand to be able to treat as null and void the votes tendered for him at the elections for $\frac{706}{48}$. Caesar, not in a position to hinder these moves, kept silence and left things to their own course.

Gradually therefore the slow course of constitutional procedure developed itself. According to custom the senate had to deliberate on the governorships of the year $\frac{705}{49}$, so far as they went to former consuls, at the beginning of $\frac{703}{51}$, so far as they went to former praetors, at the beginning of $\frac{704}{50}$; that earlier deliberation gave the first occasion to discuss the nomination of new governors for the two Gauls in the senate, and thereby the first occasion for open collision between the constitutional party pushed forward by Pompeius and the senatorial supporters of Caesar. The consul Marcus Marcellus introduced a proposal to give the two provinces hitherto administered by the proconsul Gaius Caesar from the 1st March $\frac{705}{49}$ to the two consulars who were to be provided with governorships for that year. The long-repressed indignation burst forth in a torrent through the sluice once opened; everything that the Catonians were meditating against Caesar was brought forward in these discussions. For them it was a settled point, that the right granted by exceptional law to the proconsul Caesar of announcing his candidature for the consulship in absence had been again cancelled by a subsequent decree of the people, and that the reservation inserted in the latter was invalid. The senate should in their opinion cause the same magistrate, now that the subjugation of Gaul was ended, to discharge immediately the soldiers who had served out their time. The bestowal of burgess-rights and establishment of colonies by Caesar in Upper Italy were described by them as unconstitutional and null; in further illustration of which Marcellus ordained that a respected senator of the Caesarian colony of Comum, who, even if that place had not burgess but only Latin rights, was entitled to lay claim to Roman citizenship, should receive the punishment of scourging, which was admissible only in the case of non-burgesses.

The supporters of Caesar at this time—among whom Gaius Vibius Pansa, who was the son of a man proscribed by Sulla but yet had entered on a political career, formerly an officer in Caesar's army and in this year tribune of the people, was the most notable—affirmed in the senate that both the state of things in Gaul and equity demanded not only that Caesar should not be recalled before the time, but that he should be allowed to retain the command along with the consulship; and they pointed beyond doubt to the facts, that a few years previously Pompeius had just in the same way combined the Spanish governorships with the consulate, that even at the present time, besides the important office of superintending the supply of food to the capital, he held the supreme command in Italy in addition to the Spanish, and that in fact the whole men capable of arms had been sworn in by him and had not yet been released from their oath.

The process began to take shape, but its course was not on that account more rapid. The majority of the senate, seeing the breach approaching, allowed no sitting capable of issuing a decree to take place for months; and other months in their turn were lost through the solemn procrastination of Pompeius. At length the latter broke the silence and ranged himself, in a reserved and vacillating fashion as usual but yet plainly enough, on the side of the constitutional party against his former ally. He summarily and abruptly rejected the demand of the Caesarians that their master should be allowed to conjoin the consulship and the proconsulship; this demand, he added with blunt coarseness, seemed to him no better than if a son should offer to flog his father. He approved in principle the proposal of Marcellus, in so far as he too declared that he would not allow Caesar directly to attach the consulship to the proconsulship.

He hinted, however, although without making any binding declaration on the point, that they would perhaps grant to Caesar admission to the elections for $\frac{706}{48}$ without requiring his personal announcement, as well as the continuance of his governorship at the utmost to the 13th November $\frac{705}{49}$. But in the meantime the incorrigible procrastinator consented to the postponement of the nomination of successors to the last day of February $\frac{704}{50}$, which was asked by the representatives of Caesar, probably on the ground of a clause of the Pompeio-Licinian law forbidding any discussion in the senate as to the nomination of successors before the beginning of Caesar's last year of office.

To this effect accordingly the senate decreed (29th September $\frac{703}{51}$). The filling up of the Gallic governorships was placed in the order of the day for the 1st March $\frac{704}{50}$; but even now it was attempted to break up the army of Caesar—just as had formerly been done by decree of the people with the army of Lucullus (pp. 67, 96)—by inducing his veterans to apply to the senate for their discharge. Caesar's supporters effected, indeed, as far as they constitutionally could, the cancelling of these decrees by their tribunician veto; but Pompeius very distinctly declared that the magistrates were bound unconditionally to obey the senate, and that intercessions and similar antiquated formalities should produce no change. The oligarchical party, whose organ Pompeius now made himself, betrayed not obscurely the design, in the event of a victory, of revising the constitution in their sense and removing everything which had even the semblance of popular freedom; as indeed, doubtless for this reason, it omitted to avail itself of the comitia at all in its attacks directed against Caesar. The coalition between Pompeius and the constitutional party was thus formally declared; sentence too was already evidently passed on Caesar, and the term of its promulgation was simply postponed. The elections for the following year proved thoroughly adverse to him.

During these party manœuvres of his antagonists preparatory to war, Caesar had succeeded in getting rid of the Gallic insurrection and restoring the state of peace in the whole subject territory. As early as the summer of $\frac{703}{51}$, under the convenient pretext of defending the frontier (p. 271) but evidently in token of the fact that the legions in Gaul were now beginning to be no longer needed there, he moved one of them to North Italy. He could not avoid perceiving now at any rate, if not earlier, that he would not be spared the necessity of drawing the sword against his fellow-citizens; nevertheless, as it was highly desirable to leave the legions still for a time in the barely pacified Gaul, he sought even yet to procrastinate, and, well acquainted with the extreme love of peace in the majority of the senate, did not abandon the hope of still restraining them from the declaration of war in spite of the pressure exercised over them by Pompeius. He did not even hesitate to make great sacrifices, if only he might avoid for the present open variance with the supreme governing board. When the senate (in the spring of $\frac{704}{50}$) at the suggestion of Pompeius requested both him and Caesar to furnish each a legion for the impending Parthian war (p. 318) and when agreeably to this resolution Pompeius demanded back from Caesar the legion lent to him some years before, so as to send it to Syria, Caesar complied with the double demand, because neither the opportuneness of this decree of the senate nor the justice of the demand of Pompeius could in themselves be disputed, and the keeping within the bounds of the law and of formal loyalty was of more consequence to Caesar than a few thousand soldiers. The two legions came without delay and placed themselves at the disposal of the government, but instead of sending them to the Euphrates, the latter kept them at Capua in readiness for Pompeius; and the public had once more the opportunity of comparing the manifest endeavours of Caesar to avoid a rupture with the perfidious preparations for war of his opponents.

For the discussions with the senate Caesar had succeeded in purchasing not only one of the consuls of the year, Lucius Aemilius Paullus, but above all the tribune of the people Gaius Curio, probably the most eminent among the many brilliant profligates of this epoch;[1] unsurpassed in refined elegance, in fluent and clever oratory, in dexterity of intrigue, and in that energy which in the case of vigorous but vicious characters bestirs itself only the more powerfully amid the pauses of idleness; but also unsurpassed in his dissolute life, in his talent for borrowing—his debts were estimated at 60,000,000 sesterces (£600,000)—and in his moral and political want of principle. He had previously offered himself to be bought by Caesar and had been rejected; the talent, which he thenceforward displayed in his attacks on Caesar, induced the latter subsequently to buy him up—the price was high, but the commodity was worth the money.

[1] *Homo ingeniosissime nequam* (Vellei. ii. 48).

Curio had in the first months of his tribunate of the people played the independent republican, and had as such thundered both against Caesar and against Pompeius. He availed himself with rare skill of the apparently impartial standing which this gave him, when in March $\frac{704}{50}$ the proposal as to the filling up of the Gallic governorships for the next year came up afresh for discussion in the senate; he completely approved the decree, but asked that it should be at the same time extended to Pompeius and his extraordinary commands. His arguments—that a constitutional state of things could only be brought about by the removal of all exceptional positions, that Pompeius as merely entrusted by the senate with the proconsulship could still less than Caesar refuse obedience to it, that the mere removal of one of the two generals would only increase the danger to the constitution—carried complete conviction to superficial politicians and to the public at large; and the declaration of Curio, that he intended to prevent any one-sided proceedings against Caesar by the veto constitutionally belonging to him, met with much approval in and out of the senate. Caesar declared his consent at once to Curio's proposal and offered to resign his governorship and command at any moment on the summons of the senate, provided Pompeius would do the same; he might safely do so, for Pompeius without his Italo-Spanish command was no longer to be feared. Pompeius again for that very reason could not but refuse; his reply—that Caesar must first resign, and that he meant speedily to follow the example thus set—was the less satisfactory, that he did not even specify a definite term for his retirement. Again the decision was delayed for months; Pompeius and the Catonians, perceiving the dubious humour of the majority of the senate, did not venture to bring Curio's proposal to a vote. Caesar employed the summer in establishing the state of peace in the regions which he had conquered, in holding a great review of his troops on the Scheldt, and in making a triumphal march through the province of North Italy which was entirely devoted to him; autumn found him in Ravenna, the southern frontier-town of his province.

The vote which could no longer be delayed on Curio's proposal at length took place, and exhibited the defeat of the party of Pompeius and Cato in all its extent. By 370 votes against 20 the senate resolved that the proconsuls of Spain and Gaul should both be called upon to resign their offices; and with boundless joy the good burgesses of Rome heard the glad news of the saving achievement of Curio. Pompeius was thus recalled by the senate no less than Caesar, and while Caesar was ready to comply with the command, Pompeius positively refused obedience. The presiding consul Gaius Marcellus, cousin of Marcus Marcellus and like the latter belonging to the Catonian party, addressed a severe lecture to the servile majority; and it was, no doubt, vexatious to be thus beaten in their own camp and beaten by means of a phalanx of poltroons. But where was victory to come from under a leader who, instead of shortly and distinctly dictating his orders to the senators, resorted in his old days a second time to the instructions of a professor of rhetoric, that with eloquence polished up afresh he might encounter the vigorous and brilliant talents of Curio?

The coalition, defeated in the senate, was in the most painful position. The Catonian section had undertaken to push matters to a rupture and to carry the senate along with them, and now saw their vessel stranded after a most vexatious manner on the sandbanks of the indolent majority. Their leaders had to listen in their conferences to the bitterest reproaches from Pompeius; he pointed out emphatically and with entire justice the dangers of the seeming peace; and, though it depended on himself alone to cut the knot by rapid action, his allies knew very well that they could never expect this from him, and that it was for them, as they had promised, to bring matters to a crisis. After the champions of the constitution and of senatorial government had already declared the constitutional rights of the burgesses and of the tribunes of the people to be meaningless formalities (p. 331), they now found themselves driven by necessity to treat the constitutional decisions of the senate itself in a similar manner and, as the legitimate government would not let itself be saved with its own consent, to save it against its will. This was neither new nor accidental; Sulla (iii. 330) and Lucullus (p. 58) had been obliged to carry every energetic resolution conceived by them in the true interest of the government with a high hand irrespective of it, just as Cato and his friends now proposed to do; the machinery of the constitution was in fact utterly effete, and the senate was now—as the comitia had been for centuries—nothing but a worn out wheel slipping constantly out of its track.

It was rumoured (October $\frac{704}{50}$) that Caesar had moved four legions from Transalpine into Cisalpine Gaul and stationed them at Placentia. This transference of troops was of itself within the prerogative of the governor; Curio moreover palpably showed in the senate the utter groundlessness of the rumour and they by a majority rejected the proposal of the consul Gaius Marcellus to give Pompeius on the strength of it orders to march against Caesar. Yet the said consul, in concert with the two consuls elected for $\frac{705}{49}$ who likewise belonged to the Catonian party, proceeded to Pompeius, and these three men by virtue of their own plenitude of power requested the general to put himself at the head of the two legions stationed at Capua, and to call the Italian militia to arms at his discretion. A more informal authorisation for the commencement of a civil war can hardly be conceived; but people had no longer time to attend to such secondary matters; Pompeius accepted it. The military preparations, the levies, began; in order personally to forward them, Pompeius left the capital in December $\frac{704}{50}$.

Caesar had fully attained the object of devolving the initiative of civil war on his opponents. He had, while himself keeping on legal ground, compelled Pompeius to declare war, and to declare it not as representative of the legitimate authority, but as general of an openly revolutionary minority of the senate which overawed the majority. This result was not to be reckoned of slight importance, although the instinct of the masses could not and did not deceive itself for a moment as to the fact that the war concerned other things than questions of formal law. Now, when war was declared, it was Caesar's interest to strike a blow as soon as possible. The preparations of his opponents were just beginning, and even the capital was not occupied. In ten or twelve days an army three times as strong as the troops of Caesar that were in Upper Italy could be collected at Rome; but still it was not impossible to surprise the city undefended, or even perhaps by a rapid winter campaign to seize all Italy, and to shut off the best resources of his opponents before they could make them available. The sagacious and energetic Curio, who after resigning his tribunate (10th December $\frac{704}{50}$) had immediately gone to Caesar at Ravenna, vividly represented the state of things to his master; and it hardly needed such a representation to convince Caesar that longer delay now could only be injurious. But, as he with the view of not giving his antagonists occasion to complain had hitherto brought no troops to Ravenna itself, he could for the present do nothing but despatch orders to his whole force to set out with all haste; and he had to wait till at least the one legion stationed nearest reached Ravenna. Meanwhile he sent an ultimatum to Rome, which, if useful for nothing else, by its extreme submissiveness still farther compromised his opponents in public opinion, and perhaps even, as he seemed himself to hesitate, induced them to prosecute more remissly their preparations against him. In this ultimatum Caesar dropped all the counter-demands which he formerly made on Pompeius, and offered on his own part both to resign the governorship of Transalpine Gaul, and to dismiss eight of the ten legions belonging to him, at the term fixed by the senate; he declared himself content, if the senate would leave him either the governorship of Cisalpine Gaul and Illyria with one, or that of Cisalpine Gaul alone with two, legions, not, forsooth, up to his investiture with the consulship, but till after the close of the consular elections for $\frac{706}{48}$. He thus consented to those proposals of accommodation, with which at the beginning of the discussions the senatorial party and even Pompeius himself had declared that they would be satisfied, and showed himself ready to remain in a private position from his election to the consulate down to his entering on office. Whether Caesar was in earnest with these astonishing concessions and had confidence that he should be able to carry through his game against Pompeius even after granting so much, or whether he reckoned that those on the other side had already gone too far to find in these proposals of compromise more than a proof that Caesar regarded his cause itself as lost, can no longer be with certainty determined. The probability is, that Caesar committed the fault of playing a too bold game, far rather than the worse fault of promising something which he was not minded to perform; and that, if strangely enough his proposals had been accepted, he would have made good his word.

Curio undertook once more to represent his master in the lion's den. In three days he made the journey from Ravenna to Rome. When the new consuls Lucius Lentulus and Gaius Marcellus the younger[1] assembled the senate for the first time on 1st January $\frac{705}{49}$, he delivered in a full meeting the letter addressed by the general to the senate. The tribunes of the people, Marcus Antonius, well known in the chronicle of scandal of the city as the intimate friend of Curio and his accomplice in all his follies, but at the same time known from the Egyptian and Gallic campaigns as a brilliant cavalry officer, and Quintus Cassius, Pompeius' former quaestor—the two, who were now in Curio's stead managing the cause of Caesar in Rome—insisted on the immediate reading of the despatch. The grave and clear words

[1] To be distinguished from the consul having the same name of $\frac{704}{50}$; the latter was a cousin, the consul of $\frac{705}{49}$ a brother, of the Marcus Marcellus who was consul in $\frac{703}{51}$.

in which Caesar set forth the imminence of civil war, the general wish for peace, the arrogance of Pompeius, and his own yielding disposition, with all the irresistible force of truth; the proposals for a compromise, of a moderation which doubtless surprised his own partisans; the distinct declaration that this was the last time that he should offer his hand for peace—made the deepest impression. In spite of the dread inspired by the numerous soldiers of Pompeius who flocked into the capital, the sentiment of the majority was not doubtful; the consuls could not venture to let it find expression. Respecting the proposal renewed by Caesar that both generals might be enjoined to resign their commands simultaneously, respecting all the projects of accommodation suggested by his letter, and respecting the proposal made by Marcus Coelius Rufus and Marcus Calidius that Pompeius should be urged immediately to depart for Spain, the consuls refused—as they in the capacity of presiding officers were entitled to do—to let a vote take place. Even the proposal of one of their most decided partisans who was simply not so blind to the military position of affairs as his party, Marcus Marcellus—to defer the determination till the Italian levy *en masse* could be under arms and could protect the senate—was not allowed to be brought to a vote. Pompeius caused it to be declared through his usual organ, Quintus Scipio, that he was resolved to take up the cause of the senate now or never, and that he would let it drop if they longer delayed. The consul Lentulus said in plain terms that even the decree of the senate was no longer of consequence, and that, if it should persevere in its servility, he would act of himself and with his powerful friends take the farther steps necessary. Thus overawed, the majority decreed what was commanded—that Caesar should at a definite and not distant day give up Transalpine Gaul to Lucius Domitius Ahenobarbus, and Cisalpine Gaul to Marcus Servilius Novianus, and should dismiss his army, failing which he should be esteemed a traitor. When the tribunes of Caesar's party made use of their right of veto against this resolution, not only were they, as they at least asserted, threatened in the senate-house itself by the swords of Pompeian soldiers, and forced, in order to save their lives, to flee in slaves' clothing from the capital; but the now sufficiently overawed senate treated their formally quite constitutional interference as an attempt at revolution, declared the country in danger, and in the usual forms called the whole burgesses to take up arms, and all magistrates faithful to the constitution to place themsevles at the head of the armed (7th January $\frac{705}{49}$).

Now it was enough. When Caesar was informed by the tribunes who had fled to his camp entreating protection as to the reception which his proposals had met with in the capital, he called together the soldiers of the thirteenth legion, which had meanwhile arrived from its cantonments near Tergeste (Trieste) at Ravenna, and unfolded before them the state of things. It was not merely the man of genius versed in the knowledge and skilled in the control of men's hearts, whose brilliant eloquence shone forth and glowed in this agitating crisis of his own and the world's destiny; nor merely the generous commander-in-chief and the victorious general addressing soldiers who had been called by himself to arms and for eight years had followed his banners with daily increasing enthusiasm. There spoke, above all, the energetic and consistent statesman, who had now for nine and twenty years defended the cause of freedom in good and evil times; who had braved for it the daggers of assassins and the executioners of the aristocracy, the swords of the Germans and the waves of the unknown ocean, without ever yielding or wavering; who had torn to pieces the Sullan constitution, had overthrown the rule of the senate, and had furnished the defenceless and unarmed democracy with protection and with arms by means of the struggle beyond the Alps. And he spoke, not to the Clodian public whose republican enthusiasm had been long burnt down to ashes and dross, but to the young men from the towns and villages of Northern Italy, who still felt freshly and purely the mighty influence of the thought of civic freedom; who were still capable of fighting and of dying for ideals; who had themselves received for their country in a revolutionary way from Caesar the burgess-rights which the government refused to them; whom Caesar's fall would leave once more at the mercy of the *fasces*, and who already possessed practical proofs (p. 330) of the inexorable use which the oligarchy proposed to make of these against the Transpadanes. Such were the listeners before whom the great orator set forth the facts—the thanks for the conquest of Gaul which the nobility were preparing for the general and his army; the contemptuous setting aside of the comitia; the overawing of the senate; the sacred duty of protecting with armed hand the tribunate of the people wrested five hundred years ago by their fathers, arms in hand, from the nobility, and of keeping the ancient oath which these had taken for themselves as for their children's children that they would man by man stand firm even to death for the tribunes of the people (i. 273). And then, when he—the leader and general of the popular party—summoned the soldiers of the people, now that conciliatory means had been exhausted and concession had reached its utmost limits, to follow him in the last, the inevitable, the decisive struggle against the equally hated and despised, equally perfidious and incapable, and in fact ludicrously incorrigible aristocracy—there was not an officer or a soldier who could hold back. The order was given for departure; at the head of his vanguard Caesar crossed the narrow brook which separated his province from Italy, and which the constitution forbade the proconsul of Gaul to pass. When after nine years' absence he trod once more the soil of his native land, he trod at the same time the path of revolution. "The die was cast."

CHAPTER X

BRUNDISIUM, ILERDA, PHARSALUS, AND THAPSUS

ARMS were thus to decide which of the two men who had hitherto jointly ruled Rome was now to be its sole ruler. Let us see what were the comparative resources at the disposal of Caesar and Pompeius for the impending struggle.

Caesar's power rested primarily on the wholly unlimited authority which he enjoyed within his own party. If the ideas of democracy and of monarchy met together in it, this was not the result of a coalition which had been accidentally entered into and might be accidentally dissolved; on the contrary it was involved in the very essence of a democracy without a representative constitution, that democracy and monarchy should find in Caesar at once their highest and ultimate expression. In political as in military matters throughout the first and the final decision lay with Caesar. However high the honour in which he held any serviceable instrument, it remained an instrument still; Caesar stood in his own part without confederates, surrounded only by military-political adjutants, who as a rule had risen from the army and as soldiers were trained never to ask the reason and purpose of anything, but unconditionally to obey. On this account especially, at the decisive moment when the civil war began, of all the officers and soldiers of Caesar one alone refused him obedience; and the circumstance that that one was precisely the foremost of them all, simply confirms this view of the relation of Caesar to his adherents.

Titus Labienus had shared with Caesar all the troubles of the dark times of Catilina (p. 149) as well as all the lustre of the Gallic career of victory, had regularly held independent command, and frequently led half the army; as he was the oldest, ablest, and most faithful of Caesar's adjutants, he was beyond question also highest in position and highest in honour. As late as in $\frac{704}{50}$ Caesar had entrusted to him the supreme command in Cisalpine Gaul, in order partly to put this confidential post into safe hands, partly to forward the views of Labienus in his canvass for the consulship. But from this very position Labienus entered into communication with the opposite party, resorted at the beginning of hostilities in $\frac{705}{49}$ to the head-quarters of Pompeius instead of those of Caesar, and fought through the whole civil strife with unparalleled bitterness against his old friend and master in war. We are not sufficiently informed either as to the character of Labienus or as to the special circumstances of his changing sides; but in the main his case certainly presents nothing but a further proof of the fact, that a military chief can reckon far more surely on his captains than on his marshals. To all appearance Labienus was one of those persons who combine with military efficiency utter incapacity as statesmen, and who in consequence, if they unhappily choose or are compelled to take part in politics, are exposed to those strange paroxysms of giddiness, of which the history of Napoleon's marshals supplies so many tragi-comic examples. He may probably have thought himself entitled to rank alongside of Caesar as a second chief of the democracy; and the rejection of this claim of his may have sent him over to the camp of his opponents. His case rendered for the first time apparent the whole gravity of the evil, that Caesar's treatment of his officers as adjutants without independence admitted of the rise of no men fitted to undertake a separate command in his camp, while at the same time he stood urgently in need of such men amidst the diffusion—which might easily be foreseen—of the civil war through all the provinces of the wide empire. But this disadvantage was far outweighed by that unity in the supreme leadership, which was the primary condition of all success, and a condition only to be preserved at such a cost.

This unity of leadership acquired its full power through the efficiency of its instruments. Here the army comes, first of all, into view. It still numbered nine legions of infantry or at the most 50,000 men, all of whom however had faced the enemy and two-thirds had served in all the campaigns against the Celts. The cavalry consisted of German and Noric mercenaries, whose usefulness and trustworthiness had been proved in the war against Vercingetorix. The eight years' warfare, full of varied vicissitudes against the Celtic nation—which was brave, although in a military point of view greatly inferior to the Italian—had given Caesar the opportunity of organising his army as he alone knew how to organise it. The whole efficiency of the soldier presupposes due physical vigour; in Caesar's levies more regard was had to the strength and activity of the recruits than to their means or their morals. But the serviceableness of an army, like that of any other machine, depends above all on the ease and quickness of its movements; the soldiers of Caesar attained a perfection rarely reached and probably never surpassed in their readiness for immediate departure at any time, and in the rapidity of their marching. Courage, of course, was valued above everything; Caesar practised with unrivalled mastery the art of stimulating martial emulation and the *esprit de corps*, so that the pre-eminence accorded to particular soldiers and divisions appeared even to those who were postponed as the necessary hierarchy of valour. He weaned his men from fear by not unfrequently—where it could be done without serious danger—keeping his soldiers in ignorance of an approaching conflict, and allowing them to encounter the enemy unexpectedly. But obedience was on a parity with valour. The soldier was required to do what he was bidden, without asking the reason or the object; many an aimless fatigue was imposed on him solely as a training in the difficult art of blind obedience. The discipline was strict but not harassing; it was exercised with unrelenting vigour when the soldier was in presence of the enemy; at other times, especially after victory, the reins were relaxed, and if an otherwise efficient soldier was then pleased to indulge in perfumery or to deck himself with elegant arms and the like, or even if he allowed himself to be guilty of outrages or irregularities of a very questionable kind, provided only his military duties were not immediately affected, the foolery and the crime were allowed to pass, and the general lent a deaf ear to the complaints of the provincials on such points. Mutiny on the other hand was never pardoned, either in the instigators, or even in the guilty corps itself.

But the true soldier ought to be not merely efficient, brave, and obedient, he ought to be all this willingly and spontaneously; and it is the privilege of gifted natures alone to induce the animated machine which they govern to a joyful service by means of example and of hope, and especially by the consciousness of being turned to befitting use. As the officer, who would demand valour from his troops, must himself have looked danger in the face with them, Caesar had even when general found opportunity of drawing his sword and had then used it like the best; in activity, moreover, and fatigue he was constantly far more exacting from himself than from his soldiers. Caesar took care that victory, which primarily no doubt brings gain to the general, should be associated also with personal hopes in the minds of the soldiers. We have already mentioned that he knew how to render his soldiers enthusiastic for the cause of the democracy, so far as the prosaic times still admitted of enthusiasm, and that the political equalisation of the Transpadane country—the native land of most of his soldiers—with Italy proper was proposed as one of the objects of the struggle (p. 149). Of course material recompenses were at the same time not wanting—as well special rewards for distinguished feats of arms as general rewards for every efficient soldier; the officers had their portions, the soldiers received presents, and the most lavish gifts were placed in prospect for the triumph.

Above all things Caesar as a true commander understood how to awaken in every single component element, large or small, of the mighty machine the consciousness of a befitting application. The ordinary man is destined for service, and he has no objection to be an instrument, if he feels that a master guides him. Everywhere and at all times the eagle eye of the general rested on the whole army, rewarding and punishing with impartial justice, and directing the action of each towards the course conducive to the good of all: so that there was no experimenting or trifling with the sweat and blood of the humblest, but for that very reason, where it was necessary, unconditional devotion even to death was required. Without allowing each individual to see into the whole springs of action, Caesar yet allowed each to catch such glimpses of the political and military connection of things as to secure that he should be recognised—and it may be idealised—by the soldiers as a statesman and a general. He treated his soldiers throughout, not as his equals, but as men who are entitled to demand and were able to endure the truth, and who had to put faith in the promises and the assurances of their general, without thinking of deception or listening to rumours; as comrades through long years in warfare and victory, among whom there was hardly any one that was not known to him by name and that in the course of so many campaigns had not formed more or less of a personal relation to the general; as good companions, with whom he talked and dealt confidentially and with the cheerful elasticity peculiar to him; as clients, to requite whose services, and to avenge whose wrongs and death, constituted in his view a sacred duty. Perhaps there never was an army which was more perfectly what an army ought to be—a machine able for its work and willing for its work, in the hand of a master, who transfers to it his own elasticity. Caesar's soldiers were, and felt themselves, a match for a tenfold superior force; in connection with which it should not be overlooked, that under the Roman tactics—calculated altogether for hand to hand conflict, and especially for combat with the sword—the practised Roman soldier was superior to the novice in a far higher degree than is now the case under the circumstances of modern times.[1] But still more than by the superiority of valour the adversaries of Caesar felt themselves humbled by the unchangeable and affecting fidelity with which his soldiers clung to their general. It is perhaps without a parallel in history, that when the general summoned his soldiers to follow him into the civil war, with the single exception already mentioned of Labienus, no Roman officer and no Roman soldier deserted him. The hopes of his opponents as to an extensive desertion were thwarted as ignominiously as the former attempts to break up his army like that of Lucullus (p. 331). Labienus himself appeared in the camp of Pompeius with a band doubtless of Celtic and German cavalry but without a single legionary. Indeed the soldiers, as if they would show that the war was quite as much their matter as that of their general, settled among themselves that they would give credit for the pay, which Caesar had promised to double for them at the outbreak of the civil war, to their commander up to its termination, and would meanwhile support their poorer comrades from the general means; besides, every subaltern officer equipped and paid a trooper out of his own purse.

While Caesar thus had the one thing which was needful—unlimited political and military authority and a trustworthy army ready for the fight—his power extended, comparatively speaking, over only a very limited space. It was based essentially on the province of Upper Italy. This region was not merely the most populous of all the districts of Italy, but also devoted to the cause of the democracy as its own. The feeling which prevailed there is shown by the conduct of a division of recruits from Opitergium (Oderzo in the delegation of Treviso),

[1] A centurion of Caesar's tenth legion, taken prisoner, declared to the commander-in-chief of the enemy that he was ready with ten of his men to make head against the best cohort of the enemy (500 men; *Bell. Afric.* 45). "In the ancient mode of fighting," to quote the opinion of Napoleon, "a battle consisted simply of duels; what was only correct in the mouth of that centurion, would be mere boasting in the mouth of the modern soldier." Vivid proofs of the soldierly spirit that pervaded Caesar's army are furnished by the Reports—appended to his Memoirs—respecting the African and the second Spanish wars, of which the former appears to have had as its author an officer of the second rank, while the latter is in every respect a subaltern camp-journal.

which not long after the outbreak of the war in the Illyrian waters, surrounded on a wretched raft by the war-vessels of the enemy, allowed themselves to be shot at during the whole day down to sunset without surrendering, and, such of them as had escaped the missiles, put themselves to death with their own hands during the following night. It is easy to conceive what might be expected of such a population. As they had already granted to Caesar the means of more than doubling his original army, so after the outbreak of the civil war recruits presented themselves in great numbers for the ample levies that were immediately instituted.

In Italy proper, on the other hand, the influence of Caesar was not even remotely to be compared to that of his opponents. Although he had the skill by dexterous manœuvres to put the Catonian party in the wrong, and had sufficiently commended the rectitude of his cause to all who wished for a pretext with a good conscience either to remain neutral, like the majority of the senate, or to embrace his side, like his soldiers and the Transpadanes, the mass of the burgesses naturally did not allow themselves to be misled by these things and, when the commandant of Gaul put his legions in motion against Rome, they beheld—despite all explanations as to formal law—in Cato and Pompeius the defenders of the legitimate republic, in Caesar the democratic usurper. People in general moreover expected from the nephew of Marius, the son-in-law of Cinna, the ally of Catilina, a repetition of the Marian and Cinnan horrors, a realisation of the saturnalia of anarchy projected by Catilina; and though Caesar certainly gained allies through this expectation—so that the political refugees immediately put themselves in a body at his disposal, the ruined men saw in him their deliverer, and the lowest ranks of the rabble in the capital and country towns were thrown into a ferment on the news of his advance—these belonged to the class of friends who are more dangerous than foes.

In the provinces and the dependent states Caesar had even less influence than in Italy. Transalpine Gaul indeed as far as the Rhine and the Channel obeyed him, and the colonists of Narbo as well as the Roman burgesses elsewhere settled in Gaul were devoted to him; but even in the Narbonese province the constitutional party had numerous adherents, and the newly conquered provinces were far more a burden than a benefit to Caesar in the impending civil war; in fact, for good reasons he made no use of the Celtic infantry at all in that war, and but sparing use of the cavalry. In the other provinces and the neighbouring half or wholly independent states Caesar had indeed attempted to procure for himself support, had lavished rich presents on the princes, caused great buildings to be executed in various towns, and granted to them in case of need financial and military assistance; but on the whole, of course, not much had been gained by this means, and the relations with the German and Celtic princes in the regions of the Rhine and the Danube—particularly the connection with the Noric king Voctio, so important for the recruiting of cavalry—were probably the only relations of this sort which were of any moment for him.

While Caesar thus entered the struggle only as commandant of Gaul, without other essential resources than efficient adjutants, a faithful army, and a devoted province, Pompeius began it as the *de facto* chief of the Roman commonwealth, and in full possession of all the resources that stood at the disposal of the legitimate government of the great Roman empire. But while his position was in a political and military point of view far more considerable, it was also on the other hand far less definite and firm. The unity of leadership, which resulted of itself and by necessity from the position of Caesar, was inconsistent with the nature of a coalitïon; and although Pompeius, too much of a soldier to be deceived as to its being indispensable, attempted to force it on the coalition and got himself nominated by the senate as sole and absolute generalissimo by land and sea, yet the senate itself could not be set aside nor hindered from a preponderating influence on the political, and an occasional and therefore doubly injurious interference with the military, superintendence. The recollection of the twenty years' war waged on both sides with envenomed weapons between Pompeius and the constitutional party; the feeling which vividly prevailed on both sides, and which they with difficulty concealed, that the first consequence of the victory when achieved would be a rupture between the victors; the contempt which they entertained for each other and with only too good grounds in either case; the inconvenient number of respectable and influential men in the ranks of the aristocracy and the intellectual and moral inferiority of almost all who took part in the matter—altogether produced among the opponents of Caesar a reluctant and refractory co-operation, which formed a very sad contrast to the harmonious and compact action on the other side.

While all the disadvantages incident to the coalition of powers naturally hostile were thus felt in an unusual measure by Caesar's antagonists, this coalition was certainly still a very considerable power. It had exclusive command of the sea; all ports, all ships of war, all the materials for equipping a fleet were at its disposal. The two Spains—as it were the home of the power of Pompeius just as the two Gauls were the home of that of Caesar—were faithful adherents to their master and in the hands of able and trustworthy administrators. In the other provinces also, of course with the exception of the two Gauls, the posts of the governors and commanders had during recent years been filled up with safe men under the influence of Pompeius and the minority of the senate. The client-states throughout and with great decision took part against Caesar and in favour of Pompeius. The most important princes and cities had been brought into the closest personal relations with Pompeius during the different sections of his manifold activity. In the war against the Marians, for instance, he had been the companion in arms of the kings of Numidia and Mauretania and had re-established the kingdom of the former (iii. 324); in the Mithradatic war, in addition to a number of other minor principalities temporal and spiritual, he had re-established the kingdoms of Bosporus, Armenia, and Cappadocia, and created that of Deiotarus (pp. 129, 133, 134); it was primarily at his instigation that the Egyptian war was undertaken, and it was by his adjutant that the rule of the Lagidae had been fortified afresh (p. 144). Even the city of Massilia in Caesar's own province, while indebted to the latter doubtless for various favours, was indebted to Pompeius at the time of the Sertorian war for a very considerable extension of territory (p. 199); and, besides, the ruling oligarchy there stood in natural alliance—strengthened by various mutual relations—with the oligarchy in Rome. But these personal motives and relations as well as the glory pertaining to the victor in three continents, which in these more remote parts of the empire far outshone that of the conqueror of Gaul, did perhaps less harm to Caesar in those quarters than the views and designs—which had not remained unknown to them—of the heir of Gaius Gracchus as to the necessity of uniting the dependent states and the usefulness of provincial colonisations. No one of the dependent dynasts found himself more imminently threatened by this peril than Juba king of Numidia. Not only had he years before, in the lifetime of his father Hiempsal, fallen into a vehement personal quarrel with

Caesar, but recently the same Curio, who now occupied almost the first place among Caesar's adjutants, had proposed to the Roman burgesses the annexation of the Numidian kingdom. Lastly, if matters should go so far as to lead the independent neighbouring states to interfere in the Roman civil war, the only state of real power, that of the Parthians, was practically already allied with the aristocratic party by the connection entered into between Pacorus and Bibulus (p. 320), while Caesar was far too much a Roman to league himself for party interests with the conquerors of his friend Crassus.

As to Italy the great majority of the burgesses were, as has been already mentioned, averse to Caesar—more especially, of course, the whole aristocracy with their very considerable following, but also in a not much less degree the great capitalists, who could not hope in the event of a thorough reform of the commonwealth to preserve their partisan jury-courts and their monopoly of extortion. Of equally anti-democratic sentiments were the small capitalists, the landholders and generally all classes that had anything to lose; but in these ranks of life the cares of the next rent-term and of sowing and reaping outweighed, as a rule, every other consideration.

The army at the disposal of Pompeius consisted chiefly of the Spanish troops, seven legions inured to war and in every respect reliable; to which fell to be added the divisions of troops—weak indeed, and very much scattered—which were to be found in Syria, Asia, Macedonia, Africa, Sicily, and elsewhere. In Italy there were under arms at the outset only the two legions recently given off by Caesar, whose effective strength did not amount to more than 7,000 men, and whose trustworthiness was more than doubtful, because—levied in Cisalpine Gaul and old comrades in arms of Caesar—they were in a high degree displeased at the unbecoming intrigue by which they had been made to change camps (p. 332), and recalled with longing their general who had magnanimously paid to them beforehand at their departure the presents which were promised to every soldier for the triumph. But, apart from the circumstance that the Spanish troops might arrive in Italy with the spring either by the land route through Gaul or by sea, the men of the three legions still remaining from the levies of $\frac{699}{55}$ (p. 292), as well as the Italian levy sworn to allegiance in $\frac{702}{52}$ (p. 305), could be recalled from their furlough. Including these, the number of troops standing at the disposal of Pompeius on the whole, without reckoning the seven legions in Spain and those scattered in other provinces, amounted in Italy alone to ten legions[1] or about 60,000 men, so that it was no exaggeration at all, when Pompeius asserted that he had only to stamp with his foot to cover the ground with armed men. It is true that it required some interval—though but short—to render these soldiers available; but the arrangements for this purpose as well as for the carrying out of the new levies ordered by the senate in consequence of the outbreak of the civil war were already everywhere in progress. Immediately after the decisive decree of the senate (7th January $\frac{705}{49}$), in the very depth of winter the most eminent men of the aristocracy set out to the different districts, to hasten the calling up of recruits and the preparation of arms. The want of cavalry was much felt, as for this arm they had been accustomed to rely wholly on the provinces and especially on the Celtic contingents; to make at least a beginning, three hundred gladiators belonging to Caesar were taken from the training schools of Capua and mounted—a step which however met with so general disapproval, that Pompeius again broke up this troop and levied in room of it 300 horsemen from the mounted slave-herdmen of Apulia.

The state-treasury was at a low ebb as usual; they busied themselves in supplementing the inadequate amount of cash out of the local treasuries and even from the temple-treasures of the *municipia*.

Under these circumstances the war opened at the beginning of January $\frac{705}{49}$. Of troops capable of marching Caesar had not more than a legion—5000 infantry and 300 cavalry—at Ravenna, which was by the highway some 240 miles distant from Rome; Pompeius had two weak legions—7000 infantry and a small squadron of cavalry—under the orders of Appius Claudius at Luceria, from which, likewise by the highway, the distance was just about as great to the capital. The other troops of Caesar, leaving out of account the raw divisions of recruits still in course of formation, were stationed, one half on the Saone and Loire, the other half in Belgia, while Pompeius' Italian reserves were already arriving from all sides at their rendezvous; long before even the first of the Transalpine divisions of Caesar could arrive in Italy, a far superior army could not but be ready to receive it there. It seemed folly, with a band of the strength of that of Catilina and for the moment without any effective reserve,

[1] This number was specified by Pompeius himself (Caesar, *B. C.* i. 6), and it agrees with the fact, that he lost in Italy about 60 cohorts or 30,000 men, and took 25,000 over to Greece (Caesar, *B. C.* iii. 10).

to assume the aggressive against a superior and hourly increasing army under an able general; but it was a folly in the spirit of Hannibal. If the beginning of the struggle were postponed till spring, the Spanish troops of Pompeius would assume the offensive in Transalpine, and his Italian troops in Cisalpine, Gaul, and Pompeius, a match for Caesar in tactics and superior to him in experience, was a formidable antagonist in such a campaign running its regular course. Now perhaps, accustomed as he was to operate slowly and surely with superior masses, he might be disconcerted by a wholly improvised attack; and that which could not greatly discompose Caesar's thirteenth legion after the severe trial of the Gallic surprise and the January campaign in the land of the Bellovaci (p. 263),—the suddenness of the war and the toil of a winter campaign—could not but disorganise the Pompeian corps consisting of old soldiers of Caesar or of ill-trained recruits, and still only in the course of formation.

Accordingly Caesar advanced into Italy.[1] Two highways led at that time from the Romagna to the south; the Aemilio-Cassian which led from Bononia over the Apennines to Arretium and Rome, and the Popillio-Flaminian, which led from Ravenna along the coast of the Adriatic to Fanum and was there divided, one branch running westward through the Furlo pass to Rome, another southward to Ancona and thence onward to Apulia. On the former Marcus Antonius advanced as far as Arretium, on the second Caesar himself pushed forward. Resistance was nowhere encountered; the recruiting officers of quality had no military skill, their bands of recruits were no soldiers, the inhabitants of the country towns were only anxious not to be involved in a siege. When Curio with 1500 men approached Iguvium, where a couple of thousand Umbrian recruits had assembled under the praetor Quintus Minucius Thermus, general and soldiers took to flight at the bare tidings of his approach; and similar results on a small scale everywhere ensued.

Caesar had to choose whether he would march against Rome, from which his cavalry at Arretium were already only about 130 miles distant, or against the legions encamped at Luceria.

[1] The decree of the senate was passed on the 7th January; on the 18th it had been already for several days known in Rome that Caesar had crossed the boundary (Cic. *ad Att.* vii. 10; ix. 10, 4); the messenger needed at the very least three days from Rome to Ravenna. According to this the setting out of Caesar falls about the 12th January, which according to the current reduction corresponds to the Julian 24 November $\frac{704}{50}$.

He chose the latter plan. The consternation of the opposite party was boundless. Pompeius received the news of Caesar's advance at Rome; he seemed at first disposed to defend the capital, but, when the tidings arrived of Caesar's entrance into the Picenian territory and of his first successes there, he abandoned Rome and ordered its evacuation. A panic, augmented by the false report that Caesar's cavalry had appeared before the gates, came over the world of quality. The senators, who had been informed that every one who should remain behind in the capital would be treated as an accomplice of the rebel Caesar, flocked in crowds out at the gates. The consuls themselves had so totally lost their senses, that they did not even secure the treasure; when Pompeius called upon them to fetch it, for which there was sufficient time, they returned the reply that they would deem it safer, if he should first occupy Picenum. All was perplexity; consequently a great council of war was held in Teanum Sidicinum (23rd January), at which Pompeius, Labienus, and both consuls were present. First of all proposals of accommodation from Caesar were again submitted; even now he declared himself ready at once to dismiss his army, to hand over his provinces to the successors nominated, and to become a candidate in the regular way for the consulship provided that Pompeius were to depart for Spain, and Italy were to be disarmed. The answer was, that if Caesar would immediately return to his province, they would bind themselves to procure the disarming of Italy and the departure of Pompeius by a decree of the senate to be passed in due form in the capital; perhaps this reply was intended not as a bare artifice to deceive, but as an acceptance of the proposal of compromise; it was, however, in reality the opposite. The personal conference with Pompeius desired by Caesar the former declined, and could not but decline, that he might not by the semblance of a new coalition with Caesar provoke still more the distrust already felt by the constitutional party. Concerning the management of the war it was agreed in Teanum that Pompeius should take the command of the troops stationed at Luceria, on which notwithstanding their untrustworthiness all hope depended; that he should advance with these into his own and Labienus' native country, Picenum; that he should personally call the general levy there to arms, as he had done some thirty-five years ago (iii. 312), and should attempt at the head of the faithful Picentine cohorts and the veterans formerly under Caesar to set a limit to the advance of the enemy.

Everything depended on whether Picenum would hold out until Pompeius came up to its defence. Already Caesar with his reunited army had penetrated into it along the coast road by way of Ancona. Here too the preparations were in full course; in the very northernmost Picenian town Auximum a considerable band of recruits was collected under Publius Attius Varus; but at the entreaty of the municipality Varus evacuated the town even before Caesar appeared, and a handful of Caesar's soldiers which overtook the troop not far from Auximum totally dispersed it after a brief conflict—the first in this war. In like manner soon afterwards Gaius Lucilius Hirrus with 3000 men evacuated Camerinum, and Publius Lentulus Spinther with 5000 Asculum. The men, thoroughly devoted to Pompeius, willingly for the most part left their houses and farms, and followed their leaders over the frontier; but the district itself was already lost, when the officer sent by Pompeius for the temporary conduct of the defence, Lucius Vibullius Rufus—no genteel senator, but a soldier experienced in war—arrived there; he had to content himself with taking the six or seven thousand recruits who were saved away from the incapable recruiting officers, and conducting them for the time to the nearest rendezvous.

This was Corfinium, the place of meeting for the levies in the Albensian, Marsian and Paelignian territories; the body of recruits here assembled, of nearly 15,000 men, was the contingent of the most warlike and trustworthy regions of Italy, and the flower of the army in course of formation for the constitutional party. When Vibullius arrived here, Caesar was still several days' march behind; there was nothing to prevent him from immediately starting agreeably to Pompeius' instructions and conducting the saved Picentine recruits along with those assembled at Corfinium to join the main army in Apulia. But the commandant in Corfinium was the designated successor to Caesar in the governorship of Transalpine Gaul, Lucius Domitius, one of the most narrow-minded and stubborn of the Roman aristocracy; and he not only refused to comply with the orders of Pompeius, but also prevented Vibullius from departing at least with the men from Picenum for Apulia. So firmly was he persuaded that Pompeius only delayed from obstinacy and must necessarily come up to his relief, that he scarcely made any serious preparations for a siege and did not even gather into Corfinium the bands of recruits placed in the surrounding towns. Pompeius however did not appear, and for good reasons; for, while he might perhaps apply his two untrustworthy legions as a support to the Picentine general levy, he could not with them alone offer battle to Caesar. Instead of him after a few days Caesar came (14th February). His troops had been joined in Picenum by the twelfth, and before Corfinium by the eighth, legion from beyond the Alps, and, besides these, three new legions had been formed partly from the Pompeian men that were taken prisoners or presented themselves voluntarily, partly from the recruits that were at once levied everywhere; so that Caesar before Corfinium was already at the head of an army of 40,000 men, half of whom had seen service. So long as Domitius hoped for the arrival of Pompeius, he caused the town to be defended; when the letters of Pompeius had at length undeceived him, he resolved, not forsooth to persevere at the forlorn post—by which he would have rendered the greatest service to his party—nor even to capitulate, but, while the common soldiers were informed that relief was close at hand, to make his own escape along with his noble officers during the next night. Yet he had not the judgment to carry into effect even this pretty scheme. The confusion of his behaviour betrayed him. A part of the men began to mutiny; the Marsian recruits, who held such an infamy on the part of their general to be impossible, wished to fight against the mutineers; but they too were obliged reluctantly to believe the truth of the accusation, whereupon the whole garrison arrested their staff and handed it, themselves, and the town over to Caesar (20th February). The corps in Alba, 3000 strong, and 1500 recruits assembled in Tarracina, thereupon laid down their arms, as soon as Caesar's patrols of cavalry appeared; a third division in Sulmo of 3500 men had been previously compelled to surrender.

Pompeius had given up Italy as lost so soon as Caesar had occupied Picenum; only he wished to delay his embarkation as long as possible, with the view of saving so much of his force as could still be saved. Accordingly he had slowly put himself in motion for the nearest seaport, Brundisium. Thither came the two legions of Luceria and such recruits as Pompeius had been able hastily to collect in the deserted Apulia, as well as the troops raised by the consuls and other commissioners in Campania and conducted in all haste to Brundisium; thither too resorted a number of political fugitives, including the most distinguished of the senators accompanied by their families. The embarkation began; but the vessels at hand did not suffice to transport all at once the whole multitude, which still amounted to 25,000 persons. No course remained but to divide the army. The larger half went first (4th March); with the smaller division of some 10,000 men Pompeius awaited at Brundisium the return of the fleet; for, however desirable the possession of Brundisium might be for a contingent attempt to recover Italy, they did not venture to hold the place permanently against Caesar. Meanwhile Caesar arrived before Brundisium; the siege began. Caesar attempted first of all to close the mouth of the harbour by moles and floating bridges, with a view to exclude the returning fleet; but Pompeius caused the trading vessels lying in the harbour to be armed, and managed to prevent the complete closing of the harbour until the fleet appeared, and the troops—whom Pompeius with great dexterity, in spite of the vigilance of the besiegers and the hostile feeling of the inhabitants, withdrew from the town to the last man unharmed—were carried off beyond Caesar's reach to Greece (17th March). The further pursuit, like the siege itself, failed for want of a fleet.

In a campaign of two months, without a single serious engagement, Caesar had so broken up an army of ten legions, that less than the half of it had with great difficulty escaped in a confused flight across the sea, and the whole Italian peninsula, including the capital with the state-chest and all the stores accumulated there, had fallen into the power of the victor. Not without reason did the beaten party bewail the terrible rapidity, sagacity, and energy of the "monster."

But it may be questioned whether Caesar gained or lost more by the conquest of Italy. In a military respect, no doubt, very considerable resources were now not merely withdrawn from his opponents, but rendered available for himself; even in the spring of $\frac{705}{49}$ his army embraced, in consequence of the levies *en masse* instituted everywhere, a considerable number of legions of recruits in addition to the nine old ones. But on the other hand it now became necessary not merely to leave behind a considerable garrison in Italy, but also to take measures against the closing of the transmarine traffic contemplated by his opponents who commanded the sea, and against the famine with which the capital was consequently threatened; whereby Caesar's already sufficiently complicated military task was complicated further still. Financially it was certainly of importance that Caesar had the good fortune to obtain possession of the stock of money in the capital; but the principal sources of income and particularly the revenues from the East were in the hands of the enemy, and, in consequence of the greatly increased demands for the army and the new obligation to provide for the starving population of the capital, the considerable sums which were found quickly melted away. Caesar soon found himself compelled to appeal to private credit, and, as it seemed that he could not possibly gain any long respite by this means, extensive confiscations were generally anticipated as the only remaining expedient.

More serious difficulties still were created by the political relations amidst which Caesar found himself placed on the conquest of Italy. The apprehension of an anarchical revolution was universal among the propertied classes. Friends and foes saw in Caesar a second Catilina; Pompeius believed or affected to believe that Caesar had been driven to civil war merely by the impossibility of paying his debts. This was certainly absurd; but in fact Caesar's antecedents were anything but reassuring, and still less reassuring was the aspect of the retinue that now surrounded him. Individuals of the most broken reputation, notorious personages like Quintus Hortensius, Gaius Curio, Marcus Antonius—the latter the stepson of the Catilinarian Lentulus who was executed by the orders of Cicero—were the most prominent actors in it; the highest posts of trust were bestowed on men who had long ceased even to reckon up their debts; people saw men who held office under Caesar not merely keeping dancing-girls—which was done by others also—but appearing publicly in company with them. Was there any wonder, that even grave and politically impartial men expected amnesty for all exiled criminals, cancelling of creditors' claims, comprehensive mandates of confiscation, proscription, and murder, nay, even a plundering of Rome by the Gallic soldiery?

But in this respect the "monster" deceived the expectations of his foes as well as of his friends. As soon even as Caesar occupied the first Italian town, Ariminum, he prohibited all common soldiers from appearing armed within the walls; the country towns were protected from injury throughout and without distinction, whether they had given him a friendly or hostile reception. When the mutinous garrison surrendered Corfinium late in the evening, he in the face of every military consideration postponed the occupation of the town till the following morning, solely that he might not abandon the burgesses to the nocturnal invasion of his exasperated soldiers. Of the prisoners the common soldiers, as presumably indifferent to politics, were incorporated with his own army, while the officers were not merely spared, but also freely dismissed without distinction of person and without the exaction of any promises whatever; and all which they claimed as private property was frankly given up to them, without even investigating with any strictness the warrant for their claims. Lucius Domitius himself was thus treated, and even Labienus had the money and baggage which he had left behind sent after him to the enemy's camp. In the most painful financial embarrassment the immense estates of his opponents whether present or absent were not assailed; indeed Caesar preferred to borrow from friends, rather than that he should stir up the holders of property against him even by exacting the formally admissible, but practically antiquated, land tax (iii. 371). The victor regarded only the half, and that not the more difficult half, of his task as solved with the victory; he saw the security for its duration, according to his own expression, only in the unconditional pardon of the vanquished, and had accordingly during the whole march from Ravenna to Brundisium incessantly renewed his efforts to bring about a personal conference with Pompeius and a tolerable accommodation.

But, if the aristocracy had previously refused to listen to reconciliation, the unexpected and withal so disgraceful emigration had raised their wrath to madness, and the wild vengeance breathed by the beaten contrasted strangely with the placability of the victor. The communications regularly coming from the camp of the emigrants to their friends left behind in Italy were full of projects for confiscations and proscriptions, of plans for purifying the senate and the state, compared with which the restoration of Sulla was child's play, and which even the moderate men of their own party heard with horror. The frantic passion of impotence, the wise moderation of power, produced their effect. The whole mass, in whose eyes material interests were superior to political, threw itself into the arms of Caesar. The country towns idolised "the uprightness, the moderation, the prudence" of the victor; and even opponents conceded that these testimonies of respect were meant in earnest. The great capitalists, farmers of the taxes, and jurymen, showed no special desire, after the severe shipwreck which had befallen the constitutional party in Italy, to entrust themselves farther to the same pilots; capital returned to the light, and "the rich lords resorted again to their daily task of writing their rent-rolls." Even the great majority of the senate, at least numerically speaking—for certainly but few of the nobler and more influential members of the senate were included in it—had notwithstanding the orders of Pompeius and of the consuls remained behind in Italy, and a portion of them even in the capital itself; and they acquiesced in Caesar's rule. The moderation of Caesar, well calculated even in its very semblance of excess, attained its object: the trembling anxiety of the propertied classes as to the impending anarchy was in some measure allayed. This was doubtless an incalculable gain for the future; the prevention of anarchy, and of the scarcely less dangerous alarm of anarchy, was the indispensable preliminary to the future reorganisation of the commonwealth.

But at the moment this moderation was more dangerous for Caesar than the renewal of the Cinnan and Catilinarian fury would have been; it did not convert enemies into friends, and it converted friends into enemies. Caesar's Catilinarian adherents were indignant that murder and pillage remained in abeyance; these audacious and desperate personages, some of whom were men of talent, might be expected to prove cross and untractable. The republicans of all shades, on the other hand, were neither converted nor propitiated by the leniency of the conqueror. According to the creed of the Catonian party, duty towards what they called their fatherland absolved them from every other consideration; even one who owed freedom and life to Caesar remained entitled and in duty bound to take up arms or at least to engage in plots against him. The less decided sections of the constitutional party were no doubt ready to accept peace and protection from the new monarch; nevertheless they ceased not to curse the monarchy and the monarch at heart. The more clearly the change of the constitution became manifest, the more distinctly the great majority of the burgesses—both in the capital with its keener susceptibility of political excitement, and among the more energetic population of the country and country towns—awoke to a consciousness of their republican sentiments; so far the friends of the constitution in Rome reported with truth to their brethren of kindred views in exile, that at home all classes and all persons were friendly to Pompeius. The discontented temper of all these circles was further increased by the moral pressure, which the more decided and more notable men who shared such views exercised from their very position as emigrants over the multitude of the humbler and more lukewarm. The conscience of the honourable man smote him in regard to his remaining in Italy; the half-aristocrat fancied that he was ranked among the plebeians if he did not go into exile with the Domitii and the Metelli, and even if he took his seat in the Caesarian senate of nobodies. The victor's special clemency gave to this silent opposition increased political importance; seeing that Caesar abstained from terrorism, it seemed as if his secret opponents could display their disinclination to his rule without much danger.

Very soon he experienced remarkable treatment in this respect at the hands of the senate. Caesar had begun the struggle to liberate the overawed senate from its oppressors. This was done; consequently he wished to obtain from the senate approval of what had been done, and full powers for the continuance of the war. For this purpose, when Caesar appeared before the capital (end of March) the tribunes of his party convoked for him the senate (1st April). The meeting was tolerably numerous, but the more notable of the very senators that remained in Italy were absent, including even the former leader of the servile majority Marcus Cicero and Caesar's own father-in-law Lucius Piso; and, what was worse, those who did appear were not inclined to enter into Caesar's proposals. When Caesar spoke of full power to continue the war, one of the only two consulars present, Servius Sulpicius Rufus, a very timid man who desired nothing but a quiet death in his bed, was of opinion that Caesar would deserve well of his country if he should abandon the thought of carrying the war to Greece and Spain. When Caesar thereupon requested the senate at least to be the medium of transmitting his peace proposals to Pompeius, they were not indeed opposed to that course in itself, but the threats of the emigrants against the neutrals had so terrified the latter, that no one was found to undertake the message of peace. Through the disinclination of the aristocracy to help the erection of the monarch's throne, and through the same inertness of the dignified corporation, by means of which Caesar had shortly before frustrated the legal nomination of Pompeius as generalissimo in the civil war, he too was now thwarted when making a like request. Other impediments, moreover, occurred. Caesar desired, with the view of regulating in some sort of way his position, to be named dictator; but his wish was not complied with, because such a magistrate could only be constitutionally appointed by one of the consuls, and the attempt of Caesar to buy the consul Lentulus—of which owing to the disordered condition of his finances there was a good prospect—nevertheless proved a failure. The tribune of the people Lucius

Metellus, moreover, lodged a protest against all the steps of the proconsul, and made signs as though he would protect with his person the public chest, when Caesar's men came to empty it. Caesar could not avoid in this case ordering that the inviolable person should be pushed aside as gently as possible; otherwise, he kept by his purpose of abstaining from all violent steps. He declared to the senate, just as the constitutional party had done shortly before, that he had certainly desired to regulate things in a legal way and with the help of the supreme authority; but, since this help was refused, he could dispense with it.

Without further concerning himself about the senate and the formalities of state law, he handed over the temporary administration of the capital to the praetor Marcus Aemilius Lepidus as city-prefect, and made the requisite arrangements for the administration of the provinces that obeyed him and the continuance of the war. Even amidst the din of the gigantic struggle, and with all the alluring sound of Caesar's lavish promises, it still made a deep impression on the multitude of the capital, when they saw in their free Rome the monarch for the first time exercising a monarch's prerogative and breaking open the doors of the treasury by his soldiers. But the times had gone by when the impressions and feelings of the multitude determined the course of events; it was with the legions that the decision lay, and a few painful feelings more or less were in fact of no farther moment.

Caesar hastened to resume the war. He owed his successes hitherto to the offensive, and he intended still to maintain it. The position of his antagonist was singular. After the original plan of carrying on the campaign simultaneously in the two Gauls by offensive operations from the bases of Italy and Spain had been frustrated by Caesar's aggressive, Pompeius had intended to go to Spain. There he had a very strong position. The army amounted to seven legions; a large number of Pompeius' veterans served in it, and several years of conflicts in the Lusitanian mountains had hardened soldiers and officers. Among its captains Marcus Varro indeed was simply a celebrated scholar and a faithful partisan; but Lucius Afranius had fought with distinction in the East and in the Alps, and Marcus Petreius, the conqueror of Catilina, was an officer as dauntless as he was able. While in the Further province Caesar had still various adherents from the time of his governorship there (p. 198), the more important province of the Ebro was attached by all the ties of veneration and gratitude to the celebrated general, who twenty years before had held the command in it during the Sertorian war, and after the termination of that war had organised it anew. Pompeius could evidently after the Italian disaster do nothing better than proceed to Spain with the saved remnant of his army, and then at the head of his whole force advance to meet Caesar. But unfortunately he had, in the hope of being able still to save the troops that were in Corfinium, tarried in Apulia so long that he was compelled to choose the nearer Brundisium as his place of embarkation instead of the Campanian ports. Why, master as he was of the sea and Sicily, he did not subsequently revert to his original plan, cannot be determined; probably the aristocracy after their short-sighted and distrustful fashion showed no desire to commit themselves to the Spanish troops and the Spanish population. At any rate Pompeius remained in the East, and Caesar had the option of directing his first attack either against the army which was being organised in Greece under Pompeius' own command, or against that which was ready for battle under his lieutenants in Spain. He had decided in favour of the latter course, and, as soon as the Italian campaign ended, had taken measures to collect on the lower Rhone nine of his best legions, as also 6000 cavalry—partly men individually picked out by Caesar in the Celtic cantons, partly German mercenaries—and a number of Iberian and Ligurian archers.

But at this point his opponents also had been active. Lucius Domitius, who was nominated by the senate in Caesar's stead as governor of Transalpine Gaul, had proceeded from Corfinium—as soon as Caesar had released him—along with his attendants and with Pompeius' confidant Lucius Vibullius Rufus to Massilia, and actually induced that city to declare for Pompeius and even to refuse a passage to Caesar's troops. Of the Spanish troops the two least trustworthy legions were left behind under the command of Varro in the Further province; while the five best, reinforced by 40,000 Spanish infantry—partly Celtiberian infantry of the line, partly Lusitanian and other light troops—and by 5000 Spanish cavalry, under Afranius and Petreius had, in accordance with the orders of Pompeius transmitted by Vibullius, set out to close the Pyrenees against the enemy.

Meanwhile Caesar himself arrived in Gaul and, as the commencement of the siege of Massilia still detained him in person, he immediately despatched the greater part of his troops assembled on the Rhone—six legions and the cavalry—along the great road leading by way of Narbo (Narbonne) to Rhode (Rosas) with the view of anticipating the enemy at the Pyrenees. The movement was successful; when Afranius and Petreius arrived at the passes, they found them already occupied by the Caesarians and the line of the Pyrenees lost. They then took up a position at Ilerda (Lerida) between the Pyrenees and the Ebro. This town lies twenty miles to the north of the Ebro on the right bank of one of its tributaries, the Sicoris (Segre), which was crossed by only a single solid bridge immediately at Ilerda. To the south of Ilerda the mountains which adjoin the left bank of the Ebro approach pretty close to the town; to the northward there stretches on both sides of the Sicoris a level country which is commanded by the hill on which the town is built. For an army, which had to submit to a siege, it was an excellent position; but the defence of Spain, after the occupation of the line of the Pyrenees had been neglected, could only be undertaken in earnest behind the Ebro, and, as no secure communication was established between Ilerda and the Ebro, and no bridge existed over the latter stream, the retreat from the temporary to the true defensive position was not sufficiently secured. The Caesarians established themselves above Ilerda, in the delta which the river Sicoris forms with the Cinga (Cinca), which unites with it below Ilerda; but the attack only began in earnest after Caesar had arrived in the camp (23rd June). Under the walls of the town the struggle was maintained with equal exasperation and equal valour on both sides, and with frequent alternations of success; but the Caesarians did not attain their object—which was, to establish themselves between the Pompeian camp and the town and thereby to possess themselves of the stone bridge—and they consequently remained dependent for their communication with Gaul solely on two bridges which they had hastily constructed over the Sicoris, and, as the river at Ilerda itself was too considerable to be bridged over, about eighteen or twenty miles farther up.

When the floods came on with the melting of the snow, these temporary bridges were swept away; and, as they had no vessels for the passage of the highly swollen rivers and under such circumstances the restoration of the bridges could not for the present be thought of, the Caesarian army was confined to the narrow space between the Cinca and the Sicoris, while the left bank of the Sicoris and with it the road, by which the army communicated with Gaul and Italy, were exposed almost undefended to the Pompeians, who passed the river partly by the town-bridge, partly by swimming after the Lusitanian fashion on skins. It was the season shortly before harvest; the old produce was almost used up, the new was not yet gathered, and the narrow strip of land between the two streams was soon exhausted. In the camp actual famine prevailed—the *modius* of wheat cost 50 *denarii* (£1 16*s*.)—and dangerous diseases broke out; whereas on the left bank there were accumulated provisions and varied supplies, as well as troops of all sorts—reinforcements from Gaul of cavalry and archers, officers and soldiers from furlough, foraging parties returning—in all a mass of 6000 men, whom the Pompeian attacked with superior force and drove with great loss to the mountains, while the Caesarians on the right bank were obliged to remain passive spectators of the unequal conflict. The communications of the army were in the hands of the Pompeians; in Italy the accounts from Spain suddenly ceased, and the suspicious rumours which began to circulate there were not so very remote from the truth. Had the Pompeians followed up their advantage with some energy, they could not have failed either to reduce under their power or at least to drive back towards Gaul the mass scarcely capable of resistance which was crowded together on the left bank of the Sicoris, and to occupy this bank so completely that not a man could cross the river without their knowledge. But both points were neglected; those bands were doubtless forced off with loss but neither destroyed nor completely beaten back, and the prevention of the crossing of the river was left substantially to the river itself.

Thereupon Caesar formed his plan. He ordered portable boats of a light wooden frame and osier work lined with leather, after the model of those used in the Channel among the Britons and subsequently by the Saxons, to be prepared in the camp and transported in waggons to the point where the bridges had stood. On these frail barks the other bank was reached and, as it was found unoccupied, the bridge was re-established without much difficulty; the communications were thereupon quickly restored, and the eagerly expected supplies were conveyed to the camp. Caesar's happy idea thus rescued the army from the immense peril in which it was placed. Then the cavalry of Caesar, which in efficiency far surpassed that of the enemy, began at once to scour the country on the left bank of the Sicoris; the most considerable Spanish communities between the Pyrenees and the Ebro—Osca, Tarraco, Dertosa, and others—nay, even several to the south of the Ebro, passed over to Caesar's side.

The supplies of the Pompeians were now rendered scarce through the foraging parties of Caesar and the defection of the neighbouring communities; they resolved at length to retire behind the line of the Ebro, and set themselves in all haste to form a bridge of boats over the Ebro below the mouth of the Sicoris. Caesar sought to cut off the retreat of his opponents over the Ebro and to detain them in Ilerda; but so long as the enemy remained in possession of the bridge at Ilerda and he had control of neither ford nor bridge there, he could not distribute his army over both banks of the river and could not invest Ilerda. His soldiers therefore worked day and night to lower the depth of the river by means of canals drawing off the water, so that the infantry could wade through it. But the preparations of the Pompeians to pass the Ebro were sooner finished than the arrangements of the Caesarians to invest Ilerda; when the former after finishing the bridge of boats began their march towards the Ebro along the left bank of the Sicoris, the canals of the Caesarians seemed to the general not yet far enough advanced to make the ford available for the infantry; he ordered only his cavalry to pass the stream and, by clinging to the rear of the enemy, at least to detain and harass them.

But when Caesar's legions saw in the grey morning the enemy's columns which had been retiring since midnight, they discerned with the sure instinct of experienced veterans the strategic importance of this retreat, which would compel them to follow their antagonists into distant and impracticable regions filled by hostile troops; at their own request the general ventured to lead the infantry also into the river, and although the water reached up to the shoulders of the men, it was crossed without accident. It was high time. If the narrow plain, which separated the town of Ilerda from the mountains enclosing the Ebro were once traversed and the army of the Pompeians entered the mountains, their retreat to the Ebro could no longer be prevented. Already they had, notwithstanding the constant attacks of the enemy's cavalry which greatly delayed their march, approached within five miles of the mountains, when they, having been on the march since midnight and unspeakably exhausted, abandoned their original plan of traversing the whole plain on the same day, and pitched their camp. Here the infantry of Caesar overtook them and encamped opposite to them in the evening and during the night, as the nocturnal march which the Pompeians had at first contemplated was abandoned from fear of the night-attacks of the cavalry. On the following day also both armies remained immovable, occupied only in reconnoitring the country.

Early in the morning of the third day Caesar's infantry set out, that by a movement through the pathless mountains alongside of the road they might turn the position of the enemy and bar their route to the Ebro. The object of the strange march, which seemed at first to turn back towards the camp before Ilerda, was not at once perceived by the Pompeian officers. When they discerned it, they sacrificed camp and baggage and advanced by a forced march along the highway to gain the crest of the ridge before the Caesarians. But it was already too late; when they came up, the compact masses of the enemy were already posted on the highway itself. A desperate attempt of the Pompeians to discover other routes to the Ebro over the steep mountains was frustrated by the Roman cavalry, which surrounded and cut to pieces the Lusitanian troops sent forth for that purpose. Had a battle taken place between the Pompeian army—which had the enemy's cavalry in its rear and their infantry in front, and was utterly demoralised—and the Caesarians, the issue was scarcely doubtful, and the opportunity for fighting several times presented itself; but Caesar made no use of it, and restrained, with difficulty, the impatient eagerness for combat in his soldiers sure of victory. The Pompeian army was at any rate strategically lost; Caesar avoided weakening his army and still further envenoming the bitter feud by useless bloodshed. On the very day after he had succeeded in cutting off the Pompeians from the Ebro, the soldiers of the two armies had begun to fraternise and to negotiate respecting surrender; indeed the terms asked by the Pompeians, especially as to the sparing of their officers, had been already conceded by Caesar, when Petreius with his escort consisting of slaves and Spaniards came upon the negotiators and caused the Caesarians, on whom he could lay hands, to be put to death. Caesar nevertheless sent the Pompeians who had come to his camp back unharmed, and persevered in seeking a peaceful solution. Ilerda, where the Pompeians had still a garrison and considerable magazines, became now the point which they sought to reach; but with the hostile army in front and the Sicoris between them and the fortress, they marched without coming nearer to their object. Their cavalry became gradually so afraid that the infantry had to take them into the centre and legions had to be set as the rear-guard; the procuring of water and forage became more and more difficult; they had already to kill the beasts of burden, because they could no longer feed them. At length the wandering army found itself formally inclosed, with the Sicoris in its rear and the enemy's force in front, which drew rampart and trench around it. It attempted to cross the river, but Caesar's German horsemen and light infantry anticipated it in the occupation of the opposite bank.

No bravery and no fidelity could longer avert the inevitable capitulation (2nd August $\frac{705}{49}$). Caesar granted to officers and soldiers their life and liberty, and the possession of the property which they still retained as well as the restoration of what had been already taken from them, the full value of which he undertook personally to make good to his soldiers; and not only so, but while he had compulsorily enrolled in his army the recruits captured in Italy, he honoured these old legionaries of Pompeius by the promise that no one should be compelled to enter the army against his will. He required only that each should give up his arms and repair to his home. Accordingly the soldiers who were natives of Spain, about a third of the army, were disbanded at once, while the Italian soldiers were discharged at the borders of Transalpine and Cisalpine Gaul.

Hither Spain on the breaking up of this army fell of itself into the power of the victor. In Further Spain, where Marcus Varro held the chief command for Pompeius, it seemed to him, when he learned the disaster of Ilerda, most advisable that he should throw himself into the insular town of Gades and should carry thither for safety the considerable sums which he had collected by confiscating the treasures of the temples and the property of prominent Caesarians, the not inconsiderable fleet which he had raised, and the two legions entrusted to him. But on the mere rumour of Caesar's arrival the most notable towns of the province which had been for long attached to Caesar declared for the latter and drove away the Pompeian garrisons or induced them to a similar revolt; such was the case with Corduba, Carmo, and Gades itself. One of the legions also set out of its own accord for Hispalis, and passed over along with this town to Caesar's side. When at length even Italica closed its gates against Varro, the latter resolved to capitulate.

About the same time Massilia also submitted. With rare energy the Massiliots had not merely sustained a siege, but had also kept the sea against Caesar; it was their native element, and they might hope to obtain vigorous support on it from Pompeius, who in fact had the exclusive command of it. But Caesar's lieutenant, the able Decimus Brutus, the same who had achieved the first naval victory in the Atlantic over the Veneti (p. 236), managed rapidly to equip a fleet; and in spite of the brave resistance of the enemy's crews—consisting partly of Albioecian mercenaries of the Massiliots, partly of slave-herdsmen of Domitius—he vanquished by means of his brave marines selected from the legions the stronger Massiliot fleet, and sank or captured the greater part of their ships. When a small Pompeian squadron under Lucius Nasuidis arrived from the East by way of Sicily and Sardinia in the port of Massilia, the Massiliots renewed their naval armament and sailed forth along with the ships of Nasidius against Brutus. The engagement which took place off Tauroeis (La Ciotat to the east of Marseilles) might probably have had a different result, if the vessels of Nasidius had fought with the same desperate courage which the Massiliots displayed on that day; but the flight of the Nasidians decided the victory in favour of Brutus, and the remains of the Pompeian fleet fled to Spain. The besieged were completely driven from the sea. On the landward side, where Gaius Trebonius conducted the siege, the most resolute resistance was still continued; but in spite of the frequent sallies of the Albioecian mercenaries and the skilful expenditure of the immense stores of projectiles accumulated in the city, the works of the besiegers were at length advanced up to the walls and one of the towers fell. The Massiliots declared that they would give up the defence, but desired to conclude the capitulation with Caesar himself, and entreated the Roman commander to suspend the siege operations till Caesar's arrival. Trebonius had express orders from Caesar to spare the town as far as possible; he granted the armistice desired. But when the Massiliots made use of it for an artful sally, in which they completely burnt the one half of the almost unguarded Roman works, the struggle of the siege began anew and with increased exasperation. The vigorous commander of the Romans repaired with surprising rapidity the destroyed towers and the mound; the Massiliots were now once more completely enclosed.

When Caesar on his return from the conquest of Spain arrived before their city, he found it reduced to extremities partly by the enemy's attacks, partly by famine and pestilence, and ready for the second time—on this occasion in right earnest—

to surrender on any terms. Domitius alone, remembering the indulgence of the victor which he had shamefully misused, embarked in a boat and stole through the Roman fleet, to seek a third battle-field for his implacable resentment. Caesar's soldiers had sworn to put to the sword the whole male population of the perfidious city, and vehemently demanded from the general the signal for plunder. But Caesar, mindful here also of his task of establishing Helleno-Italic civilisation in the West, was not to be coerced into furnishing a sequel to the destruction of Corinth. Massilia—the most remote from the mother-country of all those cities, once so numerous, free, and powerful, that belonged to the old Ionic mariner-nation, and almost the last in which the Hellenic seafaring life had preserved itself fresh and pure, as in fact it was the last Greek city that fought at sea—Massilia had to surrender its magazines of arms and naval stores to the victor, and lost a portion of its territory and of its privileges; but it retained its freedom and its nationality and continued, though with diminished proportions in a material point of view, to be intellectually the centre of Hellenic culture in that distant Celtic country which at this very time was attaining a new historical significance.

While thus in the western provinces the war after various critical vicissitudes was thoroughly decided at length in favour of Caesar, Spain and Massilia were subdued, and the chief army of the enemy was captured to the last man, the decision of arms had also taken place on the second arena of warfare, on which Caesar had found it necessary immediately after the conquest of Italy to assume the offensive.

We have already mentioned that the Pompeians intended to reduce Italy to starvation. They had the means of doing so in their hands. They had thorough command of the sea and laboured with great zeal everywhere—in Gades, Utica, Messana, above all in the East—to increase their fleet. They held moreover all the provinces from which the capital drew its means of subsistence: Sardinia and Corsica through Marcus Cotta, Sicily through Marcus Cato, Africa through the self-nominated commander-in-chief Titus Attius Varus and their ally Juba king of Numidia. It was indispensably needful for Caesar to thwart these plans of the enemy and to wrest from them the corn-provinces. Quintus Valerius was sent with a legion to Sardinia and compelled the Pompeian governor to evacuate the island. The more important enterprise of taking Sicily and Africa from the enemy was entrusted to the young Gaius

Curio with the assistance of the able Gaius Caninius Rebilus, who had experience in war. Sicily was occupied by him without a blow; Cato, without a proper army and not a man of the sword, evacuated the island, after having in his straightforward manner previously warned the Siceliots not to compromise themselves uselessly by an ineffectual resistance.

Curio left behind half of his troops to protect this island so important for the capital, and embarked with the other half—two legions and 500 horse—for Africa. Here he might expect to encounter more serious resistance; besides the considerable and in its own fashion efficient army of Juba, the governor Varus had formed two legions of Romans settled in Africa and also fitted out a small squadron of ten sail. With the aid of his superior fleet, however, Curio effected without difficulty a landing between Hadrumetum, where the one legion of the enemy lay along with their ships of war, and Utica, in front of which town lay the second legion under Varus himself. Curio turned against the latter, and pitched his camp not far from Utica, just where a century and a half before the elder Scipio had taken up his first winter-encampment in Africa (ii. 170). Caesar, compelled to keep together his best troops for the Spanish war, had been obliged to make up the Sicilo-African army for the most part out of the legions taken over from the enemy, more especially the war-prisoners of Corfinium; the officers of the Pompeian army in Africa, some of whom had served in the very legions that were conquered at Corfinium, now left no means untried to bring back their old soldiers who were fighting against them to their first allegiance. But Caesar had not erred in the choice of his lieutenant. Curio knew as well how to direct the movements of the army and of the fleet, as how to acquire personal influence over the soldiers; the supplies were abundant, the conflicts without exception successful.

When Varus, presuming that the troops of Curio only wanted opportunity to pass over to his side, resolved to give battle chiefly for the sake of affording them this opportunity, the result did not justify his expectations. Animated by the fiery appeal of their youthful leader, the cavalry of Curio put to flight the horsemen of the enemy, and in presence of the two armies cut down also the light infantry which had accompanied the horsemen; and emboldened by this success and by Curio's personal example, his legions advanced through the difficult ravine separating the two lines to the attack, for which the Pompeians however did not wait, but disgracefully fled back to their camp and evacuated even this in the ensuing night. The victory was so complete that Curio at once took steps to besiege Utica. When news arrived, however, that king Juba was advancing with all his forces to its relief, Curio resolved, just as Scipio had done on the arrival of Syphax, to raise the siege and to return to Scipio's former camp till reinforcements should arrive from Sicily. Soon afterwards came a second report, that king Juba had been induced by the attacks of neighbouring chiefs to turn back with his main force and was sending to the aid of the besieged merely a moderate corps under Saburra. Curio, who from his lively temperament had only with great reluctance made up his mind to rest, now set out again at once to fight with Saburra before he could enter into communication with the garrison of Utica.

His cavalry, which had gone forward in the evening, actually succeeded in surprising the corps of Saburra on the Bagradas during the night and inflicting much damage upon it; and on the news of this victory Curio hastened the march of the infantry, in order by their means to complete the defeat. Soon they perceived on the last slopes of the heights that sank towards the Bagradas the corps of Saburra, which was skirmishing with the Roman horsemen; the legions coming up helped to drive it completely down into the plain. But here the combat changed its aspect. Saburra was not, as they supposed, destitute of support; on the contrary he was not much more than five miles distant from the Numidian main force. Already the flower of the Numidian infantry and 2000 Gallic and Spanish horsemen had arrived on the field of battle to support Saburra, and the king in person with the bulk of the army and sixteen elephants was approaching. After the nocturnal march and the hot conflict there were at the moment not more than 200 of the Roman cavalry together, and these as well as the infantry, extremely exhausted by fatigue and fighting, were all surrounded, in the wide plain into which they had allowed themselves to be allured, by the continually increasing hosts of the enemy. Vainly Curio endeavoured to engage in close combat; the Libyan horsemen retreated, as they were wont, so soon as a Roman division advanced, only to pursue it when it turned. In vain he attempted to regain the heights; they were occupied and foreclosed by the enemy's horse. All was lost. The infantry was cut down to the last man. Of the cavalry a few succeeded in cutting their way through; Curio too might have probably saved himself, but he could not bear to appear without the army entrusted to him in presence of his master, and died sword in hand. Even the force which was collected in the camp before Utica, and that which guarded the fleet—which might so easily have escaped to Sicily—surrendered under the impression made by the fearfully rapid catastrophe on the following day to Varus (August or September $\frac{705}{49}$).

So ended the expedition arranged by Caesar to Sicily and Africa. It attained its object so far, since by the occupation of Sicily in connection with that of Sardinia the most urgent wants of the capital were relieved; the miscarriage of the conquest of Africa—from which the victorious party drew no farther substantial gain—and the loss of two untrustworthy legions might be got over. But the early death of Curio was an irreparable loss for Caesar, and indeed for Rome. Not without reason had Caesar entrusted the most important independent command to this young man, although he had no military experience and was notorious for his dissolute life; there was a spark of Caesar's own spirit in the fiery youth. He resembled Caesar, inasmuch as he had drained the cup of pleasure to the dregs; inasmuch as he did not become a statesman because he was an officer, but it was his political action that placed the sword in his hands; inasmuch as his eloquence was not that of rounded periods, but the eloquence of deeply felt thought; inasmuch as his mode of warfare was based on rapid action with slight means; inasmuch as his character was marked by levity and often by frivolity, by pleasant frankness and thorough life in the moment. If, as his general says of him, youthful fire and high courage carried him into incautious acts, and if he too proudly accepted death that he might not submit to be pardoned for a pardonable fault, traits of similar imprudence and similar pride are not wanting in Caesar's history also. We may regret that this exuberant nature was not permitted to work off its follies and to preserve itself for the following generation so miserably poor in talents, and so rapidly falling a prey to the dreadful rule of mediocrities.

How far these events of the war in $\frac{705}{49}$ interfered with Pompeius' general plan for the campaign, and particularly what part in that plan was assigned after the loss of Italy to the important military corps in the West, can only be determined by conjecture. That Pompeius had the intention of coming by way of Africa and Mauretania to the aid of his army fighting in Spain was simply a romantic, and beyond doubt altogether groundless, rumour circulating in the camp of Ilerda.

It is much more likely that he still kept by his earlier plan of attacking Caesar from both sides in Transalpine and Cisalpine Gaul (p. 350) even after the loss of Italy, and meditated a combined attack at once from Spain and Macedonia. It may be presumed that the Spanish army was meant to remain on the defensive at the Pyrenees till the Macedonian army in the course of organisation was likewise ready to march; whereupon both would then have started simultaneously and effected a junction according to circumstances either on the Rhine or on the Po, while the fleet, it may be conjectured, would have attempted at the same time to recover Italy proper. On this supposition apparently Caesar had first prepared himself to meet an attack on Italy. One of the ablest of his officers, the tribune of the people Marcus Antonius, commanded there with propraetorian powers. The south-eastern ports—Sipus, Brundisium, Tarentum—where an attempt at landing was first to be expected, had received a garrison of three legions. Besides this Quintus Hortensius, the degenerate son of the well-known orator, collected a fleet in the Tyrrhene Sea, and Publius Dolabella a second fleet in the Adriatic, which were to be employed partly to support the defence, partly to transport the intended expedition to Greece. In the event of Pompeius attempting to penetrate by land into Italy, Marcus Licinius Crassus, the eldest son of the old colleague of Caesar, was to conduct the defence of Cisalpine Gaul, Gaius the younger brother of Marcus Antonius that of Illyricum.

But the expected attack was long in coming. It was not till the height of summer that the conflict began in Illyria. There Caesar's lieutenant Gaius Antonius with his two legions lay in the island of Curicta (Veglia in the gulf of Quarnero), and Caesar's admiral Publius Dolabella with forty ships lay in the narrow arm of the sea between this island and the mainland. The admirals of Pompeius in the Adriatic, Marcus Octavius with the Greek, Lucius Scribonius Libo with the Illyrian division of the fleet, attacked the squadron of Dolaballa, destroyed all his ships, and cut off Antonius on his island. To rescue him, a corps under Basilus and Sallustius came from Italy and the squadron of Hortensius from the Tyrrhene Sea; but neither the former nor the latter were able to effect anything in presence of the far superior fleet of the enemy. The legions of Antonius had to be abandoned to their fate. Provisions came to an end, the troops became troublesome and mutinous; with the exception of a few divisions, which succeeded in reaching the mainland on rafts, the corps, still numbering fifteen cohorts, laid down their arms and were conveyed in the vessels of Libo to Macedonia to be there incorporated with the Pompeian army, while Octavius was left to complete the subjugation of the Illyrian coast now denuded of troops. The Dalmatae, who from the period of Caesar's governorship had been at feud with him (p. 272), the important insular town of Issa (Lissa), and other places, embraced the party of Pompeius; but the adherents of Caesar maintained themselves in Salonae (Spalato) and Lissus (Alessio), and in the former town not merely sustained with courage a siege, but when they were reduced to extremities, made a sally with such effect that Octavius raised the siege and sailed off to Dyrrhachium to pass the winter.

The success achieved in Illyricum by the Pompeian fleet, although of itself not inconsiderable, had yet but little influence on the issue of the campaign as a whole; and it appears miserably small when we consider that the performances of the land and naval forces under Pompeius' command during the whole eventful year $\frac{705}{49}$ were confined to this single feat of arms, and that from the East, where the general, the senate, the second great army, the principal fleet, the immense military and still more extensive financial resources of the antagonists of Caesar were united, no intervention at all took place at the point where it was needed in that all-decisive struggle in the West. The scattered condition of the forces in the eastern half of the empire, the method of the general never to operate except with superior masses, his awkward and tedious movements, and the discord of the coalition may perhaps explain in some measure, though not excuse, the inactivity of the land-force; but that the fleet, which commanded the Mediterranean without a rival, should have thus done nothing to affect the course of affairs—nothing for Spain, next to nothing for the faithful Massiliots, nothing to defend Sardinia, Sicily, Africa, or, if not to reoccupy Italy, at any rate to obstruct its supplies—this makes demands on our ideas of the confusion and perversity prevailing in the Pompeian camp, which we can only with difficulty meet.

The aggregate result of this campaign was corresponding. Caesar's double aggressive movement, against Spain and against Sicily and Africa, was successful in the former case completely, in the latter at least partially; while Pompeius' plan of starving Italy was thwarted in the main by the taking away of Sicily, and his general plan of campaign was frustrated completely by the destruction of the Spanish army; and in Italy only a very small portion of Caesar's defensive arrangements had come to be applied. Notwithstanding the painfully felt losses in Africa and Illyria, Caesar came forth from this first year of the war in the most decided and most decisive manner victorious.

If, however, nothing material was done from the East to obstruct Caesar in the subjugation of the West, efforts at least were made towards securing political and military consolidation there during the respite so ignominiously obtained. The great rendezvous of the opponents of Caesar was Macedonia. Thither Pompeius himself and the mass of the emigrants from Brundisium resorted; thither came the other refugees from the West: Marcus Cato from Sicily, Lucius Domitius from Massilia, but more especially a number of the best officers and soldiers of the broken-up army of Spain, with its generals Afranius and Varro at their head. In Italy emigration gradually became among the aristocrats a question not of honour merely but almost of fashion, and it obtained a fresh impulse through the unfavourable accounts which arrived regarding Caesar's position before Ilerda; not a few of the more lukewarm partisans and the political trimmers went over by degrees, and even Marcus Cicero at last persuaded himself that he did not adequately discharge his duty as a citizen by writing a dissertation on concord. The senate of emigrants at Thessalonica, where the official Rome pitched its *interim* abode, numbered nearly 200 members, including many venerable old men and almost all the consulars. But they were veritably emigrants. This Roman Coblentz presented a pitiful spectacle of the high pretensions and paltry performances of the grandees of Rome, their unseasonable reminiscences and still more unseasonable recriminations, their political perversities and financial embarrassments. It was a matter of comparatively slight moment that, while the old structure was falling to pieces, they were with the most painstaking solemnity watching over every old ornamental scroll and every speck of rust in the constitution; after all it was simply ridiculous, when the noble lords had scruples of conscience as to calling their deliberative assembly beyond the sacred soil of the city the senate, and cautiously gave it the title of the "three hundred;" [1] or when they instituted tedious investiga-

[1] As according to formal law the "legal deliberative assembly" undoubtedly, just like the "legal court," could only take place in the city itself or within the precincts, the senate of Thessalonica called itself the "three hundred" (*Bell. Afric.* 88, 90; Appian. ii. 95), not because it consisted of 300 members, but because this was the ancient normal number of senators (i. 67). It is very likely that this assembly recruited its ranks by

tions in state law as to whether and how a curiate law could be legitimately enacted elsewhere than at the Capitol.

A far worse trait was the indifference of the lukewarm and the narrow-minded stubbornness of the ultras. The former could neither be induced to act nor to keep silence. If they were asked to exert themselves in some definite way for the common good, with the inconsistency characteristic of weak people they regarded any such suggestion as a malicious attempt to compromise them still further, and either did not do what they were ordered at all or did it with half heart. At the same time of course, with their affectation of knowing better when it was too late and their over-wise impracticabilities, they proved a perpetual clog to those who were acting; their daily work consisted in criticising, ridiculing, and bemoaning every occurrence great and small, and in unnerving and discouraging the multitude by their own sluggishness and hopelessness.

While these displayed the utter prostration of weakness, the ultras on the other hand exhibited in full display its exaggerated action. With them there was no attempt to conceal that the preliminary to any negotiation for peace was the bringing over of Caesar's head; every one of the attempts towards peace, which Caesar repeatedly made even now, was tossed aside without being examined, or employed only to cover insidious attempts on the lives of the commissioners of their opponent. That the declared partisans of Caesar had jointly and severally forfeited life and property, was a matter of course; but it fared little better with those more or less neutral. Lucius Domitius, the hero of Corfinium, gravely proposed in the council of war that those senators who had fought in the army of Pompeius should come to a vote on all who had either remained neutral or had emigrated but not entered the army, and should according to their own pleasure individually acquit them or punish them by fine or even by the forfeiture of life and property. Another of these ultras formally lodged with Pompeius a charge of corruption and treason against Lucius Afranius for his defective defence of Spain. Among these deep-dyed republicans their political theory assumed almost the character of a confession of religious faith; they accordingly hated their own more lukewarm partisans and Pompeius with his personal adherents, if possible, still more than their open opponents,

equites of distinction; but, when Plutarch makes the three hundred Italian wholesale dealers (*Cato Min.* 59, 61), he has misunderstood his authority (*Bell. Afr.* 90).

and that with all the dull obstinacy of hatred which is wont to characterise orthodox theologians; and they were mainly to blame for the numberless and bitter separate quarrels which distracted the emigrant army and emigrant senate. But they did not confine themselves to words. Marcus Bibulus, Titus Labienus, and others of this clique carried out their theory in practice, and caused such officers or soldiers of Caesar's army as fell into their hands to be executed *en masse;* which, as may well be conceived, did not tend to make Caesar's troops fight with less energy. If the counter-revolution in favour of the friends of the constitution, for which all the elements were in existence (p. 357), did not break out in Italy during Caesar's absence, the reason, according to the assurance of discerning opponents of Caesar, lay chiefly in the general dread of the unbridled fury of the republican ultras after the restoration should have taken place. The better men in the Pompeian camp were in despair at this frantic behaviour. Pompeius, himself a brave soldier, spared the prisoners as far as he might and could; but he was too pusillanimous and in too awkward a position to prevent or even to punish all atrocities of this sort, as it became the commander-in-chief to do. Marcus Cato, the only man who at least carried moral consistency into the struggle, attempted with more energy to check such proceedings; he induced the emigrant senate to prohibit by a special decree the pillage of subject towns and the putting to death of a burgess otherwise than in battle. The able Marcus Marcellus had similar views. No one, indeed, knew better than Cato and Marcellus that the extreme party would carry out their valiant acts, if necessary, in defiance of all decrees of the senate. But if even now, when they had still to regard considerations of prudence, the rage of the ultras could not be tamed, people might prepare themselves after the victory for a reign of terror from which Marius and Sulla themselves would have turned away with horror; and we can understand why Cato, according to his own confession, was more afraid of the victory than of the defeat of his own party.

The management of the military preparations in the Macedonian camp was in the hands of Pompeius the commander-in-chief. His position, always troublesome and galling, had become still worse through the unfortunate events of $\frac{705}{49}$. In the eyes of his partisans he was mainly to blame for this result. This judgment was in various respects not just. A considerable part of the misfortunes endured was to be laid to the account of the perversity and insubordination of the lieutenant-generals, especially of the consul Lentulus and Lucius Domitius; from the moment when Pompeius took the head of the army, he had led it with skill and courage, and had saved at least very considerable forces from the shipwreck; that he was not a match for Caesar's altogether superior genius, which was now recognised by all, could not be fairly made matter of reproach to him. But the result alone decided men's judgment. Trusting to the general Pompeius, the constitutional party had broken with Caesar; the injurious consequences of this breach recoiled upon the general Pompeius; and, though owing to the notorious military incapacity of all the other chiefs no attempt was made to change the supreme command, yet confidence at any rate in the commander-in-chief was paralysed. To these painful consequences of the defeats endured were added the injurious influences of the emigration. Among the refugees who arrived there were certainly a number of efficient soldiers and able officers, especially those belonging to the former Spanish army; but the number of those who came to serve and fight was small, while that of the generals of quality who called themselves proconsuls and imperators with as good title as Pompeius, and of the noble lords who took part in active military service more or less reluctantly, was alarmingly great. By means of these the mode of life in the capital was introduced into the camp, not at all to the advantage of the army; the tents of these grandees were graceful bowers, the ground elegantly covered with fresh turf, the walls clothed with ivy; silver plate stood on the table, and the wine-cup often circulated there even in broad daylight. Those fashionable warriors formed a singular contrast with Caesar's dare devils, who ate coarse bread from which the former recoiled, and who, when that failed, devoured even roots and swore that they would rather chew the bark of trees than desist from the enemy. While, moreover, the action of Pompeius was hampered by the necessity of having regard to the authority of a corporation personally averse to him, this embarrassment was singularly increased when the senate of emigrants took up its abode almost in his very head-quarters and all the venom of the emigrants came to find vent in these senatorial sittings. Lastly there was nowhere any man of mark who could have thrown his own weight into the scale against all these preposterous doings. Pompeius himself was far too secondary in point of intellect for that purpose, and far too hesitating, awkward, and reserved. Marcus Cato would have had at least the requisite moral authority, and would not have lacked the good will to support Pompeius with it; but Pompeius, instead of calling him to his assistance, out of distrustful jealousy kept him in the background, and preferred for instance to commit the highly important chief command of the fleet to the utterly incapable Marcus Bibulus rather than to Cato.

While Pompeius thus treated the political aspect of his position with his characteristic perversity, and did his best to make what was already bad in itself still worse, he devoted himself on the other hand with commendable zeal to his duty of giving military organisation to the considerable but scattered forces of his party. The flower of his force was composed of the troops brought with him from Italy, but of which with the supplementary aid of the Illyrian prisoners of war and the Romans domiciled in Greece five legions in all were formed. Three others came from the East—the two Syrian legions formed from the remains of the army of Crassus, and one made up out of the two weak legions hitherto stationed in Cilicia. Nothing stood in the way of the withdrawal of these corps of occupation: because on the one hand the Pompeians had an understanding with the Parthians, and might even have had an alliance with them if Pompeius had not indignantly refused to pay them the price which they demanded for it—the cession of the Syrian province added by himself to the empire; and on the other hand Caesar's plan of despatching two legions to Syria, and inducing the Jews once more to take arms by means of the prince Aristobulus kept a prisoner in Rome, was thwarted partly by other causes, partly by the death of Aristobulus. New legions were moreover raised—one from the veteran soldiers settled in Crete and Macedonia, two from the Romans of Asia Minor. To all these fell to be added 2000 volunteers, who were derived from the remnant of the Spanish select corps and other similar sources; and, lastly, the contingents of the subjects. Pompeius like Caesar had disdained to make requisitions of infantry from them; only the Epirot, Aetolian, and Thracian militia were called out to guard the coast, and moreover 3000 archers from Greece and Asia Minor and 1200 slingers were taken up as light troops.

The cavalry again—with the exception of a noble guard, more respectable than militarily important, formed from the young aristocracy of Rome, and of the Apulian slave-herdsmen whom Pompeius had mounted (p. 349)—consisted exclusively of the contingents of the subjects and clients of Rome. The flower of it consisted of the Celts, partly from the garrison of Alexandria (p. 145), partly the contingents of king Deiotarus who in spite of his great age had appeared in person at the head of his troops, and of the other Galatian dynasts. With them were associated the excellent Thracian horsemen, who were partly brought up by their princes Sadala and Rhaskyporis, partly enlisted by Pompeius in the Macedonian province; the Cappadocian cavalry; the mounted archers sent by Antiochus king of Commagene; the contingents of the Armenians from the west side of the Euphrates under Taxiles, and from the other side under Megabates, and the Numidian bands sent by king Juba—the whole body amounted to 7000 horsemen.

Lastly the fleet of Pompeius was very considerable. It was formed partly of the Roman transports brought from Brundisium or subsequently built, partly of the war vessels of the king of Egypt, of the Colchian princes, of the Cilician dynast Tarcondimotus, of the cities of Tyre, Rhodes, Athens, Corcyra, and generally of all the Asiatic and Greek maritime states; and it numbered nearly 500 sail, of which the Roman vessels formed a fifth. Immense magazines of corn and military stores were accumulated in Dyrrhachium. The war-chest was well filled, for the Pompeians were in possession of the principal sources of the public revenue and turned to their own account the moneyed resources of the client-princes, of the senators of distinction, of the farmers of the taxes, and generally of the whole Roman and non-Roman population within their reach. Every appliance that the reputation of the legitimate government and the much-renowned protectorship of Pompeius over kings and peoples could move in Africa, Egypt, Macedonia, Greece, Western Asia and Syria, had been put in motion for the protection of the Roman republic; the report which circulated in Italy that Pompeius was arming the Getae, Colchians, and Armenians against Rome, and the designation of "king of kings" given to Pompeius in the camp, could hardly be called exaggerations. On the whole he had command over an army of 7000 cavalry and eleven legions, of which, it is true, but five at the most could be described as accustomed to war, and over a fleet of 500 sail. The temper of the soldiers, for whose provisioning and pay Pompeius manifested adequate care, and to whom in the event of victory the most abundant rewards were promised, was throughout good, in several—and these precisely the most efficient—divisions excellent; but a great part of the army consisted of newly-raised troops, the formation and training of which, however zealously it was prosecuted, necessarily required time. The force altogether was imposing, but at the same time of a somewhat motley character.

According to the design of the commander-in-chief the army and fleet were to be in the main completely united by the winter of $\frac{705-706}{49-48}$ along the coast and in the waters of Epirus. The admiral Bibulus had already arrived with 110 ships at his new head-quarters, Corcyra. On the other hand the land army, the head-quarters of which had been during the summer at Berrhoea on the Haliacmon, had not yet come up; the mass of it was moving slowly along the great highway from Thessalonica towards the west coast to the future head-quarters Dyrrhachium; the two legions, which Metellus Scipio was bringing up from Syria, remained at Pergamus in Asia for winter quarters and were expected in Europe only towards spring. They were taking time in fact for their movements. For the moment the ports of Epirus were guarded, over and above the fleet, merely by their own civic defences and the levies of the adjoining districts.

It thus remained possible for Caesar, notwithstanding the intervention of the Spanish war, to assume the offensive also in Macedonia; and he at least was not slow to act. He had long ago ordered the collection of vessels of war and transports in Brundisium, and after the capitulation of the Spanish army and the fall of Massilia had directed the greater portion of the select troops employed there to proceed to that destination. The unparalleled exertions no doubt, which were thus required by Caesar from his soldiers, thinned the ranks more than their conflicts had done, and the mutiny of one of the four oldest legions, the ninth, on its march through Placentia was a dangerous indication of the temper prevailing in the army; but Caesar's presence of mind and personal authority mastered it, and from this quarter nothing impeded the embarkation. But the want of ships, through which the pursuit of Pompeius had failed in March $\frac{705}{49}$, threatened also to frustrate this expedition. The war-vessels, which Caesar had given orders to build in the Gallic, Sicilian, and Italian ports, were not yet ready or at any rate not on the spot; his squadron in the Adriatic had been in the previous year destroyed at Curicta (p. 371); he found at Brundisium not more than twelve ships of war and scarcely transports enough to convey over at once the third part of his army—of twelve legions and 10,000 cavalry—

destined for Greece. The considerable fleet of the enemy exclusively commanded the Adriatic and especially all the harbours of the mainland and islands on its eastern coast. Under such circumstances the question presents itself, why Caesar did not instead of the maritime route choose the land route through Illyria, which relieved him from all the perils threatened by the fleet and besides was shorter for his troops, who mostly came from Gaul, than the route by Brundisium. It is true that the Illyrian country was rugged and poor beyond description; but it was traversed by other armies not long afterwards, and this obstacle can hardly have appeared insurmountable to the conqueror of Gaul. Perhaps he apprehended that during the troublesome march through Illyria Pompeius might convey his whole force over the Adriatic, whereby their parts would at once have been changed and Caesar must have taken up his position in Macedonia, while Pompeius lay in Italy; although such a rapid change was scarcely to be expected from his slow-moving antagonist. Perhaps Caesar had decided for the maritime route on the supposition that his fleet would meanwhile be brought into a condition to command respect, and, when after his return from Spain he became aware of the true state of things in the Adriatic, it might be too late to change the plan of campaign. Perhaps—and, in accordance with Caesar's quick temperament always urging him to decision, we may even say in all probability—he found himself irresistibly tempted by the circumstance that the Epirote coast was still at the moment unoccupied but would certainly be covered in a few days by the enemy, to thwart once more by a bold stroke the whole plan of his antagonist.

However this may be, on the 4th January $\frac{706}{48}$ [1] Caesar set sail with six legions greatly thinned by toil and sickness and 600 horsemen from Brundisium for the coast of Epirus. It was a counterpart to the foolhardy Britannic expedition; but at least the first throw was fortunate. The coast was reached in the middle of the Acroceraunian (Chimara) cliffs, at the little-frequented roadstead of Paleassa (Paljassa). The transports were seen both from the harbour of Oricum (creek of Avlona) where a Pompeian squadron of eighteen sail was lying, and from the head-quarters of the hostile fleet at Corcyra; but in the one quarter they deemed themselves too weak, in the other they were not ready to sail, so that the first freight was landed without hindrance. While the vessels at once returned to bring over

[1] According to the rectified calendar somewhere about the 5th Nov. $\frac{705}{49}$.

the second, Caesar on that same evening ascended the Acroceraunian mountains. His first successes were as great as the surprise of his enemies. The Epirote militia nowhere resisted; the important seaport towns of Oricum and Apollonia along with a number of smaller places were taken, and Dyrrhachium, selected by the Pompeians as their chief arsenal and filled with stores of all sorts, but only feebly garrisoned, was in the utmost danger.

But the further course of the campaign did not correspond to this brilliant beginning. Bibulus subsequently made up in some measure for the negligence, of which he had been guilty, by redoubling his exertions. He not only captured nearly thirty of the transports returning home, and caused them with every living thing on board to be burnt, but he also established along the whole district of coast occupied by Caesar, from the island Sason (Saseno) as far as the ports of Corcyra, a most careful watch, however troublesome it was rendered by the inclement season of the year and the necessity of bringing everything necessary for the guard-ships, even wood and water, from Corcyra; in fact his successor Libo—for he himself soon succumbed to the unwonted fatigues—even blockaded for a time the port of Brundisium, till the want of water again dislodged him from the little island in front of it on which he had established himself. It was not possible for Caesar's officers to convey the second portion of the army over to their general. As little did he himself succeed in the capture of Dyrrhachium. Pompeius learned through one of Caesar's peace-envoys as to his preparations for the voyage to the Epirote coast, and, thereupon accelerating his march, threw himself just at the right time into that important arsenal. The situation of Caesar was critical. Although he extended his range in Epirus as far as with his slight strength was at all possible, the subsistence of his army remained difficult and precarious, while the enemy, in possession of the magazines of Dyrrhachium and masters of the sea, had abundance of everything. With his army probably little above 20,000 strong he could not offer battle to that of Pompeius at least twice as numerous, but had to deem himself fortunate that Pompeius went methodically to work and, instead of immediately forcing a battle, took up his winter quarters between Dyrrhachium and Apollonia on the right bank of the Apsus, facing Caesar on the left, in order that after the arrival of the legions from Pergamus in the spring he might annihilate the enemy with an irresistibly superior force. Thus months passed. If the arrival of the better season, which brought to the enemy a strong additional force and the free use of his fleet, found Caesar still in the same position, he was to all appearance lost, with his weak band wedged in among the rocks of Epirus between the immense fleet and the three times superior land army of the enemy; and already the winter was drawing to a close. His sole hope still depended on the transport fleet; any attempt to steal or fight its way through the blockade was more than audacious; but after the first voluntary foolhardiness this second venture was enjoined by necessity. How desperate his situation appeared to Caesar himself is shown by his resolution—when the fleet still came not—to sail alone in a fisherman's boat through the Adriatic to Brundisium in order to fetch it; which, in reality, was only abandoned because no mariner was found to undertake the daring voyage.

But his appearance in person was not needed to induce the faithful officer who commanded in Italy, Marcus Antonius, to make this last effort for the saving of his master. Once more the transport fleet, with four legions and 800 cavalry on board, sailed from the harbour of Brundisium, and fortunately a strong south wind carried it past Libo's galleys. But the same wind, which thus saved the fleet, rendered it impossible for it to land as it was directed on the coast of Apollonia, and compelled it to sail past the camps of Caesar and Pompeius and to steer to the north of Dyrrhachium towards Lissus, which town fortunately still adhered to Caesar (p. 372). When it sailed past the harbour of Dyrrhachium, the Rhodian galleys started in pursuit, and hardly had the ships of Antonius entered the port of Lissus when the enemy's squadron appeared before it. But just at this moment the wind suddenly veered, and drove the pursuing galleys back into the open sea and partly on the rocky coast. Through the most marvellous good fortune the landing of the second freight had also been successful.

Antonius and Caesar were no doubt still some four days' march from each other, separated by Dyrrhachium and the whole army of the enemy; but Antonius happily effected the perilous march round about Dyrrhachium through the passes of the Graba Balkan, and was received by Caesar, who had gone to meet him, on the right bank of the Apsus. Pompeius, after having vainly attempted to prevent the junction of the two armies of the enemy and to force the corps of Antonius to fight by itself, took up a new position at Asparagium on the river Genusus (Uschkomobin), which flows parallel to the Apsus between the latter and the town of Dyrrhachium, and here remained once more immovable. Caesar felt himself now strong enough to give battle; but Pompeius declined it. On the other hand he succeeded in deceiving Pompeius and throwing himself unawares with his better marching troops, just as at Ilerda, between the enemy's camp and the fortress of Dyrrhachium on which it rested as a basis. The chain of the Graba Balkan, which stretching in a direction from east to west ends on the Adriatic in the narrow tongue of land at Dyrrhachium, sends off—fourteen miles to the east of Dyrrhachium—in a south-westerly direction a lateral branch which likewise turns in a crescentic form towards the sea, and the main chain and lateral branch of the mountains enclose between themselves a small plain extending round a cliff on the seashore. Here Pompeius now took up his camp, and, although Caesar's army kept the land route to Dyrrhachium closed against him, he yet with the aid of his fleet remained constantly in communication with the town and was amply and easily provided from it with everything needful; while among the Caesarians, notwithstanding strong detachments to the country lying behind, and notwithstanding all the exertions of the general to bring about an organised system of conveyance and thereby a regular supply, there was more than scarcity, and flesh, barley, nay even roots, had very frequently to take the place of the wheat to which they were accustomed.

As his phlegmatic opponent persevered in his inaction, Caesar undertook to occupy the circle of heights which enclosed the plain on the shore held by Pompeius, with the view of being able at least to arrest the movements of the superior cavalry of the enemy and to operate with more freedom against Dyrrhachium, and if possible to compel his opponent either to battle or to embarkation. Nearly the half of Caesar's troops was detached to the interior; it seemed almost Quixotic to propose with the rest virtually to besiege an army perhaps twice as strong, concentrated in position, and resting on the sea and the fleet. Yet Caesar's veterans by infinite exertions invested the Pompeian camp with a chain of posts sixteen miles long, and afterwards added, just as before Alesia, to this inner line a second outer one, to protect themselves against attacks from Dyrrhachium and against attempts to turn their position which could so easily be executed with the aid of the fleet. Pompeius attacked more than once portions of these entrenchments with a view to break if possible the enemy's line, but he did not attempt to prevent the investment by a battle; he preferred to construct in his turn a number of entrenchments around his camp, and to connect them with one another by lines. Both sides exerted themselves to push forward their trenches as far as possible, and the earthworks advanced but slowly amidst constant conflicts. At the same time skirmishing went on on the opposite side of Caesar's camp with the garrison of Dyrrhachium; Caesar hoped to get the fortress into his power by means of an understanding with some of its inmates, but was prevented by the enemy's fleet. There was incessant fighting at very different points—on one of the hottest days at six places simultaneously—and, as a rule, the tried valour of the Caesarians had the advantage in these skirmishes; once, for instance, a single cohort maintained itself in its entrenchments against four legions for several hours, till support came up. No prominent success was attained on either side; yet the effects of the investment came by degrees to be oppressively felt by the Pompeians. The stopping of the rivulets flowing from the heights into the plain compelled them to be content with scanty and bad well-water. Still more severely felt was the want of fodder for the beasts of burden and the horses, which the fleet was unable adequately to remedy; numbers of them died, and it was of but little avail that the horses were conveyed by the fleet to Dyrrhachium, because there also they did not find sufficient fodder.

Pompeius could not much longer delay to free himself from his disagreeable position by a blow struck against the enemy. He was informed by Celtic deserters that the enemy had neglected to secure the beach between his two chains of entrenchments 600 feet distant from each other by a cross-wall, and on this he formed his plan. While he caused the inner line of Caesar's entrenchments to be attacked by the legions from the camp, and the outer line by the light troops placed in vessels and landed beyond the enemy's entrenchments, a third division landed in the space left between the two lines and attacked in the rear their already sufficiently occupied defenders. The entrenchment next to the sea was taken, and the garrison fled in wild confusion; with difficulty the commander of the next trench Marcus Antonius succeeded in maintaining it and in setting a limit for the moment to the advance of the Pompeians; but, apart from the considerable loss, the outermost entrenchment along the sea remained in the hands of the Pompeians and the line was broken. Caesar the more eagerly seized the opportunity, which soon after presented itself, of attacking a Pompeian legion, which had incautiously become isolated, with the bulk of his infantry. But the attacked made valiant resistance, and, as the ground on which the fight took place had been several times employed for the encampment of larger and lesser divisions and was intersected in various directions by mounds and ditches, Caesar's right wing along with the cavalry missed entirely its way; instead of supporting the left in attacking the Pompeian legion, it got into a narrow trench that led from one of the old camps towards the river. Thus Pompeius, who came up in all haste with five legions to the aid of his troops, found the two wings of the enemy separated, and one of them in an utterly forlorn position. When the Caesarians saw his advance, a panic seized them; the whole plunged into disorderly flight; and, if the matter ended with the loss of 1000 of the best soldiers and Caesar's army did not sustain a complete defeat, this was owing simply to the circumstance that Pompeius also could not freely deploy his force on the broken ground, and to the fact that, fearing a stratagem, he at first held back his troops.

But, even as it was, these days were fraught with mischief. Not only had Caesar endured the most serious losses and forfeited at a blow his entrenchments, the result of four months of gigantic labour; he was by the recent engagements thrown back again exactly to the point from which he had set out. From the sea he was more completely driven than ever, since Pompeius' elder son Gnaeus had by a bold attack partly burnt, partly carried off, Caesar's few ships of war lying in the port of Oricum, and had soon afterwards also set fire to the transport fleet that was left behind in Lissus; all possibility of bringing up fresh reinforcements to Caesar by sea from Brundisium was thus lost. The numerous Pompeian cavalry, now released from their confinement, poured themselves over the adjacent country and threatened to render the provisioning of Caesar's army, which had always been difficult, utterly impossible. Caesar's daring enterprise of carrying on offensive operations without ships against an enemy in command of the sea and resting on his fleet had totally failed. On what had hitherto been the theatre of war he found himself in presence of an impregnable defensive position, and unable to strike a serious blow either against Dyrrhachium or against the hostile army; on the other hand it depended now solely on Pompeius whether he should proceed to attack under the most favourable circumstances an antagonist already in grave danger as to the means of subsistence. The war had arrived at a crisis. Hitherto Pompeius had, to all appearance, played the game of war without special plan, and only adjusted his defence according to the exigencies of each attack; and this was not to be censured, for the protraction of the war gave him opportunity of making his recruits capable of fighting, of bringing up his reserves, and of bringing more fully into play the superiority of his fleet in the Adriatic. The defeats of Dyrrhachium had not, it is true, that effect which Pompeius not without reason expected from them; the eminent soldierly energy of Caesar's veterans did not allow matters to come to an immediate and total breaking up of the army by hunger and mutiny; but Caesar was entirely beaten not merely in tactics but also in strategy, and it seemed as if he could neither maintain himself in his present position nor judiciously change it.

Pompeius had conquered; it was for him to assume the aggressive; and he was resolved to do so. Three different ways of rendering his victory fruitful presented themselves to him. The first and simplest was not to desist from assailing the vanquished army, and, if it departed, to pursue it. Secondly, Pompeius might leave Caesar himself and his best troops in Greece, and might cross in person, as he had long been making preparations for doing, with the main army to Italy, where the feeling was decidedly antimonarchical and the forces of Caesar, after the despatch of the best troops and their brave and trustworthy commandant to the Greek army, would not be of very much moment. Lastly, the victor might turn inland, effect a junction with the legions of Metellus Scipio, and attempt to capture the troops of Caesar stationed in the interior. The latter forsooth had, immediately after the arrival of the second cargo from Italy, despatched strong detachments to Aetolia and Thessaly to procure means of subsistence for his army, and had ordered a corps of two legions under Gnaeus Domitius Calvinus to advance on the Egnatian highway towards Macedonia, with the view of intercepting and if possible defeating in detail the corps of Scipio advancing on the same road from Thessalonica. Calvinus and Scipio had already approached within a few miles of each other, when Scipio suddenly turned southward and, rapidly crossing the Haliacmon (Jadsche Karasu) and leaving his baggage there under Marcus Favonius, penetrated into Thessaly, in order to attack with superior force Caesar's legion of recruits employed in the reduction of the country under

Lucius Cassius Longinus. But Longinus retired over the mountains towards Ambracia on the detachment under Gnaeus Calvisius Sabinus sent by Caesar to Aetolia, and Scipio could only cause him to be pursued by his Thracian cavalry, for Calvinus threatened his reserve left behind under Favonius on the Haliacmon with the same fate which he had himself destined for Longinus. So Calvinus and Scipio met again on the Haliacmon, and encamped there for a considerable time opposite to each other.

Pompeius might choose among these plans; no choice was left to Caesar. After that unfortunate engagement he entered on his retreat to Apollonia. Pompeius followed. The march from Dyrrhachium to Apollonia along a difficult road crossed by several rivers was no easy task for a defeated army pursued by the enemy; but the dexterous guidance of their general and the indestructible marching energy of the soldiers compelled Pompeius after four days' pursuit to suspend it as useless. He had now to decide between the Italian expedition and the march into the interior. However advisable and attractive the former might seem, and though various voices were raised in its favour, he preferred not to abandon the corps of Scipio, the more especially as he hoped by this march to get the corps of Calvinus into his hands. Calvinus lay at the moment on the Egnatian road at Heraclea Lyncestis between Pompeius and Scipio, and, after Caesar had retreated to Apollonia, farther distant from the latter than from the great army of Pompeius; without knowledge, moreover, of the events at Dyrrhachium and of his hazardous position, since after the successes achieved at Dyrrhachium the whole country inclined to Pompeius and the messengers of Caesar were everywhere seized. It was not till the enemy's main force had approached within a few miles of him that Calvinus learned from the accounts of the enemy's advanced posts themselves the state of things. A quick departure in a southerly direction towards Thessaly withdrew him at the last moment from imminent destruction; Pompeius had to content himself with having liberated Scipio from his position of peril. Caesar had meanwhile arrived unmolested at Apollonia. Immediately after the disaster of Dyrrhachium he had resolved if possible to transfer the struggle from the coast away into the interior, with the view of getting beyond the reach of the enemy's fleet—the ultimate cause of the failure of his previous exertions. The march to Apollonia had only been intended to place his wounded in safety and to pay his soldiers there, where his depôts were stationed; as soon as this was done, he set out for Thessaly, leaving behind garrisons in Apollonia, Oricum, and Lissus. The corps of Calvinus had also put itself in motion towards Thessaly; and Caesar could effect a junction with the reinforcements coming up from Italy, this time by the land route through Illyria—two legions under Quintus Cornificius—still more easily in Thessaly than in Epirus. Ascending by difficult paths in the valley of the Aous and crossing the mountain-chain which separates Epirus from Thessaly, he arrived at the Peneius; Calvinus was likewise directed thither, and the junction of the two armies was thus accomplished by the shortest route and that which was least exposed to the enemy. It took place at Aeginium not far from the source of the Peneius. The first Thessalian town before which the now united army appeared, Gomphi, closed its gates against it; it was quickly stormed and given up to pillage and the other towns of Thessaly terrified by this example submitted, so soon as Caesar's legions merely appeared before the walls. Amidst these marches and conflicts, and with the help of the supplies—albeit not too ample—which the region on the Peneius afforded, the traces and recollections of the calamitous days which they had passed through gradually vanished.

The victories of Dyrrhachium had thus borne not much immediate fruit for the victors. Pompeius with his unwieldy army and his numerous cavalry had not been able to follow his versatile enemy into the mountains; Caesar like Calvinus had escaped from pursuit, and the two stood united and in full security in Thessaly. Perhaps it would have been the best course if Pompeius had now without delay embarked with his main force for Italy, where success was scarcely doubtful. But in the meantime only a division of the fleet departed for Sicily and Italy. In the camp of the coalition the contest with Caesar was looked on as so completely decided by the battles of Dyrrhachium that it only remained to reap the fruits of victory, in other words, to follow out and capture the defeated army. Their former over-cautious reserve was succeeded by an arrogance still less justified by circumstances; they gave no heed to the facts, that they had, strictly speaking, failed in the pursuit, that they had to hold themselves in readiness to encounter a completely refreshed and reorganised army in Thessaly, and that there was no small risk in moving away from the sea, renouncing the support of the fleet, and following their antagonist to the battle-field chosen by himself. They were simply resolved at any price to fight with Caesar, and therefore to get at him as soon as possible and by the most convenient way. Cato took up the command in Dyrrhachium, where a garrison was left behind of eighteen cohorts, and in Corcyra, where 300 ships of war were left; Pompeius and Scipio proceeded—the former, apparently, following the Egnatian way as far as Pella and then striking into the great road to the south, the latter from the Haliacmon through the passes of Olympus—to the lower Peneius and met at Larissa.

Caesar lay to the south of Larissa in the plain—which extends between the hill-country of Cynoscephalae and the chain of Othrys and is intersected by a tributary of the Peneius, the Enipeus—on the left bank of the latter stream near the town of Pharsalus; Pompeius pitched his camp opposite to him on the right bank of the Enipeus along the slope of the heights of Cynoscephalae.[1] The entire army of Pompeius was assembled;

[1] The exact determination of the field of battle is difficult. Appian. (ii. 75) expressly places it between (New) Pharsalus (now Fersala) and the Enipeus. Of the two streams, which alone are of any importance in the question and are undoubtedly the Apidanus and Enipeus of the ancients—the Sofadhitiko and the Fersaliti—the former has its sources in the mountains of Thaumaci (Dhomoko) and the Dolopian heights, the latter in mount Othrys, and the Fersaliti alone flows past Pharsalus; now as the Enipeus according to Strabo (ix. p. 432) springs from mount Othrys and flows past Pharsalus, the Fersaliti has been most justly pronounced by Leake (*Northern Greece*, iv. 320) to be the Enipeus, and the hypothesis followed by Göler that the Fersaliti is the Apidanus is untenable. With this all the other statements of the ancients as to the two rivers agree. Only we must doubtless assume with Leake, that the river of Vlokho formed by the union of the Fersaliti and the Sofadhitiko and going to the Peneius was called by the ancients Apidanus as well as the Sofadhitiko; which, however, is the more natural, as while the Sofadhitiko probably has, the Fersaliti has not, constantly water (Leake, iv. 321). Old Pharsalus, from which the battle takes its name, must therefore have been situated between Fersala and the Fersaliti. Accordingly the battle was fought on the left bank of the Fersaliti, and in such a way that the Pompeians, standing with their faces towards Pharsalus, leaned their right wing on the river (Caesar, *B. C.* iii. 83; Frontinus, *Strat.* ii. 3, 22). The camp of the Pompeians, however, cannot have stood here, but only on the slope of the heights of Cynoscephalae, on the right bank of the Enipeus, partly because they barred the route of Caesar to Scotussa, partly because their line of retreat evidently went over the mountains above the camp towards Larissa; if they had, according to Leake's hypothesis (iv. 482), encamped to the east of Pharsalus on the left bank of the Enipeus, they could never have got to the northward through this stream, which at this very point has a deeply cut bed (Leake, iv. 469), and Pompeius must have fled to Lamia instead of Larissa. Probably therefore the Pompeians pitched their camp on the right bank of the Fersaliti, and passed the river both in order to fight and in order, after the battle, to regain their camp, whence they then moved up the slopes of Crannon and Scotussa, which culminate above the latter place in the heights of Cynoscephalae. This was not impossible. The Enipeus is a small slow-flowing rivulet, which Leake found two feet deep in November, and which in the hot season often lies quite dry (Leake,

Caesar on the other hand still expected the corps of nearly two legions formerly detached to Aetolia and Thessaly, now stationed under Quintus Fufius Calenus in Greece, and the two legions of Cornificius which were sent after him by the land route from Italy and had already arrived in Illyria. The army of Pompeius, numbering eleven legions or 47,000 men and 7000 horse, was more than double that of Caesar in infantry, and seven times as numerous in cavalry; fatigue and conflicts had so decimated Caesar's troops, that his eight legions did not number more than 22,000 men under arms, consequently not nearly the half of their normal amount. The victorious army of Pompeius provided with a countless cavalry and good magazines had provisions in abundance, while the troops of Caesar had difficulty in keeping themselves alive and only hoped for better supplies from the corn-harvest not far distant. The Pompeian soldiers, who had learned in the last campaign to know war and trust their leader, were in the best of humour. All military reasons on the side of Pompeius favoured the view, that the decisive battle should not be long delayed, seeing that they now confronted Caesar in Thessaly; and the emigrant impatience of the many noble officers and others accompanying the army doubtless had more weight than even such reasons in the council of war. Since the events of Dyrrhachium these lords regarded the triumph of their party as an ascertained fact; already there was eager strife as to the filling up of Caesar's supreme pontificate, and instructions were sent to Rome to hire houses at the Forum for the next elections. When Pompeius hesitated as to his crossing of the rivulet which separated the two armies, and which Caesar with his much weaker army did not venture to pass, this excited great indignation; Pompeius, it was alleged, delayed the battle only in order to rule somewhat longer over so many consulars and praetorians and to perpetuate his part

i. 448, and iv. 472; comp. Lucan. vi. 373), and the battle was fought in the height of summer. Further the armies before the battle lay three miles and a half from each other (Appian. *B. C.* ii. 65), so that the Pompeians could make all preparations and also properly secure the communication with their camp by bridges. Had the battle terminated in a complete rout, no doubt the retreat to and over the river could not have been executed, and doubtless for this reason Pompeius only reluctantly agreed to fight here. The left wing of the Pompeians which was the most remote from the base of retreat felt this; but the retreat at least of their centre and their right wing was not accomplished in such haste as to be impracticable under the given conditions. Caesar and his copyists are silent as to the crossing of the river, because this would place in too clear a light the eagerness for battle of the Pompeians apparent otherwise from the whole narrative, and they are also silent as to the conditions of retreat favourable for these.

of Agamemnon. Pompeius yielded; and Caesar, who under the impression that matters would not come to a battle, had just projected a mode of turning the enemy's army and for that purpose was on the point of setting out towards Scotussa, likewise arrayed his legions for battle, when he saw the Pompeians preparing to offer it to him on his bank.

Thus the battle of Pharsalus was fought on the 9th August $\frac{706}{48}$, almost on the same field where a hundred and fifty years before the Romans had laid the foundation of their dominion in the East (ii. 282). Pompeius rested his right wing on the Enipeus; Caesar opposite to him rested his left on the broken ground stretching in front of the Enipeus; the two other wings were stationed out in the plain, covered in each case by the cavalry and the light troops. The intention of Pompeius was to keep his infantry on the defensive, but with his cavalry to scatter the weak band of horsemen which, mixed after the German fashion with light infantry, confronted him, and then to take Caesar's right wing in rear. His infantry courageously sustained the first charge of that of the enemy, and the engagement there came to a stand. Labienus likewise dispersed the enemy's cavalry after a brave but short resistance, and deployed his force to the left with the view of turning the infantry. But Caesar, foreseeing the defeat of his cavalry, had stationed behind it on the threatened flank of his right wing some 2000 of his best legionaries. As the enemy's horsemen, driving those of Caesar before them, galloped along and around the line, they suddenly came upon this select corps advancing intrepidly against them and, rapidly thrown into confusion by the unexpected and unusual infantry attack,[1] they galloped at full speed from the field of battle. The victorious legionaries cut to pieces the enemy's archers now unprotected, then rushed at

[1] With this is connected the well-known direction of Caesar to his soldiers to strike at the faces of the enemy's horsemen. The infantry—which here in an altogether irregular way acted on the offensive against cavalry, who were not to be reached with the sabres—were not to throw their *pila*, but to use them as hand-spears against the cavalry and, in order to defend themselves better against these, to thrust at their faces (Plutarch, *Pomp.* 69, 71; *Caes.* 45; Appian. ii. 76, 78; Flor. ii. 12; Oros. vi. 15; erroneously Frontinus, iv. 7, 32). The anecdotical turn given to this instruction, that the Pompeian horsemen were to be brought to run away by the fear of receiving scars in their faces, and that they actually galloped off "holding their hands before their eyes" (Plutarch), collapses of itself; for it has point only on the supposition that the Pompeian cavalry had consisted principally of the young nobility of Rome, the "graceful dancers;" and this was not the case (p. 377). At the most it may be, that the wit of the camp gave to that simple and judicious military order this very irrational but certainly comic turn.

the left wing of the enemy, and began now on their part to turn it. At the same time Caesar's third division hitherto reserved advanced along the whole line to the attack. The unexpected defeat of the best arm of the Pompeian army, as it raised the courage of their opponents, broke that of the army and above all that of the general. When Pompeius, who from the outset did not trust his infantry, saw the horsemen gallop off, he rode back at once from the field of battle to the camp, without even awaiting the issue of the general attack ordered by Caesar. His legions began to waver and soon to retire over the brook into the camp, which was not accomplished without severe loss.

The day was thus lost and many an able soldier had fallen, but the army was still substantially intact, and the situation of Pompeius was far less perilous than that of Caesar after the defeat of Dyrrhachium. But while Caesar in the vicissitudes of his destiny had learned that fortune loves to withdraw herself at certain moments even from her favourites in order to be once more won back through their perseverance, Pompeius knew fortune hitherto only as the constant goddess, and despaired of himself and of her when she withdrew from him; and, while in Caesar's great nature despair only developed still mightier energies, the feebler soul of Pompeius under similar pressure sank into the infinite abyss of despondency. As once in the war with Sertorius he had been on the point of abandoning the office entrusted to him in presence of his superior opponent and of departing (p. 30), so now, when he saw the legions retire over the stream, he threw from him the fatal general's scarf, and rode off by the nearest route to the sea, to find means of embarking there. His army discouraged and leaderless—for Scipio, although recognised by Pompeius as colleague in supreme command, was yet general-in-chief only in name—hoped to find protection behind the camp-walls; but Caesar allowed it no rest; the obstinate resistance of the Roman and Thracian guard of the camp was speedily overcome, and the mass was compelled to withdraw in disorder to the heights of Crannon and Scotussa, at the foot of which the camp was pitched. It attempted by moving forward along these hills to regain Larissa; but the troops of Caesar, heeding neither booty nor fatigue and advancing by better paths in the plain, intercepted the route of the fugitives; in fact, when late in the evening the Pompeians suspended their march, their pursuers were able even to draw an entrenched line which precluded the fugitives from access to the only rivulet to be found in the neighbourhood.

So ended the day of Pharsalus. The enemy's army was not only defeated, but annihilated; 15,000 of the enemy lay dead or wounded on the field of battle, while the Caesarians missed only 200 men; the body which remained together, amounting still to nearly 20,000 men, laid down their arms on the morning after the battle; only isolated troops, including, it is true, the officers of most note, sought a refuge in the mountains; of the eleven eagles of the enemy nine were handed over to Caesar. Caesar, who on the very day of the battle had reminded the soldiers that they should not forget the fellow-citizen in the foe, did not treat the captives as Bibulus and Labienus had done; nevertheless he too found it necessary now to exercise some severity. The common soldiers were incorporated in the army, fines or confiscations of property were inflicted on the men of better rank; the senators and equites of note who were taken, with few exceptions, suffered death. The time for clemency was past; the longer the civil war lasted, the more remorseless and implacable it became.

Some time elapsed before the consequences of the 9th of August $\frac{706}{48}$ could be fully discerned. What admitted of least doubt, was the passing over to the side of Caesar of all those who had attached themselves to the party vanquished at Pharsalus merely as being the more powerful; the defeat was so thoroughly decisive, that the victor was joined by all who were not willing or were not obliged to fight for a lost cause. All the kings, peoples, and cities, which had hitherto been the clients of Pompeius, now recalled their naval and military contingents and declined to receive the refugees of the beaten party; such as Egypt, Cyrene, the communities of Syria, Phoenicia, Cilicia and Asia Minor, Rhodes, Athens, and generally the whole of the East. In fact Pharnaces king of the Bosporus pushed his officiousness so far, that on the news of the Pharsalian battle he took possession not only of the town of Phanagoria which several years before had been declared free by Pompeius, and of the dominions of the Colchian princes confirmed by him, but even of the kingdom of Little Armenia which Pompeius had conferred on king Deiotarus. Almost the sole exceptions to this general submission were the little town of Megara which allowed itself to be besieged and stormed by the Caesarians, and Juba king of Numidia, who had for long expected, and after the victory over Curio expected only with all the greater certainty, that his kingdom would be annexed by Caesar, and was thus obliged for better or for worse to abide by the defeated party.

In the same way as the client communities submitted to the victor of Pharsalus, the tail of the constitutional party—all who had joined it with half a heart or had even, like Marcus Cicero and his fellows, merely danced around the aristocracy like the witches around the Brocken—approached to make their peace with the new monarch, a peace accordingly which his contemptuous indulgence readily and courteously granted to the petitioners. But the flower of the defeated party made no compromise. All was over with the aristocracy; but the aristocrats could never become converted to monarchy. The highest revelations of humanity are perishable; the religion once true may become a lie,[1] the polity once fraught with blessing may become a curse; but even the gospel that is past still finds confessors, and if such a faith cannot remove mountains like faith in the living truth, it yet remains true to itself down to its very end, and does not depart from the realm of the living till it has dragged its last priests and its last partisans along with it, and a new generation, freed from those shadows of the past and the perishing, rules over a world that has renewed its youth. So it was in Rome. Into whatever abyss of degeneracy the aristocratic rule had now sunk, it had once been a great political system; the sacred fire, by which Italy had been conquered and Hannibal had been vanquished, continued to glow—although somewhat dim and dull—in the Roman nobility so long as that nobility existed, and rendered a cordial understanding between the men of the old *régime* and the new monarch impossible. A large portion of the constitutional party submitted at least outwardly, and recognised the monarch so far as to accept pardon from Caesar and to retire as much as possible into private life; which, however, ordinarily was not done without the mental reservation of thereby preserving themselves for a future change of things. This course was chiefly followed by the partisans of lesser note; but the able Marcus Marcellus, the same who had brought about the rupture with Caesar (p. 329), was to be found among these judicious persons and voluntarily banished himself to Lesbos. In the majority, however, of the genuine aristocracy passion was more powerful than cool reflection; along with which, no doubt, self-

[1] [I may here state once for all that in this and other passages, where Dr. Mommsen appears incidentally to express views of religion or philosophy with which I cannot be supposed to agree, I have not thought it right—as is, I believe, sometimes done in similar cases—to omit or modify any portion of what he has written. The reader must judge for himself as to the truth or value of such assertions as those given in the text.—*Tr.*]

deceptions as to success being still possible and apprehensions of the inevitable vengeance of the victor variously co-operated.

No one probably formed a judgment as to the situation of affairs with so painful a clearness, and so free from fear or hope on his own account, as Marcus Cato. Completely convinced that after the days of Ilerda and Pharsalus the monarchy was inevitable, and morally firm enough to confess to himself this bitter truth and to act upon it, he hesitated for a moment whether the constitutional party ought at all to continue a war, which would necessarily require sacrifices for a lost cause on the part of many who did not know why they offered them. And when he resolved to fight against the monarchy not for victory, but for a speedier and more honourable fall, he yet sought as far as possible to draw no one into this war who chose to survive the fall of the republic and to be reconciled to monarchy. He conceived that, so long as the republic had been merely threatened, it was a right and a duty to compel the lukewarm and bad citizen to take part in the struggle; but that now it was senseless and cruel to compel the individual to share the ruin of the lost republic. Not only did he himself discharge every one who desired to return to Italy; but when the wildest of the wild partisans, Gnaeus Pompeius the younger, insisted on the execution of these people and of Cicero in particular, it was Cato alone who by his moral authority prevented it.

Pompeius also had no desire for peace. Had he been a man who deserved to hold the position which he filled, we might suppose him to have perceived that he who aspires to a crown cannot return to the beaten track of ordinary existence, and that there is accordingly no place left on earth for one who has failed. But Pompeius was hardly too noble-minded to ask a favour, which the victor would have been perhaps magnanimous enough not to refuse to him; on the contrary, he was probably too mean to do so. Whether it was that he could not make up his mind to trust himself to Caesar, or that in his usual vague and undecided way, after the first immediate impression of the disaster of Pharsalus had vanished, he began again to cherish hope, Pompeius was resolved to continue the struggle against Caesar and to seek for himself yet another battle-field after that of Pharsalus.

Thus however much Caesar had striven by prudence and moderation to appease the fury of his opponents and to lessen their number, the struggle nevertheless went on without alteration. But the leading men had almost all taken part in the fight at Pharsalus; and, although they all escaped with the exception of Lucius Domitius Ahenobarbus, who was killed in the flight, they were yet scattered in all directions, so that they were unable to concert a common plan for the continuance of the campaign. Most of them found their way, partly through the desolate mountains of Macedonia and Illyria, partly by the aid of the fleet, to Corcyra, where Marcus Cato commanded the reserve left behind. Here a sort of council of war took place under the presidency of Cato, at which Metellus Scipio, Titus Labienus, Lucius Afranius, Gnaeus Pompeius the younger, and others were present; but the absence of the commander-in-chief and the painful uncertainty as to his fate, as well as the internal dissensions of the party, prevented the adoption of any common resolution, and ultimately each took the course which seemed to him the most suitable for himself or for the common cause. It was in fact in a high degree difficult to say among the many straws to which they might possibly cling which was the one that would keep longest above water.

Macedonia and Greece were lost by the battle of Pharsalus. It is true that Cato, who had immediately on the news of the defeat evacuated Dyrrhachium, still held Corcyra, and Rutilius Lupus the Peloponnesus, during a time for the constitutional party. For a moment it seemed also as if the Pompeians would make a stand at Patrae in the Peloponnesus; but the accounts of the advance of Calenus sufficed to frighten them from that quarter. As little was there any attempt to maintain Corcyra. On the Italian and Sicilian coasts the Pompeian squadrons despatched thither after the victories of Dyrrhachium (p. 388) had achieved not unimportant successes against the ports of Brundisium, Messana, and Vibo, and at Messana especially had burnt the whole fleet in course of being fitted out for Caesar; but the ships that were thus active, mostly from Asia Minor and Syria, were recalled by their communities in consequence of the Pharsalian battle, so that the expedition came to an end of itself. In Asia Minor and Syria there were at the moment no troops of either party, with the exception of the Bosporan army of Pharnaces which had taken possession, ostensibly on Caesar's account, of different regions belonging to his opponents. In Egypt there was still indeed a considerable Roman army, formed of the troops left behind there by Gabinius (p. 145) and thereafter recruited from Italian vagrants and Syrian or Cilician banditti; but it was self-evident and was soon officially confirmed by the recall of the Egyptian vessels, that the court of Alexandria by no means had the intention of holding firmly by the defeated party or of even placing its force of troops at their disposal. Somewhat more favourable prospects presented themselves to the vanquished in the West. In Spain Pompeian sympathies were so strong among the army as well as among the population, that the Caesarians had on that account to give up the attack which they contemplated from this quarter against Africa, and an insurrection seemed inevitable, so soon as a leader of note should appear in the peninsula. In Africa moreover the coalition, or rather Juba king of Numidia, who was the true regent there, had been arming unmolested since the autumn of $\frac{705}{49}$. While the whole East was consequently lost to the coalition by the battle of Pharsalus, it might on the other hand continue the war after an honourable manner probably in Spain, and certainly in Africa; for to claim the aid of the king of Numidia, who had for a long time been subject to the Roman community, against revolutionary fellow-burgesses was for Romans a painful humiliation doubtless, but by no means an act of treason. Those again who in this conflict of despair had no further regard for right or honour, might declare themselves beyond the pale of the law, and commence hostilities as robbers; or might enter into alliance with independent neighbouring states, and introduce the public foe into the intestine strife; or, lastly, might profess monarchy with the lips and prosecute the restoration of the legitimate republic with the dagger of the assassin.

That the vanquished should withdraw and renounce the new monarchy was at least the natural and so far the truest expression of their desperate position. The mountains and above all the seas had been in those times ever since the memory of man the asylum not only of all crime, but also of intolerable misery and of oppressed right; it was natural for Pompeians and republicans to wage a defiant war against the monarchy of Caesar, which had ejected them, in the mountains and on the seas, and especially natural for them to take up piracy on a greater scale, with more compact organisation, and with more definite aims. Even after the recall of the squadrons that had come from the East they still possessed a very considerable fleet of their own, while Caesar was as yet virtually without vessels of war; and their connection with the Dalmatae who had risen in their own interest against Caesar (p. 372), and their control over the most important seas and seaports, presented the most advantageous prospects for a naval war, especially on a small scale. As formerly Sulla's hunting out of the democrats had ended in the Sertorian insurrection, which was a conflict first waged by pirates and then by robbers and ultimately became a very serious war, so possibly, if there was in the Catonian aristocracy or among the adherents of Pompeius as much spirit and fire as in the Marian democracy, and if there was found among them a true sea-king, a commonwealth independent of the monarchy of Caesar and perhaps a match for it might arise on the still unconquered sea.

Far more serious disapproval in every respect is due to the idea of dragging an independent neighbouring state into the Roman civil war and of bringing about by its means a counter-revolution; law and conscience condemn the deserter more severely than the robber, and a victorious band of robbers finds its way back to a free and well-ordered commonwealth more easily than the emigrants who are conducted back by the public foe. Besides it was scarcely probable that the beaten party would be able to effect a restoration in this way. The only state, from which they could attempt to seek support, was that of the Parthians; and as to this it was at least doubtful whether it would make their cause its own, and very improbable that it would fight out that cause against Caesar.

The time for republican conspiracies had not yet come.

While the remnant of the defeated party thus allowed themselves to be helplessly driven about by fate, and even those who had determined to continue the struggle knew not how or where to do so, Caesar, quickly as ever resolving and quickly acting, laid everything aside to pursue Pompeius—the only one of his opponents whom he respected as an officer, and the one whose personal capture would have probably paralysed a half, and that perhaps the more dangerous half, of his opponents. With a few men he crossed the Hellespont—his single bark encountered in it a fleet of the enemy destined for the Black Sea and took the whole crews, struck as with stupefaction by the news of the battle of Pharsalus, prisoners—and as soon as the most necessary preparations were made, hastened in pursuit of Pompeius to the East. The latter had gone from the Pharsalian battle-field to Lesbos, whence he brought away his wife and his second son Sextus, and had sailed onward round Asia Minor to Cilicia and thence to Cyprus. He might have joined his partisans at Corcyra or Africa; but repugnance toward his aristocratic allies and the thought of the reception which awaited him there after the day of Pharsalus and above all after his disgraceful flight, appear to have induced him to take his own course and rather to resort to the protection of the Parthian king than to that of Cato. While he was employed in collecting money and slaves from the Roman revenue-farmers and merchants in Cyprus, and in arming a band of 2000 slaves, he received news that Antioch had declared for Caesar and that the route to the Parthians was no longer open. So he altered his plan and sailed to Egypt, where a number of his old soldiers served in the army and the situation and rich resources of the country allowed him time and opportunity to reorganise the war.

In Egypt, after the death of Ptolemy Auletes (May $\frac{703}{51}$) his children, Cleopatra about sixteen years of age and Ptolemaeus Dionysus about ten, had ascended the throne according to their father's will jointly, and as consorts; but soon the brother or rather his guardian Pothinus had driven the sister from the kingdom and compelled her to seek a refuge in Syria, whence she made preparations to get back to her paternal kingdom. Ptolemaeus and Pothinus lay with the whole Egyptian army at Pelusium for the sake of protecting the eastern frontier against her, just when Pompeius cast anchor at the Casian promontory and sent a request to the king to allow him to land. The Egyptian court, long informed of the disaster at Pharsalus, was on the point of rejecting Pompeius; but the king's tutor Theodotus pointed out that in that case Pompeius would probably employ his connections in the Egyptian army to instigate rebellion; and that it would be safer, and also preferable with regard to Caesar, if they embraced the opportunity of making away with Pompeius. Political reasonings of this sort did not readily fail of their effect among the statesmen of the Hellenic world.

Achillas the general of the royal troops and some of the former soldiers of Pompeius went off in a boat to his vessel; and invited him to come to the king and, as the water was shallow, to enter their barge. As he was stepping ashore, the military tribune Lucius Septimius stabbed him from behind, under the eyes of his wife and son, who were compelled to be spectators of the murder from the deck of their vessel, without being able to rescue or revenge (28th September $\frac{706}{48}$). On the same day on which thirteen years before he had entered the capital in triumph over Mithradates (p. 138), the man, who for a generation had been called the Great and for years had ruled Rome, died on the desert sands of the inhospitable Casian shore by the hand of one of his soldiers. A good officer, but otherwise of mediocre gifts of intellect and of heart, fate had with superhuman constancy for thirty years allowed him to solve all brilliant and toilless tasks; had permitted him to pluck all laurels planted and fostered by others; had presented to him all the conditions requisite for obtaining the supreme power—only in order to exhibit in his person an example of spurious greatness, to which history knows no parallel. Of all pitiful parts there is none more pitiful than that of passing for more than one really is; and it is the fate of monarchy that this misfortune inevitably clings to it, for barely once in a thousand years does there arise among the people a man who is a king not merely in name, but in reality. If this disproportion between semblance and reality has never perhaps been so prominently marked as in Pompeius, the fact may well excite grave reflection that it was precisely he who in a certain sense opened the series of Roman monarchs.

When Caesar following the track of Pompeius arrived in the roadstead of Alexandria, all was already over. With deep agitation he turned away when the murderer brought to his ship the head of the man who had been his son-in-law and for long years his colleague in rule, and to get whom alive into his power he had come to Egypt. The dagger of the rash assassin precluded an answer to the question, how Caesar would have dealt with the captive Pompeius; but, while the humane sympathy, which still found a place in the great soul of Caesar side by side with ambition, enjoined that he should spare his former friend, his interest also required that he should annihilate Pompeius otherwise than by the executioner. Pompeius had been for twenty years the acknowledged ruler of Rome; a dominion so deeply rooted does not perish with the ruler's death. The death of Pompeius did not break up the Pompeians, but gave to them, instead of an aged, incapable, and worn out chief, in his sons Gnaeus and Sextus two leaders, both of whom were young and active and the second was a man of decided capacity. To the newly-founded hereditary monarchy the hereditary pretendership attached itself at once like a parasite, and it was very doubtful whether by this change of persons Caesar did not lose more than he gained.

Meanwhile in Egypt Caesar had now nothing further to do, and the Romans and the Egyptians expected that he would immediately set sail and apply himself to the subjugation of Africa, and to the huge task of organisation which awaited him after the victory. But Caesar faithful to his custom—wherever he found himself in the wide empire—of finally regulating matters at once and in person, and firmly convinced that no resistance was to be expected either from the Roman garrison or from the court, being, moreover, in urgent pecuniary embarrassment, landed in Alexandria with the two amalgamated legions accompanying him to the number of 3200 men and 800 Celtic and German cavalry, took up his quarters in the royal palace, and proceeded to collect the necessary sums of money and to regulate the Egyptian succession, without allowing himself to be disturbed by the saucy remark of Pothinus that Caesar should not for such petty matters neglect his own so important affairs. In his dealing with the Egyptians he was just and even indulgent. Although the aid which they had given to Pompeius justified the imposing of a war contribution, the exhausted land was spared from this; and, while the arrears of the sum stipulated for in $\frac{695}{59}$ (p. 145) and since then only about half paid were remitted, there was required merely a final payment of 10,000,000 *denarii* (£400,000). The belligerent brother and sister were enjoined immediately to suspend hostilities, and were invited to have their dispute investigated and decided by arbitration. They submitted; the royal boy was already in the palace and Cleopatra also presented herself there. Caesar adjudged the kingdom of Egypt, agreeably to the testament of Auletes, to the intermarried brother and sister Cleopatra and Ptolemaeus Dionysus, and further gave unasked the kingdom of Cyprus—cancelling the earlier act of annexation (p. 143)—as the appanage of the second-born of Egypt to the younger children of Auletes, Arsinoe and Ptolemaeus the younger.

But a storm was secretly preparing. Alexandria was a cosmopolitan city as well as Rome, hardly inferior to the Italian capital in the number of its inhabitants, far superior to it in stirring commercial spirit, in skill of handicraft, in taste for science and art: in the citizens there was a lively national self-importance, and, if there was no political sentiment, there was at any rate a turbulent spirit, which induced them to indulge in their street riots as regularly and as heartily as the Parisians of the present day: one may conceive their feelings, when they saw the Roman general ruling in the palace of the Lagidae and their kings accepting the award of his tribunal. Pothinus and the boy-king, both as may be conceived very much discontented at once with the peremptory requisition of old debts and with the intervention in the throne-dispute which could only issue as it did in favour of Cleopatra, sent—in order to the satisfaction of the Roman demands—the treasures of the temples and the gold plate of the king with intentional ostentation to be melted at the mint; with increasing indignation the Egyptians—who were pious even to superstition, and who rejoiced in the world-renowned magnificence of their court as if it were a possession of their own—beheld the bare walls of their temples and the wooden cups on the table of their king. The Roman army of occupation also, which had been essentially denationalised by its long abode in Egypt and the many intermarriages between the soldiers and Egyptian women, and which moreover numbered a multitude of the old soldiers of Pompeius and runaway Italian criminals and slaves in its ranks, was indignant at Caesar by whose orders it had been obliged to suspend its action on the Syrian frontier, and at his handful of haughty legionaries. The tumult even at the landing, when the multitude saw the Roman axes carried into the old palace, and the numerous assassinations of his soldiers in the city, had taught Caesar the immense danger in which he was placed with his small force in presence of that exasperated multitude. But it was difficult to return on account of the north-west winds prevailing at this season of the year, and the attempt at embarkation might easily become a signal for the outbreak of the insurrection; besides, it was not the nature of Caesar to depart without having accomplished his work. He accordingly ordered up at once reinforcements from Asia, and, till these arrived, displayed throughout the utmost self-possession. Never was there greater gaiety in his camp than during this rest at Alexandria; and while the beautiful and clever Cleopatra was not sparing of her charms in general and least of all towards her judge, Caesar also appeared among all his victories to value most those won over beautiful women. It was a merry prelude to a very grave drama. Under the leadership of Achillas and, as was afterwards proved, by the secret orders of the king and his guardian, the Roman army of occupation stationed in Egypt appeared unexpectedly in Alexandria; and as soon as the citizens saw that it had come to attack Caesar, they made common cause with the soldiers.

With a presence of mind, which in some measure justifies his earlier foolhardiness, Caesar hastily collected his scattered men; seized the persons of the king and his minister; entrenched himself in the royal residence and the adjoining theatre; and gave orders, as there was no time to place in safety the war fleet stationed in the principal harbour immediately in front of the theatre, that it should be burnt and that

Pharos, the island with the light-tower commanding the harbour, should be occupied by means of boats. Thus at least a restricted position for defence was secured, and the way was kept open to procure supplies and reinforcements. At the same time orders were issued to the commandant of Asia Minor as well as to the nearest subject countries, the Syrians and Nabataeans, the Cretans and the Rhodians, to send troops and ships in all haste to Egypt. The insurrection at the head of which the princess Arsinoe and her confidant the eunuch Ganymedes had placed themselves, meanwhile had free course in all Egypt and in the greater part of the capital. In the streets of the latter there was daily fighting, but without success either on the part of Caesar in gaining freer scope and breaking through to the fresh water lake of Marea which lay behind the town, where he could have provided himself with water and forage, or on the part of the Alexandrians in acquiring superiority over the besieged and depriving them of all drinkable water; for, when the Nile canals in Caesar's part of the town had been spoiled by the introduction of salt water, drinkable water was unexpectedly found in the wells dug on the beach.

As Caesar was not to be overcome from the landward side, the exertions of the besiegers were directed to destroy his fleet and cut him off from the sea by which supplies reached him. The island with the light-house and the mole by which this was connected with the mainland divided the harbour into a western and an eastern half, which were in communication with each other through two arched openings in the mole. Caesar commanded the island and the east harbour, while the mole and west harbour were in possession of the citizens; and, as the Alexandrian fleet was burnt, his vessels sailed in and out without hindrance. The Alexandrians, after having vainly attempted to introduce fire-ships from the western into the eastern harbour, equipped with the remnant of their arsenal a small squadron and with this blocked up the way of Caesar's vessels, when these were towing in a fleet of transports with a legion that had arrived from Asia Minor; but the excellent Rhodian mariners of Caesar mastered the enemy. Not long afterwards, however, the citizens captured the lighthouse-island,[1] and from that point

[1] The loss of the lighthouse-island must, along with the description of a second naval engagement in which the Egyptian fleet beaten at Chersonesus was annihilated, have been inserted where there is now a chasm (*B. A.* 12), for the island was at first in Caesar's power (*B. C.* iii. 12; *B. A.* 8). The mole must have been constantly in the power of the enemy, for Caesar held intercourse with the island only by ships.

totally closed the narrow and rocky mouth of the east harbour for larger ships; so that Caesar's fleet was compelled to lie in the open roads before the east harbour, and his communication with the sea hung only on a weak thread. Caesar's fleet, attacked in that roadstead repeatedly by the superior naval force of the enemy, could neither shun the unequal strife, since the loss of the lighthouse-island closed the inner harbour against it, nor take its departure, for the loss of the roadstead would have debarred Caesar wholly from the sea. Though the brave legionaries, supported by the dexterity of the Rhodian sailors, had always hitherto decided these conflicts in favour of the Romans, the Alexandrians renewed and augmented their naval armaments with unwearied perseverance; the besieged had to fight as often as it pleased the besiegers, and if the former should be on a single occasion vanquished, Caesar would be totally hemmed in and probably lost.

It was absolutely necessary to make an attempt to recover the lighthouse-island. The double attack, which was made by boats from the side of the harbour and by the war vessels from the seaboard, in reality brought not only the island but also the lower part of the mole into Caesar's power; it was only at the second arch-opening of the mole that Caesar ordered the attack to be stopped, and the mole to be there closed towards the city by a transverse wall. But while a violent conflict arose around the entrenchers, the Roman troops left the lower part of the mole adjoining the island bare of defenders; a division of Egyptians landed there unexpectedly, attacked in the rear the Roman soldiers and sailors crowded together on the mole at the transverse wall, and drove the whole mass in wild confusion into the sea. A part were taken on board by the Roman ships; the most were drowned. Some 400 soldiers and a still greater number of men belonging to the fleet were sacrificed on this day; the general himself, who had shared the fate of his men, had been obliged to seek refuge in his ship, and when it sank from having been overloaded with men, he had to save himself by swimming to another. But, severe as was the loss suffered, it was amply compensated by the recovery of the lighthouse-island, which along with the mole as far as the first arch-opening remained in the hands of Caesar.

At length the longed-for relief arrived. Mithradates of Pergamus, an able warrior of the school of Mithradates Eupator, whose natural son he claimed to be, brought up by land from Syria a motley army—the Ityraeans of the prince of the Labanus

(p. 123), the Bedouins of Jamblichus, son of Sampsiceramus (p. 123), the Jews under the minister Antipater, and the contingents generally of the petty chiefs and communities of Cilicia and Syria. From Pelusium, which Mithradates had the fortune to occupy on the day of his arrival, he took the great road towards Memphis with the view of avoiding the intersected ground of the Delta and crossing the Nile before its division; during which movement his troops received manifold support from the Jewish peasants who were settled in peculiar numbers in this part of Egypt. The Egyptians, with the young king Ptolemy now at their head, whom Caesar had released to his people in the vain hope of allaying the insurrection by his means, despatched an army to the Nile to detain Mithradates on its farther bank. This army fell in with the enemy even beyond Memphis at the so-called Jews'-camp, between Onion and Heliopolis; nevertheless Mithradates, trained in the Roman fashion of manœuvring and encamping, amidst successful conflicts gained the opposite bank at Memphis. Caesar, on the other hand, as soon as he obtained news of the arrival of the relieving army, conveyed a part of his troops in ships to the end of the lake of Marea to the west of Alexandria, and marched round this lake and down the Nile to meet Mithradates advancing up the river.

The junction took place without the enemy attempting to hinder it. Caesar then marched into the Delta, whither the king had retreated, overthrew, notwithstanding the deeply cut canal in their front, the Egyptian vanguard at the first onset, and immediately stormed the Egyptian camp itself. It lay at the foot of a rising ground between the Nile—from which only a narrow path separated it—and marshes difficult of access. Caesar caused the camp to be assailed simultaneously from the front and from the flank on the path along the Nile; and during this assault ordered a third detachment to ascend unseen the heights behind the camp. The victory was complete; the camp was taken, and those of the Egyptians who did not fall beneath the sword of the enemy were drowned in the attempt to escape to the fleet on the Nile. With one of the boats, which sank overladen with men, the young king also disappeared in the waters of his native stream.

Immediately after the battle Caesar advanced at the head of his cavalry from the land-side straight into the portion of the capital occupied by the Egyptians. In mourning attire, with the images of their gods in their hands, the enemy received him and sued for peace; and his troops, when they saw him return as victor from the side opposite to that by which he had set forth, welcomed him with boundless joy. The fate of the town, which had ventured to thwart the plans of the master of the world and had brought him within a hair's breadth of destruction, lay in Caesar's hands; but he was too much of a ruler to be sensitive, and dealt with the Alexandrians as with the Massiliots. Caesar—pointing to their city severely devasted and deprived of its granaries, of its world-renowned library, and of other important public buildings on occasion of the burning of the fleet—exhorted the inhabitants in future earnestly to cultivate the arts of peace alone, and to heal the wounds which they had inflicted on themselves; for the rest, he contented himself with granting to the Jews settled in Alexandria the same rights which the Greek population of the city enjoyed, and with placing in Alexandria, instead of the previous Roman army of occupation which nominally at least obeyed the king of Egypt, a formal Roman garrison—two of the legions besieged there, and a third which afterwards arrived from Syria—under a commander nominated by himself. For this position of trust a man was purposely selected, whose birth made it impossible for him to abuse it—Rufio, an able soldier, but the son of a freedman. Cleopatra and her younger brother Ptolemaeus obtained the sovereignty of Egypt under the supremacy of Rome; the princess Arsinoe was carried off to Italy, that she might not serve once more as a pretext for insurrections to the Egyptians, who were after the Oriental fashion quite as much devoted to their dynasty as they were indifferent towards the individual dynasts; Cyprus became again a part of the Roman province of Cilicia.

This Alexandrian insurrection, insignificant as it was in itself and slight as was its intrinsic connection with the events of importance in the world's history which took place at the same time in the Roman state, had nevertheless so far a momentous influence on them that it compelled the man, who was all in all and without whom nothing could be transacted and nothing could be solved, to leave his proper tasks in abeyance from October $\frac{706}{48}$ up to March $\frac{707}{47}$ in order to fight along with Jews and Bedouins against a city rabble. The consequences of personal rule began to make themselves felt. They had the monarchy; but the wildest confusion prevailed everywhere, and the monarch was absent. The Caesarians were for the moment, just like the Pompeians, without superintendence;

the ability of the individual officers and, above all, accident decided matters everywhere.

In Asia Minor there was, at the time of Caesar's departure for Egypt, no enemy. But Caesar's lieutenant there, the able Gnaeus Domitius Calvinus, had received orders to take away again from king Pharnaces what he had without instructions wrested from the allies of Pompeius; and, as Pharnaces, an obstinate and arrogant despot like his father, perseveringly refused to evacuate Lesser Armenia, no course remained but to march against him. Calvinus had been obliged to despatch to Egypt two out of the three legions—formed out of the Pharsalian prisoners of war—left behind with him; he filled up the gap by one legion hastily gathered from the Romans domiciled in Pontus and two legions of Deiotarus exercised after the Roman manner, and advanced into Lesser Armenia. But the Bosporan army, tried in numerous conflicts with the dwellers on the Black Sea, showed itself more efficient than that of Calvinus.

In an engagement at Nicopolis the Pontic levy of Calvinus was cut to pieces and the Galatian legions ran off; only the one old legion of the Romans fought its way through with moderate loss. Instead of conquering Lesser Armenia, Calvinus could not even prevent Pharnaces from repossessing himself of his Pontic "hereditary states," and pouring forth the whole vials of his hateful sultanic caprices on their inhabitants, especially the unhappy Amisenes (winter of $\frac{706-707}{48-47}$). When Caesar in person arrived in Asia Minor and intimated to him that the service which Pharnaces had rendered to him personally by granting no help to Pompeius could not be taken into account against the injury inflicted on the empire, and that before any negotiation he must evacuate the province of Pontus and send back the property which he had pillaged, he declared himself ready to submit; nevertheless, well knowing how good reason Caesar had for hastening to the West, he made no serious preparations for the evacuation. He did not know that Caesar finished whatever he took in hand. Without negotiating further, Caesar took with him the one legion which he brought from Alexandria and the troops of Calvinus and Deiotarus, and advanced against the camp of Pharnaces at Ziela. When the Bosporans saw him approach, they boldly crossed the deep mountain-ravine which covered their front, and charged the Romans up the hill. Caesar's soldiers were still occupied in pitching their camp, and the ranks wavered for a moment;

but the veterans accustomed to war rapidly rallied and set the example for a general attack and for a complete victory (2nd August $\frac{707}{47}$). In five days the campaign was ended—an invaluable piece of good fortune at this time, when every hour was precious.

Caesar entrusted the pursuit of the king, who had gone home by way of Sinope, to Pharnaces' illegitimate brother, the brave Mithradates of Pergamus, who as a reward for the services rendered by him in Egypt received the crown of the Bosporan kingdom in room of Pharnaces. In other respects the affairs of Syria and Asia Minor were peacefully settled; Caesar's own allies were richly rewarded, those of Pompeius were in general dismissed with fines or reprimands. Deiotarus alone, the most powerful of the clients of Pompeius, was again confined to his narrow hereditary domain, the canton of the Tolistobogi. In his stead Ariobarzanes king of Cappadocia was invested with Lesser Armenia, and the tetrarchy of the Trocmi usurped by Deiotarus was conferred on the new king of the Bosporus, who was descended by the maternal side from one of the Galatian princely houses as by the paternal from that of Pontus.

In Illyria also, while Caesar was in Egypt, incidents of a very grave nature had occurred. The Dalmatian coast had been for centuries an annoyance to the Roman rule, and its inhabitants had been at open feud with Caesar from the time of his governorship; while the interior also swarmed since the time of the Thessalian war with dispersed Pompeians. Quintus Cornificius had however, with the legions that followed him from Italy, kept both the natives and the refugees in check and had at the same time sufficiently managed the difficult task of provisioning the troops in these rugged districts. Even when the able Marcus Octavius, the victor of Curicta (p. 371), appeared with part of the Pompeian fleet in these waters to wage war against Caesar by sea and land, Cornificius not only knew how to maintain himself, resting for support on the ships and the harbour of the Iadertini (Zara), but in his turn also sustained several successful engagements at sea with the fleet of his antagonist. But when the new governor of Illyria, the Aulus Gabinius recalled by Caesar from exile (p. 299), arrived by the landward route in Illyria in the winter of $\frac{706-707}{48-47}$ with fifteen cohorts and 3000 horse, the system of warfare changed. Instead of confining himself like his predecessor to war on a small scale, the bold active man undertook at once, in spite of the inclement season, an expedition with his whole force to the mountains. But the unfavourable weather, the difficulty of providing supplies, and the brave resistance of the Dalmatians, swept away the army; Gabinius had to commence his retreat, was attacked in the course of it and disgracefully defeated by the Dalmatians, and with the feeble remains of his fine army had difficulty in reaching Salonae, where he soon afterwards died. Most of the Illyrian coast towns thereupon surrendered to the fleet of Octavius; those that adhered to Caesar, such as Salonae and Epidaurus (Ragusa Vecchia), were so hard pressed by the fleet at sea and by the barbarians on land, that the surrender and capitulation of the remains of the army enclosed in Salonae seemed not far distant. Then the commandant of the depôt at Brundisium, the energetic Publius Vatinius, in the absence of ships of war caused common boats to be provided with beaks and manned with the soldiers dismissed from the hospitals, and with this extemporised war-fleet gave battle to the far superior fleet of Octavius at the island of Tauris (Torcola between Lesina and Curzola)—a battle in which, as in so many cases, the bravery of the leader and of the marines compensated for the deficiencies of the vessels, and the Caesarians achieved a brilliant victory. Marcus Octavius left these waters and proceeded to Africa (spring of $\frac{707}{47}$); the Dalmatians no doubt continued their resistance for years with great obstinacy, but it was nothing beyond a local mountain-warfare. When Caesar returned from Egypt, his resolute adjutant had already got rid of the danger that was imminent in Illyria.

All the more serious was the position of things in Africa, where the constitutional party had from the outset of the civil war ruled absolutely and had continually augmented their power. Down to the battle of Pharsalus king Juba had, strictly speaking, borne rule there; he had vanquished Curio, and his flying horsemen and his numberless archers were the main strength of the army; the Pompeian governor Varus played by his side so subordinate a part that he even had to deliver those soldiers of Curio who had surrendered to him over to the king, and had to look on while they were executed or carried away into the interior of Numidia. After the battle of Pharsalus a change took place. With the exception of Pompeius himself, hardly a man of note among the defeated party thought of flight to the Parthians. As little did they attempt to hold the sea with their united resources; the warfare waged by Marcus Octavius in the Illyrian waters was isolated, and was without permanent success. The great majority of the republicans as of the Pompeians betook themselves to Africa, where alone an honourable and constitutional warfare might still be waged against the usurper. There the fragments of the army scattered at Pharsalus, the troops that had garrisoned Dyrrhachium, Corcyra, and the Peloponnesus, the remains of the Illyrian fleet, gradually congregated; there the second commander-in-chief Metellus Scipio, the two sons of Pompeius, Gnaeus and Sextus, the political leader of the republicans Marcus Cato, the able officers Labienus, Afranius, Petreius, Octavius and others met. If the resources of the emigrants had diminished, their fanaticism had if possible increased. Not only did they continue to murder their prisoners and even the officers of Caesar under flag of truce, but king Juba, in whom the exasperation of the partisan mingled with the fury of the half-barbarous African, laid down the maxim that in every community suspected of sympathising with the enemy the burgesses ought to be extirpated and the town burnt, and even practically carried out this theory against some townships, such as the unfortunate Vaga near Hadrumetum. In fact it was solely owing to the energetic intervention of Cato that the capital of the province itself, the flourishing Utica—which, just like Carthage formerly, had been long regarded with a jealous eye by the Numidian kings—did not experience the same treatment from Juba, and that measures of precaution merely were adopted against its citizens, who certainly were not unjustly accused of leaning towards Caesar.

As neither Caesar himself nor any of his lieutenants undertook the smallest movement against Africa, the coalition had full time to acquire political and military reorganisation there. First of all, it was necessary to fill up anew the place of commander-in-chief vacant by the death of Pompeius. King Juba was not disinclined still to maintain the position which he had held in Africa up to the battle of Pharsalus; indeed he bore himself no longer as a client of the Romans but as an equal ally or even as a protector, and took it upon him, for example, to coin Roman silver money with his name and device; nay, he even raised a claim to be the sole wearer of purple in the camp, and suggested to the Roman commanders that they should lay aside their purple mantle of office. Metellus Scipio, moreover, demanded the supreme command for himself, because Pompeius had recognised him in the Thessalian campaign as on a footing of equality, more from the consideration that he was his son-in-law than on military grounds. The like demand was raised by Varus as the governor—self-nominated, it is true—of Africa, seeing that the war was to be waged in his province. Lastly the army desired for its leader the propraetor Marcus Cato. Obviously it was right. Cato was the only man who possessed the requisite devotedness, energy, and authority for the difficult office; if he was no military man, it was infinitely better to appoint as commander-in-chief a non-military man who understood how to listen to reason and make his subordinates act, than an officer of untried capacity like Varus, or one of tried incapacity like Metellus Scipio. But the decision fell at length on this same Scipio, and it was Cato himself who mainly determined that decision. He did so, not because he felt himself unequal to the task, or because his vanity found its account rather in declining than in accepting; still less because he loved or respected Scipio, with whom he on the contrary was personally at variance, and who with his notorious inefficiency had attained a certain importance merely in virtue of his position as father-in-law to Pompeius; but simply and solely because his obstinate legal formalism chose rather to let the republic go to ruin in due course of law than to save it in an irregular way. When after the battle of Pharsalus he met with Marcus Cicero at Corcyra, he had offered to hand over the command in Corcyra to the latter—who was still from the time of his Cilician administration invested with the rank of general—as the officer of higher standing according to the letter of the law, and by this readiness had driven the unfortunate advocate, who now cursed a thousand times his laurels from the Amanus, almost to despair; but he had at the same time astonished all men of any tolerable discernment. The same principles were applied now, when something more was at stake; Cato weighed the question to whom the place of commander-in-chief belonged, as if the matter had reference to a field at Tusculum, and adjudged it to Scipio. By this sentence his own candidature and that of Varus were set aside. But he it was also, and he alone, who confronted with energy the claims of king Juba, and made him feel that the Roman nobility came to him not suppliant as to the great prince of the Parthians with a view to ask aid at the hands of a protector, but as entitled to command and require aid from a subject. In the present state of the Roman forces in Africa Juba could not avoid lowering his claims to some extent; although he still carried the point with the weak Scipio, that the pay of his troops should be charged on the Roman treasury and the cession of the province of Africa should be assured to him in the event of victory.

By the side of the new general-in-chief the senate of the "three hundred" again emerged. It established its seat in Utica, and replenished its thinned ranks by the admission of the most esteemed and the wealthiest men of the equestrian order.

The warlike preparations were pushed forward, chiefly through the zeal of Cato, with the greatest energy, and every man capable of arms, even the freedman and Libyan, was enrolled in the legions; by which course so many hands were withdrawn from agriculture that a great part of the fields remained uncultivated, but an imposing result was certainly attained. The heavy infantry numbered fourteen legions, of which two were already raised by Varus, eight others were formed partly from the refugees, partly from the conscripts in the province and four were legions of king Juba armed in the Roman manner. The heavy cavalry, consisting of the Celts and Germans who arrived with Labienus and sundry others incorporated in their ranks, was, apart from Juba's squadron of cavalry equipped in the Roman style, 1600 strong. The light troops consisted of innumerable masses of Numidians riding without bridle or rein and armed merely with javelins, of a number of mounted bowmen, and a large host of archers on foot. To these fell to be added Juba's 120 elephants, and the fleet of 55 sail commanded by Publius Varus and Marcus Octavius. The urgent want of money was in some measure remedied by a self-taxation on the part of the senate, which was the more productive as the richest African capitalists had been induced to enter it. Corn and other supplies were accumulated in immense quantities in the fortresses capable of defence; at the same time the stores were as much as possible removed from the open towns. The absence of Caesar, the troublesome temper of his legions, the agitation in Spain and Italy gradually raised men's spirits and the recollection of the Pharsalian defeat began to give way to fresh hopes of victory.

The time lost by Caesar in Egypt nowhere revenged itself more severely than here. Had he proceeded to Africa immediately after the death of Pompeius, he would have found there a weak, disorganised, and frightened army and utter anarchy among the leaders; whereas there was now in Africa, owing more especially to Cato's energy, an army equal in number to that defeated at Pharsalus, under leaders of note, and under a regulated superintendence.

A peculiar evil star seemed altogether to preside over this African expedition of Caesar. He had, even before his embarkation for Egypt, arranged in Spain and Italy various measures preliminary and preparatory to the African war; but out of all there had sprung nothing but mischief. From Spain, according to Caesar's arrangement, the governor of the southern province Quintus Cassius Longinus was to cross with four legions to Africa, to form a junction there with Bogud king of West Mauretania,[1] and to advance with him towards Numidia and Africa. But that army destined for Africa included in it a number of native Spaniards and two whole legions formerly Pompeian; Pompeian sympathies prevailed in the army as in the province, and the unskilful and tyrannical behaviour of the Caesarian governor was not fitted to allay them. A formal revolt took place; troops and towns took part for or against the governor; already those who had risen against the lieutenant of Caesar were on the point of openly displaying the banner of Pompeius; already had Pompeius' elder son Gnaeus embarked from Africa for Spain to take advantage of this favourable turn, when the disavowal of the governor by the most respectable Caesarians themselves and the interference of the commander of the northern province suppressed just in right time the insurrection. Gnaeus Pompeius, who had lost time on the way with a vain attempt to establish himself in Mauretania, came too late; Gaius Trebonius, whom Caesar after his return from the East sent to Spain to relieve Cassius (autumn of $\frac{709}{45}$, met everywhere with absolute obedience. But of course amidst these blunders nothing was done from Spain to disturb the organisation of the republicans in Africa;

[1] The shape which the states in north-western Africa assumed during this period is very obscure. After the Jugurthine war Bocchus king of Mauretania ruled probably from the western sea to the port of Saldae, in what is now Morocco and Algiers (iii. 152); the princes of Tingis (Tangiers)—probably from the outset different from the Mauretanian sovereigns—who occur even earlier (Plut. *Sert.* 9), and to whom it may be conjectured that Sallust's Leptasta (*Hist.* ii. 31 Kritz) and Cicero's Mastanesosus (*In Vat.* 5, 12) belong, may have been independent within certain limits or may have held from him as feudatories; just as Syphax already ruled over many chieftains of tribes (Appian. *Pun.* 10), and about this time in the neighbouring Numidia Cirta was possessed, probably however under Juba's supremacy, by the prince Massinissa (Appian. *B. C.* iv. 54). About $\frac{672}{82}$ we find in Bocchus's tead a king called Bocut or Bogud (iii. 323), probably the son of Bocchus. From $\frac{705}{49}$ the kingdom appears divided between king Bogud who possesses the western, and king Bocchus who possesses the eastern half, and to this the later partition of Mauretania into Bogud's kingdom or the state of Tingis and Bocchus' kingdom or the state of Jol (Caesarea) refers (Plin. *H. N.* v. 2, 19; comp. *Bell. Afric.* 23).

indeed in consequence of the complications with Longinus Bogud king of West Mauretania, who was on Caesar's side and might at least have put some obstacles in the way of king Juba, had been called away with his troops to Spain.

Still more critical were the occurrences among the troops whom Caesar had caused to be collected in southern Italy, in order to his embarkation with them for Africa. They were for the most part the old legions, which had founded Caesar's throne in Gaul, Spain, and Thessaly. The spirit of these troops had not been improved by victories, and had been utterly disorganised by long repose in Lower Italy. The almost superhuman demands which the general made on them, and the effects of which were only too clearly apparent in their fearfully thinned ranks, left behind even in these men of iron a leaven of secret rancour which required only time and quiet to set their minds in a ferment. The only man who had influence over them had been absent and almost unheard-of for a year; while the officers placed over them were far more afraid of the soldiers than the soldiers of them, and overlooked in the conquerors of the world every outrage against those that gave them quarters, and every breach of discipline. When the orders to embark for Sicily arrived, and the soldier was to exchange the luxurious ease of Campania for a third campaign certainly not inferior to those of Spain and Thessaly in point of hardship, the reins, which had been too long relaxed and were too suddenly tightened, snapt asunder. The legions refused to obey till the promised presents were paid to them, scornfully repulsed the officers sent by Caesar, and even threw stones at them. An attempt to extinguish the incipient revolt by increasing the sums promised not only had no success, but the soldiers set out in masses to extort the fulfilment of the promises from the general in the capital. Several officers, who attempted to restrain the mutinous bands on the way, were slain. It was a formidable danger. Caesar ordered the few soldiers who were in the city to occupy the gates, with the view of warding off the justly apprehended pillage at least at the first onset, and suddenly appeared among the furious bands demanding to know what they wanted. They exclaimed, "discharge." In a moment the request was granted. Respecting the presents, Caesar added, which he had promised to his soldiers at his triumph, as well as respecting the lands which he had not promised to them but had destined for them, they might apply to him on the day when he and the other soldiers should triumph; in the triumph itself they could not of course participate, as having been previously discharged. The masses were not prepared for things taking this turn; convinced that Caesar could not do without them for the African campaign, they had demanded their discharge only in order that, if it were refused, they might annex their own conditions to their service. Half unsettled in their belief as to their own indispensableness; too awkward to return to their object, and to bring the negotiation which had missed its course back to the right channel; ashamed, as men, by the fidelity with which the imperator kept his word even to soldiers who had forgotten their allegiance, and by his generosity which even now granted far more than he had ever promised; deeply affected, as soldiers, when the general presented to them the prospect of their being necessarily mere civilian spectators of the triumph of their comrades, and when he called them no longer "comrades" but "burgesses"—by this very form of address, which from his mouth sounded so strangely, destroying as it were with one blow the whole pride of their past soldierly career; and, besides all this, under the spell of the man whose presence had an irresistible power—the soldiers stood for a while mute and lingering, till from all sides a cry arose that the general would once more receive them into favour and again permit them to be called Caesar's soldiers. Caesar, after having had a sufficient amount of entreaty, granted the permission; but the ringleaders in this mutiny had a third cut off from their triumphal presents. History knows no greater psychological masterpiece, and none that was more completely successful.

This mutiny operated injuriously on the African campaign, at least in so far as it considerably delayed the commencement of it. When Caesar arrived at the port of Lilybaeum destined for the embarkation, the ten legions intended for Africa were far from being fully assembled there, and it was the experienced troops that were farthest behind. Hardly however had six legions, of which five were newly formed, arrived there and the necessary war vessels and transports come forward, when Caesar put to sea with them (25th December $\frac{707}{47}$ of the uncorrected, about 8th October of the Julian, calendar). The enemy's fleet, which on account of the prevailing equinoctial gales was drawn up on the beach at the island Aegimurus in front of the bay of Carthage, did not oppose the passage; but the same storms scattered the fleet of Caesar in all directions, and, when he availed himself of the opportunity of landing not far from Hadrumetum (Susa), he could not disembark more than some

3000 men, mostly recruits, and 150 horsemen. His attempt to capture Hadrumetum strongly occupied by the enemy miscarried; but Caesar possessed himself of the two seaports not far distant from each other, Ruspina (Sahalil near Susa) and Little Leptis. Here he entrenched himself; but his position was so insecure that he kept his cavalry in the ships and the ships ready for sea and provided with a supply of water, in order to re-embark at any moment if he should be attacked by a superior force. This however was not necessary, for just at the right time the ships that had been driven out of their course arrived (3rd January $\frac{708}{46}$). On the very following day Caesar, whose army suffered in consequence of the arrangements made by the Pompeians from want of corn, undertook with three legions an expedition into the interior of the country, but was attacked on the march not far from Ruspina by the corps which Labienus had brought up to dislodge Caesar from the coast. As Labienus had exclusively cavalry and archers, and Caesar almost nothing but infantry of the line, the legions were quickly surrounded and exposed to the missiles of the enemy, without being able to retaliate or to attack with success. No doubt the deploying of the entire line relieved once more the flanks, and spirited charges saved the honour of their arms; but a retreat was unavoidable, and had Ruspina not been so near, the Moorish javelin would perhaps have accomplished the same result here as the Parthian bow at Carrhae.

Caesar, whom this day had fully convinced of the difficulty of the impending war, would not again expose his soldiers untried and discouraged by the new mode of fighting to any such attack, but awaited the arrival of his veteran legions. The interval was employed in providing some sort of compensation against the crushing superiority of the enemy in the weapons of distant warfare. The incorporation of the suitable men from the fleet as light horsemen or archers in the land army could not be of much avail. The diversions which Caesar procured were somewhat more effectual. He succeeded in bringing into arms against Juba the Gaetulian pastoral tribes wandering on the southern slope of the great Atlas towards the Sahara; for the commotions of the Marian and Sullan period had reached even to them, and their indignation against Pompeius, who had at that time made them subordinate to the Numidian kings (iii. 324), rendered them from the onset favourably inclined to the heir of the mighty Marius of whose Jugurthine campaign they had still a lively recollection. The

Mauretanian kings, Bogud in Tingis and Bocchus in Jol, were Juba's natural rivals and to a certain extent long since in alliance with Caesar. Further, there still roamed in the border-region between the kingdoms of Juba and Bocchus the last of the Catilinarians, that Publius Sittius of Nuceria (p. 158), who eighteen years before had become converted from a bankrupt Italian merchant into a Mauretanian leader of free bands, and since that time had procured for himself a name and a body of retainers amidst the Libyan quarrels. Bocchus and Sittius united fell on the Numidian land, and occupied the important town of Cirta; and their attack, as well as that of the Gaetulians, compelled king Juba to send a portion of his troops to his southern and western frontiers.

Caesar's situation, however, continued sufficiently unpleasant. His army was crowded together within a space of six square miles; though the fleet conveyed corn, the want of forage was as much felt by Caesar's cavalry as by those of Pompeius before Dyrrhachium. The light troops of the enemy remained notwithstanding all the exertions of Caesar so immeasurably superior to his, that it seemed almost impossible to carry aggressive operations into the interior even with veterans. If Scipio retired and abandoned the coast towns, he might perhaps achieve a victory like those which the vizier of Orodes had won over Crassus and Juba over Curio, and he could at least endlessly protract the war. The simplest consideration suggested this plan of campaign; even Cato, although far from a strategist, counselled its adoption, and offered at the same time to cross with a corps to Italy and to call the republicans to arms—which, amidst the utter confusion there, might very well meet with success. But Cato could only advise, not command; Scipio the commander-in-chief decided that the war should be carried on in the region of the coast. This was a blunder, not merely inasmuch as they thereby dropped a plan of war promising a sure result, but also inasmuch as the region to which they transferred the war was in dangerous agitation, and a good part of the army which they opposed to Caesar was likewise in a troublesome temper. The fearfully strict levy, the carrying off of the supplies, the devastating of the smaller townships, the feeling in general that they were being sacrificed for a cause which from the outset was foreign to them and was already lost, had exasperated the native population against the Roman republicans fighting out their last struggle of despair on African soil; and the terrorist proceedings of the latter against all communities that were but suspected of indifference (p. 410), had raised this exasperation to the most intense hatred. The African towns declared, wherever they could venture to do so, for Caesar; among the Gaetulians and the Libyans, who served in numbers among the light troops and even in the legions, desertion was spreading. But Scipio with all the obstinacy characteristic of folly persevered in his plan, marched with all his force from Utica to appear before the towns of Ruspina and Little Leptis occupied by Caesar, furnished Hadrumetum to the north and Thapsus to the south (on the promontory Râs ed Dimâs) with strong garrisons, and in concert with Juba, who likewise appeared before Ruspina with all his troops not required by the defence of the frontier, offered battle repeatedly to the enemy. But Caesar was resolved to wait for his veteran legions. As these one after another arrived and appeared on the scene of strife, Scipio and Juba lost the desire to risk a pitched battle, and Caesar had no means of compelling them to fight owing to their extraordinary superiority in light cavalry. Nearly two months passed away in marches and skirmishes in the neighbourhood of Ruspina and Thapsus, which chiefly had relation to the finding out of the concealed store-pits (silos) common in the country, and to the extension of posts. Caesar, compelled by the enemy's horsemen to keep as much as possible to the heights or to cover his flanks by entrenched lines, yet accustomed his soldiers gradually during this laborious and apparently endless warfare to the foreign mode of fighting. Friend and foe hardly recognised the rapid general in the cautious master of fence who trained his men carefully and not unfrequently in person; and they became almost puzzled by the masterly skill which displayed itself as conspicuously in delay as in promptitude of action.

At last Caesar, after being joined by his last reinforcements, made a lateral movement towards Thapsus. Scipio had, as we have said, strongly garrisoned this town, and thereby committed the blunder of presenting to his opponent an object of attack easy to be seized; to this first error he soon added the second still less excusable blunder of now for the rescue of Thapsus giving the battle, which Caesar had wished and Scipio had hitherto rightly refused, on ground which placed the decision in the hands of the infantry of the line. Immediately along the shore, opposite to Caesar's camp, the legions of Scipio and Juba appeared, the fore ranks ready for fighting, the hinder ranks occupied in forming an entrenched camp; at the same time the garrison of Thapsus prepared for a sally. Caesar's camp-guard sufficed to repulse the latter. His legions, accustomed to war, already forming a correct estimate of the enemy from the want of precision in their mode of array and their ill-closed ranks, while the entrenching was still going forward on that side, and before even the general gave the signal, compelled a trumpeter to sound for the attack, and advanced along the whole line headed by Caesar himself, who, when he saw his men advance without waiting for his orders, galloped forward to lead them against the enemy. The right wing, in advance of the other divisions, frightened the line of elephants opposed to it—this was the last great battle in which these animals were employed—by throwing bullets and arrows, so that they wheeled round on their own ranks. The covering force was cut down, the left wing of the enemy was broken, and the whole line was overthrown. The defeat was the more destructive, as the new camp of the beaten army was not yet ready and the old one was at a considerable distance; both were successively captured almost without resistance. The mass of the defeated army threw away their arms and sued for quarter; but Caesar's soldiers were no longer the same who had readily refrained from battle before Ilerda and honourably spared the defenceless at Pharsalus. The habit of civil war and the rancour left behind by the mutiny asserted their power in a terrible manner on the battle-field of Thapsus. If the hydra with which they fought always put forth new energies, if the army was hurried from Italy to Spain, from Spain to Macedonia, from Macedonia to Africa, and if the repose ever more eagerly longed for never came, the soldier sought, and not wholly without cause, the reason of this state of things in the unseasonable clemency of Caesar. He had sworn to retrieve the general's neglect, and remained deaf to the entreaties of his disarmed fellow-citizens as well as to the commands of Caesar and the superior officers. The fifty thousand corpses that covered the battle-field of Thapsus, among whom were several Caesarian officers known as secret opponents of the new monarchy, and therefore killed on this occasion by their own men, showed how the soldier procures for himself repose. The victorious army on the other hand numbered no more than fifty dead (6th April $\frac{708}{46}$).

There was as little a continuance of the struggle in Africa after the battle of Thapsus as there had been a year and a half before in the East after the defeat of Pharsalus. Cato as commandant of Utica convoked the senate, set forth how the means of defence stood, and submitted it to the decision of those assembled whether they would yield or defend themselves to the last man—only adjuring them to resolve and to act not each one for himself, but all in unison. The more courageous view found several supporters; it was proposed to manumit on behalf of the state the slaves capable of arms, which however Cato rejected as an illegal interference with private property, and suggested in its stead a patriotic appeal to the slave-owners. But soon this fit of resolution in an assembly consisting in great part of African merchants passed off, and they agreed to capitulate. Thereupon when Faustus Sulla, son of the regent, and Lucius Afranius arrived in Utica with a strong division of cavalry from the field of battle, Cato still made an attempt to hold the town through them; but he indignantly rejected their demand to let them first of all put to death the untrustworthy citizens of Utica *en masse*, and chose to let the last stronghold of the republicans fall into the hands of the monarch without resistance rather than to profane the last moments of the republic by such a massacre. After he had—partly by his authority, partly by liberal largesses—checked so far as he could the fury of the soldiery against the unfortunate Uticans; after he had with touching solicitude furnished to those who preferred not to trust themselves to Caesar's mercy the means of flight, and to those who wished to remain the opportunity of capitulating under the most tolerable conditions, so far as his ability reached; and after having thoroughly satisfied himself that he could render to no one any farther aid, he held himself released from his command, retired to his bedchamber, and plunged his sword into his breast.

Of the other fugitive leaders only a few escaped. The cavalry that fled from Thapsus encountered the bands of Sittius, and were cut down or captured by them; their leaders Afranius and Faustus were delivered up to Caesar, and, when the latter did not order their immediate execution, they were slain in a tumult by his veterans. The commander-in-chief Metellus Scipio with the fleet of the defeated party fell into the power of the cruisers of Sittius and, when they were about to lay hands on him, stabbed himself. King Juba, not unprepared for such an issue, had in that case resolved to die in a way which seemed to him befitting a king, and had caused an enormous funeral pile to be prepared in the market-place of his city Zama, which was intended to consume along with his body all his treasures and the dead bodies of the whole citizens of Zama. But the inhabitants of the town showed no desire to let themselves be employed by way of decoration for the funeral rites of the African Sardanapalus; and they closed the gates against the king when fleeing from the battle-field he appeared, accompanied by Marcus Petreius, before their city. The king—one of those natures that become savage amidst a life of dazzling and insolent enjoyment, and prepare for themselves even out of death an intoxicating feast—resorted with his companion to one of his country houses, caused a copious banquet to be served up, and at the close of the feast challenged Petreius to fight him to death in single combat. It was the victor of Catilina that received his death at the hand of the king; the latter thereupon caused himself to be stabbed by one of his slaves. The few men of eminence that escaped, such as Labienus and Sextus Pompeius, followed the elder brother of the latter to Spain and sought, like Sertorius formerly, the last refuge of robbers and pirates in the waters and the mountains of that still half-independent land.

Without resistance Caesar regulated the affairs of Africa. As Curio had already proposed, the kingdom of Massinissa was broken up. The most eastern portion or region of Sitifis was united with the kingdom of Bocchus king of East Mauretania (iii. 152), and the faithful king Bogud of Tingis was rewarded with considerable gifts. Cirta (Constantine) and the surrounding district, hitherto possessed under the supremacy of Juba by the prince Massinissa and his son Arabion, were conferred on the *condottiere* Publius Sittius that he might settle his half-Roman bands there;[1] but at the same time this district, as well as by far the largest and most fertile portion of the late Numidian kingdom, were united as "New Africa" with the older province of Africa, and the defence of the country along the coast against the roving tribes of the desert, which the republic had entrusted to a client-king, was imposed by the new monarch on the empire itself.

The struggle, which Pompeius and the republicans had undertaken against the monarchy of Caesar, thus terminated, after having lasted for four years, in the complete victory of the new monarch. No doubt the monarchy was not established for the first time on the battle-fields of Pharsalus and Thapsus; it might already be dated from the moment when Pompeius and

[1] The inscriptions of the region referred to preserve numerous traces of this colonisation. The name of the Sittii is there unusually frequent; the African township Milev bears as Roman the name *colonia Sarnensis* (Renier, *Inscr.* 1254, 2323, 2324), evidently from the Nucerian river-god Sarnus (Sueton. *Rhet.* 4).

Caesar in league had established their joint rule and overthrown the previous aristocratic constitution. Yet it was only those baptisms of blood of the 9th August $\frac{706}{48}$ and the 6th April $\frac{708}{46}$ that set aside the joint rule so opposed to the nature of absolute dominion, and conferred fixity and formal recognition on the new monarchy. Risings of pretenders and republican conspiracies might ensue and provoke new commotions, perhaps even new revolutions and restorations; but the continuity of the free republic that had been uninterrupted for five hundred years was broken through, and monarchy was established throughout the range of the Roman empire by the legitimacy of accomplished fact.

The constitutional struggle was at an end; and that it was so, was proclaimed by Marcus Cato when he fell on his sword at Utica. For many years he had been the foremost man in the struggle of the legitimate republic against its oppressors; he had continued it long after he had ceased to cherish any hope of victory. But now the struggle itself had become impossible; the republic which Marcus Brutus had founded was dead and never to be revived; what were the republicans now to do on the earth? The treasure was carried off, the sentinels were thereby relieved; who could blame them if they departed? There was more nobility, and above all more judgment, in the death of Cato than there had been in his life. Cato was anything but a great man; but with all that shortsightedness, that perversity, that dry prolixity, and those spurious phrases which have stamped him, for his own and for all time, as the ideal of unreflecting republicanism and the favourite of all who make it their hobby, he was yet the only man who honourably and courageously defended in the last struggle the great system doomed to destruction. Just because the shrewdest lie feels itself inwardly annihilated before the simple truth, and because all the dignity and glory of human nature ultimately depend not on shrewdness but on honesty, Cato has played a greater part in history than many men far superior to him in intellect. It only elevates the deep and tragic significance of his death that he was himself a fool; in truth it is just because Don Quixote is a fool that he is a tragic figure. It is an affecting fact, that on that world-stage, on which so many great and wise men had moved and acted, the fool was destined to give the epilogue. He too died not in vain. It was a fearfully striking protest of the republic against the monarchy, that the last republican went as the first monarch came—a protest which tore asunder like gossamer all that so-called constitutional character with which Caesar invested his monarchy, and exposed in all its hypocritical falsehood the shibboleth of the reconcilation of all parties, under the aegis of which despotism grew up. The unrelenting warfare which the ghost of the legitimate republic waged for centuries, from Cassius and Brutus down to Thrasea and Tacitus, nay even far later, against the Caesarian monarchy—a warfare of plots and of literature—was the legacy which the dying Cato bequeathed to his enemies. This republican opposition borrowed from Cato its whole attitude—stately, transcendental in its rhetoric, pretentiously rigid, hopeless, and faithful to death; and accordingly it began even immediately after his death to revere as a saint the man who in his lifetime was not unfrequently its laughingstock and its scandal. But the greatest of these marks of respect was the involuntary homage which Caesar rendered to him, when he made an exception to the contemptuous clemency with which he was wont to treat his opponents, Pompeians as well as republicans, in the case of Cato alone, and pursued him even beyond the grave with that energetic hatred which practical statesmen are wont to feel towards antagonists who oppose them from an ideal point of view equally dangerous and impracticable.

CHAPTER XI

THE OLD REPUBLIC AND THE NEW MONARCHY

THE new monarch of Rome, the first ruler of the whole domain of Romano-Hellenic civilisation, Gaius Julius Caesar, was in his fifty-sixth year (born 12th July $\frac{652}{102}$?) when the battle of Thapsus, the last link in a long chain of momentous victories, placed the decision of the future of the world in his hands. Few men have had their elasticity so thoroughly put to the proof as Caesar—the sole creative genius produced by Rome, and the last produced by the ancient world, which accordingly moved on in the track that he marked out for it until its sun had set. Sprung from one of the oldest noble families of Latium—which traced back its lineage to the heroes of the Iliad and the kings of Rome, and in fact to the Venus-Aphrodite common to both nations—he spent the years of his boyhood and early manhood as the genteel youth of that epoch were wont to spend them. He had tasted the sweetness as well as the bitterness of the cup of fashionable life, had recited and declaimed, had practised literature and made verses in his idle hours, had prosecuted love-intrigues of every sort, and got himself initiated into all the mysteries of shaving, curls, and ruffles pertaining to the toilette-wisdom of the day, as well as into the far more mysterious art of always borrowing and never paying. But the flexible steel of that nature was proof against even these dissipated and flighty courses; Caesar retained both his bodily vigour and his elasticity of mind and heart unimpaired. In fencing and in riding he was a match for any of his soldiers, and at Alexandria his swimming saved his life; the incredible rapidity of his journeys, which usually for the sake of gaining time were performed by night—a thorough contrast to the procession-like slowness with which Pompeius moved from one place to another—was the astonishment of his contemporaries and not the least among the causes of his success. The mind was like the body. His remarkable power of intuition revealed itself in the precision and practicability of all his arrangements, even where he gave orders without having seen with his own eyes. His memory was matchless, and it was easy for him to carry on several occupations simultaneously with equal self-possession. Although a gentleman, a man of genius, and a monarch, he had still a heart. So long as he lived, he cherished the purest veneration for his worthy mother Aurelia (his father having died early); to his wives and above all to his daughter Julia he devoted an honourable affection, which was not without reflex influence even on political affairs. With the ablest and most excellent men of his time, of high and of humble rank, he maintained noble relations of mutual fidelity, with each after his kind. As he himself never abandoned any of his partisans after the pusillanimous and unfeeling manner of Pompeius, but adhered to his friends—and that not merely from calculation—through good and bad times without wavering, several of these, such as Aulus Hirtius and Gaius Matius, gave, even after his death, noble testimonies of their attachment to him.

If in a nature so harmoniously organised there is any one trait to be singled out as characteristic, it is this—that he stood aloof from all ideology and everything fanciful. As a matter of course Caesar was a man of passion, for without passion there is no genius; but his passion was never stronger than he could control. He had had his season of youth, and song, love, and wine had taken joyous possession of his mind; but with him they did not penetrate to the inmost core of his nature. Literature occupied him long and earnestly; but, while Alexander could not sleep for thinking of the Homeric Achilles, Caesar in his sleepless hours mused on the inflections of the Latin nouns and verbs. He made verses, as everybody then did, but they were weak; on the other hand he was interested in subjects of astronomy and natural science. While wine was and continued to be with Alexander the destroyer of care, the temperate Roman, after the revels of his youth were over, avoided it entirely. Around him, as around all those whom the full lustre of woman's love has dazzled in youth, fainter gleams of it continued imperishably to linger; even in later years he had his love-adventures and successes with women, and he retained a certain foppishness in his outward appearance, or, to speak more correctly, a pleasing consciousness of his own manly beauty. He carefully covered the baldness which he keenly felt with the laurel chaplet that he wore in public in his later years, and he would doubtless have surrendered some of his victories, if he could thereby have brought back his youthful locks. But, however much even when monarch he enjoyed the society of women, he only amused himself with them, and allowed them no manner of influence over him; even his much-censured relation to queen Cleopatra was only contrived to mask a weak point in his political position (p. 401).

Caesar was thoroughly a realist and a man of sense; and whatever he undertook and achieved was pervaded and guided by the cool sobriety which constitutes the most marked peculiarity of his genius. To this he owed the power of living energetically in the present, undisturbed either by recollection or by expectation; to this he owed the capacity of acting at any moment with collected vigour, and applying his whole genius even to the smallest and most incidental enterprise; to this he owed the many-sided power with which he grasped and mastered whatever understanding can comprehend and will can compel; to this he owed the self-possessed ease with which he arranged his periods as well as projected his campaigns; to this he owed the "marvellous serenity" which remained steadily with him through good and evil days; to this he owed the complete independence, which admitted of no control by favourite or by mistress, or even by friend. It resulted, moreover, from this clearness of judgment that Caesar never formed to himself illusions regarding the power of fate and the ability of man; in his case the friendly veil was lifted up, which conceals from man the inadequacy of his working. However prudently he planned and contemplated all possibilities, the feeling was never absent from his heart that in all things fortune, that is to say accident, must bestow success; and with this may be connected the circumstance that he so often played a desperate game with destiny, and in particular again and again hazarded his person with daring indifference. As indeed occasionally men of predominant sagacity betake themselves to a pure game of hazard, so there was in Caesar's rationalism a point at which it came in some measure into contact with mysticism.

Gifts such as these could not fail to produce a statesman. From early youth, accordingly, Caesar was a statesman in the deepest sense of the term, and his aim was the highest which man is allowed to propose to himself—the political, military, intellectual, and moral regeneration of his own deeply decayed nation, and of the still more deeply decayed Hellenic nation intimately akin to his own. The hard school of thirty years' experience changed his views as to the means by which this aim was to be reached; his aim itself remained the same in the times of his hopeless humiliation and of his unlimited plenitude of power, in the times when as demagogue and conspirator he stole towards it by paths of darkness, and in those when, as joint possessor of the supreme power and then as monarch, he worked at his task in the full light of day before the eyes of the world. All the measures of a permanent king that proceeded from him at the most various times assume their appropriate places in the great building-plan. We cannot therefore properly speak of isolated achievements of Caesar; he did nothing isolated. With justice men commend Caesar the orator for his masculine eloquence, which, scorning all the arts of the advocate, like a clear flame at once enlightened and warmed. With justice men admire in Caesar the author the inimitable simplicity of the composition, the unique purity and beauty of the language. With justice the greatest masters of war of all times have praised Caesar the general, who, in a singular degree disregarding routine and tradition, knew always how to find out the mode of warfare by which in the given case the enemy was conquered, and which was consequently in the given case the right one; who with the certainty of divination found the proper means for every end; who after defeat stood ready for battle like William of Orange, and ended the campaign invariably with victory; who managed that element of warfare, the treatment of which serves to distinguish military genius from the mere ordinary ability of an officer—the rapid movement of masses—with unsurpassed perfection and found the guarantee of victory not in the massiveness of his forces but in the celerity of their movements, not in long preparation but in rapid and bold action even with inadequate means. But all these were with Caesar mere secondary matters; he was no doubt a great orator, author, and general, but he became each of these merely because he was a consummate statesman. The soldier more especially played in him altogether an accessory part, and it is one of the principal peculiarities by which he is distinguished from Alexander, Hannibal, and Napoleon, that he began his political activity not as an officer, but as a demagogue. According to his original plan he had purposed to reach his object, like Pericles and Gaius Gracchus, without force of arms, and throughout eighteen years he had as leader of the popular party moved exclusively amid political plans and intrigues—until, reluctantly convinced of the necessity for a military support, he, when already forty years of age, headed an army. It was natural that he should even afterwards remain still more statesman than general—just like Cromwell, who also transformed himself from a leader of opposition into a military chief and democratic king, and who in general, little as the Puritan hero seems to resemble the dissolute Roman, is yet in his development as well as in the objects which he aimed at and the results which he achieved of all statesmen perhaps the most akin to Caesar. Even in his mode of warfare this improvised generalship may still be recognised; the enterprises of Napoleon against Egypt and against England do not more clearly exhibit the artillery-lieutenant who had risen by service to command than the similar enterprises of Caesar exhibit the demagogue metamorphosed into a general. A regularly trained officer would hardly have been prepared, through political considerations of a not altogether stringent nature, to set aside the best-founded military scruples in the way in which Caesar did on several occasions, most strikingly in the case of his landing in Epirus. Several of his acts are therefore censurable in a military point of view; but what the general loses, the statesman gains. The task of the statesman is universal in its nature like Caesar's genius; if he undertook things the most varied and most remote one from another, they had all without exception a bearing on the one great object to which with infinite fidelity and consistency he devoted himself; and of the manifold aspects and directions of his great activity he never preferred one to another. Although a master of the art of war, he yet from statesmanly considerations did his utmost to avert the civil strife and, when it nevertheless began, to keep his laurels from the stain of blood. Although the founder of a military monarchy, he yet, with an energy unexampled in history, allowed no hierarchy of marshals or government of praetorians to come into existence. If he had a preference for any one form of services rendered to the state, it was for the sciences and arts of peace rather than for those of war.

The most remarkable peculiarity of his action as a statesman was its perfect harmony. In reality all the conditions for this most difficult of all human functions were united in Caesar. A thorough realist, he never allowed the images of the past or venerable tradition to disturb him; with him nothing was of value in politics but the living present and the law of reason, just as in grammar he set aside historical and antiquarian research and recognised nothing but on the one hand the living *usus loquendi* and on the other hand the rule of symmetry. A born ruler, he governed the minds of men as the wind drives the clouds, and compelled the most heterogeneous natures to place themselves at his service—the smooth citizen and the rough subaltern, the noble matrons of Rome and the fair princesses of Egypt and Mauretania, the brilliant cavalry-officer and the calculating banker. His talent for organisation was marvellous; no statesman has ever compelled alliances, no general has ever collected an army out of unyielding and refractory elements with such decision, and kept them together with such firmness, as Caesar displayed in constraining and upholding his coalitions and his legions; never did regent judge his instruments and assign each to the place appropriate for him with so acute an eye.

He was monarch; but he never played the king. Even when absolute lord of Rome, he retained the deportment of the party-leader; perfectly pliant and smooth, easy and charming in conversation, complaisant towards every one, it seemed as if he wished to be nothing but the first among his peers. Caesar entirely avoided the blunder of so many men otherwise on an equality with him, who have carried into politics the tone of military command; however much occasion his disagreeable relations with the senate gave for it, he never resorted to outrages such as that of the eighteenth Brumaire. Caesar was monarch; but he was never seized with the giddiness of the tyrant. He is perhaps the only one among the mighty men of the earth, who in great matters and little never acted according to inclination or caprice, but always without exception according to his duty as ruler, and who, when he looked back on his life, found doubtless erroneous calculations to deplore, but no false step of passion to regret. There is nothing in the history of Caesar's life, which even on a small scale [1] can be compared with those poetico-sensual ebullitions—such as the murder of Kleitos or the burning of Persepolis—which the history of his great predecessor in the East records. He is, in fine, perhaps the only one of those mighty men who have preserved to the end of his career the statesman's tact of discriminating between the possible and the impossible, and has not broken down in the task which for nobly gifted natures is the most difficult of all—the task of recognising, when on the pinnacle of success, its natural limits. What was possible he performed, and never left the possible good undone for the sake of the impossible better, never disdained at least to mitigate by palliatives evils

[1] The affair with Laberius, told in the well-known prologue, has been quoted as an instance of Caesar's tyrannical caprices, but those who have done so have thoroughly misunderstood the irony of the situation as well as of the poet; to say nothing of the *naïvete* of lamenting as a martyr the poet who readily pockets his honorarium.

that were incurable. But where he recognised that fate had spoken, he always obeyed. Alexander on the Hyphasis, Napoleon at Moscow, turned back because they were compelled to do so, and were indignant at destiny for bestowing even on its favourites merely limited successes; Caesar turned back voluntarily on the Thames and on the Rhine; and at the Danube and the Euphrates thought not of unbounded plans of world-conquest, but merely of carrying into effect a well-considered regulation of the frontiers.

Such was this unique man, whom it seems so easy and yet is so infinitely difficult to describe. His whole nature is transparent clearness; and tradition preserves more copious and more vivid information regarding him than regarding any of his peers in the ancient world. Of such a personage our conceptions may well vary in point of shallowness or depth, but they cannot be, strictly speaking, different; to every not utterly perverted inquirer the grand figure has exhibited the same essential features, and yet no one has succeeded in reproducing it to the life. The secret lies in its perfection. In his character as a man as well as in his place in history, Caesar occupies a position where the great contrasts of existence meet and balance each other. Of the mightiest creative power and yet at the same time of the most penetrating judgment; no longer a youth and not yet an old man; of the highest energy of will and the highest capacity of execution; filled with republican ideals and at the same time born to be a king; a Roman in the deepest essence of his nature, and yet called to reconcile and combine in himself as well as in the outer world the Roman and the Hellenic types of culture—Caesar was the entire and perfect man. Accordingly we miss in him more than in any other historical personage what are called characteristic features, which are in reality nothing else than deviations from the natural course of human development. What in Caesar passes for such at the first superficial glance is, when more closely observed, seen to be the peculiarity not of the individual, but of the epoch of culture or of the nation; his youthful adventures, for instance, were common to him with all his more gifted contemporaries of like position, his unpoetical but strongly logical temperament was the temperament of Romans in general. It formed part also of Caesar's full humanity that he was in the highest degree influenced by the conditions of time and place; for there is no abstract humanity—the living man cannot but occupy a place in a given nationality and in a definite line of culture. Caesar was a perfect man just because he more than any other placed himself amidst the currents of his time, and because he more than any other possessed the essential peculiarity of the Roman nation—practical aptitude as a citizen—in perfection: for his Hellenism in fact was only the Hellenism which had been long intimately blended with the Italian nationality. But in this very circumstance lies the difficulty, we may perhaps say the impossibility, of depicting Caesar to the life. As the artist can paint everything save only consummate beauty, so the historian, when once in a thousand years he encounters the perfect, can only be silent regarding it. For normality admits doubtless of being expressed, but it gives us only the negative notion of the absence of defect; the secret of nature, whereby in her most finished manifestations normality and individuality are combined, is beyond expression. Nothing is left for us but to deem those fortunate who beheld this perfection, and to gain some faint conception of it from the reflected lustre which rests imperishably on the works that were the creation of this great nature. These also, it is true, bear the stamp of the time. The Roman hero himself stood by the side of his youthful Greek predecessor not merely as an equal, but as a superior; but the world had meanwhile become old and its youthful lustre had faded. The action of Caesar was no longer, like that of Alexander, a joyous marching onward towards a goal indefinitely remote; he built on, and out of, ruins, and was content to establish himself as tolerably and as securely as possible within the ample but yet definite bounds once assigned to him. With reason therefore the delicate poetic tact of the nations has not troubled itself about the unpoetical Roman, and has invested the son of Philip alone with all the golden lustre of poetry, with all the rainbow hues of legend. But with equal reason the political life of nations has during thousands of years again and again reverted to the lines which Caesar drew; and the fact, that the peoples to whom the world belongs still at the present day designate the highest of their monarchs by his name, conveys a warning deeply significant and, unhappily, fraught with shame.

If the old, in every respect vicious, state of things was to be successfully got rid of and the commonwealth was to be renovated, it was necessary first of all that the country should be practically tranquillised and that the ground should be cleared from the rubbish with which since the recent catastrophe it was everywhere strewed. In this work Caesar set out from the principle of the reconciliation of the hitherto subsisting parties or, to put it more correctly—for where the antagonistic principles are irreconcilable, we cannot speak of real reconciliation—from the principle that the arena, on which the nobility and the populace had hitherto contended with each other, was to be abandoned by both parties, and that both were to meet together on the ground of the new monarchical constitution. First of all therefore all the older quarrels of the republican past were regarded as done away for ever and irrevocably. While Caesar gave orders that the statues of Sulla which had been thrown down by the mob of the capital on the news of the battle of Pharsalus should be re-erected, and thus recognised the fact that it became history alone to sit in judgment on that great man, he at the same time cancelled the last remaining effects of Sulla's exceptional laws, recalled from exile those who had been banished in the times of the Cinnan and Sertorian troubles, and restored to the children of those outlawed by Sulla their forfeited privilege of eligibility to office. In like manner all those were restored, who in the preliminary stage of the recent catastrophe had lost their seat in the senate or their civil existence through sentence of the censors or political process, especially through the impeachments raised on the basis of the exceptional laws of $\frac{702}{52}$. Those alone who had put to death the proscribed for money remained, as was reasonable, still under attainder; and Milo, the most daring *condottiere* of the senatorial party, was excluded from the general pardon.

Far more difficult than the settlement of these questions, which already belonged substantially to the past was the treatment of the parties confronting each other at the moment—on the one hand Caesar's own democratic adherents, on the other hand the overthrown aristocracy. That the former should be, if possible, still less satisfied than the latter with Caesar's conduct after the victory and with his summons to abandon the old standing-ground of party, was to be expected. Caesar himself desired doubtless on the whole the same issue which Gaius Gracchus had contemplated; but the designs of the Caesarians were no longer those of the Gracchans. The Roman popular party had been driven onward in gradual progression from reform to revolution, from revolution to anarchy, from anarchy to a war against property; they celebrated among themselves the memory of the reign of terror and now adorned the tomb of Catilina, as formerly that of the Gracchi, with flowers and garlands; they had placed themselves under Caesar's banner, because they expected him to do for them what Catilina had not been able to accomplish. But as it speedily became plain that Caesar was very far from intending to be the executor of Catilina, and that the utmost which debtors might expect from him was some alleviations of payment and modifications of procedure, indignation found loud vent in the inquiry, For whom then had the popular party conquered, if not for the people? and the rabble of this description, high and low, out of pure chagrin at the miscarriage of their politico-economic Saturnalia began first to coquet with the Pompeians, and then even during Caesar's absence of nearly two years from Italy (January $\frac{706}{48}$—autumn $\frac{707}{47}$) to instigate there a second civil war within the first.

The praetor Marcus Caelius Rufus, a good aristocrat and bad payer of debts, of some talent and much culture, as a vehement and fluent orator hitherto in the senate and in the Forum one of the most zealous champions for Caesar, proposed to the people—without being instructed from any higher quarter to do so—a law which granted to debtors a respite of six years free of interest, and then, when he was opposed in this step, proposed a second law which even cancelled all claims from loans and current house rents; whereupon the Caesarian senate deposed him from his office. It was just on the eve of the battle of Pharsalus, and the balance in the great contest seemed to incline to the side of the Pompeians; Rufus entered into communication with the old senatorian band-leader Milo, and the two contrived a counter-revolution, which inscribed on its banner partly the republican constitution, partly the cancelling of creditors' claims and the manumission of slaves. Milo left his place of exile Massilia, and called the Pompeians and the slave-herdsmen to arms in the region of Thurii; Rufus made arrangements to seize the town of Capua by armed slaves. But the latter plan was detected before its execution and frustrated by the Capuan militia; Quintus Pedius, who advanced with a legion into the territory of Thurii, scattered the band making havoc there; and the fall of the two leaders put an end to the scandal ($\frac{706}{48}$).

Nevertheless there was found in the following year ($\frac{707}{47}$) a second fool, the tribune of the people, Publius Dolabella, who, equally insolvent but far from being equally gifted with his predecessor, introduced afresh his law as to creditors' claims and house rents, and with his colleague Lucius Trebellius began on that point once more—it was the last time—the demagogic war; there were serious frays between the armed bands on both sides and various street-riots, till the commandant of Italy Marcus Antonius ordered the military to interfere, and soon afterwards Caesar's return from the East completely put an end to the preposterous proceedings. Caesar attributed to these silly attempts to revive the projects of Catilina so little importance, that he tolerated Dolabella in Italy and indeed after some time even received him again into favour. Against a rabble of this sort, who are not intent on any political question at all, but solely on a war against property—as against gangs of banditti—the mere existence of a strong government is sufficient; and Caesar was too great and too considerate to busy himself with the apprehensions which the Italian alarmists felt regarding the communists of that day, and thereby unduly to procure a false popularity for his monarchy.

While Caesar thus might leave, and actually left, the late democratic party to the process of decomposition which had already in its case advanced almost to the utmost limit, he had on the other hand, with reference to the former aristocratic party possessing a far greater vitality, to pave the way for, and initiate, its dissolution—which time alone could accomplish—by a proper combination of repression and conciliation. Among minor measures, Caesar, even from a natural sense of propriety, avoided exasperating the fallen party by empty sarcasm; he did not triumph over his conquered fellow-burgesses;[1] he mentioned Pompeius often and always with respect, and caused his statue overthrown by the people to be re-erected at the senate-house, when the latter was restored, in its earlier distinguished place. To political prosecutions after the victory Caesar assigned the narrowest possible limits. No investigation was instituted into the various communications which the constitutional party had held with nominal Caesarians; Caesar threw the piles of papers found in the enemy's head-quarters at Pharsalus and Thapsus into the fire unread, and spared himself and the country from political processes against individuals suspected of high treason. Further, all the common soldiers who had followed their Roman or provincial officers into the contest against Caesar came off with impunity. The sole exception made was in the case of those Roman burgesses, who had taken service in the army

[1] The triumph after the battle of Munda, subsequently to be mentioned, probably had reference only to the Lusitanians who served in great numbers in the conquered army.

of the Numidian king Juba; their property was confiscated by way of penalty for their treason. Even to the officers of the conquered party Caesar had granted unlimited pardon up to the close of the Spanish campaign of $\frac{705}{49}$; but he became convinced that in this he had gone too far, and that the removal at least of the leaders among them was inevitable. The rule by which he was thenceforth guided was, that every one who after the capitulation of Ilerda had served as an officer in the enemy's army or had sat in the opposition-senate, if he survived the close of the struggle, forfeited his property and his political rights, and was banished from Italy for life; if he did not survive the close of the struggle, his property at least fell to the state; but any one of these, who had formerly accepted pardon from Caesar and was once more found in the ranks of the enemy, in that case forfeited his life. These rules were however materially modified in the execution. The sentence of death was actually executed only against a very few of the numerous backsliders. In the confiscation of the property of the fallen not only were the debts attaching to the several portions of the estate as well as the claims of the widows for their dowries paid off, as was reasonable, but a portion of the paternal estate was left also to the children of the deceased. Lastly not a few of those who, in consequence of those rules were liable to punishment and confiscation of property, were at once pardoned entirely or got off with fines, like the African capitalists who were impressed as members of the senate of Utica. And even the others almost without exception got their freedom and property restored to them, if they could only prevail on themselves to petition Caesar to that effect; on several who declined to do so, such as the consular Marcus Marcellus, pardon was even conferred unasked, and ultimately in $\frac{710}{44}$ a general amnesty was issued for all who were still unrecalled.

The republican opposition submitted to be pardoned; but it was not reconciled. Discontent with the new order of things and exasperation against the unwonted ruler were general. For open political resistance there was indeed no farther opportunity—it was hardly worth taking into account, that some oppositional tribunes on occasion of the question of title acquired for themselves the republican crown of martyrdom by a demonstrative intervention against those who had called Caesar king—but republicanism found expression all the more decidedly as an opposition of opinion, and in secret agitation and plotting. Not a hand stirred when the Imperator appeared in public.

There was abundance of wall-placards and sarcastic verses full of bitter and telling popular satire against the new monarchy. When a comedian ventured on a republican allusion, he was saluted with the loudest applause. The praise of Cato formed the fashionable theme of oppositional pamphleteers, and their writings found a public all the more grateful because even literature was no longer free. Caesar indeed combated the republicans even now on their own field; he himself and his abler confidants replied to the Cato-literature with Anticatones, and the republican and Caesarian scribes fought round the dead hero of Utica like the Trojans and Hellenes round the dead body of Patroclus; but as a matter of course in this conflict—where the public thoroughly republican in its feelings was judge—the Caesarians had the worst of it. No course remained but to overawe the authors; on which account men well known and dangerous in a literary point of view, such as Publius Nigidius Figulus and Aulus Caecina, had more difficulty in obtaining permission to return to Italy than other exiles, while the oppositional writers tolerated in Italy were subjected to a practical censorship, the restraints of which were all the more annoying that the measure of punishment to be dreaded was utterly arbitrary.[1] The underground machinations of the overthrown parties against the new monarchy will be more fitly set forth in another connection. Here it is sufficient to say that risings of pretenders as well as of republicans were incessantly brewing throughout the Roman empire; that the flames of civil war kindled now by the Pompeians, now by the republicans, again burst forth brightly at various places; and that in the capital there was perpetual conspiracy against the life of the monarch. But Caesar could not be induced by these plots even to surround himself permanently with a body-guard, and usually contented himself with making known the detected conspiracies by public placards.

However much Caesar was wont to treat all things relating to his personal safety with daring indifference, he could not possibly conceal from himself the very serious danger with which this mass of malcontents threatened not merely himself but also his creations. If nevertheless, disregarding all the warning and urgency of his friends, he without deluding himself as to the implacability of the very opponents to whom he showed

[1] Any one who desires to compare the old and new hardships of authors will find opportunity of doing so in the letter of Caecina (Cicero, *Ad. Fam.* vi. 7).

mercy, persevered with marvellous composure and energy in the course of pardoning by far the greater number of them, he did so neither from the chivalrous magnanimity of a proud, nor from the sentimental clemency of an effeminate, nature, but from the correct statesmanly consideration that vanquished parties are disposed of more rapidly and with less public injury by their absorption within the state than by any attempt to extirpate them by proscription or to eject them from the commonwealth by banishment. Caesar could not for his high objects dispense with the constitutional party itself, which in fact embraced not the aristocracy merely but all the elements of a free and national spirit among the Italian burgesses; for his schemes, which contemplated the renovation of the antiquated state, he needed the whole mass of talent, culture, hereditary and self-acquired distinction, which this party embraced; and in this sense he may well have named the pardoning of his opponents the finest reward of victory. Accordingly the most prominent chiefs of the defeated parties were indeed removed, but full pardon was not withheld from the men of the second and third rank and especially of the younger generation; they were not, however, allowed to sulk in passive opposition, but were by more or less gentle pressure induced to take an active part in the new administration, and to accept honours and offices from it. As with Henry the Fourth and William of Orange, so with Caesar his greatest difficulties began only after the victory. Every revolutionary conqueror learns by experience that, if after vanquishing his opponents he would not remain like Cinna and Sulla a mere party chief, but would like Henry the Fourth and William of Orange substitute the welfare of the commonwealth for the necessarily one-sided programme of his own party, for the moment all parties, his own as well as the vanquished, unite against the new chief; and the more so, the more great and pure his idea of his new vocation. The friends of the constitution and the Pompeians, though doing homage with the lips to Caesar, bore yet in heart a grudge either at monarchy or at least at the dynasty; the degenerate democracy was in open rebellion against Caesar from the moment of its perceiving that Caesar's objects were by no means its own; even the personal adherents of Caesar murmured, when they found that their chief was establishing instead of a state of *condottieri* a monarchy equal and just towards all, and that the portions of gain accruing to them were to be diminished by the accession of the vanquished.

This settlement of the commonwealth was acceptable to no party, and had to be imposed on his associates no less than on his opponents. Caesar's own position was now in a certain sense more imperilled than before the victory; but what he lost, the state gained. By annihilating the parties and not simply sparing the partisans but allowing every man of talent or even merely of good descent to attain to office irrespective of his political past, he gained for his great building all the working power extant in the state; and not only so, but the voluntary or compulsory participation of men of all parties in the same work led the nation also over imperceptibly to the newly prepared ground. The fact that this reconciliation of the parties was for the moment only external and that they were for the present much less agreed in adherence to the new state of things than in hatred against Caesar, did not mislead him; he knew well that antagonisms lose their keenness when brought into such outward union, and that only in this way can the statesman anticipate the work of time, which alone is able finally to heal such a strife by laying the old generation in the grave. Still less did he inquire who hated him or meditated his assassination. Like every genuine statesman he served not the people for reward—not even for the reward of their love—but sacrificed the favour of his contemporaries for the blessing of posterity, and above all for the permission to save and renew his nation.

In attempting to give a detailed account of the mode in which the transition was effected from the old to the new state of things, we must first of all recollect that Caesar came not to begin, but to complete. The plan of a new polity suited to the times, long ago projected by Gaius Gracchus, had been maintained by his adherents and successors with more or less of spirit and success, but without wavering. Caesar, from the outset and as it were by hereditary right the head of the popular party, had for thirty years borne aloft its banner without ever changing or even so much as concealing his colours; he remained democrat even when monarch. As he accepted without limitation, apart of course from the preposterous projects of Catilina and Clodius, the heritage of his party; as he displayed the bitterest, even personal, hatred to the aristocracy and the genuine aristocrats; and as he retained unchanged the essential ideas of Roman democracy, viz. alleviation of the burdens of debtors, transmarine colonisation, gradual equalisation of the differences of rights among the classes belonging to the state, emancipation of the executive power from the senate: his monarchy was so little at variance with democracy, that democracy on the contrary only attained its completion and fulfilment by means of that monarchy. For his monarchy was not the Oriental despotism of divine right, but a monarchy such as Gaius Gracchus wished to found, such as Pericles and Cromwell founded—the representation of the nation by the man in whom it puts supreme and unlimited confidence. The ideas, which lay at the foundation of Caesar's work, were so far not strictly new; but to him belongs their realisation, which after all is everywhere the main matter; and to him pertains the grandeur of execution, which would probably have surprised the brilliant projector himself if he could have seen it, and which has impressed, and will always impress, every one to whom it has been presented in the living reality or in the mirror of history—to whatever historical epoch or whatever shade of politics he may belong—according to the measures of his ability to comprehend human and historical greatness, with deep and ever-deepening admiration.

At this point however it is proper expressly once for all to postulate what the historian everywhere tacitly presumes, and to protest against the custom—common to simplicity and perfidy—of using historical praise and historical censure, dissociated from the given circumstances, as phrases of general application, and in the present case of construing our judgment respecting Caesar into a judgment respecting what is called Caesarianism. It is true that the history of past centuries ought to be the instructress of the present; but not in the vulgar sense, as if one could simply by turning over the leaves discover the conjunctures of the present in the records of the past, and collect from these the symptoms for a political diagnosis and the specifics for a prescription; it is instructive only so far as the observation of earlier forms of culture reveals the organic conditions of civilisation generally—the fundamental forces everywhere alike, and the manner of their combination everywhere different—and leads and encourages men, not to unreflecting imitation, but to independent reproduction. In this sense the history of Caesar and of Roman Imperialism, with all the unsurpassed greatness of the master-worker, with all the historical necessity of the work, is in truth a more bitter censure of modern autocracy than could be written by the hand of man. According to the same law of nature, in virtue of which the smallest organism infinitely surpasses the most artistic machine, every constitution however defective which gives play to the free self-determination of a majority of citizens infinitely surpasses the most brilliant and humane absolutism; for the former is capable of development and therefore living, the latter is what it is and therefore dead. This law of nature has verified itself in the Roman absolute military monarchy and verified itself all the more completely, that, under the impulse of its creator's genius and in the absence of all material extraneous complications, that monarchy developed itself more purely and freely than any similar state. From Caesar's time, as the sequel will show and Gibbon has shown long ago, the Roman system had only an external coherence and received only a mechanical extension, while internally it became even with him utterly withered and dead. If in the early stages of the autocracy and above all in Caesar's own soul (p. 187) the hopeful dream of a combination of free popular development and absolute rule was still cherished, the government of the highly-gifted emperors of the Julian house soon taught men in a terrible form how far it was possible to hold fire and water in the same vessel. Caesar's work was necessary and salutary, not because it was or could be fraught with blessing in itself, but because—with the national organisation of antiquity, which was based on slavery and was utterly a stranger to republican-constitutional representation, and in presence of the legitimate civic constitution which in the course of five hundred years had ripened into oligarchic absolutism—absolute military monarchy was the copestone logically necessary and the least of evils. When once the slave-holding aristocracy in Virginia and the Carolinas shall have carried matters as far as their congeners in the Sullan Rome, Caesarianism will there too be legitimised in the view of the spirit of history;[1] where it appears under other conditions of development, it is at once a caricature and a usurpation. But history will not submit to curtail the true Caesar of his due honour, because her verdict may lead simplicity astray in the presence of bad Caesars, and may give to roguery occasion for lying and fraud. She too is a Bible, and if she cannot any more than the Bible hinder the fool from misunderstanding and the devil from quoting her, she too will be able to bear with, and to requite, them both.

[1] When this was written—in the year 1857—no one could foresee how soon the mightiest struggle and most glorious victory as yet recorded in human annals would save the United States from this fearful trial, and secure the future existence of an absolute self-governing freedom not to be permanently kept in check by any local Caesarianism.

The position of the new chief of the state assumed, formally, a singular shape. Caesar was invested with the dictatorship at first temporarily after the return from Spain in $\frac{705}{49}$, then after the battle of Pharsalus from the autumn of $\frac{706}{48}$ for an indefinite time, lastly after the battle of Thapsus from the 1st January $\frac{709}{45}$ as an annual office, to which he was designated at first for ten years, and ultimately in $\frac{710}{44}$ for life;[1] also with the censorship under the new title of *praefectus morum* in $\frac{708}{46}$ for three years, in $\frac{710}{44}$ for life: likewise with the consulship at first for $\frac{706}{48}$ in the usual way—this was the office, the holding of which immediately occasioned the civil war—afterwards for five, finally for ten years, once also without colleague; moreover not with the tribunate of the people indeed, but with a power similar to the tribunician in $\frac{706}{48}$ for life; then with the first place, and along with this the right of leading the vote, in the senate; lastly ($\frac{708}{46}$) with the title of Imperator for life.[2] Caesar did not need to have the supervision of worship now entrusted to him, as he already held the office of *Pontifex maximus* (p. 175); he became, however, a member of the second great priestly college of the augers. To this motley union of civil and priestly offices there was added a yet far more motley multitude of laws and decrees of the senate, which committed to Caesar the right of deciding on war and peace without consulting the senate or the people, the disposal of armies and treasures, the nomination of the provincial governors, a binding right of proposal as respected a portion of the magistrates of the city of Rome, the conducting of elections in the centuriate comitia, the right of nominating patricians, and other such extraordinary prerogatives; to say nothing of the empty honours and decorations, the conferring of the title of "father of his fatherland,"

[1] He was thus when he died ($\frac{710}{44}$) dictator for the fourth time and designated dictator for life; as he is so named in the document in Josephus, *Antiq.* xiv. 10, 7.

[2] The name *imperator* belonged in the republican period to the victorious general, and was accordingly laid aside with the surrender of the military command. Caesar bore it at first as governor of Gaul in the usual way; but the retention of the title after the termination of his generalship and the celebration of his triumph was new. So far there was certainly laid in this the ground for a distinction, as regards the title of *imperator*, between the permanent title, which was subsequently prefixed to the name, and that which was temporary and therefore capable of repetition, which was placed after the name; and we find also that Caesar, even when he had been called in the former sense Imperator once for all, was yet after the gaining of victories saluted by acclamation on the battle-field as *imperator;* he never bore the title, however, prefixed to his name, but constantly called himself and made others call him simply *Caesar imperator* (without adding any sign of repetition).

the designation of the month in which he was born by the name which it still bears of Julius, and other manifestations of the foolish tendency towards a courtly tone, which ultimately passed into the silliest adoration. Evidently an attempt was thus made—apparently by way of compromise between the new courtly devotion and the republican aversion to call the monarchy by its right name—to analyse the absolute authority of the monarch into its individual constituent elements; which in truth was as superfluous as it was logically mistaken, for absolute power by virtue of its very nature withdraws itself from all specification. That Caesar himself intended to manufacture his new kingly power out of this bundle of old and new offices and extraordinary commissions, is a conjecture more naïve than ingenious. Men of judgment will not require any proof, either that Caesar intended to engraft on the commonwealth his supreme power, not merely for a few years or even as a personal office for an indefinite period or for life somewhat like Sulla's regency, but as an essential and permanent organ—in other words, as hereditary power—or that he selected for the new institution an appropriate and simple designation; for if it is a political blunder to create names without substantial meaning, it is scarcely a less error to set up the substance of plenary power without a name. Only it is not easy to determine what was the formal shape chosen by Caesar; partly because in this period of transition the ephemeral and the permanent buildings are not clearly discriminated from each other, partly because the devotion of his clients which already anticipated the nod of their master loaded him with a multitude—offensive doubtless to himself—of decrees of confidence and laws conferring honours. Least of all did the tribunician power furnish an available expression to designate the functions of the new chief of the state, for the tribune of the people constitutionally could not command, but could only forbid others commanding. Nor could the new monarchy fitly attach itself to the consulship, on account of the collegiate character that could not well be separated from this office; Caesar too laboured evidently to degrade this hitherto supreme magistracy into an empty title, and even when he undertook it, did not ordinarily hold it for the whole year, but soon resigned it to subordinate personages. The dictatorship was practically the most prominent in point of frequency and definiteness among Caesar's many offices, evidently because Caesar employed it in the significance which it had of old in the constitutional machinery—as an extraordinary presidency for surmounting extraordinary crises. On the other hand it was far from recommending itself as the expression of the new monarchy, for it was a magistracy clothed with an exceptional and unpopular character; and it was much too narrow to embrace the new monarchy, if Caesar was invested—as seems to have been the case, and as from his earlier party position could hardly be otherwise—not with the anomalous Sullan, but with (the limit of time excepted) the ordinary republican, dictatorship.

The new name of Imperator, on the other hand, appears in every respect the appropriate formal expression to the new monarchy; just because it is new, and no definite outward occasion for its introduction is apparent. The new wine might not be put into old bottles; here is a new name for the new thing, and that name most pregnantly sums up what the democratic party had already expressed in the Gabinian law, only with less precision, as the function of its chief—the concentration of official power (*imperium*) in the hands of a popular chief independent of the senate. We find on Caesar's coins, especially those of the last period, alongside of the dictatorship the title of Imperator prevailing, and in Caesar's law as to political crimes the monarch seems to have been designated by this name; and, what is quite decisive, the authority of Imperator was given to Caesar not merely for his own person, but also for his bodily or adopted descendants. Accordingly the following times, though not immediately, connected the monarchy with the title of Imperator. To lend to this new office at once a democratic and a religious sanction, Caesar probably intended to associate with it on the one hand the tribunician power, on the other the supreme pontificate, as heirlooms, although it is only in the case of the supreme priesthood that we have express testimony to his having made it hereditary. In point of state-law the new office of Imperator was based on the position which the consuls or proconsuls occupied outside of the *pomerium*, so that not merely the military command, but the supreme judicial and consequently also the administrative power, were included in it.[1]

[1] The widely spread opinion, which sees in the imperial office of Imperator an essentially military power, namely, the dignity of general of the empire tenable for life, is entirely erroneous, and is not warranted either by the signification of the word or by the view taken by the old authorities. *Imperium* is the power of command, *imperator* is the possessor of that power; in these words as in the corresponding Greek terms κράτος, αὐτοκράτωρ so little is there implied a specific military reference, that it is on the contrary the very characteristic of the Roman official power, where it appears purely and completely, to embrace war and process—that is,

The Imperator stood to the consul in a certain measure as the latter stood to the praetor, inasmuch as their authority was similar in kind, but in case of collision, as the praetor gave way to the consul, so the consul gave way to the Imperator; which was also distinctly marked externally by the elevated imperial chair placed between the two official seats of the consuls. The authority of the Imperator was qualitatively superior to the consular-proconsular, only in so far as the former was not limited as respected time or space but was held for life and heritable and operative also in the capital; as the Imperator could not, while the consul could, be checked by colleagues of equal power; and as all the restrictions placed in course of time on the original supreme official power—especially the obligation to give place to the *provocatio* and to respect the advice of the senate—did not apply to the Imperator.

In a word, this new office of Imperator was nothing else than the primitive regal office re-established; for it was those very restrictions—as respected the temporal and local limitation of power, the collegiate arrangement, and the co-operation of the senate or the community that was necessary in certain cases—which distinguished the consul from the king (i. 246 *et seq.*). There is hardly a trait of the new monarchy which was not found in the old: the union of the supreme military, judicial, and administrative authority in the hands of the prince; a religious presidency over the commonwealth; the right of

the military and the civil power of command—as one inseparable whole. Dio says quite correctly (liii. 17; comp. xliii. 44; lii. 41) that the name Imperator was assumed by the emperors "to indicate their full power instead of the title of king and dictator (*πρὸς δήλωσιν τῆς αὐτοτελοῦς σφῶν ἐξουσίας, ἀντὶ τῆς τοῦ βασιλέως τοῦ τε δικτάτωρος ἐπικλήσεως*); for these older titles disappeared in name, but in reality the title of Imperator gives the same prerogatives (*τὸ δὲ δὴ ἔργον αὐτῶν τῇ τοῦ αὐτοκράτορος προσηγορίᾳ βεβαιοῦνται* for instance the right of levying soldiers, imposing taxes, declaring war and concluding peace, exercising the supreme authority over burgess and non-burgess in and out of the city and punishing any one at any place capitally or otherwise, and in general of assuming the prerogatives connected with the supreme *imperium* in the earliest times." It could not well be said in plainer terms, that *imperator* is nothing but a synonym for *rex*, just as *imperare* coincides with *regere*.

It is no doubt inconsistent with this view—and the circumstance seems to have primarily given rise to the conception of the imperial dignity of Imperator as a military office—that Tiberius called himself the master of his slaves, the imperator of his soldiers, the prince (*πρόκριτος, princeps*) of his fellow-burgesses (Dio, lvii. 8). But in this very statement lies its most complete confirmation; for Tiberius in fact rejected that new imperial *imperium* (Sueton. *Tib.* 26; Dio, lvii. 2; Eckhel, vi. 200) and was imperator only in the more special sense, in which this name was certainly purely military but was a mere title.

issuing ordinances with binding power; the reduction of the senate to a council of state; the revival of the patriciate and of the praefecture of the city; the peculiar quasi-hereditary character, for the constitution of Caesar, exactly like those of Cromwell and Napoleon, allowed the monarch to nominate his successor under the forms of adoption. But still more striking than these analogies is the internal similarity of the monarchy of Servius Tullius and the monarchy of Caesar; if those old kings of Rome with all their plenitude of power had yet been sovereigns of a free community and themselves the protectors of the commons against the nobility, Caesar too had not come to destroy liberty but to fulfil it, and primarily to break the intolerable yoke of the aristocracy. Nor need it surprise us that Caesar, anything but a political antiquary, went back five hundred years to find the model for a new state; for, seeing that the supreme magistracy of the Roman commonwealth had remained at all times a royalty restricted by a number of special laws, the idea of the regal office itself had by no means become obsolete. At very various periods and from very different sides —in the republican dictatorship, in the decemviral power, in the Sullan regency—there had been even during the republic a practical recurrence to it; indeed by a certain logical necessity, whenever an exceptional power seemed to be needed, the unlimited *imperium*, which was simply nothing else than the regal power, came into play in contradistinction to the usual limited *imperium*.

Lastly, outward considerations also recommended this recurrence to the former royalty. Mankind have infinite difficulty in reaching new creations, and therefore cherish the once developed forms as sacred heirlooms. Accordingly Caesar very judiciously connected himself with Servius Tullius, in the same way as subsequently Charlemagne connected himself with Caesar, and Napoleon attempted at least to connect himself with Charlemagne. He did so, not in a circuitous way and secretly, but, as well as his successors, in the most open manner possible; it was indeed the very object of this connection to find a clear, national and popular form of expression for the new state. From ancient times there stood on the Capitol the statues of those seven kings, whom the conventional history of Rome was wont to bring on the stage; Caesar ordered his own to be erected beside them as the eighth. He appeared publicly in the costume of the old kings of Alba. In his new law as to political offenders the principal variation from that of Sulla was, that there was placed alongside of the national community, and on a level with it, the Imperator as the living and personal expression of the people. In the formula used for political oaths there was added to the Jovis and the Penates of the Roman people the Genius of the Imperator. The outward badge of monarchy was, according to the view universally diffused in antiquity, the image of the monarch on the coins; from the year $\frac{710}{44}$ the head of Caesar appears on those of the Roman state.

There could accordingly be no complaint at least on the score that Caesar left the public in the dark as to his view of his position; as distinctly and as formally as possible he came forward not merely as monarch, but as very king of Rome. It is possible even, although not exactly probable, and at any rate of subordinate importance, that he had it in view to designate his official power not with the new name of Imperator, but directly with the old one of king.[1] Even in his lifetime many of his enemies as of his friends were of opinion that he intended to have himself expressly nominated king of Rome; several indeed of his most vehement adherents suggested to him in different ways and at different times that he should assume the crown; most strikingly of all, Marcus Antonius, when he as consul offered the diadem to Caesar before all the people (15th February $\frac{710}{44}$). But Caesar rejected these proposals without exception at once. If he at the same time took steps against those who made use of these incidents to stir republican opposition, it by no means follows from this that he was not in earnest

[1] On this question there may be difference of opinion; the hypothesis however that it was Caesar's intention to rule the Romans as Imperator, the non-Romans as Rex, must be simply dismissed. It is based solely on the story that in the sitting of the senate in which Caesar was assassinated a Sibylline utterance was brought forward by one of the priests in charge of the oracles, Lucius Cotta, to the effect that the Parthians could only be vanquished by a "king," and in consequence of this the resolution was adopted to commit to Caesar regal power over the Roman provinces. This story was certainly in circulation immediately after Caesar's death. But not only does it nowhere find any sort of even indirect confirmation, but it is even expressly pronounced false by the contemporary Cicero (*De Div.* ii. 54, 119) and reported by the later historians, especially by Suetonius (79) and Dio (xliv. 15) merely as a rumour which they are far from wishing to guarantee; and it is under such circumstances no better accredited by the fact of Plutarch (*Caes.* 60, 64; *Brut.* 10) and Appian. (*B. C.* ii. 110) repeating it after their wont, the former by way of anecdote, the latter methodically. But the story is not merely unattested; it is also intrinsically impossible. Even leaving out of account that Caesar had too much intellect and too much political tact to decide important questions of state after the oligarchic fashion by a stroke of the oracle-machinery, he could never think of thus formally and legally splitting up the state which he wished to reduce to a level.

with his rejection; and as little has proof been adduced that these invitations took place at his bidding, with the view of preparing the multitude for the unwonted spectacle of the Roman diadem. It may have been the uncalled-for zeal of vehement adherents alone that occasioned these incidents; it may be also, that Caesar merely permitted or even suggested the scene with Antonius, in order to put an end in as marked a manner as possible to the inconvenient gossip by a declinature made before the eyes of the burgesses and inserted by supreme command even in the calendar of the state. The probability is that Caesar, who appreciated alike the value of a convenient formal designation and the antipathies of the multitude which fasten more on the names than on the essence of things, was resolved to avoid the name of king as tainted with an ancient curse and as more familiar to the Romans of his time when applied to the despots of the East than to their own Numa and Servius, and to appropriate the substance of royalty under the title of Imperator.

But, whatever may have been the style and title, the sovereign ruler was there, and accordingly the court established itself at once with all its due accompaniments of pomp, insipidity, and emptiness. Caesar appeared in public not in the robe of the consuls which was bordered with purple stripes, but in the robe wholly of purple which was reckoned in antiquity as the proper regal attire, and received, seated on his golden chair and without rising from it, the solemn procession of the senate. The festivals in his honour commemorative of birthday, of victories, and of vows, filled the calendar. When Caesar came to the capital, his principal servants marched forth in troops to great distances so as to meet and escort him. To be near to him began to be of such importance, that the rents rose in the quarter of the city where he lived. Personal interviews with him were rendered so difficult by the multitude of individuals soliciting audience, that Caesar found himself compelled in many cases to communicate even with his intimate friends in writing, and that persons even of the highest rank had to wait for hours in the ante-chamber. People felt, more clearly than was agreeable to Caesar himself, that they no longer approached a fellow-citizen. There arose a monarchical aristocracy, which was in a remarkable manner at once new and old, and which had sprung out of the idea of casting into the shade the aristocracy of the oligarchy by that of royalty, the nobility by the patriciate. The patrician body still subsisted, although without essential privileges as an order, in the character of a close aristocratic guild (i. 298); but as it could receive no new *gentes* (i. 258) it had dwindled away more and more in the course of centuries, and in the time of Caesar there were not more than fifteen or sixteen patrician *gentes* still in existence. Caesar himself sprung from one of them, got the right of creating new patrician *gentes* conferred on the Imperator by decree of the people, and so established, in contrast to the republican nobility, the new aristocracy of the patriciate, which most happily combined all the requisites of a monarchical aristocracy—the charm of antiquity, entire dependence on the government, and total insignificance. On all sides the new sovereignty revealed itself.

Under a monarch thus practically unlimited there could hardly be room for a constitution at all—still less for a continuance of the hitherto existing commonwealth based on the legal co-operation of the burgesses, the senate, and the several magistrates. Caesar fully and definitely reverted to the tradition of the regal period; the burgess-assembly remained—what it had already been in that period—by the side of and with the king the supreme and ultimate expression of the will of the sovereign people; the senate was brought back to its original destination of giving advice to the ruler when he requested it; and lastly the ruler concentrated in his person anew the whole magisterial authority, so that there existed no independent state-official by his side any more than by the side of the kings of the earliest times.

In legislation the democratic monarch adhered to the primitive maxim of Roman state-law, that the community of the people in concert with the king convoking them had alone the power of organically regulating the commonwealth; and he had his constitutive enactments regularly sanctioned by decree of the people. The free energy and the authority half-moral, half-political, which the yea or nay of those old warrior-assemblies had carried with it, could not indeed be again instilled into the so-called comitia of this period; the co-operation of the burgesses in legislation, which in the old constitution had been extremely limited but real and living, was in the new practically an unsubstantial shadow. There was therefore no need of special restrictive measures against the comitia; many years' experience had shown that every government—the oligarchy as well as the monarch—easily kept on good terms with this formal sovereign. These Caesarian comitia were an important element in the Caesarian system and indirectly of practical significance, only in so far as they served to retain in principle the sovereignty of the people and to constitute an energetic protest against sultanism.

But at the same time—as is not only obvious of itself, but is also distinctly stated—the other maxim also of the oldest state-law was revived by Caesar himself, and not merely for the first time by his successors; viz., that what the supreme, or rather sole, magistrate commands is unconditionally valid so long as he remains in office, and that, while legislation no doubt belongs only to the king and the burgesses in concert, the royal edict is equivalent to law at least till the demission of its author.

While the democratic king thus conceded to the community of the people at least a formal share in the sovereignty, it was by no means his intention to divide his authority with what had hitherto been the governing body, the college of senators. The senate of Caesar was to be—in a quite different way from the later senate of Augustus—nothing but a supreme council of state, which he made use of for advising with him beforehand as to laws, and for the issuing of the more important administrative ordinances through it, or at least under its name—for cases in fact occurred where decrees of senate were issued, of which none of the senators recited as present at their preparation had any cognisance. There were no materal difficulties of form in reducing the senate to its original deliberative position, which it had overstepped more *de facto* than *de jure ;* but in this case it was necessary to protect himself from practical resistance, for the Roman senate was as much the headquarters of the opposition to Caesar as the Attic Areopagus was of the opposition to Pericles. Chiefly for this reason the number of senators, which had hitherto amounted at most to six hundred in its normal condition (iii. 339) and had been greatly reduced by the recent crises, was raised by extraordinary supplement to nine hundred; and at the same time, to keep it at least up to this mark, the number of quaestors to be nominated annually, that is of members annually admitted to the senate, was raised from twenty to forty.[1] The extraordinary filling up of the senate was undertaken by the monarch alone. In the case of the ordinary additions he secured to himself a permanent influence through the circumstance, that the electoral colleges were bound by law to give their votes to the first twenty candidates for the

[1] According to the probable estimate formerly assumed (iii. 339), this would yield an average aggregate number of from 1000 to 1200 senators.

quaestorship who were provided with letters of recommendation from the monarch; besides, the crown was at liberty to confer the honorary rights attaching to the quaestorship or to any office superior to it, and consequently a seat in the senate in particular, by way of exception even on individuals not qualified. The selection of the extraordinary members who were added naturally fell in the main on adherents of the new order of things, and introduced, along with *equites* of respectable standing, various dubious and plebeian personages into the proud corporation—former senators who had been erased from the roll by the censor or in consequence of a judicial sentence, foreigners from Spain and Gaul who had to some extent to learn their Latin in the senate, men lately subaltern officers who had not previously received even the equestrian ring, sons of freedmen or of such as followed dishonourable trades, and other elements of a like kind. The exclusive circles of the nobility, to whom this change in the personal composition of the senate naturally gave the bitterest offence, saw in it an intentional depreciation of the very institution itself. Caesar was not capable of such a self-destructive policy; he was as determined not to let himself be governed by his council as he was convinced of the necessity of the institute in itself. They might more correctly have discerned in this proceeding the intention of the monarch to take away from the senate its former character of an exclusive representation of the oligarchic aristocracy, and to make it once more—what it had been in the regal period—a state-council representing all classes of persons belonging to the state through their most intelligent elements, and not necessarily excluding the man of humble birth or even the foreigner; just as those earliest kings introduced non-burgesses (i. 78, 80, 256), Caesar introduced non-Italians into his senate.

While the rule of the nobility was thus set aside and its existence undermined, and while the senate in its new form was merely a tool of the monarch, autocracy was at the same time most strictly carried out in the administration and government of the state, and the whole executive was concentrated in the hands of the monarch. First of all, the Imperator naturally decided in person every question of any moment. Caesar was able to carry personal government to an extent which we puny men can hardly conceive, and which is not to be explained solely from the unparalleled rapidity and decision of his working, but has moreover its ground in a more general cause. When we see Caesar, Sulla, Gaius Gracchus, and Roman statesmen in general displaying throughout an activity which transcends our notions of human powers of working, the reason lies, not in any change that human nature has undergone since that time, but in the change which has taken place since then in the organisation of the household. The Roman house was a machine, in which even the intellectual powers of the slaves and freedmen yielded their produce to the master; a master, who knew how to govern these, worked as it were with countless minds. It was the *beau ideal* of bureaucratic centralisation; which our counting-house system strives indeed zealously to imitate, but remains as far behind the prototype as the modern power of capital is inferior to the ancient system of slavery. Caesar knew how to profit by this advantage; wherever any post demanded special confidence, we see him filling it up on principle—so far as other considerations at all permit—with his slaves, freedmen, or clients of humble birth. His works as a whole show what an organising genius like his could accomplish with such an instrument; but to the question, how the details of these marvellous feats were achieved, we have no adequate answer. Bureaucracy resembles a manufactory also in this respect, that the work done does not appear as that of the individuals who have worked at it, but as that of the manufactory which stamps it. This much only is quite clear, that Caesar had no helper at all in his work who exerted a personal influence over it or was even so much as initiated into the whole plan; he was not only the sole master-workman, but he worked also without skilled associates, merely with common labourers.

With respect to details as a matter of course in strictly political affairs Caesar avoided, so far as was at all possible, any delegation of his functions. Where it was inevitable, as especially when during his frequent absence from Rome he had need of a higher organ there, the person destined for this purpose was, significantly enough, not the legal deputy of the monarch, the prefect of the city, but a confidant without officially recognised jurisdiction, usually Caesar's banker, the cunning and pliant Phoenician merchant Lucius Cornelius Balbus from Gades. In administration Caesar was above all careful to resume the keys of the state-chest—which the senate had appropriated to itself after the fall of the regal power, and by means of which it had possessed itself of the government—and to entrust them only to those servants who with their persons were absolutely and exclusively devoted to him. In respect of ownership indeed the private means of the monarch remained, of course, strictly separate from the property of the state; but Caesar took in hand the administration of the whole financial and monetary system of the state, and conducted it entirely in the way in which he and the Roman grandees generally were wont to manage the administration of their own means and substance. For the future the levying of the provincial revenues and in the main also the management of the coinage were entrusted to the slaves and freedmen of the Imperator, and men of the senatorial order were excluded from it—a momentous step, out of which grew in course of time the important class of procurators and the "imperial household."

Of the governorships on the other hand, which, after they had handed their financial business over to the new imperial tax-receivers, were still more than they had formerly been essentially military commands, that of Egypt alone was transferred to the monarch's own retainers. The country of the Nile, in a peculiar manner geographically isolated and politically centralised, was better fitted than any other district to break off permanently under an able leader from the central power, as the attempts which had repeatedly been made by hard-pressed Italian party-chiefs to establish themselves there during the recent crisis sufficiently proved. Probably it was simply this consideration that induced Caesar not to declare the land formally a province, but to tolerate the comparatively harmless Lagidae there; and certainly for this reason the legions stationed in Egypt were not entrusted to a man belonging to the senate or in other words to the former government, but this command was, just like the posts of tax-receivers, treated as a menial office (p. 454). In general however the consideration had weight with Caesar, that the soldiers of Rome should not, like those of Oriental kings, be commanded by lackeys. It remained the rule to entrust the more important governorships to those who had been consuls, the less important to those who had been praetors; and once more, instead of the five years' interval prescribed by the law of $\frac{702}{52}$ (p. 406), the commencement of the governorship was in the ancient fashion directly annexed to the close of the official functions in the city. On the other hand the distribution of the provinces among the qualified candidates, which had hitherto been arranged sometimes by decree of the people or senate, sometimes by concert among the magistrates or by lot, passed to the monarch. And, as the consuls were frequently induced to abdicate before the end of the year and to make room for after-elected consuls (*consules suffecti*); as, moreover, the number of praetors annually nominated was raised from eight to sixteen, and the nomination of half of them was entrusted to the Imperator in the same way as that of the half of the quaestors; and, lastly, as there was reserved to the Imperator the right of nominating, if not titular consuls, at any rate titular praetors and titular quaestors: Caesar secured a sufficient number of candidates acceptable to him for filling up the governorships. Their recall remained of course left to the discretion of the regent as well as their nomination; as a rule it was assumed that the consular governor should not remain more than two years, nor the praetorian more than one year, in the province.

Lastly, so far as concerns the administration of the city which was his capital and residence, the Imperator evidently intended for a time to entrust this also to magistrates similarly nominated by him. He revived the old city-lieutenancy of the regal period (i. 64); on different occasions he committed during his absence the administration of the capital to one or more such lieutenants nominated by him without consulting the people and for an indefinite period, who united in themselves the functions of all the administrative magistrates and possessed even the right of coining money with their own name, although of course not with their own effigy. In $\frac{707}{47}$ and in the first nine months of $\frac{709}{45}$ there were, moreover, neither praetors nor curule aediles nor quaestors; the consuls too were nominated in the former year only towards its close, and in the latter Caesar was even consul without a colleague. This looks altogether like an attempt to revive completely the old regal authority within the city of Rome, as far as the limits enjoined by the democratic past of the new monarch; in other words, of magistrates additional to the king himself, to allow only the prefect of the city during the king's absence and the tribunes and plebeian aediles appointed for protecting popular freedom to continue in existence, and to abolish the consulship, the censorship, the praetorship, the curule aedileship, and the quaestorship.[1] But Caesar subsequently departed from this; he neither accepted the royal title himself, nor did he cancel those venerable names interwoven with the glorious history of the republic. The consuls, praetors, aediles, tribunes, and quaestors retained

[1] Hence accordingly the cautious turns of expression on the mention of these magistracies in Caesar's laws; *cum censor aliusve quis magistratus Romae populi censum aget* (*L. Jul. mun.* l. 144); *praetor isve quei Romae iure deicundo praeerit* (*L. Rubr.* often); *quaestor urbanus queive aerario praeerit* (*L. Jul. mun.* l. 37 etc.).

substantially their previous formal powers; nevertheless their position was totally altered. It was the political idea lying at the foundation of the republic that the Roman empire was identified with the city of Rome, and in consistency with it the municipal magistrates of the capital were treated throughout as magistrates of the empire. In the monarchy of Caesar that view and this consequence of it fell into abeyance; the magistrates of Rome formed thenceforth only the first among the many municipalities of the empire, and the consulship in particular became a purely titular post, which preserved a certain practical importance only in virtue of the reversion of a higher governorship annexed to it. The fate, which the Roman community had been wont to prepare for the vanquished, now by means of Caesar befell itself; its sovereignty over the Roman empire was converted into a limited communal freedom within the Roman state. That at the same time the number of the praetors and quaestors was doubled has been already mentioned; the same course was followed with the plebeian aediles, to whom two new "corn-aediles" (*aediles Ceriales*) were added to superintend the supplies of the capital. The appointment to those offices remained with the community, and was subject to no restriction as respected the consuls, tribunes of the people, and plebeian aediles; we have already adverted to the fact, that the Imperator reserved a right of proposal binding on the electors as regards the half of the praetors, curule aediles, and quaestors to be annually nominated. In general the ancient and sacred palladia of popular freedom were not touched; which, of course, did not prevent the individual refractory tribune of the people from being seriously interfered with and, in fact, deposed and erased from the roll of senators.

As the Imperator was thus, for all the more general and more important questions, his own minister; as he controlled the finances by his servants, and the army by his adjutants; as the old republican state-magistracies were again converted into municipal magistracies of the city of Rome; and as in addition to all this he acquired the right of himself nominating his successor—the autocracy was sufficiently established.

In the spiritual hierarchy on the other hand Caesar, although he issued a detailed law respecting this portion of the state-economy, made no material alteration, except that he attached the supreme pontificate and the augurship to the person of the regent; and, partly in connection with this, one new stall was created in each of the three supreme colleges, and three new stalls in the fourth college of the banquet-masters. If the Roman state-hierarchy had hitherto served as a support to the ruling oligarchy, it might render precisely the same service to the new monarchy. The conservative religious policy of the senate was transferred to the new kings of Rome; when the strictly conservative Varro published about this time his "Antiquities of Divine Things," the great fundamental repository of Roman state-theology, he could dedicate it to the *Pontifex Maximus* Caesar. The faint lustre which the worship of Jovis was still able to impart shone round the newly established throne; and the old national faith became in its last stages the instrument of a Caesarian papacy, which, however, was from the outset but hollow and feeble.

In judicial matters, first of all, the old regal jurisdiction was re-established. As the king had originally been judge in criminal and civil causes, without being legally bound in the former to respect an appeal to the prerogative of mercy in the people, or in the latter to commit the decision of the question in dispute to jurymen; so Caesar claimed the right of bringing capital causes as well as private processes for sole and final decision to his own bar, and disposing of them in the event of his presence personally, in the event of his absence by the city-lieutenant. In fact we find him, quite after the manner of the ancient kings, now sitting in judgment publicly in the Forum of the capital on Roman burgesses accused of high treason, now holding a judicial inquiry in his house regarding the client princes accused of the like crime; so that the only privilege, which the Roman burgesses had as compared with the other subjects of the king, seems to have consisted in the publicity of the judicial procedure. But this resuscitated supreme jurisdiction of the kings, although Caesar discharged its duties with impartiality and care, could only from the nature of the case find practical application in exceptional cases.

For the usual procedure in criminal and civil causes the former republican mode of administering justice was substantially retained. Criminal causes were still disposed of as formerly before the different jury-commissions entitled to deal with the several crimes, civil causes partly before the court of inheritance or, as it was commonly called, of the *centumviri*, partly before the single *judices*; the superintendence of judicial proceedings was as formerly conducted in the capital chiefly by the praetors, in the provinces by the governors. Political crimes too continued even under the monarchy to be referred to a jury-commission; the new ordinance, which Caesar issued respecting them, specified the acts legally punishable with precision and in a liberal spirit which excluded all prosecution of opinions, and it fixed as the penalty not death, but banishment. As respects the selection of the jurymen, whom the senatorial party desired to see chosen exclusively from the senate and the strict Gracchans exclusively from the equestrian order, Caesar, faithful to the principle of reconciling the parties, left the matter on the footing of the compromise-law of Cotta (p. 90), but with the modification—for which the way was probably prepared by the law of Pompeius of $\frac{699}{55}$ (p. 298)—that the *tribuni aerarii* who came from the lower ranks of the people were set aside; so that there was established a rating for jurymen of at least 400,000 sesterces (£4000), and senators and equites now divided the functions of jurymen which had so long been an apple of discord between them.

The relations of the regal and the republican jurisdiction were on the whole co-ordinate, so that any cause might be initiated as well before the king's bar as before the competent republican tribunal, the latter of course in the event of collision giving way; if on the other hand the one or the other tribunal had pronounced sentence, the cause was thereby finally disposed of. But in another way the new king acquired the power of revising under certain circumstances a judicial sentence. The tribune of the people might interfere so as to cancel—like any other official act—the sentence pronounced by jurymen under the direction of a magistrate; unless where special exceptional laws excluded the tribunician intercession—which was the case with the jury-courts of the *centumviri* and of the different criminal commissions instituted by recent laws. With the exception of these sentences, accordingly, the Imperator might by virtue of his tribunician power annul any judgment of jurymen, and particularly any decision in the ordinary private process before civil jurymen, and might then by virtue of his supreme judicial prerogative order the cause to be discussed anew before himself. Thus Caesar established,[1] by the side of his regal tribunal of first and sole jurisdiction which was co-ordinate with the former ordinary tribunals, a regal appellate jurisdiction; and thereby originated the legal form of appeal to

[1] These rules certainly cannot be fully proved to have existed anterior to Augustus; but, as all the elements of this remarkable judicial reform are implied in the powers of the Imperator as arranged by Caesar, we may be allowed to refer their origin to him.

a court of higher resort, which was thoroughly foreign to the earlier procedure, and which was to be so important for the succeeding, and even for modern, times.

Certainly these innovations, the most important of which—the introduction of the principle of appeal—cannot even be reckoned absolutely an improvement, by no means healed thoroughly the evils from which the Roman administration of justice was suffering. Criminal procedure cannot be sound in any slave state, inasmuch as the task of proceeding against slaves lies, if not *de jure*, at least *de facto* in the hands of the master. The Roman master, as may readily be conceived, punished throughout the crime of his serf, not as a crime, but only so far as it rendered the slave useless or disagreeable to him; slave criminals were merely drafted off somewhat like oxen addicted to goring, and, as the latter were sold to the butcher, so were the former sold to the fighting-booth. But even the criminal procedure against free men, which had been from the outset and always in great part continued to be a political process, had amidst the disorder of the last generations become transformed from a grave lawsuit into a faction-fight to be fought out by means of favour, money, and violence. The blame rested jointly on all that took part in it, on the magistrates, the jury, the parties, even the public who were spectators; but the most incurable wounds were inflicted on justice by the doings of the advocates. In proportion as the parasitic plant of Roman forensic eloquence flourished, all positive ideas of right became broken up; and the distinction, so difficult of apprehension by the public, between opinion and evidence was in reality expelled from the Roman criminal practice. "A plain simple defendant," says a Roman advocate of much experience at this period, "may be accused of any crime at pleasure which he has or has not committed, and will be certainly condemned." Numerous pleadings in criminal causes have been preserved to us from this epoch; there is hardly one of them which makes even a serious attempt to fix the crime in question and to put into proper shape the proof or counterproof.[1] That the contemporary civil procedure was likewise in various

[1] *Plura enim multo*, says Cicero in his treatise *De Oratore* (ii. 42, 178), primarily with reference to criminal trials, *homines indicant odio aut amore aut cupiditate aut iracundia aut dolore aut laetitia aut spe aut timore aut errore aut aliqua permotione mentis, quam veritate aut praescripto aut iuris norma aliqua aut iudicii formula aut legibus.* On this accordingly are founded the further instructions which he gives for advocates entering on their profession.

respects unsound we need scarcely mention; it too suffered from the effects of the party politics mixed up with all things, as for instance in the process of Publius Quinctius ($\frac{671-673}{83-81}$), where the most contradictory decisions were given according as Cinna or Sulla had the ascendancy in Rome; and the advocates, frequently non-jurists, produced here also intentionally and unintentionally abundance of confusion. But it was implied in the nature of the case, that party mixed itself up with such matters only by way of exception, and that here the quibbles of advocates could not so rapidly or so deeply break up the ideas of right; accordingly the civil pleadings which we possess from this epoch, while not according to our stricter ideas effective compositions for their purpose, are yet of a far less libellous and far more juristic character than the contemporary speeches in criminal causes. If Caesar permitted the curb imposed on the eloquence of advocates by Pompeius (p. 305) to remain, or even rendered it more severe, there was at least nothing lost by this; and much was gained, when better selected and better superintended magistrates and jurymen were nominated and the palpable corruption and intimidation of the courts came to an end. But the sacred sense of right and the reverence for the law, which it is difficult to destroy in the minds of the multitude, it is still more difficult to reproduce. Though the legislator did away with various abuses, he could not heal the root of the evil; and it might be doubted whether time, which cures everything curable, would in this case bring relief.

The Roman military system of this period was nearly in the same condition as the Carthaginian at the time of Hannibal. The governing classes furnished only the officers; the subjects, plebeians and provincials, formed the army. The general was, financially and militarily, almost independent of the central government, and, whether in fortune or misfortune, substantially left to himself and to the resources of his province. Civic and even national spirit had vanished from the army, and the *esprit de corps* was alone left as a bond of inward union. The army had ceased to be an instrument of the commonwealth; in a political point of view it had no will of its own, but it was doubtless able to adopt that of the master who wielded it; in a military point of view it sank under the ordinary miserable leaders into a disorganised useless rabble, but under a right general it attained a military perfection which the burgess army could never reach. The class of officers especially had deeply degenerated. The higher ranks, senators and equites, grew more and more unused to arms. While formerly there had been a zealous competition for the posts of staff officers, now every man of equestrian rank, who chose to serve, was sure of a military tribuneship, and several of these posts had even to be filled with men of humbler rank; and any man of quality at all who still served sought at least to finish his term of service in Sicily or some other province where he was sure not to face the enemy. Officers of ordinary bravery and efficiency were stared at as prodigies; as to Pompeius especially, his contemporaries practised a military idolatry which in every respect compromised them. The staff, as a rule, gave the signal for desertion and for mutiny; in spite of the culpable indulgence of the commanders proposals for the cashiering of officers of rank were daily occurrences. We still possess the picture—drawn not without irony by Caesar's own hand—of the state of matters at his head-quarters when orders were given to march against Ariovistus, of the cursing and weeping, and preparing of testaments, and presenting even of requests for furlough. In the soldiery not a trace of the better classes could any longer be discovered. In law the general obligation to bear arms still subsisted; but the levy took place in the most irregular and unfair manner; numerous persons liable to serve were wholly passed over, while those once levied were retained thirty years and longer beneath the eagles. The Roman burgess-cavalry now merely vegetated as a sort of mounted noble guard, whose perfumed cavaliers and exquisite high-bred horses only played a part in the festivals of the capital; the so-called burgess-infantry was a troop of mercenaries swept together from the lowest ranks of the burgess-population; the subjects furnished the cavalry and the light troops exclusively, and came to be more and more extensively employed also in the infantry. The posts of centurions in the legions, on which in the mode of warfare of that time the efficiency of the divisions essentially depended, and to which according to the national military constitution the soldier served his way upward with the pike, were now not merely regularly conferred according to favour, but were not unfrequently sold to the highest bidder. In consequence of the bad financial management of the government and the venality and fraud of the great majority of the magistrates, the payment of the soldiers was extremely defective and irregular.

The necessary consequence of this was, that in the ordinary course of things the Roman armies pillaged the provincials, mutinied against their officers, and ran off in presence of the enemy; instances occurred where considerable armies, such as the Macedonian army of Piso in $\frac{697}{57}$ (p. 272), were without any proper defeat utterly ruined, simply by this misconduct. Capable leaders on the other hand, such as Pompeius, Caesar, Gabinius, formed doubtless out of the existing materials able and efficient, and to some extent exemplary, armies; but these armies belonged far more to their general than to the commonwealth. The still more complete decay of the Roman marine—which, moreover, had remained an object of antipathy to the Romans and had never been fully nationalised—scarcely requires to be mentioned. Here too, in all directions, everything that could be ruined had been reduced to ruin under the oligarchic government.

The reorganisation of the Roman military system by Caesar was substantially limited to the tightening and strengthening of the reins of discipline, which had been relaxed under the negligent and incapable supervision previously subsisting. The Roman military system seemed to him neither to need, nor to be capable of, radical reform; he accepted the elements of the army, just as Hannibal had accepted them. The enactment of his municipal ordinance that, in order to the holding of a municipal magistracy or sitting in the municipal council before the thirtieth year, three years' service on horseback—that is, as officer—or six years' service on foot should be required, proves indeed that he wished to attract the better classes to the army; but it proves with equal clearness that amidst the ever-increasing prevalence of an unwarlike spirit in the nation he himself held it no longer possible to associate the holding of an honorary office with the fulfilment of the time of service unconditionally as hitherto. This very circumstance serves to explain why Caesar made no attempt to re-establish the Roman burgess-cavalry. The levy was better arranged, the time of service was regulated and abridged; otherwise matters remained on the footing that the infantry of the line were raised chiefly from the lower orders of the Roman burgesses, the cavalry and the light infantry from the other subjects. That nothing was done for the reorganisation of the fleet, is surprising.

It was an innovation—hazardous beyond doubt even in the view of its author—to which the untrustworthy character of the cavalry furnished by the subjects compelled him (p. 252), that Caesar for the first time deviated from the old Roman system of never fighting with mercenaries, and incorporated in the cavalry hired foreigners, especially Germans. Another innovation was the appointment of adjutants of the legion with praetorian powers (*legati legionis pro praetore*). Hitherto the military tribunes, nominated partly by the burgesses, partly by the governor concerned, had led the legions in such a way that six of them were placed over each legion, and the command alternated among these; a single commandant of the legion was appointed by the general only as a temporary and extraordinary measure. In subsequent times on the other hand those colonels or adjutants of legions appear as a permanent and organic institution, and as nominated no longer by the governor whom they obey, but by the supreme command in Rome; both changes seem referable to Caesar's arrangements connected with the Gabinian law (p. 98). The reason for the introduction of this important intervening step in the military hierarchy must be sought partly in the necessity for a more energetic centralisation of the command, partly in the felt want of able superior officers, partly and chiefly in the design of providing a counterpoise to the governor by associating with him one or more colonels nominated by the Imperator.

The most essential change in the military system consisted in the institution of a permanent military head in the person of the Imperator, who, superseding the previous unmilitary and in every respect incapable governing corporation, united in his hands the whole control of the army, and thus converted it from a direction which for the most part was merely nominal into a real and energetic supreme command. We are not properly informed as to the position which this supreme command occupied towards the special commands hitherto omnipotent in their respective spheres. Probably the analogy of the relation subsisting between the praetor and the consul or the consul and the dictator served generally as a basis, so that, while the governor in his own right retained the supreme military authority in his province, the Imperator was entitled at any moment to take it away from him and assume it for himself or his delegates, and, while the authority of the governor was confined to the province, that of the Imperator, like the regal and the earlier consular authority, extended over the whole empire. Moreover it is extremely probable that now the nomination of the officers, both the military tribunes and the centurions, so far as it had hitherto belonged to the governor,[1] as well as the nomination of the new adjutants of the legion, passed directly into the hands of the Imperator; and in like

[1] With the nomination of a part of the military tribunes by the burgesses (ii. 303) Caesar—in this also a democrat—did not meddle.

manner even now the arrangement of the levies, the bestowal of leave of absence, and the more important criminal cases, may have been submitted to the judgment of the commander-in-chief. With this limitation of the powers of the governors and with the regulated control of the Imperator, there was no great room to apprehend in future either that the armies might be utterly disorganised or that they might be converted into retainers personally devoted to their respective officers.

But, however decidedly and urgently the circumstances pointed to military monarchy, and however distinctly Caesar took the supreme command exclusively for himself, he was nevertheless not at all inclined to establish his authority by means of, and on, the army. No doubt he deemed a standing army necessary for his state, but only because from its geographical position it required a comprehensive regulation of the frontiers and permanent frontier garrisons. Partly at earlier periods, partly during the recent civil war, he had worked at the tranquillising of Spain, and had established strong positions for the defence of the frontier in Africa along the great desert, and in the north-west of the empire along the line of the Rhine. He occupied himself with similar plans for the countries on the Euphrates and on the Danube. Above all he designed an expedition against the Parthians, to avenge the day of Carrhae; he had destined three years for this war, and was resolved to settle accounts with these dangerous enemies once for all and not less cautiously than thoroughly. In like manner he had projected the scheme of attacking Boerebistas king of the Getae, who was greatly extending his power on both sides of the Danube (p. 273), and of protecting Italy in the north-east by border-districts similar to those which he had created for it in Gaul. On the other hand there is no evidence at all that Caesar contemplated like Alexander an indefinite career of victory; it is said indeed that he had intended to march from Partia to the Caspian and from this to the Black Sea and then along its northern shores to the Danube, to annex to the empire all Scythia and Germany as far as the Northern Ocean—which according to the notions of that time was not so very distant from the Mediterranean—and to return home through Gaul; but no authority at all deserving of credit vouches for the existence of these fabulous projects. In the case of a state which, like the Roman state of Caesar, already included a mass of barbaric elements difficult to be controlled, and had still for centuries to come more than enough to do with their assimilation, such conquests, even granting their military practicability, would have been simply blunders far more brilliant and far worse than the Indian expedition of Alexander. Judging both from Caesar's conduct in Britain and Germany and from the conduct of those who became the heirs of his political ideas, it is in a high degree probable that Caesar with Scipio Aemilianus called on the gods not to increase the empire, but to preserve it, and that his schemes of conquest were confined to a settlement of the frontier—measured, it is true, by his own great scale—which should secure the line of the Euphrates and, instead of the very variable and militarily useless boundary of the empire on the north-east, should establish and render defensible the line of the Danube.

But, if it remains a mere probability that Caesar ought not to be designated a world-conqueror in the same sense as Alexander and Napoleon, it is quite certain that his design was not to rest his new monarchy primarily on the support of the army nor generally to place the military authority above the civil, but to incorporate it with, and as far as possible subordinate it to, the civil commonwealth. The invaluable pillars of a military state, those old and far-famed Gallic legions, were honourably dissolved just on account of the incompatibility of their *esprit de corps* with a civil commonwealth, and their glorious names were only perpetuated in newly-founded civic communities. The soldiers presented by Caesar with allotments of land on their discharge were not, like those of Sulla, settled together—as it were militarily—in colonies of their own, but, especially when they settled in Italy, were isolated as much as possible and scattered throughout the peninsula; except in the case of the portions of the Campanian land that remained at his disposal, where an aggregation of the old soldiers of Caesar could not be avoided. Caesar sought to solve the difficult task of keeping the soldiers of a standing army within the sphere of civil life, partly by retaining the former arrangement which prescribed merely certain years of service, and not a service strictly constant, that is, uninterrupted by any dismissal; partly by the already mentioned shortening of the term of service, which occasioned a speedier change in the personal composition of the army; partly by the regular settlement of the soldiers who had served out their time as agricultural colonists; partly and principally by keeping the army aloof from Italy and generally from the proper seats of the civil and political life of the nation, and directing the soldier to the points, where according to the opinion of the great king he was alone in his place—to the frontier stations, that he might ward off the extraneous foe.

The true criterion also of the military state—the development of, and the privileged position assigned to, the corps of guards—is not to be met with in the case of Caesar. Although as respects the army on active service the institution of a special body-guard for the general had been already long in existence (iii. 190), in Caesar's system it fell completely into the background; his praetorian cohort seems to have essentially consisted merely of orderly officers or non-military attendants, and never to have been a proper select corps, consequently never an object of jealousy to the troops of the line. While Caesar thus as general practically dropped the body-guard, he still less as king tolerated a guard round his person. Although constantly beset by lurking assassins and well aware of it, he yet rejected the proposal of the senate to institute a select guard; dismissed, as soon as things grew in some measure quiet, the Spanish escort which he had made use of at first in the capital, and contented himself with the retinue of lictors sanctioned by traditional usage for the Roman supreme magistrates.

However much of the ideal of his party and of his youth—the founding of a Periclean government in Rome not by virtue of the sword, but by virtue of the confidence of the nation—Caesar had been obliged to abandon in the struggle with realities, he retained even now the fundamental idea of founding no military monarchy with an energy to which history scarcely supplies a parallel. Certainly this too was an impracticable ideal—it was the sole illusion, in regard to which the earnest longing of that vigorous mind was more powerful than its clear judgment. A government, such as Caesar had in view, was not merely of necessity very much based on his personal influence, and so liable to perish with the death of its author just as the kindred creations of Pericles and Cromwell with the death of their founders; but, amidst the deeply disorganised state of the nation, it was not at all credible that the eighth king of Rome would succeed even for his lifetime in ruling, as his seven predecessors had ruled, his fellow-burgesses merely by virtue of law and justice, and as little probable that he would succeed in incorporating the standing army—after it had during the last civil war learned its power and unlearned its reverence—once more as a duly subordinate element in civil society. To any one who calmly considered to what extent reverence for the law had disappeared from the lowest as from the highest ranks of society, the former hope must have seemed almost a dream; and, if with the Marian reform of the military system the soldier generally had ceased to be a citizen (iii. 191), the Campanian mutiny and the battle-field of Thapsus showed with fatal clearness the nature of the support which the army now lent to the law. Even the great democrat could only with difficulty and imperfectly hold in check the powers which he had unchained; thousands of swords still flew at his signal from the scabbard, but they no longer returned to the scabbard at his signal. Fate is mightier than genius. Caesar desired to become the restorer of the civil commonwealth, and became the founder of the military monarchy which he abhorred; he overthrew the *régime* of aristocrats and bankers in the state, only to put a military *régime* in their place, and the commonwealth continued as before to be tyrannised and turned to profit by a privileged minority. And yet it is a privilege of the highest natures thus creatively to err. The brilliant attempts of great men to realise the ideal, though they do not reach their aim, form the best treasure of nations. It was owing to the work of Caesar that the Roman military state did not become a police-state till after the lapse of several centuries, and that the Roman Imperators, however little they otherwise resembled the great founder of their sovereignty, yet employed the soldier in the main not against the citizen but against the public foe, and esteemed both nation and army too highly to place the latter as constable over the former.

The regulation of financial matters occasioned comparatively little difficulty in consequence of the solid foundations which the immense magnitude of the empire and the exclusion of the system of credit supplied. If the state had hitherto found itself in perpetual financial embarrassment, the fault was far from chargeable on the inadequacy of the state revenues; on the contrary these had of late years immensely increased. To the earlier aggregate income, which is estimated at 200,000,000 sesterces (in round numbers £2,000,000) there were added 85,000,000 sesterces (£850,000) by the erection of the provinces of Bithynia-Pontus and Syria; which increase, along with the other newly opened up or augmented sources of income, especially from the constantly increasing produce of the taxes on luxuries, far outweighed the loss of the Campanian rents. Besides, immense sums had been brought from extraordinary sources into the exchequer through Lucullus, Metellus, Pompeius, Cato, and others. The cause of the financial embarrassments rather lay partly in the increase of the ordinary and extraordinary expenditure, partly in the disorder of management. Under the former head, the distribution of corn to the multitude of the capital claimed exorbitant sums; through the extension given to it by Cato in $\frac{691}{63}$ (p. 174) the yearly expenditure for that purpose amounted to 30,000,000 sesterces (£300,000) and after the abolition in $\frac{696}{58}$ of the compensation hitherto paid, it swallowed up even a fifth of the state revenues. The military budget also had risen, since the garrisons of Cilicia, Syria, and Gaul had been added to those of Spain, Macedonia, and the other provinces. Among the extraordinary items of expenditure must be named in the first place the great cost of fitting out fleets, on which, for example, five years after the great razzia of $\frac{687}{67}$, 34,000,000 sesterces (£340,000) were expended at once. Add to this the very considerable sums which were consumed in wars and warlike preparations; such as 18,000,000 sesterces (£180,000) paid at once to Piso merely for the outfit of the Macedonian army, 24,000,000 sesterces (£240,000) even annually to Pompeius for the maintenance and pay of the Spanish army, and similar sums to Caesar for the Gallic legions. But considerable as were these demands made on the Roman exchequer it would still have been able probably to meet them, had not its administration once so exemplary been affected by the universal laxity and dishonesty of this age; the payments of the treasury were often suspended merely because of the neglect to call up its outstanding claims. The magistrates placed over it, two of the quaestors—young men annually changed—contented themselves at the best with inaction; among the official staff of clerks and others, formerly so justly held in high esteem for its integrity, the worst abuses now prevailed, more especially since such posts had come to be bought and sold.

As soon however as the threads of Roman state-finance were concentrated no longer as hitherto in the senate, but in the cabinet of Caesar, new life, stricter order, and more compact connection at once pervaded all the wheels and springs of that great machine. The two institutions, which originated with Gaius Gracchus and ate like a gangrene into the Roman financial system—the leasing of the direct taxes, and the distributions of grain—were partly abolished, partly remodelled. Caesar wished not like his predecessor to hold the nobility in check by the banker-aristocracy and the populace of the capital, but to set them aside and to deliver the commonwealth from all parasites whether high or low; and therefore he went in these two important questions not with Gaius Gracchus, but with the oligarch Sulla. The leasing system was allowed to continue for the indirect taxes, in the case of which it was very old and —under the maxim of Roman financial administration, which was retained inviolable also by Caesar, that the levying of the taxes should at any cost be kept simple and readily manageable —absolutely could not be dispensed with. But the direct taxes were thenceforth universally either treated, like the African and Sardinian deliveries of corn and oil, as contributions in kind to be directly supplied to the state, or converted, like the revenues of Asia Minor, into fixed money payments, in which case the collection of the several sums payable was entrusted to the tax-districts themselves.

The corn distributions in the capital had hitherto been looked on as a profitable prerogative of the community which ruled and, because it ruled, had to be fed by its subjects. This infamous principle was set aside by Caesar; but it could not be overlooked that a multitude of wholly destitute burgesses had been protected solely by these largesses of food from starvation. In this aspect Caesar retained them. While according to the Sempronian ordinance renewed by Cato every Roman burgess settled in Rome had possessed a legal claim to bread-corn without payment, this list of recipients, which had at last risen to the number of 320,000, was reduced by the exclusion of all individuals having means or otherwise provided for to 150,000, and this number was fixed once for all as the maximum number of recipients of free corn; at the same time an annual revision of the list was ordered, so that the places vacated by removal or death might be filled up with the most needful among the applicants. By this conversion of the political privilege into a provision for the poor, a principle remarkable in a moral as well as in a historical point of view came for the first time into living operation. Civil society but slowly and gradually attains to a perception of the interdependence of interests; in earlier antiquity the state doubtless protected its members from the public enemy and the murderer, but it was not bound to protect the totally helpless fellow-citizen from the worse enemy, want, by affording the needful means of subsistence. It was the Attic civilisation which first developed, in the Solonian and subsequent legislation, the principle that it is the duty of the community to provide for its invalids and for the poor generally; and it was Caesar that first developed what in the restricted compass of Attic life had remained a municipal matter into an organic institution of state, and transformed an arrangement which was a burden and a disgrace to the commonwealth into the first of those institutions—in modern times equally numerous and beneficial—where the infinite depth of human compassion contends with the infinite depth of human misery.

In addition to these fundamental reforms a thorough revision of the income and expenditure took place. The ordinary items of income were everywhere regulated and fixed. Exemption from taxation was conferred on not a few communities and even on whole districts, whether indirectly by the bestowal of the Roman or Latin franchise, or directly by special privilege; it was obtained, *e.g.* by all the Sicilian communities [1] in the former, by the town of Ilion in the latter way. Still greater was the number of those whose proportion of tribute was lowered; the communities in Further Spain, for instance, already after Caesar's governorship had on his suggestion a reduction of tribute granted to them by the senate, and now the deeply oppressed province of Asia had not only the levying of its direct taxes facilitated, but also a third of them wholly remitted. The newly added taxes, such as those of the communities subdued in Illyria and above all of the Gallic communities—which latter together paid annually 40,000,000 sesterces (£400,000)—were fixed throughout on a low scale. It is true on the other hand that various towns such as Little Leptis in Africa, Sulci in Sardinia, and several Spanish communities, had their tribute raised by way of penalty for their conduct during the last war. The very lucrative Italian harbour-tolls abolished in the recent times of anarchy (p. 184) were re-established all the more readily that this tax fell essentially on luxuries imported from the East. To these new or revived sources of ordinary income were added the sums which accrued by extraordinary means, especially in consequence of the civil war, to the victor—the booty collected in Gaul; the stock of cash in the capital; the treasures taken from the Italian and Spanish temples; the sums raised in the shape of forced loan, compulsory present, or fine, from the dependent communities and dynasts, and the pecuniary penalties imposed in a similar way by judicial sentence, or simply by

[1] This follows from the very fact that Sicily obtained Latin rights; but Varro also directly attests the discontinuance of the Sicilian *decumae* in a treatise published after Cicero's death (*De R. R. 2 praef.*) where he names—as the corn-provinces whence Rome derives her subsistence—only Africa and Sardinia, no longer Sicily.

sending an order to pay, on individual wealthy Romans; and above all things the proceeds from the estates of his defeated opponents. How productive these sources of income were, we may learn from the fact, that the fine of the African capitalists who sat in the opposition-senate alone amounted to 100,000,000 sesterces (£1,000,000) and the price paid by the purchasers of the property of Pompeius to 70,000,000 sesterces (£700,000). This course was necessary, because the power of the beaten nobility rested in great measure on their colossal wealth and could only be effectually broken by imposing on them the defrayment of the costs of the war. But the odium of the confiscations was in some measure mitigated by the fact that Caesar directed their proceeds solely to the benefit of the state, and, instead of overlooking after the manner of Sulla any act of fraud in his favourites, exacted the purchase-money with rigour even from his most faithful adherents such as Marcus Antonius.

In the expenditure a diminution was in the first place obtained by the considerable restriction of the largesses of grain. The distribution of corn to the poor of the capital which was retained, as well as the kindred supply of oil for the Roman baths newly introduced by Caesar, were at least in great part charged once for all on the contributions in kind from Sardinia and especially from Africa, and were thereby wholly or for the most part kept separate from the exchequer. On the other hand the regular expenditure for the military system was increased partly by the augmentation of the standing army, partly by the raising of the pay of the legionary from 480 sesterces (£5) to 900 (£9) annually. Both steps were in fact indispensable. There was a total want of any real defence for the frontiers, and an indispensable preliminary to it was a considerable increase of the army; and the doubling of the pay, although employed doubtless by Caesar to attach his soldiers to him (p. 344), was not introduced as a permanent alteration on that account. The former pay of $1\frac{1}{3}$ sesterces ($3\frac{1}{4}$*d.*) per day had been fixed in very ancient times, when money had an altogether different value from that which it had in the Rome of Caesar's day; it could only have been retained down to a period when the common day-labourer in the capital earned by the labour of his hands daily on an average 3 sesterces ($7\frac{1}{2}$*d.*), because in those times the soldier entered the army not for the sake of the pay, but chiefly for the sake of the—in great measure illicit—perquisites of military service. The first condition in order to a serious reform in the military system, and to the getting rid of those irregular gains of the soldier which formed a burden mostly on the provincials, was an increase suitable to the times in the regular pay; and the fixing of it at 2½ sesterces (6½*d.*) may be regarded as equitable, while the great burden thereby imposed on the treasury was a necessary, and in its consequences a very beneficial step.

Of the amount of the extraordinary expenses which Caesar had to undertake or voluntarily undertook, it is difficult to form any conception. The wars themselves consumed enormous sums; and sums perhaps not less were required to fulfil the promises which Caesar had been obliged to make during the civil war. It was a bad example and one unhappily not lost sight of in the sequel, that every common soldier received for his participation in the civil war 20,000 sesterces (£200), every burgess of the multitude in the capital for his non-participation in it 300 sesterces (£3) as an addition to his aliment; but Caesar, after having once under the pressure of circumstances pledged his word, was too much of a king to abate from it. Besides, Caesar answered innumerable demands of honourable liberality, and put into circulation immense sums for building more especially, which had been shamefully neglected during the financial distress of the last times of the republic—the cost of his buildings executed partly during the Gallic campaigns, partly afterwards, in the capital was reckoned at 160,000,000 (£1,600,000). The general result of the financial administration of Caesar is expressed in the fact that, while by sagacious and energetic reforms and by a right combination of economy and liberality he amply and fully met all equitable claims, nevertheless in March $\frac{710}{44}$ there lay in the public treasury 700,000,000, and in his own 100,000,000 sesterces (together £8,000,000)—a sum which exceeded by tenfold the amount of cash in the treasury in the most flourishing times of the republic (ii. 311).

But the task of breaking up the old parties and furnishing the new commonwealth with an appropriate constitution, an efficient army, and well-ordered finances, difficult as it was, was not the most difficult part of Caesar's work. If the Italian nation was really to be regenerated, it required a reorganisation which should transform all parts of the great empire—Rome, Italy, and the provinces—to the very foundation. Let us endeavour here also to delineate the old state of things, as well as the beginnings of a new and more tolerable time.

The good stock of the Latin nation had long since wholly disappeared from Rome. It is implied in the very nature of the case, that a capital loses its municipal and even its national stamp more quickly than any subordinate community. There the upper classes speedily withdraw from urban public life, in order to find their home rather in the state as a whole than in a single city; there are inevitably concentrated the foreign settlers, the fluctuating population of travellers on pleasure or business, the mass of the indolent, lazy, criminal, financially and morally bankrupt, and for that very reason cosmopolitan, rabble. All this pre-eminently applied to Rome. The opulent Roman frequently regarded his house in town merely as a lodging. When the urban municipal offices were converted into imperial magistracies; when the urban *comitia* became the assembly of burgesses of the empire; and when smaller self-governing tribal or other associations were not tolerated within the capital: all proper communal life ceased for Rome. From the whole compass of the widespread empire people flocked to Rome, for speculation, for debauchery, for intrigue, for accomplishment in crime, or even for the purpose of hiding there from the eye of the law.

These evils arose in some measure necessarily from the very nature of a capital; others more accidental and perhaps still more grave were associated with them. There has never perhaps existed a great city so thoroughly destitute of the means of support as Rome; importation on the one hand, and domestic manufacture by slaves on the other, rendered any free industry from the outset impossible there. The injurious consequences of the radical evil pervading the polities of antiquity in general —the slave-system—were more conspicuous in the capital than anywhere else. Nowhere were such masses of slaves accumulated as in the city palaces of the great families or of wealthy upstarts. Nowhere were the nations of the three continents mingled as in the slave population of the capital—Syrians, Phrygians and other half-Hellenes with Libyans and Moors, Getae and Iberians with the daily-increasing influx of Celts and Germans. The demoralisation inseparable from the absence of freedom, and the terrible inconsistency between formal and moral right, were far more glaringly apparent in the case of the half or wholly cultivated—as it were genteel—city-slave than in that of the rural serf who tilled the field in chains like the fettered ox. Still worse than the masses of slaves were those who had been *de jure* or simply *de facto* released from slavery— a mixture of mendicant rabble, and extremely rich parvenus, no longer slaves and not yet fully burgesses, economically and even legally dependent on their master and yet with the pretensions of free men; these freedmen were peculiarly attracted towards the capital, where gain of various sorts was to be had and the retail traffic as well as the minor handicrafts were almost wholly in their hands. Their influence on the elections is expressly attested; and that they took a leading part in the street riots, is very evident from the ordinary signal by means of which these were as it were proclaimed by the demagogues—the closing of the shops and places of sale.

Moreover, the government not only did nothing to counteract this corruption of the population of the capital, but even encouraged it for the benefit of their selfish policy. The judicious rule of law, which prohibited persons condemned for a capital offence from dwelling in the capital, was not carried into effect by the negligent police. The police-supervision of the association and clubs of the rabble, so urgently required, was at first neglected, and afterwards (p. 278) even declared punishable as a restriction inconsistent with the freedom of the people. The popular festivals had been allowed so to increase that the seven ordinary ones alone—the Roman, the Plebeian, those of the Mother of the Gods, of Ceres, of Apollo, of Flora (ii. 386) and of Victoria—lasted altogether sixty-two days; and to these were added the gladiatorial games and numerous other extraordinary amusements. The duty of providing grain at low prices—which was unavoidably necessary with such a proletariate living wholly from hand to mouth—was treated with the most unscrupulous frivolity, and the fluctuations in the price of bread-corn were of a fabulous and incalculable description.[1] Lastly, the distributions of grain formed an official invitation to the whole burgess-proletariate who were destitute of food and indisposed for work to take up their abode in the capital.

The seed sown was bad, and the harvest corresponded. The system of clubs and bands in the sphere of politics, the worship of Isis and similar pious extravagances in that of religion, had their root in this state of things. People were constantly in prospect of a dearth, and not unfrequently in utter famine. Nowhere was a man less secure of his life than in the capital; murder professionally prosecuted by banditti was the single trade peculiar to it; the alluring of the victim to Rome was the

[1] In Sicily, the country of production, the *modius* was sold within a few years at two and at twenty sesterces; from this we may guess what must have been the fluctuations of price in Rome, which subsisted on transmarine corn and was the seat of speculators.

preliminary to his assassination; no one ventured into the country in the vicinity of the capital without an armed retinue. Its outward condition corresponded to this inward disorganisation, and seemed a keen satire on the aristocratic government. Nothing was done for the regulation of the stream of the Tiber; excepting that they caused the only bridge, with which they still made shift (iii. 381), to be constructed of stone at least as far as the Tiber-island. As little was anything done toward the levelling of the city on the seven hills, except where perhaps the accumulation of rubbish had effected some improvement. The streets ascended and descended narrow and angular, and were wretchedly kept; the footpaths were small and ill paved. The ordinary houses were built of bricks negligently and to a giddy height, mostly by speculative builders on account of the small proprietors; by which means the former became prodigiously rich, and the latter were reduced to beggary. Like isolated islands amidst this sea of wretched buildings were seen the splendid palaces of the rich, which curtailed the space for the smaller houses just as their owners curtailed the burgess-rights of smaller men in the state, and beside whose marble pillars and Greek statues the decaying temples, with their images of the gods still in great part carved of wood, made a melancholy figure. A police-supervision of streets, of river-banks, of fires, or of building was almost unheard of; if the government troubled itself at all about the inundations, conflagrations, and falls of houses which were of yearly occurrence, it was only to ask from the state-theologians their report and advice regarding the true import of such signs and wonders. If we try to conceive to ourselves a London with the slave-population of New Orleans, with the police of Constantinople, with the non-industrial character of the modern Rome, and agitated by politics after the fashion of the Paris in 1848, we shall acquire an approximate idea of the republican glory, the departure of which Cicero and his associates in their sulky letters deplore.

Caesar did not deplore, but he sought to help so far as help was possible. Rome remained, of course, what it was—a cosmopolitan city. Not only would the attempt to give to it once more a specially Italian character have been impracticable; it would not have suited Caesar's plan. Just as Alexander found for his Graeco-Oriental empire an appropriate capital in the Hellenic, Jewish, Egyptian, and above all cosmopolitan Alexandria, so the capital of the new Romano-Hellenic universal empire, situated at the meeting-point of the East and the West, was to be not an Italian community, but the denationalised capital of many nations. For this reason Caesar tolerated the worship of the newly-settled Egyptian gods alongside of Father Jovis, and granted even to the Jews the free exercise of their strangely foreign ritual in the very capital of the empire. However offensive was the motley mixture of the parasitic—especially the Helleno-Oriental—population in Rome, he nowhere opposed its extension; it is significant, that at his popular festivals for the capital he caused dramas to be performed not merely in Latin and Greek, but also in other languages, probably in Phoenician, Hebrew, Syrian, or Spanish.

But, while Caesar accepted with the full consciousness of what he was doing the fundamental character of the capital as he found it, he yet worked energetically at the improvement of the lamentable and disgraceful state of things prevailing there. Unhappily the primary evils were the least capable of being eradicated. Caesar could not abolish slavery with its train of national calamities; it must remain an open question, whether he would in the course of time have attempted at least to limit the slave population in the capital, as he undertook to do so in another field. As little could Caesar conjure into existence a free industry in the capital; yet the great building-operations remedied in some measure the want of means of support there, and opened up to the proletariate a source of small but honourable gain. On the other hand Caesar laboured energetically to diminish the mass of the free proletariate. The constant influx of persons brought by the corn-largesses to Rome was, if not wholly stopped,[1] at least very materially restricted by the conversion of these largesses into a provision for the poor limited to a fixed number. The ranks of the existing proletariate were thinned on the one hand by the tribunals which were instructed to proceed with unrelenting rigour against the rabble, on the other hand by a comprehensive transmarine colonisation; of the 80,000 colonists, whom Caesar sent beyond the seas in the few years of his government, a very great portion must have been taken from the lower ranks of the population of the capital; most of the Corinthian settlers indeed were freedmen. But

[1] It is a fact not without interest that a political writer of later date but much judgment, the author of the letters addressed in the name of Sallust to Caesar, gives the latter the advice to transfer the corn distribution of the capital to the several *municipia*. There is good sense in the admonition; as indeed similar ideas obviously prevailed in the noble municipal provision for orphans under Trajan.

this must have been more than a mere temporary arrangement; Caesar, convinced like every other man of sense that the only true remedy for the misery of the proletariate consisted in a well-regulated system of colonisation, and placed by the condition of the empire in a position to realise it to an almost unlimited extent, must have had the design of permanently continuing the process, and so opening up a constant means of abating an evil which was constantly reproducing itself. Measures were further taken to set bounds to the serious fluctuations in the price of the most important means of subsistence in the markets of the capital. The newly-organised and liberally-administered finances of the state furnished the means for this purpose, and two newly-nominated magistrates, the corn aediles (p. 454) were charged with the special supervision of the contractors and of the market of the capital.

The club system was checked, more effectually than was possible through prohibitive laws, by the change of the constitution; inasmuch as with the republic and the republican elections and tribunals the corruption and violence of the electioneering and judicial *collegia*—and generally the political Saturnalia of the *canaille*—came to an end of themselves. Moreover the combinations called into existence by the Clodian law were broken up, and the whole system of association was placed under the superintendence of the governing authorities. With the exception of the ancient guilds and associations, of the religious unions of the Jews, and of other specially excepted categories, for which a simple intimation to the senate seems to have sufficed, the permission to constitute a permanent society with fixed times of assembling and standing deposits was made dependent on a concession to be granted by the senate after the consent of the monarch had been obtained.

To this was added a stricter administration of criminal justice and an energetic police. The laws, especially as regards the crime of violence, were rendered more severe; and the irrational regulation of the republican law, that the convicted criminal was entitled to withdraw himself from a part of the penalty which he had incurred by self-banishment, was with reason set aside. The detailed regulations, which Caesar issued regarding the police of the capital, are in great part still preserved; and all who choose may convince themselves that the Imperator did not disdain to insist on the house proprietors putting the streets into repair and paving the footpath in its whole breadth with hewn stones, and to issue appropriate enactments regarding the carrying of litters and the driving of waggons, which from the nature of the streets were only allowed to move freely through the capital in the evening and by night. The supervision of the local police remained as hitherto chiefly with the four aediles, who were instructed now at least, if not earlier, each to superintend a distinctly marked-off police district within the capital.

Lastly, building in the capital, and the provision connected therewith, of institutions for the public benefit, received from Caesar—who combined in himself the love for building of a Roman and of an organiser—a sudden stimulus, which not merely put to shame the mismanagement of the recent anarchic times, but also left all that the Roman aristocracy had done in their best days as far behind as the genius of Caesar surpassed the honest endeavours of the Marcii and Aemilii. It was not merely by the extent of the buildings in themselves and the magnitude of the sums expended on them that Caesar excelled his predecessors; but a genuine statesmanly perception of what was for the public good distinguishes what Caesar did for the public institutions of Rome from all similar services. He did not build, like his successors, temples and other splendid structures, but he relieved the market-place of Rome—in which the burgess-assemblies, the seats of the chief courts, the exchange, and the daily business as well as the daily idleness, still were crowded together—at any rate from the assemblies and the courts by constructing for the former a new *comitium*, the Saepta Julia in the Campus Martius, and for the latter a separate place of judicature, the Forum Julium between the Capitol and Palatine. Of a kindred spirit is the arrangement originating with him, by which there were supplied to the baths of the capital annually three million pounds of oil, mostly from Africa, and they were thereby enabled to furnish to the bathers the oil required for the anointing of the body gratuitously—a measure of cleanliness and sanitary police which, according to the ancient dietetics based substantially on bathing and anointing, was highly judicious.

But these noble arrangements were only the first steps towards a complete remodelling of Rome. Projects were already formed for a new senate-house, for a new magnificent bazaar, for a theatre to rival that of Pompeius, for a public Latin and Greek library after the model of that recently destroyed at Alexandria—the first institution of the sort in Rome—lastly for a temple of Mars, which was to surpass all that had hitherto existed in riches and glory. Still more brilliant was the idea of altering the whole lower course of the Tiber and of conducting it from the present Ponte Molle—instead of between the Campus Vaticanus and the Campus Martius to Ostia—round the Campus Vaticanus and the Janiculum across the Pomptine marshes to the port of Tarracina. By this gigantic plan three objects would have been accomplished at once: the extremely limited facilities for building in the capital would have been enlarged by substituting the Campus Vaticanus now transferred to the left bank of the Tiber for the Campus Martius, and employing the latter spacious field for public and private edifices; the Pomptine marshes and the Latin coast generally would have been drained; and the capital would have been supplied with a safe seaport, the want of which was so painfully felt. It seemed as if the Imperator would remove mountains and rivers, and venture to contend with nature herself.

Much however as the city of Rome gained by the new order of things in commodiousness and magnificence, its political supremacy was, as we have already said, lost to it irrecoverably through that very change. The idea that the Roman state should coincide with the city of Rome had indeed in the course of time become more and more unnatural and preposterous; but the maxim had been so intimately blended with the essence of the Roman republic, that it could not perish before the republic itself. It was only in the new state of Caesar that it was, with the exception perhaps of some legal fictions, completely set aside, and the community of the capital was placed legally on a level with all other municipalities; indeed Caesar—here as everywhere endeavouring not merely to regulate the thing, but also to call it officially by the right name—issued his Italian municipal ordinance, beyond doubt purposely, at once for the capital and for the other urban communities. We may add that Rome, just because it was incapable of a living communal character as a capital, was even essentially inferior to the other municipalities of the imperial period. The republican Rome was a den of robbers, but it was at the same time the state; the Rome of the monarchy, although it began to embellish itself with all the glories of the three continents and to glitter in gold and marble, was yet nothing in the state but a royal residence in connection with a poor-house, or in other words a necessary evil.

While in the capital the only object aimed at was to get rid of palpable evils by police ordinances on the greatest scale, it was a far more difficult task to remedy the deep disorganisation of Italian society. Its radical misfortunes were those which we previously noticed in detail—the disappearance of the agricultural, and the unnatural increase of the mercantile, population—with which an endless train of other evils were associated. The reader will not fail to remember what was the state of Italian agriculture. In spite of the most earnest attempts to check the annihilation of the small holdings, farm-husbandry was scarcely any longer the predominant species of economy during this epoch in any region of Italy proper, with the exception perhaps of the valleys of the Apennines and Abruzzi. As to the management of estates, no material difference is perceptible between the Catonian system formerly set forth (ii. 342-351) and that described to us by Varro, except that the latter shows the traces for better and for worse of the progress of fashionable life in Rome. "Formerly," says Varro, "the barn on the estate was larger than the manor-house; now it is wont to be the reverse." In the domains of Tusculum and Tibur, on the shores of Tarracina and Baiae—where the old Latin and Italian farmers had sown and reaped—there now rose in barren splendour the villas of the Roman nobles, some of which covered the space of a moderate-sized town with their appurtenances of garden-grounds and aqueducts, fresh and salt water ponds for the preservation and breeding of river and marine fishes, nurseries of snails and slugs, game-preserves for keeping hares, rabbits, stags, roes, and wild boars, and aviaries in which even cranes and peacocks were kept. But the luxury of a great city enriches also many an industrious hand, and supports more poor than philanthropy with its expenditure of alms. Those aviaries and fishponds of the grandees were of course under ordinary circumstances a very costly indulgence. But this system was carried to such an extent and prosecuted with so much keenness, that *e.g.* the stock of a pigeon-house was valued at 100,000 sesterces (£1000); a methodical system of fattening had sprung up, and the manure got from the aviaries became of importance in agriculture; a single bird-dealer was able to furnish at once 5000 fieldfares—for they knew how to rear these also—at three denarii (2*s.*) each, and a single possessor of a fishpond 2000 *muraenae*; and the fishes left behind by Lucius Lucullus brought 40,000 sesterces (£400). As may readily be conceived, under such circumstances any one who followed this occupation industriously and intelligently might obtain very large profits with a comparatively small outlay of capital. A small bee-breeder of this period sold from his thyme-garden not larger than an acre in the neighbourhood of Falerii honey to an average annual amount of at least 10,000 sesterces (£100). The rivalry of the growers of fruit was carried so far, that in elegant villas the fruit-chamber lined with marble was not unfrequently fitted up at the same time as a dining-room, and sometimes fine fruit acquired by purchase was exhibited there as of home growth. At this period the cherry from Asia Minor and other foreign fruit-trees were first planted in the gardens of Italy. The vegetable gardens, the beds of roses and violets in Latium and Campania, yielded rich produce, and the "market for dainties" (*forum cupedinis*) by the side of the Via Sacra, where fruits, honey, and chaplets were wont to be exposed for sale, played an important part in the life of the capital. Generally the management of estates, worked as they were on the planter-system, had reached in an economic point of view a height scarcely to be surpassed. The valley of Rieti, the region round the Fucine lake, the districts on the Liris and Volturnus, and indeed Central Italy in general, were as respects husbandry in the most flourishing condition; even certain branches of industry, which were suitable accompaniments of the management of an estate by means of slaves, were taken up by intelligent landlords, and, where the circumstances were favourable, inns, weaving factories, and especially brick-works were constructed on the estate. The Italian producers of wine and oil in particular not only supplied the Italian markets, but carried on also in both articles a considerable business of transmarine exportation. A homely professional treatise of this period compares Italy to a great fruit-garden; and the pictures which a contemporary poet gives of his beautiful native land, where the well-watered meadow, the luxuriant corn-field, the pleasant vine-covered hill are fringed by the dark line of the olive-trees—where the "ornament" of the land, smiling in varied charms, cherishes the loveliest gardens in its bosom and is itself wreathed round by food-producing trees—these descriptions, evidently faithful pictures of the landscape daily presented to the eye of the poet, transplant us into the most flourishing districts of Tuscany and Terra di Lavoro. The pastoral husbandry, it is true, which for reasons formerly explained was always spreading farther especially in the south and south-east of Italy, was in every respect a retrograde movement; but it too participated to a certain degree in the general progress of agriculture; much was done for the improvement of the breeds, *e.g.* asses for breeding brought 60,000 sesterces

(£600), 100,000 (£1000), and even 400,000 (£4000). The solid Italian husbandry obtained at this period, when the general development of intelligence and abundance of capital rendered it fruitful, far more brilliant results than ever the old system of small cultivators could have given; and was carried even already beyond the bounds of Italy, for the Italian agriculturist turned to account large tracts in the provinces by raising cattle and even cultivating corn.

In order to show what dimensions money-dealing assumed by the side of this estate-husbandry unnaturally prospering over the ruin of the small farmers, how the Italian merchants vying with the Jews poured themselves into all the provinces and client-states of the kingdom, and how all capital ultimately flowed to Rome, it will be sufficient, after what has been already said, to point to the single fact that in the money-market of the capital the regular rate of interest at this time was six per cent., and consequently money there was cheaper by a half than it was on an average elsewhere in antiquity.

In consequence of this economic system based both in its agrarian and mercantile aspects on masses of capital and on speculation, there arose a most fearful disproportion in the distribution of wealth. The often used and often abused phrase of a commonwealth composed of millionnaires and beggars applies perhaps nowhere so completely as to the Rome of the last age of the republic; and nowhere perhaps has the essential maxim of the slave-state—that the rich man who lives by the exertions of his slaves is necessarily respectable, and the poor man who lives by the labour of his hands is necessarily vulgar—been recognised with so terrible a precision as the undoubted principle underlying all public and private intercourse.[1] A real

[1] The following exposition in Cicero's treatise *De Officiis* (i. 42) is characteristic: *Jam de artificiis et quaestibus, qui liberales habendi, qui sordidi sint, haec fere accepimus. Primum improbantur ii quaestus, qui in odia hominum incurrunt, ut portitorum, ut feneratorum. Illiberales autem et sordidi quaestus mercenariorum omnium, quorum operae, non artes emuntur. Est autem in illis ipsa merces auctoramentum servitutis. Sordidi etiam putandi, qui mercantur a mercatoribus quod statim vendant, nihil enim proficiant, nisi admodum mentiantur. Nec vero est quidquam turpius vanitate. Opificesque omnes in sordida arte versantur; nec enim quidquam ingenuum habere potest officina. Minimeque artes eae probandae, quae ministrae sunt voluptatum,*

"*Cetarii, lanii, coqui, fartores, piscatores,*"

ut ait Terentius. Adde huc, si placet, unguentarios, saltatores, totumque ludum talarium. Quibus autem artibus aut prudentia major inest, aut non mediocris utilitas quaeritur, ut medicina, ut architectura, ut doctrina rerum honestarum, eae sunt iis, quorum ordini conveniunt, honestae. Mercatura

middle class in our sense of the term there was not, as indeed no such class can exist in any fully developed slave-state; what appears as if it were a good middle class and is so in a certain measure, is composed of those rich men of business and landholders who are so uncultivated or so highly cultivated as to content themselves within the sphere of their activity and to keep aloof from public life. Of the men of business—a class, among whom the numerous freedmen and other upstarts, as a rule, were seized with the giddy fancy of playing the man of quality—there were not very many who showed so much judgment. A model of this sort was the Titus Pomponius Atticus frequently mentioned in the accounts of this period. He acquired an immense fortune partly from the great estate-farming which he prosecuted in Italy and Epirus, partly from his money-transactions which ramified throughout Italy, Greece, Macedonia, and Asia Minor; but at the same time he continued to be throughout the simple man of business, did not allow himself to be seduced into soliciting office or even into monetary transactions with the state, and, equally remote from the avaricious niggardliness and from the prodigal and burdensome luxury of his time—his table, for instance, was maintained at a daily cost of 100 sesterces (£1)—contented himself with an easy existence appropriating to itself the charms of a country and a city life, the pleasures of intercourse with the best society of Rome and Greece, and all the enjoyments of literature and art.

More numerous and more solid were the Italian landholders of the old type. Contemporary literature preserves in the description of Sextus Roscius, who was murdered amidst the proscriptions of $\frac{673}{81}$, the picture of such a rural nobleman (*pater familias rusticanus*); his wealth, estimated at 6,000,000 sesterces (£60,000), is mainly invested in his thirteen landed estates; he attends to the management of it in person systematically and

autem, si tenuis est, sordida putanda est; sin magna et copiosa, multa undique apportans, multaque sine vanitate impertiens, non est admodum vituperanda; atque etiam, si satiata quaestu, vel contenta potius; ut saepe ex alto in portum, ex ipso portu in agros se possessionesque contulerit, videtur optimo jure posse laudari. Omnium autem rerum, ex quibus aliquid acquiritur, nihil est agricultura melius, nihil uberius, nihil dulcius, nihil homine libero dignius. According to this the respectable man must, in strictness, be a landowner; the trade of a merchant becomes him only so far as it is a means to this ultimate end; science as a profession is suitable only for the Greeks and for Romans not belonging to the ruling classes, who by this means may purchase at all events a certain toleration of their personal presence in genteel circles. It is a thoroughly developed aristocracy of planters, with a strong infusion of mercantile speculation and a slight shading of general culture.

with enthusiasm; he comes seldom or never to the capital, and, when he does appear there, by his clownish manners he contrasts not less with the polished senator than the innumerable hosts of his uncouth rural slaves with the elegant train of domestic slaves in the capital. Far more than the circles of the nobility with their cosmopolitan culture and the mercantile class at home everywhere and nowhere, these landlords and the "country towns" to which they essentially gave tone (*municipia rusticana*) preserved as well the discipline and manners as the pure and noble language of their fathers. The order of landlords was regarded as the flower of the nation; the speculator, who has made his fortune and wishes to appear among the notables of the land, buys an estate and seeks, if not to become himself the squire, at any rate to rear his son with that view. We meet the traces of this class of landlords wherever a national movement appears in politics and wherever literature puts forth any fresh growth; from it the patriotic opposition to the new monarchy drew its best strength; to it belonged Varro, Lucretius, Catullus; and nowhere perhaps does the comparative freshness of this landlord-life come more characteristically to light than in the graceful Arpinate introduction to the second book of Cicero's treatise *De Legibus*—a green oasis amidst the fearful desert of that equally empty and voluminous writer.

But the cultivated class of merchants and the vigorous order of landlords were far overgrown by the two classes that gave tone to society—the mass of beggars, and the world of quality proper. We have no statistical figures to indicate precisely the relative proportions of poverty and riches for this epoch; yet we may here perhaps again recall the expression which a Roman statesman employed some fifty years before (iii. 130)—that the number of families of firmly established riches among the Roman burgesses did not amount to 2000. The burgess-body had since then become different; but clear indications attest that the disproportion between poor and rich had remained at least as great. The increasing impoverishment of the multitude shows itself only too plainly in their crowding to the corn-largesses and to enlistment in the army; the corresponding increase of riches is attested expressly by an author of this generation, when, speaking of the circumstances of the Marian period, he describes an estate of 2,000,000 sesterces (£20,000) as "riches according to the circumstances of that day;" and the statements which we find as to the property of individuals lead to the same conclusion. The extremely rich

Lucius Domitius Ahenobarbus promised to twenty thousand soldiers four *iugera* of land each out of his own property; the estate of Pompeius amounted to 70,000,000 sesterces (£700,000) that of Aesopus the actor to 20,000,000 (£200,000); Marcus Crassus, the richest of the rich, possessed at the outset of his career, 7,000,000 (£70,000), at its close, after lavishing enormous sums on the people, 170,000,000 sesterces (£1,700,000). The effect of such poverty and such riches was on both sides an economic and moral disorganisation outwardly different, but at bottom of the same character. If the common man was saved from starvation only by support from the resources of the state, it was the necessary consequence of this mendicant misery —although it also reciprocally appears as a cause of it—that he addicted himself to the beggar's laziness and to the beggar's good cheer. The Roman plebeian was fonder of gazing in the theatre than of working; the taverns and brothels were so frequented that the demagogues found their special account in gaining the possessors of such establishments over to their interests. The gladiatorial games—which revealed, at the same time that they fostered, the worst demoralisation of the ancient world—had become so flourishing that a lucrative business was done in the sale of the programmes for them; and it was at this time that the horrible innovation was adopted by which the decision as to the life or death of the vanquished became dependent, not on the law of duel or on the pleasure of the victor, but on the caprice of the onlooking public, and according to its signal the victor either spared or transfixed his prostrate antagonist. The trade of fighting had so risen or freedom had so fallen in value, that the intrepidity and the emulation, which were lacking on the battle-fields of this age, were universal in the armies of the arena, and, where the law of the duel required, every gladiator allowed himself to be stabbed mutely and without shrinking; that in fact free men not unfrequently sold themselves to the contractors for board and wages as gladiatorial slaves. The plebeians of the fifth century had also suffered want and famine, but they had not sold their freedom; and still less would the jurisconsults of that period have lent themselves to pronounce the equally immoral and illegal contract of such a gladiatorial slave "to let himself be chained, scourged, burnt, or killed without opposition, if the laws of the institution should so require" by means of unbecoming juristic subtleties as a contract lawful and actionable.

In the world of quality such things did not occur, but at bottom it was hardly different, and least of all better. In doing nothing the aristocrat boldly competed with the proletarian; if the latter lounged on the pavement, the former lay in bed till far on in the day. Extravagance prevailed here as unbounded as it was devoid of taste. It was lavished on politics and on the theatre, of course to the corruption of both; the consular office was purchased at an incredible price—in the summer of $\frac{700}{54}$ the first voting-division alone was paid 10,000,000 sesterces (£100,000)—and all the pleasure of the man of culture in the drama was spoilt by the insane luxury of decoration. Rents in Rome appear to have been on an average four times as high as in the country towns; a house there was once sold for 15,000,000 sesterces (£150,000). The house of Marcus Lepidus (consul in $\frac{676}{78}$) which was at the time of the death of Sulla the finest in Rome, did not rank a generation afterwards even as the hundredth on the list of Roman palaces. We have already mentioned the extravagance practised in the matter of country-houses; we find that 4,000,000 sesterces (£40,000) were paid for such a house, which was valued chiefly for its fishpond; and the thoroughly fashionable grandee now needed at least two villas—one in the Sabine or Alban mountains near the capital, and a second in the vicinity of the Campanian baths—and in addition if possible a garden immediately outside of the gates of Rome. Still more irrational than these villa-palaces were the palatial sepulchres, several of which still existing at the present day attest what a lofty pile of masonry the rich Roman needed in order to die as became his rank. Fanciers of horses and dogs too were not wanting; 24,000 sesterces (£240) was no uncommon price for a showy horse. They indulged in furniture of fine wood—a table of African cypress-wood cost 1,000,000 sesterces (£10,000); in dresses of purple stuffs or transparent gauzes accompanied by an elegant adjustment of their folds before the mirror—the orator Hortensius is said to have brought an action of damages against a colleague because he ruffled his dress in a crowd; in precious stones and pearls, which first at this period took the place of the far more beautiful and more artistic ornaments of gold—it was already utter barbarism, when at the triumph of Pompeius over Mithradates the image of the victor appeared wrought wholly of pearls, and when the sofas and the shelves in the dining-hall were silver-mounted and even the kitchen-utensils were made of silver. In a similar spirit the collectors of this period took out the artistic medallions from the old silver cups, to set them anew in vessels of gold. Nor was there any lack of luxury also in travelling. "When the governor travelled," Cicero tells us as to one of the Sicilian governors, "which of course he did not in winter, but only at the beginning of spring—not the spring of the calendar but the beginning of the season of roses—he had himself conveyed, as was the custom with the kings of Bithynia, in a litter with eight bearers, sitting on a cushion of Maltese gauze stuffed with rose-leaves, with one garland on his head and a second twined round his neck, applying to his nose a little smelling-bag of fine linen, with minute meshes, filled with roses; and thus he had himself carried even to his bedchamber."

But no sort of luxury flourished so much as the coarsest of all—the luxury of the table. The whole villa arrangements and the whole villa life had ultimate reference to dining; not only had they different dining-rooms for winter and summer, but dinner was served in the picture-gallery, in the fruit-chamber, in the aviary, or on a platform erected in the deer-park, around which, when the bespoken "Orpheus" appeared in theatrical costume and blew his flourish, the duly trained roes and wild boars congregated. Such was the care bestowed on decoration; but amidst all this the reality was by no means forgotten. Not only was the cook a graduate in gastronomy, but the master himself often acted as the instructor of his cooks. The roast had been long ago thrown into the shade by marine fishes and oysters; now the Italian river-fishes were utterly banished from good tables, and Italian delicacies and Italian wines were looked on as almost vulgar. Now even at the popular festivals there were distributed, besides the Italian Falerian, three sorts of foreign wine—Sicilian, Lesbian, Chian, while a generation before it had been sufficient even at great banquets to send round Greek wine once; in the cellar of the orator Hortensius there was found a stock of 10,000 jars (at 33 quarts) of foreign wine. It was no wonder that the Italian wine growers began to complain of the competition of the wines from the Greek islands. No naturalist could ransack land and sea more zealously for new animals and plants than the epicures of that day ransacked them for new culinary dainties.[1] The

[1] We have still (Macrobius, iii. 13) the bill of fare of the banquet, which Mucius Lentulus Niger gave before $\frac{691}{63}$ on entering on his pontificate, and of which the pontifices—Caesar included—the Vestal Virgins, and some other priests and ladies nearly related to them partook. Before the dinner proper came sea-hedgehogs; fresh oysters as many as the guests wished; large mussels; sphondyli; fieldfares with asparagus; fattened fowls;

circumstance of the guest taking an emetic after a banquet, to avoid the consequences of the varied fare set before him, no longer created surprise. Debauchery of every sort became so systematic and aggravated that it found its professors, who earned a livelihood by serving as instructors of the youth of quality in the theory and practice of vice.

It will not be necessary to dwell longer on this confused picture, so monotonous in its variety; and the less so, that the Romans were far from original in this respect, and confined themselves to exhibiting a copy of the Helleno-Asiatic luxury still more exaggerated and stupid than their model. Plutos naturally devours his children as well as Kronos; the competition for all these mostly worthless objects of fashionable longing so forced up prices, that those who swam with the stream found the most colossal estate melt away in a short time, and even those, who only for credit's sake joined in what was most necessary, saw their inherited and firmly-established wealth rapidly undermined. The canvass for the consulship, for instance, was the usual highway to ruin for houses of distinction; and nearly the same description applies to the games, the great buildings, and all those other pleasant but doubtless expensive pursuits. The princely wealth of that period is only surpassed by its still more princely liabilities; Caesar owed about $\frac{692}{62}$, after deducting his assets, 25,000,000 sesterces (£250,000); Marcus Antonius, at the age of twenty-four, 6,000,000 sesterces (£60,000), fourteen years afterwards 40,000,000 (£400,000); Curio owed 60,000,000 (£600,000); Milo 70,000,000 (£700,000). That those extravagant habits of the Roman world of quality rested throughout on credit, is shown by the fact that the rate of interest in Rome was once suddenly raised from four to eight per cent. through the borrowing of the different competitors for the consulship. Insolvency, instead of leading in due time to a meeting of creditors or at any

oyster and mussel pasties; black and white sea-acorns; sphondyli again; glycimarides; sea-nettles; becaficoes; roe-ribs; boar's ribs; fowls dressed with flour; becaficoes; purple shell-fish of two sorts. The dinner itself consisted of sow's udder; boar's-head; fish-pasties; boar-pasties; ducks; boiled teals; hares; roasted fowls; starch-pastry; Pontic pastry.

These are the college-banquets regarding which Varro (*De R. R.* iii. 2, 16) says that they forced up the price of all delicacies. Varro in one of his satires enumerates the following as the most notable foreign delicacies: peacocks from Samos; grouse from Phrygia; cranes from Melos; kids from Ambracia; tunny fishes from Chalcedon; muraenas from the Straits of Gades; ass-fishes (? *aselli*) from Pessinus; oysters and scallops from Tarentum; sturgeons (?) from Rhodes; *scarus*-fishes (?) from Cilicia; nuts from Thasos; dates from Egypt; acorns from Spain.

rate to a liquidation which might at least place matters once more on a clear footing, was ordinarily prolonged by the debtor as much as possible; instead of selling his property and especially his landed estates, he continued to borrow and to present the semblance of riches, till the crash only became the worse and the winding-up yielded a result like that of Milo, in which the creditors obtained somewhat above four per cent. of the sums for which they ranked. Amidst this startlingly rapid transition from riches to bankruptcy and this systematic swindling, nobody of course gained so much as the cool banker, who knew how to give and refuse credit. The relations of debtor and creditor thus returned almost to the same point at which they had stood in the worst times of the social crises of the fifth century; the nominal landowners held virtually by sufferance of their creditors; the debtors were either in servile subjection to their creditors, so that the humbler of them appeared like freedmen in the creditor's train and those of higher rank spoke and voted even in the senate at the nod of their creditor-lord; or they were ready to make war on property itself, and either to intimidate their creditors by threats or to get rid of them by conspiracy and civil war. On these relations was based the power of Crassus; out of them arose the insurrections—whose motto was "a clear sheet"—of Cina (iii. 243, 306) and still more definitely of Catilina, of Coelius, of Dolabella, entirely resembling the battles between those who had and those who had not, which a century before agitated the Hellenic world (ii. 274). That amidst so rotten an economic condition every financial or political crisis should occasion the most dreadful confusion, was to be expected from the nature of the case; we need hardly mention that the usual phenomena—the disappearance of capital, the sudden depreciation of landed estates, innumerable bankruptcies, and an almost universal insolvency—made their appearance now during the civil war, just as they had done during the Social and Mithradatic wars (iii. 386).

Under such circumstances, as a matter of course, morality and family life were treated as antiquated things among all ranks of society. To be poor was not merely the sorest disgrace and the worst crime, but the only disgrace and the only crime: for money the statesman sold the state, and the burgess sold his freedom; the post of the officer and the vote of the juryman were to be had for money; for money the lady of quality surrendered her person as well as the common courtesan; falsifying of documents and perjuries had become so common that in a popular poet of this age an oath is called "the plaster for debts." Men had forgotten what honesty was; a person who refused a bribe was regarded not as an upright man, but as a personal foe. The criminal statistics of all times and countries will hardly furnish a parallel to the dreadful picture of crimes—so varied, so horrible, and so unnatural—which the trial of Aulus Cluentius unrolls before us in the bosom of one of the most respectable families of an Italian country town.

But while at the bottom of the national life the slime was thus constantly accumulating more and more deleteriously and deeply, so much the more smooth and glittering was the surface, overlaid with the varnish of polished manners and universal friendship. All the world interchanged visits; so that in the houses of quality it was necessary to admit the persons presenting themselves every morning for the levee in a certain order fixed by the master or occasionally by the attendant in waiting, and to give audience only to the more notable one by one, while the rest were more summarily admitted partly in groups, partly in a body at the close—a distinction which Gaius Gracchus, in this too the first founder of the new monarchy, is said to have introduced. The interchange of letters of courtesy was carried to as great an extent as the visits of courtesy; "friendly" letters flew over land and sea between persons who had neither personal relations nor business with each other, whereas proper and formal business-letters scarcely occur except where the letter is addressed to a corporation. In like manner invitations to dinner, the customary new year's presents, the domestic festivals, were divested of their proper character and converted almost into public ceremonials; even death itself did not release the Roman from these attentions to his countless "neighbours," but in order to die with due respectability he had to provide each of them at any rate with a keepsake. Just as in certain circles of our mercantile world the genuine intimacy of family ties and family friendships had so totally vanished from the Rome of that day that the whole intercourse of business and acquaintance could be garnished with forms and flourishes of affection which had lost all meaning, and thus by degrees the reality came to be superseded by that spectral shadow of "friendship" which holds by no means the least place among the various evil spirits brooding over the proscriptions and civil wars of this age.

An equally characteristic feature in the brilliant decay of this period was the emancipation of women. In an economic point of view the women had long since made themselves independent (ii. 384); in the present epoch we even meet with solicitors acting specially for women, who officiously lend their aid to solitary rich ladies in the management of their property and their lawsuits, make an impression on them by their knowledge of business and law, and thereby procure for themselves ampler perquisites and legacies than other loungers on the exchange. But it was not merely from the economic guardianship of father or husband that women felt themselves emancipated. Love-intrigues of all sorts were constantly in progress. The ballet-dancers (*mimae*) were quite a match for those of the present day in the variety of their pursuits and the skill with which they followed them out; their primadonnas, Cytheris and the like, pollute even the pages of history. But their, as it were, licensed trade was very materially injured by the free art of the ladies of aristocratic circles. Liaisons in the first houses had become so frequent, that only a scandal altogether exceptional could make them the subject of special talk; a judicial interference seemed now almost ridiculous. An unparalleled scandal, such as Publius Clodius produced in $\frac{693}{61}$ at the women's festival in the house of the Pontifex Maximus, although a thousand times worse than the occurrences which fifty years before had led to a series of capital sentences (iii. 409), passed almost without investigation and wholly without punishment. The watering-place season—in April, when political business was suspended and the world of quality congregated in Baiae and Puteoli—derived its chief charm from the relations licit and illicit which, along with music and song and elegant breakfasts on board or on shore, enlivened the gondola voyages. There the ladies held absolute sway; but they were by no means content with this domain which rightfully belonged to them; they also acted as politicians, appeared in party conferences, and took part with their money and their intrigues in the wild coterie-proceedings of the time. Any one who beheld these female statesmen performing on the stage of Scipio and Cato and saw at their side the young fop—as with smooth chin, delicate voice, and mincing gait, with headdress and neckerchiefs, frilled robe, and women's sandals he copied the loose courtesan—might well have a horror of the unnatural world, in which the sexes seemed as though they wished to change parts. What ideas as to divorce prevailed in the circles of the aristocracy may be discerned in the conduct of their best and most moral hero Marcus Cato, who did not hesitate to separate from his wife at the request of a friend desirous to marry her, and as little scrupled on the death of this friend to marry the same wife a second time. Celibacy and childlessness became more and more common, especially among the upper classes. While among these marriage had for long been regarded as a burden which people took upon them at the best in the public interest (ii. 409; iii. 394), we now encounter even in Cato and those who shared Cato's sentiments the maxim to which Polybius a century before traced the decay of Hellas (iii. 42), that it is the duty of a citizen to keep great wealth together and therefore not to beget too many children. Where were the times, when the designation "children-producer" (*proletarius*) had been a term of honour for the Roman?

In consequence of such a social condition the Latin stock in Italy underwent an alarming diminution, and its fair provinces were overspread partly by parasitic immigrants, partly by sheer desolation. A considerable portion of the population of Italy flocked to foreign lands. Already the aggregate amount of talent and of working power, which the supply of Italian magistrates and Italian garrisons for the whole domain of the Mediterranean demanded, transcended the resources of the peninsula, especially as the elements thus sent abroad were in great part lost for ever to the nation. For the more that the Roman community grew into an empire embracing many nations, the more the governing aristocracy lost the habit of looking on Italy as their exclusive home; while of the men levied or enlisted for service a considerable portion perished in the many wars, especially in the bloody civil war, and another portion became wholly estranged from their native country by the long period of service, which sometimes lasted for a generation. In like manner with the public service, speculation kept a portion of the landholders and almost the whole body of merchants all their lives or at any rate for a long time out of the country, and the demoralising itinerant habits of the latter in particular estranged them altogether from civic existence in the mother country and from the various restraints of family life. As a compensation for these, Italy obtained on the one hand the proletariate of slaves and freedmen, on the other hand the craftsmen and traders flocking thither from Asia Minor, Syria, and Egypt, who flourished chiefly in the capital and still more in the seaport towns of Ostia, Puteoli, and Brundisium (iii. 399). In the largest and most important part of Italy however, there was not even such a substitution of impure elements for pure; but the population was visibly on the decline.

Especially was this true of the pastoral districts such as Apulia, the chosen land of cattle-breeding, which is called by contemporaries the most deserted part of Italy, and of the region around Rome, where the Campagna was annually becoming more desolate under the constant reciprocal action of the retrograde agriculture and the increasing malaria. Labici, Gabii, Bovillae once cheerful little country towns, were so decayed, that it was difficult to find representatives of them for the ceremony of the Latin festival. Tusculum, although still one of the most eminent communities of Latium, consisted almost solely of some families of rank who lived in the capital but retained their native Tusculan franchise, and was far inferior in the number of burgesses entitled to vote even to small communities in the interior of Italy. The stock of men capable of arms in this district, on which Rome's ability to defend herself had once mainly depended, had so totally vanished, that people read with astonishment and perhaps with horror the accounts of the annals—sounding fabulous in comparison with things as they stood—respecting the Aequian and Volscian wars. Matters were not so bad everywhere, especially in the other portions of Central Italy and in Campania; nevertheless, as Varro complains, "the once populous cities of Italy" in general "stood desolate."

It is a dreadful picture—this picture of Italy under the rule of the oligarchy. There was nothing to bridge over or soften the fatal contrast between the world of the beggars and the world of the rich. The more clearly and painfully this contrast was felt on both sides—the giddier the height to which riches rose, the deeper the abyss of poverty yawned—the more frequently, amidst that changeful world of speculation and playing at hazard, were individuals tossed from the bottom to the top and again from the top to the bottom. The wider the chasm by which the two worlds were externally divided, the more completely they coincided in the like annihilation of family life—which is yet the germ and core of all nationality—in the like laziness and luxury, the like unsubstantial economy, the like unmanly dependence, the like corruption differing only in its scale, the like criminal demoralisation, the like longing to begin the war with property. Riches and misery in close league drove the Italians out of Italy, and filled the peninsula partly with swarms of slaves, partly with awful silence. It is a terrible picture, but not one peculiar to Italy; wherever the government of capitalists in a slave-state has fully developed itself, it has desolated God's fair world in the same way. As rivers glisten in different colours, but a common sewer everywhere looks like itself, so the Italy of the Ciceronian epoch resembles substantially the Hellas of Polybius and still more decidedly the Carthage of Hannibal's time, where in exactly similar fashion the all-powerful rule of capital ruined the middle class, raised trade and estate-farming to the highest prosperity, and ultimately led to a—hypocritically whitewashed—moral and political corruption of the nation. All the arrant sins that capital has been guilty of against nation and civilisation in the modern world, remain as far inferior to the abominations of the ancient capitalist-states as the free man, be he ever so poor, remains superior to the slave; and not until the dragon-seed of North America ripens, will the world have again similar fruits to reap.

These evils, under which the national economy of Italy lay prostrate, were in their deepest essence irremediable, and so much of them as still admitted of remedy depended essentially for its amendment on the people and on time; for the wisest government is as little able as the most skilful physician to give freshness to the corrupt juices of the organism, or to do more in the case of the deeper-rooted evils than to prevent those accidents which obstruct the remedial power of nature in its working. The peaceful energy of the new rule even of itself furnished such a preventive, for by its means some of the worst excrescences were done away, such as the artificial pampering of the proletariate, the impunity of crimes, the purchase of offices, and various others. But the government could do something more than simply abstain from harm. Caesar was not one of those over-wise people who refuse to embank the sea, because forsooth no dike can defy some sudden influx of the tide. It is better, if a nation and its economy follow spontaneously the path prescribed by nature; but, seeing that they had got out of this path, Caesar applied all his energies to bring back by special intervention the nation to its home and family life, and to reform the national economy by law and decree.

With a view to check the continued absence of the Italians from Italy and to induce the world of quality and the merchants to establish their homes in their native land, not only was the term of service for the soldiers shortened, but men of senatorial rank altogether prohibited from taking up their abode out of Italy except when on public business, while the other Italians of marriageable age (from the twentieth to the fortieth year) were enjoined not to be absent from Italy for more than three consecutive years. In the same spirit Caesar had already in his first consulship on founding the colony of Capua kept specially in view fathers who had several children (p. 188); and now as Imperator he proposed extraordinary rewards for the fathers of numerous families, while he at the same time as supreme judge of the nation treated divorce and adultery with a vigour according to Roman ideas unparalleled.

Nor did he even think it beneath his dignity to issue a detailed law as to luxury—which, among other points, cut down extravagance in building at least in one of its most irrational forms, that of sepulchral monuments; restricted the use of purple robes and pearls to certain times, ages, and classes, and totally prohibited it in grown-up men; fixed a maximum for the expenditure of the table; and directly forbade a number of luxurious dishes. Such ordinances doubtless were not new; but it was a new thing that the "master of morals" seriously insisted on their observance, superintended the provision-markets by means of paid overseers, and ordered that the tables of men of rank should be examined by his officers and the forbidden dishes on them should be confiscated. It is true that by such theoretical and practical instructions in moderation as the new monarchical police gave to the fashionable world hardly more could be accomplished than the compelling luxury to retire somewhat more into concealment; but, if hypocrisy is the homage which vice pays to virtue, under the circumstances of the times even a semblance of propriety enforced by police measures was a step towards improvement not to be despised.

The measures of Caesar for the better regulation of Italian monetary and agricultural relations were of a graver character and promised greater results. The first question here related to temporary enactments respecting the scarcity of money and the debt-crisis generally. The law called forth by the outcry as to locked-up capital—that no one should have on hand more than 60,000 sesterces (£600) in gold and silver cash—was probably only issued to allay the indignation of the blind public against the usurers; the form of publication, which proceeded on the fiction that this was merely the renewed enforcing of an earlier law that had fallen into oblivion, shows that Caesar was ashamed of this enactment, and it can hardly have passed into actual application. A far more serious question was the treatment of the pending claims for debt, the complete remission of which was vehemently demanded from Caesar by the party which called itself by his name. We have already mentioned that he did not yield to this demand (p. 433); but two important concessions were made to the debtors, and that as early as $\frac{705}{49}$. First, the interest in arrear was struck off,[1] and that which was paid was deducted from the capital. Secondly, the creditor was compelled to accept the movable and immovable property of the debtor in lieu of payment at the estimated value which his effects had before the civil war and the general depreciation which it had occasioned. The latter enactment was not unreasonable; if the creditor was to be looked on *de facto* as the owner of the property of his debtor to the amount of the sum due to him, it was doubtless proper that he should bear his share in the general depreciation of the property. On the other hand the cancelling of the payments of interest made or outstanding —which practically amounted to this, that the creditors lost, besides the interest itself, on an average 25 per cent. of what they were entitled to claim as capital at the time of the issuing of the law—was in fact nothing else than a partial concession of that cancelling of creditor's claims springing out of loans for which the democrats had clamoured so vehemently; and, however bad may have been the conduct of the usurers, it is not possible thereby to justify the universal and retrospective abolition of all claims for interest without distinction. In order at least to understand it, we must recollect how the democratic party stood towards the question of interest. The legal prohibition against taking interest, which the old plebeian opposition had extorted in $\frac{412}{342}$ (i. 300), had no doubt been practically disregarded by the nobility which controlled the civil procedure by means of the praetorship, but had still remained since that period formally valid; and the democrats of the seventh century, who regarded themselves throughout as the continuers of that old agitation as to privilege and social position (p. 163), had maintained the illegality of payment of interest at any time, and even already practically enforced that principle, at least temporarily, in the confusion of the Marian period (iii. 243). It is not credible that Caesar shared the crude views of his party on the interest question; the fact, that in his account of the matter of liquidation he mentions the enactment as to the surrender of the property of the debtor in lieu of payment

[1] This is not stated by our authorities, but it necessarily follows from the permission to deduct the interest paid by cash or assignation (*si quid usurae nomine numeratum aut perscriptum fuisset*; Sueton. *Caes.* 42), as paid contrary to law, from the capital.

but is silent as to the cancelling of the interest, is perhaps a tacit self-reproach. But he was, like every party-leader, dependent on his party and could not directly repudiate the traditional maxims of the democracy in the question of interest; the more especially when he had to decide this question, not as the all-powerful conqueror of Pharsalus, but even before his departure for Epirus. But, while he permitted perhaps rather than originated this violation of legal order and of property, it is certainly his merit that that monstrous demand for the annulling of all claims arising from loans was rejected; and it may perhaps be looked on as a saving of his honour, that the debtors were far more indignant at the—according to their view extremely unsatisfactory—concession given to them than the injured creditors, and made under Caelius and Dolabella those foolish and (as already mentioned) speedily frustrated attempts to extort by riot and civil war what Caesar refused to them.

But Caesar did not confine himself to helping the debtor at the moment; he did what as legislator he could permanently to keep down the fearful omnipotence of capital. First of all the great legal maxim was proclaimed, that freedom is not a possession commensurable with property, but an eternal right of man, of which the state is entitled judicially to deprive the criminal alone, not the debtor. It was Caesar, who, perhaps stimulated in this case also by the more humane Egyptian and Greek legislation, especially that of Solon,[1] introduced this principle—diametrically opposed to the maxims of the earlier ordinances as to debt—into the common law, where it has since retained its place undisputed. According to Roman law the debtor unable to pay became the slave of his creditor (i. 160). The Poetelian law no doubt had allowed a debtor, who had become unable to pay through temporary embarrassments, not through genuine insolvency, to save his personal freedom by the cession of his property (i. 301); nevertheless for the really insolvent that principle of law, though doubtless modified in secondary points, had been in substance retained unaltered for five hundred years; a direct recourse to the debtor's estate only occurred exceptionally, when the debtor had died or had forfeited his burgess-rights or could not be found. It was

[1] The Egyptian royal laws (Diodorus, i. 79) and likewise the legislation of Solon (Plutarch, *Sol.* 13, 15) forbade bonds in which the loss of the personal liberty of the debtor was made the penalty of non-payment; and at least the latter imposed on the debtor in the event of bankruptcy no more than the cession of his whole assets.

Caesar who first gave an insolvent the right—on which our modern bankruptcy regulations are based—of formally ceding his estate to his creditors, whether it might suffice to satisfy them or not, so as to save at all events his personal freedom although with diminished honorary and political rights, and to begin a new financial existence, in which he could only be sued on account of claims proceeding from the earlier period and not protected in the liquidation, if he could pay them without renewed financial ruin.

While thus the great democrat had the imperishable honour of emancipating personal freedom in principle from capital, he attempted moreover to impose a police limit on the excessive power of capital by usury-laws. He did not affect to disown the democratic antipathy to stipulations for interest. For Italian money-dealing there was fixed a maximum amount of the loans at interest to be allowed in the case of the individual capitalist, which appears to have been proportioned to the Italian landed estate belonging to each, and perhaps amounted to half its value. Transgressions of this enactment were, after the fashion of the procedure prescribed in the republican usury-laws, treated as criminal offences and sent before a special jury-commission. If these regulations were successfully carried into effect, every Italian man of business would be compelled to become at the same time an Italian landholder, and the class of capitalists subsisting merely on their interest would disappear wholly from Italy. Indirectly too the no less injurious category of insolvent landowners who practically managed their estates merely for their creditors was by this means materially curtailed, inasmuch as the creditors, if they desired to continue their lending business, were compelled to buy for themselves. From this very fact besides it is plain that Caesar wished by no means simply to renew that naïve prohibition of interest by the old popular party, but on the contrary to allow the taking of interest within certain limits. It is very probable however that he did not confine himself to that injunction—which applied merely to Italy—of a maximum amount of sums to be lent, but also, especially with respect to the provinces, prescribed maximum rates for interest itself. The enactments—that it was illegal to take higher interest than 1 per cent. per month, or to take interest on arrears of interest, or in fine to make a judicial claim for arrears of interest to a greater amount than a sum equal to the capital—were, probably also after the Graeco-

Egyptian model,[1] first introduced in the Roman empire by Lucius Lucullus for Asia Minor and retained there by his better successors; soon afterwards they were transferred to other provinces by edicts of the governors, and ultimately at least part of them was provided with the force of law in all provinces by a decree of the Roman senate of $\frac{704}{50}$. The fact that these Lucullan enactments afterwards appear in all their compass as imperial law and so became the basis of the Roman and indeed of modern legislation as to interest, may perhaps be traceable to an ordinance of Caesar.

Hand in hand with these efforts to guard against the ascendancy of capital went the endeavours to bring back agriculture to the path which was most advantageous for the commonwealth. For this purpose the improvement of the administration of justice and of police was very essential. Hitherto nobody in Italy had been sure of his life and of his movable or immovable property; Roman *condottieri* for instance, at the intervals when their gangs were not helping to manage the politics of the capital, applied themselves to robbery in the forests of Etruria or rounded off the country estates of their paymasters by fresh acquisitions; but this sort of club-law was now at an end; and in particular the agricultural population of all classes must have felt the beneficial effects of the change. The plans of Caesar for great works also, which were not at all limited to the capital, were intended to tell in this respect; the construction, for instance, of a convenient high road from Rome through the passes of the Apennines to the Adriatic was designed to stimulate the internal traffic of Italy, and the lowering the level of the Fucine lake to benefit the Marsian farmers. But Caesar also sought by more direct measures to influence the state of Italian husbandry. The Italian graziers were required to take at least a third of their herdsmen from freeborn adults, whereby brigandage was checked and at the same time a source of gain was opened to the free proletariate. In the agrarian question Caesar who already in his first consulship had been in a position to regulate it (p. 188), more judicious than Tiberius Gracchus, did not seek to restore the farmer-system at any price, even at that of a revolution—concealed under juristic clauses—directed against property;

[1] At least the latter rule occurs in the old Egyptian royal laws (Diodorus, i. 79). On the other hand the Solonian legislation knows no restrictions on interest, but on the contrary expressly allows interest to be fixed of any amount at pleasure.

by him on the contrary, as by every other genuine statesman, the security of that which is property or is at any rate regarded by the public as property was esteemed as the first and most inviolable of all political maxims, and it was only within the limits assigned by this maxim that he sought to accomplish the elevation of the Italian small holdings, which appeared to him as a vital question for the nation. Even as it was, there was much still left for him in this respect to do. Every private right, whether it was called property or designated as heritable possession, whether traceable to Gracchus or to Sulla, was unconditionally respected by him. On the other hand Caesar, after he had in his strictly economical fashion—which tolerated no waste and no negligence even on a small scale—instituted a general revision of the Italian titles to property by the revived commission of twenty (p. 190), destined the whole actual domain land of Italy (including a considerable portion of the lands that were in the hands of spiritual guilds but legally belonged to the state) for distribution in the Gracchan fashion, so far, of course, as it was fitted for agriculture; the Apulian summer and the Samnite winter pastures belonging to the state continued to be domain; and it was at least the design of the Imperator, if these domains should not suffice, to procure the additional land requisite by the purchase of Italian estates from the public funds. In the selection of the new farmers provision was naturally made first of all for the veteran soldiers, and as far as possible the burden, which the levy imposed on the mother country, was converted into a benefit by the fact that Caesar gave the proletarian, who was levied from it as a recruit, back to it as a farmer; it is remarkable also that the desolate Latin communities, such as Veii and Capena, seem to have been especially provided with new colonists. The regulation of Caesar that the new owners should not be entitled to alienate the lands received by them till after twenty years, was a happy medium between the full bestowal of the right of alienation, which would have brought the larger portion of the distributed land speedily back into the hands of the great capitalists, and the permanent restrictions on free trade in land which Tiberius Gracchus (iii. 85, 91, 125) and Sulla (iii. 336, iv. 83) had enacted, both equally in vain.

Lastly, while the government thus energetically applied itself to remove the diseased, and to strengthen the sound, elements of the Italian national life, the newly-regulated municipal system—which had but recently developed itself out of the crisis of the Social War in and alongside of the state-economy (iii. 354)—was intended to communicate to the new absolute monarchy the communal life which was compatible with it, and to impart to the sluggish circulation of the noblest elements of public life once more a quickened action. The leading principles in the two municipal ordinances issued in $\frac{705}{49}$ for Cisalpine Gaul and in $\frac{709}{45}$ for Italy,[1] the latter of which remained the fundamental law for all succeeding times, are apparently, first, the strict purifying of the urban corporations from all immoral elements, while yet no trace of political police occurs; secondly, the utmost restriction of centralisation and the utmost freedom of movement in the communities, to which there was even now reserved the election of magistrates and a limited civil and criminal jurisdiction. The general police enactments, such as the restrictions on the right of association (p. 475), came, it is true, into operation also here.

Such were the ordinances by which Caesar attempted to reform the Italian national economy. It is easy both to show their insufficiency, seeing that they allowed a multitude of evils still to exist, and to prove that they operated in various respects injuriously by imposing restrictions, some of which were very severely felt, on freedom of trade. It is still easier to show that the evils of the Italian national economy generally were incurable. But in spite of this the practical statesman will admire the work as well as the master-workman. It was no small achievement, that in circumstances where a man like Sulla, despairing of remedy, had contented himself with a mere formal reorganisation, the evil was seized in its proper seat and grappled with there; and we may well conclude that Caesar with his reforms came as near to the measure of what was possible as it was given to a statesman and a Roman to come. He could not and did not expect from them the regeneration of Italy; but he sought on the contrary to attain this in a very different way, for the right apprehension of which it is necessary first of all to review the condition of the provinces as Caesar found them.

The provinces, which Caesar found in existence, were fourteen in number: seven European—the Further and the Hither Spain, Transalpine Gaul, Italian Gaul with Illyricum, Macedonia with Greece, Sicily, Sardinia with Corsica; five Asiatic—Asia, Bithynia and Pontus, Cilicia with Cyprus, Syria, Crete; and two African—Cyrene and Africa. To these Caesar added

[1] Of both laws considerable fragments still exist.

three new ones by the erection of the two new governorships of Lugdunese Gaul and Belgia (p. 266) and by constituting Illyria a separate province.[1]

In the administration of these provinces oligarchic misrule reached a point which, notwithstanding various noteworthy performances in this line, no second government has ever attained at least in the West, and which according to our ideas it seems no longer possible to surpass. Certainly the responsibility for this rests not on the Romans alone. Almost everywhere before their day the Greek, Phoenician, or Asiatic rule had already driven out of the nations the higher spirit and the sense of right and of liberty belonging to better times. It was doubtless hard, that every accused provincial was bound, when asked, to appear personally in Rome to answer for himself; that the Roman governor interfered at pleasure in the administration of justice and the management of the dependent communities, pronounced capital sentences, and cancelled transactions of the municipal council; and that in case of war he treated the militia as he chose and often infamously, as *e.g.* when Cotta at the siege of the Pontic Heraclea assigned to the militia all the posts of danger to save his Italians, and on the siege not going according to his wish, ordered the heads of his engineers to be laid at his feet. It was doubtless hard, that no rule of morality or of penal justice was longer binding on the Roman administrators and their train, and that violent outrages, rapes, and murders with or without form of law were of daily occurrence in the provinces. But these things were at least nothing new; almost everywhere men had long been accustomed to be treated like slaves, and it signified little in the long run whether a Carthaginian overseer, a Syrian satrap, or a Roman proconsul acted as the local tyrant. Their material well-being, almost the only thing for which the provincials still cared, was far less disturbed by those occurrences, which although numerous in proportion to the many tyrants yet affected merely isolated individuals, than by the financial exactions pressing heavily on all, which had never previously been prosecuted with such energy.

The Romans now gave fearful proof of their old mastery of finance in this field. We have already endeavoured to

[1] As according to Caesar's ordinance annually sixteen propraetors and two proconsuls divided the governorships among them, and the latter remained two years in office (p. 453), we might conclude that he intended to bring the number of provinces in all up to twenty. Certainty is, however, the less attainable as to this, seeing that Caesar perhaps designedly instituted fewer offices than candidatures.

describe the Roman system of provincial oppression in its modest and rational foundations as well as in its growth and corruption (iii. 372-379); as a matter of course, the latter went on increasing. The ordinary taxes became far more oppressive from the inequality of their distribution and from the preposterous system of levying them than from their high amount. As to the burden of quartering troops, Roman statesmen themselves expressed the opinion that a town suffered nearly to the same extent when a Roman army took up winter quarters in it as when an enemy took it by storm. While the taxation in its original character had been an indemnification for the burden of military defence undertaken by Rome, and the community paying tribute had thus a right to remain exempt from ordinary service, garrison-service was now—as is attested *e.g.* in the case of Sardinia—for the most part imposed on the provincials, and even in the ordinary armies, besides other duties, the whole heavy burden of the cavalry-service was devolved on them. The extraordinary contributions demanded—such as, the deliveries of grain for little or no compensation to benefit the proletariate of the capital; the frequent and costly naval armaments and coast-defences in order to check piracy; the task of supplying works of art, wild beasts, or other demands of the insane Roman luxury in the theatre and the chase; the military requisitions in case of war—were just as frequent as they were oppressive and incalculable. A single instance may show how far things were carried. During the three years' administration of Sicily by Gaius Verres the number of farmers in Leontini fell from 84 to 32, in Motya from 187 to 86, in Herbita from 252 to 120, in Agyrium from 250 to 80; so that in four of the most fertile districts of Sicily 59 per cent. of the landholders preferred to let their fields lie fallow than to cultivate them under this *régime.* And these landholders were, as their small number shows and as is expressly stated, not at all small farmers, but respectable planters and in great part Roman burgesses!

In the client states the forms of taxation were somewhat different, but the burdens themselves were if possible still worse, since in addition to the exactions of the Romans there came those of the native courts. In Cappadocia and Egypt the farmer as well as the king was bankrupt; the former was unable to satisfy the tax-collector, the latter was unable to satisfy his Roman creditor. Add to these the exactions, properly so called, not merely of the governor himself, but also of his "friends," each of whom fancied that he had as it were a draft on the governor and a title accordingly to return from the province a made man. The Roman oligarchy in this respect exactly resembled a gang of robbers, and followed out the plundering of the provincials in a professional and business-like manner; the able members of the gang set to work not too nicely, for they had in fact to share the spoil with the advocates and the jurymen, and the more they stole, they did so the more securely. The notion of honour in theft too was already developed; the big robber looked down on the little, and the latter on the mere thief, with contempt; any one, who had been once for a wonder condemned, boasted of the high figure of the sums which he was proved to have exacted. Such was the behaviour in the provinces of the successors of those men who had been accustomed to bring home nothing from their administration but the thanks of the subjects and the approbation of their fellow-citizens.

But still worse, if possible, and still less subject to any control was the havoc committed by the Italian men of business among the unhappy provincials. The most lucrative portions of the landed property and the whole commercial and monetary business in the provinces were concentrated in their hands. The estates in the transmarine regions, which belonged to Italian grandees, were exposed to all the misery of management by stewards, and never saw their owner; excepting possibly the hunting-parks, which occur as early as this time in Transalpine Gaul with an area amounting to nearly twenty square miles. Usury flourished as it had never flourished before. The small landowners in Illyricum, Asia, and Egypt managed their estates even in Varro's time in great part practically as the debtor-slaves of their Roman or non-Roman creditors, just as the plebeians in former days for their patrician lords. Cases occurred of capital being lent even to urban communities at four per cent. per month. It was no unusual thing for an energetic and influential man of business to get either the title of envoy [1] given to him by the senate or that of officer by the governor, and, if possible, to have men put at his service for the better prosecution of his affairs; a case is narrated on credible authority, where one of these honourable martial bankers on account of a claim against the town of Salamis in Cyprus kept its municipal council blockaded in the town-house, until five of the members had died of hunger.

[1] This is the so-called "free embassy" (*libera legatio*), namely an embassy without any proper public errand.

To these two modes of oppression, each of which by itself was intolerable and which were always becoming better arranged to work into each other's hands, were added the general calamities, for which the Roman government was also in great part, at least indirectly, responsible. In the various wars a large amount of capital was dragged away from the country and a larger amount destroyed sometimes by the barbarians, sometimes by the Roman armies. Owing to the worthlessness of the Roman land and maritime police, brigands and pirates swarmed everywhere. In Sardinia and the interior of Asia Minor brigandage was endemic; in Africa and Further Spain it became necessary to fortify all buildings constructed outside of the city-enclosures with walls and towers. The fearful evil of piracy has been already described in another connection (p. 37). The panaceas of the prohibitive system, with which the Roman governor was wont to interpose when scarcity of money or dearth occurred, as under such circumstances they could not fail to do—the prohibition of the export of gold or grain from the province—did not mend the matter. The communal affairs were almost everywhere embarrassed, in addition to the general distress, by local disorders and frauds of the public officials.

Where such grievances afflicted communities and individuals not temporarily but for generations with an inevitable, steady, and yearly-increasing oppression, the best regulated public and private economy could not but succumb to them, and the most unspeakable misery could not but extend over all the nations from the Tagus to the Euphrates. "All the communities," it is said in a treatise published as early as $\frac{684}{70}$, "are ruined;" the same truth is specially attested as regards Spain and Narbonese Gaul, the very provinces which, comparatively speaking, were still in the most tolerable economic position. In Asia Minor even towns like Samos and Halicarnassus stood almost empty; legal slavery seemed here a haven of rest compared with the torments to which the free provincial succumbed, and even the patient Asiatic had become, according to the descriptions of Roman statesmen themselves, weary of life. Any one who desires to fathom the depths to which man can sink in the criminal infliction, and in the no less criminal endurance, of all conceivable injustice, may altogether from the criminal records of this period the wrongs which Roman grandees could perpetrate and Greeks, Syrians, and Phoenicians could suffer. Even the statesmen of Rome herself publicly and frankly conceded that the Roman name was unutterably odious through all Greece and Asia; and, when the burgesses of the Pontic Heraclea on one occasion put to death the whole of the Roman tax-collectors, the only matter for regret was that such things did not occur oftener.

The Optimates scoffed at the new master who went in person to inspect his "farms" one after the other; in reality the condition of the several provinces demanded all the earnestness and all the wisdom of one of those rare men, who redeem the name of king from being regarded by the nations as merely a conspicuous example of human insufficiency. The wounds inflicted had to be healed by time; Caesar took care that they might be so healed, and that there should be no fresh inflictions.

The system of administration was thoroughly remodelled. The Sullan proconsuls and propraetors had been in their provinces essentially sovereign and practically subject to no control; those of Caesar were the well-disciplined servants of a stern master, who from the very unity and life-tenure of his power sustained a more natural and more tolerable relation to the subjects than those numerous, annually changing, petty tyrants. The governorships were no doubt still distributed among the annually retiring two consuls and sixteen praetors, but, as the Imperator directly nominated eight of the latter and the distribution of the provinces among the competitors depended solely on him (p. 453), they were in reality bestowed by the Imperator. The functions also of the governors were practically restricted. The superintendence of the administration of justice and the administrative control of the communities remained in their hands; but their command was paralysed by the new supreme command in Rome and its adjutants associated with the governor (p. 461), and the raising of the taxes was probably even now committed in the provinces substantially to imperial officials (p. 453), so that the governor was thenceforward surrounded with an auxiliary staff which was absolutely dependent on the Imperator in virtue either of the laws of the military hierarchy or of the still stricter laws of domestic discipline. While hitherto the proconsul and his quaestor had appeared as if they were members of a gang of robbers despatched to levy contributions, the magistrates of Caesar were present to protect the weak against the strong; and, instead of the previous worse than useless control of the equestrian or senatorian tribunals, they had to answer for themselves at the bar of a just and unrelenting monarch. The law as to exactions, the enactments of which Caesar had already in his first consulate made more stringent, was applied by him against the chief commandants in the provinces with an inexorable severity going even beyond its letter; and the tax-officers, if indeed they ventured to indulge in an injustice, atoned for it to their master, as slaves and freedmen according to the cruel domestic law of that time were wont to atone.

The extraordinary public burdens were reduced to the right proportion and the actual necessity; the ordinary burdens were materially lessened. We have already mentioned the comprehensive regulation of taxation (p. 466); the extension of the exemptions from tribute, the general lowering of the direct taxes, the limitation of the system of *decumae* to Africa and Sardinia, the complete setting aside of middlemen in the collection of the direct taxes, were most beneficial reforms for the provincials. That Caesar after the example of one of his greatest democratic predecessors, Sertorius (p. 20), wished to free the subjects from the burden of quartering troops and to insist on the soldiers erecting for themselves permanent encampments resembling towns, cannot indeed be proved; but he was, at least, after he had exchanged the part of pretender for that of king, not the man to abandon the subject to the soldier; and it was in keeping with his spirit, when the heirs of his policy created such military camps, and then converted them into towns which formed rallying-points for Italian civilisation amidst the barbarian frontier districts.

It was a task far more difficult than the checking of official irregularities, to deliver the provincials from the oppressive ascendancy of Roman capital. Its power could not be directly broken without applying means which were still more dangerous than the evil; the government could for the time being abolish only isolated abuses—as when Caesar for instance prohibited the employment of the title of state-envoy for financial purposes—and meet manifest acts of violence and palpable usury by a sharp application of the general penal laws and of the laws as to usury, which extended also to the provinces (p. 496); but a more radical cure of the evil was only to be expected from the reviving prosperity of the provincials under a better administration. Temporary enactments, to relieve the insolvency of particular provinces, had been issued on several occasions in recent times. Caesar himself had in $\frac{694}{60}$ when governor of Further Spain assigned to the creditors two-thirds of the income of their debtors in order to pay themselves from that source.

Lucius Lucullus likewise when governor of Asia Minor had directly cancelled a portion of the arrears of interest which had swelled beyond measure and had for the remaining portion assigned to the creditors a fourth part of the produce of the lands of their debtors, as well as a suitable proportion of the profits accruing to them from house-rents or slave-labour. We are not expressly told that Caesar after the civil war instituted similar general liquidations of debt in the provinces; yet from what has just been remarked and from what was done in the case of Italy (p. 496), it can hardly be doubted that Caesar likewise directed his efforts towards this object, or at least that it formed part of his plan.

While thus the Imperator, as far as lay within human power, relieved the provincials from the oppressions of the magistrates and capitalists of Rome, it might at the same time be with certainty expected from the government to which he imparted fresh vigour, that it would scare off the wild border-peoples and disperse the freebooters by land and sea, as the rising sun chases away the mist. However the old wounds might still smart, with Caesar there appeared for the sorely tortured subjects the dawn of a more tolerable epoch, the first intelligent and humane government that had appeared for centuries, and a policy of peace which rested not on cowardice but on strength. Well might the subjects in particular mourn along with the best Romans by the bier of the great liberator.

But this abolition of existing abuses was not the main matter in Caesar's provincial reform. In the Roman republic, according to the view of the aristocracy and democracy alike, the provinces had been nothing but—what they were frequently called—country-estates of the Roman people, and they were employed and worked out as such. This view had now passed away. The provinces as such were gradually to disappear, in order to prepare for the renovated Helleno-Italic nation a new and more spacious home, of whose several component parts no one existed merely for the sake of another but all for each and each for all; the new existence in the renovated home, the fresher, broader, grander national life, was of itself to overbear the sorrows and wrongs of the nation for which there was no help in the old Italy. These ideas, as is well known, were not new. The emigration from Italy to the provinces that had been regularly going on for centuries had long since, though unconsciously on the part of the emigrants themselves, paved the way for such an extension of Italy. The first who in a systematic way guided the Italians to settle beyond the bounds of Italy was Gaius Gracchus, the creator of the Roman democratic monarchy, the author of the Transalpine conquests, the founder of the colonies of Carthage and Narbo. Then the second statesman of genius produced by the Roman democracy, Quintus Sertorius, began to introduce the barbarous Occidentals to Latin civilisation; he gave to the Spanish youth of rank the Roman dress, and urged them to speak Latin and to acquire the higher Italian culture at the training institution founded by him in Osca. When Caesar entered on the government, a large Italian population—though, in great part, lacking stability and concentration—already existed in all the provinces and client-states. To say nothing of the formally Italian towns in Spain and southern Gaul, we need only recall the numerous troops of burgesses raised by Sertorius and Pompeius in Spain by Caesar in Gaul, by Juba in Numidia, by the constitutional party in Africa, Macedonia, Greece, Asia Minor, and Crete; the Latin lyre—ill-tuned doubtless—on which the town-poets of Corduba as early as the Sertorian war sang the praises of the Roman generals; and the translations of Greek poetry valued on account of their very elegance of language, which the earliest extra-Italian poet of note, the Transalpine Publius Terentius Varro of the Aude, published shortly after Caesar's death.

On the other hand the interpenetration of the Latin and Hellenic character was, we might say, as old as Rome. On occasion of the union of Italy the conquering Latin nation had assimilated to itself all the other conquered nationalities, excepting only the Greek, which was received just as it stood without any attempt at external amalgamation. Wherever the Roman legionary went, the Greek schoolmaster, no less a conqueror in his own way, followed; at an early date we find famous teachers of the Greek language settled on the Guadalquivir, and Greek was as well taught as Latin in the institute at Osca. The higher Roman culture itself was in fact nothing else than the proclamation of the great gospel of Hellenic manners and art in the Italian idiom; against the modest pretension of the civilising conquerors to proclaim it first of all in their own language to the barbarians of the West the Hellene at least could not loudly protest. Already the Greek everywhere—and, most decidedly, just where the national feeling was purest and strongest, on the frontiers threatened by barbaric denationalisation, *e.g.*, in Massilia, on the north coast of the Black Sea, and on the Euphrates and Tigris—descried the protector and avenger of

Hellenism in Rome; and in fact the foundation of towns by Pompeius in the far East resumed after an interruption of centuries the beneficent work of Alexander.

The idea of an Italo-Hellenic empire with two languages and a single nationality was not new—otherwise it would have been nothing but a blunder; but the development of it from floating projects to a firmly-grasped conception, from scattered initial efforts to the laying of a secure and concentrated foundation, was the work of the third and greatest of the democratic statesmen of Rome.

The first and most essential condition for the political and national levelling of the empire was the preservation and extension of the two nations destined to joint dominion, along with the absorption as rapidly as possible of the barbarian races, or those termed barbarian, existing by their side. In a certain sense we might no doubt name along with Romans and Greeks a third nationality, which vied with them in ubiquity in the world of that day, and was destined to play no insignificant part in the new state of Caesar. We speak of the Jews. This remarkable people, yielding and yet tenacious, was in the ancient as in the modern world everywhere and nowhere at home, and everywhere and nowhere powerful. The successors of David and Solomon were of hardly more significance for the Jews of that age than Jerusalem for those of the present day; the nation found doubtless for its religious and intellectual unity a visible rallying-point in the petty kingdom of Jerusalem, but the nation itself consisted not merely of the subjects of the Hasmonaeans, but of the innumerable bodies of Jews scattered through the whole Parthian and the whole Roman empire. Within the cities of Alexandria especially and of Cyrene the Jews formed special communities administratively and even locally distinct, not unlike the "Jews' quarters" of our towns, but with a freer position and superintended by a "master of the people" as superior judge and administrator. How numerous even in Rome the Jewish population was already before Caesar's time, and how closely at the same time the Jews even then kept together as fellow-countrymen, is shown by the remark of an author of this period, that it was dangerous for a governor to offend the Jews in his province, because he might then certainly reckon on being hissed after his return by the populace of the capital. Even at this time the predominant business of the Jews was trade; the Jewish trader moved everywhere with the conquering Roman merchant then, in the same way as he afterwards accompanied the Genoese and the Venetian, and capital flowed in on all hands to the Jewish, by the side of the Roman, merchants. At this period too we encounter the peculiar antipathy of the Occidentals towards this so thoroughly Oriental race and their foreign opinions and customs. This Judaism, although not the most pleasing feature in the nowhere pleasing picture of the mixture of nations which then prevailed, was nevertheless an historical element developing itself in the natural course of things, which the statesmen could neither ignore nor combat, and which Caesar on the contrary, just like his predecessor Alexander, with correct discernment of the circumstances, fostered as far as possible. While Alexander, by laying the foundation of Alexandrian Judaism, did not much less for the nation than its own David by building the temple of Jerusalem, Caesar also advanced the interests of the Jews in Alexandria and in Rome by special favours and privileges, and protected in particular their peculiar worship against the Roman as well as against the Greek local priests. The two great men of course did not contemplate placing the Jewish nationality on an equal footing with the Hellenic or Italo-Hellenic. But the Jew who has not like the Occidental received the Pandora's gift of political organisation, and stands substantially in a relation of indifference to the state; who moreover is as reluctant to give up the essence of his national idiosyncrasy as he is ready to clothe it with any nationality at pleasure and to adapt himself up to a certain degree to foreign habits—the Jew was for this very reason as it were made for a state which was to be built on the ruins of a hundred living polities and to be endowed with a somewhat abstract and, from the outset, weakened nationality. In the ancient world also Judaism was an effective leaven of cosmopolitanism and of national decomposition, and to that extent a specially privileged member in the Caesarian state, the polity of which was really nothing but a citizenship of the world, and the nationality of which was really nothing but humanity.

But the Latin and Hellenic nationalities continued to be exclusively the positive elements of the new citizenship. The distinctively Italian state of the republic was thus at an end; but the rumour that Caesar was ruining Italy and Rome on purpose to transfer the centre of the empire to the Greek East and to make Ilion or Alexandria its capital, was nothing but a piece of talk—very easy to be accounted for, but also very silly—of the angry nobility. On the contrary, in Caesar's organisations the Latin nationality always retained the ascendancy; as is indicated in the very fact that he issued all his enactments in Latin, although those destined for the Greek-speaking countries were at the same time issued in Greek. In general he arranged the relations of the two great nations in his monarchy just as his republican predecessors had arranged them in the united Italy; the Hellenic nationality was protected where it existed, the Italian was extended as far as circumstances permitted, and the inheritance of the races to be absorbed was destined for it. This was necessary, because an entire equalising of the Greek and Latin elements in the state would in all probability have in a very short time occasioned that catastrophe which Byzantinism brought about several centuries later; for the Greek element was superior to the Roman not merely in all intellectual aspects, but also in the measure of its predominance, and it had within Italy itself in the hosts of Hellenes and half-Hellenes who migrated compulsorily or voluntarily to Italy an endless number of apostles apparently insignificant, but whose influence could not be estimated too highly. To mention only the most conspicuous phenomenon in this respect, the rule of Greek lackeys over the Roman monarchs is as old as the monarchy. The first in the equally long and repulsive list of these personages is the confidential servant of Pompeius, Theophanes of Mytilene, who by his power over his weak master contributed probably more than any one else to the outbreak of the war between Pompeius and Caesar. Not wholly without reason he was after his death treated with divine honours by his countrymen; he commenced, forsooth, the *valet de chambre* government of the imperial period which in a certain measure was just a dominion of the Hellenes over the Romans. The government had accordingly every reason not to encourage by its direct action the extension of Hellenism at least in the West; but the Greek element, wherever it existed, was preserved and protected. However political crises might suggest to the Imperator the demolition of the strong pillars of Hellenism in the West and in Egypt, Massilia and Alexandria were neither destroyed nor denationalised. If Sicily was not simply relieved of the presence of the *decumae* but had its communities invested with Latin rights, which was probably meant to be followed in due time by full equalisation with Italy, Caesar's design beyond doubt was not to Latinise Sicily, but to attach that glorious island—which nature had destined not so much to be an appendage to Italy, as to be the finest of its provinces—to the association of the Italian com munities, under retention of its Hellenic nationality, just like Neapolis and Rhegium.

On the other hand the Roman element was promoted by the government through colonisation and Latinising with all vigour and at the most various points of the kingdom. The principle, which originated no doubt from a bad combination of formal law and brute force, but was inevitably necessary in order to deal freely with the nations destined to destruction—that all the soil in the provinces not ceded by special act of the government to communities or private persons was the property of the state, and the holder of it for the time being had merely an heritable possession on sufferance and revocable at any time—was retained by Caesar and raised by him from a democratic party-theory to a fundamental principle of monarchical law.

Gaul, of course, fell to be primarily dealt with in the extension of Roman nationality. Cisalpine Gaul obtained throughout—what a great part of the inhabitants had long enjoyed—political equalisation with the leading country by the admission of the Transpadane communities into the Roman burgess-union, which had for long been assumed by the democracy as accomplished (pp. 4, 293) and was now ($\frac{705}{49}$) finally accomplished by Caesar. Practically this province had already completely Latinised itself during the forty years which had elapsed since the bestowal of Latin rights. The exclusives might ridicule the broad and gurgling accent of the Celtic Latin, and miss "an undefined something of the grace of the capital" in the Insubrian or Venetian, who as Caesar's legionary had conquered for himself with his sword a place in the Roman Forum and even in the Roman senate. Nevertheless Cisalpine Gaul with its dense chiefly agricultural population was even before Caesar's time practically an Italian country, and remained for centuries the true asylum of Italian manners and Italian culture; indeed the teachers of Latin literature found nowhere else out of the capital so much encouragement and approbation.

While Cisalpine Gaul was thus substantially merged in Italy, the place which it had hitherto occupied was taken by the old Transalpine province, which had been converted by the conquests of Caesar from a frontier into an inland province, and which by its vicinity as well as by its climate was fitted beyond all other regions to become in due course of time likewise an Italian land. Thither principally, according to the old aim of the transmarine settlements of the Roman democracy, was the stream of Italian emigration directed. There the ancient colony of Narbo was reinforced by new settlers, and four new burgess-colonies were instituted at Baeterrae (Beziers) not far from Narbo, at Arelate (Arles) and Arausio (Orange) on the Rhone, and at the new seaport Forum Julii (Fréjus); while the names assigned to them at the same time preserved the memory of the brave legions which had annexed northern Gaul to the empire.[1] The townships not furnished with colonists appear, at least for the most part, to have been led on towards Romanisation in the same way as Transpadane Gaul in former times (iii. 234) by the bestowal of Latin rights; in particular Nemausus (Nîmes), as the chief place of the territory taken from the Massiliots in consequence of their revolt against Caesar (p. 367), was converted from a Massiliot village into a Latin urban community, and endowed with a considerable territory and even with the right of coinage.[2] While Cisalpine Gaul thus advanced from the preparatory stage to full equality with Italy, the Narbonese province advanced at the same time into that preparatory stage; just as previously in Cisalpine Gaul, the most considerable communities there had the full franchise, the rest Latin rights.

In the other non-Greek and non-Latin regions of the empire, which were still more remote from the influence of Italy and the process of assimilation, Caesar confined himself to the establishment of several centres for Italian civilisation such as Narbo had hitherto been in Gaul, in order by their means to pave the way for a future complete equalisation. Such pre-

[1] Narbo was called the colony of the Decimani, Baeterrae of the Septimani, Forum Julii of the Octavani, Arelate (and besides this the Latin colony of Ruscino) of the Sextani, Arausio of the Secundani. The ninth legion is wanting, because it had disgraced its number by the mutiny of Placentia (p. 379). That the colonists of these colonies belonged to the legions from which they took their names, is not stated and is not credible the veterans themselves were, at least the great majority of them, settled in Italy (p. 463). Cicero's complaint, that Caesar "had confiscated whole provinces and districts at a blow" (*De Off.* ii. 7, 27; comp. *Philipp.* xiii. 15, 31, 32) relates beyond doubt, as its close connection with the censure of the triumph over the Massiliots proves, to the confiscations of land made on account of these colonies in the Narbonese province and primarily to the losses of territory imposed on Massilia.

[2] We are not expressly informed from whom the Latin rights of the non-colonised townships of this region and especially of Nemausus proceeded. But Caesar himself (*B. C.* i. 35) virtually states that Nemausus up to $\frac{705}{49}$ was a Massiliot village; as according to Livy's account (Dio, xli. 25; Flor. ii. 13; Oros. vi. 15) this very portion of territory was taken from the Massiliots by Caesar; and lastly as even on pre-Augustan coins and then in Strabo the town appears as a community of Latin rights, Caesar alone can have been the author of this bestowal of Latinity. As to Ruscino (Roussillon near Perpignan) and other communities in Narbonese Gaul which early attained a Latin constitution, we can only conjecture that they received it contemporarily with Nemausus.

liminary foundations can be pointed out in all the provinces of the empire, with the exception of the poorest and least important of all, Sardinia. How Caesar proceeded in Northern Gaul, we have already set forth (p. 266); the Latin language obtained there general official recognition, though not yet employed for all branches of public intercourse, and the colony of Noviodunum (Nyon) arose on the Leman lake as the most northerly town with an Italian constitution.

In Spain, which was probably at that time the most densely peopled country of the Roman empire, Caesarian colonists, so far as we see, were settled only in the important Helleno-Iberian seaport town of Emporiae by the side of the old population. On the other hand the ancient and wealthy mercantile city of Gades, whose municipal system Caesar even when praetor had remodelled suitably to the times, now obtained from the Imperator the full rights of the Italian *municipia* ($\frac{705}{49}$) and became —what Tusculum had been in Italy (i. 345)—the first extra-Italian community not founded by Rome which was admitted into the Roman burgess-union. Some years afterwards ($\frac{709}{45}$) similar rights were conferred also on some other Spanish communities, and Latin rights probably on still more.

In Africa the project, which Gaius Gracchus had not been allowed to bring to an issue, was now carried out, and on the spot where the city of the hereditary foes of Rome had stood, 3000 Italian colonists and a great number of the tenants on lease and sufferance resident in the Carthaginian territory were settled; and the new "Venus-colony," the Roman Carthage, throve with amazing rapidity under the singularly favourable circumstances of the locality. Utica, hitherto the capital and first commercial town in the province, had already been in some measure compensated beforehand, apparently by the bestowal of Latin rights, for the revival of its superior rival. In the Numidian territory newly annexed to the empire the important Cirta and the other communities assigned to the Roman *condottiere* Publius Sittius for himself and his troops (p. 421) obtained the rights of Roman military colonies. The stately provincial towns indeed, with the insane fury of Juba and of the desperate remnant of the constitutional party had converted into ruins, did not revive so rapidly as they had been reduced to ashes, and many a ruinous site recalled long afterwards this fatal period; but the two new Julian colonies, Carthage and Cirta, became and continued to be the centres of Africano-Roman civilisation.

In the desolate land of Greece, Caesar, besides other plans such as the institution of a Roman colony in Buthrotum (opposite Corfu), busied himself above all with the restoration of Corinth. Not only was a considerable burgess-colony conducted thither, but a plan was projected for cutting through the isthmus, so as to avoid the dangerous circumnavigation of the Peloponnesus and to make the whole traffic between Italy and Asia pass through the Corintho-Saronic gulf. Lastly, even in the remote Hellenic East the monarch called into existence Italian settlements; on the Black Sea, for instance, at Heraclea and Sinope, which towns the Italian colonists shared, as in the case of Emporiae, with the old inhabitants; on the Syrian coast, in the important port of Berytus, which like Sinope obtained an Italian constitution; and even in Egypt, where a Roman station was established on the lighthouse-island commanding the harbour of Alexandria.

Through these ordinances the Italian municipal freedom was carried into the provinces in a manner far more comprehensive than had been previously the case. The communities of full burgesses—that is, all the towns of the Cisalpine province and the burgess-colonies and burgess-*municipia* scattered in Transalpine Gaul and elsewhere—were on an equal footing with the Italian, in so far as they administered their own affairs, and even exercised a somewhat limited jurisdiction; while on the other hand the more important processes came before the Roman authority competent to deal with them—as a rule, the governor of the province.[1] The formally autonomous Latin and the other emancipated communities—including now those of Narbonese Gaul, all those of Sicily, so far as they were not burgess-communities, and a considerable number also in the other provinces—had not merely free administration, but

[1] That no community of full burgesses had more than limited jurisdiction, is certain. But the fact, which is distinctly apparent from the Caesarian municipal ordinance for Cisalpine Gaul, is a surprising one—that the processes lying beyond municipal competency from this province went not before its governor, but before the Roman praetor; for in other cases the governor is in his province quite as much representative of the praetor who administers justice between burgesses as of the praetor who administers justice between burgess and non-burgess, and is thoroughly competent to determine all processes. Beyond doubt this is a remnant of the arrangement before Sulla, under which in the whole continental territory as far as the Alps the urban magistrates alone were competent, and thus all the processes there, where they exceeded municipal competency, necessarily came before the praetors in Rome. In Narbo again, Gades, Carthage, Corinth, the processes in such a case went certainly to the governor concerned; as indeed even from practical considerations the carrying of a suit to Rome could not well be thought of.

probably unlimited jurisdiction; so that the governor was only entitled to interfere there by virtue of his—certainly very arbitrary—administrative control. No doubt even earlier there had been communities of full burgesses within the provinces of governors, such as Aquileia, Ravenna, Narbo, and whole governors' provinces, such as Cisalpine Gaul, had consisted of communities with Italian constitution; but it was, if not in law, at least in a political point of view a singularly important innovation, that there was now a province which as well as Italy was peopled solely by Roman burgesses,[1] and that others promised to become such.

With this disappeared the first great practical distinction that separated Italy from the provinces; and the second—that ordinarily no troops were stationed in Italy, while they were stationed in the provinces—was likewise in the course of disappearing; troops were now stationed only where there was a frontier to be defended, and the commandants of the provinces in which this was not the case, such as Narbo and Sicily, were officers only in name. The formal contrast between Italy and the provinces, which had at all times depended on other distinctions (ii. 62), continued certainly still to subsist—Italy being the sphere of the civil jurisdiction and of the consuls and praetors while the provinces were districts under the jurisdiction of martial law and subject to proconsuls and propraetors, but the procedure according to civil and according to martial law had for long been practically coincident, and the different titles of the magistrates signified little after the one Imperator was over all.

In all these various municipal foundations and ordinances—which are traceable at least in plan, if not perhaps all in execution, to Caesar—a definite system is apparent. Italy was converted from the mistress of the subject peoples into the mother of the renovated Italo-Hellenic nation. The Cisalpine province completely equalised with the mother-country was a promise and a guarantee that, in the monarchy of Caesar just as in the healthier times of the republic, every Latinised district

[1] It is difficult to see why the bestowal of the Roman franchise on a province collectively, and the continuance of a provincial administration for it, should be usually conceived as contrasts excluding each other. Besides, Cisalpine Gaul notoriously obtained the *civitas* at latest in $\frac{705}{49}$, while it remained a province as long as Caesar lived and was only united with Italy after his death (Dio, xlviii. 12); the governors also can be pointed out down to $\frac{711}{43}$. The very fact that the Caesarian ordinance never designates the country as Italy, but as Cisalpine Gaul, ought to have led to the right view.

might expect to be placed on an equal footing by the side of its elder sisters and of the mother herself. On the threshold of full national and political equalisation with Italy stood the adjoining lands, the Greek Sicily and the south of Gaul, which was rapidly becoming Latinised. In a more remote stage of preparation stood the other provinces of the empire, in which, just as hitherto in southern Gaul Narbo had been a Roman colony, the great maritime cities—Emporiae, Gades, Carthage, Corinth, Heraclea in Pontus, Sinope, Berytus, Alexandria—now became Italian or Helleno-Italian communities, the centres of an Italian civilisation even in the Greek East, the fundamental pillars of the future national and political equalisation of the empire. The rule of the urban community of Rome over the shores of the Mediterranean was at an end; in its stead came the new Mediterranean state, and its first act was to atone for the two greatest outrages which that urban community had perpetrated on civilisation. While the destruction of the two greatest marts of commerce in the Roman dominions marked the turning point at which the protectorate of the Roman community degenerated into political tyrannising over, and financial exaction from, the subject lands, the prompt and brilliant restoration of Carthage and Corinth marked the foundation of the new great commonwealth which was to train up all the regions on the Mediterranean to national and political equality, to union in a genuine state. Well might Caesar bestow on the city of Corinth in addition to its far-famed ancient name the new one of "Honour to Julius" (LAVS JVLI).

While thus the new united empire was furnished with a national character, which doubtless necessarily lacked individuality and was rather an inanimate product of art than a fresh growth of nature, it further had need of unity in those institutions which express the general life of nations—in constitution and administration, in religion and jurisprudence, in money, measures, and weights; as to which, of course, local diversities of the most varied character were quite compatible with essential union. In all these departments we can only speak of the initial steps, for the thorough formation of the monarchy of Caesar into an unity was the work of the future and all that he did was to lay the foundation for the building of centuries. But of the lines, which the great man drew in these departments, several can still be recognised; and it is more pleasing to follow him here, than in the task of reconstruction from the ruins of the nationalities.

As to constitution and administration, we have already noticed elsewhere the most important elements of the new unity—the transition of the sovereignty from the municipal council of Rome to the sole master of the Mediterranean monarchy; the conversion of that municipal council into a supreme imperial council representing Italy and the provinces; above all, the transference—now commenced—of the Roman, and generally of the Italian, municipal organisation to the provincial communities. This latter course—the bestowal of Latin, and thereafter of Roman, rights on the communities ripe for full admission to the united state—gradually of itself brought about uniform communal arrangements. In one respect alone this process could not be waited for. The new empire needed immediately an institution which should place before the government at a glance the principal bases of administration—the proportions of population and property in the different communities—in other words an improved census. First the census of Italy was reformed. Hitherto, strange to say, it had been always held exclusively in the capital, to the annoyance of the burgesses and to the injury of business. According to Caesar's ordinance[1] in future, when a census took place in the Roman community, there were to be simultaneously registered by the highest authority in each Italian community the name of every municipal burgess and that of his father or manumitter, his district, his age, and his property; and these lists were to be furnished to the Roman censor early enough to enable him to complete in proper time the general list of Roman burgesses and of Roman property. That it was Caesar's intention to introduce similar institutions also in the provinces is attested partly by the measurement and survey of the whole empire ordered by him, partly by the nature of the arrangement itself; for it in fact furnished the general instrument appropriate for procuring, as well in the Italian as in the non-Italian communities of the state, the information requisite for the central administration. Evidently here too it was Caesar's intention to revert to the traditions of the earlier republican times, and to reintroduce the census of the empire, which the earlier republic had effected—essentially in the same way as Caesar effected the Italian—by analogous extension of the institution of the urban censorship with its set terms and other essential rules

[1] That this was a change introduced by Caesar, and not possibly an enactment already made in consequence of the Social War, should never have been doubted (Cic. *Verr. act.* i. 18, 54 and elsewhere).

to all the subject communities of Italy and Sicily (i. 418, ii. 63). This had been one of the first institutions which the torpid aristocracy allowed to drop, and in this way deprived the supreme governing authority of any general view of the resources in men and taxation at its disposal and consequently of all possibility of an effective control (ii. 319). The indications still extant, and the very connection of things, show irrefragably that Caesar made preparations to renew the general census that had been obsolete for centuries.

We need scarcely say that in religion and in jurisprudence no thorough levelling could be thought of; yet with all toleration towards local faiths and municipal statutes the new state needed a common worship consonant to the Italo-Hellenic nationality and a general code of law superior to the municipal statutes. It needed them; for *de facto* both were already in existence. In the field of religion men had for centuries been busied in fusing together the Italian and Hellenic worships partly by external adoption, partly by internal adjustment of their respective conceptions of the gods; and owing to the pliant formless character of the Italian gods, there had been no great difficulty in resolving Jupiter into Zeus, Venus into Aphrodite, and so every essential idea of the Latin faith into its Hellenic counterpart. The Italo-Hellenic religion stood forth in its outlines ready-made; how much in this very department men were conscious of having gone beyond the specifically Roman point of view and advanced towards an Italo-Hellenic quasi-nationality, is shown by the distinction made in the already mentioned theology of Varro between the "common" gods, that is, those acknowledged by Romans and Greeks, and the special gods of the Roman community.

So far as concerns the field of criminal and police law, where the government more directly interferes and the necessities of the case are substantially met by a judicious legislation, there was no difficulty in attaining, in the way of legislative action, that degree of material uniformity which certainly was in this department needful for the unity of the empire. In the civil law again, where the initiative belongs to commercial intercourse and merely the formal shape to the legislator, the code for the united empire, which the legislator certainly could not have created, had been already long since developed naturally by commercial intercourse itself. The Roman urban law was still indeed legally based on the embodiment of the Latin national law contained in the Twelve Tables. Later laws had doubtless introduced various improvements of detail suited to the times, among which the most important was probably the abolition of the old inconvenient mode of commencing a process through standing forms of declaration by the parties (i. 154) and the substitution of an instruction to the single juryman drawn up in writing by the presiding magistrate (*formula*); but in the main the popular legislation had only piled upon that venerable foundation an endless chaos of special laws long since in great part antiquated and forgotten, which can only be compared to the English statutes at large. The attempts to impart to them scientific shape and system had certainly rendered the tortuous paths of the old civil law accessible, and thrown light upon them (iii. 445); but no Roman Blackstone could remedy the fundamental defect, that an urban code composed four hundred years ago with its equally diffuse and confused supplements was now to serve as the law of a great state.

Commercial intercourse provided for itself a more thorough remedy. The lively commerce between Romans and non-Romans had long ago developed in Rome an international private law (*ius gentium;* i. 157), that is to say, a body of maxims especially relating to commercial matters, according to which Roman judges pronounced judgment, when a cause could not be decided either according to their own or any other national code and they were compelled—setting aside the peculiarities of Roman, Hellenic, Phoenician and other law—to revert to the common perceptions of right underlying all commercial dealings. The formation of the newer law proceeded on this basis. In the first place as a standard for the legal dealings of Roman burgesses with each other, it *de facto* substituted for the old urban law, which had become practically useless, a new code based in substance on a compromise between the national law of the Twelve Tables and the international law or so-called law of nations. The former was essentially adhered to, though of course with modifications suited to the times, in the law of marriage, family, and inheritance; whereas in all regulations which concerned dealings with property, and consequently in reference to ownership and contracts, the international law was the standard; in these matters indeed various important arrangements were borrowed even from local provincial law, such as the legislation as to usury (p. 496), and the institution of *hypotheca*. Through whom, when, and how this comprehensive innovation came into existence, whether at once or gradually, whether through one or several authors, are questions to which we cannot furnish a satisfactory answer. We know only that this reform, as was natural, proceeded in the first instance from the urban court; that it was first embodied in the instructions annually issued by the *praetor urbanus*, when entering on office, for the guidance of the parties in reference to the most important maxims of law to be observed in the judicial year then beginning (*edictum annuum* or *perpetuum praetoris urbani*); and that, although various preparatory steps towards it may have been taken in earlier times, it certainly only attained its completion in this epoch. The new code was theoretic and abstract, inasmuch as the Roman view of law had therein divested itself of such of its national peculiarities as it had become aware of; but it was at the same time practical and positive, inasmuch as it by no means faded away into the dim twilight of general equity or even into the pure nothingness of the so-called law of nature, but was applied by definite functionaries for definite concrete cases according to fixed rules, and was not merely capable of, but had already essentially received, a statutory embodiment in the urban edict. This code moreover corresponded in matter to the wants of the time, in so far as it furnished the more convenient forms required by the increase of commerce for legal procedure, for acquisition of property, and for conclusion of contracts. Lastly, it had already in the main become subsidiary law throughout the compass of the Roman empire, inasmuch as—while the manifold local statutes were retained for those legal relations which were not directly commercial, as well as for local transactions between members of the same legal district—dealings relating to property between subjects of the empire belonging to different legal districts were regulated throughout after the model of the urban edict, though not applicable *de jure* to these cases, both in Italy and in the provinces. The law of the urban edict had thus essentially the same position in that age which the Roman law has occupied in our political development; this also is, so far as such opposites can be combined, at once abstract and positive; this also recommended itself by its (compared with the earlier legal code) flexible forms of intercourse, and took its place by the side of the local statutes as universal auxiliary law. But the Roman legal development had an essential advantage over ours in this, that the denationalised legislation appeared not, as with us, prematurely and by artificial birth, but at the right time and agreeably to nature.

Such was the state of the law as Caesar found it. When he projected the plan for a new code, it is not difficult to divine his intentions. This code could only comprehend the law of Roman burgesses, and could be a general code for the empire merely so far as a code of the ruling nation suitable to the times could not but of itself become general subsidiary law throughout the compass of the empire. In criminal law, if the plan embraced this at all, there was needed only a revision and adjustment of the Sullan ordinances. In civil law, for a state whose nationality was strictly humanity, the necessary and only possible formal shape was to invest that urban edict, which had already spontaneously grown out of lawful commerce, with the security and precision of statute-law. The first step towards this had been taken by the Cornelian law of $\frac{687}{67}$, when it enjoined the judge to keep to the maxims set forth at the beginning of his magistracy and not arbitrarily to administer other law (p. 148)—a regulation, which may well be compared with the law of the Twelve Tables, and which became almost as significant for the fixing of the latter urban law as that collection for the fixing of the earlier. But although after the Cornelian decree of the people the edict was no longer subordinate to the judge, but the judge was by law subject to the edict; and though the new code had practically dispossessed the old urban law in judicial usage as in legal instruction—every urban judge was still free at his entrance on office absolutely and arbitrarily to alter the edict, and the law of the Twelve Tables with its additions still always outweighed formally the urban edict, so that in each individual case of collision the antiquated rule had to be set aside by arbitrary interference of the magistrate and therefore, strictly speaking, by violation of formal law. The subsidiary application of the urban edict in the court of the *praetor peregrinus* at Rome and in the different provincial judicatures was entirely subject to the arbitrary pleasure of the individual presiding magistrate. It was evidently necessary to set aside definitively the old urban law, so far as it had not been transferred to the newer, and in the case of the latter to set suitable limits to its arbitrary alteration by each individual urban judge, possibly also to regulate its subsidiary application by the side of the local statutes. This was Caesar's design, when he projected the plan for his code; for it could not have been otherwise. The plan was not executed; and thus that troublesome state of transition in Roman jurisprudence was perpetuated till this necessary reform was accomplished six centuries afterwards, and then but imperfectly, by one of the successors of Caesar, the emperor Justinian.

Lastly, in money, measures, and weights the substantial equalisation of the Latin and Hellenic systems had long been in progress. It was very ancient so far as concerned the definitions of weight and the measures of capacity and of length indispensable for trade and commerce (i. 207), and in the monetary system little more recent than the introduction of the silver coinage (ii. 358). But these older equations were not sufficient, because in the Hellenic world itself the most varied metrical and monetary systems subsisted side by side; it was necessary, and formed part doubtless of Caesar's plan, now to introduce everywhere in the new united empire, so far as this had not been done already, Roman money, Roman measures, and Roman weights in such a manner that they alone should be reckoned by in official intercourse, and that the non-Roman systems should be restricted to local currency or placed in a —once for all regulated—ratio to the Roman. The action of Caesar, however, can only be pointed out in two of the most important of these departments, the monetary system and the calendar.

The Roman monetary system was based on the two precious metals circulating side by side and in a fixed relation to each other, gold being given and taken according to weight,[1] silver in the form of coin; but practically in consequence of the extensive transmarine intercourse the gold far preponderated over the silver. Whether the acceptance of Roman silver money was not even at an earlier period obligatory throughout the empire, is uncertain; at any rate uncoined gold essentially supplied the place of imperial money throughout the Roman territory, the more so as the Romans had prohibited the coining of gold in all the provinces and client-states, and the *denarius* had, in addition to Italy, *de jure* or *de facto* naturalised itself in Cisalpine Gaul, in Sicily, in Spain and various other places, especially in the West (iii. 390). But the imperial coinage begins with Caesar. Exactly like Alexander, he marked the foundation of the new monarchy embracing the civilised world by the fact that the only metal forming an universal medium obtained

[1] The gold pieces, which Sulla (iii. 388) and contemporarily Pompeius caused to be struck, both in small quantity, do not invalidate this proposition; for they probably came to be taken solely by weight just like the golden Phillippei which were in circulation even down to Caesar's time. They are certainly remarkable, because they anticipate the Caesarian imperial gold just as Sulla's regency anticipated the new monarchy.

the first place in the coinage. The greatness of the scale on which the new Caesarian gold piece (20*s.* 7*d.* according to the present value of the metal) was immediately coined, is shown by the fact that in a single treasure buried seven years after Caesar's death there were found 80,000 of these pieces. It is true that financial speculations may have exercised a collateral influence in this respect.[1] As to the silver money, the exclusive rule of the Roman *denarius* in all the West, for which the foundation had previously been laid, was finally established by Caesar, when he definitely closed the only Occidental mint that still competed in silver currency with the Roman, that of Massilia. The coining of silver or copper small money was still permitted to a number of Occidental communities; three-quarter *denarii* were struck by some Latin communities of southern Gaul, half *denarii* by several cantons in northern Gaul, copper small coins in various instances even after Caesar's time by communes of the West; but this small money was throughout coined after the Roman standard, and its acceptance moreover was probably obligatory only in local dealings. Caesar does not seem any more than the earlier government to have contemplated the regulation with a view to unity of the monetary system of the East, where great masses of coarse silver money—much of which too easily admitted of being debased or worn away—and to some extent even, as in Egypt, a copper coinage akin to our paper money were in circulation, and the Syrian commercial cities would have felt very severely the want of their previous national coinage corresponding to the Mesopotamian currency. We find here subsequently the arrangement that the *denarius* has everywhere legal currency and is the only medium of official reckoning,[2] while the local coins have legal currency within their limited range but according to a tariff unfavourable for them as compared with the *denarius*.[3]

[1] It appears to wit, that in earlier times the claims of the state-creditors payable in silver could not be paid against their will in gold according to its legal ratio to silver; whereas it admits of no doubt, that from Caesar's time the gold piece had to be taken without opposition for 100 silver sesterces. This was just at that time the more important, as in consequence of the great quantities of gold put into circulation by Caesar it stood for a time in the currency of trade 25 per cent. below the legal ratio.

[2] There is probably no inscription of the Imperial period, which specifies sums of money otherwise than in Roman coin.

[3] Thus the Attic *drachma*, although sensibly heavier than the *denarius*, was yet reckoned equal to it; the *tetradrachmon* of Antioch, weighing on an average 15 grammes of silver, was made equal to 3 Roman *denarii*, which only weigh about 12 grammes; the *cistophorus* of Asia Minor was according to the value of silver above 3, according to the legal tariff = $2\frac{1}{2}$ *denarii*; the Rhodian half *drachma* according to the value of silver = $\frac{3}{4}$, according to the legal tariff = $\frac{5}{8}$ of a *denarius*, and so on.

This was probably not introduced all at once, and in part perhaps may have preceded Caesar; but it was at any rate the essential complement of the Caesarian arrangement as to the imperial coinage, whose new gold piece found its immediate model in the almost equally heavy coin of Alexander and was doubtless calculated especially for circulation in the East.

Of a kindred nature was the reform of the calendar. The republican calendar, which strangely enough was still the old decemviral calendar—an imperfect adoption of the *octaeteris* that preceded Meton (i. 466)—had by a combination of wretched mathematics and wretched administration come to anticipate the true time by sixty-seven whole days, so that *e.g.* the festival of Flora was celebrated on the 11th July instead of the 28th April. Caesar finally removed this evil, and with the help of the Greek mathematician Sosigenes introduced the Italian farmer's year regulated according to the Egyptian calendar of Eudoxus, as well as a rational system of intercalation, into religious and official use; while at the same time the beginning of the year on the 1st March of the old calendar was abolished, and the date of the 1st January—fixed at first as the term for changing the supreme magistrates and, in consequence of this, long since predominant in civil life—was assumed as the calendar period for commencing the year. Both changes came into effect on the 1st January 709 of the city, 45 B.C., and along with them the use of the Julian calendar so named after its author, which long after the fall of the monarchy of Caesar remained the regulative standard of the civilised world and in the main is so still. By way of explanation there was added in a detailed edict a star-calendar derived from the Egyptian astronomical observations and transferred—not indeed very skilfully—to Italy, which fixed the rising and setting of the stars named according to days of the calendar.[1] In this domain also the Roman and Greek worlds were thus placed on a par.

Such were the foundations of the Mediterranean monarchy of Caesar. For the second time in Rome the social question had reached a crisis, at which the antagonisms not only ap-

[1] The identity of this edict drawn up perhaps by Marcus Flavius (Macrob. *Sat.* i. 14, 2) and the alleged treatise of Caesar De Stellis, is shown by the joke of Cicero (Plutarch, *Caes.* 59) that now the Lyre rises according to edict.

Moreover it was known even before Caesar, that the solar year of 365 days 6 hours, which was the basis of the Egyptian calendar, and which he made the basis of his, was somewhat too long. The most exact calculation of the tropical year which the ancient world was acquainted with, that of Hipparchus, put it at 365 d. 5 h. 52′ 12″; the true length is 365 d. 5 h. 48′48″.

peared to be, but actually were, in form of their exhibition, insoluble and, in their expression, irreconcilable. On the first occasion Rome had been saved by the fact that Italy was merged in Rome and Rome in Italy, and in the new enlarged and altered home those old antagonisms were not reconciled, but fell into abeyance. Now Rome was once more saved by the fact that the countries of the Mediterranean were merged in it or became prepared for merging; the war between the Italian poor and rich, which in the old Italy could only end with the destruction of the nation, had no longer a battle-field or a meaning in the Italy of three continents. The Latin colonies closed the gap which threatened to swallow up the Roman community in the fifth century; the deeper chasm of the seventh century was filled by the Transalpine and transmarine colonisations of Gaius Gracchus and Caesar. For Rome alone history not merely performed miracles, but also repeated its miracles, and twice cured the internal crisis, which in the state itself was incurable, by regenerating the state. There was doubtless much corruption in this regeneration; as the union of Italy was accomplished over the ruins of the Samnite and Etruscan nations, so the Mediterranean monarchy built itself on the ruins of countless states and tribes once living and vigorous; but it was a corruption out of which sprang a fresh growth, part of which remains green at the present day. What was pulled down for the sake of the new building, was merely the secondary nationalities which had long since been marked out for destruction by the levelling hand of civilisation. Caesar wherever he came forward as a destroyer, only carried out the pronounced verdict of historical development; but he protected the germs of culture, where and as he found them, in his own land as well as among the sister nation of the Hellenes. He saved and renewed the Roman element; and not only did he spare the Greek element, but with the same self-relying genius with which he accomplished the renewed foundation of Rome he undertook also the regeneration of the Hellenes, and resumed the interrupted work of the great Alexander, whose image, we may well believe, never was absent from Caesar's soul. He solved these two great tasks not merely side by side, but the one by means of the other. The two great essentials of humanity—general and individual development, or state and culture—once in embryo united in those old Graeco-Italians feeding their flocks in primeval simplicity far from the coasts and islands of the Mediterranean, had become dissevered when these were parted into Italians and Hellenes, and had thenceforth remained apart for many centuries. Now the descendant of the Trojan prince and the Latin king's daughter created out of a state without distinctive culture and a cosmopolitan civilisation a new whole, in which state and culture again met together at the acme of human existence in the rich fulness of blessed maturity and worthily filled the sphere appropriate to such an union.

The outlines have thus been set forth, which Caesar drew for this work, according to which he laboured himself, and according to which posterity—for many centuries confined to the paths which this great man marked out—endeavoured to prosecute the work, if not with the intellect and energy, yet on the whole in accordance with the intentions, of the illustrious master. Little was finished; much was merely begun. Whether the plan was complete, those who venture to vie in thought with such a man may decide; we observe no material defect in what lies before us—every single stone of the building enough to make a man immortal, and yet all combining to form one harmonious whole. Caesar ruled as king of Rome for five years and a half, not half as long as Alexander; in the intervals of seven great campaigns, which allowed him to stay not more than fifteen months altogether[1] in the capital of his empire, he regulated the destinies of the world for the present and the future, from the establishment of the boundary-line between civilisation and barbarism down to the removal of the rain-pools in the streets of the capital, and yet retained time and composure enough attentively to follow the prize-pieces in the theatre and to confer the chaplet on the victor with improvised verses. The rapidity and precision with which the plan was executed prove that it had been long meditated thoroughly and all its parts settled in detail; but, even thus, they remain not much less wonderful than the plan itself. The outlines were laid down and thereby the new state was defined for all coming time; the boundless future alone could complete the structure. So far Caesar might say, that his object was attained; and this was probably the meaning of the words which were sometimes heard to fall from him—that he had lived long enough. But precisely because the building was an

[1] Caesar stayed in Rome in April and Dec. $\frac{705}{49}$, on each occasion for a few days; from Sept. to Dec. $\frac{707}{47}$; some four months in the autumn of the year of fifteen months $\frac{708}{46}$, and from Oct. $\frac{709}{45}$ to March $\frac{710}{44}$.

endless one, the master as long as he lived restlessly added stone to stone, with always the same dexterity and always the same elasticity busy at his work, without ever overturning or altering, just as if there were for him merely a to-day and no to-morrow. Thus he worked and created as never any mortal did before or after him; and as a worker and creator he still, after wellnigh two thousand years, lives in the memory of the nations—the first, and the unique, Imperator Caesar.

CHAPTER XII

RELIGION, CULTURE, LITERATURE, AND ART

In the development of religion and philosophy no new element appeared during this epoch. The Romano-Hellenic state-religion and the Stoic state-philosophy inseparably combined with it were not merely a convenient instrument for every government—oligarchy, democracy, or monarchy—but altogether indispensable, because it was just as impossible to construct the state wholly without religious elements as to discover any new state-religion adapted to form a substitute for the old. So the besom of revolution swept doubtless at times very roughly through the cobwebs of the augural bird-lore (p. 190); nevertheless the rotten machine creaking at every joint survived the earthquake which swallowed up the republic itself, and preserved its insipidity and its arrogance without diminution for transference to the new monarchy. As a matter of course, it fell more and more into disfavour with all those who manifested freedom of judgment. Towards the state-religion indeed public opinion maintained an attitude essentially indifferent; it was on all sides recognised as an institution of political convenience, and no one specially troubled himself about it with the exception of political and antiquarian literati. But towards its philosophical sister there gradually sprang up among the unprejudiced public that hostility, which the empty and yet perfidious hypocrisy of set phrases never fails in the long run to awake. That a presentiment of its own worthlessness began to dawn on the Stoa itself, is shown by its attempt artificially to infuse into itself some fresh spirit in the way of syncretism. Antiochus of Ascalon (flourishing about $\frac{675}{79}$), who professed to have amalgamated the Stoic and Platonic-Aristotelian systems into one organic unity, in reality so far succeeded that his misshapen doctrine became the fashionable philosophy of the conservatives of his time and was conscientiously studied by the genteel dilettanti and literati of Rome. Every one who displayed intellectual vigour, opposed the Stoa or ignored it. It was principally antipathy towards the boastful and tiresome Roman Pharisees, coupled doubtless with the increasing disposition to take refuge from practical life in indolent apathy or empty irony, that occasioned during this epoch the extension of the system of Epicurus to a larger circle and the naturalisation of the Cynic philosophy of Diogenes in Rome. However stale and poor in thought the former might be, a philosophy, which did not seek the way to wisdom through an alteration of traditional terms but contented itself with those in existence, and throughout recognised only the perceptions of sense as true, was always better than the terminological jingle and the hollow conceptions of the Stoic wisdom; and the Cynic philosophy was of all the philosophical systems of the times in so far by much the best, as its system was confined to the having no system at all, and sneering at all systems and all systematisers. In both fields war was waged against the Stoa with zeal and success; for serious men, the Epicurean Lucretius preached with the full accents of heartfelt conviction and of holy zeal against the Stoical faith in the Gods and Providence and the Stoical doctrine of the immortality of the soul; for the great public ready to laugh, the Cynic Varro hit the mark still more sharply with the flying darts of his extensively-read satires. While thus the ablest men of the older generation made war on the Stoa, the younger generation again, such as Catullus, stood in no inward relation to it at all, and passed a far sharper censure on it by completely ignoring it.

But, if in the present instance a faith no longer believed was maintained out of political convenience, they amply made up for this in other respects. Unbelief and superstition, different hues of the same historical phenomenon, went in the Roman world of that day hand in hand, and there was no lack of individuals who in themselves combined both—who denied the gods with Epicurus, and yet prayed and sacrificed before every shrine. Of course only the gods that came from the East were still in vogue, and, as the men continued to flock from the Greek lands to Italy, so the gods of the East migrated in ever-increasing numbers to the West. The importance of the Phrygian cultus at that time in Rome is shown both by the polemical tone of the older men such as Varro and Lucretius, and by the poetical glorification of it in the fashionable Catullus, which concludes with the characteristic request that the goddess may deign to turn the heads of others only, and not that of the poet himself.

A fresh addition was the Persian worship, which is said to have first reached the Occidentals through the medium of the pirates who met on the Mediterranean from the East and from the West: the oldest seat of this cultus in the West is stated to have been Mount Olympus in Lycia. That in the adoption of Oriental worships in the West such higher speculative and moral elements as they contained were generally allowed to drop, is strikingly evinced by the fact that Ahuramazda, the supreme god of the pure doctrine of Zarathustra, remained virtually unknown in the West, and adoration there was especially directed to that god who had occupied the first place in the old Persian national religion and had been transferred by Zarathustra to the second—the sun-god Mithra.

But the brighter and gentler celestial forms of the Persian religion did not so rapidly gain a footing in Rome as the wearisome mystical host of the grotesque divinities of Egypt—Isis the mother of nature with her whole train, the constantly dying and constantly reviving Osiris, the gloomy Sarapis, the taciturn and grave Harpocrates, the dog-headed Anubis. In the year when Clodius emancipated the clubs and conventicles ($\frac{696}{58}$), and doubtless in consequence of this very emancipation of the populace, that host even prepared to make its entry into the old stronghold of the Roman Jupiter in the Capitol, and it was with difficulty that the invasion was prevented and the inevitable temples were banished at least to the suburbs of Rome. No worship was equally popular among the lower orders of the population in the capital: when the senate ordered the temples of Isis constructed within the ring-wall to be pulled down, no labourer ventured to lay the first hand on them, and the consul Lucius Paullus was himself obliged to apply the first stroke of the axe ($\frac{704}{50}$); a wager might be laid, that the more lax any woman was, the more piously she worshipped Isis. That the casting of lots, the interpretation of dreams, and similar liberal arts supported their professors, was a matter of course. The casting of horoscopes was already a scientific pursuit; Lucius Tarutius of Firmum, a respectable and in his own way learned man, a friend of Varro and Cicero, with all gravity cast the nativity of kings Romulus and Numa and of the city of Rome itself, and for the edification of the credulous on either side confirmed by means of his Chaldaean and Egyptian wisdom the accounts of the Roman annals.

But by far the most remarkable phenomenon in this domain was the first attempt to reconcile crude faith with speculative thought, the first appearance of those tendencies, which we are accustomed to describe as Neo-Platonic, in the Roman world.

Their oldest apostle there was Publius Nigidius Figulus, a Roman of rank belonging to the strictest section of the aristocracy, who filled the praetorship in $\frac{696}{58}$ and died in $\frac{709}{45}$ as a political exile beyond the bounds of Italy. With astonishing copiousness of learning and still more astonishing strength of faith he created out of the most dissimilar elements a philosophico-religious structure, the singular outline of which he probably developed still more in his oral discourses than in his theological and physical writings. In philosophy, seeking deliverance from the skeletons of the current systems and abstractions, he recurred to the neglected fountain of the pre-Socratic philosophy, to whose ancient sages thought had still presented itself with sensuous vividness. The researches of physical science—which, suitably treated, afford even now so excellent a handle for mystic delusion and pious sleight of hand, and in antiquity with its more defective insight into physical laws lent themselves still more easily to such objects—played in this case, as may readily be conceived, a considerable part. His theology was based essentially on that strange medley, in which Greeks of a kindred spirit had intermingled Orphic and other very old or very new indigenous wisdom with Persian, Chaldaean, and Egyptian secret doctrines, and with which Figulus incorporated the quasi-results of the Tuscan investigations into nothing and of the indigenous lore touching the flight of birds, so as to produce further harmonious confusion. The whole system obtained its consecration—political, religious, and national—from the name of Pythagoras, the ultra-conservative statesman whose supreme principle was "to promote order and to check disorder," the miracle-worker and necromancer, the primeval sage who was a native of Italy, who was interwoven even with the legendary history of Rome, and whose statue was to be seen in the Roman Forum. As birth and death are kindred with each other, so—it seemed—Pythagoras was to stand not merely by the cradle of the republic as friend of the wise Numa and colleague of the sagacious mother Egeria, but also by its grave as the last protector of the sacred bird-lore. But the new system was not merely marvellous, it also worked marvels; Nigidius announced to the father of the subsequent emperor Augustus, on the very day when the latter was born, the future greatness of his son; nay the prophets conjured up spirits for the credulous, and, what was of more moment, they pointed out to them the places where their lost money lay. The new-and-old wisdom, such as it was, made a profound impression on its contemporaries; men of the highest rank, of the greatest learning, of the most solid ability, belonging to very different parties—the consul of $\frac{700}{54}$ Appius Claudius, the learned Marcus Varro, the brave officer Publius Vatinius—took part in the citation of spirits, and it even appears that a police interference was necessary against the proceedings of these societies. These last attempts to save the Roman theology like the similar efforts of Cato in the field of politics, produce at once a comical and a melancholy impression; we may smile at the creed and its propagators, but still it is a grave matter when able men begin to addict themselves to absurdity.

The training of youth followed, as may naturally be supposed, the course of bilingual humane culture chalked out in the previous epoch, and the general culture also of the Roman world conformed more and more to the forms established for that purpose by the Greeks. Even the bodily exercises advanced from ball-playing, running, and fencing to the more artistically developed Greek gymnastic contests; though there were not yet any public institutions for gymnastics, in the principal country-houses the *palaestra* was already to be found by the side of the bath-rooms. The manner in which the cycle of general culture had changed in the Roman world during the course of a century, is shown by a comparison of the encyclopaedia of Cato (ii. 440) with the similar treatise of Varro "concerning the school-sciences." As constituent elements of non-professional culture, there appear in Cato the art of oratory, the sciences of agriculture, of law, of war, and of medicine; in Varro—according to probable conjecture—grammar, logic or dialectics, rhetoric, geometry, arithmetic, astronomy, music, medicine, and architecture. Consequently in the course of the seventh century the sciences of war, jurisprudence, and agriculture had been converted from general into professional studies. On the other hand in Varro the Hellenic education appears already in all its completeness: by the side of the course which had so long remained distinctively Hellenic, of geometry, arithmetic, astronomy, and music.[1] That astronomy more especially, which in the nomenclature of the stars gratified the thoughtless erudite dilettantism of the age and in its relations to astrology ministered to the prevailing religious delusions,

[1] These form, as is well known, the so-called seven liberal arts, which, with this distinction between the three species of discipline earlier naturalised in Italy and the four subsequently received, maintained their position throughout the middle ages.

was regularly and zealously studied by the youth in Italy, can be proved also otherwise; the astronomical didactic poems of Aratus, among all the works of Alexandrian literature, found earliest admittance into the instruction of Roman youth. To this Hellenic course there was added the study of medicine retained from the older Roman education, and lastly that of architecture so indispensable to the Roman of rank at this period, who instead of cultivating the ground built houses and villas.

In comparison with the previous epoch the Greek as well as the Latin training improved in extent and in scholastic strictness quite as much as it declined in purity and in refinement. The increasing eagerness after the knowledge of Greek gave to instruction of itself an erudite character. To explain Homer or Euripides was after all no great art; teachers and scholars found their account better in handling the Alexandrian poems, which, besides, were in their spirit far more congenial to the Roman world of that day than the genuine Greek national poetry, and which, if they were not quite so venerable as the Iliad, possessed at any rate an age sufficiently respectable to pass as classics with schoolmasters. The erotic poems of Euphorion, the "Causes" of Callimachus and his "Ibis," the comically obscure "Alexandra" of Lycophron contained in rich abundance rare vocables (*glossae*) suitable for being extracted and interpreted, sentences laboriously involved and difficult of analysis, prolix digressions full of mystic combinations of antiquated myths—in fact, a store of cumbersome erudition of all sorts. Education required exercises more and more difficult; these productions, in great part model efforts of schoolmasters, were excellently adapted to be lessons for model scholars. Thus the Alexandrian poems took a permanent place in Italian scholastic instruction, especially as trial-themes and certainly promoted knowledge, although at the expense of taste and of discretion. The same unhealthy appetite for culture moreover impelled the Roman youths to derive their Hellenism as much as possible from the fountain-head. The courses of the Greek masters in Rome sufficed only for initiation; every one who wished to be able to converse heard lectures on Greek philosophy at Athens, and on Greek rhetoric at Rhodes, and made a literary and artistic tour through Asia Minor, where the old art-treasures of the Hellenes were still in great measure to be found on the spot, and the cultivation of the fine arts had been continued, although somewhat mechanically; whereas the more distant Alexandria, especially celebrated as the seat of the exact sciences, was far more rarely the point whither young men desirous of culture directed their travels.

The progress of Latin instruction was similar to the Greek. This in part resulted from the mere reflex influence of the Greek, from which it in fact essentially borrowed its methods and its stimulants. Moreover, the state of politics, the impulse to ascend the orator's platform in the Forum which the democratic agitation communicated to a daily enlarging circle, contributed not a little to the diffusion and increase of oratorical exercises; "wherever one casts his eyes," says Cicero, "every place is full of rhetoricians." Besides, the writings of the sixth century, the farther they receded into the past, began to be more decidedly regarded as classical texts of the golden time of Latin literature, and thereby gave a greater preponderance to the instruction which was essentially concentrated upon them. Lastly, the immigration and spreading of barbarian elements from many quarters and the incipient Latinising of extensive Celtic and Spanish districts, naturally gave to Latin grammar and Latin instruction a higher importance than they could have had, so long as Latium alone spoke Latin; the teacher of Latin literature had from the outset a different position in Comum and Narbo than he had in Praeneste and Ardea. Yet the aggregate result was a falling off rather than an improvement of culture. The ruin of the Italian country towns, the extensive intrusion of foreign elements, the political, economic, and moral deterioration of the nation, above all, the distracting civil wars inflicted more injury on the language than all the schoolmasters of the world could repair. The closer contact with the Hellenic culture of the present, the more decided influence of the loquacious Athenian wisdom and of the rhetoric of Rhodes and Asia Minor, supplied to the Roman youth just the very elements that were most pernicious in Hellenism. The propagandist mission which Latium undertook among the Celts, Iberians, and Libyans—proud as the task was—could not but have the like consequences for the Latin language as the Hellenising of the East had had for the Hellenic. The fact that the Roman public of this period applauded the well arranged and rhythmically balanced periods of the orator, and any offence in language or metre cost the actor dear, doubtless shows that the insight into the mother tongue which was the reflection of scholastic training was becoming the common possession of a daily widening circle. But at the same time contemporaries capable of judging complain that the Hellenic culture in Italy about $\frac{690}{64}$ was at a far lower level than it had been a generation before; that opportunities of hearing pure and good Latin were but rare, and these chiefly from the mouth of elderly cultivated ladies; that the tradition of genuine culture, the good old Latin mother wit, the Lucilian polish, the cultivated circle of readers of the Scipionic age were gradually disappearing. The circumstance that the term *urbanitas*, and the idea of a polished national culture which it expressed, arose during this period, proves, not that it was in the ascendant, but that it was on the wane, and that people were keenly alive to the absence of this *urbanitas* in the language and the habits of the Latinised barbarians or barbarised Latins. Where we still meet with the urbane tone of conversation, as in Varro's Satires and Cicero's Letters, it is an echo of the old fashion which was not yet so obsolete in Reate and Arpinum as in Rome.

Thus the previous culture of youth remained substantially unchanged, except that—not so much from its own deterioration as from the general decline of the nation—it was productive of less good and more evil than in the preceding epoch. Caesar initiated a revolution also in this department. While the Roman senate had first combated and then at the most had simply tolerated culture, the government of the new Italo-Hellenic empire, whose essential character in fact was *humanitas*, could not but adopt measures to stimulate it after the Hellenic fashion. If Caesar conferred the Roman franchise on all teachers of the liberal sciences and all the physicians of the capital, we may discover in this step a paving of the way in some degree for those institutions in which subsequently the higher bilingual culture of the youth of the empire was provided for on the part of the state, and which form the most significant expression of the new state of *humanitas*; and if Caesar had further resolved on the establishment of a public Greek and Latin library in the capital and had already nominated the most learned Roman of the age, Marcus Varro, as principal librarian, this implied unmistakably the design of opening up the cosmopolitan monarchy to cosmopolitan literature.

The development of the language during this period turned on the distinction between the classical Latin of cultivated society and the vulgar language of common life. The former itself was a product of the distinctively Italian culture; even in the Scipionic circle "pure Latin" had become the cue, and the mother tongue was spoken, no longer in entire *naïveté*, but in conscious contradistinction to the language of the great multitude. This epoch opens with a remarkable reaction against the classicism which had hitherto exclusively prevailed in the higher language of conversation and accordingly also in literature—a reaction which had inwardly and outwardly a close connection with the reaction of a similar nature in Greece. Just about this time the rhetor and romance-writer Hegesias of Magnesia and the numerous rhetors and literati of Asia Minor who attached themselves to him began to rebel against the orthodox Atticism. They demanded full recognition for the language of life, without distinction, whether the word or the phrase originated in Attica or in Caria and Phrygia; they themselves spoke and wrote not for the taste of learned cliques, but for that of the great public. There could be no reasonable dispute as to the principle; but certainly the result could not be better than was the public of Asia Minor of that day, which had totally lost the taste for chasteness and purity of production, and longed only after the showy and brilliant. To say nothing of the spurious forms of art that sprang out of this tendency—especially the romance and the history assuming the form of romance—the very style of these Asiatics was, as may readily be conceived, abrupt and without modulation and finish, minced and effeminate, full of tinsel and bombast, thoroughly vulgar and affected; "any one who knows Hegesias," says Cicero, "knows what silliness is."

Yet this new style found its way also into the Latin world. When the Hellenic fashionable rhetoric, after having at the close of the previous epoch obtruded into the Latin instruction of youth (iii. 416), took at the beginning of the present period the final step and mounted the Roman rostra in the person of Quintus Hortensius ($\frac{640-704}{114-50}$), the most celebrated pleader of the Sullan age, it adhered closely even in the Latin idiom to the bad Greek taste of the time; and the Roman public, no longer having the pure and chaste culture of the Scipionic age, naturally applauded with zeal the innovator who knew how to give to vulgarism the semblance of an artistic performance. This was of great importance. As in Greece the battles of language were always waged at first in the schools of the rhetoricians, so in Rome the forensic oration to a certain extent even more than literature set the standard of style, and accordingly there was combined, as it were of right, with the leadership of the bar the prerogative of giving the tone to the fashionable mode of speaking and writing. The Asiatic vulgarism of

Hortensius thus dislodged classicism from the Roman platform and partly also from literature. But the fashion soon changed once more in Greece and in Rome. In the former it was the Rhodian school of rhetoricians, which, without reverting to all the chaste severity of the Attic style, attempted to strike out a middle course between it and the modern fashion: if the Rhodian masters were not too particular as to the internal correctness of their thinking and speaking, they at least insisted on purity of language and style, on the careful selection of words and phrases, and the thorough modulation of sentences.

In Italy it was Marcus Tullius Cicero ($\frac{648-711}{106-43}$) who, after having in his early youth gone along with the Hortensian manner, was brought by hearing the Rhodian masters and by his own more matured taste to better paths, and thenceforth addicted himself to strict purity of language and the thorough periodic arrangement and modulation of his discourse. The models of language, which in this respect he followed, he found especially in those circles of the higher Roman society which had suffered but little or not at all from vulgarism; and, as was already said, there were still such, although they were beginning to disappear. The earlier Latin and the good Greek literature, however considerable was the influence of the latter, more especially on the rhythm of his oratory, were in this matter only of secondary moment: this purifying of the language was by no means a reaction of the language of books against that of conversation, but a reaction of the language of the really cultivated against the jargon of spurious and partial culture. Caesar, in the department of language also the greatest master of his time, expressed the fundamental idea of Roman classicism, when he enjoined that in speech and writing every foreign word should be avoided, as rocks are avoided by the mariner; the poetical and the obsolete word of the older literature was rejected as well as the rustic phrase or that borrowed from the language of common life, and more especially the Greek words and phrases which, as the letters of this period show, had to a very great extent found their way into conversational language. Nevertheless this scholastic and artificial classicism of the Ciceronian period stood to the Scipionic as repentance to innocence, or the French of the classicists under Napoleon to the model French of Molière and Boileau; while the former classicism had sprung out of the full freshness of life, the latter as it were caught just in right time the last breath of a race perishing beyond recovery. Such as it was, it rapidly diffused itself. With the leadership of the bar the dictatorship of language and taste passed from Hortensius to Cicero, and the varied and copious authorship of the latter gave to this classicism—what it had hitherto lacked—extensive prose texts. Thus Cicero became the creator of the modern classical Latin prose, and Roman classicism attached itself throughout and altogether to Cicero as a stylist; it was to the stylist Cicero, not to the author, still less to the statesman, that the extravagant panegyrics—yet not made up wholly of verbiage—applied, with which the most gifted representatives of classicism, such as Caesar and Catullus, loaded him.

They soon went farther. What Cicero did in prose, was carried out in poetry towards the end of the epoch by the new Roman school of poets, which modelled itself on the Greek fashionable poetry, and in which the man of most considerable talent was Catullus. Here too the higher language of conversation dislodged the archaic reminiscences which hitherto to a large extent prevailed in this domain, and as Latin prose submitted to the Attic rhythm, so Latin poetry submitted gradually to the strict or rather painful metrical laws of the Alexandrines; *e.g.* from the time of Catullus, it is no longer allowable at once to begin a verse and to close a sentence begun in the verse preceding with a monosyllabic word or a dissyllabic one not specially weighty.

At length science stepped in, fixed the law of language, and developed its rule, which was no longer determined by experience, but asserted the claim to determine experience. The endings of declension, which hitherto had in part been variable, were now to be once for all fixed; *e.g.* of the genitive and dative forms hitherto current side by side in the so-called fourth declension (*senatuis* and *senatus*, *senatui* and *senatu*) Caesar recognised exclusively as valid the contracted forms (*us* and *u*). In orthography various changes were made, to bring the written more fully into correspondence with the spoken language; thus the *u* in the middle of words like *maxumus* was replaced after Caesar's precedent by *i*; and of the two letters which had become superfluous, *k* and *q*, the removal of the first was effected, and that of the second was at least proposed. The language was, if not yet stereotyped, in the course of becoming so; it was not yet indeed passively dominated by the rule, but it had already become conscious of its influence. That this action in the department of Latin grammar derived generally its spirit and method from the Greek, and not only so, but that the Latin language was also directly rectified in accordance with Greek precedent, is shown, for example, by the treatment of the final *s*, which till towards the close of this epoch had received at pleasure sometimes the value of a consonant, sometimes that of a vowel, but was treated by the new-fashioned poets throughout, as in Greek, as a consonantal termination. This regulation of language is the proper domain of Roman classicism; in the most various ways, and for that very reason all the more significantly, the rule is inculcated and the offence against it rebuked by the coryphaei of classicism, by Cicero, by Caesar, even in the poems of Catullus; whereas the older generation expresses itself with natural keenness of feeling respecting the revolution which had affected the field of language as remorselessly as the field of politics.[1] But while the new classicism—that is to say, the standard Latin governed by rule and as far as possible placed on a parity with the standard Greek—which arose out of a conscious reaction against the vulgarism intruding into higher society and even into literature, acquired literary fixity and systematic shape, the latter by no means evacuated the field. Not only do we find it naïvely employed in the works of secondary personages who have drifted into the ranks of authors merely by accident, as in the account of Caesar's second Spanish war, but we shall meet it also with an impress more or less distinct in literature proper, in the mime, in the semi-romance, in the aesthetic writings of Varro; and it is a significant circumstance, that it maintains itself precisely in the most national departments of literature, and that truly conservative men, like Varro, take it into protection. Classicism was based on the death of the Italian language as monarchy on the decline of the Italian nation; it was completely consistent that the men, in whom the republic was still living, should continue to accord its rights to the living language, and for the sake of its comparative vitality and nationality should tolerate its aesthetic defects. Thus then the linguistic opinions and tendencies of this epoch are everywhere divergent; by the side of the old-fashioned poetry of Lucretius appears the thoroughly modern poetry of Catullus, by the side of Cicero's well-modulated period stands the sentence of Varro intentionally disdaining all subdivision. The field of language likewise mirrors the distraction of the age.

In the literature of this period we are first of all struck by the outward increase, as compared with the former epoch, of

[1] Thus Varro (*De R. R.* i. 2) says: *ab aeditimo, ut dicere didicimus a patribus nostris; ut corrigimur ab recentibus urbanis, ab aedituo.*

literary effort in Rome. It was long since the literary activity of the Greeks flourished no more in the free atmosphere of civic independence, but only in the scientific institutions of the larger cities and especially of the courts. Left to depend on the favour and protection of the great, and dislodged from the former seats of the Muses[1] by the extinction of the dynasties of Pergamus ($\frac{621}{133}$), Cyrene ($\frac{658}{96}$), Bithynia ($\frac{679}{75}$), and Syria ($\frac{690}{64}$) and by the waning splendour of the court of the Lagidae—moreover, since the death of Alexander the Great, necessarily cosmopolitan and at least quite as much strangers among the Egyptians and Syrians as among the Latins—the Hellenic literati began more and more to turn their eyes towards Rome. Among the host of Greek attendants with which the Roman of quality at this time surrounded himself, the philosopher, the poet, and the memoir-writer played conspicuous parts by the side of the cook, the boy-favourite, and the jester. We meet with literati of note in such positions; the Epicurean Philodemus, for instance, was installed as domestic philosopher with Lucius Piso consul in $\frac{696}{58}$, and occasionally edified the initiated with his clever epigrams on the coarse Epicureanism of his patron. From all sides the most notable representatives of Greek art and science migrated in daily increasing numbers to Rome, where literary gains were now more abundant than anywhere else. Among those thus mentioned as settled in Rome we find the physician Asclepiades whom king Mithra-

[1] The dedication of the poetical description of the earth which passes under the name of Scymnus is remarkable in reference to those relations. After the poet has declared his purpose of preparing in the favourite Menandrian measure a sketch of geography intelligible for scholars and easy to be learned by heart, he dedicates—as Apollodorus dedicated his similar historical compendium to Attalus Philadelphus king of Pergamus

ἀθάνατον ἀπονέμοντα δόξαν 'Αττάλῳ
τῆς πραγματείας ἐπιγραφὴν εἰληφότι—

his manual to Nicomedes III. king ($\frac{663}{91}$?—$\frac{679}{75}$) of Bithynia:

ἐγὼ δ' ἀκούων, διότι τῶν νῦν βασιλέων
μόνος βασιλικὴν χρηστότητα προσφέρεις,
πεῖραν ἐπεθύμησ' αὐτὸς ἐπ' ἐμαυτοῦ λαβεῖν
καὶ παραγενέσθαι καὶ τί βασιλεύς ἐστ' ἰδεῖν.
διὸ τῇ προθέσει σύμβουλον ἐξελεξάμην
. . . . τὸν 'Απόλλωνα τὸν Διδυμῆ . . . .
οὗ δὴ σχεδὸν μάλιστα καὶ πεπεισμένος
πρὸς σὴν κατὰ λόγον ἧκα (κοινὴν γὰρ σχεδόν
τοῖς φιλομαθοῦσιν ἀναδέδειχας) ἑστίαν.

dates vainly endeavoured to draw away from thence into his service; the universalist in learning, Alexander of Miletus, termed Polyhistor; the poet Parthenius from Nicaea in Bithynia; Posidonius of Apamea in Syria equally celebrated as a traveller, teacher, and author, who at a great age migrated in $\frac{703}{51}$ from Rhodes to Rome; and various others. A house like that of Lucius Lucullus was a seat of Hellenic culture and a rendezvous for Hellenic literati almost like the Alexandrian Museum; Roman resources and Hellenic connoisseurship had gathered in these halls of wealth and science an incomparable collection of statues and paintings of earlier and contemporary masters, as well as a library as carefully selected as it was magnificently fitted up, and every person of culture and especially every Greek was welcome there—the master of the house himself was often seen walking up and down the beautiful colonnade in philological or philosophical conversation with one of his learned guests. No doubt these Greeks brought along with their rich treasures of culture their preposterousness and servility to Italy; one of these learned wanderers for instance, the author of the "Art of Flattery," Aristodemus of Nysa (about $\frac{700}{54}$) recommended himself to his masters by demonstrating that Homer was a native of Rome!

In the same measure as the pursuits of the Greek literati prospered in Rome, literary activity and literary interest increased among the Romans themselves. Even Greek composition, which the stricter taste of the Scipionic age had totally set aside, now revived. The Greek language was now universally current, and a Greek treatise found a quite different public from a Latin one; therefore Romans of rank, such as Lucius Lucullus, Marcus Cicero, Titus Atticus, Quintus Scaevola (tribune of the people in $\frac{700}{54}$), like the kings of Armenia and Mauretania, published occasionally Greek prose and even Greek verses. Such Greek authorship however by native Romans remained a secondary matter and almost an amusement; the literary as well as the political parties of Italy all coincided in adhering to their Italian nationality, only more or less pervaded by Hellenism. Nor could there be any complaint at least as to want of activity in the field of Latin authorship. There was a flood of books and pamphlets of all sorts, and above all of poems, in Rome. Poets swarmed there, as they did only in Tarsus or Alexandria; poetical publications had become the standing juvenile sin of livelier natures, and even then the writer was reckoned fortunate whose youthful poems compassionate oblivion withdrew from criticism. Any one who understood the art, wrote without difficulty at a sitting his five hundred hexameters in which no schoolmaster found anything to censure, but no reader discovered anything to praise. The female world also took a lively part in these literary pursuits; the ladies did not confine themselves to dancing and music, but by their spirit and wit ruled conversation and talked excellently on Greek and Latin literature; and, when poetry laid siege to a maiden's heart, the beleaguered fortress not unfrequently capitulated likewise in graceful verses. Rhythms became more and more the fashionable plaything of the big children of both sexes; poetical epistles, joint poetical exercises and competitions among good friends, were of common occurrence, and towards the end of this epoch institutions were already opened in the capital, at which unfledged Latin poets might learn verse-making for money. In consequence of the large consumption of books the machinery for the manufacture of copies was substantially perfected, and publication was effected with comparative rapidity and cheapness; bookselling became a respectable and lucrative trade, and the bookseller's shop a usual meeting-place of men of culture. Reading had become a fashion, nay a mania; at table, where coarser pastimes had not already intruded, reading was regularly introduced, and any one who meditated a journey seldom forgot to pack up a travelling library. The superior officer was seen in the camp-tent with the obscene Greek romance, the statesman in the senate with the philosophical treatise, in his hands. Matters accordingly stood in the Roman state as they have stood and will stand in every state where the citizens read "from the threshold to the closet." The Parthian vizier was not far wrong, when he pointed out to the citizens of Seleucia the romances found in the camp of Crassus, and asked them whether they still regarded the readers of such books as formidable opponents.

The literary tendency of this age was varied and could not be otherwise, for the age itself was divided between the old and the new modes. The same tendencies which came into conflict on the field of politics, the national-Italian tendency of the conservatives, the Helleno-Italian or, if the term be preferred, cosmopolitan tendency of the new monarchy, fought their battles also on the field of literature. The former attached itself to the older Latin literature, which in the theatre, in the school, and in erudite research assumed more and more the character of classical. With less taste and stronger party tendencies than the Scipionic epoch showed, Ennius, Pacuvius, and especially Plautus were now exalted to the skies. The leaves of the Sibyl rose in price, the fewer they became; the relatively greater nationality and relatively greater productiveness of the poets of the sixth century were never more vividly felt than in this epoch of finished Epigonism, which in literature as decidedly as in politics looked up to the century of the Hannibalic warriors as to the golden age that had now unhappily passed away beyond recall. No doubt there was in this admiration of the old classics no small portion of the same hollowness and hypocrisy which are characteristic of the conservatism of this age in general; and here too there was no want of trimmers. Cicero for instance, although in prose one of the chief representatives of the modern tendency, revered nevertheless the older national poetry nearly with the same antiquarian respect which he paid to the aristocratic constitution and the augural discipline; "patriotism requires," we find him saying, "that we should rather read a notoriously wretched translation of Sophocles than the original." While thus the modern literary tendency cognate to the democratic monarchy numbered secret adherents enough even among the orthodox admirers of Ennius, there were not wanting already bolder judges, who treated the native literature as disrespectfully as the senatorial politics. Not only did they resume the strict criticism of the Scipionic epoch and give weight to Terence only in order to condemn Ennius and still more the Ennianists, but the younger and bolder men went much farther and ventured already—though only as yet in heretical revolt against literary orthodoxy—to call Plautus a rude jester and Lucilius a bad verse-smith. This modern tendency attached itself not to the native authorship, but rather to the more recent Greek literature or the so-called Alexandrinism.

We cannot avoid saying at least so much respecting this remarkable aftergrowth of Hellenic language and art as is requisite for the understanding of the Roman literature of this and the later epochs. The Alexandrian literature was based on the decline of the pure Hellenic idiom, which from the time of Alexander the Great was superseded in daily life by an inferior jargon deriving its origin from the contact of the Macedonian dialect with various Greek and barbarian tribes; or, to speak more accurately, the Alexandrian literature sprang out of the ruin of the Hellenic nation generally, which had to perish, and did perish, in its national individuality in order to establish the universal monarchy of Alexander and the empire of Hellenism. Had Alexander's universal empire continued to subsist, the former national and popular literature would have been succeeded by a cosmopolitan literature Hellenic merely in name, essentially denationalised and called into life in a certain measure by royal patronage, but at all events ruling the world; but, as the state of Alexander was unhinged by his death, the germs of the literature corresponding to it rapidly perished. Nevertheless the Greek nation with all that it had possessed—with its nationality, its language, its art—belonged to the past. It was only in a comparatively narrow circle not of men of culture—for such, strictly speaking, no longer existed—but of men of erudition that the Greek literature was still cherished even when dead; that the rich inheritance which it had left was inventoried with melancholy pleasure or arid refinement of research; and that the living sense of sympathy or the dead erudition was elevated into a semblance of productiveness. This posthumous productiveness constitutes the so-called Alexandrinism. It is essentially similar to that literature of scholars, which, keeping aloof from the living Romanic nationalities and their vulgar idioms, grew up during the fifteenth and sixteenth centuries among a cosmopolitan circle of erudite philologers—as an artificial aftergrowth of the departed antiquity; the contrast between the classical and the vulgar Greek of the period of the Diadochi is doubtless less strongly marked, but is not, properly speaking, different from that between the Latin of Manutius and the Italian of Macchiavelli.

Italy had hitherto been in the main disinclined towards Alexandrinism. Its season of comparative brilliance was the period shortly before and after the first Punic war; yet Naevius, Ennius, Pacuvius and generally the whole body of the national Roman authors down to Varro and Lucretius in all branches of poetical production, not excepting even the didactic poem, attached themselves, not to their Greek contemporaries or very recent predecessors, but without exception to Homer, Euripides, Menander and the other masters of the living and national Greek literature. Roman literature was never fresh and national; but, as long as there was a Roman people, its authors instinctively sought for living and national models, and copied, if not always to the best purpose or the best authors, at least such as were original. The Greek literature which sprang up after Alexander found its first imitators—for the slight attempts of the Marian age (iii. 435) can scarcely be taken into account—

among the contemporaries of Cicero and Caesar; and now the Roman Alexandrinism spread with singular rapidity. In part this arose from external causes. The increased contact with the Greeks, especially the frequent journeys of the Romans into the Hellenic provinces and the assemblage of Greek literati in Rome, naturally procured a public even among the Italians for the Greek literature of the day, for the epic and elegiac poetry, epigrams, and Milesian tales current at that time in Greece. Moreover, as we have already stated (p. 533), the Alexandrian poetry had its established place in the instruction of the Italian youth; and thus reacted on Latin literature all the more, since the latter continued to be essentially dependent at all times on the Hellenistic school-training. We find in this respect even a direct connection of the new Roman with the new Greek literature; the already mentioned Parthenius, one of the better known Alexandrian elegists, opened, apparently about $\frac{700}{54}$, a school for literature and poetry in Rome, and the excerpts are still extant in which he supplied one of his noble pupils with materials for Latin elegies of an erotic and mythological nature according to the well known Alexandrian receipt. But it was by no means simply such accidental occasions which called into existence the Roman Alexandrinism; it was on the contrary a product—perhaps not pleasing, but thoroughly inevitable—of the political and national development of Rome. On the one hand, as Hellas resolved itself into Hellenism, so now Latium resolved itself into Romanism; the national development of Italy became overgrown and was merged in Caesar's Mediterranean empire, just as the Hellenic development in the Eastern empire of Alexander. On the other hand, as the new empire rested on the fact that the mighty streams of Greek and Latin nationality, after having flowed in parallel channels for many centuries, now at length coalesced, the Italian literature had not merely as hitherto to seek its groundwork generally in the Greek, but also to put itself on a level with the Greek literature of the present, or in other words with Alexandrinism. With the scholastic Latin, with the closed number of classics, with the exclusive circle of classic-reading *urbani*, the national Latin literature was dead and at an end; there arose instead of it a thoroughly degenerate, artificially fostered, imperial literature, which did not rest on any definite nationality, but proclaimed in two languages the universal gospel of humanity, and was dependent in point of spirit throughout and consciously on the old Hellenic, in point of language partly on this, partly on the old Roman popular literature. This was no improvement. The Mediterranean monarchy of Caesar was doubtless a grand and—what is more—a necessary creation; but it had been called into life by an arbitrary superior will, and therefore there was nothing to be found in it of the fresh popular life, of the overflowing national vigour, which are characteristic of younger, more limited, and more natural commonwealths, and which the Italian state of the sixth century had still been able to exhibit. The ruin of the Italian nationality accomplished in the creation of Caesar, nipped the promise of literature. Every one who has any sense of the close affinity between art and nationality will always turn back from Cicero and Horace to Cato and Lucretius; and nothing but the schoolmaster's view of history and of literature—which has acquired, it is true, in this department the sanction of prescription—could have called the epoch of art beginning with the new monarchy pre-eminently the golden age. But while the Romano-Hellenic Alexandrinism of the age of Caesar and Augustus must be deemed inferior to the older, however imperfect, national literature, it is on the other hand as decidedly superior to the Alexandrinism of the age of the Diadochi as Caesar's enduring structure to the ephemeral creation of Alexander. We shall have afterwards to show that the Augustan literature, compared with the kindred literature of the period of the Diadochi, was far less a literature of philologers and far more an imperial literature than the latter, and therefore had a far more permanent and far more general influence in the upper circles of society than the Greek Alexandrinism.

Nowhere was the prospect more lamentable than in dramatic literature. Tragedy and comedy had already before the present epoch become inwardly extinct in the Roman national literature. New pieces were no longer performed. That the public still in the Sullan age expected to see such, appears from the reproductions—belonging to this epoch—of Plautine comedies with the titles and names of the persons altered, with reference to which the managers well added that it was better to see a good old piece than a bad new one. From this the step was not great to that entire surrender of the stage to the dead poets, which we find in the Ciceronian age, and to which Alexandrinism made no opposition. Its productiveness in this department was worse than none. Real dramatic composition the Alexandrian literature never knew; the spurious drama alone, which was written primarily for reading and not for exhibition, could be introduced by it into Italy, and soon accordingly these dramatic iambics began to be quite as prevalent in Rome as in Alexandria, and the writing of tragedy in particular began to figure among the regular diseases of adolescence. We may form a pretty accurate idea of the quality of these productions from the fact that Quintus Cicero, in order homoeopathically to beguile the weariness of winter quarters in Gaul, composed four tragedies in sixteen days.

In the "picture of life" or mimus alone the last still vigorous product of the national literature, the Atellan farce, became engrafted with the ethological offshoots of Greek comedy, which Alexandrinism cultivated with greater poetical vigour and better success than any other branch of poetry. The mimus originated out of the dances in character to the flute, which had long been usual, and which were performed sometimes on other occasions, *e.g.* for the entertainment of the guests during dinner, but more especially in the pit of the theatre during the intervals between the acts. It was not difficult to form out of these dances—in which the aid of speech had doubtless long since been occasionally employed—by means of the introduction of a more organised plot and a regular dialogue little comedies, which were yet essentially distinguished from the earlier comedy and even from the farce by the facts, that the dance and the lasciviousness inseparable from such dancing continued in this case to play a chief part, and that the mimus, as belonging properly not to the boards but to the pit, threw aside all ideal scenic effects, such as masks for the face and theatrical buskins, and—what was specially important—admitted of the female characters being represented by women. This new mimus, which first seems to have come on the stage of the capital about $\frac{672}{82}$, soon swallowed up the national harlequinade, with which it indeed in the most essential respects coincided, and was employed as the usual interlude and especially as afterpiece along with the other dramatic performances.[1] The plot was of course still more indifferent, loose,

[1] Cicero testifies that the mimus in his time had taken the place of the Atellana (*Ad Fam.* ix. 16); with this accords the fact, that the *mimi* and *mimae* first appear about the Sullan epoch (*Ad Her.* i. 14, 24; ii. 13, 19; Atta, *Fr.* 1 Ribbeck; Plin. *H. N.* vii. 48, 158; Plutarch, *Sull.* 2, 36). The designation *mimus*, however, is sometimes inaccurately applied to the comedian generally. Thus the *mimus* who appeared at the festival of Apollo in $\frac{542-543}{212-211}$ (Festus under *salva res est;* comp. Cicero, *De Orat.* ii. 59, 242) was evidently nothing but an actor of the *palliata*, for there was at this period no room in the development of the Roman theatre for real mimes in the later sense.

With the mimus of the classical Greek period—prose dialogues, in which

and absurd than in the harlequinade; if it was only sufficiently chequered, so that the beggar suddenly became a Croesus and so forth, they did not remonstrate with the poet who instead of untying the knot cut it to pieces. The subjects were chiefly of an amorous nature, mostly of the licentious sort; for example, poet and public without exception took part against the husband, and poetical justice consisted in the derision of good morals. The artistic charm depended wholly, as in the Atellana, on the portraiture of the manners of common and low life; in which rural pictures are laid aside for those of the life and doings of the capital, and the sweet rabble of Rome—just as in the similar Greek pieces the rabble of Alexandria—is summoned to applaud its own likeness. Many subjects are taken from the life of tradesmen; there appear the—here also inevitable—"Fuller," then the "Ropemaker," the "Dyer," the "Saltman," the "Female Weavers," the "Rascal;" other pieces give sketches of character, as the "Forgetful," the "Braggart," the "Man of 100,000 sesterces;"[1] or pictures of other lands, the "Etruscan Woman," the "Gauls," the "Cretan," "Alexandria;" or descriptions of popular festivals, as the "Compitalia," the "Saturnalia," "Anna Perenna," the "Hot Baths;" or parodies of mythology, as the "Voyage to the Underworld," the "Arvernian Lake." Apt nicknames and short commonplaces which were easily retained and applied were welcome; but every piece of nonsense was of itself privileged; in this preposterous world Bacchus is applied to for water and the fountain-nymph for wine. Isolated examples even of the political allusions formerly so strictly prohibited in the Roman theatre are found in these mimes.[2] As regards metrical form, these poets gave themselves, as they tell us, "but moderate trouble with the versification;" the language abounded, even in the pieces prepared for publication, with vulgar expressions and low figures. The mime was,

genre pictures, particularly of a rural kind, were presented—the Roman mimus had no especial relation.

[1] With the possession of this sum, which constituted the qualification for the first voting-class and subjected the inheritance to the Voconian law, the boundary line was crossed which separated inferior (*tenuiores*) from respectable people. Therefore the poor client of Catullus (xxiii. 26) beseeches the gods to help him to this fortune.

[2] In the "Descensus ad Inferos" of Laberus all sorts of people come forward, who have seen wonders and signs; to one there appeared a husband with two wives, whereupon a neighbour is of opinion that this is still worse than the vision, recently seen by a soothsayer in a dream, of six aediles. Caesar forsooth desired—according to the talk of the time—to introduce polygamy in Rome (Suetonius, *Caes.* 82) and he nominated in reality six aediles instead of four. One sees from this that Laberius understood how to exercise the fool's privilege and Caesar how to permit the fool's freedom.

it is plain, in substance nothing but the former farce; with this exception, that the character-masks and the standing scenery of Atella as well as the rustic impress are dropped, and in their room the life of the capital in its boundless liberty and licence is brought on the stage. Most pieces of this sort were doubtless of a very fugitive nature and made no pretension to a place in literature; but the mimes of Laberius, full of pungent delineation of character and in point of language and metre exhibiting the hand of a master, maintained their ground in it; and even the historian must regret that we are no longer permitted to compare the drama of the republican death-struggle in Rome with its great attic counterpart.

With the worthlessness of dramatic literature the increase of scenic spectacles and of scenic pomp went hand in hand. Dramatic representations obtained their regular place in the public life not only of the capital but also of the country towns; the former also now at length acquired by means of Pompeius a permanent theatre ($\frac{699}{55}$; see p. 282), and the Campanian custom of stretching canvas over the theatre for the protection of the actors and spectators during the performance, which in ancient times always took place in the open air, now likewise found admission to Rome ($\frac{676}{78}$). As at that time in Greece it was not the—more than pale—Pleiad of the Alexandrian dramatists, but the classic drama, above all the tragedies of Euripides, which amidst the amplest development of scenic resources kept the stage, so in Rome at the time of Cicero the tragedies of Ennius, Pacuvius, and Accius, and the comedies of Plautus were those chiefly produced. While the latter had been in the previous period supplanted by the more tasteful but in point of comic vigour far inferior Terence, Roscius and Varro, or in other words dramatic art and antiquarian scholarship, co-operated to procure for him a resurrection similar to that which Shakespeare experienced at the hands of Garrick and Johnson; but even Plautus had to suffer from the degenerate susceptibility and the impatient haste of an audience spoilt by the short and slovenly farces, so that the managers found themselves compelled to excuse the length of the Plautine comedies and even perhaps to make omissions and alterations. The more limited the stock of plays, the more the activity of the managing and executive staff as well as the interest of the public was directed to the scenic representation of the pieces. There was hardly any more lucrative trade in Rome than that of the actor and the dancing-girl of the first rank. The princely estate of the tragic actor Aesopus has been already mentioned (p. 483); his still more celebrated contemporary Roscius (iii. 431) estimated his annual income at 600,000 sesterces (£6000)[1] and the dancer Dionysia estimated hers at 200,000 sesterces (£2000). At the same time immense sums were expended on decorations and costume; now and then trains of six hundred mules in harness crossed the stage, and the Trojan theatrical army was employed to present to the public a tableau of the nations vanquished by Pompeius in Asia. The music which accompanied the delivery of the inserted choruses likewise obtained a greater and more independent importance; as the wind sways the waves, says Varro, so the skilful flute-player sways the minds of the listeners with every modulation of melody. It accustomed itself to the use of quicker time, and thereby compelled the player to more lively action. Musical and dramatic connoisseurship was developed; the *habitué* recognised every tune by the first note, and knew the texts by heart; every fault in the music or recitation was severely censured by the audience. The state of the Roman stage in the time of Cicero vividly reminds us of the modern French theatre. As the Roman mime corresponds to the loose tableaux of the pieces of the day, nothing being too good and nothing too bad for either the one or the other, so we find in both the same traditionally classic tragedy and comedy, which the man of culture is in duty bound to admire or at least to applaud. The multitude is satisfied, when it meets its own reflection in the face, and admires the decorative pomp and receives the general impression of an ideal world in the drama; the man of higher culture concerns himself at the theatre not with the piece, but only with its artistic representation. Moreover the Roman histrionic art oscillated in its different spheres, just like the French, between the cottage and the drawing-room. It was nothing unusual for the Roman dancing-girls to throw off at the finale the upper robe and to give a dance in undress for the benefit of the public; but on the other hand in the eyes of the Roman Talma the supreme law of his art was, not the truth of nature, but symmetry.

In recitative poetry metrical annals after the model of those of Ennuis seem not to have been wanting; but they were perhaps sufficiently criticised by that graceful vow of his mistress of which Catullus sings—that the worst of the bad heroic poems should be

[1] He obtained from the state for every day on which he acted 1,000 *denarii* (£40) and besides this the pay for his company. In later years he declined the honorarium for himself.

presented as a sacrifice to holy Venus, if she would only bring back her lover from his vile political poetry to her arms.

Indeed in the whole field of recitative poetry at this epoch the older national-Roman tendency is represented only by a single work of note, which, however, is altogether one of the most important poetical products of Roman literature. It is the didactic poem of Titus Lucretius Carus ($\frac{655-699}{99-55}$) "Concerning the Nature of Things," whose author, belonging to the best circles of Roman society, but taking no part in public life whether from weakness of health or from disinclination, died in the prime of manhood shortly before the outbreak of the civil war. As a poet he attached himself decidedly to Ennius and thereby to the classical Greek literature. Indignantly he turns away from the "hollow Hellenism" of his time, and professes himself with his whole soul and heart to be the scholar of the "chaste Greeks," as indeed even the sacred earnestness of Thucydides has found no unworthy echo in one of the best-known sections of this Roman poem. As Ennius draws his wisdom from Epicharmus and Euhemerus, so Lucretius borrows the form of his representation from Empedocles, "the most glorious treasure of the richly endowed Sicilian isle;" and, as to the matter, gathers "all the golden words together from the rolls of Epicurus," "who outshines other wise men as the sun obscures the stars." Like Ennius, Lucretius disdains the mythological lore with which poetry was overloaded by Alexandrinism, and requires nothing from his reader but a knowledge of the legends generally current.[1] In spite of the modern purism which rejected foreign words from poetry, Lucretius prefers to use, as Ennius had done, a significant Greek word in place of a feeble and obscure Latin one. The old Roman alliteration, the want of mutual adjustment between the divisions of the verse and those of the sentence, and generally the older modes of expression and composition, are still frequently found in Lucretius' rhythms, and although he handles the verse more melodiously than Ennius, his hexameters move not, as those of the modern poetical school, with a lively grace like the rippling brook, but with a stately slowness like the stream of liquid gold. Philosophically and practically also Lucretius leans throughout on Ennius, the only indigenous poet whom his poem

[1] Such an individual apparent exception as Panchaea, the land of incense (ii. 417), is to be explained from the circumstance that this had passed from the romance of the Travels of Euhemerus already perhaps into the poetry of Ennius, at any rate into the poems of Lucius Manlius (iii. 435; Plin. *H. N.* xi. 2, 4), and thence was well known to the public for which Lucretius wrote.

celebrates. The confession of faith of the singer of Rudiae (ii. 425)—

Ego deum genus esse semper dixi et dicam caelitum,
Sed eos non curare opinor, quid agat humanum genus—

describes completely the religious standpoint of Lucretius, and not unjustly for that reason he himself terms his poem as it were the continuation of Ennius:—

Ennius ut noster cecinit, qui primus amoeno
Detulit ex Helicone perenni fronde coronam,
Per gentis Italas hominum quae clara clueret.

Once more—and for the last time—the poem of Lucretius is resonant with the whole poetic pride and the whole poetic earnestness of the sixth century, in which, amidst the images of the formidable Carthaginian and the glorious Scipiad, the imagination of the poet is more at home than in his own degenerate age.[1] To him too his own song "gracefully welling out of the abundance of feeling" sounds, as compared with the common poems, "like the brief song of the swan compared with the cry of the crane;"—with him too the heart swells, listening to the melodies of its own invention, with the hope of illustrious honours—just as Ennius forbids the men to whom he "gave from the depth of the heart a foretaste of fiery song," to mourn at his, the immortal singer's, tomb.

It is a remarkable fatality, that this man of extraordinary talents, far superior in originality of poetic endowments to most if not to all his contemporaries, fell upon an age in which he felt himself strange and forlorn, and in consequence of this made the most singular mistake in the selection of a subject. The system of Epicurus, which converts the universe into a great vortex of atoms and undertakes to explain the origin and end of the world as well as all the problems of nature and of life in a purely mechanical way, was doubtless somewhat less silly than the conversion of myths into history which was attempted by Euhemerus and after him by Ennius; but it was not an ingenious or a fresh system, and the task of poetically unfolding this mechanical view of the world was of such a nature that never probably did poet expend life and art on a more ungrateful theme. The philosophic reader censures in the Lucretian poem

[1] This naively appears in the description of war, in which the tempests that destroy armies, and the hosts of elephants that trample down those who are on their own side—pictures, that is, from the Punic wars—appear as if they belong to the immediate present. Comp. ii. 41; v. 1226, 1303, 1339.

the omission of the finer points of the system, the superficiality especially with which controversies are presented, the defective division, the frequent repetitions, with quite as good reason as the poetical reader frets at the mathematics put into rhythm which makes a great portion of the poem absolutely unreadable. In spite of these incredible defects, before which every man of mediocre talent must inevitably have succumbed, this poet might justly boast of having carried off from the poetic wilderness a new chaplet such as the Muses had not yet bestowed on any; and it was by no means merely the occasional similitudes, and the other inserted descriptions of mighty natural phenomena and yet mightier passions, which acquired for the poet this chaplet. The genius which marks the view of life as well as the poetry of Lucretius depends on his unbelief, which came forward and was entitled to come forward with the full victorious power of truth, and therefore with the full vigour of poetry, in opposition to the prevailing hypocrisy or superstition.

Humana ante oculos foede cum vita jaceret
In terris oppressa gravi sub religione,
Quae caput a caeli regionibus ostendebat
Horribili super aspectu mortalibus instans,
Primum Graius homo mortalis tendere contra
Est oculos ausus primusque obsistere contra.
Ergo vivida vis animi pervicit, et extra
Processit longe flammantia moenia mundi
Atque omne immensum peragravit mente animoque.

The poet accordingly was zealous to overthrow the gods, as Brutus had overthrown the kings, and "to release nature from her stern lords." But it was not against the long ago collapsed throne of Jovis that these flaming words were hurled; just like Ennius, Lucretius fights practically above all things against the wild foreign faiths and superstitions of the multitude, the worship of the Great Mother for instance and the childish lightning-lore of the Etruscans. Horror and antipathy towards that terrible world in general, in which and for which the poet wrote, suggested his poem. It was composed in that hopeless time when the rule of the oligarchy had been overthrown and that of Caesar had not yet been established, in the sultry years during which the outbreak of the civil war was awaited with long and painful suspense. If we seem to perceive in its unequal and restless utterance that the poet daily expected to see the wild tumult of revolution break forth over himself and his work, we must not with reference to his view of men and things forget amidst what men, and in prospect of what things, that view had its origin. In

Hellas at the epoch of Alexander the Great it was a current saying, and one profoundly felt by all the best men, that the best thing of all was not to be born, and the next best to die. Of all views of the world possible to a tender and poetically organised mind in the kindred Caesarian age this was the noblest and the most ennobling, that it is a benefit for man to be released from a belief in the immortality of the soul and thereby from the evil dread of death and of the gods which malignantly steals over men like terror creeping over children in a dark room; that, as the sleep of the night is more refreshing than the trouble of the day, so death, eternal repose from all hope and fear, is better than life, as indeed the gods of the poet themselves are nothing, and have nothing, but an eternal blessed rest; that the pains of hell torment man, not after life, but during its course, in the wild and unruly passions of his throbbing heart; that the task of man is to attune his soul to equanimity, to esteem the purple no higher than the warm dress worn at home, rather to remain in the ranks of those that obey than to press into the confused crowd of candidates for the office of ruler, rather to lie on the grass beside the brook than to take part under the golden ceiling of the rich in emptying his countless dishes. This philosophico-practical tendency is the true ideal essence of the Lucretian poem and is only overlaid, not choked, by all the dreariness of its physical demonstrations. Essentially on this rests its comparative wisdom and truth. The man who with a reverence for his great predecessors and a vehement zeal, to which this century elsewhere knew no parallel, preached such doctrine and embellished it with the charm of art, may be termed at once a good citizen and a great poet. The didactic poem concerning the Nature of Things, however much it may challenge censure, has remained one of the brilliant stars in the poorly illuminated expanse of Roman literature; and with reason the greatest of German philologists chose the task of making the Lucretian poem once more readable as his last and most masterly work.

Lucretius, although his poetical vigour as well as his art was admired by his cultivated contemporaries, yet remained—of late growth as he was—a master without scholars. In the Hellenic fashionable poetry on the other hand there was no lack at least of scholars, who exerted themselves to emulate the Alexandrian masters. With true tact the more gifted of the Alexandrian poets avoided larger works and the pure forms of poetry—the drama, the epos, the lyric; the most pleasing and successful performances consisted with them, just as with the new Latin poets, in "short-winded" tasks, and especially in such as belonged to the domains bordering on the pure forms of art, more especially to the wide field intervening between narrative and song. Multifarious didactic poems were written. Small half heroic, half erotic epics were great favourites, and especially an erudite sort of love-elegy peculiar to this autumnal summer of Greek poetry and characteristic of the philological source whence it sprang, in which the poet more or less arbitrarily interwove the description of his own feelings, chiefly amatory, with epic shreds from the cycle of Greek legend. Festal lays were diligently and ingeniously manufactured; in general, owing to the want of spontaneous poetical feeling, the occasional poem preponderated and especially the epigram, of which the Alexandrians produced excellent specimens. The poverty of materials and the want of freshness in language and rhythm, which inevitably cleave to every literature not national, men sought as much as possible to conceal under odd themes, far-fetched phrases, rare words and artificial versification, and generally under the whole apparatus of philological and antiquarian erudition and technical dexterity.

Such was the gospel which was preached to the Roman boys of this period, and they came in crowds to hear and to practise it; already (about $\frac{700}{54}$) the love poems of Euphorion and similar Alexandrian poetry formed the ordinary reading and the ordinary pieces for declamation of the cultivated youth.[1] The literary revolution took place; but it yielded in the first instance with rare exceptions only premature or unripe fruits. The number of the "new-fashioned poets" was legion, but poetry was rare and Apollo was compelled, as always when so many throng towards Parnassus, to make very short work. The long poems never were worth anything, the short ones seldom. Even in this literary age the poetry of the day had become a public nuisance; it sometimes happened that one's friend would send home to him by way of mockery as a festal present a pile of trashy verses fresh from the bookseller's shop, whose value was at once betrayed by the elegant binding and the smooth paper. A real public, in the sense in which national literature has a

[1] "No doubt," says Cicero (*Tusc.* iii. 19, 45) in reference to Ennius, "the glorious poet is despised by our reciters of Euphorion." "I have safely arrived," he writes to Atticus (vii. 2 *init.*), "as a most favourable north wind blew for us across from Epirus. This spondaic line you may, if you choose, sell to one of the new-fashioned poets as your own" (*ita belle nobis flavit ab Epiro lenissumus Onchesmites. Hunc σπονδειάζοντα si cui voles τῶν νεωτέρων pro tuo vendito*).

public, was wanting to the Roman Alexandrians as well as to the Hellenic; it was thoroughly the poetry of a clique or rather cliques, whose members clung closely together, abused intruders, read and criticised among themselves the new poems, sometimes also quite after the Alexandrian fashion celebrated the successful productions in fresh verses, and variously sought to secure for themselves by clique-praises a spurious and ephemeral renown. A notable teacher of Latin literature, himself poetically active in this new direction, Valerius Cato appears to have exercised a sort of scholastic patronage over the most distinguished men of this circle, and to have pronounced final decision on the relative value of the poems. As compared with their Greek models, these Roman poets evince throughout a want of freedom, sometimes a schoolboy dependence; most of their products must have been simply the austere fruits of a school poetry still occupied in learning and by no means yet dismissed as mature. Inasmuch as in language and in measure they adhered to the Greek patterns far more closely than ever the national Latin poetry had done, a greater correctness and consistency in language and metre were certainly attained; but it was at the expense of the flexibility and fullness of the national idiom. As respects the subject-matter, under the influence partly of effeminate models, partly of an immoral age, amatory themes acquired a surprising preponderance little conducive to poetry; but the favourite metrical compendia of the Greeks were also in various cases translated, such as the astronomical treatise of Aratus by Cicero, and, either at the end of this or more probably at the commencement of the following period, the geographical manual of Eratosthenes by Publius Varro of the Aude and the physico-medicinal manual of Nicander by Aemilius Macer. It is neither to be wondered at nor regretted that of this countless host of poets but few names have been preserved to us; and even these are mostly mentioned merely as curiosities or as once upon a time great; such as the orator Quintus Hortensius with his "five hundred thousand lines" of tiresome obscenity, and the somewhat more frequently mentioned Laevius, whose *Erotopaegnia* attracted a certain interest only by their complicated measures and affected phraseology. Even the small epic of Smyrna by Gaius Helvius Cinna (†$\frac{710}{44}$?), much as it was praised by the clique, bears both in its subject—the incestuous love of a daughter for her father—and in the nine years' toil bestowed on it the worst characteristics of the time.

Those poets alone of this school constitute an original and

pleasing exception, who knew how to combine with its neatness and its versatility of form the national elements of worth still existing in the republican life, especially in that of the country-towns. To say nothing here of Laberius and Varro, this description applies especially to the three poets already mentioned above (p. 300) of the republican opposition, Marcus Furius Bibaculus ($\frac{652-691}{102-63}$), Gaius Licinius Calvus ($\frac{672-706}{82-48}$), and Quintus Valerius Catullus ($\frac{667-c.\ 700}{87-54}$). Of the two former, whose writings have perished, we can indeed only conjecture this; respecting the poems of Catullus we can still form a judgment. He too depends in subject and form on the Alexandrians. We find in his collection translations of pieces of Callimachus, and these not altogether the very good, but the very difficult. Among the original pieces, we meet with elaborately-turned fashionable poems, such as the over-artificial Galliambics in praise of the Phrygian Mother; and even the poem, otherwise so beautiful, of the marriage of Thetis has been artistically spoiled by the truly Alexandrian insertion of the complaint of Ariadne in the principal poem. But by the side of these school-pieces we meet with the melodious lament of the genuine elegy, the festal poem in the full pomp of individual and almost dramatic execution, above all, the freshest miniature-painting of cultivated social life, the pleasant and very unreserved amatory adventures of which half the charm consists in prattling and poetising about the mysteries of love, the delightful life of youth with full cups and empty purses, the pleasures of travel and of poetry, the Roman and still more frequently the Veronese anecdote of the town, and the humorous jest amidst the familiar circle of friends. But not only does Apollo touch the lyre of the poet, he wields also the bow; the winged dart of sarcasm spares neither the tedious verse-maker nor the provincial who corrupts the language, but it hits none more frequently and more sharply than the potentates by whom the liberty of the people is endangered. The short-lined and merry metres, often enlivened by a graceful refrain, are of finished art and yet free from the repulsive smoothness of the manufactory. These poems lead us alternately to the valleys of the Nile and the Po; but the poet is incomparably more at home in the latter. His poems are based on Alexandrian art doubtless, but at the same time on the distinctive feelings of a burgess and a burgess in fact of a rural town, on the contrast of Verona with Rome, on the contrast of the homely municipal with the high-born lords of the senate who usually maltreat their humble friends—as that contrast was probably felt more vividly than anywhere else in Catullus' home, the flourishing and comparatively vigorous Cisalpine Gaul. The most beautiful of his poems reflect the sweet pictures of the Lago di Garda, and hardly could any man of the capital have written a poem like the deeply pathetic one on his brother's death, or the excellent genuinely homely festal hymn for the marriage of Manlius and Aurunculeia. Catullus, although dependent on the Alexandrian masters and in the midst of the fashionable and clique poetry of that age, was yet not merely a good scholar among many mediocre and bad ones, but himself as much superior to his masters as the burgess of a free Italian community was superior to the cosmopolitan Hellenic man of letters. Eminent creative vigour indeed and high poetic intentions we may not look for in him; he is a richly gifted and graceful but not a great poet, and his poems are, as he himself calls them, nothing but "pleasantries and trifles." Yet when we find not merely his contemporaries electrified by these fugitive songs, but the art-critics of the Augustan age also characterising him along with Lucretius as the most important poet of this epoch, his contemporaries as well as their successors were completely right. The Latin nation has produced no second poet in whom the artistic substance and the artistic form appear in so symmetrical perfection as in Catullus; and in this sense the collection of the poems of Catullus is certainly the most perfect which Latin poetry as a whole can show.

Lastly, poetry in a prose form begins in this epoch. The law of genuine *naïve* as well as conscious art, which had hitherto remained unchangeable—that the poetical subject-matter and the metrical setting should go together—gave way before the intermixture and disturbance of all kinds and forms of art, which is one of the most significant features of this period. As to romances indeed nothing farther is to be noticed, than that the most famous historian of this epoch, Sisenna, did not esteem himself too good to translate into Latin the much-read Milesian tales of Aristides—licentious fashionable novels of the most stupid sort.

A more original and pleasing phenomenon in the debatable border-land between poetry and prose was the aesthetic writings of Varro, who was not merely the most important representative of Latin philologico-historical research, but one of the most fertile and most interesting authors in *belles-lettres*. Descended from a plebeian *gens* which had its home in the Sabine land, but had belonged for the last two hundred years to the Roman senate, strictly reared in antique discipline and decorum,[1] and already at the beginning of this epoch a man of maturity, Marcus Terentius Varro of Reate ($\frac{638-727}{116-27}$) belonged in politics, as a matter of course, to the constitutional party, and bore an honourable and energetic part in its doings and sufferings. He supported it, partly in literature—as when he combated the first coalition, the "three-headed monster," in pamphlets; partly in more serious warfare, where we found him in the army of Pompeius as commandant of Further Spain (p. 359). When the cause of the republic was lost, Varro was destined by his conqueror to be librarian of the library which was to be formed in the capital. The troubles of the following period drew the old man once more into their vortex, and it was not till seventeen years after Caesar's death, in the eighty-ninth year of his well-occupied life, that death called him away.

The aesthetic writings, which have made him a name, were brief essays, some in simple prose and of graver contents, others humorous sketches the prose groundwork of which was inlaid with various poetical effusions. The former were the "philosophico-historical dissertations" (*Logistorici*), the latter the Menippean Satires. In neither case did he follow Latin models, and the *Satura* of Varro in particular was by no means based on that of Lucilius. In fact the Roman *Satura* in general was not properly a fixed species of art, but only indicated negatively the fact that the "multifarious poem" was not to be included under any of the recognised forms of art; and accordingly the *Satura*-poetry assumed in the hands of every gifted poet a different and peculiar character. It was rather in the pre-Alexandrian Greek poetry that Varro found the models for his more severe as well as for his lighter aesthetic works; for the graver dissertations, in the dialogues of Heraclides of Heraclea on the Black Sea (†about $\frac{450}{300}$), for the satires, in the writings of Menippus of Gadara in Syria (flourishing about $\frac{475}{280}$). The choice was significant. Heraclides, stimulated as an author by Plato's philosophical dialogues, had amidst the brilliance of their form totally lost sight of the scientific contents and made the poetico-fabulistic dress the main matter; he was an agreeable and largely-read author, but far from a philosopher. Menippus was quite as

[1] "For me when a boy," he somewhere says, "there sufficed a single rough coat and a single under-garment, shoes without stockings, a horse without a saddle; I had no daily warm bath, and but seldom a river-bath." On account of his personal valour he obtained in the Piratic war, where he commanded a division of the fleet, the naval crown.

little a philosopher, but the most genuine literary representative of that philosophy whose wisdom consisted in denying philosophy and ridiculing philosophers, the cynical wisdom of Diogenes; a comic teacher of serious wisdom, he proved by examples and merry sayings that except an upright life everything is vain in earth and heaven, and nothing more vain than the disputes of so-called sages. These were the true models for Varro, a man full of old Roman indignation at the pitiful times and full of old Roman humour, by no means destitute withal of plastic talent, but as to everything which presented the appearance not of palpable fact, but of idea or even of system, utterly stupid, and perhaps the most unphilosophical among the unphilosophical Romans.[1] But Varro was no slavish pupil. The impulse and in general the form he derived from Heraclides and Menippus; but his was a nature too individual and too decidedly Roman not to keep his imitative creations essentially independent and national.

For his grave dissertations, in which a moral maxim or other subject of general interest is handled, he disdained in his framework to approximate to the Milesian tales, as Heraclides had done, and so to serve up to the reader even childish little stories like those of Abaris and of the maiden reawakened to life after being seven days dead. But seldom he borrowed the dress from the nobler myths of the Greeks, as in the essay "Orestes or concerning Madness;" history ordinarily afforded him a worthier frame for his subjects, more especially the contemporary history of his country, so that these essays became, as they were called, *laudationes* of esteemed Romans, above all of the Coryphaei of the constitutional party. Thus the dissertation "concerning Peace" was at the same time a memorial of Metellus Pius, the last in the brilliant series of successful generals of the senate; that "concerning the Worship of the Gods" was at the same time destined to preserve the memory of the highly-respected Optimate and Pontifex Gaius Curio; the essay "on Fate" was connected with Marius, that "on the Writing of History" with Sisenna the first historian of this epoch, that

[1] There is hardly anything more childish than Varro's scheme of all the philosophies, which in the first place summarily declares all systems that do not propose the happiness of man as their ultimate aim to be non-existent, and then reckons the number of philosophies conceivable under this supposition as two hundred and eighty-eight. The able man was unfortunately too much a scholar to confess that he neither could nor would be a philosopher, and accordingly as such throughout life he performed a blind dance—not altogether becoming—between the Stoa, Pythagoreanism, and Diogenism.

"on the Beginnings of the Roman Stage" with the princely giver of scenic spectacles Scaurus, that "on Numbers" with the highly-polished Roman banker Atticus. The two philosophico-historical essays "Laelius or concerning Friendship," "Cato or concerning Old Age," which Cicero wrote probably after the model of those of Varro, may give us some approximate idea of Varro's half didactic, half narrative, treatment of these subjects.

The Menippean satire was handled by Varro with equal originality of form and contents; the bold mixture of prose and verse is foreign to the Greek original, and the whole intellectual contents are pervaded by Roman idiosyncrasy—one might say, by a savour of the Sabine soil. These satires like the essays already noticed handle some moral or other theme adapted to the larger public, as is shown by the several titles—*Columnae Herculis*, περὶ Δόξης; Εὗρεν ἡ Λοπὰς τὸ Πῶμα, περὶ Γεγαμηκότων; *Est Modus Matulae*, περὶ Μέθης; "*Papiapapae*, περὶ Ἐγκωμίων." The plastic dress, which in this case might not be wanting, is of course but seldom borrowed from the history of his native country, as in the satire *Serranus*, περὶ Αρχαιρεσιῶν. The dog-world of Diogenes on the other hand plays, as might be expected, a great part; we meet with the Κυνίστωρ, the Κυνορρήτωρ, the Ἱπποκύων, the Ὑδροκύων, the Κυνοδιδασκαλικόν, and others of a like kind. Mythology is also laid under contribution for comic purposes; we find a *Prometheus Liber*, an *Ajax Stramenticius*, a *Hercules Socraticus*, a *Sesqueulixes* who had spent not merely ten but fifteen years in wanderings. The outline of the dramatic or romantic framework is still discoverable from the fragments in some pieces, such as the *Prometheus Liber*, the *Sexagessis*, the *Manius*; it appears that Varro frequently, perhaps regularly, narrated the tale as his own experience; *e.g.* in the *Manius* the *dramatis personae* go to Varro and discourse to him "because he was known to them as a bookmaker." As to the poetical value of this dress we are no longer allowed to form any certain judgment; there still occur in our fragments several very charming sketches full of wit and liveliness—thus in the "*Prometheus Liber*" the hero after the loosing of his chains opens a manufactory of men, in which Goldshoe the rich (*Chrysosandalos*) bespeaks for himself a maiden, of milk and finest wax, such as the Milesian bees gather from various flowers, a maiden without bones and sinews, without skin or hair, pure and polished, slim, smooth, tender, charming. The life-breath of this poetry is polemics—not so much the political warfare of party, such as Lucilius and Catullus practised, but the general moral antagonism of the stern elderly man to the unbridled and perverse youth, of the scholar living in the midst of his classics to the loose and slovenly, or at any rate in point of tendency reprobate, modern poetry,[1] of the good burgess of the ancient type to the new Rome in which the Forum, to use Varro's language, was a pigsty and Numa, if he turned his eyes towards his city, would see no longer a trace of his wise regulations. In the constitutional struggle Varro did what seemed to him the duty of a citizen; but his heart was not in such partisan agitation—"why," he complains on one occasion, "do ye call me from my pure life into the filth of your senate-house?" He belonged to the good old time, when the talk savoured of onions and garlic, but the heart was sound. His warfare against the hereditary foes of the genuine Roman spirit, the Greek philosophers, was only a single aspect of this old-fashioned opposition to the spirit of the new times; but it resulted both from the nature of the Cynical philosophy and from the temperament of Varro, that the Menippean lash was very specially plied round the ears of the philosophers and put them accordingly into proportional alarm—it was not without palpitation that the philosophic scribes of the time transmitted to the "severe man" their newly issued treatises. Philosophising is verily no art. With the tenth part of the trouble with which a master rears his slave to be a professional baker, he trains himself to be a philosopher; no doubt, when the baker and the philosopher both come under the hammer, the artist of pastry goes off a hundred times dearer than the philosopher. Singular people, these philosophers! One enjoins that corpses be buried in honey—it is a fortunate circumstance that his desire is not complied with, otherwise where would any honey-wine be left? Another thinks that

[1] On one occasion he writes, "*Quintiporis Clodii foria ac poemata ejus gargaridians dices; O fortuna, O fors fortuna!*" And elsewhere, "*Cum Quintipor Clodius tot comoedias sine ulla fecerit Musa, ego unum libellum non 'edolem' ut ait Ennius?*" This not otherwise known Clodius must have been in all probability a wretched imitator of Terence, as those words sarcastically laid at his door "*O fortuna, O fors fortuna!*" are found occurring in a Terentian comedy.

The following description of himself by a poet in Varro's Ὄνος Λύρας,

Pacuvi discipulus dicor, porro is fuit Enni,
Ennius Musarum; Pompilius clueor

might aptly parody the introduction of Lucretius (p. 551), to whom Varro as a declared enemy of the Epicurean system cannot have been well disposed, and whom he never quotes.

men grow out of the earth like cresses. A third has invented a world-borer (Κοσμοτορύνη) by which the earth will some day be destroyed.

Postremo, nemo aegrotus quicquam somniat
Tam infandum, quod non aliquis dicat philosophus.

It is ludicrous to observe how a Long-beard—by which is meant an etymologising Stoic—cautiously weighs every word in goldsmith's scales; but there is nothing that surpasses the genuine philosophers' quarrel—a Stoic boxing-match far excels any encounter of athletes. In the satire *Marcopolis*, περὶ ἀρχῆς, when Marcus created for himself a Cloud-Cuckoo-Home after his own heart, matters fared, just as in the Attic comedy, well with the peasant, but ill with the philosopher; the *Celer*-δι'-ἑνὸς-λήμματος-λόγος, son of Antipater the Stoic, beats in the skull of his opponent—evidently the philosophic *Dilemma*—with the mattock.

With this morally polemic tendency and this talent for embodying it in caustic and picturesque expression, which, as the dress of dialogue given to the books on Husbandry written in his eightieth year shows, never forsook him down to extreme old age, Varro most happily combined an incomparable knowledge of the national manners and language, which is embodied in the philological writings of his old age after the manner of a commonplace-book, but displays itself in his Satires in all its direct fulness and freshness. Varro was in the best and fullest sense of the term a local antiquarian, who from the personal observation of many years knew his nation in its former idiosyncrasy and seclusion as well as in its modern state of transition and dispersion, and had supplemented and deepened his direct knowledge of the national manners and national language by the most comprehensive investigation of historical and literary archives. His partial deficiency in rational judgment and learning—in our sense of the words—was compensated for by his clear intuition and the poetry which lived within him. He sought neither after antiquarian notices nor after rare antiquated or poetical words;[1] but he was himself an old and old-fashioned man and almost a rustic, the classics of his nation were his favourite and long-familiar companions; how could it fail that many details of the manners of his forefathers which he loved above all and especially knew should be narrated in his writings,

[1] He himself once aptly says, that he had no special fondness for antiquated words, but frequently used them, and that he was very fond of poetical words, but did not use them.

and that his discourse should abound with proverbial Greek and Latin phrases, with good old words preserved in the Sabine conversational language, with reminiscences of Ennius, Lucilius, and above all of Plautus? We should not judge as to the prose style of these aesthetic writings of Varro's earlier period by the standard of his work on Language written in his old age and probably published in an unfinished state, in which certainly the clauses of the sentence are arranged on the thread of the relative like thrushes on a string; but we have already observed that Varro rejected on principle the effort after a chaste style and Attic periods (p. 537), and his aesthetic essays, while destitute of the mean bombast and the spurious tinsel of vulgarism, were yet written after an unclassic and even slovenly fashion, in sentences rather directly joined on to each other than regularly subdivided. The poetical pieces inserted on the other hand show not merely that their author knew how to mould the most varied measures with as much mastery as any of the fashionable poets, but that he had a right to include himself among those to whom a god has granted the gift of "banishing cares from the heart by song and sacred poesy."[1]

[1] The following description is taken from the *Marcipor* ('Slave of Marcus').

Repente noctis circiter meridiem
Cum pictus aer fervidis late ignibus
Caeli chorean astricen ostenderet,
Nubes aquali, frigido velo leves
Caeli cavernas aureas subduxerant,
Aquam vomentes inferam mortalibus.
Ventique frigido se ab axe eruperant,
Phrenetici septentrionum filii,
Secum ferentes tegulas, ramos, syrus.
At nos caduci, naufragi, ut ciconiae
Quarum bipennis fulminis plumas vapor
Perussit, alte maesti in terram cecidimus.

In the Ἀνθρωπόπολις we find the lines:

Non fit thesauris, non auro pectu' solutum ;
Non demunt animis curas ac religiones
Persarum montes, non atria diviti' Crassi.

But the poet was successful also in a lighter vein. In the *Est Modus Matulae* there stood the following elegant commendation of wine:—

Vino nihil iucundius quisquam bibit.
Hoc aegritudinem ad medendam invenerunt,
Hoc hilaritatis dulce seminarium,
Hoc continet coagulum convivia.

And in the Κοσμοτορύνη the wanderer returning home thus concludes his address to the sailors:—

Detis habenas animae leni,
Dum nos ventus flamine sudo
Suavem ad patriam perducit.

The sketches of Varro no more created a school than the didactic poem of Lucretius; to the more general causes which prevented this there falls to be added their thoroughly individual stamp, which was inseparable from the greater age, from the rusticity, and even from the peculiar learning of their author. But the grace and humour of the Menippean satires above all, which seem to have been in number and importance far superior to Varro's graver works, captivated his contemporaries as well as those in after times who had any relish for originality and national spirit; and even we, who are no longer permitted to read them, may still from the fragments preserved discern in some measure that the writer "knew how to laugh and how to jest in moderation." And as the last breath of the good spirit of the old burgess-times ere it departed, as the latest fresh growth which the national Latin poetry put forth, the Satires of Varro deserved that the poet in his poetical testament should commend these his Menippean children to every one "who had at heart the prosperity of Rome and of Latium;" and they accordingly retain an honourable place in the literature as in the history of the Italian people.[1]

[1] The sketches of Varro have so uncommon historical and even poetical significance, and are yet, in consequence of the fragmentary shape in which information regarding them has reached us, known to so few and so irksome to study, that we may be allowed to give in this place a résumé of some of them with the few restorations indispensable for making them readable.

The satire *Manius* (Early Up!) describes the management of a rural household. "Manius summons his people to rise with the sun, and in person conducts them to the scene of their labours. The youths make their own bed, which labour renders soft to them, and supply themselves with waterpot and lamp. Their drink is the clear fresh spring, their fare bread, and onions as a relish. Everything prospers in house and field. The house is no work of art; but an architect might learn symmetry from it. Care is taken of the field, that it shall not be left disorderly and waste, or go to ruin through slovenliness and neglect; in return the grateful Ceres wards off damage from the produce, that the high-piled sheaves may gladden the heart of the husbandman. Here hospitality still holds good; every one who has but imbibed mother's milk is welcome. The bread-pantry and wine-vat and the store of sausages on the rafters, lock and key are at the service of the traveller, and piles of food are set before him; contented sits the sated guest, looking neither before nor behind, dozing by the hearth in the kitchen. The warmest double-wool sheep-skin is spread as a couch for him. Here people still as good burgesses obey the righteous law, which neither out of envy injures the innocent, nor out of favour pardons the guilty. Here they speak no evil against their neighbours. Here they trespass not with their feet on the sacred hearth, but honour the gods with devotion and with sacrifices, throw to the familiar spirit his little bit of flesh into his appointed little dish, and when the master of the household dies, accompany the bier with the same prayer with which those of his father and of his grandfather were borne forth."

In another satire there appears a "Teacher of the Old" (Γεροντοδιδά-

The critical writing of history, after the manner in which the Attic authors wrote the national history in their classic period and in which Polybius wrote the history of the world, was never properly developed in Rome. Even in the field most adapted for it—the representation of contemporary and of recently past events—there was nothing, on the whole, but more or less inadequate attempts; in the epoch especially from Sulla to Caesar the not very important contributions, which the previous epoch had to show in this field—the labours of Antipater and Asellius—were barely even equalled. The only work of note belonging to this field, which arose in the present epoch, was the history of the Social and Civil Wars by Lucius Cornelius Sisenna (praetor in $\frac{676}{78}$). Those who had read it testify that it far excelled in liveliness and readableness the old dry chronicles, but was written withal in a style thoroughly impure and even degenerating into puerility; as indeed the few remaining frag-

σκαλος), of whom the degenerate age seems to stand more urgently in need than of the teacher of youth, and he explains how "once everything in Rome was chaste and pious," and now all things are so entirely changed. "Do my eyes deceive me, or do I see slaves in arms against their masters? —Formerly every one who did not present himself for the levy, was sold on the part of the state into slavery abroad; now the censor who allows cowardice and everything to pass is called [by the aristocracy ii. 306, iii. 348, iv. 90, 305] a great citizen, and earns praise because he does not seek to make himself a name by annoying his fellow-citizens.—Formerly the Roman husbandman had his beard shaven once every week; now the rural slave cannot have it fine enough.—Formerly one saw on the estates a corn-granary, which held ten harvests, spacious cellars for the wine-vats and corresponding wine-presses; now the master keeps flocks of peacocks, and causes his doors to be inlaid with African cypress-wood.—Formerly the matron turned the spindle with the hand and kept at the same time the pot on the hearth in her eye, that the pottage might not be singed; now," it is said in another satire, "the daughter begs her father for a pound of precious stones and the wife her husband for a bushel of pearls.—Formerly a newly-married husband was silent and bashful; now the wife surrenders herself to the first coachman that comes.—Formerly the blessing of children was woman's pride; now if her husband desires for himself children, she replies: Knowest thou not what Ennius says?

Ter sub armis malim vitam cernere
Quam semel modo parere.—

Formerly the wife was quite content, when the husband once or twice in the year gave her a trip in the uncushioned waggon;" now, he could add (comp. Cicero, *Pro Mil.* 21, 55), the wife sulks if her husband goes to his country estate without her, and the travelling lady is attended to the villa by the fashionable host of Greek menials and the choir.—In a treatise of a graver kind, "Catus or the Training of Children," Varro not only instructs the friend who had asked him for advice on that point, regarding the gods who were according to old usage to be sacrificed to for the children's welfare, but, referring to the more judicious mode of rearing children among the Persians and to his own strictly spent youth, he warns against over-feeding and over-sleeping, against sweet bread and fine fare—the whelps, the old

ments exhibit a paltry painting in detail of the horrible,[1] and a number of words newly coined or derived from the language of conversation. When it is added that the author's model and, so to speak, the only Greek historian familiar to him was Clitarchus, the author of a biography of Alexander the Great oscillating between history and fiction in the manner of the semi-romance which bears the name of Curtius, we shall not hesitate to recognise in Sisenna's celebrated historical work, not a product of genuine historical criticism and art, but the first Roman essay in that hybrid mixture of history and romance so much a favourite with the Greeks, which desires to make the groundwork of facts life-like and interesting by means of fictitious details and thereby makes it insipid and untrue; and it will no longer excite surprise that we meet with the same Sisenna as translator of Greek fashionable romances (p. 558).

That the prospect should be still more lamentable in the field of the general annals of the city and even of the world, is implied in the nature of the case. The increasing activity of antiquarian research induced the expectation that the current narrative

man thinks, are now fed more judiciously than the children—and likewise against the enchantresses' charms and blessings, which in cases of sickness so often take the place of consulting the physician. He advises to keep the girls at embroidery, that they may afterwards understand how to judge properly of embroidered and textile work, and not to allow them to put off the child's dress too early; he warns against carrying boys to the gladiatorial games, in which the heart is early pardoned and cruelty learned.—In the "Man of Sixty Years" Varro appears as a Roman Epimenides who had fallen asleep when a boy of ten and awoke again after half a century. He is astonished to find instead of his smooth-shorn boy's head an old bald pate with an ugly snout and savage bristles like a hedgehog; but he is still more astonished at the change in Rome. Lucrine oysters, formerly a wedding dish, are now every-day fare; for which, accordingly, the bankrupt glutton silently prepares the incendiary torch. While formerly the father disposed of his boy, now the disposal is transferred to the latter: he disposes, forsooth, of his father by poison. The comitium had become an exchange, the criminal trial a mine of gold for the jurymen. No law is any longer obeyed save only this one, that nothing is given for nothing. All virtues have vanished; in their stead the awakened man is saluted by the impiety, perfidy, lewdness of the new denizens. "Alas for thee, Marcus, with such a sleep and such an awakening!"—The sketch resembles the Catilinarian epoch, shortly after which (about $\frac{697}{57}$) the old man must have written it, and there lay a truth in the bitter turn at the close; where Marcus, properly reproved for his unseasonable accusations and antiquarian reminiscences, is—with a mock application of a primitive Roman custom—dragged as an useless old man to the bridge and thrown into the Tiber. There was certainly no longer room for such men in Rome.

[1] "The innocent," so ran a speech, "thou draggest forth, trembling in every limb, and on the high margin of the river's bank in the dawn of the morning" [thou causest them to be slaughtered]. Several such phrases, that might be inserted without difficulty in a commonplace novel, occur.

would be rectified from documents and other trustworthy sources; but this hope was not fulfilled. The more and the deeper men investigated, the more clearly it became apparent what a task it was to write a critical history of Rome. The difficulties even, which opposed themselves to investigation and narration, were immense; but the most dangerous obstacles were not those of a literary kind. The conventional early history of Rome, as it had now been narrated and believed for at least ten generations (i. 457), was most intimately mixed up with the civil life of the nation; and yet in any thorough and honest inquiry not only had details to be modified here and there, but the whole building had to be overturned as much as the Franconian primitive history of king Pharamund or the British of king Arthur. An inquirer of conservative views, such as was Varro for instance, could have no wish to put his hand to such a work; and if a daring freethinker had undertaken it, an outcry would have been raised by all good citizens against this worst of all revolutionaries, who was preparing to deprive the constitutional party even of their past. Thus philological and antiquarian research deterred from the writing of history rather than conduced towards it. Varro and the more sagacious men in general evidently gave up the task of annals as hopeless; at the most they arranged, as did Titus Pomponius Atticus, the official and gentile lists in unpretending tabular shape—a work by which the synchronistic Graeco-Roman chronology was finally brought into the shape in which it was conventionally fixed for posterity. But the manufacture of city-chronicles of course did not suspend its activity; it continued to supply its contributions both in prose and verse to the great library written by *ennui* for *ennui*, while the makers of the books, in part already freedmen, did not trouble themselves at all about research properly so called. Such of these writings as are noticed—not one of them is preserved—seem to have been not only of a wholly secondary character, but in great part even pervaded by interested falsification. It is true that the chronicle of Quintus Claudius Quadrigarius (about $\frac{676}{78}$?) was written in an old-fashioned but good style, and studied at least a commendable brevity in the representation of the fabulous period. Gaius Licinius Macer (+as late praetor in $\frac{688}{66}$), father of the poet Calvus (p. 557) and a zealous democrat, laid claim more than any other chronicler to documentary research and criticism, but his *libri lintei* and other matters peculiar to him are in the highest degree suspicious, and an interpolation of the whole annals for purposes of a democratic character—an interpolation of a very extensive kind, and which has passed over in part to the latter annalists—is probably traceable to him. Lastly, Valerius Antias excelled all his predecessors in prolixity as well as in puerile story-telling. The falsification of numbers was here systematically carried out down even to contemporary history, and the primitive history of Rome was elaborated once more from one form of insipidity to another; for instance the narrative of the way in which the wise Numa according to the instructions of the nymph Egeria caught the gods Faunus and Picus with wine, and the beautiful conversation thereupon held by the same Numa with the god Jupiter, cannot be too urgently recommended to all worshippers of the so-called legendary history of Rome in order that, if possible, they may believe these things—of course, in substance. It would have been a marvel if the Greek novel-writers of this period had allowed such materials, made as if for their use, to escape them. In fact there were not wanting Greek literati, who worked up the Roman history into romances; such a composition, for instance, was the Five Books "Concerning Rome" of the Alexander Polyhistor already mentioned among the Greek literati living in Rome (p. 540), a preposterous mixture of vapid historical tradition and trivial, principally erotic, fiction. He, it may be conjectured, took the first steps towards filling up the five hundred years, which were wanting to bring the destruction of Troy and the origin of Rome into the chronological connection required by the fables on either side, with one of those lists of kings without achievements which were unhappily familiar to the Egyptian and Greek chroniclers; for, to all appearance, it was he that launched into the world the kings Aventinus and Tiberinus and the Alban *gens* of the Silvii, whom the following times accordingly did not neglect to furnish in detail with name, period of reigning, and, for the sake of greater definiteness, also a portrait.

Thus from various sides the historical romance of the Greeks finds its way into Roman historiography; and it is more than probable that not the least portion of what we are accustomed now-a-days to call tradition of the Roman primitive times proceeds from sources of the stamp of Amadis of Gaul and the chivalrous romances of Fouqué—an edifying consideration, which may be commended to those who have a relish for the humour of history and who know how to appreciate the comical aspect of the piety still cherished in certain circles of the nineteenth century for king Numa.

A novelty in the Roman literature of this period is the appearance of universal history or, to speak more correctly, of Roman and Greek history conjoined, alongside of the native annals. Cornelius Nepos (*c.* $\frac{650}{100}$—*c.* $\frac{725}{30}$) first supplied an universal chronicle (published before $\frac{700}{54}$) and a general collection of biographies—arranged according to certain categories—of Romans and Greeks distinguished in politics or literature or of men at any rate who exercised influence on the Roman or Greek history. These works are of a kindred nature with the universal histories which the Greeks had for a considerable time been composing; and these very Greek world-chronicles, such as that of Kastor son-in-law of the Galatian king Deiotarus, concluded in $\frac{698}{56}$, now began to include in their range the Roman history which previously they had neglected. These works certainly attempted, just like Polybius, to substitute the history of the Mediterranean world for the more local one; but that which in Polybius was the result of a grand and clear conception and deep historical feeling was in these chronicles rather the product of the practical exigencies of school and self-instruction. These general chronicles, treatises for scholastic instruction or manuals for reference, and the whole literature therewith connected which subsequently became very copious in the Latin language also, can hardly be reckoned as belonging to artistic historical composition; and Nepos himself in particular was a mere compiler distinguished neither by spirit nor even by symmetrical plan.

The historiography of this period is certainly remarkable and in a high degree characteristic, but it is as far from pleasing as the age itself. The interpenetration of Greek and Latin literature is in no field so clearly apparent as in that of history; here the respective literatures become earliest equalised in matter and form, and the conception of Helleno-Italic history as an unity, in which Polybius was so far in advance of his age, was now learned by Greek and Roman boys at school. But while the Mediterranean state had found an historian before it had become conscious of its own existence, now, when that consciousness had been attained, there did not arise either among the Greeks or among the Romans any man who was able to give to it adequate expression. "There is no such thing," says Cicero, "as Roman historical composition;" and, so far as we can judge, this is no more than the simple truth. The man of research turns away from writing history, the writer of history turns away from research; historical literature oscillates between the schoolbook and the romance. All the species of pure art—epos, drama, lyric poetry, history—are worthless in this worthless world; but in no species is the intellectual decay of the Ciceronian age reflected with so terrible a clearness as in its historiography.

The minor historical literature of this period displays on the other hand, amidst many insignificant and forgotten productions, one treatise of the first rank—the Memoirs of Caesar, or rather the Military Report of the democratic general to the people from whom he had received his commission. The most finished section, and that which alone was published by the author himself, describing the Celtic campaigns down to $\frac{702}{52}$, is evidently designed to justify as well as possible before the public the formally unconstitutional enterprise of Caesar in conquering a great country and constantly increasing his army for that object without instructions from the competent authority; it was written and given forth in $\frac{703}{51}$, when the storm broke out against Caesar in Rome and he was summoned to dismiss his army and answer for his conduct.[1] The author of this vindication writes, as he himself says, entirely as an officer and carefully avoids extending his military report to the hazardous departments of political organisation and administration. His incidental and partisan treatise cast in the form of a military report is itself a piece of history like the bulletins of Napoleon,

[1] That the treatise on the Gallic war was published all at once, has been long conjectured; the distinct proof that it was so, is furnished by the mention of the equalisation of the Boii and the Haedui already in the first book (c. 28) whereas the Boii still appear in the seventh (c. 10) as tributary subjects of the Haedui, and evidently only obtained equal rights with their former masters on account of their conduct and that of the Haedui in the war against Vercingetorix. On the other hand any one who attentively follows the history of the time will find in the expression as to the Milonian crisis (vii. 6) a proof that the treatise was published before the outbreak of the civil war; not because Pompeius is there praised, but because Caesar there approves the exceptional laws of $\frac{702}{52}$ (p. 304). This he might and could not but do, so long as he sought to bring about a peaceful accommodation with Pompeius (p. 332), but not after the rupture, when he reversed the condemnations that took place on the basis of those laws injurious for him (p. 432). Accordingly the publication of this treatise has been quite rightly placed in $\frac{703}{51}$.

The tendency of the work, we discern most distinctly in the constant, often—most decidedly, doubtless, in the case of the Aquitanian expedition, iii. 11—not successful, justification of every single act of war as a defensive measure which the state of things had rendered inevitable. That the adversaries of Caesar censured his attacks on the Celts and Germans above all as unprovoked, is well known (Sueton. *Caes*. 24).

but it is not, and was not intended to be, an historical work in the true sense of the word; the objective form which the narrative assumes is that of the magistrate, not that of the historian. But in this modest character the work is masterly and finished, more than any other in all Roman literature. The narrative is always terse and never scanty, always simple and never careless, always of transparent vividness and never strained or affected. The language is completely pure from archaisms and from vulgarisms—the type of the modern *urbanitas*. In the Books concerning the Civil War we seem to feel that the author had desired to avoid war and could not avoid it, and perhaps also that in Caesar's soul, as in every other, the period of hope was purer and fresher than that of fulfilment; but over the treatise on the Gallic war there is diffused a bright serenity, a simple charm, which are no less unique in literature than Caesar is in history.

Of a kindred nature were the letters interchanged between the statesmen and literati of this period, which were carefully collected and published in the following epoch; such as the correspondence of Caesar himself, of Cicero, Calvus, and others. They can still less be included among strictly literary performances; but this literature of correspondence was a rich storehouse for historical as for all other research, and the most faithful mirror of an epoch in which so much of the worth of past times and so much spirit, cleverness, and talent were evaporated and dissipated in trifling.

A journalist literature in the modern sense was never formed in Rome; literary warfare continued to be confined to the writing of pamphlets and, along with this, to the custom generally diffused at that time of annotating the notices destined for the public in places of resort with the pencil or the pen. On the other hand subordinate persons were employed to note down the events of the day and news of the city for the absent men of quality; and Caesar as early as his first consulship took fitting measures for the immediate publication of an extract of the transactions of the senate. From the private journals of those Roman penny-a-liners and these official current reports there arose a sort of news-sheet for the capital (*acta diurna*), in which the *résumé* of the business discussed before the people and in the senate, and births, deaths, and such like were recorded. This became a not unimportant source for history, but remained without proper political as without literary significance.

To subsidiary historical literature belongs of right also the composition of orations. The speech whether written down or not, is in its nature ephemeral and does not belong to literature; but it may, like the report and the letter, and indeed still more readily than these, come to be included, through the significance of the moment and the power of the mind from which it springs, among the permanent treasures of the national literature. Thus in Rome the records of orations of a political tenor delivered before the burgesses or the jurymen had for long played a great part in public life; and not only so, but the speeches of Gaius Gracchus in particular were justly reckoned among the classical Roman writings. But in this epoch a singular change occurred on all hands. The composition of political speeches was on the decline like political speaking itself. The political speech in Rome, as generally in the ancient polities, reached its culminating point in the discussions before the burgesses; there the orator was not fettered, as in the senate, by corporate considerations and burdensome forms, nor, as in the judicial addresses, by the interests—in themselves foreign to politics—of the accusation and defence; there alone his heart swelled proudly before the whole great and mighty Roman people hanging on his lips. But all this was now gone. Not as though there was any lack of orators or of the publishing of speeches delivered before the burgesses; on the contrary political authorship only now waxed copious, and it began to become a standing complaint at table that the host incommoded his guests by reading before them his latest orations. Publius Clodius had his speeches to the people issued as pamphlets, just like Gaius Gracchus; but two men may do the same thing without producing the same effect. The more important leaders even of the opposition, especially Caesar himself, did not often address the burgesses, and no longer published the speeches which they delivered; indeed they partly sought for their political fugitive writings another form than the traditional one of *contiones*, in which respect more especially the writings praising and censuring Cato (p. 436) are remarkable. This is easily explained. Gaius Gracchus had addressed the burgesses; now men addressed the populace; and as the audience, so was the speech. No wonder that the reputable political author shunned a dress which implied that he had directed his words to the crowd assembled in the Forum.

While the composition of orations thus declined from its former literary and political value in the same way as all branches of literature which were the natural growth of the national life, there began at the same time a singular, non-political, literature of pleadings. Hitherto the Romans had known nothing of the idea that the address of an advocate as such was destined not only for the judges and the parties, but also for the literary edification of contemporaries and posterity; no advocate had written down and published his pleadings, unless they were possibly at the same time political orations, and in so far were fitted to be circulated as party writings, and this had not occurred very frequently. Even Quintus Hortensius ($\frac{640-704}{114-50}$), the most celebated Roman advocate in the first years of this period, published but few speeches and these apparently only such as were wholly or half political. It was his successor in the leadership of the Roman bar, Marcus Tullius Cicero ($\frac{648-711}{106-43}$) who was from the outset quite as much author as forensic orator; he published his pleadings regularly, even when they were not at all or but remotely connected with politics. This was a token, not of progress, but of an unnatural and degenerate state of things. In Athens also the appearance of non-political pleadings among the forms of literature was a sign of debility; and it was doubly so in Rome, which did not like Athens by a sort of necessity produce this malformation through an exaggerated pursuit of rhetoric, but borrowed it from abroad arbitrarily and in antagonism to the better traditions of the nation. Yet this new species of literature came rapidly into vogue, partly because it had various points of contact and coincidence with the earlier authorship of political orations, partly because the unpoetic, dogmatical, rhetorising temperament of the Romans offered a favourable soil for the new seed, as indeed at the present day the speeches of advocates and even a sort of literature of law-proceedings are of some importance in Italy.

Thus oratorical authorship emancipated from politics was naturalised in the Roman literary world by Cicero. We have already had occasion several times to mention this many-sided man. As a statesman without insight, opinion, or purpose, he figured successively as democrat, as aristocrat, and as a tool of the monarchs, and was never more than a short-sighted egotist. Where he exhibited the appearance of action, the questions to which his action applied had, as a rule, just reached their solution; thus he came forward in the trial of Verres against the senatorial *judicia* when they were already set aside; thus he was silent at the discussion on the Gabinian, and acted as a champion of the Manilian, law; thus he thundered against

Catilina when his departure was already settled, and so forth. He was valiant in opposition to sham attacks, and he knocked down many walls of pasteboard with a loud din; no serious matter was ever, either in good or evil, decided by him, and the execution of the Catilinarians in particular was far more due to his acquiescence than to his instigation. In a literary point of view we have already noticed that he was the creator of the modern Latin prose (p. 537); his importance rests on his mastery of style, and it is only as a stylist that he shows confidence in himself. In the character of an author, on the other hand, he stands quite as low as in that of a statesman. He essayed the most varied tasks, sang the great deeds of Marius and his own petty achievements in endless hexameters, beat Demosthenes off the field with his speeches, and Plato with his philosophic dialogues; and time alone was wanting for him to vanquish also Thucydides. He was in fact so thoroughly a dabbler, that it was pretty much a matter of indifference to what work he applied his hand. By nature a journalist in the worst sense of that term—abounding, as he himself says, in words, poor beyond all conception in ideas—there was no department in which he could not with the help of a few books have rapidly got up by translation or compilation a readable essay. His correspondence mirrors most faithfully his character. People are in the habit of calling it interesting and clever; and it is so, as long as it reflects the urban or villa life of the world of quality; but where the writer is thrown on his own resources, as in exile, in Cilicia, and after the battle of Pharsalus, it is stale and empty as was ever the soul of a feuilletonist banished from his familiar circles. It is scarcely needful to add that such a statesman and such a *littérateur* could not, as a man, exhibit aught else than a thinly varnished superficiality and heartlessness. Must we still describe the orator? The great author is also a great man; and in the great orator more especially conviction or passion flows forth with a clearer and more impetuous stream from the depths of the breast than in the scantily-gifted many who merely count and are nothing. Cicero had no conviction and no passion; he was nothing but an advocate, and not a good one. He understood how to set forth his narrative of the case with piquancy of ancedote, to excite, if not the feeling, at any rate the sentimentality of his hearers, and to enliven the dry business of legal pleading by cleverness or witticisms mostly of a personal sort; his better orations, though they are far from coming up to the free gracefulness and the sure point of the most excellent compositions of this sort, for instance the Memoirs of Beaumarchais, yet form easy and agreeable reading. But while the very advantages just indicated will appear to the serious judge as advantages of very dubious value, the absolute want of political discernment in the orations on constitutional questions and of juristic deduction in the forensic addresses, the egotism forgetful of its duty and constantly losing sight of the cause while thinking of the advocate, the dreadful barrenness of thought in the Ciceronian orations must revolt every reader of feeling and judgment.

If there is anything wonderful in the case, it is in truth not the orations, but the admiration which they excited. As to Cicero every unbiassed person will soon make up his mind: Ciceronianism is a problem, which in fact cannot be properly solved, but can only be resolved into the greater mystery of human nature—language and the effect of language on the mind. Inasmuch as the noble Latin language, just before it perished as a national idiom, was once more as it were comprehensively grasped by that dexterous stylist and deposited in his copious writings, something of the power which language exercises, and of the piety which it awakens, was transferred to the unworthy vessel. The Romans possessed no great Latin prose-writer; for Caesar was, like Napoleon, only incidentally an author. Was it to be wondered at that, in the absence of such an one, they should at least honour the genius of the language in the great stylist? and that, like Cicero himself Cicero's readers also should accustom themselves to ask not what, but how he had written? Custom and the schoolmaster then completed what the power of language had begun.

Cicero's contemporaries however were, as may readily be conceived, far less involved in this strange idolatry than many of their successors. The Ciceronian manner ruled no doubt throughout a generation the Roman advocate-world, just as the far worse manner of Hortensius had done; but the most considerable men, such as Caesar, kept themselves always aloof from it, and among the younger generation there arose in all men of fresh and living talent the most decided opposition to that hybrid and feeble rhetoric. They found Cicero's language deficient in precision and chasteness, his jests deficient in liveliness, his arrangement deficient in clearness and articulate division, and above all his whole eloquence wanting in the fire which makes the orator. Instead of the Rhodian eclectics men began to recur to the genuine Attic orators, especially to Lysias and Demosthenes, and sought to naturalise a more vigorous and masculine eloquence in Rome. Representatives of this tendency were, the solemn but stiff Marcus Junius Brutus ($\frac{669-712}{85-42}$); the two political partisans Marcus Caelius Rufus ($\frac{672-706}{82-48}$; p. 433) and Gaius Scribonius Curio ($+\frac{705}{49}$; pp. 333, 370)—both as orators full of spirit and life; Calvus well known also as a poet ($\frac{672-706}{82-48}$), the literary coryphaeus of this younger group of orators; and the earnest and conscientious Gaius Asinius Pollio ($\frac{678-757}{76-4}$). Undeniably there was more taste and more spirit in this younger oratorical literature than in the Hortensian and Ciceronian put together; but we are not able to judge how far, amidst the storms of the revolution which rapidly swept away the whole of this richly gifted group with the single exception of Pollio, those better germs attained development. The time allotted to them was but too brief. The new monarchy began by making war on freedom of speech, and soon wholly suppressed the political oration (p. 340). Thenceforth the subordinate species of the pure advocate-pleading was doubtless still retained in literature; but the higher art and literature of oratory, which thoroughly depend on political excitement, perished with the latter of necessity and for ever.

Lastly there sprang up in the aesthetic literature of this period the artistic treatment of subjects of professional science in the form of the stylistic dialogue, which had been very extensively in use among the Greeks and had been already employed also in isolated cases among the Romans (iii. 442). Cicero especially made various attempts at presenting rhetorical and philosophical subjects in this form and making the professional manual a suitable book for reading. His chief writings are the *De Oratore* (written in $\frac{699}{55}$), to which the history of Roman eloquence (the dialogue *Brutus* written in $\frac{708}{46}$) and other minor rhetorical essays were added by way of supplement; and the treatise *De Republicâ* (written in $\frac{700}{54}$), with which the treatise *De Legibus* (written in $\frac{702}{52}$?) after the model of Plato is brought into connection. They are no great works of art, but undoubtedly they are the works in which the excellences of the author are most, and his faults least, conspicuous. The rhetorical writings are far from coming up to the didactic chasteness of form and precision of thought of the Rhetoric dedicated to Herennius, but they contain instead a store of practical forensic experience and forensic anecdotes of all sorts easily and tastefully set forth, and in fact solve the problem of combining didactic instruction with amusement. The treatise *De*

Republicâ carries out, in a singular mongrel compound of history and philosophy, the leading idea that the existing constitution of Rome is substantially the ideal state-organisation sought for by philosophers; an idea indeed just as unphilosophical as unhistorical, and besides not even peculiar to the author, but which, as may readily be conceived, became and remained popular. The scientific groundwork of these rhetorical and political writings of Cicero belongs of course entirely to the Greeks, and many of the details also, such as the grand concluding effect in the treatise *De Republicâ*, the Dream of Scipio, are directly borrowed from them; yet they possess comparative originality, inasmuch as the elaboration shows throughout Roman local colouring, and the proud consciousness of political life, which the Roman was certainly entitled to feel as compared with the Greeks, makes the author even confront his Greek instructors with a certain independence. The form of Cicero's dialogue is doubtless neither the genuine interrogative dialectics of the best Greek artificial dialogue nor the genuine conversational tone of Diderot or Lessing; but the great groups of advocates gathering around Crassus and Antonius and of the older and younger statesmen of the Scipionic circle furnish a lively and effective framework, fitting channels for the introduction of historical references and anecdotes, and convenient resting-points for the scientific discussion. The style is quite as elaborate and polished as in the best-written orations, and so far more pleasing than these, since the author does not often in this field make a vain attempt at pathos.

While these rhetorical and political writings of Cicero with a philosophic colouring are not devoid of merit, the compiler on the other hand completely failed, when in the involuntary leisure of the last years of his life ($\frac{709-710}{45-44}$) he applied himself to philosophy proper, and with equal pevishness and precipitation composed in a couple of months a philosophical library. The receipt was very simple. In rude imitation of the popular writings of Aristotle, in which the form of dialogue was employed chiefly for the setting forth and criticising of the different older systems, Cicero stitched together the Epicurean, Stoic, and Syncretist writings handling the same problem, as they came or were given to his hand, into a so-called dialogue. And all that he did on his own part was, to supply an introduction prefixed to the new book from the ample collection of prefaces for future works which he had beside him; to impart a certain popular character, inasmuch as he interwove Roman examples and references, and sometimes digressed to subjects irrelevant but more familiar to the writer and the reader, such as the treatment of the deportment of the orator in the *De Officiis;* and to exhibit that sort of bungling which a man of letters, who has not attained to philosophic thinking or even to philosophic knowledge, and who works rapidly and boldly, shows in the reproduction of dialectic trains of thought. In this way no doubt a multitude of thick tomes might very quickly come into existence—" They are copies," wrote the author himself to a friend who wondered at his fertility; " they give me little trouble, for I supply only the words and these I have in abundance." Against this nothing further could be said; but any one who seeks classical productions in works so written can only be advised to study in literary matters a becoming silence.

Of the sciences only a single one manifested vigorous life, that of Latin philology. The scheme of linguistic and antiquarian research within the domain of the Latin race, planned by Stilo, was carried out especially by his disciple Varro on the grandest scale. There appeared comprehensive elaborations of the whole stores of the language, more especially the extensive grammatical commentaries of Figulus and the great work of Varro *De Lingua Latina;* monographs on grammar and the history of the language, such as Varro's writings on the usage of the Latin language, on synonyms, on the age of the letters, on the origin of the Latin tongue; scholia on the older literature, especially on Plautus; works of literary history, biographies of poets, investigations into the earlier drama, into the scenic division of the comedies of Plautus, and into their genuineness. Latin archaeology, which embraced the whole older history and the ritual law apart from practical jurisprudence, was comprehended in Varro's " Antiquities of Things Human and Divine," which was and for all times remained the fundamental treatise on the subject (published between $\frac{687}{67}$ and $\frac{709}{45}$). The first portion, " Of Things Human," described the primeval age of Rome, the divisions of city and country, the sciences of the years, months, and days, lastly, the public transactions at home and in war; in the second half, " Of Things Divine," the state-theology, the nature and significance of the colleges of experts, of the holy places, of the religious festivals, of sacrificial and votive gifts, and lastly of the gods themselves were summarily unfolded. Moreover, besides a number of monographs—*e.g.* on the descent of the Roman people, on the Roman *gentes* descended from Troy, on the tribes—there was added, as a larger and more independent supplement, the treatise "Of the Life of the Roman people"—a remarkable attempt at a history of Roman manners, which sketched a picture of the state of domestic life, finance, and culture in the regal, the early republican, the Hannibalic, and the most recent period. These labours of Varro were based on an empiric knowledge of the Roman world and its adjacent Hellenic domain more various and greater in its kind than any other Roman either before or after him possessed—a knowledge to which living observation and the study of literature alike contributed. The eulogy of his contemporaries was well deserved, that Varro had enabled his countrymen—strangers in their own world—to know their position in their native land, and had taught the Romans who and where they were. But criticism and system will be sought for in vain. His Greek information seems to have come from somewhat confused sources, and there are traces that even in the Roman field the writer was not free from the influence of the historical romance of his time. The matter is doubtless inserted in a convenient and symmetrical framework, but not classified or treated methodically; and with all his efforts to bring tradition and personal observation into harmony, the scientific labours of Varro are not to be acquitted of a certain implicit faith in tradition or of an unpractical scholasticism.[1] The connection with Greek philology consists in the imitation of its defects more than of its excellences; for instance, the basing of etymologies on mere similarity of sound both in Varro himself and in the other philologists of this epoch runs into pure guesswork and often into downright absurdity.[2] In its empiric confidence and copiousness as well as in its empiric inadequacy and want of method the Varronian vividly reminds us of the English national philology, and just like the latter, finds its centre in the study of the older drama. We have already observed that the

[1] A remarkable example is the general exposition regarding cattle in the treatise on Husbandry (ii. 1) with the nine times nine subdivisions of the doctrine of cattle-rearing, with the "incredible but true" fact that the mares at Olisipo (Lisbon) become pregnant by the wind, and generally with its singular mixture of philosophical, historical, and agricultural notices.

[2] Thus Varro derives *facere* from *facies*, because he who makes anything gives to it an appearance, *volpes*, the fox, after Stilo from *volare pedibus* as the flying-footed; Gaius Trebatius, a philological jurist of this age, derives *sacellum* from *sacra cella*, Figulus *frater* from *fere alter*, and so forth. This practice, which appears not merely in isolated instances but as a main element of the philological literature of this age, presents a very great resemblance to the mode in which till recently comparative philology was prosecuted, before insight into the organism of language put a stop to the occupation of the empirics.

monarchical literature developed the rules of language in contradistinction to this linguistic empiricism (p. 602). It is in a high degree significant that there stands at the head of the modern grammarians no less a man than Caesar himself, who in his treatise on Analogy (given forth between $\frac{696}{58}$ and $\frac{704}{50}$) first undertook to bring free language under the power of law.

Alongside of this extraordinary stir in the field of philology the small amount of activity in the other sciences is surprising. What appeared of importance in philosophy—such as Lucretius' representation of the Epicurean system in the poetical child-dress of the pre-Socratic philosophy, and the better writings of Cicero—produced its effects and found its audience not through its philosophic contents, but in spite of these solely through its aesthetic form; the numerous translations of Epicurean writings and the Pythagorean works, such as Varro's great treatise on the Elements of Numbers and the still more copious one of Figulus concerning the Gods, had beyond doubt neither scientific nor formal value.

Even the professional sciences were but feebly cultivated. Varro's Books on Husbandry written in the form of dialogue are no doubt more methodical than those of his predecessors Cato and Saserna—on which accordingly he drops many a side glance of censure—but have on the whole proceeded more from the study than, like those earlier works, from living experience. Of the juristic labours of Varro and of Servius Sulpicius Rufus (consul in $\frac{703}{51}$) hardly aught more can be said, than that they contributed to the dialectic and philosophical embellishment of Roman jurisprudence. And there is nothing farther here to be mentioned, except perhaps the three books of Gaius Matius on cooking, pickling, and making preserves—so far as we know, the earliest Roman cookery-book, and, as the work of a man of rank, certainly a phenomenon deserving of notice. That mathematics and physics were stimulated by the increased Hellenistic and utilitarian tendencies of the monarchy, is apparent from their growing importance in the instruction of youth (p. 532) and from various practical applications; under which, besides the reform of the calendar (p. 524), may perhaps be included the appearance of wall-maps at this period, the technical improvements in shipbuilding and in musical instruments, designs and buildings like the aviary specified by Varro, the bridge of piles over the Rhine executed by the engineers of Caesar, and even two semicircular stages of boards arranged for being pushed together, and employed first separately as two theatres and then jointly as an amphitheatre. The public exhibition of foreign natural curiosities at the popular festivals was not unusual; and the descriptions of remarkable animals, which Caesar had embodied in the reports of his campaigns, show that, had an Aristotle appeared, he would have again found his patron-prince. But such literary performances as are mentioned in this department are essentially associated with Neopythagoreanism, such as the comparison of Greek and Barbarian, *i.e.* Egyptian, celestial observations by Figulus, and his writings concerning animals, winds, and generative organs. After Greek physical research generally had swerved from the Aristotelian effort to find amidst the several facts their law, and had more and more passed into an empiric and mostly uncritical observation of the external and surprising in nature, natural science when coming forward as a mystical philosophy of nature, instead of enlightening and stimulating, could only still more stupefy and paralyse; and in presence of such a method it was better to rest satisfied with the platitude which Cicero delivers as Socratic wisdom, that the investigation of nature either seeks after things which nobody can know, or after such things as nobody needs to know.

If, in fine, we cast a glance at art, we discover here the same unpleasant phenomena which pervade the whole mental life of this period. Building on the part of the state was virtually brought to a total stand amidst the scarcity of money that marked the last age of the republic. We have already spoken of the luxury in building of the Roman grandees; the architects learned in consequence of this to be lavish of marble—the coloured sorts such as the yellow Numidian (Giallo antico) and others came into vogue at this time, and the marble-quarries of Luna (Carrara) were now employed for the first time—and began to inlay the floors of the rooms with mosaic work, to panel the walls with slabs of marble, or to paint the compartments in imitation of marble—the first steps towards the subsequent fresco painting. But art was not a gainer by this lavish magnificence.

In the arts of design connoisseurship and collecting were always on the increase. It was a mere affectation of Catonian simplicity, when an advocate spoke before the jurymen of the works of art "of a certain Praxiteles;" every one travelled and inspected, and the trade of the art-ciceroni, or, as they were then called, the *exegetae*, was none of the worst. Ancient works of art were formally hunted after—statues and pictures less, it is true, than, in accordance with the rude character of Roman luxury, artistically wrought furniture and ornaments of all sorts for the room and the table. As early as that age the old Greek tombs of Capua and Corinth were ransacked for the sake of the bronze and earthenware vessels which had been placed in the tomb along with the dead. For a small statuette of bronze 40,000 sesterces (£400) were paid, and 200,000 (£2000) for a pair of costly carpets; a well wrought bronze cooking machine came to cost more than an estate. In this barbaric hunting after art the rich amateur was, as might be expected, frequently cheated by those who supplied him; but the economic ruin of Asia Minor in particular so exceedingly rich in artistic products brought many really ancient and rare ornaments and works of art into the market, and from Athens, Syracuse, Cyzicus, Pergamus, Chios, Samos, and other ancient seats of art, everything that was for sale and very much that was not migrated to the palaces and villas of the Roman grandees. We have already mentioned what treasures of art were to be found within the house of Lucullus, who indeed was accused, perhaps not unjustly, of having gratified his interest in the fine arts at the expense of his duties as a general. The amateurs of art crowded thither as they crowd at present to the Villa Borghese, and complained even then of such treasures being confined to the palaces and country houses of the grandees, where they could be seen only with difficulty and after special permission from the possessor. The public buildings on the other hand were far from filled in like proportion with famous works of Greek masters, and in many cases there still stood in the temples of the capital nothing but the old images of the gods carved in wood. As to the exercise of art there is virtually nothing to report; there is hardly mentioned by name from this period any Roman sculptor or painter except a certain Arellius, whose pictures rapidly went off not on account of their artistic value, but because the cunning reprobate furnished in his pictures of the goddesses faithful portraits of his mistresses for the time being.

The importance of music and dancing increased in public as in domestic life. We have already set forth how theatrical music and the dancing-piece attained to an independent standing in the development of the stage at this period (p. 549); we may add that now in Rome itself representations were very frequently given by Greek musicians, dancers, and declaimers on the public stage—such as were usual in Asia Minor and generally in the whole Hellenic and Hellenising world.[1] To these fell to be added the musicians and dancing-girls, who exhibited their arts to order at table and elsewhere, and the special choirs of stringed and wind instruments and singers which were no longer rare in noble houses. But that even the world of quality itself played and sang with diligence, is shown by the very adoption of music into the cycle of the generally recognised subjects of instruction (p. 532); as to dancing, it was, to say nothing of women, made matter of reproach even against consulars that they exhibited themselves in dancing performances amidst a small circle.

Towards the end of this period, however, there appears with the commencement of the monarchy the beginning of a better time also in art. We have already mentioned the mighty stimulus which building in the capital received, and building

[1] Such "Greek entertainments" were very frequent not merely in the Greek cities of Italy, especially in Naples (Cic. *pro Arch.* 5, 10; Plut. *Brut.* 21), but even now also in Rome (iii. 445; Cic. *Ad Fam.* vii. 1, 3; *Ad Att.* xvi. 5, 1; Sueton. *Caes.* 39; Plut. *Brut.* 21). When the well-known epitaph of Licinia Eucharis fourteen years of age, which probably belongs to the end of this period, makes this "girl well instructed and taught in all arts by the Muses themselves" shine as a dancer in the private exhibitions of noble houses and appear first in public on the Greek stage (*modo nobilium ludos decoravi choro, et Graeca in scaena prima populo apparui*), this doubtless can only mean that she was the first girl that appeared on the public Greek stage in Rome; as generally indeed it was not till this epoch that women began to come forward publicly in Rome (p. 547). These "Greek entertainments" in Rome seem not to have been properly scenic, but rather to have belonged to the category of composite exhibitions—primarily musical and declamatory—such as were not of rare occurrence in subsequent times also in Greece (Welcker, *Griech. Trag.* S. 1277). This view is supported by the prominence of flute-playing in Polybius (xxx. 13) and of dancing in the account of Suetonius regarding the armed dances from Asia Minor performed at Caesar's games and in the epitaph of Eucharis; the description also of the *citharoedus* (*Ad Her.* iv. 47, 60; comp. Vitruv. v. 5, 7) must have been derived from such "Greek entertainments." The combination of these representations in Rome with Greek athletic combats is significant (Polyb. *l. c.*; Liv. xxxix. 22). Dramatic recitations were by no means excluded from these mixed entertainments, since among the players whom Lucius Anicius caused to appear in $\frac{587}{167}$ in Rome, tragedians are expressly mentioned; there was however no exhibition of plays in the strict sense, but either whole dramas, or perhaps still more frequently pieces taken from them, were declaimed or sung to the flute by single artists. This must accordingly have been done also in Rome; but to all appearance for the Roman public the main matter in these Greek games was the music and dancing, and the text probably had little more significance for them than the texts of the Italian opera for the Londoners and Parisians of the present day. Those composite entertainments with their confused medley were far better suited for the Roman public, and especially for exhibitions in private houses, than proper scenic performances in the Greek language; the view that the latter also took place in Rome cannot be refuted, but can as little be proved.

throughout the empire was destined to receive, through Caesar. Even in the cutting of the dies of the coins there appears about $\frac{700}{54}$ a remarkable change; the stamping, hitherto for the most part rude and negligent, is thenceforward managed with more delicacy and care.

We have reached the end of the Roman republic. We have seen it rule for five hundred years in Italy and in the countries on the Mediterranean; we have seen it brought to ruin in politics and morals, religion and literature, not through outward violence, but through inward decay, and thereby making room for the new monarchy of Caesar. There was in the world, as Caesar found it, much of the noble heritage of past centuries and an infinite abundance of pomp and glory, but little spirit, still less taste, and least of all true delight in life. It was indeed an old world; and even the richly-gifted patriotism of Caesar could not make it young again. The dawn does not return till after the night has fully set in and run its course. But yet with him there came to the sorely harassed people on the Mediterranean a tolerable evening after the sultry noon; and when at length after a long historical night a new day dawned once more for the peoples, and fresh nations in free self-movement commenced their race towards new and higher goals, there were found among them not a few, in which the seed sown by Caesar had sprung up, and which were and are indebted to him for their national individuality.

throughout the empire was destined to receive, through Caesar. Even in the cutting of the dies of the coins there appears about 708 a remarkable change; the stamping, hitherto for the most part rude and negligent, is thenceforward managed with more delicacy and care.

We have reached the end of the Roman republic. We have seen it rule for five hundred years in Italy and in the countries on the Mediterranean; we have seen it brought to ruin in politics and morals, religion and literature, not through outward violence, but through inward decay, and thereby making room for the new monarchy of Caesar. There was in the world, as Caesar found it, much of the noble heritage of past centuries and an infinite abundance of pomp and glory, but little spirit, still less taste, and least of all true delight in life. It was indeed an old world; and even the richly-gifted patriotism of Caesar could not make it young again. The dawn does not return till after the night has fully set in and run its course. But yet with him there came to the sorely harassed people on the Mediterranean a tolerable evening after the sultry noon; and when at length after a long historical night a new day dawned once more for the peoples, and fresh nations in free self-movement commenced their race towards new and higher goals, there were found among them not a few in which the seed sown by Caesar had sprung up, and which were and are indebted to him for their national individuality.

INDEX

MADE AT THE TEMPLE PRESS LETCHWORTH IN GREAT BRITAIN

EVERYMAN'S LIBRARY

A CLASSIFIED LIST OF THE 954 VOLUMES

In each of the thirteen classifications in this list (except BIOGRAPHY) the volumes are arranged alphabetically under the *authors' names*, but Anthologies and works by various hands are listed under titles. Where authors appear in more than one section, a cross-reference is given, viz.: (*See also* FICTION). The number at the end of each item is the number of the volume in the series.
All the volumes are obtainable in the standard Cloth binding; selected volumes obtainable in Leather are marked L.

BIOGRAPHY

Audubon the Naturalist, Life and Adventures of. By R. Buchanan. 601
Baxter (Richard), Autobiography of. Ed. by Rev. J. M. Lloyd Thomas. 868
Beaconsfield (Lord), Life of. By J. A. Froude. 666
Berlioz (Hector), Life of. Translated by Katherine F. Boult. 602
Blackwell (Dr Elizabeth): Pioneer Work for Women. With an Introduction by Mrs Fawcett. 667
Brontë (Charlotte), Life of. By Mrs Gaskell. Intro. by May Sinclair. 318
(*See also* FICTION)
Browning (Robert), Life of. By E. Dowden. 701
(*See also* POETRY AND DRAMA)
Burns (Robert), Life of. By J. G. Lockhart. Intro. by E. Rhys. 156
(*See also* POETRY AND DRAMA)
Buxton (Sir Thomas Fowell), Memoirs of. Ed. by Charles Buxton. 773
L Byron's Letters. Introduction by André Maurois. 931
(*See also* POETRY AND DRAMA)
Carey (William), Life of: Shoemaker and Missionary. By George Smith. 395
Carlyle's Letters and Speeches of Cromwell. 3 vols. 266-8
" Reminiscences. 875 (*See also* ESSAYS *and* HISTORY)
Cellini's (Benvenuto) Autobiography. 51
Cibber's (Colley) An Apology for his Life. 668
Columbus, Life of. By Sir Arthur Helps. 332
Constable (John), Memoirs of. By C. R. Leslie, R.A. 563
Cowper (William), Selected Letters of. Intro. by W. Hadley, M.A. 774
(*See also* POETRY AND DRAMA)
De Quincey's Reminiscences of the Lake Poets. Intro. by E. Rhys. 163
(*See also* ESSAYS)
De Retz (Cardinal): Memoirs. By Himself. 2 vols. 735-6
Dickens (Charles), Life of. By John Forster. Introduction by G. K. Chesterton. 2 vols. 781-2 (*See also* FICTION)
Disraeli (Benjamin), Life of. By J. A. Froude. 666
Evelyn's Diary. 2 vols. Introduction by G. W. E. Russell. 220-1
Fox (George), Journal of. Text revised by Norman Penney. 754
Franklin's (Benjamin) Autobiography. 316
Gibbon (Edward), Autobiography of. 511 (*See also* HISTORY)
Gladstone, Life of. By G. W. E. Russell (' Onlooker '). 661
Goethe, Life of. By G. H. Lewes. Intro. by Havelock Ellis. 269
Hastings (Warren), Life of. By Capt. L. J. Trotter. 452
Hodson of Hodson's Horse. By Capt. L. J. Trotter. 401
Hutchinson (Col.), Memoirs of. Intro. Monograph by F. P. G. Guizot. 317
L Johnson (Dr Samuel), Life of. By James Boswell. 2 vols. 1-2
" " Lives of the Poets. 770-1 (*See also* TRAVEL)
Keats (John), Life and Letters of. By Lord Houghton. Introduction by R. Lynd. 801 (*See also* POETRY AND DRAMA)
Lamb (Charles), Letters of. 2 vols. 342-3
(*See also* ESSAYS *and* FOR YOUNG PEOPLE)
Lincoln (Abraham), Life of. By Henry Bryan Binns. 783 (*See also* ORATORY)
Mahomet, Life of. By Washington Irving. Intro. Prof. E. V. Arnold. 513

Issued February 1940

BIOGRAPHY—*continued*

Mazzini, Life of. By Bolton King, M.A. 562
Mozart, Life of. By Edward Holmes. Intro. by Ernest Newman. 564
Napoleon, Life of. By J. G. Lockhart. 3
Nelson, Life of. By Robert Southey. 52
Newcastle (First Duke of), Life of, and other writings. By the Duchess of Newcastle. 722
Outram (Sir J.), The Bayard of India. By Capt. L. J. Trotter. 396
L **Pepys's Diary.** Lord Braybrooke's 1854 ed. 2 vols. 53–4
Plutarch's Lives of Noble Greeks and Romans. Dryden's Translation. Revised, with Introduction, by Arthur Hugh Clough. 3 vols. 407–9
Rousseau, Confessions of. 2 vols. 859–60
Scott (Sir Walter), Life of (abridged). By J. G. Lockhart. 55
Scott's Lives of the Novelists. Introduction by George Saintsbury. 331
(*See also* FICTION *and* POETRY)
Seebohm (Frederic): The Oxford Reformers. 665
Shakespeare, Life and Work of. By Oliphant Smeaton. 514
(*See also* POETRY AND DRAMA)
Swift's Journal to Stella. Newly deciphered and edited by J. K. Moorhead. Introduction by Sir Walter Scott. 757
(*See also* ESSAYS *and* FICTION)
Vasari's Lives of the Painters. Trans. by A. B. Hinds. 4 vols. 784–7
Voltaire's Life of Charles XII. Introduction by Rt Hon. J. Burns. 270
(*See also* FICTION)
Walpole (Horace), Selected Letters of. Intro. by W. Hadley, M.A. 775
Wellington, Life of. By G. R. Gleig. 341
Wesley's Journal. 4 vols. Intro. by Rev. F. W. Macdonald. 105–8
Woolman's (John) Journal and Other Papers. Introduction by Vida D. Scudder. 402

CLASSICAL

Æschylus' Lyrical Dramas. Translated by Professor J. S. Blackie. 62
Aristophanes' The Frogs, The Clouds, The Thesmophorians. 516
" **The Acharnians, The Knights, and The Birds.** Frere's Translation. Introduction by John P. Maine. 344
Aristotle's Politics. Introduction by A. D. Lindsay. 605
" **Poetics, etc., and Demetrius on Style, etc.** Edited by Rev. T. A. Moxon. 901 (*See also* PHILOSOPHY)
Caesar's The Gallic War and Other Commentaries. Translated by W. A. McDevitte. 702
Cicero's Essays and Select Letters. Intro. Note by de Quincey. 345
Epictetus, Moral Discourses, etc. Elizabeth Carter's Translation. Edited by W. H. D. Rouse, M.A. 404
Euripides' Plays in 2 vols. Introduction by V. R. Reynolds. Translated by M. Wodhull and R. Potter, with Shelley's 'Cyclops' and Dean Milman's 'Bacchanals.' 63, 271
Herodotus. Rawlinson's Translation, omitting his Essays, and Appendices. Edited, with Intro., by E. H. Blakeney, M.A. 2 vols. 405–6
L **Homer's Iliad.** Lord Derby's Translation. 453
L " **Odyssey.** William Cowper's Translation. 454
Horace. Complete Poetical Works. 515
Hutchinson's (W. M. L.) The Muses' Pageant. 3 vols. 581, 606, and 671
Livy's History of Rome. Vols. I–VI. Translated by Rev. Canon Roberts. 603, 669, 670, 749, 755, and 756
Lucretius: On the Nature of Things. Translated by W. E. Leonard. 750
L **Marcus Aurelius' Meditations.** Introduction by W. H. D. Rouse. 9
Plato's Dialogues. 2 vols. Introduction by A. D. Lindsay. 456–7
L " **Republic.** Translated, with an Introduction, by A. D. Lindsay. 64
Plutarch's Moralia. 20 Essays translated by Philemon Holland. 565
Sophocles' Dramas. Translated by Sir G. Young, Bart. 114
Thucydides' Peloponnesian War. Crawley's Translation. 455
Virgil's Æneid. Translated by E. Fairfax-Taylor. 161
" **Eclogues and Georgics.** Translated by T. F. Royds, M.A. 222
Xenophon's Cyropaedia. Translation revised by Miss F. M. Stawell. 672

ESSAYS AND BELLES-LETTRES

Anthology of Prose. Compiled and Edited by Miss S. L. Edwards. 675
Arnold's (Matthew) Essays. Introduction by G. K. Chesterton. 115
„ „ Study of Celtic Literature, and other Critical Essays, with Supplement by Lord Strangford, etc. 458
(*See also* POETRY)
Bacon's Essays. Introduction by Oliphant Smeaton. 10
(*See also* PHILOSOPHY)
Bagehot's Literary Studies. 2 vols. Intro. by George Sampson. 520–1
Belloc's (Hilaire) Stories, Essays, and Poems. 948
Brown's Rab and his Friends, etc. 116
Burke's Reflections on the French Revolution and contingent Essays. Introduction by A. J. Grieve, M.A. 460
(*See also* ORATORY)
Canton's (William) The Invisible Playmate, W. V., Her Book, and In [Memory of W. V. 566
(*See also* FOR YOUNG PEOPLE)
Carlyle's Essays. 2 vols. With Notes by J. Russell Lowell. 703–4
„ Past and Present. Introduction by R. W. Emerson. 608
„ Sartor Resartus and Heroes and Hero Worship. 278
(*See also* BIOGRAPHY *and* HISTORY)
Castiglione's The Courtier. Translated by Sir Thomas Hoby. Introduction by W. H. D. Rouse. 807
L Century of Essays, A. An Anthology of English Essayists. 653
Chesterfield's (Lord) Letters to his Son. 823
L Chesterton's (G. K.) Stories, Essays, and Poems. 913
Coleridge's Biographia Literaria. Introduction by Arthur Symons. 11
„ Essays and Lectures on Shakespeare, etc. 162
(*See also* POETRY)
L De la Mare's (Walter) Stories, Essays, and Poems. 940
De Quincey's (Thomas) Opium Eater. Intro. by Sir G. Douglas. 223
„ „ The English Mail Coach and Other Writings. Introduction by S. Hill Burton. 609
(*See also* BIOGRAPHY)
Dryden's Dramatic Essays. With an Introduction by W. H. Hudson. 568
Elyot's Gouernour. Intro. and Glossary by Prof. Foster Watson. 227
L Emerson's Essays. First and Second Series. 12
L „ Nature, Conduct of Life, Essays from the 'Dial.' 322
„ Representative Men. Introduction by E. Rhys. 279
„ Society and Solitude and Other Essays. 567
(*See also* POETRY)
Florio's Montaigne. Introduction by A. R. Waller, M.A. 3 vols. 440–2
Froude's Short Studies. Vols. I and II. 13, 705
(*See also* HISTORY *and* BIOGRAPHY)
Gilfillan's Literary Portraits. Intro. by Sir W. Robertson Nicoll. 348
Goethe's Conversations with Eckermann. Intro. by Havelock Ellis. 851. (*See also* FICTION *and* POETRY)
Goldsmith's Citizen of the World and The Bee. Intro. by R. Church. 902
(*See also* FICTION *and* POETRY)
Hamilton's The Federalist. 519
Hazlitt's Lectures on the English Comic Writers. 411
„ The Round Table and Shakespeare's Characters. 65
„ Spirit of the Age and Lectures on English Poets. 459
„ Table Talk. 321
„ Plain Speaker. Introduction by P. P. Howe. 814
Holmes's Autocrat of the Breakfast Table. 66
„ Poet at the Breakfast Table. 68
„ Professor at the Breakfast Table. 67
L Hudson's (W. H.) A Shepherd's Life. Introduction by Ernest Rhys. 926
Hunt's (Leigh) Selected Essays. Introduction by J. B. Priestley. 829
L Huxley's (Aldous) Stories, Essays, and Poems. 935
Irving's Sketch Book of Geoffrey Crayon. 117
(*See also* BIOGRAPHY *and* HISTORY)
L Lamb's Essays of Elia. Introduction by Augustine Birrell. 14
(*See also* BIOGRAPHY *and* FOR YOUNG PEOPLE)

ESSAYS AND BELLES-LETTRES—*continued*

Landor's Imaginary Conversations and Poems: A selection. Edited with Introduction by Havelock Ellis. 890
Lowell's (James Russell) Among My Books. 607
Macaulay's Essays. 2 vols. Introduction by A. J. Grieve, M.A. 225–6
" Miscellaneous Essays and The Lays of Ancient Rome. 439
(*See also* HISTORY *and* ORATORY)
Machiavelli's Prince. Special Trans. and Intro. by W. K. Marriott. 280
(*See also* HISTORY)
Martinengo-Cesaresco (Countess): Essays in the Study of Folk-Songs. 673
Mazzini's Duties of Man, etc. Introduction by Thomas Jones, M.A. 224
Milton's Areopagitica, etc. Introduction by Professor C. E. Vaughan. 795
(*See also* POETRY)
L Mitford's Our Village. Edited, with Intro., by Sir John Squire. 927
Montagu's (Lady) Letters. Introduction by R. Brimley Johnson. 69
Newman's On the Scope and Nature of University Education, and a paper on Christianity and Scientific Investigation. Introduction by Wilfred Ward. 723
(*See also* PHILOSOPHY)
Osborne's (Dorothy) Letters to Sir William Temple. Edited and connotated by Judge Parry. 674
Penn's The Peace of Europe. Some Fruits of Solitude, etc. 724
Prelude to Poetry, The. Edited by Ernest Rhys. 789
Reynold's Discourses. Introduction by L. March Phillipps. 118
Rhys's New Book of Sense and Nonsense. 813
Rousseau's Emile. Translated by Barbara Foxley. 518
(*See also* PHILOSOPHY AND THEOLOGY)
Ruskin's Crown of Wild Olive and Cestus of Aglaia. 323
" Elements of Drawing and Perspective. 217
" Ethics of the Dust. Introduction by Grace Rhys. 282
" Modern Painters. 5 vols. Introduction by Lionel Cust. 208–12
" Pre-Raphaelitism. Lectures on Architecture and Painting, Academy Notes, 1855–9, and Notes on the Turner Gallery. Introduction by Laurence Binyon. 218
L " Sesame and Lilies, The Two Paths, and The King of the Golden River. Introduction by Sir Oliver Lodge. 219
" Seven Lamps of Architecture. Intro. by Selwyn Image. 207
" Stones of Venice. 3 vols. Intro. by L. March Phillipps. 213–15
" Time and Tide with other Essays. 450
" Unto This Last. The Political Economy of Art. 216
(*See also* FOR YOUNG PEOPLE)
Spectator, The. 4 vols. Introduction by G. Gregory Smith. 164–7
Spencer's (Herbert) Essays on Education. Intro. by C. W. Eliot. 504
Sterne's Sentimental Journey and Journal and Letters to Eliza. Intro. by George Saintsbury. 796
(*See also* FICTION)
Stevenson's In the South Seas and Island Nights' Entertainments. 769
L " Virginibus Puerisque and Familiar Studies of Men and Books. 765
(*See also* FICTION, POETRY, *and* TRAVEL)
Swift's Tale of a Tub, The Battle of the Books, etc. 347
(*See also* BIOGRAPHY *and* FICTION)
Swinnerton's (Frank) The Georgian Literary Scene. 943
Table Talk. Edited by J. C. Thornton. 906
Taylor's (Isaac) Words and Places, or Etymological Illustrations of History, Ethnology, and Geography. Intro. by Edward Thomas. 517
Thackeray's (W. M.) The English Humorists and The Four Georges. Introduction by Walter Jerrold. 610
(*See also* FICTION)
Thoreau's Walden. Introduction by Walter Raymond. 281
Trench's On the Study of Words and English Past and Present. Introduction by George Sampson. 788
Tytler's Essay on the Principles of Translation. 168
Walton's Compleat Angler. Introduction by Andrew Lang. 70

FICTION

Aimard's The Indian Scout. 428
Ainsworth's (Harrison) Old St Paul's. Intro. by W. E. A. Axon. 522
" " The Admirable Crichton. Intro. by E. Rhys. 804
L " " The Tower of London. 400
" " Windsor Castle. 709
" " Rookwood. Intro. by Frank Swinnerton. 870
American Short Stories of the Nineteenth Century. Edited by John Cournos. 840
L Austen's (Jane) Emma. Introduction by R. B. Johnson. 24
" " Mansfield Park. Introduction by R. B. Johnson. 23
" " Northanger Abbey and Persuasion. Introduction by R. B. Johnson. 25
L " " Pride and Prejudice. Introduction by R. B. Johnson. 22
L " " Sense and Sensibility. Intro. by R. B. Johnson. 21
Balzac's (Honoré de) Atheist's Mass. Preface by George Saintsbury. 229
" " Catherine de Médici. Introduction by George Saintsbury. 419
" " Christ in Flanders. Introduction by George Saintsbury. 284
" " Cousin Pons. Intro. by George Saintsbury. 463
" " Eugénie Grandet. Intro. by George Saintsbury. 169
" " Lost Illusions. Intro. by George Saintsbury. 656
" " Old Goriot. Intro. by George Saintsbury. 170
" " The Cat and Racket, and Other Stories. 349
" " The Chouans. Intro. by George Saintsbury. 285
" " The Country Doctor. Intro. George Saintsbury. 530
" " The Country Parson. 686
" " The Quest of the Absolute. Introduction by George Saintsbury. 286
" " The Rise and Fall of César Birotteau. 596
" " The Wild Ass's Skin. Intro. George Saintsbury. 26
" " Ursule Mirouët. Intro. by George Saintsbury. 733
Barbusse's Under Fire. Translated by Fitzwater Wray. 798
L Bennett's (Arnold) The Old Wives' Tale. 919
L Blackmore's (R. D.) Lorna Doone. 304
L Borrow's Lavengro. Introduction by Thomas Seccombe. 119
" Romany Rye. 120
(*See also* TRAVEL)
Brontë's (Anne) The Tenant of Wildfell Hall and Agnes Grey. 685
L " (Charlotte) Jane Eyre. Introduction by May Sinclair. 287
L " " Shirley. Introduction by May Sinclair. 288
" " The Professor. Introduction by May Sinclair. 417
" " Villette. Introduction by May Sinclair. 351
L " (Emily) Wuthering Heights. 243
Burney's (Fanny) Evelina. Introduction by R. B. Johnson. 352
Butler's (Samuel) Erewhon and Erewhon Revisited. Introduction by Desmond MacCarthy. 881
" " The Way of All Flesh. Intro. by A. J. Hoppé. 895
Collins' (Wilkie) The Woman in White. 464
L Conrad's Lord Jim. Introduction by R. B. Cunninghame Grahame. 925
L Converse's (Florence) Long Will. 328
Dana's (Richard H.) Two Years before the Mast. 588
Daudet's Tartarin of Tarascon and Tartarin of the Alps. 423
Defoe's Fortunes and Misfortunes of Moll Flanders. Intro. by G. A. Aitken [837
" Captain Singleton. Introduction by Edward Garnett. 74
" Journal of the Plague Year. Introduction by G. A. Aitken. 289
" Memoirs of a Cavalier. Introduction by G. A. Aitken. 283
(*See also* FOR YOUNG PEOPLE)

CHARLES DICKENS' WORKS. Each volume with an Intro. by G. K. Chesterton.

American Notes. 290
L Barnaby Rudge. 76
L Bleak House. 236
Child's History of England. 291
L Christmas Books. 239
L Christmas Stories. 414
L David Copperfield. 242
L Dombey and Son. 240
Edwin Drood. 725
L Great Expectations. 234

FICTION—*continued*

CHARLES DICKENS' WORKS—*continued*

Hard Times. 292
L Little Dorrit. 293
L Martin Chuzzlewit. 241
L Nicholas Nickleby. 238
L Old Curiosity Shop. 173
L Oliver Twist. 233
Our Mutual Friend. 294
L Pickwick Papers. 235
Reprinted Pieces. 744
Sketches by Boz. 237
L Tale of Two Cities. 102
Uncommercial Traveller. 536

Disraeli's Coningsby. Introduction by Langdon Davies. 535

Dostoevksy's (Fyodor) Crime and Punishment. Introduction by Laurence Irving. 501

" " Letters from the Underworld and Other Tales. Translated by C. J. Hogarth. 654

" " Poor Folk and the Gambler. Translated by C. J. Hogarth. 711

" " The Possessed. Introduction by J. Middleton Murry. 2 vols. 861–2

" " The House of the Dead, or Prison Life in Siberia. Introduction by Madame Stepniak. 533

" " The Brothers Karamazov. Translated by Constance Garnett. 2 vols. 802–3

" " The Idiot. 682

Du Maurier's (George) Trilby. Introduction by Sir Gerald du Maurier. With the original illustrations. 863

Dumas' Black Tulip. Introduction by Ernest Rhys. 174
" Chicot the Jester. 421
" Le Chevalier de Maison Rouge. Intro. by Julius Bramont. 614
" Marguerite de Valois ('La Reine Margot'). 326
L " The Count of Monte Cristo. 2 vols. 393–4
" The Forty-Five. 420
L " The Three Musketeers. 81
" The Vicomte de Bragelonne. 3 vols. 593–5
L " Twenty Years After. Introduction by Ernest Rhys. 175

Edgar's Cressy and Poictiers. Introduction by Ernest Rhys. 17
" Runnymede and Lincoln Fair. Intro. by L. K. Hughes. 320
(*See also* FOR YOUNG PEOPLE)

Edgeworth's Castle Rackrent and The Absentee. 410

L Eliot's (George) Adam Bede. 27
" " Felix Holt. 353
" " Middlemarch. 2 vols. 854–5
L " " Mill on the Floss. Intro. Sir W. Robertson Nicoll. 325
" " Romola. Introduction by Rudolf Dircks. 231
L " " Scenes of Clerical Life. 468
" " Silas Marner. Introduction by Annie Matheson. 121

L English Short Stories. An Anthology. 743

Erckmann-Chatrian's The Conscript and Waterloo. 354
" " The Story of a Peasant. Translated by C. J. Hogarth. 2 vols. 706–7

Fenimore Cooper's The Deerslayer. 77
" " The Last of the Mohicans. 79
" " The Pathfinder. 78
" " The Pioneers. 171
" " The Prairie. 172

Ferrier's (Susan) Marriage. Introduction by H. L. Morrow. 816

Fielding's Amelia. Intro. by George Saintsbury. 2 vols. 852–3
" Jonathan Wild, and The Journal of a Voyage to Lisbon. Introduction by George Saintsbury. 877
" Joseph Andrews. Introduction by George Saintsbury. 467
" Tom Jones. Intro. by George Saintsbury. 2 vols. 355–6

Flaubert's Madame Bovary. Translated by Eleanor Marx-Aveling. Introduction by George Saintsbury. 808
" Salammbô. Translated by J. S. Chartres. Introduction by Professor F. C. Green. 869

French Short Stories of the 19th and 20th Centuries. Selected, with an Introduction by Professor F. C. Green. 896

L Galsworthy's (John) The Country House. 917

FICTION—*continued*

Galt's Annals of a Parish. Introduction by Baillie Macdonald. 427
Gaskell's (Mrs) Cousin Phillis, etc. Intro. by Thos. Seccombe. 615
L " Cranford. 83
" Mary Barton. Introduction by Thomas Seccombe. 598
" Sylvia's Lovers. Intro. by Mrs. Ellis Chadwick. 524
Ghost Stories. Edited by John Hampden. 952
(*See also* POETRY AND DRAMA)
Gleig's (G. R.) The Subaltern. 708
Goethe's Wilhelm Meister. Carlyle's Translation. 2 vols. 599–600
(*See also* ESSAYS *and* POETRY)
Gogol's (Nicol) Dead Souls. Translated by C. J. Hogarth. 726
" " Taras Bulba and Other Tales. 740
L Goldsmith's Vicar of Wakefield. Introduction by J. M. D. 295
(*See also* ESSAYS *and* POETRY)
Goncharov's Oblomov. Translated by Natalie Duddington. 878
Gorki's Through Russia. Translated by C. J. Hogarth. 741
Harte's (Bret) Luck of Roaring Camp and other Tales. 681
L Hawthorne's The House of the Seven Gables. Intro. Ernest Rhys. 176
" The Scarlet Letter. 122
" The Blithedale Romance. 592
" The Marble Faun. Intro. by Sir Leslie Stephen. 424
" Twice Told Tales. 531
(*See also* FOR YOUNG PEOPLE)
L Hugo's (Victor) Les Misérables. Intro. by S. R. John. 2 vols. 363–4
L " " Notre Dame. Introduction by A. C. Swinburne. 422
" " Toilers of the Sea. Introduction by Ernest Rhys. 509
Italian Short Stories. Edited by D. Pettoello. 876
James's (G. P. R.) Richelieu. Introduction by Rudolf Dircks. 357
L James's (Henry), The Turn of the Screw and The Aspern Papers. 912
Jefferies's (Richard) After London *and* Amaryllis at the Fair. Intro. by David Garnett. 951
(*See also* FOR YOUNG PEOPLE)
Kingsley's (Charles) Alton Locke. 462
L " " Hereward the Wake. Intro. by Ernest Rhys. 296
" " Hypatia. 230
L " " Westward Ho! Introduction by A. G. Grieve. 20
" " Yeast. 611
(*See also* POETRY *and* FOR YOUNG PEOPLE)
" (Henry) Geoffrey Hamlyn. 416
" " Ravenshoe. 28
L Lawrence's (D. H.) The White Peacock. 914
Lever's Harry Lorrequer. Introduction by Lewis Melville. 177
L Loti's (Pierre) Iceland Fisherman. Translated by W. P. Baines. 920
Lover's Handy Andy. Introduction by Ernest Rhys. 178
L Lytton's Harold. Introduction by Ernest Rhys. 15
L " Last Days of Pompeii. 80
" Last of the Barons. Introduction by R. G. Watkin. 18
" Rienzi. Introduction by E. H. Blakeney, M.A. 532
(*See also* TRAVEL)
MacDonald's (George) Sir Gibbie. 678
(*See also* ROMANCE)
Manning's Mary Powell and Deborah's Diary. Introduction by Katherine Tynan (Mrs Hinkson). 324
" Sir Thomas More. Introduction by Ernest Rhys. 19
Marryat's Jacob Faithful. 618
L " Mr Midshipman Easy. Introduction by R. B. Johnson. 82
" Percival Keene. Introduction by R. Brimley Johnson. 358
" Peter Simple. Introduction by R. Brimley Johnson. 232
" The King's Own. 580
(*See also* FOR YOUNG PEOPLE)
L Maugham's (Somerset) Cakes and Ale. 932
Maupassant's Short Stories. Translated by Marjorie Laurie. Introduction by Gerald Gould. 907
Melville's (Herman) Moby Dick. Introduction by Ernest Rhys. 179

FICTION—*continued*

Melville's (Herman) Omoo. Introduction by Ernest Rhys. 297
L „ „ Typee. Introduction by Ernest Rhys. 180
L Meredith's (George) The Ordeal of Richard Feverel. 916
Mérimée's Carmen, with Prévost's Manon Lescaut. Intro. by Philip [Henderson. 834
Mickiewicz's (Adam) Pan Tadeusz. 842
Modern Short Stories. Edited by John Hadfield. 954
L Moore's (George) Esther Waters. 933
Mulock's John Halifax, Gentleman. Introduction by J. Shaylor. 123
Neale's (J. M.) The Fall of Constantinople. 655
Paltock's (Robert) Peter Wilkins; or, The Flying Indians. Introduction by A. H. Bullen. 676
Pater's Marius the Epicurean. Introduction by Osbert Burdett. 903
Peacock's Headlong Hall and Nightmare Abbey. 327
L Poe's Tales of Mystery and Imagination. Intro. by Padraic Colum. 336
(*See also* POETRY)
Prévost's Manon Lescaut, with Mérimée's Carmen. Introduction by [Philip Henderson. 834
L Priestley's Angel Pavement. 938
Pushkin's (Alexander) The Captain's Daughter and Other Tales. Trans. by Natalie Duddington. 898
Quiller-Couch's (Sir Arthur) Hetty Wesley. 864
Radcliffe's (Ann) Mysteries of Udolpho. Intro. by R. Austin Freeman. [2 vols. 865–6
L Reade's (C.) The Cloister and the Hearth. Intro. by A. C. Swinburne. 29
„ Peg Woffington and Christie Johnstone. 299
Richardson's (Samuel) Pamela. Intro. by G. Saintsbury. 2 vols. 683–4
„ „ Clarissa. Intro. by Prof. W. L. Phelps. 4 vols. 882–5
Russian Authors, Short Stories from. Trans. by R. S. Townsend. 758
Sand's (George) The Devil's Pool and François the Waif. 534
Scheffel's Ekkehard: a Tale of the Tenth Century. 529
Scott's (Michael) Tom Cringle's Log. 710

SIR WALTER SCOTT'S WORKS:

Abbot, The. 124
Anne of Geierstein. 125
Antiquary, The. 126
Black Dwarf and Legend of Montrose. 128
Bride of Lammermoor. 129
Castle Dangerous and the Surgeon's Daughter. 130
Count Robert of Paris. 131
Fair Maid of Perth. 132
Fortunes of Nigel. 71
Guy Mannering. 133
Heart of Midlothian, The. 134
Highland Widow and Betrothed. 127
L Ivanhoe. Intro. Ernest Rhys. 16
L Kenilworth. 135
Monastery, The. 136
Old Mortality. 137
Peveril of the Peak. 138
Pirate, The. 139
Quentin Durward. 140
Redgauntlet. 141
Rob Roy. 142
St. Ronan's Well. 143
Talisman, The. 144
Waverley. 75
Woodstock. Intro. by Edward Garnett. 72

(*See also* BIOGRAPHY *and* POETRY)

Shchedrin's The Golovlyov Family. Translated by Natalie Duddington. Introduction by Edward Garnett. 908
Shelley's (Mary Wollstonecraft) Frankenstein. 616
Sheppard's Charles Auchester. Intro. by Jessie M. Middleton. 505
Shorter Novels, Vol. I. Elizabethan and Jacobean. Edited by Philip Henderson. 824
„ „ Vol. II. Jacobean and Restoration. Edited by Philip Henderson. 841
„ „ Vol. III. Eighteenth Century (Beckford's Vathek, Walpole's Castle of Otranto, and Dr. Johnson's Rasselas). 856
Sienkiewicz (Henryk). Tales from. Edited by Monica M. Gardner. 871
Smollett's Peregrine Pickle. 2 vols. 838–9
„ Roderick Random. Introduction by H. W. Hodges. 790
Stendhal's Scarlet and Black. Translated by C. K. Scott Moncreiff. 2 vols. 945–6
L Sterne's Tristram Shandy. Introduction by George Saintsbury. 617
(*See also* ESSAYS)

FICTION—*continued*

L Stevenson's Dr Jekyll and Mr Hyde. The Merry Men, and Other Tales.
L „ The Master of Ballantrae and The Black Arrow. 764 [767
L „ Treasure Island and Kidnapped. 763
„ St. Ives. Introduction by Ernest Rhys. 904
(*See also* ESSAYS, POETRY, *and* TRAVEL)
Surtees' Jorrocks' Jaunts and Jollities. 817
Swift's Gulliver's Travels. Unabridged Edition, with contemporary maps. Introduction by Harold Williams. 60
L Tales of Detection. Edited, with Introduction, by Dorothy L. Sayers. 928
Thackeray's Rose and the Ring and other stories. Intro. Walter Jerrold.
„ Esmond. Introduction by Walter Jerrold. 73 [359
„ Newcomes. Introduction by Walter Jerrold. 2 vols. 465–6
„ Pendennis. Intro. by Walter Jerrold. 2 vols. 425–6
„ Roundabout Papers. 687
L „ Vanity Fair. Introduction by Hon. Whitelaw Reid. 298
„ Virginians. Introduction by Walter Jerrold. 2 vols. 507–8
(*See also* ESSAYS)
L Tolstoy's Anna Karenina. Trans. by Rochelle S. Townsend. 2 vols. 612–13
„ Childhood, Boyhood, and Youth. Trans. by C. J. Hogarth. 591
„ Master and Man, and other Parables and Tales. 469
„ War and Peace. 3 vols. 525–7
Trollope's (Anthony) Barchester Towers. 30
„ „ Dr. Thorne. 360
„ „ Framley Parsonage. Intro. by Ernest Rhys. 181
„ „ The Golden Lion of Granpère. Introduction by Sir Hugh Walpole. 761
„ „ The Last Chronicles of Barset. 2 vols. 391–2
„ „ Phineas Finn. Intro. by Sir Hugh Walpole. 2 vols.
„ „ The Small House at Allington. 361 [832–3
„ „ The Warden. Introduction by Ernest Rhys. 182
Turgenev's Fathers and Sons. Translated by C. J. Hogarth. 742
„ Liza. Translated by W. R. S. Ralston. 677
„ Virgin Soil. Translated by Rochelle S. Townsend. 528
L Voltaire's Candide and Other Tales. 936
L Walpole's (Hugh) Mr Perrin and Mr Traill. 918
L Well's (H. G.) The Time Machine and The Wheels of Chance. 915
Whyte-Melville's The Gladiators. Introduction by J. Mavrogordato. 523
Wood's (Mrs Henry) The Channings. 84
Woolf's (Virginia) To the Lighthouse. Intro. by D. M. Hoare. 949
Yonge's (Charlotte M.) The Dove in the Eagle's Nest. 329
„ „ The Heir of Redclyffe. Intro. Mrs Meynell. 362
(*See also* FOR YOUNG PEOPLE)
Zola's (Emile) Germinal. Translated by Havelock Ellis. 897

HISTORY

Anglo-Saxon Chronicle, The. Translated by James Ingram. 624
Bede's Ecclesiastical History, etc. Introduction by Vida D. Scudder. 479
Burnet's History of His Own Times. 85
L Carlyle's French Revolution. Introduction by H. Belloc. 2 vols. 31–2
(*See also* BIOGRAPHY *and* ESSAYS)
Creasy's Decisive Battles of the World. Introduction by E. Rhys. 300
De Joinville (*See* Villehardouin)
Duruy's (Jean Victor) A History of France. 2 vols. 737–8
Finlay's Byzantine Empire. 33
„ Greece under the Romans. 185
Froude's Henry VIII. Intro. by Llewellyn Williams, M.P. 3 vols. 372–4
„ Edward VI. Intro. by Llewellyn Williams, M.P., B.C.L. 375
„ Mary Tudor. Intro. by Llewellyn Williams, M.P., B.C.L. 477
„ History of Queen Elizabeth's Reign. 5 vols. Completing Froude's 'History of England,' in 10 vols. 583–7
(*See also* ESSAYS *and* BIOGRAPHY)
Gibbon's Decline and Fall of the Roman Empire. Edited, with Introduction and Notes, by Oliphant Smeaton, M.A. 6 vols. 434–6, 474–6
(*See also* BIOGRAPHY)

HISTORY—*continued*

Green's Short History of the English People. Edited and Revised by L. Cecil Jane, with an Appendix by R. P. Farley, B.A. 2 vols. 727–8
Grote's History of Greece. Intro. by A. D. Lindsay. 12 vols. 186–97
Hallam's (Henry) Constitutional History of England. 3 vols. 621–3
Holinshed's Chronicle as used in Shakespeare's Plays. Introduction by Professor Allardyce Nicoll. 800
Irving's (Washington) Conquest of Granada. 478
(*See also* ESSAYS *and* BIOGRAPHY)
Josephus' Wars of the Jews. Introduction by Dr Jacob Hart. 712
Lutzow's Bohemia: An Historical Sketch. Introduction by President T. G. Masaryk. Revised edition. 432
Macaulay's History of England. 3 vols. 34–6
(*See also* ESSAYS *and* ORATORY)
Maine's (Sir Henry) Ancient Law. 734
Merivale's History of Rome. (An Introductory vol. to Gibbon.) 433
Mignet's (F. A. M.) The French Revolution. 713
Milman's History of the Jews. 2 vols. 377–8
Mommsen's History of Rome. Translated by W. P. Dickson, LL.D. With a review of the work by E. A. Freeman. 4 vols. 542–5
Motley's Dutch Republic. 3 vols. 86–8
Parkman's Conspiracy of Pontiac. 2 vols. 302–3
Paston Letters, The. Based on edition of Knight. Introduction by Mrs Archer-Hind, M.A. 2 vols. 752–3
Pilgrim Fathers, The. Introduction by John Masefield. 480
L Pinnow's History of Germany. Translated by M. R. Brailsford. 929
Political Liberty, The Growth of. A Source-Book of English History. Arranged by Ernest Rhys. 745 [M.A. 2 vols. 397–8
Prescott's Conquest of Mexico. With Introduction by Thomas Seccombe.
,, Conquest of Peru. Intro. by Thomas Seccombe, M.A. 301
Sismondi's Italian Republics. 250
Stanley's Lectures on the Eastern Church. Intro. by A. J. Grieve. 251
Tacitus. Vol. I. Annals. Introduction by E. H. Blakeney. 273
,, Vol. II. Agricola and Germania. Intro. E. H. Blakeney. 274
Thierry's Norman Conquest. Intro. by J. A. Price, B.A. 2 vols. 198–9
Villehardouin and De Joinville's Chronicles of the Crusades. Translated, with Introduction, by Sir F. Marzials, C.B. 333
Voltaire's Age of Louis XIV. Translated by Martyn P. Pollack. 780

ORATORY

Anthology of British Historical Speeches and Orations. Compiled by Ernest Rhys. 714
Bright's (John) Speeches. Selected with Intro. by Joseph Sturge. 252
Burke's American Speeches and Letters. 340. (*See also* ESSAYS)
Demosthenes: Select Orations. 546
Fox (Charles James): Speeches (French Revolutionary War Period). Edited with Introduction by Irene Cooper Willis, M.A. 759
Lincoln's Speeches, etc. Intro. by the Rt Hon. James Bryce. 206
(*See also* BIOGRAPHY)
Macaulay's Speeches on Politics and Literature. 399
(*See also* ESSAYS *and* HISTORY)
Pitt's Orations on the War with France. 145

PHILOSOPHY AND THEOLOGY

L A Kempis' Imitation of Christ. 484
Ancient Hebrew Literature. Being the Old Testament and Apocrypha. Arranged by the Rev. R. B. Taylor. 4 vols. 253–6
Aristotle, The Nicomachean Ethics of. Translated by D. P. Chase. Introduction by Professor J. A. Smith. 547
(*See also* CLASSICAL)
Bacon's The Advancement of Learning. 719 (*See also* ESSAYS)
Berkeley's (Bishop) Principles of Human Knowledge, New Theory of Vision. With Introduction by A. D. Lindsay. 483

PHILOSOPHY AND THEOLOGY—*continued*

Boehme's (Jacob) The Signature of All Things, with Other Writings. Introduction by Clifford Bax. 569
Browne's Religio Medici, etc. Intro. by Professor C. H. Herford. 92
Bunyan's Grace Abounding and Mr Badman. Introduction by G. B. Harrison. 815 (*See also* ROMANCE)
Burton's (Robert) Anatomy of Melancholy. Introduction by Holbrook Jackson. 3 vols. 886–8
Butler's Analogy of Religion. Introduction by Rev. Ronald Bayne. 90
Descartes' (René) A Discourse on Method. Translated by Professor John Veitch. Introduction by A. D. Lindsay. 570
L Ellis' (Havelock) Selected Essays. Introduction by J. S. Collis. 930
L Gore's (Charles) The Philosophy of the Good Life. 924
Hindu Scriptures. Edited by Dr Nicol Macnicol. Introduction by Rabindranath Tagore. 944
Hobbes' Leviathan. Edited, with Intro. by A. D. Lindsay, M.A. 691
Hooker's Ecclesiastical Polity. Intro. by Rev. H. Bayne. 2 vols. 201–2
Hume's Treatise of Human Nature, and other Philosophical Works. Introduction by A. D. Lindsay, M.A. 2 vols. 548–9
James (William): Selected Papers on Philosophy. 739
Kant's Critique of Pure Reason. Translated by J. M. D. Meiklejohn. Introduction by A. D. Lindsay, M.A. 909
Keble's The Christian Year. Introduction by J. C. Shairp. 690
King Edward VI. First and Second Prayer Books. Introduction by the Right Rev. Bishop of Gloucester. 448
L Koran, The. Rodwell's Translation. 380
Latimer's Sermons. Introduction by Canon Beeching. 40
Law's Serious Call to a Devout and Holy Life. 91
Leibniz's Philosophical Writings. Selected and trans. by Mary Morris. Introduction by C. R. Morris, M.A. 905
Locke's Two Treatises of Civil Government. Introduction by Professor William S. Carpenter. 751
Malthus on the Principles of Population. 2 vols. 692–3
Mill's (John Stuart) Utilitarianism, Liberty, Representative Government. With Introduction by A. D. Lindsay, M.A. 482
„ Subjection of Women. (*See* Wollstonecraft, Mary, *under* SCIENCE)
More's Utopia. Introduction by Judge O'Hagan. 461
New Testament. Arranged in the order in which the books came to the Christians of the First Century. 93
Newman's Apologia pro Vita Sua. Intro. by Dr Charles Sarolea. 636 (*See also* ESSAYS)
Nietzsche's Thus Spake Zarathustra. Trans. by A. Tille and M. M. Bozman. [892
Paine's Rights of Man. Introduction by G. J. Holyoake. 718
Pascal's Pensées. Translated by W. F. Trotter. Introduction by T. S. Eliot. 874
Ramayana and the Mahabharata, The. Translated by Romesh Dutt, [C.I.E. 403
Renan's Life of Jesus. Introduction by Right Rev. Chas. Gore, D.D. 805
Robertson's (F. W.) Sermons on Christian Doctrine, and Bible Subjects. Each Volume with Introduction by Canon Burnett. 3 vols. 37–9 (*Note: No.* 37 *is out of print.*)
Robinson's (Wade) The Philosophy of Atonement and Other Sermons. Introduction by Rev. F. B. Meyer. 637
Rousseau's (J. J.) The Social Contract, etc. 660. (*See also* ESSAYS)
St Augustine's Confessions. Dr Pusey's Translation. 200
L St Francis: The Little Flowers, and The Life of St. Francis. 485
Seeley's Ecce Homo. Introduction by Sir Oliver Lodge. 305
Selection from St Thomas Aquinas. Edited by The Rev. Father M. C. D'Arcy. 953
Spinoza's Ethics, etc. Translated by Andrew J. Boyle. With Introduction by Professor Santayana. 481
Swedenborg's (Emmanuel) Heaven and Hell. 379
„ „ The Divine Love and Wisdom. 635
„ „ The Divine Providence. 658
L „ „ The True Christian Religion. 893

POETRY AND DRAMA

Anglo-Saxon Poetry. Edited by Professor R. K. Gordon. 794
Arnold's (Matthew) Poems, 1840–66, including Thyrsis. 334
Ballads, A Book of British. Selected by R. B. Johnson. 572
Beaumont and Fletcher, The Select Plays of. Introduction by Professor Baker, of Harvard University. 506
Björnson's Plays. Vol. I. The Newly Married Couple. Leonardo, A Gauntlet. Trans. by R. Farquharson Sharp. 625
„ „ Vol. II. The Editor, The Bankrupt, and The King. Translated by R. Farquharson Sharp. 696
Blake's Poems and Prophecies. Introduction by Max Plowman. 792
Browning's Poems, 1833–44. Introduction by Arthur Waugh. 41
„ „ 1844–64. 42
„ The Ring and the Book. Intro. by Chas. W. Hodell. 502
L Burns' Poems and Songs. Introduction by J. Douglas. 94
Byron's Poetical and Dramatic Works. 3 vols. 486–8
Calderon: Six Plays, translated by Edward FitzGerald. 819
L Chaucer's Canterbury Tales. Edited by Principal Burrell, M.A. 307
Coleridge, Golden Book of. Edited by Stopford A. Brooke. 43
(*See also* Essays)
Cowper (William). Poems of. Edited by H. I'Anson Fausset. 872
(*See also* Biography)
Dante's Divine Comedy (Cary's Translation). Specially edited by Edmund Gardner. 308
Donne's Poems. Edited by H. I'Anson Fausset. 867
Dryden's Poems. Edited by Bonamy Dobree. 910
Eighteenth-Century Plays. Edited by John Hampden. 818
Emerson's Poems. Introduction by Professor Bakewell, Yale, U.S.A. 715
L English Religious Verse. Edited by G. Lacey May. 937
L Everyman and other Interludes, including eight Miracle Plays. Edited by Ernest Rhys. 381
L FitzGerald's (Edward) Omar Khayyám and Six Plays of Calderon. 819
Goethe's Faust. Parts I and II. Trans. and Intro. by A. G. Latham. 335
(*See also* Essays *and* Fiction)
L Golden Book of Modern English Poetry, The. Edited by Thomas Caldwell. 921
Golden Treasury of Longer Poems, The. Edited by Ernest Rhys. 746
Goldsmith's Poems and Plays. Introduction by Austin Dobson. 415
(*See also* Essays *and* Fiction)
Gray's Poems and Letters. Introduction by John Drinkwater. 628
Hebbel's Plays. Translated with an Introduction by Dr C. K. Allen. 694
Heine: Prose and Poetry. 911
Herbert's Temple. Introduction by Edward Thomas. 309
Herrick's Hesperides and Noble Numbers. Intro. by Ernest Rhys. 310
L Ibsen's Brand. Translated by F. E. Garrett. 716
„ Ghosts, The Warriors at Helgeland, and An Enemy of the People. Translated by R. Farquharson Sharp. 552
„ Lady Inger of Ostraat, Love's Comedy, and The League of Youth. Translated by R. Farquharson Sharp. 729
„ Peer Gynt. Translated by R. Farquharson Sharp. 747
„ A Doll's House, The Wild Duck, and The Lady from the Sea. Translated by R. Farquharson Sharp. 494
„ The Pretenders, Pillars of Society, and Rosmersholm. Translated by R. Farquharson Sharp. 659
Jonson's (Ben) Plays. Intro. by Professor Schelling. 2 vols. 489–90
Kalidasa: Shakuntala. Translated by Professor A. W. Ryder. 629
L Keats' Poems. 101
Kingsley's (Charles) Poems. Introduction by Ernest Rhys. 793
(*See also* Fiction *and* For Young People)
L Langland's (William) Piers Plowman. 571
Lessing's Laocoon, Minna von Barnhelm, and Nathan the Wise. 843
L Longfellow's Poems. Introduction by Katherine Tynan. 382
Marlowe's Plays and Poems. Introduction by Edward Thomas. 383

POETRY AND DRAMA—*continued*

L Milton's Poems. Introduction by W. H. D. Rouse. 384
(*See also* ESSAYS)
Minor Elizabethan Drama. Vol. I. Tragedy. Selected, with Introduction, by Professor Thorndike. Vol. II. Comedy. 491–2
L Minor Poets of the 18th Century. Edited by H. I'Anson Fausset. 844
Minor Poets of the 17th Century. Edited by R. G. Howarth. 873
L Modern Plays. 942
Molière's Comedies. Introduction by Prof. F. C. Green. 2 vols. 830–1
New Golden Treasury, The. An Anthology of Songs and Lyrics. 695
Old Yellow Book, The. Introduction by Charles E. Hodell. 503
Omar Khayyám (The Rubáiyát of). Trans. by Edward FitzGerald. 819
L Palgrave's Golden Treasury. Introduction by Edward Hutton. 96
Percy's Reliques of Ancient English Poetry. 2 vols. 148–9
Poe's (Edgar Allan) Poems and Essays. Intro. by Andrew Lang. 791
(*See also* FICTION)
Pope (Alexander): Collected Poems. Introduction by Ernest Rhys. 760
Proctor's (Adelaide A.) Legends and Lyrics. 150
Restoration Plays, A Volume of. Introduction by Edmund Gosse. 604
Rossetti's Poems and Translations. Introduction by E. G. Gardner. 627
Scott's Poems and Plays. Intro. by Andrew Lang. 2 vols. 550–1
(*See also* BIOGRAPHY *and* FICTION)
L Shakespeare's Comedies. 153
L Historical Plays, Poems, and Sonnets. 154
L Tragedies. 155
Shelley's Poetical Works. Introduction by A. H. Koszul. 2 vols. 257–8
L Sheridan's Plays. 95
Spenser's Faerie Queene. Intro. by Prof. J. W. Hales. 2 vols. 443–4
" Shepherd's Calendar and Other Poems. Edited by Philip Henderson. 879
Stevenson's Poems–A Child's Garden of Verses, Underwoods, Songs of Travel, Ballads. 768 (*See also* ESSAYS, FICTION, *and* TRAVEL)
L Tchekhov. Plays and Stories. 941
Tennyson's Poems. Vol. I. 1830–56. Introduction by Ernest Rhys. 44
" " Vol. II. 1857–70. 626
Twenty One-Act Plays. Selected by John Hampden. 947
Webster and Ford. Plays. Selected, with Introduction, by Dr G. B. Harrison. 899
Whitman's (Walt) Leaves of Grass (I), Democratic Vistas, etc. 573
Wilde (Oscar), Plays, Prose Writings, and Poems. 858
Wordsworth's Shorter Poems. Introduction by Ernest Rhys. 203
" Longer Poems. Note by Editor. 311

REFERENCE

Atlas of Ancient and Classical Geography. Many coloured and line Maps; Historical Gazetteer, Index, etc. 451
Biographical Dictionary of English Literature. 449
Biographical Dictionary of Foreign Literature. 900
Dates, Dictionary of. 554
Dictionary of Quotations and Proverbs. 2 vols. 809–10
Everyman's English Dictionary. 776
Literary and Historical Atlas. I. Europe. Many coloured and line Maps; full Index and Gazetteer. 496
" " " II. America. Do. 553
" " " III. Asia. Do. 663
" " " IV. Africa and Australia. Do. 662
Non-Classical Mythology, Dictionary of. 632
Reader's Guide to Everyman's Library. Revised edition, covering the first 950 vols. 889
Roget's Thesaurus of English Words and Phrases. 2 vols. 630–1
Smith's Smaller Classical Dictionary. Revised and Edited by E. H. Blakeney, M.A. 495
Wright's An Encyclopaedia of Gardening. 555

ROMANCE

Aucassin and Nicolette, with other Medieval Romances. 497
Boccaccio's Decameron. (Unabridged.) Translated by J. M. Rigg. Introduction by Edward Hutton. 2 vols. 845–6
L Bunyan's Pilgrim's Progress. Introduction by Rev. H. E. Lewis. 204
Burnt Njal, The Story of. Translated by Sir George Dasent. 558
Cervantes' Don Quixote. Motteux's Translation. Lockhart's Introduction. 2 vols. 385–6
Chrétien de Troyes: Eric and Enid. Translated, with Introduction and Notes, by William Wistar Comfort. 698
French Medieval Romances. Translated by Eugene Mason. 557
Geoffrey of Monmouth's Histories of the Kings of Britain. 577
Grettir Saga, The. Newly Translated by G. Ainslie Hight. 699
Gudrun. Done into English by Margaret Armour. 880
Guest's (Lady) Mabinogion. Introduction by Rev. R. Williams. 97
Heimskringla: The Olaf Sagas. Translated by Samuel Laing. Introduction and Notes by John Beveridge. 717
„ Sagas of the Norse Kings. Translated by Samuel Laing. Introduction and Notes by John Beveridge. 847
Holy Graal, The High History of the, 445
Kalevala. Introduction by W. F. Kirby, F.L.S., F.E.S. 2 vols. 259–60
Le Sage's The Adventures of Gil Blas. Intro. by Anatole Le Bras. 2 vols.
MacDonald's (George) Phantastes: A Faerie Romance. 732 [437–8
(*See also* FICTION)
Malory's Le Morte d'Arthur. Intro. by Professor Rhys. 2 vols. 45–6
L Morris (William): Early Romances. Introduction by Alfred Noyes. 261
„ „ The Life and Death of Jason. 575
Morte d'Arthur Romances, Two. Introduction by Lucy A. Paton. 634
Nibelungs, The Fall of the. Translated by Margaret Armour. 312
Rabelais' The Heroic Deeds of Gargantua and Pantagruel. Introduction by D. B. Wyndham Lewis. 2 vols. 826–7
Wace's Arthurian Romance. Translated by Eugene Mason. Layamon's Brut. Introduction by Lucy A. Paton. 578

SCIENCE

Boyle's The Sceptical Chymist. 559
Darwin's The Origin of Species. Introduction by Sir Arthur Keith. 811
(*See also* TRAVEL) [E. F. Bozman. 922
L Eddington's (Sir Arthur) The Nature of the Physical World. Intro. by
Euclid: the Elements of. Todhunter's Edition. Introduction by Sir Thomas Heath, K.C.B. 891
Faraday's (Michael) Experimental Researches in Electricity. 576
Galton's Inquiries into Human Faculty. Revised by Author. 263
George's (Henry) Progress and Poverty. 560
Hahnemann's (Samuel) The Organon of the Rational Art of Healing. Introduction by C. E. Wheeler. 663
Harvey's Circulation of the Blood. Introduction by Ernest Parkyn. 262
Howard's State of the Prisons. Introduction by Kenneth Ruck. 835
Huxley's Essays. Introduction by Sir Oliver Lodge. 47
„ Select Lectures and Lay Sermons. Intro. Sir Oliver Lodge. 498
Lyell's Antiquity of Man. With an introduction by R. H. Rastall. 700
Marx's (Karl) Capital. Translated by Eden and Cedar Paul. Introduction by G. D. H. Cole. 2 vols. 848–9
Miller's Old Red Sandstone. 103
Owen's (Robert) A New View of Society, etc. Intro. by G. D. H. Cole. 799
L Pearson's (Karl) The Grammar of Science. 939
Ricardo's Principles of Political Economy and Taxation. 590
Smith's (Adam) The Wealth of Nations. 2 vols. 412–13
Tyndall's Glaciers of the Alps and Mountaineering in 1861. 98
White's Selborne. Introduction by Principal Windle. 48
Wollstonecraft (Mary), The Rights of Woman, with John Stuart Mill's The Subjection of Women. 825

TRAVEL AND TOPOGRAPHY

A Book of the 'Bounty.' Edited by George Mackaness. 950
Anson's Voyages. Introduction by John Masefield. 510
Bates' Naturalist on the Amazon. With Illustrations. 446
Belt's The Naturalist in Nicaragua. Intro. by Anthony Belt, F.L.S. 561
Borrow's (George) The Gypsies in Spain. Intro. by Edward Thomas. 697
„ „ The Bible in Spain. Intro. by Edward Thomas. 151
„ „ Wild Wales. Intro. by Theodore Watts-Dunton. 49
(*See also* FICTION)
Boswell's Tour in the Hebrides with Dr Johnson. 387
(*See also* BIOGRAPHY)
Burton's (Sir Richard) First Footsteps in East Africa. 500
Cobbett's Rural Rides. Introduction by Edward Thomas. 2 vols. 638–9
Cook's Voyages of Discovery. 99
Crèvecoeur's (H. St John) Letters from an American Farmer. 640
Darwin's Voyage of the Beagle. 104
(*See also* SCIENCE)
Defoe's Tour through England and Wales. Introduction by G. D. H. [Cole. 820–1
(*See also* FICTION)
Dennis' Cities and Cemeteries of Etruria. 2 vols. 183–4
Dufferin's (Lord) Letters from High Latitudes. 499
Ford's Gatherings from Spain. Introduction by Thomas Okey. 152
Franklin's Journey to the Polar Sea. Intro. by Capt. R. F. Scott. 447
Giraldus Cambrensis: Itinerary and Description of Wales. 272
Hakluyt's Voyages. 8 vols. 264, 265, 313, 314, 338, 339, 388, 389
Kinglake's Eothen. Introduction by Harold Spender, M.A. 337
Lane's Modern Egyptians. With many Illustrations. 315
Mandeville's (Sir John) Travels. Introduction by Jules Bramont. 812
Park (Mungo): Travels. Introduction by Ernest Rhys. 205
Peaks, Passes, and Glaciers. Selected by E. H. Blakeney, M.A. 778
L Polo's (Marco) Travels. Introduction by John Masefield. 306
Roberts' The Western Avernus. Intro. by Cunninghame Grahame. 762
Speke's Discovery of the Source of the Nile. 50
L Stevenson's An Inland Voyage, Travels with a Donkey, and Silverado [Squatters. 766
(*See also* ESSAYS, FICTION, *and* POETRY)
Stow's Survey of London. Introduction by H. B. Wheatley, 589
Wakefield's Letter from Sydney and Other Writings on Colonization. 828
Waterton's Wanderings in South America. Intro. by E. Selous. 772
Young's Travels in France and Italy. Intro. by Thomas Okey. 720

FOR YOUNG PEOPLE

Aesop's and Other Fables: An Anthology from all sources. 657
Alcott's Little Men. Introduction by Grace Rhys. 512
L „ Little Women and Good Wives. Intro. by Grace Rhys. 248
Andersen's Fairy Tales. Illustrated by the Brothers Robinson. 4
„ More Fairy Tales. Illustrated by Mary Shillabeer. 822
Annals of Fairyland. The Reign of King Oberon. 365
„ „ The Reign of King Cole. 366
Asgard and the Norse Heroes. Translated by Mrs Boult. 689
Baker's Cast up by the Sea. 539
Ballantyne's Coral Island. 245
„ Martin Rattler. 246
„ Ungava. Introduction by Ernest Rhys. 276
L Browne's (Frances) Granny's Wonderful Chair. Intro. by Dollie Radford. [112
Bulfinch's (Thomas) The Age of Fable. 472
„ „ Legends of Charlemagne. Intro. by Ernest Rhys. 556
L Canton's A Child's Book of Saints. Illustrated by T. H. Robinson. 61
(*See also* ESSAYS)
L Carroll's Alice in Wonderland, Through the Looking-Glass, etc. Illustrated by the Author. Introduction by Ernest Rhys. 836
Clarke's Tales from Chaucer. 537
Collodi's Pinocchio; the Story of a Puppet. 538

FOR YOUNG PEOPLE—*continued*

Converse's (Florence) The House of Prayer. 923
(*See also* FICTION)
Cox's (Sir G. W.) Tales of Ancient Greece. 721
Defoe's Robinson Crusoe. Illustrated by J. A. Symington. 59
(*See also* FICTION)
Dodge's (Mary Mapes) Hans Brinker; or, The Silver Skates. 620
Edgar's Heroes of England. 471
(*See also* FICTION)
Ewing's (Mrs) Jackanapes, Daddy Darwin's Dovecot, illustrated by R. Caldecott, and The Story of a Short Life. 731
" " Mrs Overtheway's Remembrances. 730
Fairy Gold. Illustrated by Herbert Cole. 157
Fairy Tales from the Arabian Nights. Illustrated. 249
Froissart's Chronicles. 57
Gatty's Parables from Nature. Introduction by Grace Rhys. 158
Grimm's Fairy Tales. Illustrated by R. Anning Bell. 56
Hawthorne's Wonder Book and Tanglewood Tales. 5
(*See also* FICTION)
Howard's Rattlin the Reefer. Introduction by Guy Pocock. 857
L Hughes' Tom Brown's School Days. Illustrated by T. Robinson. 58
Ingelow's (Jean) Mopsa the Fairy. Illustrated by Dora Curtis. 619
Jefferies's (Richard) Bevis, the Story of a Boy. Intro. by Guy Pocock. [850
Kingsley's Heroes. Introduction by Grace Rhys. 113
" Madam How and Lady Why. Introduction by C. I. Gardiner, M.A. 777
" Water Babies and Glaucus. 277
(*See also* POETRY *and* FICTION)
Kingston's Peter the Whaler. 6
" Three Midshipmen. 7
L Lamb's Tales from Shakespeare. Illustrated by A. Rackham.
(*See also* BIOGRAPHY *and* ESSAYS)
Lear (and Others): A Book of Nonsense. 806
Marryat's Children of the New Forest. 247
" Little Savage. Introduction by R. Brimley Johnson. 159
" Masterman Ready. Introduction by R. Brimley Johnson. 160
" Settlers in Canada. Introduction by R. Brimley Johnson. 370
" (Edited by) Rattlin the Reefer. 857
(*See also* FICTION)
Martineau's Feats on the Fjords, etc. Illustrated by A. Rackham. 429
Mother Goose's Nursery Rhymes. Illustrated. 473
Poetry Book for Boys and Girls. Edited by Guy Pocock. 894
Reid's (Mayne) The Boy Hunters of the Mississippi. 582
" " The Boy Slaves. Introduction by Guy Pocock. 797
Ruskin's The Two Boyhoods and Other Passages. 688
(*See also* ESSAYS)
L Sewell's (Anna) Black Beauty. Illustrated by Lucy Kemp-Welch. 748
Spyri's (Johanna) Heidi. Illustrations by Lizzie Lawson. 431
L Story Book for Boys and Girls. Edited by Guy Pocock. 934
Stowe's Uncle Tom's Cabin. 371
Swiss Family Robinson. Illustrations by Chas. Folkard. 430
Verne's (Jules) Abandoned. 50 Illustrations. 368
" " Dropped from the Clouds. 50 Illustrations. 367
L " " Five Weeks in a Balloon and Around the World in Eighty Days. Translated by Arthur Chambers and P. Desages. [779
L " " Twenty Thousand Leagues Under the Sea. 319
" " The Secret of the Island. 50 Illustrations. 369
Yonge's (Charlotte M.) The Book of Golden Deeds. 330
" " The Lances of Lynwood. Illus. by Dora Curtis. [579
" " The Little Duke. Illustrated by Dora Curtis. 470
(*See also* FICTION)

Made in Great Britain at The Temple Press, Letchworth, Herts (N 279)